Lecture Notes in Computer Science   11114

Commenced Publication in 1973
Founding and Former Series Editors:
Gerhard Goos, Juris Hartmanis, and Jan van Leeuwen

More information about this series at http://www.springer.com/series/7412

Leszek J. Chmielewski · Ryszard Kozera
Arkadiusz Orłowski · Konrad Wojciechowski
Alfred M. Bruckstein · Nicolai Petkov (Eds.)

Computer Vision and Graphics

International Conference, ICCVG 2018
Warsaw, Poland, September 17–19, 2018
Proceedings

 Springer

Editors
Leszek J. Chmielewski ⓘ
Faculty of Applied Informatics
  and Mathematics
Warsaw University of Life Sciences
Warsaw, Poland

Ryszard Kozera ⓘ
Faculty of Applied Informatics
  and Mathematics
Warsaw University of Life Sciences
Warsaw, Poland

Arkadiusz Orłowski ⓘ
Faculty of Applied Informatics
  and Mathematics
Warsaw University of Life Sciences
Warsaw, Poland

Konrad Wojciechowski
Institute of Computer Science
Silesian University of Technology
Gliwice, Poland

and

Polish-Japanese Academy of Information
  Technology
Warsaw, Poland

Alfred M. Bruckstein
Technion, Israel Institute of Technology
Haifa, Israel

Nicolai Petkov ⓘ
University of Groningen
Groningen, The Netherlands

ISSN 0302-9743   ISSN 1611-3349   (electronic)
Lecture Notes in Computer Science
ISBN 978-3-030-00691-4   ISBN 978-3-030-00692-1   (eBook)
https://doi.org/10.1007/978-3-030-00692-1

Library of Congress Control Number: 2018954669

LNCS Sublibrary: SL6 – Image Processing, Computer Vision, Pattern Recognition, and Graphics

This Springer imprint is published by the registered company Springer Nature Switzerland AG
The registered company address is: Gewerbestrasse 11, 6330 Cham, Switzerland

Preface

The International Conference on Computer Vision and Graphics, organized since 2002, is the continuation of The International Conferences on Computer Graphics and Image Processing, GKPO, held in Poland every second year from 1990 to 2000. The founder and organizer of these conferences was Prof. Wojciech Mokrzycki. The main objective of ICCVG is to provide an environment for the exchange of ideas between researchers in the closely related domains of computer vision and computer graphics.

ICCVG 2018 brought together 108 authors. The proceedings contain 45 papers, each accepted on the grounds of merit and relevance confirmed by three independent reviewers. The number of papers is smaller than in the previous years because we have greatly increased the quality requirements in the reviewing process.

ICCVG 2018 was organized by the Association for Image Processing, Poland (Towarzystwo Przetwarzania Obrazów – TPO), the Faculty of Applied Informatics and Mathematics, Warsaw University of Life Sciences (WZIM SGGW), together with the Faculty of Information Science, West Pomeranian University of Technology (WI ZUT), Szczecin, and the Polish-Japanese Academy of Information Technology (PJATK) as the supporting organizers.

The Association for Image Processing integrates the Polish community working on the theory and applications of computer vision and graphics. It was formed between 1989 and 1991.

The Faculty of Applied Informatics and Mathematics (WZIM), established in 2008 at the Warsaw University of Life Sciences (SGGW), which celebrates its 10th anniversary this year, offers programs of study in Informatics as well as in Informatics and Econometrics. Its location at the leading life sciences university in Poland is the source of opportunities for valuable research at the border of applied information sciences, agribusiness, forestry, furniture and wood industry, veterinary medicine, and the broadly understood domains of biology and economy.

We would like to thank all the members of the Scientific Committee, as well as the additional reviewers, for their help in ensuring the high quality of the papers. We would also like to thank Grażyna Domańska-Żurek for her excellent work on technically editing the proceedings, and Dariusz Frejlichowski, Bartosz Świderski, Henryk Palus, Grzegorz Gawdzik, Halina Paluszkiewicz-Schaitter, Dominika Rudaś, Beata Sztab, and Aneta Ryńska for their engagement in the conference organization and administration.

September 2018

Leszek J. Chmielewski
Ryszard Kozera
Arkadiusz Orłowski
Konrad Wojciechowski
Alfred M. Bruckstein
Nicolai Petkov

Organization

- Association for Image Processing (TPO)
- Faculty of Applied Informatics and Mathematics,
  Warsaw University of Life Sciences (WZIM SGGW)
- Polish-Japanese Academy of Information Technology (PJATK)
- Faculty of Computer Science and Information Technology,
  West Pomeranian University of Technology (WI ZUT)
- Springer, *Lecture Notes in Computer Science* (LNCS)

Conference General Chairs

Leszek J. Chmielewski, Poland
Ryszard Kozera, Poland
Arkadiusz Orłowski, Poland
Konrad Wojciechowski, Poland

Scientific Committee

Ivan Bajla, Slovakia
Gunilla Borgefors, Sweden
Nadia Brancati, Italy
M. Emre Celebi, USA
Leszek Chmielewski, Poland
Dmitry Chetverikov, Hungary
Piotr Czapiewski, Poland
László Czúni, Hungary
Silvana Dellepiane, Italy
Marek Domański, Poland
Mariusz Flasiński, Poland
Paweł Forczmański, Poland
Dariusz Frejlichowski, Poland
Maria Frucci, Italy
André Gagalowicz, France
Duncan Gillies, UK
Samuel Morillas Gómez, Spain
Ewa Grabska, Poland
Diego Gragnaniello, Italy
Marcin Iwanowski, Poland

Adam Jóźwik, Poland
Heikki Kälviäinen, Finland
Andrzej Kasiński, Poland
Włodzimierz Kasprzak, Poland
Bertrand Kerautret, France
Nahum Kiryati, Israel
Reinhard Klette, New Zealand
Przemysław Klęsk, Poland
Józef Korbicz, Poland
Marcin Korzeń, Poland
Ryszard Kozera, Poland
Hans-Jörg Kreowski, Germany
Adam Krzyżak, Canada
Juliusz L. Kulikowski, Poland
Marek Kurzyński, Poland
Bogdan Kwolek, Poland
Y. B. Kwon, South Korea
Bart Lamiroy, France
Piotr Lech, Poland
Anna Lewandowska, Poland

Contents

3D and Stereo Image Processing

Low-Level and Middle-Level Image Processing

Medical Image Analysis

Motion Analysis and Tracking

Human Face, Gestures and Action Analysis

Security and Protection

Pattern Recognition and New Concepts in Classification

Computer Graphics, Perception and Image Quality

Hemispherical Gaussians for Accurate Light Integration

Julian Meder[1,2]([✉]) and Beat Brüderlin[1]

[1] TU Ilmenau, Helmholtzplatz 5, 98693 Ilmenau, Germany
Julian.Meder@tu-ilmenau.de
[2] 3DInteractive GmbH, Am Vogelherd 10, 98693 Ilmenau, Germany

Abstract. In real-time computer graphics, approximations are often used to allow for interactive virtual scene rendering. Concerning the on-line lighting of such scenes, an approach getting increased recognition is to approximate the light in every direction of the hemisphere of a surface point using suitable mathematical distribution functions, such as the well-known Spherical Gaussian. A drawback of this distribution is that current methods using it are inaccurate and do not reflect the correct lighting integral over the surface hemisphere. We show new and more accurate convolution of a Spherical Gaussian with a clamped cosine distribution. In short, we propose a closed form approximation of the hemispherical integral of such a distribution in an arbitrary hemisphere. While our use case is the approximation of the hemispherical lighting situation, we believe that our general formulation of the hemispherical integral of a Spherical Gaussian can also be useful in other areas.

1 Introduction

Calculating the lighting of a virtual scene is still one of the most challenging problems in interactive computer graphics. Here, the idealized expectations of a realistic scene clash with the reality of available hardware resources and necessitate many approximations to at least show plausible results mimicking the physically accurate. With Spherical Harmonics [9] complex light situations started to get approximated using mathematical distributions precomputed off-line and evaluated on-line. In recent years, we observe a trend where approximating complex lighting situations on-the-fly into comparable distributions becomes increasingly popular. Therefore, we came to study such distributions more closely.

Our main contributions described in this paper include a novel approximation of the integral of a Spherical Gaussian distribution in a selected hemisphere. The approximation can be used generally when dealing with these distributions. Based on this, we additionally propose a more precise convolution of a Spherical Gaussian with a cosine factor, the latter being often encountered in lighting calculations. This use case will be explained in more detail in the next section while the remainder of this paper is organized as follows: Sect. 3 defines Spherical Gaussians as they are used in this paper and Sect. 4 gives a summary of work

© Springer Nature Switzerland AG 2018
L. J. Chmielewski et al. (Eds.): ICCVG 2018, LNCS 11114, pp. 3–15, 2018.
https://doi.org/10.1007/978-3-030-00692-1_1

related to using distributions approximating lighting in general and Spherical Gaussians in particular. Afterwards, Sect. 5 motivates our new approximations and derives them. Finally, Sect. 6 shows empirical comparisons and Sect. 7 concludes this paper.

2   Approximating the Rendering Equation

The task of calculating lighting in computer graphics is the solution of the so called rendering equation [5]:

$$L_o(x, \omega_o) = L_e(x, \omega_o) + \int_{\Omega_n^+} L_i(\omega) f_r(x, \omega, \omega_o)(\omega \circ n) d\omega \qquad (1)$$

Essentially, radiance reflected from a surface point x in direction ω_o is the self-emitted radiance $L_e(x, \omega_o)$, i.e. if x is a light source itself, and the integral over all possible directions ω of incoming radiance $L_i(\omega)$ weighted by the bidirectional reflectance distribution function (BRDF) f_r and the cosine between ω and the surface normal n ($\circ$ being the dot product). We denote the hemisphere over x in direction n as Ω_n^+, i.e. where $(\omega \circ n)$ is greater or equal to 0, Ω_n^- as the hemisphere in inverse direction of n, i.e. where $(\omega \circ n)$ is less than 0, and Ω as the whole sphere.

In our use case we ignore self-emittance L_e and approximate (1) as

$$L_o(x, \omega_o) \approx \int_{\Omega_n^+} G(x, \omega)(\omega \circ n) d\omega \qquad (2)$$

meaning we assume the incoming light times the BRDF can be well approximated as some distribution $G(x, \omega)$, which we chose to be a Spherical Gaussian and compute on-line from a fully dynamic lighting environment. The remaining problem is an efficient and accurate convolution of this distribution with the cosine factor.

3   Spherical Gaussians

A Spherical Gaussian we use in Sect. 2 in the rendering equation is evaluated in a normalized direction ω and defined as

$$G(\mu, \lambda, \phi, \omega) = \mu e^{\lambda(\phi \circ \omega - 1)}, \qquad (3)$$

where μ is its color value in our case, λ its sharpness and ϕ its normalized direction. This distribution has a simple analytical integral over the whole sphere of possible directions Ω [12]:

$$\mu A(\lambda) = \int_{\Omega} G(\mu, \lambda, \phi, \omega) d\omega = \mu \frac{2\pi}{\lambda}(1 - e^{-2\lambda}). \qquad (4)$$

Multiplication of two Spherical Gaussians $G(\mu_1, \lambda_1, \phi_1, \omega)$ and $G(\mu_2, \lambda_2, \phi_2, \omega)$ simply yields a new Spherical Gaussian $G(\mu_3, \lambda_3, \phi_3, \omega)$ with

$$\lambda_3 = \|\lambda_1\phi_1 + \lambda_2\phi_2\|$$
$$\phi_3 = \frac{\lambda_1\phi_1 + \lambda_2\phi_2}{\lambda_3} \qquad (5)$$
$$\mu_3 = \mu_1\mu_2 e^{\lambda_3 - \lambda_2 - \lambda_1}.$$

Respective derivations can be found in [14].

4   Related Work

One of the major foundations concerning the application of mathematical distributions as the lighting approximation has been established by Sloan et al. [9] with their work on Spherical Harmonics. The distributions themselves were precomputed off-line back then, but evaluation during interactive runtime was very efficient due to the mathematical properties of Spherical Harmonics. They have since been used many times, recently even completely during runtime in the works of Kaplanyan et al. [6], using them as representations for light in discrete volumes of the scene, propagating through the whole volume grid, and Jendersie et al. [4], approximating the hemispherical light of a discrete set of selected scene points and interpolating it over the geometry.

In contrast, Spherical Gaussians have been investigated in an interactive environment by Green et al. [3], who approximated the transport function, i.e. $f_r(x, \omega, \omega_o)(\omega \circ n)$ from Eq. (2), as a weighted mix of Spherical Gaussians. Comparable to Sloan et al. [9], Tsai et al. used Spherical Gaussians during a general evaluation of spherical radial basis functions for precomputed radiance transfer [13]. Yan et al. found an efficient algorithm to render translucent objects under Spherical Gaussian Lights accurately [17]. Xu et al. used Spherical Gaussians to approximate the whole sphere of environmental light during interactive hair rendering [15]. In similar fashion, Tokuyoshi converted Reflective Shadow Maps (RSMs) [1] to a small set of Spherical Gaussian Lights and used them to interactively render convincing diffuse and glossy reflections, even supporting caustics [11]. This work was later extended for more meaningful filtering of the RSM via kernel-based importance sampling [12].

5   Hemispherical Gaussian Lighting

Because we compute distribution G in (2) dynamically on-line, we decided against Spherical Harmonics [9] in favor of Spherical Gaussians. Due to the effective value ranges of Spherical Harmonics being constrained to certain parts of the unit sphere, a weighted sum of base functions is always used instead of a single one. While determining the necessary weights is comparatively easy in a formal sense [8], it involves the evaluation of each chosen base function with each hemispherical light sample. In practice, only a small number of base functions is used when performing all computations on-line [4,6].

Accumulating the lighting situation into a Spherical Gaussian has been shown to be more efficient by Tokuyoshi [11] when using Toksvig's method [10] as the required costly divisions are independent of the number of hemispherical samples. Also, with Spherical Harmonics it is difficult to represent distributions with notably dominant or high frequency directions [3,7]. Spherical Gaussians in contrast allow to define said dominant direction directly (see Sect. 3).

5.1   Cosine Convolution

Now given the Spherical Gaussian distributions we actually have two problems while solving Eq. (2):

1. Achieving convolution only around the positive hemisphere Ω_n^+
2. Accurate integration of a Spherical Gaussian multiplied with a cosine

The first problem is directly given through the rendering Eq. (1). For the second problem, no analytical solution is known [15]. A common approximation, for example employed by [12,14,17], is assuming the dot product as a constant and using the following closed form solution:

$$
\begin{aligned}
\int_{\Omega_n^+} & G(\mu,\lambda,\phi,\omega)(\omega \circ n)d\omega \\
& \approx \max(0,\phi \circ n)\int_{\Omega} G(\mu,\lambda,\phi,\omega)d\omega \\
& = \max(0,\phi \circ n)\mu A(\lambda)
\end{aligned}
\tag{6}
$$

(a)   (b)

Fig. 1. Assuming a constant cosine: (a) Many scattered lights or close area lights create notable wrong shading compared to (b) the ground truth.

This approximation only works for sufficient sharpness λ, as it implies the directional distribution of the Spherical Gaussian being narrow enough to be seen as constant. In other words the distribution is interpreted as a single directional light.

This is not a given in our use case however, as the Spherical Gaussian potentially represents many lights scattered across the hemisphere or large area light sources close to the respective pixel's surface (see Fig. 1).

Another solution proposed by Tokuyoshi [12] is to represent the dot product as a Spherical Gaussian and integrate over the whole sphere:

$$\int_{\Omega_n^+} G(\mu, \lambda, \phi, \omega)(\omega \circ n)d\omega$$
$$\approx \int_{\Omega} G(\mu, \lambda, \phi, \omega)G(1, 2, n, \omega)d\omega \tag{7}$$
$$= \int_{\Omega} G(\mu', \lambda', \phi', \omega)d\omega = \mu' A(\lambda').$$

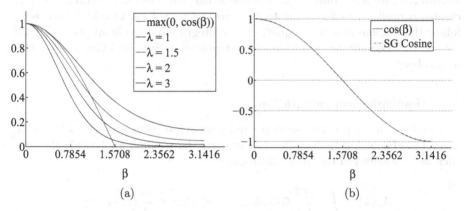

Fig. 2. Comparing the cosine with its Spherical Gaussian approximations: (a) No matter the chosen sharpness, a section of the function's image is either too low or too high compared to the positive clamped cosine. (b) Our approximation follows the slope of the non-clamped cosine.

Therefore, the Spherical Gaussian multiplication (5) and subsequent analytical integral (4) can be used. However, as Fig. 2a shows, the image of the cosine approximation differs remarkably from the real positive clamped cosine and in dependence of the chosen sharpness can either be too low or too high, resulting in overly dark or bright lighting.

We still believe the approximation of the cosine term as a Spherical Gaussian to be a good start for further investigation. After some experiments, we found that a Spherical Gaussian with a similar distribution as a cosine is indeed easily achievable using a modified formulation with an additional parameter α:

$$G(\mu_{cos}, \lambda_{cos}, \phi_{cos}, \alpha_{cos}, \omega) = G(\mu_{cos}, \lambda_{cos}, \phi_{cos}, \omega) - \alpha_{cos} \tag{8}$$

Automatic non-linear curve fitting this distribution to a standard cosine via Matlab resolved the parameters to $\mu_{cos} = 32.7080$, $\lambda_{cos} = 0.0315$ and $\alpha_{cos} = 31.7003$

with a RMSE of 0.0059. ϕ_{cos} is chosen to be the surface normal n. Figure 2b shows a comparison of this approximation with the cosine in range $[0; \pi]$. With this, we can now accurately convolve the Spherical Gaussian lighting distribution with a quasi-cosine analogous to Eq. (7). Integration over Ω would still be easily given by

$$
\begin{aligned}
&\int_{\Omega_n^+} G(\mu, \lambda, \phi, \omega)(\omega \circ n) d\omega \\
&\approx \int_{\Omega} G(\mu, \lambda, \phi, \omega) G(\mu_{cos}, \lambda_{cos}, \alpha_{cos}, n, \omega) d\omega \\
&= \int_{\Omega} G(\mu', \lambda', \phi', \omega) d\omega - \int_{\Omega} G(\mu, \lambda, \phi, \omega) \alpha_{cos} d\omega \\
&= \mu' A(\lambda') - \mu \alpha_{cos} A(\lambda).
\end{aligned}
\tag{9}
$$

However, as we now convolve with a cosine-like distribution integrating over Ω creates cancellation effects due to negative cosine values. Our idea here is to follow the original rendering equation and integrate only in hemisphere Ω_n^+. Of course, this necessitates a solution for integrating a Spherical Gaussian in this hemisphere.

5.2   Hemispherical Integration

Our findings in the previous section require us to integrate a Spherical Gaussian in a selected hemisphere. Some specific integrals have simple analytical solutions, such as its integral in the upper hemisphere Ω_ϕ^+

$$
A_u(\lambda) = \int_0^{2\pi} \int_0^{\frac{\pi}{2}} G(\lambda, \phi, \omega) \sin(\theta) d\theta d\varphi = \frac{2\pi}{\lambda}(1 - e^{-\lambda}),
\tag{10}
$$

in the lower hemisphere Ω_ϕ^- rotated 180° away from ϕ

$$
A_b(\lambda) = \int_0^{2\pi} \int_{\frac{\pi}{2}}^{\pi} G(\lambda, \phi, \omega) \sin(\theta) d\theta d\varphi = \frac{2\pi}{\lambda} e^{-2\lambda}(e^\lambda - 1)
\tag{11}
$$

and in the hemisphere rotated by 90° away from ϕ

$$
A_m(\lambda) = \int_0^{\pi} \int_0^{\pi} G(\lambda, \phi, \omega) \sin(\theta) d\theta d\varphi = \frac{\pi}{\lambda}(1 - e^{-2\lambda})
\tag{12}
$$

We obtained these solutions by using symbolic integration via Matlab. μ will be omitted for all further derivations as by its constant nature it can be pulled out of the integral immediately. For these and all following equations we denote $\omega = \left(\sin(\theta)\cos(\varphi), \sin(\theta)\sin(\varphi), \cos(\theta)\right)^T$ in spherical coordinates.

Generally, we can express the integral over some hemisphere rotated away from the original upper hemisphere by rotating ω in (10) by some angle β. In our use case, β is given by $acos(\phi \circ n)$, i.e. the angle between the Spherical Gaussian's direction and the surface normal. As Spherical Gaussians are isotropic

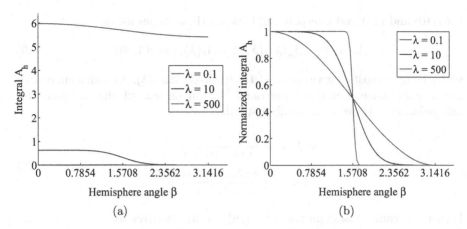

Fig. 3. Plots of numerical integration values A_h in dependence on β: (a) Absolute values and (b) curves normalized to $[0; 1]$.

in distribution, we assume w.l.o.g. that the rotation occurs around the local x axis. Therefore the rotation is given through the matrix

$$M(\beta) = \begin{pmatrix} 1 & 0 & 0 \\ 0 & \cos(\beta) & \sin(\beta) \\ 0 & -\sin(\beta) & \cos(\beta) \end{pmatrix} \tag{13}$$

Inserting this rotation into (10) and w.l.o.g. assuming $\phi = (0,0,1)^T$ yields

$$\begin{aligned} A_h(\lambda, \beta) &= \int_0^{2\pi} \int_0^{\frac{\pi}{2}} G(\lambda, (0,0,1)^T, M\omega) \sin(\theta) d\theta d\varphi \\ &= \int_0^{2\pi} \int_0^{\frac{\pi}{2}} e^{\lambda(\cos(\beta)\cos(\theta) - \sin(\beta)\sin(\phi)\sin(\theta) - 1)} \sin(\theta) d\theta d\varphi \end{aligned} \tag{14}$$

Unfortunately, we did not find a direct analytical solution for A_h. We therefore investigated the integral numerically to look for possible closed form approximations. When plotting the discrete values of A_h in relation to β as in Fig. 3a and additionally normalizing the curves to an image range of $[0; 1]$ as in Fig. 3b some interesting observations can be made:

- The integral values vary smoothly and decrease monotonically from A_u ($\beta = 0$) to A_b ($\beta = \pi$) passing through A_m when $\beta = \frac{\pi}{2}$.
- The function shape appears to be dependent on λ. It becomes cosine-like as λ approaches zero and step-like, when λ approaches infinity.
- The function seems to be mirrored by an axis passing through A_m.

These observations substantiate the suspicion of a logistic curve [2] for us. We therefore hypothesize, that the integral of a Spherical Gaussian over an arbitrary hemisphere can be well approximated by calculating A_u and A_b following

Eqs. (10) and (11) and interpolating between these values using

$$A_h(\lambda, \beta) \approx A_u(\lambda)s(\lambda, \beta) + A_b(\lambda)(1 - s(\lambda, \beta)),\qquad(15)$$

with s being a logistic curve over $\cos(\beta)$ with steepness $t(\lambda)$. As such a curve does not have an image of $[0; 1]$ in input range $[0; \pi]$ in general, which is necessary for interpolation (15), we additionally normalize it:

$$s'(\lambda, \beta) = \frac{1}{e^{\cos(\beta)t(\lambda)} + 1}$$
$$s(\lambda, \beta) = \frac{s'(\lambda, \beta) - s'(\lambda, \pi)}{s'(\lambda, 0) - s'(\lambda, \pi)}\qquad(16)$$

For ease of computation on the GPU (16) can be rewritten as

$$s(\lambda, \beta) = \frac{e^{t(\lambda)}e^{t(\lambda)\cos(\beta)} - 1}{(e^{t(\lambda)} - 1)(e^{t(\lambda)\cos(\beta)} + 1)}$$
$$= \frac{ab - 1}{(a - 1)(b + 1)}, a = e^{t(\lambda)}, b = e^{t(\lambda)\cos(\beta)}.\qquad(17)$$

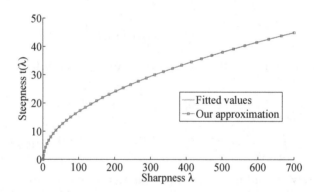

Fig. 4. Curve fitted steepness values $t(\lambda)$ compared to our closed form approximation

With this approximation, we were able to accurately fit the hemispherical integrals depending on λ and β with RMSEs given in Sect. 6.1.

What remains is a closed form approximation for the steepness $t(\lambda)$. Again, looking at the values resulting from non-linear curve fitting shown in Fig. 4 we recognize the familiar shape of a square root. Indeed, different modifications of the square root gave us good fits to the curve in Fig. 4 and we ultimately used the solution given in the next section.

Algorithm 1. Approximate Hemispherical Gaussian Convolution

---

function $A_h(\lambda, \cos(\beta))$

$\quad t \leftarrow \sqrt{\lambda} \frac{1.6988\lambda^2 + 10.8438\lambda}{\lambda^2 + 6.2201\lambda + 10.2415}$

$\quad a \leftarrow e^t$

$\quad b \leftarrow e^{t\cos(\beta)}$

$\quad s \leftarrow \frac{ab-1}{(a-1)(b+1)}$

$\quad$ **return** $A_b(\lambda)(1-s) + A_u(\lambda)s$

end function

function SG_COSINE_CONVOLVE(μ, λ, ϕ, n)

$\quad \mu_{cos} \leftarrow 32.7080$

$\quad \lambda_{cos} \leftarrow 0.0315$

$\quad \alpha_{cos} \leftarrow 31.7003$

$\quad \lambda' \leftarrow \|\lambda_{cos}n + \lambda\phi\|$

$\quad \phi' \leftarrow \frac{\lambda_{cos}n + \lambda\phi}{\lambda'}$

$\quad \mu' \leftarrow \mu_{cos}\mu e^{\lambda' - \lambda - \lambda_{cos}}$

$\quad$ **return** $\mu' A_h(\lambda', \phi' \circ n) - \mu\alpha_{cos}A_h(\lambda, \phi \circ n)$

end function

5.3   Final Algorithms

Using the findings of the previous section, the cosine approximation (8) and the Spherical Gaussian multiplication (5) we can now closely approximate convolution (2). Algorithm 1 summarizes both this and our method for calculating the general hemispherical integral A_h.

Clearly, our approach is more costly than the approximations we referred to in Sect. 5.1, involving a total of 4 individual Spherical Gaussian integral evaluations plus the additional overhead for the two hemispherical approximations. However, as the next section will prove empirically, it carries more overall accuracy and shows a more generalized behavior when applying it to our use case. Also, as $A_u(\lambda)$ and $A_b(\lambda)$ are mainly composed of identical factors Algorithm 1 can be heavily optimized to avoid unnecessary recalculations.

6   Evaluation

6.1   Approximation Error

In this section, we evaluate our and other approximations against the ground truth given by numerical integration over $\beta \in [0; \pi]$ for a range of different sharpness values λ. We both show the absolute error between the curves and a relative error by normalizing the curves to an image range of $[0; 1]$, the latter giving a better comparison of the integral shapes.

Figure 5 shows the positive result of using our accurate cosine representation combined with our novel hemispherical integration. While the other approximations show significantly increasing error values, especially when λ approaches 0,

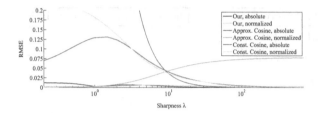

Fig. 5. Comparison between the RMSE values to the ground truth numerical integral when using either of the two existing cosine convolution approximations or our approximation (see Sect. 5.1).

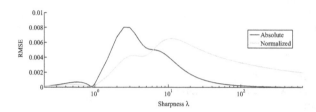

Fig. 6. RMSE values for our hemispherical integral approximation compared to the numerical integral.

our approximation remains a good fit overall. Our method additionally matches the shape of the integral closely for the most part, as is evident when comparing the normalized curves.

We did not find any other works proposing a general approximation for the integral of a Spherical Gaussian over an arbitrary hemisphere. Therefore, for the sake of completeness we include the RMSEs of our general hemispherical integral approximation in Fig. 6 for further reference.

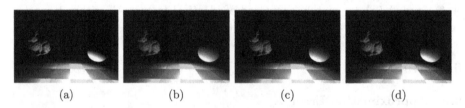

Fig. 7. (a) Under conditions of broad hemispherical lighting, the assumption of the constant cosine breaks down, but (b) the errors of the approximate cosine are not easily noticeable in this case. (c) Our solution is a close match to (d) the brute force ground truth. (Bunny model ©Stanford University)

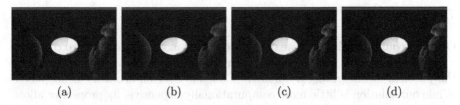

(a)   (b)   (c)   (d)

Fig. 8. (a) Assuming the cosine factor to be constant works in situations of narrow hemispherical lighting while (b) using the approximate cosine wrongly shows brighter results. (c) Again, our solution is a close match to (d) the brute force ground truth (Bunny model ©Stanford University).

6.2 Visual and Speed Comparison

For the visual comparison, we use gathering on a Reflective Shadow Map [1] into a Spherical Gaussian distribution per surface point. The final lighting is then calculated using either of the approximations from Sect. 5.1.

The approximation of the rendering integral as in Eq. (6), assuming the constant cosine, behaves as expected from its underlying assumptions: It shows good results when the lighting situation is narrowly distributed over the hemisphere (Fig. 8a) and unsuitable results for broad hemispherical lighting (Fig. 7a). The less accurate Spherical Gaussian cosine approximation of Tokuyoshi [12] shows brighter results than the ground truth in both situations, while perceptively being a little less recognizable in the broad lighting situation (see Figs. 7b and 8b), as the longer tail of the distribution causes higher integral values.

Comparing these with our approximation in Figs. 7c and 8c shows results close to the ground truth solution in Figs. 8d and 7d. This yields the conclusion that we propose a more generalized solution for this particular use case.

Table 1. Computation time per frame averages (ms)

Method	Resolution			
	1280 × 720	1920 × 1080	2560 × 1600	3840 × 2400
Constant Cosine	4.90	5.56	6.30	10.59
Approximate Cosine	5.07	5.78	6.73	11.70
Ours	5.29	6.22	7.43	13.83

Our qualitative comparison in Sect. 5.3 already predicted that our increased precision comes at the cost of performance. However, as Table 1 shows our testing environment remains real-time capable when we replace the previous methods with our novel approach. Indeed, the increase in processing time is negligible compared to the removal of the noticeable visual errors of the other methods.

7   Conclusion

Over the course of this paper we developed both a more accurate way to convolve a Spherical Gaussian with a cosine factor and a novel general approximation to the problem of integrating a Spherical Gaussian over an arbitrary hemisphere. While our solution is little more computationally expensive, its properties allow a more generalized application. In addition, our generalized hemispherical integration method is not constricted to problems in computer graphics, but may be applied in other areas where Spherical Gaussians are employed.

For future work, we will investigate a direct closed form approximation of integral (2), as this can yield a cheaper and potentially even more accurate solution. Furthermore, we find the idea of integrating anisotropic Spherical Gaussians [16] over arbitrary hemispheres to be a very interesting research direction.

References

1. Dachsbacher, C., Stamminger, M.: Reflective shadow maps. In: Proceedings of the 2005 Symposium on Interactive 3D Graphics and Games, pp. 203–231. I3D 2005. ACM, New York (2005). http://doi.acm.org/10.1145/1053427.1053460
2. Garnier, J., Quetelet, A.: Correspondance mathématique et physique. No. 10, Impr. d'H. Vandekerckhove (1838). https://books.google.de/books?id=8GsEAAAAYAAJ
3. Green, P., Kautz, J., Matusik, W., Durand, F.: View-dependent precomputed light transport using nonlinear Gaussian function approximations. In: Proceedings of the 2006 Symposium on Interactive 3D Graphics and Games, pp. 7–14, I3D 2006. ACM, New York (2006). http://doi.acm.org/10.1145/1111411.1111413
4. Jendersie, J., Kuri, D., Grosch, T.: Precomputed illuminance composition for real-time global illumination. In: Proceedings of the 20th ACM SIGGRAPH Symposium on Interactive 3D Graphics and Games, pp. 129–137, I3D 2016. ACM, New York (2016). http://doi.acm.org/10.1145/2856400.2856407
5. Kajiya, J.T.: The rendering equation. SIGGRAPH Comput. Graph. **20**(4), 143–150 (1986). http://doi.acm.org/10.1145/15886.15902
6. Kaplanyan, A., Dachsbacher, C.: Cascaded light propagation volumes for real-time indirect illumination. In: Proceedings of the 2010 ACM SIGGRAPH Symposium on Interactive 3D Graphics and Games, pp. 99–107, I3D 2010. ACM, New York (2010). http://doi.acm.org/10.1145/1730804.1730821
7. Ng, R., Ramamoorthi, R., Hanrahan, P.: All-frequency shadows using non-linear wavelet lighting approximation. ACM Trans. Graph. **22**(3), 376–381 (2003). http://doi.acm.org/10.1145/882262.882280
8. Sloan, P.P.: Stupid spherical harmonics (SH) tricks. In: GDC 2008 (2008)
9. Sloan, P.P., Kautz, J., Snyder, J.: Precomputed radiance transfer for real-time rendering in dynamic, low-frequency lighting environments. ACM Trans. Graph. **21**(3), 527–536 (2002). http://doi.acm.org/10.1145/566654.566612
10. Toksvig, M.: Mipmapping normal maps. J. Graph. Tools **10**(3), 65–71 (2005). https://doi.org/10.1080/2151237X.2005.10129203
11. Tokuyoshi, Y.: Virtual spherical Gaussian lights for real-time glossy indirect illumination. Comput. Graph. Forum **34**(7), 89–98 (2015). http://dx.doi.org/10.1111/cgf.12748

12. Tokuyoshi, Y.: Modified filtered importance sampling for virtual spherical Gaussian lights. Comput. Vis. Media **2**(4), 343–355 (2016). https://doi.org/10.1007/s41095-016-0063-3
13. Tsai, Y.T., Shih, Z.C.: All-frequency precomputed radiance transfer using spherical radial basis functions and clustered tensor approximation. In: ACM SIGGRAPH 2006 Papers, pp. 967–976, SIGGRAPH 2006. ACM, New York (2006). http://doi.acm.org/10.1145/1179352.1141981
14. Xu, K., Cao, Y.P., Ma, L.Q., Dong, Z., Wang, R., Hu, S.M.: A practical algorithm for rendering interreflections with all-frequency BRDFS. ACM Trans. Graph. **33**(1), 10:1–10:16 (2014). http://doi.acm.org/10.1145/2533687
15. Xu, K., Ma, L.Q., Ren, B., Wang, R., Hu, S.M.: Interactive hair rendering and appearance editing under environment lighting. ACM Trans. Graph. **30**(6), 173:1–173:10 (2011). http://doi.acm.org/10.1145/2070781.2024207
16. Xu, K., Sun, W.L., Dong, Z., Zhao, D.Y., Wu, R.D., Hu, S.M.: Anisotropic spherical Gaussians. ACM Trans. Graph. **32**(6), 209:1–209:11 (2013). http://doi.acm.org/10.1145/2508363.2508386
17. Yan, L.Q., Zhou, Y., Xu, K., Wang, R.: Accurate translucent material rendering under spherical Gaussian lights. Comput. Graph. Forum **31**(7pt2), 2267–2276 (2012). http://dx.doi.org/10.1111/j.1467-8659.2012.03220.x

Gaze-Dependent Screen Space Ambient Occlusion

Radosław Mantiuk$^{(\boxtimes)}$

West Pomeranian University of Technology,
Szczecin al. Piastów 17, 70–310 Szczecin, Poland
`rmantiuk@zut.edu.pl`

Abstract. The screen space ambient occlusion (SSAO) is a fast global illumination technique, which approximates interreflections between rendered objects. Due to its simplicity, it is often implemented in commercial computer games. However, despite the fact that SSAO calculations take a few milliseconds per frame, a significant computation load is added to the total rendering time. In this work we propose a technique, which accelerates the SSAO calculations using information about observer's gaze direction captured by the eye tracker. The screen region surrounding the observer's gaze position is rendered with maximum quality, which is reduced gradually for higher eccentricities. The SSAO quality is varying by changing the number of samples that are used to approximate the SSAO occlusion shadows. The reduced sampling results in almost two-fold acceleration of SSAO with negligible deterioration of the image quality.

1 Introduction

In the Phong reflection model, diffuse and specular reflections are varying due to observer and lights positions, but ambient light is constant. Having this assumptions, we miss the interreflections between rendered objects. Adding *ambient occlusion* (AO) for varying ambient light creates very convincing soft shadows, that combined with direct lighting give realistic images [1, Sect. 9.2]. The AO technique is faster in comparison to the full global illumination solutions, however, it still needs demanding resources to achieve high quality renderings. An approximation of this technique, called *screen space ambient occlusion* (SSAO) [15] simulates local occlusions in real time. However, the accuracy of approximation strongly depends on the sampling density, which in turn limits its applications. It is especially a drawback in the game engine, in which the rendering time spent for AO computation should use only a fraction of the frame time because other calculations determine the quality of the gameplay. Thus, further acceleration of the SSAO computations is a desirable task which has significant impact on the overall quality of the real-time computer graphics.

In this work we present a gaze-dependent screen space ambient occlusion technique in which information about human viewing direction is employed to vary accuracy of the occlusion factors. The screen region surrounding the

© Springer Nature Switzerland AG 2018
L. J. Chmielewski et al. (Eds.): ICCVG 2018, LNCS 11114, pp. 16–27, 2018.
https://doi.org/10.1007/978-3-030-00692-1_2

observer's gaze position is rendered with maximum precision, decreasing gradually towards parafoveal and peripheral regions. The idea of this solution is based on the directional characteristic of the human visual system (HVS). People see the high frequency details only in a small viewing angle subtended 2–3° of the field of view. In this range, people see with a resolution of up to 60 cycles per angular degree, but for a 20-degree viewing angle, this sensitivity is reduced even ten times [8].

The accuracy of the occlusion factors is determined by the number of samples used to calculate these factors. In practice, less samples results in ragged edges of the SSAO shadows. However, this aliasing artifacts are barely visible by humans in peripheral regions of vision. In other words, image deterioration caused by low sampling in the SSAO technique can be clearly visible only in high frequency regions. Number of samples in SSAO can be gradually reduced with distance to a gaze point what significantly speeds-up rendering. We use the *eye tracker* to capture the *human gaze point*. Then, sampling is reduced with eccentricity (deviations from the axis of vision) along the curve determined by the gaze-dependent contrast sensitivity function (GD-CSF) [5]. This perceptual function models loss of contrast sensitivity with *eccentricity*. It can be used to determine the maximum special frequency visible for humans for an arbitrary viewing angle.

Section 2 gives background information on the screen-space ambient occlusion technique and outlines the previous work. Section 3 is focused on our gaze-dependent extension of SSAO and shows how sampling can be reduced without noticeable image deterioration. Section 4 presents the results of the perceptual experiment in which we evaluate the perceptual visibility of the image deteriorations.

2 Background and Previous Work

Screen space ambient occlusion (SSAO) is a rendering technique for approximating the global illumination in real time [15]. For every pixel on the screen, the depths of surrounding pixels are analyzed to compute the amount of occlusion, which is proportional to the depth difference between a current pixel and a sampled pixel.

We implemented the *normal-oriented hemisphere* SSAO technique [20]. The hemisphere is oriented along the surface normal at the pixel. The samples from the hemisphere are projected into screen space to get the coordinates into the depth buffer. If the sample position is behind this sample depth (i.e. inside geometry), it contributes to the occlusion factor. The procedure is repeated for every pixel in image to generate the map of occlusion factors (also called the *occlusion shadows*, see example in Fig. 1). This map forms a characteristic shadowing of ambient light, which is visible as a high frequency information in characteristic regions of the scene (e.g. at corners, close to complex objects, etc.). The shadows are blended with the pixel colors computed based on the Phong lighting equation. Wherein, frequency of the shadows is often higher than variability of the Phong ambient shading.

Fig. 1. Map of occlusion shadows generated by the normal-oriented hemisphere SSAO technique.

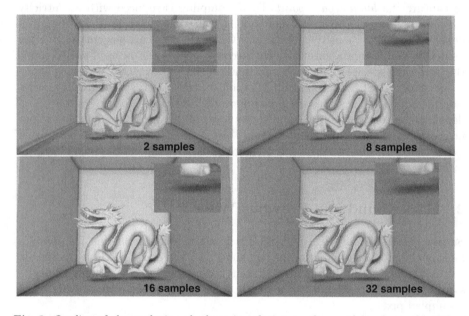

Fig. 2. Quality of the occlusion shadows in relation to the number of samples. The image deterioration is especially visible in the insets.

In SSAO the screen space computations are performed rather than tracing new rays in 3-dimensional space as it is done in the original Ambient Occlusion (AO) technique [23]. The AO algorithm generates better results than SSAO, but its complexity prevents the use of AO in the game engines and generally in the real time computer graphics. Even gaze-dependent extension of AO proposed in [9] offers rendering of up to 1–2 frames per second at full GPU load.

The SSAO method introduces a number of visible artifacts like z-fighting caused by the limited resolution of the Z-buffer or unrealistic darkening of the objects resulting from applying an arbitrary sampling radius around the pixel (see details in [3, 7, 15]). However, the most problematic is a noise and banding in occlusion shadows caused by too few number of samples (see examples in Fig. 2). To avoid noise visibility, hundreds of samples per pixel should be generated. This is too much for the game engines, for which the trade-off between accuracy and computational complexity is required. The number of samples is reduced to 32, while using the bilateral filtering, which is still time consuming. We noticed that fewer samples from these 32, even with the low-pass filtering, results in perceivable quality deterioration of the ambient occlusion shadows and should not be used in the practical applications.

In the following section we propose a technique, which reduces number of samples in the peripheral region of vision without visible degradation of the image quality. This type of image synthesis is called *foveated rendering*. The foveated rendering was proposed to accelerate the ray casting by Murphy et al. [16]. Günter et al. [6] presented a rendering engine, which generates three low-resolution images corresponding to the different fields of view. Then, the wide-angle images are magnified and combined with non-scaled image of the area surrounding the gaze point. Thus, the number of processed pixels can be reduced by 10–15 times, while ensuring the deterioration of image quality invisible for observer. Another foveated rendering technique proposed by Stengel et al. [19] aimed to reduce shading complexity in the deferred shading technique [1]. The spatial sampling is constant for the whole image but the material shaders are simplified for peripheral pixels. According to the authors, this technique reduces the shading time up to 80%. The foveated rendering was also proposed for real time tone mapping [10, 13].

3   Gaze-Dependent Rendering of SSAO

In the gaze-dependent SSAO technique the high frequency spatial sampling is performed in the region of interest. The further from the gaze point, the less detailed ambient factor is rendered saving computation time, while the use of eye tracker leaves observer with a feeling that the sampling is fully detailed. The outline of our gaze-dependent SSAO system is presented in Fig. 3. Observer's gaze position on the screen of the display is captured by the eye tracker (see Sect. 3.3). At the same time, the 3D scene is rendered using the Phong lighting model. Then, the ambient occlusions are calculated using varying number of samples (see Sect. 3.2). Frequency of sampling depends on the angular distance between a pixel and position of the gaze point (see Sect. 3.1). Finally, the occlusions are blended with the color image and displayed in real time on the screen.

3.1   Gaze-Dependent Contrast Sensitivity Function

The fundamental relationship describing the behavior of the human visual system is the contrast sensitivity function (CSF) [2]. It shows the dependence

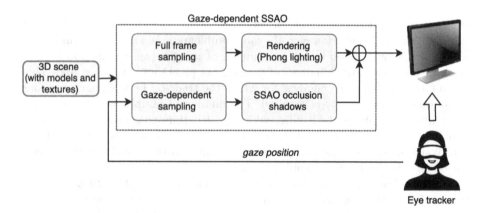

Fig. 3. Gaze-dependent screen space ambient occlusion rendering system.

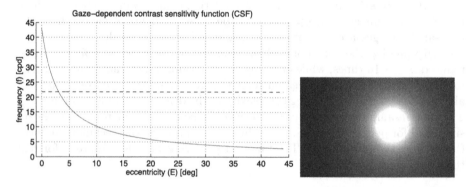

Fig. 4. Left: the most recognizable stimulus frequency as a function of eccentricity expressed (the dashed line shows the maximum frequency of our display). Right: Region-of-interest mask for an image of 1920×1080 pixel resolution (gaze position at $(1000, 500)$), brighter area depicts higher frequency of HVS. The white spot surrounding the gaze position shows an area, in which the maximum resolution of the display is reached.

between the threshold contrast visibility and the frequency of the stimulus. For a frequencies of about 4 cpd (cycles-per-degree), people are the most sensitive to contrast, i.e. they will see the pattern despite the slight differences in the brightness of its individual motifs. The CSF can be used to e.g. better compress the image by removing the high frequency details that would not be seen by humans.

An extension of the CSF, called the gaze-dependent CSF (GD-CSF), is measured for stimuli observed in various viewing angles. Following Peli et al. [5], we model the contrast sensitivity C_t for spatial frequency f at an eccentricity E with the equation:

$$C_t(E, f) = C_t(0, f) * exp(kfE), \tag{1}$$

where k determines how fast sensitivity drops off with eccentricity (the k value is ranged from 0.030 to 0.057). $C_t(0, f)$ is the contrast sensitivity for the foveal vision (equivalent to CSF). The plot of this function is presented in Fig. 4 (left).

Based on GD-CSF, for a range of eccentricities, the most recognizable stimulus frequency can be modeled by the equation [21]:

$$f_c(E) = E_1 * E_2/(E_2 + E), \tag{2}$$

where f_c denotes cut-off spatial frequency (above this frequency observer cannot identify the pattern), E_2 is retinal eccentricity at which the spatial frequency cut-off drops to half its foveal maximum ($E_1 = 43.1$), and $E_2 = 3.118$ (see details in [22]). An example region-of-interest mask computed for our display based on the above formula is presented in the right image in Fig. 4. Applying this mask, one can sample an image with varying frequency generating less samples for the peripheral regions of vision.

3.2   Region-of-Interest Sampling

In the SSAO technique, a number of samples located in the hemisphere oriented along the surface normal at the pixel is analyzed (see Sect. 2 for details). For pixels distant from the gaze point, we reduce a number of samples in the hemisphere according to Eq. 2. For each pixel in the image the eccentricity E expressed in degrees of the viewing angle is calculated. This transformation must take into account the position of the gaze point as well as physical dimensions of the display, its resolution and viewing distance. Resulting frequency $f_c(E)$ is normalized to <0, 1> and mapped to a number of samples ranging from 2 to 32. The example ambient occlusion maps generated for varying number of samples are presented in Fig. 5.

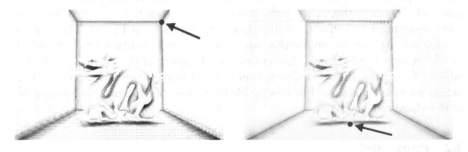

Fig. 5. The occlusion shadows with the gaze-dependent reduction of the sampling frequency. The blue arrows point the location of the gaze points. The deterioration of shadows is clearly visible in the areas farther from the gaze points. (Color figure online)

3.3   Eye Tracking

Accuracy of the eye tracking plays a crucial role in our GD-SSAO setup, because even small deviations from the actual gaze position can make the peripheral image deteriorations visible for observer. Eye tracker captures the gaze position indicated by temporary location of the pupil centre [11]. This data must be filtered because saccadic movements of the eye make the gaze position unstable [4]. A typical filtration is based on the *fixation algorithms*, that analyze velocity and/or dispersion of the gaze points and estimates the average gaze position for a time window [17]. However, the fixation techniques are also prone to accuracy errors and cannot be directly used in our system because of flickering they generate [12]. We found that temporal pooling of the fixation points generates satisfactory results. In our setup a 250 Hz eye tracker is used which frequency allowed to average 4 gaze point locations per frame. In cases of persons "incompatible" with the eye tracker (i.e. receiving significant calibration error) we increase the size of the high frequency sampling area by scaling the $f_c(E)$ value (multiplying by a number greater than one). This solution eliminates visible flickering of the occlusion shadows, however, also reduces the achieved rendering speed-up.

4   Experimental Evaluation

The main goal of the experiment was to evaluate how reduction of the SSAO sampling affects the quality of the rendered animation. We wanted to test if the peripheral image deteriorations are visible for observers. In this Section we also present a performance boost achieved due to reduced SSAO sampling.

4.1   Stimuli

In the experiment we used the Stanford dragon model[1] enclosed in the 5-walls box and Sibenik cathedral scene[2]. Three camera poses were selected for each scene resulting in 6 different images (see selected shots in Fig. 8). The images were static because we notice that an animation focuses observers's attention on object movements rather than evaluation of quality of the ambient occlusion effect. Please note, that this assumption leads to more conservative results. The image deteriorations should be less visible in the case of dynamic images because of the visual masking effect.

4.2   Procedure

We asked observer to carefully watch two images presented one by one on the screen in random order. One of these images was rendered with the full frame

---

[1] The Stanford dragon is a test model created with a Cyberware 3030 Model Shop (MS) Color 3D Scanner at Stanford University (100040 triangles).

[2] The Sibenik cathedral is a project by Marko Dabrovic (www.RNA.HR, 80841 triangles).

SSAO with 32 samples per pixel (we called it the reference image). The second image was rendered using our GD-SSAO technique with the gaze point captured by eye tracker. Each image was presented for 10 s and after this time observer were asked to assess the image quality on the 10-points Likert scale ranging from significant deteriorated image (score 0) to excellent quality (score 10). This procedure was repeated for 6 pairs of images twice, resulting in 24 images being evaluated (2 scenes x 3 camera poses x 2 repetitions x 2 images in a pair).

4.3 Participants

The experiment was repeated for 9 observers (aged between 21 and 24 years old, 7 males and 2 females). All of them had normal or corrected to normal vision. No session took longer than 10 min. The participants were naïve about the purpose of the experiment. The eye tracker were calibrated at the beginning of the session. Observer did not know if it was used while watching a given image.

4.4 Apparatus and Performance Tests

The experiment was conducted in a darkened room. Observers sit in the front of the 22-in. LCD display with the screen dimensions of 51×28.5 cm, and the native resolution of 1920×1080 pixels. To achieve the rendering framerate of 30 Hz for the full frame SSAO (32 samples per each pixel), we reduced the image resolution to 1280×720 pixels. A distance from observer's eyes to the display screen was restricted to 65 cm with a chin rest. We use SMI RED250 [18] eye tracker working with accuracy close to $1°$. Our GD-SSAO renderer was run on PC equipped with 2.66 GHz Intel Xenon W3520 CPU with 8 GB of RAM, Windows 7 64bit OS, and a GPU NVIDIA QUADRO 4000 graphics card.

For the full frame SSAO, our system was able to render 30 fps (frames-per-second) for Sibenik scene, and 35.5 fps for the Stanford Dragon. For GD-SSAO the performance increased to the average frame-rate of 47.7 fps for Sibienik and 54.7 fps for Stanford Dragon (1.59-times and 1.56-times acceleration, respectively).

Please note, that the frame-rate depends on location of the gaze point because sampling in image regions corresponding with the complex geometry of the scene is more challenging than for flat regions. For the Stanford Dragon scene the higher frame rates were achieved when observer looks at the corners of the box because the dragon was sampled with the lower frequency. For this scene the frame-rate varied from 48.8 fps to 63.2 fps. For Sibenik scene, it varied from 40.4 fps for observer looking at the centre of the screen, to 52.3 fps for the top-right corner.

It is also worth noting that acceleration in the GD-SSAO technique is related to resolution of the rendered image. Due to hardware limitation, we has to reduce this resolution to 1280×720 pixels. For the full HD or 4k resolution displays the performance boost will be correspondingly greater.

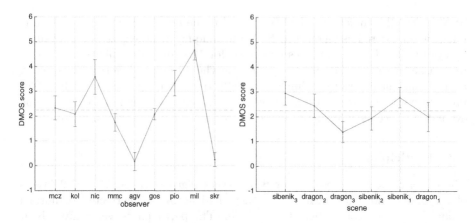

Fig. 6. Results of the quality evaluation for individual observers (left) and scene shots (right). The dashed horizontal line depicts average DMOS value. The error bars show standard error of mean. (Color figure online)

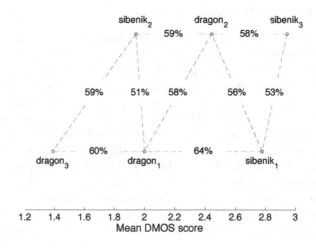

Fig. 7. Ranking graph illustrating lack of the statistically significant difference between tested scenes.

4.5 Quality Evaluation

To evaluate if the peripheral image deterioration was visible for observers we calculated the difference mean opinion score (DMOS) as a difference between the scores given for the reference full-frame SSAO rendering and for GD-SSAO with eye tracker. The score of zero would suggest that observers did not see any difference between techniques, while DMOS = 10 would mean the full disagreement for the GD-SSAO. The DMOS score computed based on the results of our experiment, averaged over all observers and all pairs of images, is equal to 2.25

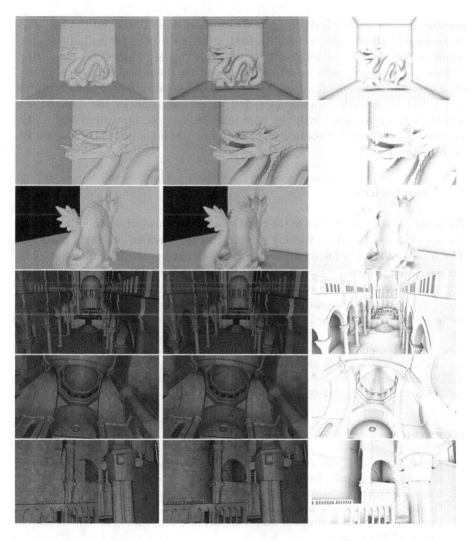

Fig. 8. Images used in the experiment. Left column presents images rendered based on the Phong shading. The ambient occlusions were added in the middle column. Column on the right shows corresponding ambient occlusion maps.

(std = 2.04), which suggests that observes noticed the quality deterioration when using eye tracker but this deterioration was negligible.

Figure 6 shows the DMOS scores for individual observers (left) and individual scene shots (right). The variation of the scores could suggest that there are different opinions between observers and for different scenes. Therefore, we perform the multiple-comparison test, which identifies statistical difference in ranking tests. After [14], the results of this analysis are presented as the ranking of the mean DMOS score for tested scene (see Fig. 7). The scenes are ordered according to increasing DMOS value, with the smallest DMOS on the left. The percentages indicate the probability that an average observer will choose the scene on the right as better than the scene on the left. If the line connecting two samplings is red and dashed, it indicates that there is no statistical difference between this pair of scenes. The probabilities close to 50% usually result in the lack of statistical significance. For higher probabilities the dashed-lines will start to be replaced with the blue lines but, as can be seen in Fig. 7, the multiple-comparison test confirms lack of the significant statistical difference for all tested scenes.

5   Conclusion

We proposed a novel concept of the SSAO technique, in which a rendering speed-up was achieved based on varying sampling of the ambient occlusion shadows. The results of the conducted experiments show that people can experience only a slight deterioration of image quality in comparison to the full frame SSAO. We argue that this deterioration is caused rather by the eye tracking temporal lag than the reduced sampling. In future work we plan to repeat the experiment using better rendering hardware and higher image resolution.

Acknowledgement. In this work we used partial results of Andrzej Czajkowski master thesis. We would like to thank you our former student for his excellent work. The project was partially funded by the Polish National Science Centre (grant number DEC-2013/09/B/ST6/02270).

References

1. Akenine-Möller, T., Haines, E., Hoffman, N.: Real-Time Rendering, 3rd edn. A. K. Peters Ltd., Natick (2008)
2. Barten, P.G.J.: Contrast Sensitivity of the Human Eye and Its Effects on Iimage Quality. SPIE Press, Bellingham (1999)
3. Bunnell, M.: Dynamic ambient occlusion and indirect lighting. In: GPU Gems 2. Addison Wesley (2005)
4. Duchowski, A.T.: Eye Tracking Methodology: Theory and Practice, 2nd edn. Springer, London (2007). https://doi.org/10.1007/978-1-84628-609-4
5. Eli Peli, J.Y., Goldstein, R.B.: Image invariance with changes in size: the role of peripheral contrast thresholds. JOSA A 8(11), 1762 (1991)
6. Guenter, B., Finch, M., Drucker, S., Tan, D., Snyder, J.: Foveated 3D graphics. ACM Trans. Graph. 31(6), 164:1–164:10 (2012)
7. Hegeman, K., Premoze, S., Ashikhmin, M., Drettakis, G.: Approximate ambient occlusion for trees. In: Proceedings of ACM Symposium in Interactive 3D Graphics and Games (I3D 2006), pp. 41–48 (2006)
8. Loschky, L.C., McConkie, G.W., Yang, J., Miller, M.E.: The limits of visual resolution in natural scene viewing. Vis. Cogn. 12, 1057–1092 (2005)
9. Mantiuk, R., Janus, S.: Gaze-dependent ambient occlusion. In: Bebis, G., et al. (eds.) ISVC 2012. LNCS, vol. 7431, pp. 523–532. Springer, Heidelberg (2012). https://doi.org/10.1007/978-3-642-33179-4_50

10. Mantiuk, R.: Gaze-dependent tone mapping for HDR video. In: Chalmers, A., Campisi, P., Shirley, P., Olaizola, I. (eds.) High Dynamic Range Video Concepts, Technologies and Applications, vol. 10, pp. 189–199. Academic Press (2016)

11. Mantiuk, R.: Accuracy of high-end and self-build eye-tracking systems. In: Kobayashi, S., Piegat, A., Pejaś, J., El Fray, I., Kacprzyk, J. (eds.) ACS 2016. AISC, vol. 534, pp. 216–227. Springer, Cham (2017). https://doi.org/10.1007/978-3-319-48429-7_20

12. Mantiuk, R., Bazyluk, B., Mantiuk, R.K.: Gaze-driven object tracking for real time rendering. Comput. Graph. Forum **32**(2), 163–173 (2013). https://doi.org/10.1111/cgf.12036, http://diglib.eg.org/EG/CGF/volume32/issue2/v32i2pp163-173.pdf

13. Mantiuk, R., Markowski, M.: Gaze-dependent tone mapping. In: Kamel, M., Campilho, A. (eds.) ICIAR 2013. LNCS, vol. 7950, pp. 426–433. Springer, Heidelberg (2013). https://doi.org/10.1007/978-3-642-39094-4_48

14. Mantiuk, R.K., Tomaszewska, A., Mantiuk, R.: Comparison of four subjective methods for image quality assessment. Comput. Graph. Forum **31**(8), 2478–2491 (2012)

15. Mittring, M.: Finding next gen-cryengine 2. In: SIGGRAPH 2007 Advanced Real-Time Rendering in 3D Graphics and Games Course Notes (2007)

16. Murphy, H.A., Duchowski, A.T., Tyrrell, R.A.: Hybrid image/model-based gaze-contingent rendering. ACM Trans. Appl. Percept. (TAP) **5**(4), 22 (2009)

17. Salvucci, D.D., Goldberg, J.H.: Identifying fixations and saccades in eye-tracking protocols. In: Proceedings of the 2000 Symposium on Eye Tracking Research & Applications (ETRA), New York, pp. 71–78 (2000)

18. SMI: RED250 Technical Specification, sensoMotoric Instruments GmbH (2009)

19. Stengel, M., Magnor, M.: Gaze-contingent computational displays: boosting perceptual fidelity. IEEE Signal Process. Mag. **33**(5), 139–148 (2016)

20. Vardis, K., Papaioannou, G., Gaitatzes, A.: Multi-view ambient occlusion with importance sampling. In: Proceedings of the ACM SIGGRAPH Symposium on Interactive 3D Graphics and Games, I3D 2013, pp. 111–118 (2013)

21. Yang, J., Coia, T., Miller, M.: Subjective evaluation of retinal-dependent image degradations. In: Proceedings of PICS 2001: Image Processing, Image Quality, Image Capture Systems, pp. 142–147. Society for Imaging Science and Technology (2001)

22. Yang, J., Qi, X., Makous, W.: Zero frequency masking and a model of contrast sensitivity. Vis. Res. **35**, 1965 (1995)

23. Zhukov, S., Iones, A., Kronin, G.: An ambient light illumination model. In: Drettakis, G., Max, N. (eds.) Rendering Techniques '98. Eurographics, pp. 45–56. Springer, Vienna (1998). https://doi.org/10.1007/978-3-7091-6453-2_5

A Fast Algorithm for Quaternion-Based 4D Rotation

Aleksandr Cariow, Galina Cariowa, and Dorota Majorkowska-Mech[(✉)]

Faculty of Computer Science and Information Technology,
West Pomeranian University of Technology Szczecin, Szczecin, Poland
dmajorkowska@wi.zut.edu.pl

Abstract. In this work, a fast algorithm for quaternion-based 4D rotation is presented which reduces the number of underlying real multiplications. Performing a quaternion-based rotation using rotation matrix takes 32 multiplications and 60 additions of real numbers while the proposed algorithm can compute the same result in only 16 real multiplications (or multipliers - in hardware implementation case) and 56 additions.

1 Introduction

Quaternion rotation is a powerful tool for rotating vectors in 3D and 4D. As a result, it has been used in various fields of science [1] and engineering including navigation, orbital mechanics of satellites, robotics [2], autonomous vehicles [3,4], digital signal and image processing [5–12], computer graphics and machine vision [13,14], wireless communications [15], public-key cryptography [16], crystallographic texture analysis, etc. Using unit quaternions is a most natural, elegant, and practical way to describe a rotation in 4-dimensional space. However, the direct applying of quaternions for rotation in 4D space requires a relatively large amount of computation. For that reason, this operation is usually implemented via multiplication of a vector by so-called "rotation matrix", which is simply calculated based on the coefficients of the quaternion [17–19]. Nevertheless, even this way requires a relatively large amount of computation. In the rest of this article, we will show a new algorithm that requires fewer calculations than the algorithm that uses a rotation matrix.

2 Preliminary Remarks

A point in 4-dimensional space with Cartesian coordinates (u, x, y, z) may be represented by a quaternion $P = u + xi + yj + zk$, where $ij = k$, $jk = i$, $ki = j$, $ji = -k$, $kj = -i$, $ik = -j$ and $i^2 = j^2 = k^2 = -1$. Let $L = a + bi + cj + dk$ and $R = p + qi + rj + sk$ be unit quaternions $(a^2 + b^2 + c^2 + d^2 = 1, p^2 + q^2 + r^2 + s^2 = 1)$. In quaternion language we can interpret the 4D rotation as follows [17]:

$$u' + x'i + y'j + z'k = (a + bi + cj + dk)(u + xi + yj + zk)(p + qi + rj + sk). \quad (1)$$

© Springer Nature Switzerland AG 2018
L. J. Chmielewski et al. (Eds.): ICCVG 2018, LNCS 11114, pp. 28–37, 2018.
https://doi.org/10.1007/978-3-030-00692-1_3

In the matrix-vector form the Eq. (1) can be rewritten as follows:

$$\mathbf{y}_4 = \mathbf{L}_4 \mathbf{R}_4 \mathbf{x}_4 \tag{2}$$

where

$$\mathbf{L}_4 = \begin{bmatrix} a & -b & -c & -d \\ b & a & -d & c \\ c & d & a & -b \\ d & -c & b & a \end{bmatrix}, \quad \mathbf{R}_4 = \begin{bmatrix} p & -q & -r & -s \\ q & p & s & -r \\ r & -s & p & q \\ s & r & -q & p \end{bmatrix},$$

and

$$\mathbf{x}_4 = [u, x, y, z]^\mathrm{T}, \quad \mathbf{y}_4 = [u', x', y', z']^\mathrm{T}.$$

Direct implementation of the calculations in accordance with these equations requires 32 multiplications and 24 additions of real numbers. It is well known, that the product of the matrices included in expression (2) can be calculated in advance. Then we obtain:

$$\begin{bmatrix} u' \\ x' \\ y' \\ z' \end{bmatrix} = \begin{bmatrix} a & -b & -c & -d \\ b & a & -d & c \\ c & d & a & -b \\ d & -c & b & a \end{bmatrix} \begin{bmatrix} p & -q & -r & -s \\ q & p & s & -r \\ r & -s & p & q \\ s & r & -q & p \end{bmatrix} \begin{bmatrix} u \\ x \\ y \\ z \end{bmatrix} = \begin{bmatrix} a_{00} & a_{01} & a_{02} & a_{03} \\ a_{10} & a_{11} & a_{12} & a_{13} \\ a_{20} & a_{21} & a_{22} & a_{23} \\ a_{30} & a_{31} & a_{32} & a_{33} \end{bmatrix} \begin{bmatrix} u \\ x \\ y \\ z \end{bmatrix}$$

where

$$\begin{array}{ll} a_{00} = ap - bq - cr - ds, & a_{01} = -aq - bp + cs - dr, \\ a_{02} = -ar - bs - cp + dq, & a_{03} = -as + br - cq - dp, \\ a_{10} = bp + aq - dr + cs, & a_{11} = -bq + ap + ds + cr, \\ a_{12} = -br + as - dp - cq, & a_{13} = -bs - ar - dq + cp, \\ a_{20} = cp + dq + ar - bs, & a_{21} = -cq + dp - as - br, \\ a_{22} = -cr + ds + ap + bq, & a_{23} = -cs - dr + aq - bp, \\ a_{30} = dp - cq + br + as, & a_{31} = -dq - cp - bs + ar, \\ a_{32} = -dr - cs + bp - aq, & a_{33} = -ds + cr + bq + ap. \end{array}$$

It is easy to see that the calculation of the entries of the rotation matrix requires 16 conventional multiplications and 48 additions. Multiplication of a vector by this matrix requires 16 more multiplications and 12 additions. Thus, 32 multiplications and 60 additions are required to rotate the point in 4D space. A fully parallel implementation of the rotation operation requires 32 multipliers and 60 adders. A multiplier is the most critical block, so reducing the number of multipliers is essential. We will show how this can be done.

3   The Algorithm

The idea is that both the matrix $\mathbf{L}_4$ and the matrix $\mathbf{R}_4$ in expression (2) can be decomposed as an algebraic sum of a symmetric Toeplitz matrix and another matrix which has many zero entries. The Toeplitz matrix is shift-structured and a number of algorithms exist for fast matrix-vector multiplication. For instance, the matrix can be diagonalized using the fast Hadamard transform (FHT) and thus matrix-vector products can be computed efficiently. To compute the product $\mathbf{R}_4\mathbf{x}_4$ let us multiply the first row of $\mathbf{R}_4$ by (-1). This transformation is done in order to present a modified in this manner matrix as an algebraic sum of the block-symmetric Toeplitz-type matrix and some sparse matrix, i.e. matrix containing only a small number of nonzero entries. We can easily see that this transformation leads to minimize the computational complexity of the final algorithm. Then we can rewrite the product $\mathbf{R}_4\mathbf{x}_4$ in the following form [20]:

$$\mathbf{z}_4 = \mathbf{R}_4\mathbf{x}_4 = \bar{\mathbf{I}}_4(\hat{\mathbf{R}}_4 - 2\check{\mathbf{R}}_4)\mathbf{x}_4 \tag{3}$$

were

$$\hat{\mathbf{R}}_4 = \begin{bmatrix} p\,q\,r\,s \\ q\,p\,s\,r \\ r\,s\,p\,q \\ s\,r\,q\,p \end{bmatrix}, \quad \check{\mathbf{R}}_4 = \begin{bmatrix} p\,0\,0\,0 \\ 0\,0\,0\,r \\ 0\,s\,0\,0 \\ 0\,0\,q\,0 \end{bmatrix}, \quad \bar{\mathbf{I}}_4 = \begin{bmatrix} -1\,0\,0\,0 \\ 0\,1\,0\,0 \\ 0\,0\,1\,0 \\ 0\,0\,0\,1 \end{bmatrix} \text{ and } \mathbf{z}_4 = [z_0, z_1, z_2, z_3]^{\mathrm{T}}.$$

In this case the matrix-vector product $\hat{\mathbf{R}}_4\mathbf{x}_4$ (with Toeplitz-type matrix) can now be calculated using one of the well-known fast algorithms. Indeed, it is easy to see that $\hat{\mathbf{R}}_4$ has the following structure:

$$\hat{\mathbf{R}}_4 = \left[\begin{array}{c|c} \mathbf{A}_2 & \mathbf{B}_2 \\ \hline \mathbf{B}_2 & \mathbf{A}_2 \end{array} \right],$$

where

$$\mathbf{A}_2 = \begin{bmatrix} p\,q \\ q\,p \end{bmatrix}, \quad \mathbf{B}_2 = \begin{bmatrix} r\,s \\ s\,r \end{bmatrix}.$$

Then we can calculate the product of $\hat{\mathbf{R}}_4\mathbf{x}_4$ with the following decomposition:

$$\hat{\mathbf{R}}_4\mathbf{x}_4 = (\mathbf{H}_2 \otimes \mathbf{I}_2)\frac{1}{2}[(\mathbf{A}_2 + \mathbf{B}_2) \oplus (\mathbf{A}_2 - \mathbf{B}_2)](\mathbf{H}_2 \otimes \mathbf{I}_2)\mathbf{x}_4 \tag{4}$$

where

$$\mathbf{A}_2 + \mathbf{B}_2 = \begin{bmatrix} p+r\,q+s \\ q+s\,p+r \end{bmatrix}, \quad \mathbf{A}_2 - \mathbf{B}_2 = \begin{bmatrix} p-r\,q-s \\ q-s\,p-r \end{bmatrix}, \quad \mathbf{H}_2 = \begin{bmatrix} 1\,\ \ 1 \\ 1\,-1 \end{bmatrix} -$$

is the order 2 Hadamard matrix, $\mathbf{I}_N$ - is the order N identity matrix, and $\otimes$, $\oplus$ - denote the tensor product and direct sum of two matrices, respectively [20,21]. It is easy to see that the matrices $\mathbf{A}_2 + \mathbf{B}_2$ and $\mathbf{A}_2 - \mathbf{B}_2$ possess structures that provide "good" decompositions too. Therefore, similar to the previous case, we can write:

$$\mathbf{A}_2 + \mathbf{B}_2 = \mathbf{H}_2\left\{ \frac{1}{2}[(p+r+q+s) \oplus (p+r-q-s)] \right\}\mathbf{H}_2,$$

$$\mathbf{A}_2 - \mathbf{B}_2 = \mathbf{H}_2\left\{ \frac{1}{2}[(p-r+q-s) \oplus (p-r-q+s)] \right\}\mathbf{H}_2.$$

Combining partial decompositions in a single procedure we can rewrite (4) as follows:

$$\hat{\mathbf{R}}_4\mathbf{x}_4 = \mathbf{W}_4^{(0)}\mathbf{W}_4^{(1)}\mathbf{D}_4^{(1)}\mathbf{W}_4^{(1)}\mathbf{W}_4^{(0)}\mathbf{x}_4 \tag{5}$$

where

$$\mathbf{W}_4^{(0)} = \mathbf{H}_2 \otimes \mathbf{I}_2 = \begin{bmatrix} 1 & 0 & 1 & 0 \\ 0 & 1 & 0 & 1 \\ 1 & 0 & -1 & 0 \\ 0 & 1 & 0 & -1 \end{bmatrix}, \quad \mathbf{W}_4^{(1)} = \mathbf{I}_2 \otimes \mathbf{H}_2 = \begin{bmatrix} 1 & 1 & 0 & 0 \\ 1 & -1 & 0 & 0 \\ 0 & 0 & 1 & 1 \\ 0 & 0 & 1 & -1 \end{bmatrix},$$

$$\mathbf{D}_4^{(1)} = \mathrm{diag}(s_0, s_1, s_2, s_3),$$

$$s_0 = \frac{1}{4}(p + r + q + s), \quad s_1 = \frac{1}{4}(p + r - q - s),$$

$$s_2 = \frac{1}{4}(p - r + q - s), \quad s_3 = \frac{1}{4}(p - r - q + s).$$

It is easy to see that the diagonal entries of the matrix $\mathbf{D}_4^{(1)}$ can be calculated using the following matrix-vector procedure:

$$\mathbf{d}_4 = \frac{1}{4}\mathbf{W}_4^{(1)}\mathbf{W}_4^{(0)}\mathbf{r}_4 \tag{6}$$

where

$$\mathbf{d}_4 = [s_0, s_1, s_2, s_3]^{\mathrm{T}}, \quad \mathbf{r}_4 = [p, q, r, s]^{\mathrm{T}}.$$

Unfortunately, the computational complexity of the product $2\check{\mathbf{R}}_4\mathbf{x}_4$ cannot be reduced and this product is calculated directly, without any tricks. Combining the calculations for both matrices in a single procedure we finally obtain:

$$\mathbf{z}_4 = \mathbf{R}_4\mathbf{x}_4 = \bar{\mathbf{I}}_4\mathbf{\Sigma}_{4\times8}\mathbf{W}_8^{(2)}\mathbf{W}_8^{(1)}\mathbf{D}_8^{(1)}\mathbf{W}_8^{(1)}\mathbf{W}_8^{(0)}\mathbf{P}_{8\times4}\mathbf{x}_4 \tag{7}$$

where

$$\mathbf{P}_{8\times4} = \mathbf{1}_{2\times1} \otimes \mathbf{I}_4 = \begin{bmatrix} 1 & 0 & 0 & 0 \\ 0 & 1 & 0 & 0 \\ 0 & 0 & 1 & 0 \\ 0 & 0 & 0 & 1 \\ 1 & 0 & 0 & 0 \\ 0 & 1 & 0 & 0 \\ 0 & 0 & 1 & 0 \\ 0 & 0 & 0 & 1 \end{bmatrix}, \quad \mathbf{1}_{2\times1} = [1, 1]^{\mathrm{T}},$$

$$\mathbf{W}_8^{(0)} = (\mathbf{H}_2 \otimes \mathbf{I}_2) \oplus \mathbf{P}_4^{(0)} = \left[\begin{array}{cccc:cccc} 1 & 0 & 1 & 0 & & & & \\ 0 & 1 & 0 & 1 & & \mathbf{0}_4 & & \\ 1 & 0 & -1 & 0 & & & & \\ 0 & 1 & 0 & -1 & & & & \\ \hdashline & & & & 1 & 0 & 0 & 0 \\ & \mathbf{0}_4 & & & 0 & 0 & 0 & 1 \\ & & & & 0 & 1 & 0 & 0 \\ & & & & 0 & 0 & 1 & 0 \end{array}\right], \quad \mathbf{P}_4^{(0)} = \begin{bmatrix} 1 & 0 & 0 & 0 \\ 0 & 0 & 0 & 1 \\ 0 & 1 & 0 & 0 \\ 0 & 0 & 1 & 0 \end{bmatrix},$$

$$\mathbf{W}_8^{(1)} = (\mathbf{I}_2 \otimes \mathbf{H}_2) \oplus \mathbf{I}_4 = \left[\begin{array}{cc:cc:cccc} 1 & 1 & & & & & & \\ 1 & -1 & \mathbf{0}_2 & & & \mathbf{0}_4 & & \\ \hdashline & & 1 & 1 & & & & \\ \mathbf{0}_2 & & 1 & -1 & & & & \\ \hdashline & & & & 1 & 0 & 0 & 0 \\ & \mathbf{0}_4 & & & 0 & 1 & 0 & 0 \\ & & & & 0 & 0 & 1 & 0 \\ & & & & 0 & 0 & 0 & 1 \end{array}\right],$$

$$\mathbf{D}_8^{(1)} = \mathrm{diag}(s_0, s_1, s_2, s_3, s_4, s_5, s_6, s_7),$$

$$s_4 = 2p, \ s_5 = 2r, \ s_6 = 2s, \ s_7 = 2q,$$

and s_0, s_1, s_2, s_3 are the diagonal entries of the matrix $\mathbf{D}_4^{(1)}$,

$$\mathbf{W}_8^{(2)} = (\mathbf{H}_2 \otimes \mathbf{I}_2) \oplus \mathbf{I}_4 = \left[\begin{array}{cccc:cccc} 1 & 0 & 1 & 0 & & & & \\ 0 & 1 & 0 & 1 & & \mathbf{0}_4 & & \\ 1 & 0 & -1 & 0 & & & & \\ 0 & 1 & 0 & -1 & & & & \\ \hdashline & & & & 1 & 0 & 0 & 0 \\ & \mathbf{0}_4 & & & 0 & 1 & 0 & 0 \\ & & & & 0 & 0 & 1 & 0 \\ & & & & 0 & 0 & 0 & 1 \end{array}\right],$$

$$\mathbf{\Sigma}_{4\times 8} = (\bar{\mathbf{1}}_{1\times 2} \otimes \mathbf{I}_4) = \left[\begin{array}{cccc:cccc} 1 & 0 & 0 & 0 & -1 & 0 & 0 & 0 \\ 0 & 1 & 0 & 0 & 0 & -1 & 0 & 0 \\ 0 & 0 & 1 & 0 & 0 & 0 & -1 & 0 \\ 0 & 0 & 0 & 1 & 0 & 0 & 0 & -1 \end{array}\right], \quad \bar{\mathbf{1}}_{1\times 2} = [1, -1].$$

It is easy to see that the diagonal entries of the matrix $\mathbf{D}_8^{(1)}$ can be calculated using the following matrix-vector procedure:

$$\mathbf{d}_8^{(1)} = \hat{\mathbf{D}}_8 \mathbf{W}_8^{(1)} \mathbf{W}_8^{(3)} \mathbf{P}_{8\times 4} \mathbf{r}_4 \tag{8}$$

where

$$d_8^{(1)} = [s_0, s_1, s_2, s_3, s_4, s_5, s_6, s_7]^T,$$

$$\hat{D}_8 = \text{diag}\left(\frac{1}{4}, \frac{1}{4}, \frac{1}{4}, \frac{1}{4}, 2, 2, 2, 2\right),$$

$$W_8^{(3)} = (H_2 \otimes I_2) \oplus P_4^{(1)} = \begin{bmatrix} \begin{array}{cccc} 1 & 0 & 1 & 0 \\ 0 & 1 & 0 & 1 \\ 1 & 0 & -1 & 0 \\ 0 & 1 & 0 & -1 \end{array} & 0_4 \\ 0_4 & \begin{array}{cccc} 1 & 0 & 0 & 0 \\ 0 & 0 & 1 & 0 \\ 0 & 0 & 0 & 1 \\ 0 & 1 & 0 & 0 \end{array} \end{bmatrix}, \quad P_4^{(1)} = \begin{bmatrix} 1 & 0 & 0 & 0 \\ 0 & 0 & 1 & 0 \\ 0 & 0 & 0 & 1 \\ 0 & 1 & 0 & 0 \end{bmatrix}.$$

To obtain $y_4 = L_4 z_4$, where $z_4 = R_4 x_4$ is regarded as being computed earlier, we will act in the same way as before. Namely, we multiply the first row of L_4 by (-1). Then it is easy to see that the matrix-vector product $L_4 z_4$ can be represented in the following form:

$$y_4 = L_4 z_4 = \bar{I}_4 (\hat{L}_4 - 2\check{L}_4) z_4 \tag{9}$$

were

$$\hat{L}_4 = \begin{bmatrix} a & b & c & d \\ b & a & d & c \\ c & d & a & b \\ d & c & b & a \end{bmatrix}, \quad \check{L}_4 = \begin{bmatrix} a & 0 & 0 & 0 \\ 0 & 0 & d & 0 \\ 0 & 0 & 0 & b \\ 0 & c & 0 & 0 \end{bmatrix}.$$

It is easy to see that we are dealing again with the same matrix structures. Thus, in this case, all the previous steps related to the synthesis of the algorithm for calculating the product $R_4 x_4$ can be repeated for calculating the product $L_4 z_4$ too. By analogy with the previous one, we can write:

$$y_4 = L_4 z_4 = \bar{I}_4 \Sigma_{4 \times 8} W_8^{(2)} W_8^{(1)} D_8^{(2)} W_8^{(1)} W_8^{(3)} P_{8 \times 4} z_4. \tag{10}$$

The diagonal entries of the matrix $D_8^{(2)} = \text{diag}(c_0, c_1, c_2, c_3, c_4, c_5, c_6, c_7)$ can be calculated using the following matrix-vector procedure:

$$d_8^{(2)} = \hat{D}_8 W_8^{(1)} W_8^{(0)} P_{8 \times 4} l_4 \tag{11}$$

where $l_4 = [a, b, c, d]^T$, $d_8^{(2)} = [c_0, c_1, c_2, c_3, c_4, c_5, c_6, c_7]^T$ and

$$c_0 = \frac{1}{4}(a + c + b + d), \quad c_1 = \frac{1}{4}(a + c - b - d),$$

$$c_2 = \frac{1}{4}(a - c + b - d), \quad c_3 = \frac{1}{4}(a - c - b + d),$$

$$c_4 = 2a, \quad c_5 = 2d, \quad c_6 = 2b, \quad c_7 = 2c.$$

Thus, we can describe the final procedure for computing the vector $\mathbf{y}_4$ as follows:

$$\mathbf{y}_4 = \bar{\mathbf{I}}_4 \Sigma_{4\times8} \mathbf{W}_8^{(2)} \mathbf{W}_8^{(1)} \mathbf{D}_8^{(2)} \mathbf{W}_8^{(1)} \mathbf{W}_8^{(3)} \mathbf{P}_{8\times4} \bar{\mathbf{I}}_4 \Sigma_{4\times8} \mathbf{W}_8^{(2)} \mathbf{W}_8^{(1)} \mathbf{D}_8^{(1)} \mathbf{W}_8^{(1)} \mathbf{W}_8^{(0)} \mathbf{P}_{8\times4} \mathbf{x}_4. \quad (12)$$

Realization of computations in accordance with (12) requires 16 multiplications and 56 additions of real numbers.

Figure 1 shows a data flow diagram representation of the rationalized algorithm for computation of coordinates of the rotated vector and Fig. 2 shows a data flow diagram of the process for calculating the nonzero entries of the diagonal matrices $\mathbf{D}_8^{(1)}$ and $\mathbf{D}_8^{(2)}$. In this paper, data flow diagrams are oriented from left to right. Straight lines in the figures denote the operations of data transfer. Points, where lines converge, denote summation (the dash-dotted lines indicate the subtraction operation). We use the usual lines without arrows on purpose, so as not to clutter the picture. The circles in these figures show the operation of multiplication by a number (variable or constant) inscribed inside a circle. In turn, the rectangles indicate the matrix-vector multiplications with the (2×2)-Hadamard matrices.

From an examination of Fig. 2 it can be seen that the algorithm contains the multiplication by numbers, which are different powers of two. These operations are reduced to ordinary shifts to the left (or right) on a number of positions. Because of the ease of implementation, these operations are usually not taken into account when assessing the computational complexity.

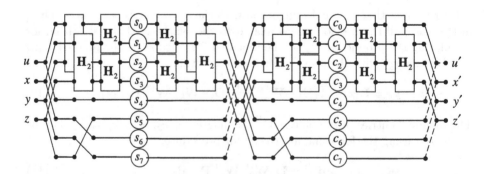

Fig. 1. Data flow diagram of the rationalized algorithm for computation coordinates of the rotated vector in 4D space.

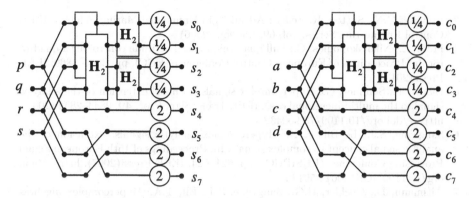

Fig. 2. Data flow diagram of the process for calculating the nonzero entries of the diagonal matrices $\mathbf{D}_8^{(1)}$ and $\mathbf{D}_8^{(2)}$.

4 Conclusion

The article presents a new algorithm for 4D spatial rotation. To reduce computational complexity, we utilized algorithmic tricks, which we used earlier in the fast algorithm for multiplying quaternions [22]. Our algorithm contains twice fewer multiplications in comparison with the naive way of implementing computations and almost as many additions as the naive algorithm. This results in a reduction in hardware implementation cost and allows the effective use of parallelization of computations. Reducing the number of multiplications is especially important in the design of specialized onboard VLSI processors because minimizing the number of necessary multipliers also reduces the power dissipation and lowers the implementation cost of the entire system. It is known that the implementation complexity of an embedded multiplier grows quadratically with operand size, while the implementation complexity of a binary adder increases linearly with operand size. Therefore a hardware multiplier is more complicated unit than an adder and occupies much more chip area than the adder. Even if the VLSI chip already contains embedded multipliers, as it happens in the case of modern FPGAs, their number is always limited. This means that if the implemented algorithm has a large number of multiplications, the synthesized processor may not always fit into the chip and the problem of reducing the number of multipliers still remains relevant.

References

1. Yefremov, A.P.: Quaternions: algebra, geometry and physical theories. Hypercomplex Numbers Geom. Phys. **1**, 104–119 (2004)
2. Hu, C., Meng, M.Q.-H., Mandal, M., Liu, P.X.: Robot rotation decomposition using quaternions. In: Proceedings of the 2006 IEEE International Conference on Mechatronics and Automation, pp. 1158–1163. IEEE Press (2006). https://doi.org/10.1109/ICMA.2006.257789

3. Roberts, G.N., Sutton, R., (eds.): Advances in Unmanned Marine Vehicles. IEEE Control Engineering Series, vol. 69, London (2006)
4. Fresk, E., Nikolakopoulos, G.: Full quaternion based attitude control for a quadrotor. In: Proceedings of European Control Conference (ECC), pp. 3864–3869. IEEE Press (2013)
5. Bülow, T., Sommer, G.: Hypercomplex signals - a novel extension of the analytic signal to the multidimensional case. IEEE Trans. Sign. Proc. **49**, 2844–2852 (2001). https://doi.org/10.1109/78.960432
6. Sangwine, S.J., Le Bihan, N.: Hypercomplex analytic signals: extension of the analytic signal concept to complex signals. In: Proceedings of 15th European Signal Processing Conference (EUSIPCO), pp. 621–624. IEEE Press (2007). https://doi.org/10.1109/ICIP.2001.959190
7. Alfsmann, D., Göckler, H.G., Sangwine, S.J., Ell, T.A.: Hypercomplex algebras in digital signal processing: benefits and drawbacks (Tutorial). In: Proceedings of 15th European Signal Processing Conference (EUSIPCO), pp. 1322–1326. IEEE Press (2007)
8. Pei, S.-C., Ding, J.-J., Chang, J.-H.: Color pattern recognition by quaternion correlation. In: Proceedings of IEEE International Conference on Image Processing, pp. 847–849. IEEE Press (2001). https://doi.org/10.1109/ICIP.2001.959190
9. Pei, S.-C., Ding, J.-J., Chang, J.-H.: Efficient implementation of quaternion fourier transform, convolution, and correlation by 2-D complex FFT. IEEE Trans. Sign. Proc. **49**, 2783–2797 (2001). https://doi.org/10.1109/78.960426
10. Ell, T.A.: Quaternion-Fourier transforms for analysis of two-dimensional linear time-invariant partial differential systems. In: Proceedings of the 32nd IEEE Conference on Decision and Control, pp. 1830–1841. IEEE Press (1993). https://doi.org/10.1109/CDC.1993.325510
11. Witten, B., Shragge, J.: Quaternion-based signal processing. In: Proceedings of 2006 SEG Annual Meeting, pp. 2862–2865. Society of Exploration Geophysicists Press (2006)
12. Bayro-Corrochano, E.: The theory and use of the quaternion wavelet transform. J. Math. Imaging Vis. **24**, 19–35 (2006). https://doi.org/10.1007/s10851-005-3605-3
13. Vince, J.: Quaternions for Computer Graphics. Springer, London (2011). https://doi.org/10.1007/978-0-85729-760-0
14. Hanson, A.J.: Visualizing Quaternions. The Morgan Kaufmann Series in Interactive 3D Technology. Elsevier Inc., New York (2006)
15. Wysocki, B.J., Wysocki, T.A., Seberry, J.: Modeling dual polarization wireless fading channels using quaternions. In: Joint IST Workshop on Mobile Future, 2006 and the Symposium on Trends in Communications. SympoTIC 2006, pp. 68–71. IEEE Press (2006). https://doi.org/10.1109/TIC.2006.1708024
16. Malekian, E., Zakerolhosseini, A., Mashatan, A.: QTRU: quaternionic version of the NTRU public-key cryptosystems. ISC Int. J. Inf. Secur. **3**, 29–42 (2011)
17. Mebius, J.E.: A matrix-based proof of the quaternion representation theorem for four-dimensional rotations. arXiv:math/0501249 (2005)
18. Weiner, J.L., Wilkens, G.R.: Quaternions and rotations in E^4. Am. Math. Monthly **112**, 69–76 (2005)
19. Angeles, J.: Fundamentals of Robotic Mechanical Systems: Theory, Methods, and Algorithms. Springer, Switzerland (2006). https://doi.org/10.1007/978-3-319-01851-5
20. Cariow, A.: Strategies for the synthesis of fast algorithms for the computation of the matrix-vector products. J. Sig. Process. Theor. Appl. **3**, 1–19 (2014). https://doi.org/10.7726/jspta.2014.1001

21. Steeb, W.-H., Hardy, Y.: Matrix Calculus and Kronecker Product: A Practical Approach to Linear and Multilinear Algebra. World Scientific Publishing Company (2011)
22. Ţariova, G., Ţariov, A.: Aspekty algorytmiczne redukcji liczby bloków mnożących w układzie do obliczania iloczynu dwóch kwaternionów [Algorithmic aspects of multiplication block number reduction in a two quaternion hardware multiplier]. Pomiary Automatyka Kontrola **56**, 688–690 (2010). (in Polish)

A Study on Image Comparison Metrics for Atmospheric Scattering Phenomenon Rendering

Tomasz Gałaj$^{(\boxtimes)}$ and Adam Wojciechowski

Institute of Information Technology, Łódź University of Technology, Łódź, Poland
`tomasz.galaj@edu.p.lodz.pl`, `adam.wojciechowski@p.lodz.pl`

Abstract. Though reference image quality can be calculated with several, well established, comparison methods, images synthesizing light atmospheric scattering phenomenon require adequate evaluation approaches. Current metrics concentrate mainly on noise ratio, entropy or simple pixels correlation coefficients. Thus methods require images strict adequacy in structure and position of their components. On the other hand, light atmospheric scattering renders, synthesized with different methods, should concentrate on their structural representation and possible color gradients rather than direct correspondence of individual pixels. The paper presents a study on image comparison methods in a context of light atmospheric scattering phenomenon. We have focused on several, most popular image comparison metrics like Pearson Correlation Coefficient (PCC), Structural Similarity (SSIM), Multi-Scale Structural Similarity (MS-SSIM) and Perceptual Difference (PD). We compare this metrics in terms of clear sky synthesis problem and try to select the most relevant metrics for the stated phenomenon. The conclusion and discussion provides a handful of suggestions concerning phenomenon related metrics selection.

1 Introduction

Rendering of a light atmospheric scattering phenomenon is a very time consuming task which requires a lot of computations, even on the most modern GPUs. It becomes a crucial aspect affecting performance and perception quality [5] of contemporary games and virtual environments [7]. Many authors [1,2,4,13] have developed fast and quite accurate methods to provide visually acceptable and reliable sky renders. However telling which synthetic image of the generated clear (without clouds) sky is better and why, is not a trivial problem. Therefore, there is a need for elaboration of objective, problem dedicated, metrics that can compare two synthetic sky images and tell which image is more accurate and has the lowest error.

The exemplary rendered images of the sunset skies are shown in Fig. 1. We can observe that gradients in the presented images are very non-uniform. In some image regions they are subtle and images differences are very small while in some

L. J. Chmielewski et al. (Eds.): ICCVG 2018, LNCS 11114, pp. 38–47, 2018.
https://doi.org/10.1007/978-3-030-00692-1_4

other regions (especially at the horizon) differences are highly perceptible. In this case, we need a very precise and sensitive metric that will catch these non-uniform changes, at different image resolutions [14] and image specific segments [6,15,20].

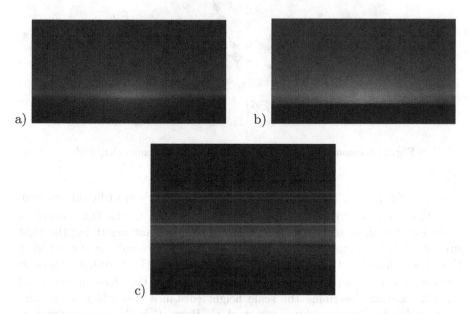

Fig. 1. Example images presenting synthetic clear sky images rendered by means of (a) midpoint rule integration, (b) Bruneton's model [1], (c) Elek's model [4].

In the following sections we describe how authors of selected light atmospheric scattering rendering methods evaluated resulting images. Next we describe experiments on light scattering phenomenon renders evaluation with selected quality metrics. Then we discuss the obtained results and conclude with selection of the most appropriate metric to the presented problem. Moreover, we provide a set of suggestions applicable to light atmospheric scattering phenomenon in terms of image quality metrics selection.

2 Related Work

Light atmospheric scattering rendering is usually computed by means of numerical integration of Eq. 1 (called Light Transport Equation [9]) for each pixel within current digital camera field of view. The camera viewing volume originates in point P_a and is oriented along camera viewing direction (vector $\overrightarrow{V}$ in Fig. 2).

$$I_v(\lambda) = I_s(\lambda)K(\lambda)F(\theta,g)\int_{P_a}^{P_b}(e^{\frac{-h(P)}{H_0}} \cdot e^{-t(PP_c,\lambda)-t(PP_a,\lambda)})dP \qquad (1)$$

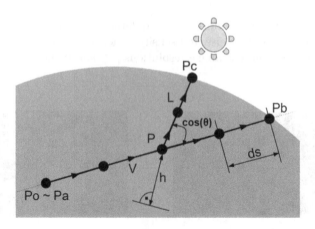

Fig. 2. Schematic of how the single scattering is being calculated.

In the Eq. 1, term P_a is the location of the observer's eye (digital camera), $\vec{V}$ is the observer's view direction, $\vec{L}$ is the direction to the light source, λ is the wavelength of scattered light. $I_s(\lambda)$ is the constant describing the light intensity, $K(\lambda)$ is a constant describing the amount of molecules at the sea level, $F(\theta, g)$ is a phase function (e.g. Henyey-Greenstein phase function), θ is an angle between vector $\vec{V}$ and $\vec{L}$, g is the asymmetry factor of the phase function and H_0 is a constant describing the scale height (distance over which a quantity of air molecules decreases by a factor of e). Point P is the sample point at altitude h, P_b is the intersection point of vector $\vec{V}$ and the atmosphere. P_c is the intersection point of the vector coming from $\vec{L}$ and the atmosphere. What is more, function $t(P_a P_b, \lambda)$ describes the optical depth (transmittance) and is expressed with Eq. 2. We also assume that all sun light rays are parallel.

$$t(P_a P_b, \lambda) = 4\pi K(\lambda) \int_{P_a}^{P_b} e^{\frac{-h(P)}{H_0}} dP \qquad (2)$$

Researchers that tackled the problem of the light atmospheric scattering synthesis, calculated the Eq. 1 using various numerical methods (the most frequently used method is Trapezoidal Rule) and then intended to validate the obtained results. It will be described further in this section.

Nishita et al. [11,12] were the first who developed a method to efficiently calculate the Eq. 1 as to create synthetic images of the clear sky. For each pixel, they numerically computed the integral along the corresponding view ray. To avoid computing the double integral, Nishita et al. computed the first transmittance term incrementally, while evaluating the outer integral, and precomputed the second transmittance term in a 2D lookup table. Their method did not enable user to change atmosphere's density (e.g. to visualize different planet's sky) due to pre-computed values in a lookup table. Unfortunately, they did not use any validation method or metric to objectively tell how good their method is.

They just showed the NASDA's photographs [11] as a reference and were theoretically discussing the differences between rendered images and reference photographs.

Bruneton et al. [1] created the first method of calculating the atmospheric scattering equation, including single and multiple scattering [1] terms, using precomputed (using 4D table) values of the atmospheric scattering equation. The rendering results validation method relied on comparing the relative luminance of renders obtained using their method, and images obtained using the CIE clear sky model (it is a physically accurate model which is controlled by two illuminance values [3]). So far, this is the most scientific approach to objectively tell how good is the Bruneton's method in area of simulating the light atmospheric scattering as it refers to physically accurate sky model.

Elek [4] enhanced the Bruneton's method. Instead of using 4D lookup table, he was able to store all of the required data in a 3D lookup table. Unfortunately, he did not validate the obtained results in terms of quality of the clear sky renders. He only focused on time and memory complexity of his algorithm.

Bruneton [2] created a framework to evaluate 8 clear sky rendering methods. He compared these methods with the ground truth data with the *libRadtran* library. He compared, among others, fisheye renderings, absolute luminance, relative luminance, chromaticity and relative mean square error of provided images. So far, this is the most scientific approach to evaluate the clear sky models and the most accurate since it compares the highest number of parameters of each method with the ground truth data [10].

The methods of the light atmospheric scattering calculation, give very interesting insight into efficient rendering of light atmospheric scattering phenomenon, but it is very hard to tell which method gives the best results and why. It is mainly due to the fact that the authors of the discussed methods neglected rendering quality metrics. They have used very basic image comparison metrics to compare their results with the reference. They did not take into account other image features (apart from the relative luminance) like image structure or contrast. In the following sections we will try to fill this hole by verifying selected quality metrics for comparing synthetic renders of different quality. The reference images were generated using the same numerical integration method - Trapezoidal Rule, but with different integration and camera settings.

3 Image Quality Comparative Metrics

We have selected four metrics to compare the quality of the source image with the reference image. These metrics were especially used in the *image processing* applications (e.g. monitoring image compression quality). However, these metrics are not so popular in the field of modeling and rendering the light atmospheric scattering phenomenon.

The image comparison metrics, that we have chosen these are: Pearson Correlation Coefficient (PCC) [8], Structural Similarity (SSIM) [17], Multi-Scale Structural Similarity (MS-SSIM) [16] and Perceptual Difference (PD) [19].

PCC metric is a measure of linear correlation between two variables X and Y. In our case variable X contains the relative luminance values of the reference image, and variable Y contains the luminance values of the compared image. PCC is described with Eq. 3, where $cov(X,Y)$ is the covariance of the variables X and Y, σ_X is the standard deviation of X and σ_Y is the standard deviation of Y.

$$\rho_{X,Y} = \frac{cov(X,Y)}{\sigma_X \sigma_Y} \tag{3}$$

To calculate the luminance values of the RGB images we use Eq. 4, where R, G and B - are respectively the red, blue and green channel of the source image.

$$Y(R,G,B) = 0.2126R + 0.7152G + 0.0722B \tag{4}$$

SSIM is a metric for assessing the quality of images on various windows (regions) of an image. To calculate SSIM metric value, for a reference window x (of the reference image) and source window y (of the source image) of size NxN pixels, we use Eq. 5, where μ_x and μ_y are the averages of x and y, σ_{xy} is the covariance of x and y, σ_x^2 and σ_y^2 are the variances of x and y, $c_1 = (k_1 L)^2$ and $c_2 = (k_2 L)^2$ are the two variables to stabilize the division with weak denominator, L is the dynamic range of the pixel values (typically it is defined as $2^{bitsperpixel} - 1$), and $k_1 = 0.01$ and $k_2 = 0.03$. This is a perception-based model that considers the structural information of the image, while also taking into account luminance and contrast features of the image. This metric, in its base concept, is an improvement to *Mean Square Error* and *Peak Signal-to-Noise Ratio* metrics which estimate only an absolute errors.

$$SSIM(x,y) = \frac{(2\mu_x \mu_y + c_1)(2\sigma_{xy} + c_2)}{(\mu_x^2 + \mu_y^2 + c_1)(\sigma_x^2 + \sigma_y^2 + c^2)} \tag{5}$$

MS-SSIM metric is an improvement of SSIM. The concept and equation is the same as for the SSIM, but MS-SSIM performs the assessment over multiple scales (we use 5 scales, where the next scale is the half of the previous one) of the source image. It has been shown that MS-SSIM performs equally good or better than SSIM metric [16].

PD metric is a fully perceptually based image comparison method, that was designed especially for rendering systems. The authors of this metric needed a metric to tell them if the new changes applied to light rendering algorithms were better or worse than the previous version of the algorithm. This way, they could easily tell how optimizations applied to the rendering algorithms affected the final image. Within several steps authors describe comparison procedure. First RGB reference and source images are converted to XYZ and CIE-Lab color spaces. Then they use Laplacian pyramids to compute spatial frequencies presented in the image. Next the Contrast Sensitivity Function is being computed and finally they perform two tests to mark images as different if any of these tests fail. More in-depth information about this metric can be found in the Yee's paper [19].

4   Light Atmospheric Scattering Integration Method

To compare the usability of the selected image comparison metrics, initially we had to generate some sets of reference images and some source images that will be compared with the reference. As a reference we decided to use the images computed using Trapezoidal Rule (with better accuracy - using 500 integration samples on the viewing ray $\overrightarrow{V}$, and 250 integration samples on the light ray $\overrightarrow{L}$), which is used by most of the above mentioned atmospheric scattering methods.

As a source images we used images that were computed using lower number of numerical integration steps (which gave us images with lower quality) than the reference image. The compared images were calculated with lower accuracy using 90 and 16 integration samples on the viewing ray $\overrightarrow{V}$; 45 and 8 integration samples on the light ray $\overrightarrow{L}$.

What is more, we have also generated the reference and source images with the same quality, but the camera's orientation was slightly different (not so noticeable to the human eye) - it was rotated around camera vertical axis to the right, by 1°.

Finally, we compared the reference images with the corresponding source images using PCC, SSIM, MS-SSIM and PD metrics.

The renders (Fig. 3) were obtained using Intel Core i5 4200H CPU and the rendered images' resolution was fixed to 512x512. Parameters (constants) of the Eq. 1 were the same for all the images. The number of integration samples for the reference image was 500 on the viewing ray $\overrightarrow{V}$, and 250 on the light ray $\overrightarrow{L}$). For the compared images we used lower accuracy using 90 and 16 integration samples on the viewing ray $\overrightarrow{V}$ and on the light ray $\overrightarrow{L}$ we used 45 and 8 integration samples. To obtain the shifted image (Fig. 3a and b), we rotated camera to the right, by 1°.

5   Results

Figure 3 shows generated set of images for different perspectives (position of the camera in relation to sky horizon) that were compared using above mentioned metrics. Left column contains the reference images, middle (besides first row) and right columns contain the source images.

Moreover, Table 1 presents the comparison results for each metric (PCC, SSIM, MS-SSIM and PD) for the images set from Fig. 3 and Table 2 presents the performance (time in seconds) results for each comparison result from Table 1.

In Fig. 3, we can see that images are mostly the same. It is practically very difficult to tell the differences between the reference and source images. Hence, it is necessary to compare the obtained results using image comparison metrics - to see if we get closer or further away the reference images.

In Table 1, we have the results of conducted experiment. For each metric there are two results (besides the rotated view) that were retrieved from comparison. Left result comes from comparing the highest with middle accuracy (90 view ray and 45 light ray integration samples). Right result comes from comparing

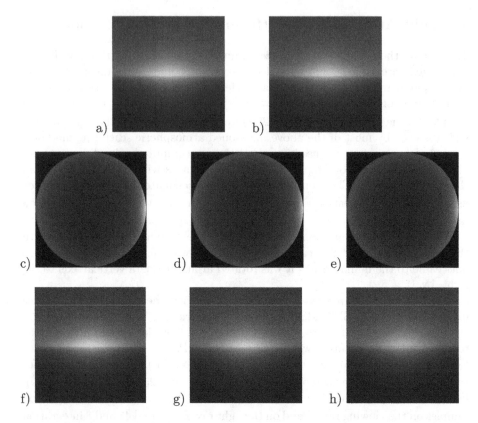

Fig. 3. Tested images: (a), (b) - *Rotated views*; (c), (d), (e) - *Fisheye views*; (f), (g), (h) - *Surface views*. Images (a) and (b) present the same image, generated with the same number of integration samples, but in the b) the camera was rotated right by 1 degree. Images (c) and (f) present the reference images with the highest accuracy. Images (d) and (g) present the images with middle accuracy. Images (e) and (h) present the images with the lowest accuracy.

the highest with the lowest accuracy (16 view ray and 8 light ray integration samples).

We can notice, that for the *rotated views*, which are practically indistinguishable for a human eye, MS-SSIM returned the lowest score, which tells us that this metric is vulnerable more to image shifts/rotations than other metrics. PD metric returned maximum value what means that both images are the same (according to this metric), where in fact they are not. PCC and SSIM metrics returned results very close to 1.0. Obtained results suggest that PD metric might be the best for general image description and is resistant to slight images/camera transformations.

Table 1. Results obtained from comparison of the reference images and source images. For each metric there are two results (besides rotated view). Left result comes from comparing the highest with middle accuracy. Right result comes from comparing the highest with the lowest accuracy.

View	Metric							
	PCC		SSIM		MS-SSIM		PD	
Rotated view	0.99924		0.99820		0.92776		1.00000	
Fisheye view	0.99994	0.99834	0.99967	0.99590	0.98620	0.90062	0.99966	0.99968
Surface view	0.99985	0.99271	0.99856	0.97797	0.94965	0.90116	1.00000	0.86229

Table 2. Performance (time in seconds) results of each considered metric. Presented results correspond directly to the comparison results from Table 1.

View	Metric							
	PCC		SSIM		MS-SSIM		PD	
Rotated view	0.03245		0.05309		0.30890		1.40303	
Fisheye view	0.03438	0.03251	0.05302	0.05277	0.30709	0.30745	1.40498	2.64664
Surface view	0.02185	0.02479	0.04310	0.04355	0.30057	0.30370	0.26127	1.77245

For the *surface views*, PD metric again did not noticed any difference between reference (Fig. 3f) and source (Fig. 3g) image. However, for the Fig. 3h image PD metric recognized more differences than other metrics. MS-SSIM noticed difference in both source images. For PCC metric both source images are roughly the same as the reference. SSIM metric recognized more differences than PCC and still less than MS-SSIM.

For the *fisheye views*, the results are similar to the *surface views* with the difference in case of PD metric, which returned very similar results for both source images. MS-SSIM returned higher result for the source image with middle quality. PCC and SSIM metrics still cannot tell the big difference between reference and source images.

6   Conclusions

Taking into account the results of the conducted experiment we can say that for objective comparison of the light scattering phenomenon synthetic images, which have very subtle differences two metrics become predominant and preferably should be used: these are PD and MS-SSIM. PD metric takes into account HSV color model and may catch the differences more robustly than the other metrics. Whereas MS-SSIM not only takes into account luminance, contrast and structure of the image, but also downscaled versions of the original image.

To conclude, the task of objective comparison of two synthetic images, which comprise light scattering simulations is not trivial. We think, that it is an interesting area of research that should be further studied, however objective metrics for comparison of rendered images become an indispensable tool for reliable evaluation of renders.

References

1. Bruneton, E., Neyret, F.: Precomputed atmospheric scattering. Comput. Graph. Forum **27**(4), 1079–1086 (2008)
2. Bruneton, E.: A qualitative and quantitative evaluation of 8 clear sky models. IEEE Trans. Vis. Comput. Graph. **23**(12), 2641–2655 (2017)
3. Darula, S., Kittler, R.: CIE general sky standard defining luminance distributions. In: Proceedings eSim, pp. 11–13 (2002)
4. Elek, O.: Rendering parameterizable planetary atmospheres with multiple scattering in real-time. In: Proceedings of the Central European Seminar on Computer Graphics. Citeseer (2009)
5. Fornalczyk, K., Napieralski, P., Szajerman, D., Wojciechowski, A., Sztoch, P., Wawrzyniak, J.: Stereoscopic image perception quality factors. Int. J. Microelectron. Comput. Sci. **6**(1), 15–22 (2015). Proceedings of MIXDES International Conference
6. Karasulu, B., Balli, S.: Image segmentation using fuzzy logic, neural networks and genetic algorithms: survey and trends. Mach. Graph. Vis. **19**(4), 367–409 (2010)
7. Wojciechowski, A.: Camera navigation support in a virtual environment. Bull. Pol. Acad. Sci.: Tech. Sci. **61**(4), 871–884 (2013)
8. Goshtasby, A.A.: Similarity and dissimilarity measures. Image Registration, pp. 7–66. Springer, London (2012). https://doi.org/10.1007/978-1-4471-2458-0_2
9. Guzek, K., Napieralski, P.: Rendering participating media with streamed photon mapping. J. Appl. Comput. Sci. **24**(1), 7–15 (2016)
10. Kider Jr., J.T., Knowlton, D., Newlin, J., Li, Y.K., Greenberg, D.P.: A framework for the experimental comparison of solar and skydome illumination. ACM Trans. Graph. (TOG) **33**(6), 180 (2014)
11. Sirai, T.N.T., Nakamae, K.T.E.: Display of the earth taking into account atmospheric scattering. In: SIGGRAPH 93: Conference Proceedings, 1–6 August 1993, p. 175. Addison-Wesley Longman, July 1993
12. Nishita, T., Dobashi, Y., Kaneda, K., Yamashita, H.: Display method of the sky color taking into account multiple scattering. Pac. Graph. **96**, 117–132 (1996)
13. O'Neil, S.: Accurate atmospheric scattering. GPU Gems **2**, 253–268 (2005)
14. Peleshko, D., Rak, T., Peleshko, M., Izonin, I., Batyuk, D.: Two-frames image superresolution based on the aggregate divergence matrix. In: IEEE 1st International Conference on Data Stream Mining & Processing, pp. 235–238 (2016)
15. Polyakova, M., Krylov, V., Volkova, N.: The methods of image segmentation based on distributions and wavelet transform. In: IEEE 1st International Conference on Data Stream Mining & Processing, pp. 243–247 (2016)
16. Wang, Z., Simoncelli, E. P., Bovik, A.C.: Multiscale structural similarity for image quality assessment. In: Conference Record of the Thirty-Seventh Asilomar Conference on Signals, Systems and Computers, vol. 2, pp. 1398–1402. IEEE, November 2003

17. Wang, Z., Bovik, A.C., Sheikh, H.R., Simoncelli, E.P.: Image quality assessment: from error visibility to structural similarity. IEEE Trans. Image Process. **13**(4), 600–612 (2004)
18. Ward, G.J.: The RADIANCE lighting simulation and rendering system. In: Proceedings of the 21st Annual Conference on Computer Graphics and Interactive Techniques, pp. 459–472. ACM, July 1994
19. Yee, H.: Perceptual metric for production testing. J. Graph. Tools **9**(4), 33–40 (2004)
20. Youssef, B.A.: Image segmentation using streamlines analogy. Mach. Graph. Vis. **19**(1), 19–31 (2010)

Graphical Interface Design for Chatbots for the Needs of Artificial Intelligence Support in Web and Mobile Applications

Mateusz Modrzejewski$^{(\boxtimes)}$ and Przemysław Rokita

Division of Computer Graphics, Institute of Computer Science,
The Faculty of Electronics and Information Technology,
Warsaw University of Technology, Nowowiejska 15/19, 00-665 Warsaw, Poland
{M.Modrzejewski,P.Rokita}@ii.pw.edu.pl

Abstract. The interest in the topic of conversational agents has been continuously rising for the past few years, as the technology itself has proved to have multiple practical applications. This paper discusses the design principles for graphical interfaces of conversational agents implemented for the needs of any branch of business that may benefit from the introduction of such solutions, including customer service, healthcare, sales and various types of services. Requirements are defined according to current trends in application design, including the use on mobile devices. The paper presents a survey on solutions fulfilling the mentioned requirements and discusses emerging issues. The paper also describes and proposes a reply scenario model suitable for the needs of implementing a flexible graphical interface for a modern chatbot-based system.

Keywords: Conversational agents · Chatbots · Graphical interfaces
AI · Graphics in business applications · Graphical design

1 Introduction

Chatbots have long been an important topic for artificial intelligence [1]: developed language is one of the greatest achievements of human kind and one the most basic means of our communication. It is no wonder that creating an artificial intelligence able of communicating intelligently with us in natural language would be a scientific milestone. As the great philosopher Ludwig Wittgenstein once stated, *"The limits of my language mean the limits of my world."* [2] - AI is yet far from having the language comprehension that we possess, but efforts are being made constantly.

The Loebner's Prize [3] is an annual competition for chatbots creation. Chatbots are put under a specific version of the Turing test, where human judges determine whether their conversation partner is human or AI. The Loebner's Prize has been a motor for the development of NLP, with specific tools like AIML [4] and ChatScript [5,6] evolving along the way. The chatbots submitted

© Springer Nature Switzerland AG 2018
L. J. Chmielewski et al. (Eds.): ICCVG 2018, LNCS 11114, pp. 48–56, 2018.
https://doi.org/10.1007/978-3-030-00692-1_5

for the Loebner's Prize are designed in a way to imitate human conversation capabilities and the test itself is varies in terms of requirements and topics - nevertheless, the graphical design of these bots is irrelevant, as only the "brain" itself is put under judgement [7].

On the other hand, the market has seen an increasing need for chatbots in sectors like AI-aided customer support, management, information exchange, trades, healthcare [8], news, media and other services [9]. Conversational interfaces are seen as faster, easier to learn and more user-friendly than conventional mechanisms. Therefore, the application of chatbots seems to be a separate problem from the main branch of chatbot development, as the usages and requirements differ heavily from the original, Loebner's Prize approach. Here chatbots can bee seen rather as a blend of the classic, Loebner's Prize chatbot with various question-answering functionalities contained within a user-friendly interface. The interface itself serves not only as a view for the application, but defines the communication model between the human user and the AI.

Apart from the business aspect, chatbots are currently being embedded as a key element of many modern computer programs, including games. An extremely interesting example of a highly developed chatbot interface can be seen in the game *Event [0]* by Ocelot Society, where the player plays as an astronaut on an abandoned space station and communicates with a sentient AI by a network of terminals [10,11]. The gameplay can be furthered only by conversation with the AI, as it controls all the locks and mechanisms on the station. The game has received a fair amount of attention and critical praise, winning numerous game industry prizes (Fig. 1).

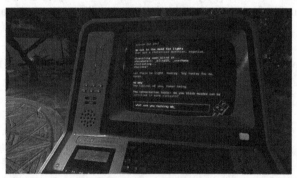

Fig. 1. Conversation with the AI in *Event [0]* (Ocelot Society, 2016)

2   Requirements

When defining the requirements for the graphical interface of a chatbot-based AI system, we need to consider the following questions [13]:

- *what will the chatbot be used for?*
- *how will the chatbot be provided to the user? Via SMS-like messaging? Mobile devices? A web interface? An internal desktop application?*

– *what conveniences will be provided to the user by the chatbot's interface?*
– *what scope of understanding and competence should the chatbot have?*
– *how relevant are the chatbot's conversation capabilities to its purpose?*

A survey regarding chatbots uses in business has been carried out by Usurv in May 2016 [12] on a nationally representative sample of 1,000 UK adults. The survey allows to clearly identify the main needs of the market, as seen by the predicted usages of chatbots, shown in Table 1.

Table 1. Predicted usages of chatbots [12]

#	Usage	Replies (%)
1	Quick emergency answers	46
2	Forwarding to appropriate human	40
3	Buy basic items (clothes, food)	33
4	Complaint resolution	26
5	Mailing list or service subscription	24
6	Bookings or reservations	24
7	Providing detailed answers and explanations	20

The other provided replies include paying bills, expensive purchases and purchase inspiration. The emerging conclusion is further supported by the analysis of expected benefits from utilizing chatbots as intelligent business-aid, as shown in Table 2.

Table 2. Most expected benefits from the usage of chatbots [12]

#	Benefit	Replies (%)
1	Getting 24-h service	68
2	Quick answers to simple questions	64
3	Getting an instant response	51
4	Convenience for you	50
5	Ease of communication	37
6	Ability to easily register a complaint	28
7	Efficient complaint resolution	18

The audience also raised concerns about the comprehensive capabilities of the chatbots, as "Poor question understanding" was chosen the number one barrier to chatbot usage with 55% of the respondents saying so.

The interesting conclusion therefore is that the most common requirement is speed and providing aid in simple, repetitive tasks - advanced problem solving capabilities, although also desired, have a much lower priority. Therefore, it can be clearly stated, that advanced NLP mechanisms will not always be the solution to the problem, as inside of the narrow domain [14], the chatbot will mostly operate on keywords and rely upon correct identification of the user's intent and entities regarding that intent. One of the most important factors to consider, though, will be the interface of the chatbot and it's capabilities of providing quick, clean methods and clearly steering the conversation when needed.

3   Design Principles

The design principles for engaging chatbots rely mostly on the interface design and scripting. The widely accepted standard is a text message (SMS) application or Facebook Messenger type of design [15–18]. An example may be seen as in Fig. 2.

Fig. 2. Example of a mobile chat application.

The two main modules of the applications are the "contacts view" and the "chat view". The former stores and displays the recent conversations that the user has had, while the latter displays the current conversation. The layout of the modules follows the modern principles of creating very simple, clean interfaces with a minimal number of active controls on-screen. Another trend is to use responsive layout - many modern tools and libraries (like, for instance, Bootstrap [19] or Vaadin [20]) provide support for this type of interfaces.

Most modern chat applications designed for humans allow to embed audio clips and images into the messages, which opens up additional possibilities: a small UI control, like a date selector or a choice input field, may be embedded is the bot's message as well. This allows to further reduce the number of active elements on-screen, as the control will receive the user's attention only for the time of interaction and will be quickly and elegantly scrolled away in the further ensuing conversation. The controls can be specialized in order to increase the convenience of providing additional input data needed to answer the input query. Whenever answering the question requires a set of data to be retrieved, charts and diagrams may be generated and embedded into the reply as well, if only they are handled correctly by the chatbot's brain.

Multi-bot [21] systems are also an interesting way of handling multiple topics: each time a specialized question is asked by the user, a dispatcher bot "invites" one of his friends to the conversation. The new bot acts as an additional party of the conversation, asks additional questions if needed and provides the final answer to the user. The conversation then returns to a basic one-on-one model. This approach may not be implemented as so in the brain of the chatbot, but such enhancement of the user's experience may be appropriate and desired within a particular domain of interest.

3.1   Personality

The final user experience consists not only of the correct answers, but also the style of the conversation [17,18]. In modern culture, internet conversations make heavy use of emojis, commonly known visual running gags ("memes"), internet slang and so on. Users often type quick, short messages and it is not uncommon to write a single thought across a few messages. We may therefore design the bot's personality in a way that makes it less robotic and more appealing to the user. Slackbot [22] is a great example of a bot that has gained wide acceptance in the users community, as it provides a near perfect blend of functionality, convenience and personality (Fig. 3).

Some of the techniques used to provide personality to a chatbot are:

- simulating human internet conversations according to the chat platform itself, for instance by using emojis to communicate reactions and thoughts,
- delaying the replies by a very short time in order to simulate the typing process (possibly with a floating "three dots" message, similar to the ones that are displayed when having a regular conversation in popular applications),
- using the context of the conversation to add basic human traits, like remembering a problem that was solved before or introducing changes to the conversation style according to the conversation style of the user.

Obviously, some applications of chatbots will require a much stronger personality (like the volatile AI in the aforementioned *Event [0]* game, where an emotion matrix is utilized in order to activate and deactivate certain dialogue options during gameplay), but the user's experience of even a basic chatbot used for scheduling meeting can be easily enhanced with simple techniques like clever scripting and clear interface design.

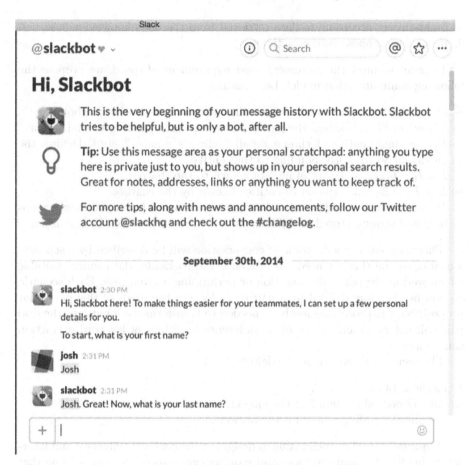

Fig. 3. Slackbot onboarding [22].

4   Proposition of Reply Scenario Interface Model

As stated before, in the classic approach, the chatbot's brain defines scripts for
its conversation capabilities. The scripts vary according to the used technology
and complexity: for instance, environments like ChatScript use ontologies and
allow to define and group the scripts into topics, concepts and highly advances
sequences. This is further used to better interpret the user's input and provide
a very human-like answer.

Specific domain chatbots [14] with business applications, on the other hand,
rely on the following general algorithm:

1. read user input,
2. identify user's intent and the corresponding entities,
3. if needed, ask for any missing parts of the query,
4. gather data necessary to build answer,

5. build answer according to data retrieved from the bot's knowledge base,
6. if suitable, propose further actions.

In order to meet the aforementioned requirement of speed, we propose the following communication model. Let's assume:

- I_i - a single intent, which defines the basic actions of the chatbot ("get", "show" etc.) and defines the particular words corresponding to that intent.
- E_j - a single entity of chosen detail ("client's number" etc.). Defines the particular words corresponding to that entity,
- $I = I_1 \cup I_2 \cup ...$ - the set of intents known to the chatbot,
- $E = E_1 \cup E_2 \cup ...$ - the set of entities known by the chatbot,
- P - the set of parameters needed to answer the query (most commonly, numbers and strings, stored in different data sources or provided by the user);

Therefore, each specific topic of conversation will be described by a separate scenario, as the chatbot needs to reference the particular data source suitable for answering the particular question or performing a given task. Each scenario S_x will be therefore defined by a pair of I_i, E_j. For the needs of this particular proposition, the processing methods needed to transform the input into the said pair will not be described, as many different algorithms of keyword extraction can be used.

The scenario should therefore define:

1. methods of acquiring P,
2. data D needed for building the answer,
3. the initial building blocks for the answer A,

Acquiring P is the crucial issue in designing the chatbot's interface and interaction model - the main purpose and requirement is speed, and we assume that the users do not have time to learn the questions formats that are "understood best by the chatbot". Instead, we want the chatbot to recognize the user's intent as fast as possible upon short input messages and then ask for any additional data, according to the way a regular conversation with a human being would occur.

Because the intent and entity clearly define the chatbot's action, we can acquire each of the parameters P_x by small reply messages within the scenario. Each of this messages asks the user for an additional piece of relevant data. The set of available reply messages, R_P can also be defined by the designer, as they will be common for many of the scenarios ("Please provide the date", "Please choose topic of complaint" etc.). Each of the replies existing in the model may be then translated into the controller and view of the system, equipped with convenient, specialized, user friendly UI components. The retrieved parameters are then used for answer-specific data retrieval mechanisms, according to the knowledge base implementation. Finally, the answer is built out of A, completed with the data retrieved from the knowledge base.

The structure of this model may be demonstrated as in Fig. 4.

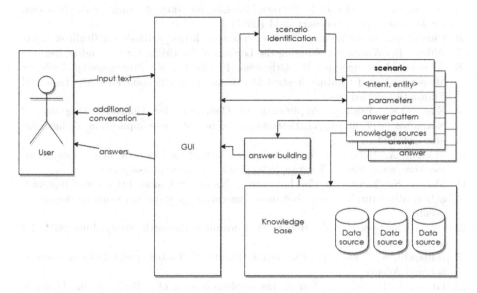

Fig. 4. Communication provided by the scenario-based model

5   Conclusions

In this paper we have discussed and analyzed the requirements and design principles for modern business applications of chatbots within graphical interfaces. We
have also proposed a flexible model of communication and conversation designed
for the particular needs of closed domain chatbots within such interfaces. As the
market and interest in applying chatbot technology rises [23,24], we believe
that natural language will eventually become a key part of our communication
with artificial intelligence. We are also positive that the development of natural
language technology will inspire the development of UI design. Certain functionalities will be resolved with the introduction of a conversational interface,
allowing the graphical elements to focus on the more difficult aspects of data
input, organisation and presentation.

References

1. Wiezenbaum, J.: ELIZA - a computer program for the study of natural language
   communication between man and machine. Commun. ACM **9**(1), 36–45 (1966)
2. Wittgenstein, L.: Tractatus Logico-Philosophicus (5.6) (1922)
3. Bradeško, L., Mladeni, D.: A Survey of Chatbot Systems through a Loebner Prize
   Competition (2012)

 4. AIML language for Chatbots, A.L.I.C.E. foundation. http://www.alicebot.org/aiml.html
 5. Wilcox, B.: Beyond Facade: Pattern Matching for Natural Language Applications, for Telltale Games, February 2011 (2011)
 6. ChatScript - Bruce Wilcox's GitHub repository. https://github.com/bwilcox-1234/
 7. Wilcox, B., Wilcox, S.: Winning the Loebner's, for Brillig Understanding Inc
 8. Abashev, A., Grigoryev, R., Grigorian, K., Boyko, V.: Programming Tools for Messenger-Based Chatbot System Organization: Implication for Outpatient and Translational Medicines
 9. Kiat, O.K.: Business Application of ChatBots, for Chatbots Magazine, 2 November 2017. https://chatbotsmagazine.com/business-application-of-chatbots-afb952cfdb93
10. Meehan, A.: Hello chatbot, can we play a game? for vice.com. https://waypoint.vice.com/en_us/article/kwzyan/hello-chatbot-can-we-play-a-game
11. Mohov, S.: Turning a Chatbot into a Narrative Game. https://archives.nucl.ai/recording/turning-a-chatbot-into-a-narrative-game-language-interaction-in-event0/
12. clvr.co/chatbots, CHAT BOTS! A Consumer Research Study–June 2016 for mycleveragency.com
13. Radziwill, N., Benton, M.: Evaluating Quality of Chatbots and Intelligent Conversational Agents
14. Ghose, S., Barua, J.J.: Toward the implementation of a Topic specific Dialogue based Natural Language Chatbot as an Undergraduate Advisor
15. Honap, S.: Designing a service chatbot, for booking.design. https://booking.design/designing-a-service-chatbot-f121455b8da7
16. Amunwa, J.: Let's Talk About Text: A Chatbot Design Guide, for Telepathy. https://www.dtelepathy.com/blog/design/lets-talk-about-text-a-chatbot-design-guide
17. Kulawik, A.: Making Chatbots Talk - Writing Conversational UI Scripts Step by Step, for UXCollective. https://uxdesign.cc/making-chatbots-talk-writing-conversational-ui-scripts-step-by-step-62622abfb5cf
18. Martin, J.: Chatbot Design Trends 2018, for Chatbots Magazine. https://chatbotsmagazine.com/chatbot-design-trends-2018-253fb356d3a3
19. Boostrap home page. www.getbootstrap.com
20. Vaadin home page. www.vaadin.com
21. Candello, H., Pinhanez, C.: Designing the user experience of a multi-bot conversational system
22. Weissberg, J.: Onboarding in Slack. http://blog.outbound.io/slack-kills-at-onboarding-heres-how-they-do-it
23. Abdul-Kader, S.A., Wood, J.: Survey on chatbot design techniques in speech conversation systems. Int. J. Adv. Comput. Sci. Appl. (IJACSA) 6(7) (2015)
24. Ask, J.A., Facemire, M., Hogan, A.: The State Of Chatbots. Forrester.com report 20 October 2016 (2016)

Algorithms for Random Maps Generation and Their Implementation as a Python Library

Marian Rusek(ID), Rafał Jusiak, and Waldemar Karwowski(✉)(ID)

Faculty of Applied Informatics and Mathematics,
Warsaw University of Life Sciences – SGGW, Warsaw, Poland
{marian_rusek,waldemar_karwowski}@sggw.pl

Abstract. Random map generation has application in strategy computer games, terrain simulators, and other areas. In this paper basic assumptions of a library for random maps generation are presented. It uses both value noise and diamond square computer graphics algorithms, as well as newly invented algorithms for biomes creation and river generation. Complete library implementation with an example use in a separate application is explained in detail. Basic issues related to developing programming libraries and random map generations are also discussed.

1 Introduction

Nowadays the generation of random maps has many applications. The most popular are definitely computer games. One such game is Minecraft, where the key element of the game is a randomly generated area where the whole gameplay takes place. The player can freely explore and modify the entire world. This game, however, would not be so attractive to the player, if not unlimited size of generated games worlds were possible. Game worlds, although they are generated by algorithms, give the impression of truly existing sites. Each newly generated world in this game differs from the others, but preserves the familiar life rules of nature. Another example of the game with implemented terrain generator is Civilization. Although user can play on a map reminiscent of an Earth's map, game on a random map is also possible. These maps, as in the previous example, despite the random generation, look realistic.

The goal of this work was to create a simple-to-use development tool intended to generate random maps. Special algorithms to generate biomes, or climate are developed. Algorithms for rivers generation taking into account sea level and terrain height are also designed. The rest of this paper is organized as follows: in Sect. 2 the algorithms and methods for map generation are discussed. In Sect. 3 the biomes and river generation algorithms are presented. In Sect. 4 implementation of the algorithm in Python library is described as well as sample results of the algorithms are presented. Summary and final remarks are formulated in Sect. 5.

© Springer Nature Switzerland AG 2018
L. J. Chmielewski et al. (Eds.): ICCVG 2018, LNCS 11114, pp. 57–67, 2018.
https://doi.org/10.1007/978-3-030-00692-1_6

2   Procedural Map Generation

Procedural content generation is a popular method in game programming. It refers to the automatic or semi-automatic generation of game content. Procedural content generation comes in many game elements, because there are many types of game content that can be generated (such as levels, adventures, characters, weapons, scenes, histories). Moreover there are many ways in which the content can be generated. Some of them are based on methods from artificial intelligence or computational intelligence, such as constraint satisfaction, planning, evolutionary computation, or based on fractals [18]. In [17] the five main categories that a content generator can fall into are listed: generation as optimization, generation as constraint satisfaction, generation with grammars, generation as content selection, and generation as a constructive process. There are various reasons for procedural content generation. One of the most common reasons is removing the repeatability of the scene. If game designers provide possibility of automatic creation of nearly infinite amounts of content, the player can replay the game many times and do not get bored. There are many other motivations for using procedural generation, such as speeding up game development, saving human designer effort and cost, saving memory or secondary storage space, or enabling completely new types of games. Survey of procedural content generation is presented in [8].

Procedural map generation is a kind of content generation devoted to creating terrain data algorithmically without manual graphics. According to the previous remarks most obvious reason is that by generating a fresh map each time the game is played, the life-span of the game is extended. Procedural map generation techniques can be classified according to their resulting content such as terrains, continents, roads, rivers, cities etc. [4]. Additionally each technique can be classified as assisted or not assisted, highlighting the need of human interaction or guidance in order to produce content using the referenced technique. The most common is a random generation method to provide the diversity of the resulting maps. For example a simple way of generating map is to start with sea, set randomly small islands, and grow them out in random directions by doing a few steps. Certain features on land, such as forest, desert or grass area, can be created in the same way. Other approaches involve using fractals [12], in [3] review of fractal based methods for building visually-rich and fully-realistic natural environments is made. Many methods are based on planar mesh, in particular to improve rendering, algorithms use LOD (Level of Detail) meshes for terrain generation. There are many types of meshes: based on triangles, squares, regular or irregular polygons, Voronoi diagrams and others. To improve generated map the mesh density should be increased. Generally new nodes are set between existing nodes and appropriate values have to be set at new nodes. Such methods are called midpoint displacement methods. In [12] many midpoint displacement methods are discussed; midpoint displacement constructions for the paraboloids, random midpoint displacements with a sharply non-Gaussian displacements' distribution or random landscapes without creases. Generalized Stochastic Subdivision was discussed in [11]. In [13] diamond-square method also known as the random midpoint displacement fractal, is described. The diamond-square algorithm works by iteratively subdividing areas of space and offsetting the midpoint by random amounts. Such algorithms are most commonly used with height maps to generate, for example, believable mountains. An advantage of this family of algorithms is that they are so fast that they can often be used for real-time terrain generation [14]. Of course starting data do not have to be random, a step-by-step process for downloading and creating terrain from real world USGS elevation data is described [15]. A separate group of procedural generation methods starts from random noise. Noise functions are used in general to generate clouds; the most realistic results are obtained with Perlin noise [16]. However algorithms based on noise are useful for terrain generation too [7,19]. The classical method for generating rivers is a part of height-map generation algorithm. The algorithm generates a terrain model around a precomputed set of ridge lines and rivers network is presented in [1]. First, it is used a rapid method that generates the ridges and rivers network. Then, an extension of the basic midpoint displacement method is applied for generating fractal terrain model around a pre-filled ridges and rivers network. Terrain generation using concepts from hydrology is discussed in [6], issues connected with river network generation are presented in [20]. Example of software tool for dynamic run-time map generation is described in [2], other example of procedural map generator for a real-time strategy game is discussed in [10]. There are many programs for scenery generation which use described above algorithms, most popular is Terragen.

3   Terrain, Biomes and Rivers Generation Algorithms

Since our goal was to generate terrain, biomes and rivers, it was necessary to develop a suitable algorithm. To generate terrain two methods mentioned in the previous section were adopted. The first method was based on value noise, the second one on diamond square algorithm. In both at the beginning a two-dimensional array is created. Heights are implemented as integer values that are in the range $(0, k)$, where 0 corresponds to very deep water and k means highest mountain peaks. Value k limits the number of colours possible to use during rendering, we later take k equal to 255.

Value noise method is based on algorithm presented in [19] and works as follows. First random values between 0 and 1 according to uniform distribution are set to every element of two-dimensional array. Next, to maintain regular map shapes, a step called turbulence is taken exactly as described in [19]. The turbulence involves connecting the generated noise layers, resulting in larger clusters of fields with smaller differences between adjacent values. During turbulence bilinear interpolation is used for smoothing. The process results in an increasing blurring and creates a more natural look of terrain.

Diamond square method is adopted according to description presented in [5], and is based on completely different rule than the previously described value noise algorithm. During iteration random values are generated in the 4 corners of the square, than diamond and square steps are performed. In the diamond step, for each square in the array the midpoint is set with value equal to the average of the four corner points plus a random value. In the square step for each diamond in the array, the midpoint of that diamond is set to the average of the four corner points plus a random value. In our implementation random value is taken with uniform distribution between -1.6 and 1.6 and is times by step size. Two-dimensional array has to be square array and because at every step area is divided into four sub squares size d should be equal to 2^n+1, where n is a natural number. When all the steps are completed and the entire array is filled with the correct values, the smoothing stage is determined. The value in cell is set to the average of it and all values in cells around it, one repetition of smoothing was sufficient in our case. At the end of the algorithm, a two-dimensional array of generated values is standardized, i.e., values are set between 0 and 255.

Biomes depend mainly on the temperature and can be created with the same algorithms as the terrain. Temperatures can also be implemented as integer values that are in the range $(0, 255)$, where 0 is the highest temperature, and 255 is the lowest. This gives formally good results, but not realistic compared to real world climate maps, since the average temperature does not distribute randomly. An alternative to this solution may be to use a temperature-generating algorithm, for example depending on the distance to the equator (that is, if the map is represented as a two-dimensional array, the middle row represents equator). The following algorithm was designed. At the beginning of algorithm the middle row is selected. Because size should be equal to $2^n + 1$ every column can be divided into equator value and two half columns, north and south, with size 2^{n-1}. Then for every column, equator value is set to 0 (maximal temperature) and each half column is generated randomly with normal distribution with mean equal to 130 and standard deviation equal to 60. North half of column is sorted ascending, south part of column is sorted descending. This operation causes the equator to have high temperature values, while approaching the poles the temperature decreases significantly. When all columns are populated, the values in resulting two dimensional array are smoothing, which is the last step in generating the biomes. Smoothing simply counts average value from all neighbours of point. Thanks to this stage the bordering points are closer to each other, making the map look more realistic. Smoothing can be performed repeatedly, in our case two times gave fairly good results.

In order to implement the generation of rivers, it was decided to design dedicated algorithm. Generally the problem was simplified to designate a random path in the Cartesian system between points S (start) and T (target). Starting at point S, the path should always be generated by approaching the T point. At every step path should slightly change its direction, however it cannot create a loop. The sign(x) function used below can takes three values: -1 for $x < 0$, 0 for $x = 0$ and 1 for $x > 0$. The following algorithm fulfills listed conditions:

1: We have a Cartesian system with points with integer coordinates (pixels).
2: Start point is marked $S(s_1, s_2)$ and target point $T(t_1, t_2)$.
3: Path L is a list consisting of one point S.

4: Current point $C(c_1, c_2)$ at the beginning is equal to S

5: **while** $C \neq T$ **do**

6:     Vector $V[s_1 - c_1, s_2 - c_2]$ is counted.

7:     With the sign function the values $k = \text{sign}(s_1 - c_1)$ and $l = \text{sign}(s_2 - c_2)$ are determined.

8:     **if** $k \neq 0 \wedge l \neq 0$ **then**

9:         we draw one vector $u[u_1, u_2]$ from $[k, 0], [k, l], [0, l]$

10:    **else**

11:        we start with a set of vectors $W = [k+l, k+l], [k, l], [k-l, l-k]$

12:        for every w from W we check

13:        **if** $C + w$ belongs to L **then**

14:           $W = W - w$

15:        **end if**

16:        we draw one vector $u[u_1, u_2]$ from W

17:    **end if**

18:    We add drawn vector u to point C: $c_1 = c_1 + u_1$ and $c_2 = c_2 + u_2$

19:    Modified C is added to path L

20: **end while**

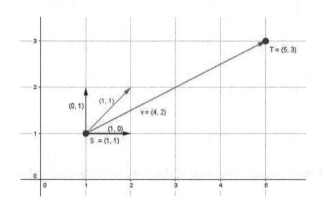

Fig. 1. Start of the river generation algorithm

We can illustrate sample steps of our algorithm. Assume that at start we have $S(1, 1)$ and $T(5, 3)$, C is equal to S and $L = (1, 1)$. Vector $V = [4, 2]$, it means that $k = 1$ and $l = 1$. We have to draw from vectors $[1, 0]; [1, 1]; [0, 1]$ (Fig. 1). Assume that vector $u = [1, 1]$ was drawn, then $C = (2, 2)$ and $L = (1, 1), (2, 2)$. Now vector $V = [3, 1]$, it means that $k = 1$ and $l = 1$. We have to draw from vectors $[1, 0]; [1, 1]; [0, 1]$ (Fig. 2). Assume that vector $u = [0, 1]$ was drawn, then $C = (2, 3)$ and $L = (1, 1), (2, 2), (2, 3)$. Now vector $V = [3, 0]$, it means that $k = 1$ and $l = 0$. We have to draw from vectors $[1, 1]; [1, 0]; [1, -1]$ (Fig. 3). Algorithm is continued up to when the point T is reached.

Now we prove that the river generation algorithm is always converging to the target point. Let $d(C, T)$ be Manhattan distance between current point and

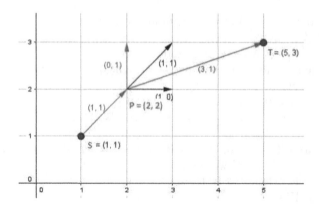

Fig. 2. Sample second step of the river generation algorithm

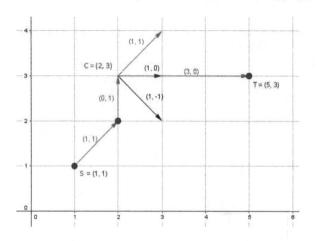

Fig. 3. Sample third step of the river generation algorithm

target point. It is easy to observe that if $k \neq 0$ and $l \neq 0$, then $d(C,T)$ decreases by 1 or 2 after one step. Particular situation for $l = 1$ and $k = 1$ is presented in Fig. 4a), all other situations for $k \neq 0$ and $l \neq 0$ are analogous. Possible next current points are colored in red. We see that $d(C,T) = d(P_1,T) + 1$, $d(C,T) = d(P_2,T) + 2$, $d(C,T) = d(P_3,T) + 1$. We have to note that in this case P_2 can be equal to T. If $k = 0$ or $l = 0$ and $d(C,T) > 1$, then $d(C,T)$ decreases by 1 or 2 after two subsequent steps. Particular situation for $l = 0$ and $k = 1$ is presented in Fig. 4b), other situations are analogous. Possible next current points are colored in red. We see that $d(C,T) = d(P_1,T) + 1$, $d(C,T) = d(P_2,T) + 1$, $d(C,T) = d(P_3,T) + 2$, $d(C,T) = d(P_4,T) + 1$. We can achieve P_1 in two steps with paths: $C - A - P_1$ and $C - B - P_1$. Analogously we have for P_2: $C - A - P_2$ and $C - P_1 - P_2$; for P_3: $C - A - P_3$, $C - B - P_3$, and $C - P_1 - P_3$; for P_4: $C - B - P_4$ and $C - P_1 - P_4$. We have to note that in this case P_3 can be equal to T.

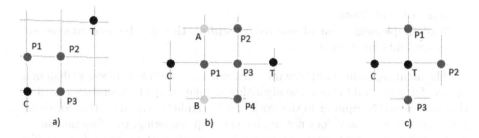

Fig. 4. Choosing next current point in the river generation algorithm

It remains to justify the situation when $k = 0$ or $l = 0$ and $d(C, T) = 1$. Particular case of $l = 0$ and $d(C, T) = 1$ is presented in Fig. 4c), all other situations for $d(C, T) = 1$ and $l = 0$ or $d(C, T) = 1$ and $k = 0$ are analogous. We can list all possible paths: $C - T$, $C - P_1 - T$, $C - P_1 - P_2 - T$, $C - P_1 - P_2 - P_3 - T$, $C - P_3 - T$, $C - P_3 - P_2 - T$ and $C - P_3 - P_2 - P_1 - T$. Because for every next current candidate we check if it belongs to L there is no possibility of looping. The presented algorithm has become the basis for the method of generating rivers in the library described in the next section.

4   Library of Algorithms in Python

Python is now a very popular programming language. In Python it is also possible to develop games. A special library PyMap has been prepared by authors to help game programmer create maps [9]. The purpose of this library is to provide the possibility of generating random maps without special knowledge of this issue, and make the use of the library as simple as possible in practice. The only technical requirement for a programmer is the knowledge of Python and object-oriented programming. The core functionality of the library is of course the possibility of generating a random map. However, the library should include functionality to extent maps generations by new algorithms in the future. Moreover user interface has to provide parametrizations of methods and add practical facilities for the programmer who is using it. The functionalities contained in the library are the following:

- The ability to choose an algorithm that will generate a random terrain map. Moreover provide an abstract base class `BaseAlgorithm`, whereby a programmer can implement his or her own algorithm by creating a subclass after it.
- Generate biomes or climate zones (desert, temperate and arctic) in random areas of the map.
- Possibility to choose a random grain, so by selecting the same value twice will generate an identical map.
- Select the dimension of the map.
- The possibility of setting the percentage water level relative to the entire map surface and the average temperature.

– Generation of rivers.
– Ready implementations of selected algorithms that can be used to generate terrain and climate on the map.

The main algorithms implemented in the library are value noise and diamond square, for maps and biomes, the algorithm simulating the temperature distribution relative to the equator in the world, and in addition the algorithm for rivers generation. The library does not implement map rendering, this functionality a programmer must implement separately, for example with external libraries like PySide (based on QT C++ libraries).

Each map consists of two layers—the terrain layer and the temperature layer to give possibility to generate physical and climate properties together. There is `BasePointsLayer` class and classes derived from it: `TerrainLayer` and `TemperatureLayer`. They have been separated due to the fact that if persons wishing to develop a library for their own needs, for example, to add city creation algorithm, they may add a new special layer that will store only cities spread unevenly across the map. Process of generation is the following. During starting a parameter specifying the water level is passed for the `TerrainLayer` class, in turn for the `TemperatureLayer` class analogously the parameter governing the average temperature is set. The `BaseAlgorithm` class was created for two reasons: firstly, because of the similarity in implementation of all terrain and temperature algorithms, secondly, in order to maintain transparent code and to allow users to overwrite this class in the future, not worrying about changing the implementation of other key library classes. The implementation of the river generator is contained in a separate class, independent of `BaseAlgorithm`, even though it affects the terrain layer.

The constructor of the `DiamondSquareAlgorithm` class verifies first of all whether the given dimensions match the condition so that their value is equal to $2^n + 1$, where n is a natural number. In our Python Library, to simplify future rendering with external libraries, terrain height values (0–255) are projected into six levels (number of levels can be customized). Sea depth is represented only with two levels: deep and shallow water, but mainland elevations with four levels: sand, plain, heights and mountain. Library defines six colors separate for each level. We have to note that such casting additionally smooths terrain values. Value noise and diamond square algorithms are also used to generate temperature, but because the user might want to use a different kind of biomes generation, the two versions are implemented: algorithm for generating the equator with Poles (`PolesAndEquatorAlgorithm` class); algorithm that simply return a given kind of biome on the whole map according to temperature factor (desert, temperate or arctic). The `TemperatureLayer` class casts temperature values (0–255) into three types: 0 corresponds to the desert climate), 1 corresponds to the temperate climate and 2 correspond to arctic climate. For each type of biome table of colors corresponding to different heights on the map was defined. An example application in Python was implemented, which uses PyMap library and renders generated maps with PySide package [9]. The sample results of algorithm that generate particular biomes, rendered with PySide library, are presented in the (Fig. 5).

Fig. 5. Sample arctic, desert and temperate biomes

We decided to create the terrain first and later the river. Consequently, in order to make the river run more realistic, the river generation should consider such factor like the height of the terrain. The starting point should be the mountain point and the end point has to be the sea or another river. According to this assumption we modified river generation algorithm presented in the previous section. To generate the realistic river run, the following three lists are needed. River points list, empty at the beginning, stores the points of the created river (the points where the all new river water is located); water points list stores all the points in which water is shallow (i.e., points of possible river estuaries); mountain points list stores all the points where the terrain is adequately high, or in other words—the area where the mountains are located (i.e., points of possible river sources). Due to the fact that the map can be generated without mountains then if the mountains are not found, all points where there are at least hills are assigned to the mountain points list. The algorithm first finds the starting point in the mountains by randomizing it from the mountain points list and then selecting an end point from the water points list. Alternatively it is possible to chose start and end point by user, but end point should belongs to shallow water and start point height should be bigger than end point height. Since the height of the river decreases over sea level, the current height parameter is defined, which initially takes the height value of starting point. At each iteration of the algorithm, the current height is stored at each new generated point of the river to prevent the next step from generating a higher position than the previous point. The main algorithm loop performs the following steps:

1. Calculation of the vectors from the currently considered point to the destination point (i.e. 3 possible vectors according to the algorithm described in the previous section).
2. Removing from calculated vectors impossible directions in which the river cannot be directed form current point (i.e. destination point height is bigger than current height).
3. Drawing one of the possible variants and designating a new point in which the river runs. In the case where a river cannot be generated because no possible variants, the algorithm is interrupted and the river is not formed.

4. Checking if current point has shallow water height, if yes loop is finishing otherwise continuing with step 1.

The algorithm is implemented in `RiverGenerator` class. Its constructor takes as argument start point, end point and thickness. If start point is none, then a random point from list of highest points is chosen, if end point is none, then a random point from list of shallow water points is chosen. Sample generated rivers, rendered with PySide library, are presented on the (Fig. 6).

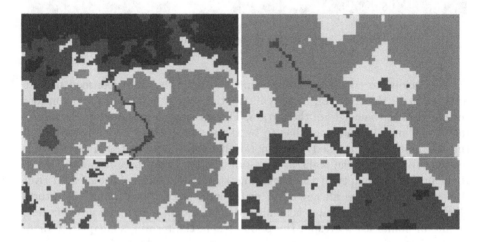

Fig. 6. Examples of generated rivers

5   Conclusion

The sample application shows that obtained results are promising. Two algorithms, i.e., value noise and diamond square, chosen to generate terrains, turned out to be a good choice. They give satisfactory results after a few improvements. Algorithms for biome generation based on them, produced fairly natural maps. In addition, the algorithm to generate a stream of rivers works quite well too. The Python language proved to be a very good choice when implementing PyMap library due to its flexibility and simplicity. The most important advantage of the PyMap library is its openness to the next modifications due to the clear separation of its key elements (layers, algorithms and builders). Example application created with PyMap and PySide library works fairly good. The future research requires the preparation more advanced biomes algorithms which take account for example lakes, forests, agricultural areas, cities etc.

References

1. Belhadj F., Audibert P.: Modeling landscapes with ridges and rivers. In: Proceedings of the 3rd International Conference on Computer Graphics and Interactive Techniques, Australasia and South East Asia, pp. 447–450 (2005)

2. Bhojan, A., Wong, H.W.: ARENA - dynamic run-time map generation for multi-player shooters. In: Pisan, Y., Sgouros, N.M., Marsh, T. (eds.) ICEC 2014. LNCS, vol. 8770, pp. 149–158. Springer, Heidelberg (2014). https://doi.org/10.1007/978-3-662-45212-7_19
3. Boiangiu, C., Morosan, A.G., Stan, M.: A fractal world: building visually-rich and fully-realistic natural environments. Int. J. Math. Comput. Simul. **10**, 100–111 (2016)
4. De Carli, D.M., Bevilacqua, F., Pozzer, C.T., d'Ornellas, M.: A survey of procedural content generation techniques suitable to game development. In: Brazilian Symposium on Games and Digital Entertainment, SBGAMES, pp. 26–35 (2011)
5. Fournier, A.: Computer rendering of stochastic models. Commun. ACM **25**(6), 371–384 (1982)
6. Génevaux, J., Galin, É., Guérin, É., Peytavie, A., Beneš, B.: Terrain generation using procedural models based on hydrology. ACM Trans. Graph. **32**(4), 143 (2013)
7. Gonzalez, V.P.: The Book of Shaders. https://thebookofshaders.com/. Accessed 14 Mar 2018
8. Hendrikx, M., Meijer, S., Van Der Velden, J., Iosup, A.: Procedural content generation for games: a survey. ACM Trans. Multimedia Comput. Commun. Appl. **9**(1), 1 (2013)
9. Jusiak R.: Implementation of library for random maps generation, M.Sc thesis, Warsaw University of Life Sciences (2017)
10. Lara-Cabrera, R., Cotta, C., Fernández-Leiva, A.: Procedural map generation for a RTS game. In: 13th International Conference on Intelligent Games and Simulation, GAME-ON (2012)
11. Lewis, J.P.: Generalized stochastic subdivision. ACM Trans. Graph. **6**(3), 167–190 (1987)
12. Mandelbrot, B.: Fractal landscapes without creases and with rivers. In: Peitgen, H., Saupe, D. (eds.) The Science of fractal images, pp. 243–260. Springer-Verlag, New York (1988)
13. Miller, G.S.P.: The definition and rendering of terrain maps. In: ACM SIGGRAPH Computer Graphics, vol. 20 (4), pp. 39–48 (1986)
14. Olsen, J.: Realtime procedural terrain generation, University of Southern Denmark. Technical Report (2004)
15. Parberry, I.: Designer worlds: procedural generation of infinite terrain from real-world elevation data. J. Comput. Graph. Tech. (JCGT) **3**(1), 74–85 (2014)
16. Perlin, K.: An image synthesizer. ACM SIGGRAPH Comput. Graph. **19**(3), 287–296 (1985)
17. Smith, G.: Understanding procedural content generation: a design-centric analysis of the role of PCG in games. In: Proceedings of the 2014 ACM Conference on Computer-Human Interaction (2014)
18. Togelius, J., Preuss, M., Beume, N., et al.: Controllable procedural map generation via multiobjective evolution. Genet. Program. Evolvable Mach. **14**(2), 245–277 (2013)
19. Vandevenne, L.: Texture Generation using Random Noise. http://lodev.org/cgtutor/randomnoise.html. Accessed 14 Mar 2018
20. Zhang, H., Qu, D., Hou, Y., Gao, F., Huang, F.: Synthetic modeling method for large scale terrain based on hydrology. IEEE Access **4**, 6238–6249 (2016)

Modeling and Rendering of Volumetric Clouds in Real-Time with Unreal Engine 4

Łukasz Nowak[1]([⊠])(iD), Artur Bąk[1]([⊠])(iD), Tomasz Czajkowski[2],
and Konrad Wojciechowski[1]

[1] Polish-Japanese Academy of Information Technology, Warsaw, Poland
{lnowak,abak,konradw}@pjwstk.edu.pl
[2] Orka Postproduction Studio, Warsaw, Poland

Abstract. Simulation of realistic clouds is a difficult task that graphic designers have been trying to achieve for many years. Clouds are necessary for video games and animated movies with outdoor scenes.

Unreal Engine 4, currently one of the most advanced game engines, offers various solutions for implementing such effects. In this paper, we present the effective methods for obtaining realistic real-time clouds in Unreal Engine 4 and provide some new extensions to make the result even better. The methods described are suitable for modeling and rendering both a single cloud and the entire sky filled with clouds. Amongst proposed techniques are modeling clouds by using noise functions, modeling by using a simplified simulation of cloud forming phenomena, rendering by using Ray marching technique and using fluid simulation to allow interaction of clouds with other objects on the scene.

Keywords: Clouds · Volume rendering · Unreal Engine 4 · Real-time

1 Introduction

Clouds are a significant part of the sky, which we can observe every day. This is why adding them to our virtual skies noticeably improves their realism. Game developers and animated movie makers, being conscious of this, used various techniques to draw clouds on screen. Creating virtual clouds is not always an easy task and it is still researched, now for over 40 years. The difficulty level of making clouds depends on how important they are in our product. If we want to create a video game whose action is settled only on the ground level, we could limit ourselves to simple tricks which make sky look convincing for the player. But when we are making an aircraft simulator or an animated movie we could be forced to use more advanced methods, especially if achieving real-time operation is necessary.

In this paper, we would like to present the results of our research on obtaining realistic volumetric clouds working in real-time using Epic Games' Unreal

© Springer Nature Switzerland AG 2018
L. J. Chmielewski et al. (Eds.): ICCVG 2018, LNCS 11114, pp. 68–78, 2018.
https://doi.org/10.1007/978-3-030-00692-1_7

Engine 4 game engine [20]. Some of the methods described have already been implemented and used by us in Unreal Engine 4, while others are proposals that we are going to try to implement and test in the future.

Next section presents existing tools and previous work done in field of creation of volumetric clouds. Section 3 describes our approach and is divided into five areas (modeling, rendering, lighting, shadows and interaction with other objects) where we presents methods used or considered by us. Section 3 also contains brief explanation of Unreal Engine 4 terminology and cloud forming process. Section 4 presents current results of our approach and in Sect. 5 future works related to our system can be found.

2 Previous Work

As mentioned earlier, research on generating clouds by computer started many years ago and it is still going on. At the beginning of our research, complete solutions for Unreal Engine 4 were sought. There is one commercial solution for generating sky filled with volumetric clouds and with weather system that has integration with Unreal Engine 4 through editor plugin, Simul's trueSKY [16]. trueSKY may give good visual results and is undoubtedly great solution for creating realistic skies but it does not suit all of our needs. It is proprietary and closed, it cannot be used for creating single cloud, and it does not offer any support for interaction between clouds and other objects on the scene.

Other commercial software that was considered for cloud creation is NVIDIA's Flow [17] from GameWorks suite. Flow allows creating volumetric fire and smoke with fluid simulation built-in in real-time. It has integration with Unreal Engine 4 through custom modifications in engine source code. Unfortunately, again, Flow does not meet all of our expectations as it is non-deterministic and its integration with Unreal Engine 4 has a few flaws concerning lighting and shadows (rendered volume does not cast shadows and other objects on the scene cannot cast shadow on volume). Another disadvantage is that it is a closed source software.

There are also a few hobbyistic projects aiming for volumetric clouds creation presented and discussed mostly on the official Unreal Engine 4 forum [14], two of them are worth mentioning, [18,19]. Both of them are not released for public.

Finally, there is a content plugin for Unreal Engine 4 created by Epic Games' principal technical artist Ryan Brucks, which contains Blueprint scripts and materials implementing ray marching rendering technique and fluid simulation with possibility of user interaction in two dimensions. Plugin is available at [15]. We currently use some solutions included in this plugin and several methods proposed by Brucks, which are described on his personal web page, [11,12]. From now on this plugin will be called *ShaderBits plugin* in the rest of this paper.

Leaving Unreal Engine 4 and focusing on general research on creating clouds, a few works are worth mentioning. First of them is the Master's thesis of Taxén [4], which describes in detail the physical processes related to cloud forming and also presents different types of clouds modeling. A practical example of using Perlin noise for clouds modeling was presented in [7]. In [2] a proposition of modeling algorithm inspired by clouds forming phenomena was presented. [1] describes clouds modeling method based on [2], which is closer to a simplified simulation of clouds forming phenomena.

In NVIDIA's GPU Gems books, the subject of fluid simulation in real-time was raised. [5,6,9] from respectively first, second and third volume of GPU Gems, describe algorithms for fluid simulation based on Navier-Stokes equations and flow simulation with complex boundaries. Fluid simulation in ShaderBits plugin is actually based on [5].

Another important subject in terms of rendering is lighting. A brief description of light scattering in clouds is in [4]. Approximation of light scattering in clouds was proposed by Harris in [8].

Finally, two works based on released video games are also notable. In [3], we can see an approach for real-time atmospheric effects existing in Crytek's CryEngine 2 [21]. SIGGRAPH 2015 presentation of Guerrilla Games [10] presents a complete pipeline of volumetric clouds creation in their video game including the results of their research and approach for both modelling using noise and rendering by ray marching technique.

3   Overwiev of Methods Used in Our System

This section describes the methods already used in our system and methods that could be implemented and tested by us in Unreal Engine 4.

3.1   Brief Overview of Unreal Engine 4 Terminology

In order to fully understand the solutions proposed and presented in this paper a knowledge of basic terminology existing in Unreal Engine 4 may be required. Unreal Engine 4 is a complex game engine and offers a lot of possibilities. Most important tool in Unreal Engine 4 (UE4 for short) is Editor, a complete tool for game creation. UE4 Editor, which will be also called just *editor* for the rest of this paper, allows creating and setting of maps, materials, Blueprint scripts and many other content.

Map in Unreal Engine 4 is name for scene or level.

UE4's material, which will be called just *material*, will be considered as a pixel shader in this paper. In fact, materials are more complex and can additionally act as vertex or geometry shader. Materials can be created and edited in Material Editor which is a part of Unreal Engine 4 Editor. Material Editor is a graphical tool in which we create material by dragging and dropping blocks, performing various operations (e.g. addition or subtraction), called nodes. We also have possibility to create our own nodes, which are known as Material Functions. Material can be applied on mesh to change its appearance.

Blueprint Visual Scripting is another important part of Unreal Engine 4. It is a complete object-oriented gameplay scripting system. Blueprint scripts can be created and edited in editor, and similarly to materials they are created visually by dragging and dropping blocks responsible for various operations.

Render Target is a special type of texture on which we can draw in runtime. As an example, we can draw the materials content on this texture. From now on the term *rendering to texture* will stand for drawing material to Render Target in the rest of paper.

Objects on scene in Unreal Engine 4 are called *actors*.

3.2   Brief Description of Cloud Forming Process

Clouds consists of very small water droplets with radius of approximately 50 μm or ice crystals. When floating up in troposphere, the water vapour (which e.g. comes from sea or ocean heated by sun) gets cooled, as the temperature in the atmosphere drops with increase of altitude. When the vapour temperature drops to a certain level called a *dew point* due to condensation or deposition, it is changed to water droplets or ice crystals. Water droplets combined together form a cloud that we could see on the sky. When the water droplet in the cloud grow, it could become too heavy, change into a rain drop and fall from the cloud to the ground.

Most of the clouds we can see on the sky can be divided to 10 basic types based on appearance and altitude. Brief presentation of these 10 types can be found at third section of [1].

3.3   Modeling

Our system for creating volumetric clouds in Unreal Engine 4 consists of two parts, modeling and rendering. Modeling is a process of which the result is cloud (or clouds) density data. Usually, density data is stored in 3D textures, but unfortunately Unreal Engine 4 does not support 3D textures. Known workaround for this limitation is proposed in [11] use of, so called, *pseudo volume textures*. The pseudo volume texture is a regular 2D texture containing slices of volume arranged in a grid. Each slice consists of volume density data at a particular height. An example of such a pseudo volume texture is shown in Fig. 1. The more slices in pseudo volume texture, the more detailed will be rendered volumetric object, but also it will take more time to process the texture in the material.

Although one can create such a texture procedurally in a tool like Houdini and export it to the editor, we focused on methods for generating pseudo volume textures without user interaction and the need for external software. We consider two methods of modeling, using the noise function and running a simulation based on a simplified cloud forming phenomena. Unreal Engine 4 material editor contains a built-in node named *Noise*, which generates the noise for given (on node input) position vector. Noise node has a few parameters possible to tweak where most important of them is *Function*, which allows to select the used noise function. Available functions are *Simplex*, *Gradient*, *Fast Gradient* and *Voronoi*. Each function has its own complexity, which significantly affects the frame rate. The most simple and fastest function is Fast Gradient and the most complex

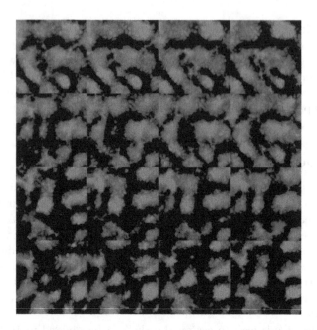

Fig. 1. Example pseudo volume texture with 4×4 grid of slices.

and slowest is Voronoi. Using the Noise node we can create a material that can be used for generation of pseudo volume texture by drawing it to the Render Target. In such material, either only one Noise node can be used or a few Noise nodes with different parameters values can be combined. Mixing several Noise nodes or using complex functions is not possible in real-time if we need to render our material to texture in every frame, e.g. if we want to animate our clouds depending on time. The possible solution can be a one-time generation of the noise texture with expensive functions like Voronoi and passing it to the material drawn every time to Render Target as a parameter. Then the material calculated every frame would contain only the Noise nodes using cheap functions like Fast Gradient. Material generating density texture by noise may require additional operations to make the clouds looking more natural and resemble actual clouds of a given type.

The second method of generating the density pseudo volume texture with clouds is the use of algorithms inspired by the cloud forming phenomena. Performing an exact simulation of all physical phenomena is not possible and would be too complex to calculate in real-time. This is why the algorithms considered by us for implementing in Unreal Engine 4 are very simplified comparing to natural processes. At the moment we have not implemented any of such algorithms yet but in the future we plan to implement the ones described in [1,2]. To achieve a scene with volumetric clouds in real-time using these algorithms, the implementation of them in material (processed on GPU) may be necessary. One possible approach is using the pseudo volume texture to store the simulation grid. Such a texture would be created and populated with initial values in Blueprint script (executed on CPU) and then processed in the material performing the simulation in each next frame. Texture channels can be used to store up to four parameters of grid cell in a single texture.

3.4 Rendering

We use a ray marching method implemented according to [12] for rendering clouds in our system. The Ray marching algorithm is implemented in a separate material. Such material is then applied to the mesh, which was chosen to contain clouds. Method presented in [12] and used by us is suited for cube-shaped meshes. The general idea of the ray marching method consists of "shooting" rays from every pixel of the mesh (with ray marching material applied) and moving through them with constant step defined by the user. At each step, operations defining this pixel colour are executed, e.g. the amount of absorbed light is added up. Number of steps is finite and defined by user. Usually, the end condition for a given pixel is the execution of all number of steps. Graphical presentation of ray marching technique is presented in Fig. 2.

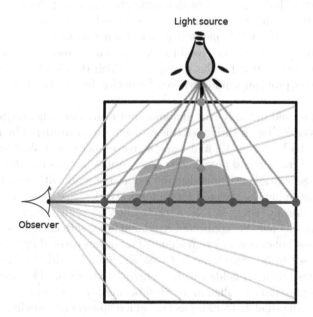

Fig. 2. Brief overview of ray marching technique. At every step (marked by red circles) of ray coming from observer or more precisely mesh' pixel, additional steps (green circles) to light source are performed for volume shading calculation. (Color figure online)

3.5 Lighting

Implementation of a lighting model based strictly on the real world can be difficult and impossible in real-time. This is due to how the light scatters in the cloud. The most difficult task is the approximation of in-scattering existing in the cloud (multiple scattering of light inside the cloud). We currently use the lighting model proposed in [12], which implements only out-scattering. It gives a decent visual result but we consider implementation of more realistic looking solution. Similar approach was presented in [2] and extension of that method in [8].

3.6 Shadows

For obtaining a shadow of the cloud we created a simple material with *Blend mode* (material parameter) set to *Masked*, which takes the pseudo volume texture as a parameter. The material calculates the shape of the cloud based on the pseudo volume texture by summing the density values from its every slice in a given position. Such material is then applied on the regular UE4 plane mesh. The plane mesh is set to not be visible, but casts its shadow. Thanks to the usage of Masked Blend Mode, the shadow shape matches the cloud shape. The shadow shape calculated in this material is in fact a projection of the cloud to the XY plane. One drawback of this method results from this fact, the created cloud shadow will always present the cloud in the XY plane projection independently of the light direction. But for the scenario in which the clouds are high in the atmosphere, this problem would not even be noticeable by the observer in most cases.

The cloud should not only cast shadows, but also allow other objects to cast their shadows on it. Two solutions of this problem were considered by us, using a distance field shadow as in [12] and using a custom per object shadow map presented in [13]. First method gives good visual results but has one drawback, the distance field generation in Unreal Engine 4 does not work with *Skeletal meshes*, i.e. meshes containing the skeleton for animations. We have found a workaround for this limitation by using *sockets*. Sockets allow to connect any mesh to specific Skeletal mesh bone. We connected regular spheres with changed scale and/or rotation to some bones in a way that shape of mesh was covered by these spheres. Spheres were set to be not visible but cast shadow. As added spheres are not Skeletal meshes, distance fields can be generated for them. This way we have obtained an approximated shadow of Skeletal mesh on volumetric cloud. This method allows the shadow to move as the added spheres are moving along with the bones to which they are connected while the Skeletal mesh is playing animation. One inconvenience of this workaround is that additional spheres must be added and connected to bones manually in Unreal Engine 4 editor. The second method of achieving the shadows of other objects on clouds, i.e. using custom per object shadow map, was implemented in UE4 according to [13]. Although this method does not have a problem with various types of meshes (e.g. Skeletal meshes) it has other significant drawbacks. The first drawback is a poor performance compared to the previous method. The second drawback is the necessity of making the shadows softer to look more realistic on cloud that may impact the performance even more. Another problem are graphical artifacts like distortion or disappearance of shadow when object casting it is moved away from the cloud (as it could not be captured by *Scene Capture* component). Because of these drawbacks we decided to use the first of described methods, i.e. distance fields shadows.

3.7   Interaction with Other Objects on Scene

In most of video games, the player does not interact directly with the clouds and even in most aircraft simulators, flying through the clouds does not change their appearance. However such feature could be desired e.g. in animated movie. This is why we used a fluid simulation for allowing other objects on the scene to reshape cloud by e.g. flying through it. The ShaderBits plugin contains the fluid simulation based on [5] implemented in materials, where each stage of simulation is implemented in a separate material. Unfortunately, by default, the interaction works only for 2 dimensions. We have modified it to work in 3 dimensions with volumetric objects. As such simulation is computationally expensive, we use it only with the single cloud at this moment. Figure 3 presents an example effect of fluid simulation in cloud.

Fig. 3. Fluid simulation in cloud. Left: before sphere moved into cloud
Middle: after sphere moved through cloud
Right: after few passes of sphere through cloud

4   Results

The results of our work are slightly different for creation of one cloud and multiple clouds, which can fill the sky. Our setup for single cloud consists of an actor

Blueprint script and materials for ray marching, fluid simulation stages and cloud shadow. Appropriate parameters in Blueprint script allow to set the ray marching material, the cloud density pseudo volume texture or material for generating one, the pseudo volume texture dimensions and various settings for fluid simulation. Interaction with other objects on the scene is limited to only one object at this time. Figure 3 presents the single cloud with fluid simulation.

For multiple clouds, which can fill the sky, we have very similar setup. Again, it consists of the actor Blueprint script and materials for ray marching, pseudo volume texture generation and clouds shadow. As mentioned in subsection dedicated to modeling, we currently use the noise functions for generating pseudo volume texture. We do not use the fluid simulation for multiple clouds setup. In Fig. 4 the sample sky created by our system using Fast Gradient noise function is presented.

Fig. 4. Sky filled with volumetric clouds modeled by Fast Gradient noise function. Images taken from various viewing angles and time.

All of presented results were achieved on Unreal Engine 4.19.2 in 1920 × 1080 pixels resolution running on desktop computer with Intel Core i7-5820K CPU, 64 GB of RAM and NVIDIA GeForce GTX 970 video card. The frame rate of performed simulations resolves around 25 frames per second.

5   Future Work

Although we managed to generate clouds, our system is still incomplete and further research is necessary. First, our cloud modeling by noise needs to be improved for achieving clouds more resembling existing in nature clouds of various types. In terms of cloud modeling we are also planning implementation of methods in [1,2]. For rendering, the ray marching technique will be used but improvements in lighting area, especially approximation of multiple scattering will be researched. We also consider enhancements in the fluid simulation methods used by us to allow more complex simulation boundaries and support more than one object at time.

Acknowledgements. This work has been supported by the National Centre for Research and Development, Poland, in the frame of Operational Programme Smart Growth 2014–2020 within Sectoral Programme GAMEINN, POIR.01.02.00-00-0115/16 "Innovative use of computer game engine in order to reduce costs and time of production of animated film".

References

1. Miyazaki R., Yoshida S., Dobashi Y., Nishita T.: A method for modeling clouds based on atmospheric fluid dynamics (2001)
2. Dobashi Y., Kaneda K., Yamashita H., Okita T., Nishita T.: A simple, efficient method for realistic animation of clouds (2000)
3. Wenzel C.: Advanced real-time rendering in 3D graphics and games, chapt. 6, Real-time atmospheric effects in games (2006)
4. Taxén, G.: Cloud Modeling for Computer Graphics (1999)
5. Harris, M., Fernando, R. (eds.): GPU Gems, chapt. 38, Fast Fluid Dynamics Simulation on the GPU. Addison-Wesley Professional (2004). ISBN 978-0321228321
6. Li, W., Fan, Z., Wei, X., Kaufman, A., Pharr, M. (eds.): GPU Gems 2, chap. 47, Flow Simulation with Complex Boundaries. Addison-Wesley Professional (2005). ISBN: 978-0321335593
7. Man P.: Generating and real-time rendering of cloud (2006)
8. Harris M.: Real-time cloud rendering for games (2002)
9. Crane, K., Llamas, I., Tariq, S., Nguyen, H. (eds.): GPU Gems 3, chap. 30, Real-Time Simulation and Rendering of 3D Fluids. Addison-Wesley Professional (2007). ISBN 978-0321515261
10. Schneider A., Vos N.: The real-time volumetric cloudscapes of Horizon - Zero Dawn (2015)
11. Brucks R.: Authoring pseudo volume textures. http://shaderbits.com/blog/authoring-pseudo-volume-textures (2016). Accessed 17 July 2018
12. Brucks R.: Creating a volumetric ray marcher. http://shaderbits.com/blog/creating-volumetric-ray-marcher (2016). Accessed 17 July 2018
13. Brucks R.: Custom per object shadowmaps using blueprints. http://shaderbits.com/blog/custom-per-object-shadowmaps-using-blueprints (2016). Accessed 17 July 2018
14. Unreal Engine 4 Forums. https://forums.unrealengine.com/. Accessed 17 July 2018

15. Training Livestream - Realtime Simulation and Volume Modelling Experiments (Unreal Engine 4 forum thread). https://forums.unrealengine.com/unreal-engine/events/116634-training-livestream-realtime-simulation-and-volume-modelling-experiments-may-2-live-from-epic. Accessed 17 July 2018
16. Simul trueSKY Web Page. https://simul.co/truesky/. Accessed 17 July 2018
17. NVIDIA Flow Web Page. https://developer.nvidia.com/nvidia-flow. Accessed 17 July 2018
18. Volumetric cloud system overview (Unreal Engine 4 forum thread). https://forums.unrealengine.com/community/community-content-tools-and-tutorials/32639-volumetric-cloud-system-overview. Accessed 17 July 2018
19. Working on Volumetric Clouds in UE4. https://80.lv/articles/working-on-volumetric-clouds-in-ue4/. Accessed 17 July 2018
20. Unreal Engine 4 Web Page. https://www.unrealengine.com/. Accessed 17 July 2018
21. CryEngine 2 Web Page. http://www.crytek.com/cryengine/cryengine2/overview. Accessed 17 July 2018

Real-Time Simulation of Animated Characters Crowd in Unreal Engine 4

Michał Rosenbeiger[1]([✉]), Artur Bąk[1][ID], and Tomasz Czajkowski[2]

[1] Polish-Japanese Academy of Information Technology, Warsaw, Poland
{michalr,abak}@pjwstk.edu.pl
[2] Orka Postproduction Studio, Warsaw, Poland

Abstract. Realistic crowd simulation is still not an easy task in computer animation and computer games domain, especially when it has to be done in real-time and no post-processing correction is possible. The goal of this paper is to analyze and compare the algorithms of crowd behavior and collision avoidance available in Unreal Engine 4, which is one of the most popular game engines. We addressed various methods: natively implemented in the engine, requiring their own implementation and requiring the use of external software. We found one of the natively implemented algorithms, Detour Crowd, as the most useful in terms of quality and flexibility to extend, so as a consequence we use it as a base for our own improvements of engine functionality to achieve more believable movement of actors in crowd simulation. These improvements are also addressed by the paper.

Keywords: Crowds · Detour Crowd · Unreal Engine 4 · Real-time

1 Introduction

While the basics of artificial intelligence used for characters in simulations are commonly known, using them in a realistic manner remains a subject of many studies to this day. The problem is especially demanding when the simulation has to be done in real-time without the possibility of correction during the post-processing. As a result, there are many different solutions whose goal is to represent the actors movement in a dense crowd. They may focus more or less on various aspects like path generation, collision avoidance or addition of animations to achieve this goal.

One of the most popular game engines, Unreal Engine 4, has a built-in implementation of the basic version of Reciprocal Velocity Obstacle avoidance algorithm and Detour Crowd for the purposes of simulating movements of groups of actors in real-time. These algorithms represent medium quality on their own, but have s relatively large room for improvement. Aside from them, there are also many other available crowd simulation methods of varying quality.

This article will focus on the analysis of available methods and algorithms as well as on expanding solutions available in Unreal Engine 4 to improve the realism of its built-in crowd simulation.

© Springer Nature Switzerland AG 2018
L. J. Chmielewski et al. (Eds.): ICCVG 2018, LNCS 11114, pp. 79–88, 2018.
https://doi.org/10.1007/978-3-030-00692-1_8

The second section will expand on solutions and algorithms already available on the market or as an Open Source. Then, in the third section the changes applied to the Detour Crowd algorithm will be described. The results of the modification will be presented in the fourth section. The fifth section will focus on current and future research.

2 Previous Work

In this section, currently available methods and algorithms for simulating crowds will be listed and shortly described. Some of them, especially the ones already included in Unreal Engine 4, will include additional presentations presented in the form of screen captures.

2.1 Simple AI

For the purposes of later comparisons, simple AI Controllers have been tested using the most basic pathing algorithm available in Unreal Engine 4 with behavior trees without any use of complex avoidance and crowd simulation elements (Fig. 1).

Fig. 1. Crowd using simple AI locked on the door entrance.

It is especially visible in tests that, while this method actually does work acceptably well for small number of actors, it has major problems during tests with bigger ones. The characters have a problem with the crowd avoidance and moving through narrow passages. Groups of characters trying to move through a door get stuck on one another when actors' target points, and thus also their calculated paths through the doors, overlap while the algorithm has no collision avoidance to try to find an alternate path. This problem can be solved to some extent by controlling the spawning or activating of actors in order to avoid situation, where the paths would collide.

Trying to have two groups of characters moving through each other always results in at least partial deadlock, where characters try to follow their paths through the crowd coming from the opposite direction.

The only real advantage of using such simple AI is to ensure a complete predictability of the characters' movements.

2.2 Reciprocal Velocity Obstacle

Reciprocal Velocity Obstacle (hereinafter referred to as RVO) is an extension of the Velocity Obstacle Algorithm, which calculates the eponymous velocity obstacle for every actor in the group by taking into account the velocities of nearby actors and calculating the range of velocities that could cause collisions and should be avoided [1]. RVO improves on that algorithm by taking into account the fact that other actors also use the same avoidance algorithm, which results in smaller velocity obstacles and avoiding needless oscillatory motions [2]. This algorithm still tends to avoid obstacles in a large distance so it is particularly effective for medium-sized crowds in small spaces. Large crowds in small spaces however make this algorithm inefficient as they cannot keep their distances.

The algorithm is implemented in the Unreal Engine and can easily be used with simple AI controllers similar to ones described in the previous subsection to visibly improve their performance (Fig. 2).

Fig. 2. Two crowds intersecting using RVO (left) and simple AI without RVO (right).

As mentioned previously, RVO is particularly effective for large crowd moving through narrow passages without deadlocking on one another. However during the tests, situations of deadlocking still happened when a very narrow passage is used, which sometimes puts all velocity obstacles in it, disallowing any actors to pass. Nevertheless, compared to non-velocity-obstacle algorithms it is relatively rare and happens only in extreme cases.

There is a large and visible distance that actors tend to keep between one another. This may give the crowd some kind of realism but may be problematic for cases where dense crowds are a preferable option. Compared to other algorithms, RVO is not the fastest one – it makes much longer for two crowds to intersect and switch positions with each other. This may or may not be preferable depending on the case in which algorithm is used.

A major problem of this algorithm in the Unreal Engine are distinctive side-way sliding motions of the actors when they are pushed aside by others' moving velocity obstacles causing unnatural movement without affecting the animations. This problem could be potentially reduced by lowering the density of the crowd, which would lower the chance of collisions; by trying to force special animations when characters are moving sideways; or by trying to force actors to rotate when they are pushed.

There were multiple reports of actors, coded with controllers using RVO, blocking in walls and objects when ignoring the navigation meshes. These were not confirmed during the tests, but the possibility of these problems happening should still be taken into consideration.

2.3 Reciprocal Velocity Obstacle 2

The University of North Carolina at Chapel Hill created two improved versions of the RVO library. First of these is RVO2. It was created in order to improve efficiency for very large crowds and to decrease needless movement of actors when the crowd is not very dense. The library uses Optimal Reciprocal Collision Avoidance (ORCA) [4]. It is available as an Open Source C++ library under Apache license. While possible, the integration of library with Unreal Engine may take a lot of time. There have been attempts to integrate the library with the Unreal Development Kit [5], but not the Unreal Engine 4 as yet.

Characters do better at moving in large groups through narrow passages. However, the problem with actors sliding when pushed aside by one another persists and may cause problems.

2.4 Hybrid Reciprocal Velocity Obstacle

Hybrid Reciprocal Velocity Obstacle (HRVO) is another alternative modification to RVO library also made by The University of North Carolina at Chapel Hill. HRVO in a way combines the RVO algorithm with standard VO algorithm reducing the amount of sidetracking of actors when prioritizing the avoidance over the attempt to keep the desired velocity [3]. This prevents the actors from moving in large distance between one another. Its creator describes it as able to achieve an oscillation-free and collision-free actor movement [6]. This avoidance algorithm was created mainly with an intention of use for robots. With this groups of robots, assuming that each of them uses the algorithm, can avoid each other seamlessly with a great precision [7]. This may render it suboptimal for the case of implementing crowds in the Unreal Engine 4, but the tests of the algorithm on virtual agents seem to give very good effects [8]. This algorithm is also efficient in avoiding static obstacles.

2.5   Detour Crowd

Detour Crowd is another algorithm, built-in in Unreal Engine 4, designed to simulate the movement of crowds. It is a part of the recastnavigation project by Mikko Mononen, although without the use of recast to generate navigation meshes.

The implementation of the Detour Crowd controller is much better in the Unreal Engine than it is the case with the RVO. It properly rotates the characters in all cases and prevents unnatural movements. It seems especially useful for very dense crowds. It is also very easy to implement albeit requires a bit more configuration than others. In order to use it in Unreal Engine, characters, that are expected to use it, need to have Pawn with a controller that inherits from DetourCrowdAIController class. This can be done both as a C++ or a Blueprint class. Usage of the controller is similar to regular one, it requires proper Behavior Tree with a correct leaf with a "Move To." instruction.

Algorithm creates a set number of subdivided, concentric rings, where each subdivision is weighted. Numbers of rings and their subdivisions are set through algorithm parameters. Each subdivision is weighted according to obstacles, other agents, and weights set through parameters, which include preferences for keeping close to expected direction on an obstacle-less course, preference for not changing velocity, preference not to move sideways if possible to dodge the obstacle or to minimize and preference to avoid collisions. Then algorithm calculates the optimal path through the points with lowest weights in a manner similar to A* (Fig. 3).

Fig. 3. Example of generated rings shown in debug mode.

Aside from the weights, many other parameters are available for configuration including maximum number of agents included to the crowd, maximum distance between them, maximum numbers of nearest agents and static obstacles taken into consideration by the algorithm for each actor, as well as intervals between updating the path and checking whether the actor is still correctly on th navigation mesh.

The implementation of Detour Crowd in Unreal Engine 4 is supposed to work correctly with RVO enabled for its controllers, but using them in this manner is not recommended as the algorithms may collide with each other (Fig. 4).

Fig. 4. Two crowds intersecting using Detour Crowd (left) and RVO (right).

Compared to the crowd using the RVO alone, actors using Detour Crowd keep much lower distances from one another allowing two main groups to intersect with each other on much smaller space. On the top of that properly configured groups using detour crowd controllers split into small, neat groups. This is not the case with controllers using just RVO, as it only provides avoidance, without any additional crowd interactions. The movement with RVO is way more chaotic and this results in both groups taking much longer time to intersect.

Compared to a simple AI, the problem with the deadlocking in narrow passages still persists when generated paths of multiple actors align and they try to cross the passage at the same time. This problem however, to a greater or lesser extent, seems to concern all tested inbuilt algorithms in Ureal Engine 4, thus a way to prevent such situations seems to be most efficient way of solving this problem. On the other hand, as mentioned before, there is a major positive side of the detour crowd algorithm, which is efficiency of groups of actors moving through each other. This also applies to avoiding static obstacles so as long as the actors are prevented from taking similar paths at the same place and time, detour crowd would prove to be more efficient in such cases despite RVO being more reliable otherwise.

In spite of the persisting deadlocking problem, the implementation of Detour Crowd in Unreal Engine has the least problem compared to using simple AI with RVO and doesn't require any additional implementations. Thus it has been decided that this will be used as a basis for simulations set as the goal of this project.

2.6   Anima 3

Anima is a tool created by Axyz-design to generate animated crowds and export them to FBX files and then, optionally, to the Unreal Engine 4. While this program is not applicable for real-time crowd simulation in the game engine itself, it sets a high standard for crowds simulations on its own. The movement of the generated crowds is very smooth and optimized. The actors' models are optionally randomized and have additional animations that result in the crowd appearing more realistic to an observer. The only downside would be the fact that the actors follow patch in a very mechanical way, with low degree of randomness. The real-time simulation this article pursues should aim to incorporate the positive features of Anima generator in its own ways.

3 Improvements Used in Our System

In this section, implemented fixes and improvements to crowds using Detour Crowd algorithm are listed.

3.1 Minor Fixes to Improve Responsiveness of the Crowd

Multiple minor fixes were applied to the performance of default Detour Crowd controller and the actors to reduce bugs during the simulations. First of them was the lowering of the characters' tick interval to 0.2 to prevent actors from stuttering when changing paths in real time on every update. At the same the interval could not be too high as it would reduce the effectiveness of the whole algorithm.

Another change was the reduction of rotation rate of the characters' meshes to 180 degrees per second. This prevented unnatural rotations when the actor's target was abruptly changed. This change also required to set the rotation to be oriented to the movement while disabling the change of rotations by the controller. This way the controller could operate independently and optimize actors' paths as often as needed without causing them to instantly turn around.

Additionally, the acceleration was adjusted to realistic levels to prevent the actors from starting and stopping too abruptly.

3.2 Reducing the Possibility of Characters Deadlocking

The main issue to resolve when implementing crowds using Detour Crowd is to prevent the actors from deadlocking on one another, when too many actors try to move through narrow spaces. Aside from that, any changes that could improve the way two crowds pass through each others would be welcome, especially if amount of occurrences where two or more actors stay in one place waiting for others to move could be reduced.

These problems have been addressed in multiple ways. Firstly, the Detour Crowd parameters, mainly weights, were adjusted. The most important parameters in this case would be Current Velocity Weight, which was lowered in order to make actors more "willing" to change direction when encountering an obstacle, as well as Side Bias Weight, which was increased to balance out by preventing actors from moving sideways when not necessary.

Next improvement was meant to decrease concentration of actors when moving towards the same target. This was resolved by adding an option to set an area around common target where each actor will assign a random point to itself. Effects of this are particularly apparent in wide areas, where otherwise actors would not try to spread across the road, as a real crowd would, but instead concentrate on the shortest way to the destination, resulting not only in lower realism, but also in possible increased prevalence of mutual blocking and slowing between the actors.

Finally, an optional delay was added between actors' spawning. This decreases the chances of multiple actors trying to move through a narrow passage and deadlocking, when the configuration is correct. Additionally delays improve the quality of simulations where constant stream of actors is required, e.g. when actors are walking on the sidewalk of the street.

3.3   Additional Target Changes During Simulation

While not necessary to improve performance additional target selection was implemented to expand the crowd simulations' possibilities. First of these was the addition of optional re-rolling of target when an actor arrives at its destination. This allows actors at the destination to act more realistically as a crowd after the main movement to their respective targets. It is especially useful for simulating massive numbers of people exiting building, which in real world results in chaotic movements around the square in front of the main door.

The target is not completely random but relies on placement and rotation of the actor on the area designated for selecting random targets. This is to prevent actor from abruptly change directions when selecting new target.

Moreover switching targets between the initial target and the starting point was added. This allows simulation of crowd moving on sidewalks or similar paths to not require despawning and respawning actors at the ends of the path, when they are not visible.

3.4   Randomization of Character Meshes and Animations

As crowd simulation chosen as the goal of this study should imitate a real crowd as much as possible, character meshes were randomized from meshes provided by the user. This allows to create a much more realistic simulation with various agents spawning and moving along with the crowd.

On top of it the additional random animations were added to play when actors slow down or stop to increase the immersion.

4   Results

After fixes a properly configured crowd should not deadlock or, provided it is not too limited in terms of the navigation space e.g. in a very narrow corridor, slow down when passing each other from opposite directions. Tests show it is usually the case, however there is still a field for improvement as far as the density required for a seamless movement goes (Fig. 5).

Quality of the randomization of character meshes and animations is good, but would gain a lot if many more meshes and animations are used, as it would present the possibilities of this solution to the full extent. As it stands now, it is

Fig. 5. Crowd of actors runs out of the building without any blocks, then proceeds to randomly change targets and play animations.

representative enough for tests yet not presenting the full extent of possibilities this solution provides.

The randomization of actors' targets seems to work very well, and re-rolling targets after reaching the goal has achieved its goal of emulating crowd exiting the building quite well. Depending on how the adjustable speed and probability of animations are set, the movements may resemble these of children leaving school or just regular people leaving a building suddenly in large quantities.

Minor adjustment including but not limited to rotation rate and limited acceleration did surprisingly good job to improve visual quality and realism of the movement and improve the immersion for a viewer or player.

5   Current and Future Plans

Currently, the efforts are being undertaken in order for the actors to try to pass the ones coming from the opposite direction from the same side, i.e. to encourage a right-hand or a left-hand traffic between the actors. This would not only make the crowd movement more realistic, but also improve the flow of the crowd reducing blocking and slowing down of actors to the absolute minimum.

Next, research will be undertaken to add full determinism to the simulation, where given the same conditions crowd will always act in the same manner. Currently the movement of actors is still partially random as a result of the internal structure of the engine, which may be unfavorable for the user.

Acknowledgements. This work has been supported by the National Centre for Research and Development, Poland, in the frame of Operational Programme Smart Growth 2014-2020 within Sectoral Programme GAMEINN, POIR.01.02.00-00-0115/16 "Innovative use of computer game engine in order to reduce costs and time of production of animated film".

References

1. van den Berg, J., Lin, M.C., Manocha, D.: Reciprocal velocity obstacles for real-time multi-agent navigation. In: Proceedings IEEE International Conference on Robotics and Automation (ICRA), pp. 1928–1935 (2008)
2. van den Berg, J., Patil, S., Sewall, J., Manocha, D., Lin, M.C.: Interactive navigation of individual agents in crowded environments. In: Proceedings ACM SIGGRAPH Symposium Interactive 3D Graphics and Games, Redwood City, California, pp. 139–147, 15–17 February 2008
3. Snape, J., Guy, S.J., Lin, M.C., Manocha, D.: Reciprocal collision avoidance and multi-agent navigation for video games. AAAI Technical report WS-12-10 (2012)
4. van den Berg, J., Guy, S.J., Lin, M., Manocha, D.: Reciprocal n-body collision avoidance. In: Pradalier, C., Siegwart, R., Hirzinger, G. (eds.) Robotics Research: The 14th International Symposium ISRR, Springer Tracts in Advanced Robotics, vol. 70, pp. 3–19. Springer, Heidelberg (2011)
5. RVO2 Library Integration with Unreal Development Kit. http://gamma.cs.unc.edu/RVO2-UDK/. Accessed 20 July 2018
6. Snape, J., van den Berg, J., Guy, S.J., Manocha, D.: The hybrid reciprocal velocity obstacle. IEEE Trans. Robot. **27**(4), 696–706 (2011)
7. Snape, J., van den Berg, J., Guy, S.J., Manocha, D.: Independent navigation of multiple mobile robots with hybrid reciprocal velocity obstacles. In: Proceedings IEEE/RSJ International Conference Intelligent Robots and Systems, St. Louis, Missouri, pp. 5917–5922 (2009)
8. HRVO Library in Mason. https://www.youtube.com/watch?v=9xhlyaqt8jo. Accessed 20 July 2018

Object Classification and Features

Plane Object-Based High-Level Map Representation for SLAM

Pavel Gritsenko[2], Igor Gritsenko[2], Askar Seidakhmet[2], and Bogdan Kwolek[1(✉)]

[1] AGH University of Science and Technology,
30 Mickiewicza, 30-059 Kraków, Poland
bkw@agh.edu.pl
[2] Al-Farabi Kazakh National University,
Prospect al-Farabi 71, Almaty, Kazakhstan
lickro@mail.ru
http://home.agh.edu.pl/~bkw/contact.html

Abstract. High-level map representation providing object-based understanding of the environment is an important component for SLAM. We present a novel algorithm to build plane object-based map representation upon point cloud that is obtained in real–time from RGB-D sensors such as Kinect. On the basis of segmented planes in point cloud we construct a graph, where a node and edge represent a plane and its real intersection with other plane, respectively. After that, we extract all trihedral angles (corners) represented by 3rd order cycles in the graph. Afterwards, we execute systematic aggregation of trihedral angles into object such as trihedral angles of the same plane-based object have common edges. Finally, we classify objects using simple subgraph patterns and determine their physical sizes. Our experiments figured out that the proposed algorithm reliably extracts objects, determines their physical sizes and classifies them with a promising performance.

1 Introduction

Recent progress in development of robotics has increased capabilities such as mobility and autonomy. Navigating in unknown environments requires a SLAM (Simultaneous Localization and Mapping) system or module. The SLAM problem can be posed as the metaphorical chicken-and-egg dilemma: a robot in order to determine its current location needs an accurate map. However, in order to incrementally build a map, it should have estimate of its position within the map. The SLAM problem is related to two questions: "where am I?" (localization), and "what does the environment look like?" (mapping). The currently utilized formulation of SLAM has its origins in the seminal work [11].

A robust SLAM algorithm is an essential component for any mobile robot to navigate through an unstructured environment. The SLAM problem has been one of the most popular research topics in mobile robotics for the last two decades and several approaches have been proposed [4]. In [5], authors argue that developments in the area of SLAM are entering the third era - "robust–perception

© Springer Nature Switzerland AG 2018
L. J. Chmielewski et al. (Eds.): ICCVG 2018, LNCS 11114, pp. 91–102, 2018.
https://doi.org/10.1007/978-3-030-00692-1_9

age". The key requirements for the new age SLAM system are as follows: (1) Robust Performance; (2) High-Level Understanding; (3) Resource Awareness; (4) Task-Driven Perception.

In this paper, we propose an algorithm to build high-level map representation in order to extend capabilities of state-of-the-art SLAM algorithms in order to match the requirements mentioned above. At present, most of RGB-D SLAM systems relies on point clouds or truncated signed distance function (TSDF). The first crucial drawback is that these representations require substantial amount of memory. Even in case of mapping a simple environment, like an empty room, in both mentioned representations the memory requirements grow very fast with scene complexity and time, which makes impossible to use them in long-term operation and leads to noncompliance with the key requirements of third era SLAM systems – robust performance and resource awareness.

2   Relevant Work and Our Contribution

2.1   Relevant Work

Compact map requiring small amount of memory is an essential component of any SLAM system for long term operation and operation in a large environment. There are number of works that were devoted to constructing compact maps on the basis of geometric primitives like points, lines, and planes [3,17,23,24, 28]. SLAM system using plane-to-plane correspondences was presented in [28], whereas the problem of unknown correspondences was investigated in [17]. One of the major shortcomings of plane-based methods [3,17,23,28] is insufficient number of non-parallel planes. This problem is partially solved in [24] by using additional laser scanner with large FOV, but with an additional cost and system complexity. In line-based SLAM it is hard to obtain line correspondences because the RGB-D data from 3D sensors like Kinect is noisy and includes missing depth values [23]. An exemplar point-based RGB-D mapping system is presented in [11]. It is based on seeking for three point-to-point correspondences using RGB and depth map stream to find an initial estimate of the pose using RANSAC, which is further handled and improved by ICP algorithm.

It is worth noting that despite remarkable progress in constructing a compact map, almost all SLAM systems include little semantic information to the map [5]. There are three main ways to construct high-level map representation and to provide semantics to a mobile robot [5]. The first kind of solutions treat the SLAM as a first step and then add semantics to produced map. The first attempt consisted in building classical geometric map using a 2D laser scanner [15]. Then associative Markov network was used to fuse the classified semantic places from each robot pose. A later work was quite similar, but it concentrated on 3D maps that were constructed off-line from RGB-D sequences [14]. The first on-line version was developed by Pronobis et al. [19]. After that, object recognition in videos has been supported by a monocular SLAM system [18]. The second group of approaches extract semantics in advance and then take advantage of prior knowledge including semantic classes or objects, their geometry, in order to improve the mapping quality. The first attempts focused on monocular SLAM with sparse features [7] and a dense map representation [8]. The first successful RGB-D SLAM was developed by Salas-Moreno et al. [21]. The third kind of approaches combine extraction of semantics and SLAM and do it simultaneously. The first successful approach was achieved by Flint et al. [9], where a model leveraging the Manhattan world assumption has been utilized. In a later work, estimation of camera parameters and objects using both geometric and semantic information has been investigated [1]. Despite achieving improvement in the performance of object recognition, this approach is considered to be impractical for on-line robot operation because of execution time (about 20 min per image pair) and limited number of objects that can be processed. The complexity of the algorithm was gradually reduced in [13] using late fusion of semantic information and metric map. However, the system still works only in off-line. The first success in constructing on-line system with object recognition and adding semantic information to the scene has been achieved in [26] through the use of stereo cameras and a dense map representation.

2.2 Differences with Relevant Approaches

Our approach differs in several aspects from the relevant work. The first key difference is that our system does not decompose point cloud into set of separate primitives, but it aggregates planes into objects and builds a complex representation consisting of plane-based objects and point clouds representing objects of complex shapes, see Fig. 1.

The second difference is that our algorithm reconstructs plane-based objects of any type consisting of any number of faces, and thus it differs from RANSAC,

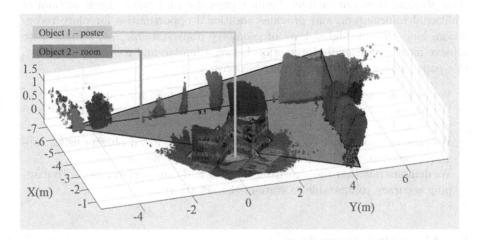

Fig. 1. Plane object-based high-level map representation on the point cloud reconstructed from 907 frames, represented by open TUM RGB-D dataset [22] (rgbd_dataset_freiburg3_structure_texture_far).

which extracts only objects of predefined shape. The third difference is that our high-level map representation is capable of reconstructing plane-based object of any size (room, floor, building) from sequence of frames, i.e. it adds object parts frame-by-frame. We will show that our map representation gradually reduces memory consumption by dozens of times with respect to point cloud-based representation. The fourth difference is that our algorithm allows to use all state-of-the-art closed-form solutions [6, 10, 16, 20, 25, 29] to determine the robot pose. Closed form solutions do not assume any motion model and are more reliable comparatively to the most popular state-of-the-art ICP algorithm [2]. The use of trihedral angles (corners) to represent plane-based objects stands for this ability. The trihedral angle allows to use all three types of primitives: point, line, plane, see also Fig. 1, as well as point-to-point [25], line-to-line [29], plane-to-plane [10], point-to-line [16], point-to-plane [20], and line-to-plane [6] correspondences and their closed-form solutions. From one hand any of such solutions can be used at a time. From the other hand, any combination of several solutions can be used [27]. This gradually increases the robustness of the proposed algorithm. Additionally, closed-form solutions are obtained in one iteration and require less computational resources than ICP. Therefore, the fourth difference refers to resource awareness.

It is worth noting that the fifth difference lies in classification of plane-based objects using a graph. The algorithm is based on graph patterns instead of ANN, RANSAC or other complex and computationally expensive algorithm. It is simple, fast and computationally very cheap, which makes possible real-time or close to real-time execution on ARM processors.

Another crucial point is that none of state-of-the-art representations provide high-level information about the environment to allow a robot to distinguish between objects, their sizes and types [5]. With the ability to extract objects and their physical sizes, our high-level map representation provides great amount of additional information, and provides additional opportunities for place recognition, loop closure, higher level of geometry understanding, i.e. semantics to achieve more user-friendly interaction between human and robot. In summary, this paper makes the following contributions:

- We present a novel plane object-based high-level map representation.
- We present an efficient algorithm to find real intersections (edges) between planes and to determine their sizes.
- We present an efficient algorithm to classify plane-based objects using sub-graph patterns, which is fast and computationally effective.
- We demonstrate that the algorithm achieves real-time performance with mapping accuracy comparable to state-of-the-art algorithms.

3   Algorithm Overview

Figure 2 shows step–by–step transition from simple point cloud to classified plane–based object representation with sizes (edge lengths). Actually the whole

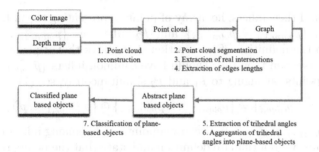

Fig. 2. Diagram representing transition from colored point cloud to classified plane object-based high-level map representation.

algorithm consists of seven major steps. In the first step, it acquires RGB-D data stream consisting of a pair of a color image and a depth map. After that, on the basis of the RGB-D stream and intrinsic calibration parameters we reconstruct colored point cloud. Such a colored point cloud becomes an initial map representation of the perceived scene. In the next step a plane segmentation from initial point cloud on the basis of M-estimator SAmple Consensus (MSAC) is executed. Then, real planes intersections as well as their lengths are determined. On the basis of the segmented planes and their intersections a graph is constructed. This results in the second map representation, which consists of plane equations and point clouds representing objects of complex shape (not plane-based objects). Due to the substitution of point clouds representing plane equations the map representation becomes compact. The next step comprises extraction of trihedral angles that are represented by 3rd order cycles from the constructed graph (Fig. 3). After extracting the trihedral angles, their aggregation can be achieved assuming that trihedral angles of the same plane-based object have common edges. Finding common edges for trihedral angles is done using the constructed graph, which is fast and computationally effective. Through aggregating all trihedral angles having common edges we obtain abstract plane-based objects. This means that in this step we have a structure describing which planes belong to which object, the number of such objects, theirs sizes, but no types. Therefore, we call this representation as abstract plane-based objects, see Fig. 2. In the last step the classification is executed. The classification algorithm is based on matching graph patterns with a subgraph from the extracted graph. The resulting algorithm is simple, fast and effective.

4 Proposed Algorithm

4.1 Determining Physical Object Size

Let's consider how to extract real intersection of two planes and its length. Let's assume that we have planes: $P_1 = A_1x + B_1y + C_1z + D_1$ and $P_2 = A_2x + B_2y + C_2z + D_2$. According to the algorithm presented in Fig. 2, after point cloud segmentation we determine the plane intersections. Therefore, after this step we have planes and their inliers, i.e. array of points representing them. Let's denote P_1 inliers as $\{p_{plane1,1} \cdots p_{plane1,i}\}$ and P_2 inliers as $\{p_{plane2,1} \cdots p_{plane2,i}\}$. According to the definition of intersection that states that if planes P_1 and P_2 have real intersection then they should have common inliers $\{p_{edge,1} \cdots p_{edge,i}\}$, i.e. array of points belonging to P_1 and P_2 simultaneously, see (1):

$$\{p_{edge,1} \cdots p_{edge,i}\} = \{p_{plane1,1} \cdots p_{plane1,i}\} \cap \{p_{plane2,1} \cdots p_{plane2,i}\} \quad (1)$$

However, $p_{edge,1} \cdots p_{edge,i} = \emptyset$, because a point can be among inliers of only single plane. Thus, we reformulate definition and state that the points representing real intersection $p_{edge,1} \cdots p_{edge,i}$ will be simultaneously close to planes P_1 and P_2. Therefore, we calculate point-to-plane distance for both sets of inliers to both planes on the basis of (2)–(5).

$$\{d_{plane1-plane1,1} \cdots d_{plane1-plane1,i}\} = |A_1 p_{plane1,i,x} + B_1 p_{plane1,i,y} \quad (2)$$
$$+ C_1 p_{plane1,i,z} + D_1| * (A_1^2 + B_1^2 + C_1^2)^{1/2}$$
$$\{d_{plane1-plane2,1} \cdots d_{plane1-plane2,i}\} = |A_2 p_{plane1,i,x} + B_2 p_{plane1,i,y} \quad (3)$$
$$+ C_2 p_{plane1,i,z} + D_2| * (A_2^2 + B_2^2 + C_2^2)^{1/2}$$
$$\{d_{plane2-plane2,1} \cdots d_{plane2-plane2,i}\} = |A_2 p_{plane2,i,x} + B_2 p_{plane2,i,y} \quad (4)$$
$$+ C_2 p_{plane2,i,z} + D_2| * (A_2^2 + B_2^2 + C_2^2)^{1/2}$$
$$\{d_{plane2-plane1,1} \cdots d_{plane2-plane1,i}\} = |A_1 p_{plane2,i,x} + B_1 p_{plane2,i,y} \quad (5)$$
$$+ C_1 p_{plane2,i,z} + D_1| * (A_1^2 + B_1^2 + C_1^2)^{1/2}$$

After that we determine all points that have the distance to both planes smaller than d_{thresh} and grater than d_{min}. d_{min} is used to deal with noise.

In order to define edge length d_{edge} we took two points from $p_{edge,1} \cdots p_{edge,i}$ with maximum distance to each other. Actually, the distance between the points represents diagonal length $d_{diagonal}$ of the cylinder of radius d_{thresh}. Thus, the edge length is determined according to (6):

$$4 * d_{tresh}^2 + d_{edge}^2 = d_{diagonal}^2 \quad (6)$$

4.2   Aggregation of Planes into Object

After determining the plane intersections we can construct a graph whose node and edge represent a plane and its real intersection with other plane, respectively. This graph allows us to find in a fast manner all trihedral angles as 3rd order cycles in the graph, see Fig. 3. Afterwards, we make assumption that all trihedral angles of the same plane-based object have common edges.

This assumption allow us to extract plane-based objects. Trihedral angle is represented by three planes, see Fig. 3, so let's denote it by indexes of planes. For example, trihedral angle 2-3-7 has common faces with 2-9-7, 2-6-3, 3-7-5. Therefore, they belong to the same plane-based object. In the same time, the trihedral angle 2-9-7 has common edge with 2-9-6, and 5-9-7 so that all these (2-3-7, 2-6-3, 2-9-7, 3-7-5, 2-9-6, 5-9-7) trihedral angles belong to the same plane-based object. This way the aggregation is capable of adding trihedral angles, angle-by-angle.

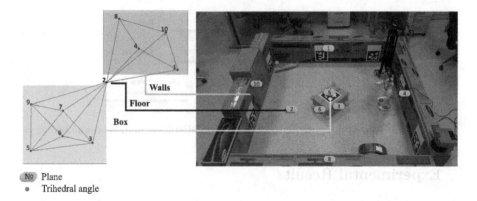

Nº Plane
● Trihedral angle

Fig. 3. The graph representing scene of the sequence 2 – a box in a simple room with four walls, which are observed by Nao humanoid robot.

4.3   Classification of Objects

After all plane-based objects are extracted, a classification step can be executed. It is based on splitting the graph into sub-graphs (for instance plane two in Fig. 3), and then matching the predefined patterns, see Fig. 4.

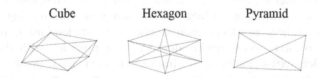

Fig. 4. Predefined patterns to match objects in the graph representation.

4.4   Merging Plane Object-Based High-Level Map Representation

Merging a pair of plane object-based high-level map representation is done using a graph representation. At first, data association is done and plane-to-plane correspondence is found on the basis of matching normals as well as distances between the considered planes. After that, a transformation matrix between frames is computed using closed-form solution for plane-to-plane correspondence [12]. The transformation matrix is further refined by a ICP algorithm. After that, the frames are aligned. Then using the plane-to-plane correspondence we merge graph representations. We assume that each edge length is the longest one from corresponding edges in pair of frames. This way the graph is reconstructed. Finally, we reinitialize the plane-based object structure and the classification, see Fig. 5.

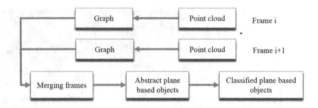

Fig. 5. Algorithm of merging plane object-based high-level map representations.

5   Experimental Results

Our system is conceived to work with any RGB-D sensor. In the experiments we utilized Kinect 1 and ASUS Xtion sensors. They work at a frame rate of 30 Hz and provides color stream and depth map at a resolution of 640 × 480 pixels. The system has been tested on two sequences. The first sequence is available in open collection of Kinect (RGB+D) datasets with 6D ground truth recorded by the TUM CV group [22], (rgbd_dataset_freiburg3_structure_texture_far). It includes 907 frames with synchronized color image, depth map, accelerometer data and ground-truth for each step. The dataset has been recorded with frame–rate of 30 Hz and sensor resolution of 640 × 480 pixels. The ground-truth trajectory was obtained using high-accuracy motion-capture system consisting of eight high-speed tracking cameras (100 Hz). Figure 6 depicts results that were achieved in constructing plane object-based high-level map representation using hand-held Kinect. Figure 6a shows results of reconstruction of point cloud using color image, depth map and intrinsic calibration data that are provided with the dataset. Figure 6b depicts extraction of planes from the reconstructed point cloud using MSAC. Figure 6c shows results of systematic aggregation of trihedral angles into objects.

We merged point clouds that were reconstructed step-by-step from color images and depth map, using ground–truth trajectory. We determined the merged point clouds for frames number 200, 400 and 907.

As can be seen in Fig. 6a, there is substantial level of noise in the point cloud. Despite this the segmentation step is successful, see Fig. 6b. As can be seen in Fig. 6b–c, the proposed algorithm for extraction of real intersections of planes from point cloud generated satisfactory results. Its is worth noting that the poster stands on the floor and its planes have real intersections with it. Despite that the floor has also intersections with the room planes, the system correctly extracted two different plane-based objects (poster and room) that are represented on Fig. 6c by different colors (green and red, respectively). However, we have no ability to estimate edge length error because there is no data in the TUM dataset for object sizes. We have determined object sizes for our dataset.

The second RGB-D sequence[1] has been recorded using the ASUS Xtion Pro Live that has been mounted on the Nao humanoid robot. In the discussed sce-

---

[1] Available at: http://bit.ly/ICCVG2018.

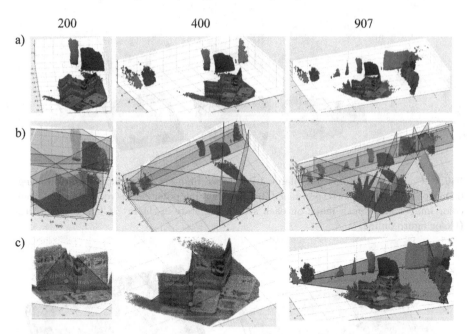

Fig. 6. An example of constructing plane object-based high-level map representation using hand-held Kinect. (a) Reconstructed point cloud using color image, depth map and intrinsic calibration data of the Kinect from TUM RGB-D dataset. (b) Results of extracting planes from reconstructed point cloud using MSAC. (c) Results of systematic aggregation of trihedral angles into objects. Green points of the graph stand for centers of trihedral angles. Edges of trihedral angles are represented by black line segments. (Color figure online)

nario the Nao robot made a circle of the radius 0.7 m in 24 steps. In each step, RGB, depth and ground-truth data were recorded, see Fig. 8. Ground-truth position has been determined using 2D LIDAR (SICK LMS 200 laser scanner), see Fig. 3. This dataset has been utilized in an experiment comprising constructing high-level map representations for each frame and merging them frame-by-frame. Figure 7 compares point cloud that was reconstructed frame-by-frame using state-of-the-art ICP algorithm with plane object-based high-level map representation that was reconstructed frame-by-frame on the basis of direct-estimate of plane-to-plane correspondence [12], see Fig. 7b.

It is worth noting that trihedral angle allows us to use all three types of basic geometric primitives: point, line and plane (Fig. 1). However, it is an open problem how to combine transformation matrices that are obtained on the basis of different closed form solutions for our high-level map representation. Actually, in the discussed experiment we have employed plane-to-plane [10] correspondence to find the transformation matrix between frames. Our system consumes about 60 times less amount of memory than state-of-the-art point cloud, see high level-

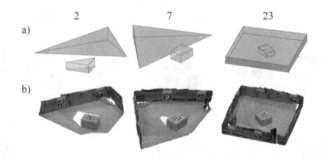

Fig. 7. Comparison of merging plane object-based high-level map representation using 6 DoF plane-to-plane correspondence (b) with merging point clouds reconstructed from color images and depth maps on each step using state-of-the-art ICP algorithm (a). (Color figure online)

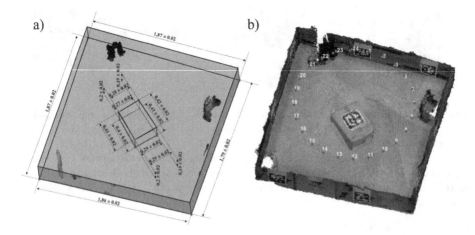

Fig. 8. Comparison of memory consumption of plane object-based high-level map representation for SLAM with point cloud. High-level map representation with estimated object sizes and errors (a) Ground truth trajectory (green points) in (b) has been determined using LMS 200 SICK laser scanner while the path (red points) has been estimated on the basis of visual odometry and our high level map representation. (Color figure online)

map representation on Fig. 8a. The discussed figure depicts also the estimated object sizes as well as the estimated path with respect to ground-truth path.

Comparing estimated object sizes for box and walls (see Fig. 8) to its ground truth values (box height = 0.19 m, box width = 0.29 m, box length = 0.38 m, room width = room length = 1.88 m) we obtained the average error of 0.02 m.

6   Conclusions

We presented a novel algorithm for constructing plane object-based high-level map representation for SLAM. It achieves promising performance on point clouds acquired by Kinect and ASUS Xtion sensors and provides reliable extraction of plane-based objects, their dimensions and types. In future work we plan to extend the system and use all combinations of primitives for calculating 6 DoF robot pose.

Acknowledgment. This work was partially supported by Polish National Science Center (NCN) under a research grant 2014/15/B/ST6/02808 as well as by PhD program of the Ministry of Science and Education of the Republic of Kazakhstan.

References

1. Bao, S., Bagra, M., Chao, Y., Savarese, S.: Semantic structure from motion with points, regions, and objects. In: IEEE Conference on Computer Vision and Pattern Recognitoin, pp. 2703–2710 (2012)
2. Besl, P., McKay, N.: A method for registration of 3-D shapes. IEEE Trans. Pattern Anal. Mach. Intell. **14**(2), 239–256 (1992)
3. Bodis-Szomoru, A., Riemenschneider, H., Van-Gool, L.: Efficient edge-aware surface mesh reconstruction for urban scenes. Comput. Vis. Image Underst. **66**, 91–106 (2015)
4. Bresson, G., Alsayed, Z., Yu, L., Glaser, S.: Simultaneous localization and mapping: a survey of current trends in autonomous driving. IEEE Trans. Intell. Veh. **2**(3), 194–220 (2017)
5. Cadena, C., et al.: Past, present, and future of simultaneous localization and mapping: Toward the robust-perception age. IEEE Trans. Robot. **32**(6), 1309–1332 (2016)
6. Chen, H.: Pose determination from line-to-plane correspondences: existence condition and closed-form solutions. IEEE Trans. Pattern Anal. Mach. Intell. **13**(6), 530–541 (1991)
7. Civera, J., Galvez-Lopez, D., Riazuelo, L., Tardos, J., Montiel, J.: Towards semantic SLAM using a monocular camera. In: Intelligent Robots and Systems (IROS), pp. 1277–1284 (2011)
8. Dame, A., Prisacariu, V., Ren, C., Reid, I.: Dense reconstruction using 3D object shape priors. In: IEEE Conference Computer Vision and Pattern Recognition, pp. 1288–1295 (2013)
9. Flint, A., Murray, D., Reid, I.: Manhattan scene understanding using monocular, stereo, and 3D features. In: International Conference on Computer Vision, pp. 2228–2235 (2011)
10. Grimson, W., Lozano-Perez, T.: Model-based recognition and localization from sparse range or tactile data. Int. J. Robot. Res. **3**(3), 3–35 (1984)
11. Henry, P., Krainin, M., Herbst, E., Ren, X., Fox, D.: RGB-D mapping: using depth cameras for dense 3D modeling of indoor environments. In: International Symposium Experimental Robotics (ISER), pp. 477–491 (2010)
12. Khoshelham, K.: Direct 6-DoF pose estimation from point-plane correspondences. In: International Conference on Digital Image Computing: Techniques and Applications (DICTA), pp. 1–6 (2015). https://doi.org/10.1109/DICTA.2015.7371253

13. Kundu, A., Li, Y., Dellaert, F., Li, F., Rehg, J.M.: Joint semantic segmentation and 3D reconstruction from monocular video. In: Fleet, D., Pajdla, T., Schiele, B., Tuytelaars, T. (eds.) ECCV 2014. LNCS, vol. 8694, pp. 703–718. Springer, Cham (2014). https://doi.org/10.1007/978-3-319-10599-4_45

14. Lai, K., Bo, L., Fox, D.: Unsupervised feature learning for 3D scene labeling, pp. 3050–3057. IEEE, September 2014

15. Mozos, M., Triebel, R., Jensfelt, P., Axel, R., Burgard, W.: Supervised semantic labeling of places using information extracted from sensor data. Robot. Auton. Syst. **55**(5), 391–402 (2007)

16. Nister, D.: A minimal solution to the generalised 3-point pose problem. In: IEEE Conference Computer Vision and Pattern Recognition (CVPR), pp. 560–567, June 2004

17. Pathak, K., Birk, A., Vaskevicius, N., Poppinga, J.: Fast registration based on noisy planes with unknown correspondences for 3-D mapping. IEEE Trans. Rob. **26**(3), 424–441 (2010)

18. Pillai, S., Leonard, J.: Monocular SLAM supported object recognition. In: Robotics Science and Systems Conference, pp. 310–319 (2015)

19. Pronobis, A., Jensfelt, P.: Large-scale semantic mapping and reasoning with heterogeneous modalities. In: IEEE International Conference on Robotics and Automation, pp. 3515–3522, May 2012

20. Ramalingam, S., Taguchi, Y.: A theory of minimal 3D point to 3D plane registration and its generalization. Int. J. Comput. Vis. **102**, 73–90 (2012)

21. Salas-Moreno, R., Newcombe, R., Strasdat, H., Kelly, P., Davison, A.: SLAM++: simultaneous localisation and mapping at the level of objects. In: IEEE Conference Computer Vision and Pattern Recognition, pp. 1352–1359 (2013)

22. Sturm, J., Engelhard, N., Endres, F., Burgard, W., Cremers, D.: A benchmark for the evaluation of RGB-D SLAM systems. In: Proceedings of the International Conference on Intelligent Robot Systems (IROS), pp. 573–580 (2012)

23. Taguchi, Y., Jian, Y., Ramalingam, S., Feng, C.: Point-plane SLAM for handheld 3D sensors. In: IEEE International Conference on Robotics and Automation (ICRA), pp. 5182–5189, May 2013

24. Trevor, A., Rogers, J., Christensen, H.: Planar surface SLAM with 3D and 2D sensors. In: IEEE International Conference Robotics Automation (ICRA), pp. 3041–3048, May 2012

25. Umeyama, S.: Least-squares estimation of transformation parameters between two point patterns. IEEE Trans. Pattern Anal. Mach. Intell. **13**(4), 376–380 (1991)

26. Vineet, V., et al.: Incremental dense semantic stereo fusion for large-scale semantic scene reconstruction. In: International Conference on Robotics and Automation, pp. 75–82 (2015)

27. Walker, M., Shao, L., Volz, R.: Estimating 3-D location parameters using dual number quaternions. CVGIP: Image Underst. **54**(3), 358–367 (1991)

28. Weingarten, J., Siegwart, R.: 3D SLAM using planar segments. In: IEEE/RSJ International Conference Intelligent Robots and Systems (IROS), pp. 3062–3067, October 2006

29. Zhang, Z., Faugeras, O.: Determining motion from 3D line segment matches: a comparative study. Image Vis. Comput. **9**(1), 10–19 (1991)

Level-Set Based Algorithm for Automatic Feature Extraction on 3D Meshes: Application to Crater Detection on Mars

Nicole Christoff[1,2(✉)], Agata Manolova[2], Laurent Jorda[3], Sophie Viseur[4], Sylvain Bouley[5], and Jean-Luc Mari[1]

[1] Aix Marseille Univ, Université de Toulon, CNRS, LIS, Marseille, France
nicole.christoff@univ-amu.fr
[2] Faculty of Telecommunications, Technical University of Sofia, blvd. Kliment Ohridski 8, 1796 Sofia, Bulgaria
[3] Aix-Marseille Université, CNRS, LAM UMR 7326, Marseille, France
[4] Aix-Marseille Université, CNRS, IRD, CEREGE UM 34, Marseille, France
[5] Université Paris-Sud, CNRS, GEOPS UMR 8148, Orsay, France

Abstract. The knowledge of the origin and development of all bodies in the solar system begins with understanding the geologic history and evolution of the universe. The only approach for dating celestial body surfaces is by the analysis of the crater impact density and size. In order to facilitate this process, automatic approaches have been proposed for the impact craters detection. In this article, we propose a novel approach for detecting craters' rims. The developed method is based on a study of the Digital Elevation Model (DEM) geometry, represented as a 3D triangulated mesh. We use curvature analysis, in combination with a fast local quantization method to automatically detect the craters' rims with artificial neural network. The validation of the method is performed on Barlow's database.

Keywords: Geometric features · 3D mesh
Automated crater detection · Curvature analysis · Neural network
Mars

1 Introduction

Impact craters are topographic features on planetary surfaces formed by the hypervelocity impact of asteroids and meteorites. These impacts trigger the apparition of craters of different diameters, depending on the energy involved in the collision. They are dominant, very common geographic features on all hard-surface bodies in the solar system and can be over time accumulated on slow erosion surfaces, such those of the Moon and Mars. To determine the age of different surfaces, Neukum *et al.* proposed for instance sizes and frequencies of impact craters to be used [13]. In planetary sciences, the detection of impact craters is a key problem, but it still implies a large effort each time a data set is

© Springer Nature Switzerland AG 2018
L. J. Chmielewski et al. (Eds.): ICCVG 2018, LNCS 11114, pp. 103–114, 2018.
https://doi.org/10.1007/978-3-030-00692-1_10

acquired by a spacecraft. The commonly used method is still a manual detection by expert. This task is highly time consuming, because of the increasing amount of imaging data. For example, in the case of Mars, Barlow *et al.* have been identified only kilometer-sized craters [2], while the Context Camera onboard the Mars Reconnaissance Orbiter acquires an imaging data with the resolution 6 m per pixel [12]. This, together with the advancements in image processing, has implied new efforts to develop automatic *Crater Detection Algorithms* (CDAs). The crater spatial frequency and their morphology will facilitate the understanding of the active degradation process over time and the dating of a planetary surface.

Our contribution is the development of a new approach that uses all the information about the topography including frequencies and morphology of the crater.

The article is organized as follows: in Sect. 2, some of the existing approaches related to crater detection are briefly described. In Sect. 3, we describe the environmental data, then the core of this approach is described in Sect. 4. Section 5 is dedicated to the results and discussion of the proposed method. Conclusions are given in Sect. 6.

2   Related Work

Urbach and Stepinski, Meng *et al.* and Wang *et al.* [14,28,29] have developed an automatic detection method, but they rely on the use of images or DEMs [26,29], which are 2.5D data. The current state of technology gives the possibility of approaches based on 3D mesh processing, but such methods are scarce [24]. The approaches can be also distinguished according to whether they use: the texture [1], the value of elevation [3] and/or the curvature [24]. Other authors combine imagery data and the DEM data in detecting craters [11].

In planetary science, to achieve higher levels of crater detection rate, machine learning is used. Bandeira *et al.*, Jin and Zhang use in their works "AdaBoost" or "Boosting algorithms", but they propose an image-based crater detection technique [1,8] where the elevation information is partially lost. Stepinski *et al.* use the same approach [26], but their algorithm works for detection of craters from topographic data. The method of Salamunićcar and Lončarić is applied directly onto DEM data [22]. They propose a "Support Vector Machines" approach to detect crater rims. An image processing techniques on Mars DEM data obtained by the Mars Orbiter Laser Altimeter (MOLA) instrument is used by Di *et al.* [6]. In the two-dimensional DEM, they uses a boosting algorithm to detect square features. For the training step, Haar-like, local binary pattern (LBP) and scaled Haar-like are used to extract relevant features. To test the method, the algorithm is applied to three local DEMs of Mars. A local terrain analysis and the Circular Hough Transform (CHT) are exploited to delimit the craters rim. They are applied on those square regions, which are classified as being craters regions by the classifier. However, this is not full 3D method and it could not detect densely distributed, overlapped and heavily degraded craters [6].

3   Data Preparation

Data preparation consists of an analysis of the DEM geometry of Mars, represented as a 3D triangulated mesh.

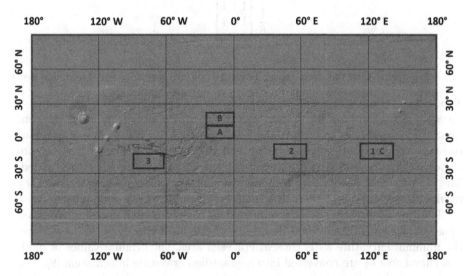

Fig. 1. The map of Mars with selected regions, used in this article. The areas A, B and C are the regions, from which the training set is constructed and the areas 1, 2 and 3 are the validation region for the proposed approach.

3.1   Input Data

The source data is presented as point cloud, stored in Polygon File Format, from which the 3D mesh is crated. For this work, the input data consist of MOLA data [30], at a scale of 128 pixels per degree, or $\sim$ 463 m at the equator. It is centered at $(0°, 0°)$ and represents the equidistant cylindrical projection. Five areas were chosen for the training (A, B and C) and tree for the validation (1, 2 and 3) (Fig. 1), with geographic coordinates as shown in Table 1.

Table 1. Information about the training and testing sites.

	Top	Bottom	Left	Right	Block size	Area (km²)
Site A	$0.00°$	$13.00°N$	$25.00°W$	$0.01°W$	3200×1665	$1,142,158$
Site B	$13.00°N$	$26.00°N$	$25.00°W$	$0.01°W$	3200×1665	$1,142,158$
Site 1	$7.57°S$	$18.42°S$	$114°E$	$142°E$	3585×1389	$1,067,464$
Site 2	$8.05°S$	$18.89°S$	$37.69°E$	$65.69°E$	3583×1386	$1,064,565$
Site 3	$14.85°S$	$25.69°S$	$88.87°W$	$61.26°W$	3534×1386	$1,050,006$

The noise, due to the scanning process is eliminated, by calculation of the quantile of the distribution for values lying outside the interval in only 5% of cases [19]. To preserve the spatial neighborhood relationships of pixel values, an adaptive 2D linear filter is applied:

$$\frac{1}{8} \begin{bmatrix} 1 & 1 & 1 \\ 1 & 0 & 1 \\ 1 & 1 & 1 \end{bmatrix}$$

3.2 Discrete Curvatures on a Triangle Mesh for Crater Description

The proposed approach can be applied on any topographic data types. In mesh processing, the curvatures are used as indicators of information about the concavity or convexity of a surface along its principal directions. In our precious research, the maximal, minimal, mean and Gaussian curvatures at a vertex are respectively estimated [4]. For comparison, the DEM data was also investigated. The experimental results with five different classifiers show that better accuracy results are obtained over the features selected from the grey scale image.

The impact craters are characterized by a circular depression surrounded by a circular ridge. As a good descriptor of the local concavity of the surface, the minimal curvature k_2 is chosen. For each area, the original values of minimal curvatures k_2 are converted into a quantified grayscale information [9]. The minimum and maximum values $k_{2,min}$ and $k_{2,max}$ are calculated and quantified between 0 and 255. These gray levels are actually RGB colors mapped to a lower range of values. The values of k_2 are represented as a grid of pixels containing the grayscale curvature $k_{2,G}$. The output images of this preprocessing step are hereafter called "$k_{2,G}$-images".

In this study, the Barlow Database [2] is used. Due to a shift between the catalog and MOLA topography, all possible errors in the position of the crater are manually corrected. For each training area, a sub-window of the $k_{2,G}$ image around all the craters in the Barlow catalog is extracted as positive samples. A sub-window about 1.5 times the diameter of the crater (see [6]) plus a constant c is automatically extracted around its central position. According to the average difference calculated after the manual corrections, the $c = 5$ pixels is chosen to manage the errors of the position of the centers.

In addition to these sub-windows, we automatically select an equivalent number of "background" images at random locations with sizes between 2 and 100 pixels, as negative samples. We manually removed all samples containing craters.

All the sub-windows should be resampled to create a normalized window of 20 × 20 pixels. Bandeira et al. and Di et al. use the bilinear interpolation [1,6]. The others, as De Croon and Izzo and Szabo et al. use bicubic interpolation [5,27]. It is generally considered preferable as it retains some semblance of sharpness, due to the use of more data for the calculation. In this paper, the bicubic interpolation is used also, because it creates smoother curves than bilinear interpolation, and introduces fewer artifacts that stand out as conspicuous deteriorating the apparent quality of the mesh. In comparison with the bilinear interpolation, the bicubic interpolation increases a little the computational complexity. All the sub-windows are resampled by bicubic interpolation to create a normalized window of 20 × 20 pixels, hereafter called *Area*.

4   Level-Set Algorithm Description

After the data preparation, the algorithm continues with the proposed level-set method for feature extraction on the minimal curvature k_2. This information is fed into the neural network to perform an automatic detection of the regions of interest. From all positive outputs, CHT is applied for the crater rims extraction.

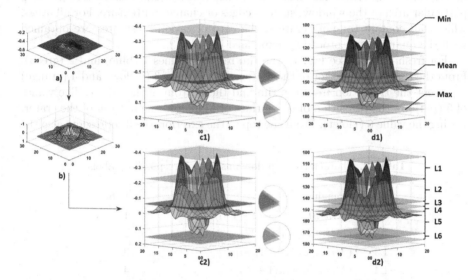

Fig. 2. Quantization method. On the 3D triangulated mesh (a), the minimal curvature is estimated (b). It is further resized using bicubic interpolation (c2) and those values are converted into a quantified grayscale information $k_{2,G}$ between 0 and 255 (d2). For visual comparison, (c1) represents bilinear interpolated (b) and (d1) is its $k_{2,G}$ representation. For each region, the local *Min*, *Mean* and *Max* values are calculated and the 6 characterization domains are label via Table 2.

4.1   Feature Extraction

A reduced number of grey levels with a proper quantization method significantly reduce the dimensionality, while improving the accuracy of a classification system [17]. The idea behind the algorithm is the separation of each area into zones, as a dimensionality reduction, but still keeping the crater information. The crater rim is higher than the bottom of the crater and the ratio between the height of the rim and the depth is larger for a fresh crater than for a degraded one. Typically, in nature, there are no two identical craters. We propose a fast quantization method depending on the calculated *Mean*, *Max* and *Min* values for a given Area.

Figure 2 describes the feature extraction method of crater present in the Barlow catalog. Figure 2 (a) is the mesh representation of a neighborhood of a small fresh crater, after the denoising filter; (b) is the computed minimal curvature k_2 of the same crater. Applying the level repartition on (c2) (or (c1)), the transition between the crater rim and the surface of Mars, the surface itself and the slope of the bottom are lost. The (d2) is the grayscale representation of values on (c2). Having those assumptions, we cannot give absolute values. That is why we introduce a treshold P. According to the goal of this article and after experimental testing with different values, with $P = 0.03$ we obtain a better description of all crater features. The values reveal certain characteristics of a particular area of the window, such as edges or changes in texture. For all areas, which can contain (or not) craters, the categorization attributes are obtained with the quantization procedure explained in Table 2.

For fresh craters (see Fig. 3), the rim receives values 1 (blue) and 2 (green). From the top to the interior of the crater: the values of 3 (yellow) and 4 (orange) represent the transition from the rim and the bottom of the crater. The values of 5 (red) are the transition of the surface of Mars and the bottom of the crater, having the value 6 (violet). From the top to the exterior: the 3 represents also the

Table 2. Characterization domains and corresponding labels.

Level	Domains	Label
L1	$[Min, Mean(1 - (1 - P))/2]$	1
L2	$((Mean(1 - P) + Min)/2, Mean(1 - P)]$	2
L3	$(Mean(1 - P), Mean]$	3
L4	$(Mean, Mean(1 + P)]$	4
L5	$(Mean(1 + P), Max(1 - P)]$	5
L6	$(Max(1 - P), Max]$	6

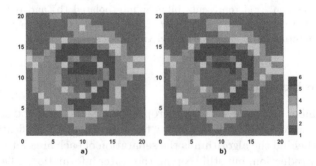

Fig. 3. Fresh crater: (a) result after linear interpolation and (b) after bilinear interpolation. (Color figure online)

transition from the rim and the surface of Mars. The craters ejecta is labelled with 4 (orange). The surface of Mars is labelled with 5. Regarding the ratio radius/depth of the crater and the level of the degradation, it is possible some values to not be present.

4.2 Multilayer Perceptron (MLP) Classification

In this article, for the classification task, a classical feedforward multilayer perceptron with supervised learning [10] is used. The input consists of the feature vectors, calculated in Subsect. 4.1. 1505 positive samples (containing craters) and equal number negative samples (not containing craters) are used. To find the optimal number of the hidden nodes, the growing algorithm for artificial neural network is used [10]. After several tests, subject to the error calculated, the n has increased to 50. As activation function, the conjugate back propagation gradient is used during the training of the network as the best compromise between quality classification and performance according to Moller [15]. To insure no overfitting of the validation results, due to the optimization of the data [7], 10 fold cross validation is used [10].

4.3 Crater Regions Detection

Sliding a detection window in the $k_{2,G}$ determines the crater regions after the training of the neural network. We detect craters of different sizes, resizing the $k_{2,G}$ by building a pyramid from it. The size of each layer is downscaled to 1.2^{-1} times the size of the previous layer. The first layer in the pyramid is the original $k_{2,G}$ and the last is the smallest crater region with a width and height no less than 20 pixels. In each layer a window of 20×20 pixels is slid by 3 pixels each time to scan the minimal curvature $k_{2,G}$. The region within the window is recorded to calculate the local Max, $Mean$ and Min values, to label the defined in Table 2 domains and after that classified into the crater or non crater region.

4.4 Craters Contour Extraction

For all classified as craters regions, a Circular Hough Transform technique [16] is applied over the corresponding k_2 images. The purpose of this feature extraction technique is to draw potential circles from imperfect image inputs, by voting in the Hough parameter space. Then in an accumulator matrix, selecting local maxima, gives the position and the radius of the circle.

In this work, to save time and memory cost, the parameters are directly indicated, depending on the polarity of the object, which adapts the circle. The local darkest points of the three dimensional accumulator provide the position and radius of the craters. The radius $\in$ [5, 10] to obtain crater coordinates and rim in the sub-window 20×20. The accumulator gives the completeness of the circle. The minimal threshold value is set to 0.1 in order to reduce the false positive circles. The estimated center coordinates and diameter of the circles are readjusted and resized according to the coordinates of the map.

4.5 Crater Matching

During the CHT, due to the existing multiple layers and the sliding window, a same crater can be assigned with a slightly different center coordinates and/or radius. Those duplicates are detected and deleted. To determine if two entries from the obtained crater list are the same or are different, Salamunićcar and Lončarić propose automated process of matching [21]. They propose a matching relative process for two craters, Crater 1 and Crater 2. From the stored crater list, where X, Y are the coordinates of the crater centers and R is the radius, any two craters are considered to belong to the same crater if they satisfy Eqs. 1 and 2:

$$f_{diff} = max(\frac{r_1}{r_2} - 1, \frac{d}{r_2}) \tag{1}$$

$$f_{diff} < f_c \tag{2}$$

Salamunićcar and Lončarić introduce the definition for a measure of crater difference f_{diff} [21]. The r_1 and r_2 are respectively the radiuses of Crater 1 and Crater 2, where $r_1 \geq r_2$. The distance between the crater centers is marked by d and $f_c \geq 0$ is craters difference factor. In Fig. 4, the particular cases for f_{diff} are shown: $f_{diff} = 0.25$ (a), $f_{diff} = 0.50$ (b), $f_{diff} = 1.00$ (c). The $f_{diff} = \frac{r_1}{r_2} - 1 = \frac{d}{r_2}$ is satisfied for case (c).

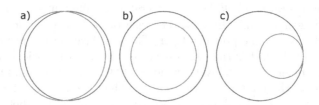

Fig. 4. "Similar" craters according to their relative area of overlap. The red circle is Crater 1 and the green circle Crater 2. Courtesy of Salamunićcar and Lončarić [21]. (Color figure online)

The crater matching was done after each layer. In a case of a match, the new information for the crater is calculated, according to the following equations:

$$x_{cr} = (\frac{x_1 + x_2}{2}); \qquad y_{cr} = (\frac{y_1 + y_2}{2}); \qquad r_{cr} = (\frac{r_1 + r_2}{2}) \tag{3}$$

For the final crater list (the crater list with all craters from all layers), in the case of a match, the information about the bigger radius is stored.

5 Results and Discussion

To evaluate the performance of the method, the quality factors of detection percentage ($D = 100 \times (\frac{TP}{TP+FN})$), quality percentage ($Q = 100 \times (\frac{TP}{TP+FP+FN})$)

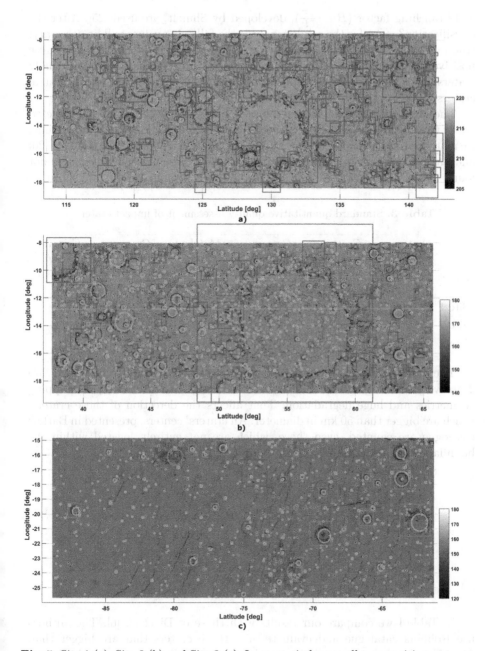

Fig. 5. Site 1 (a), Site 2 (b) and Site 3 (c). In green circles are all true positive craters, matched with at least one of the four catalogues. In blue are all craters, manually labelled as being craters. In green rectangles are the matched craters with those in the Barlow catalogue. Red rectangles are those, which are omitted by our method. Red circles represent the wrong detected craters. (Color figure online)

and branching factor ($B = \frac{FP}{TP}$), developed by Shufelt, are used [25]. After the classification? stage for the results analysis the following values will be necessary: true positive (TP), which stands for the number of real detected craters, false positives (FP) stands for the number detected craters that are not actually craters and FN stands for the number of false negative detections (omitted real craters).

The same criteria, explained in Subsect. 4.5, is employed to match a detected crater to a crater in the Barlow catalogue. To validate all craters and to save time, we matched our craters with three more catalogues: Radionova [18], Robbins [20] and Salamunićcar [23]. Experts manually verified those craters, which were not found in any catalogue. In Fig. 5 and Table 3, the obtained results are shown.

Table 3. Standard quantitative quality assessment of impact craters.

	Craters in the Barlow catalogue	Craters using our approach	Craters correctly detected (TP)	Matched craters	Craters omitted (FN)	Craters falsely detected (FP)
Site 1	499	1142	987	336	163	155
Site 2	432	1844	1434	311	121	410
Site 3	202	982	708	188	14	274

The performance of our method in the three test sites differs. Site 1 and Site 2 are very challenging, because of the wide range of crater sizes, overlapping geometries and huge degradation. That affects the detection of those craters, which are bigger than 50 km in diameter. All craters' centers, presented in Barlow catalogue are counted, even those, which are not entirely located within the boundaries of each area.

Table 4. Comparison with Di's CDA.

	Our approach			Di's approach		
	D (%)	B	Q (%)	D (%)	B	Q (%)
Site 1	85.8	0.16	75.6	76	0.16	68
Site 2	92.2	0.29	73.0	76	0.14	69
Site 3	98.1	0.39	71.1	90	0.15	79

In Table 4 we compare our results with those of Di *et al.* [6]. The authors use Robbins catalogue and evaluate only those craters that are bigger than 6*km*. For the three sites, we obtain a better detection percentage and a better quality for Site 1 and Site 2. For Site 1, we have the same branching factor as Di *et al.*; however, for Site 2 and 3, Di *et al.* obtains better branching factor (small is better). For Site 1, Di *et al.* obtain slightly better results than Bue and Stepinski CDA [3], who have achieved $D = 76\%$, $B = 0.29$ and $Q = 61\%$[6]. For his validation, Bue and Stepinski use Barlow catalog as we do.

6 Conclusion and Future Work

In this article, we have presented a new approach for CDA. It is an original combination between differential estimators on a surface mesh and a machine learning algorithm. This approach produces better results compared to other popular methods. It can also be used to detect more generic round shapes on meshes.

The detection performance of our method is influenced by the crater distribution complexity of each area. However, in comparison with other CDA, we obtain better detection percentages and quality factors. As future work we plan to try with a more dense mesh, to extract more geometric features for the detected craters and to classify them in different categories (fresh, old, etc.).

References

1. Bandeira, L., Ding, W., Stepinski, T.: Detection of sub-kilometer craters in high resolution planetary images using shape and texture features. Adv. Space Res. **49**(1), 64–74 (2012)
2. Barlow, N.G.: Crater size-frequency distributions and a revised Martian relative chronology. Icarus **75**(2), 285–305 (1988)
3. Bue, B., Stepinski, T.F.: Machine detection of martian impact craters from digital topography data. IEEE Trans. Geosci. Remote Sens. **45**(1), 265–274 (2007)
4. Christoff, N., Manolova, A., Jorda, L., Mari, J.-L.: Feature extraction and automatic detection of Martian impact craters from 3D meshes. In: 13th International Conference on Advanced Technologies, Systems and Services in Telecommunications (TELSIKS), 18–20 October 2017, Nis, Serbia, pp. 211–214 (2017)
5. De Croon, G.C.H.E., Izzo, D., Schiavone, G.: Time-to-contact estimation in landing scenarios using feature scales. Acta Futura **5**, 73–82 (2012)
6. Di, K., Li, W., Yue, Z., Sun, Y., Liu, Y.: A machine learning approach to crater detection from topographic data. Advances in Space Research **54**(11), 2419–2429 (2014)
7. Stenzel, O.: Gradient index films and multilayers. The Physics of Thin Film Optical Spectra. SSSS, vol. 44, pp. 163–180. Springer, Cham (2016). https://doi.org/10.1007/978-3-319-21602-7_8
8. Jin, S., Zhang, T.: The automatic detection of impact craters on Mars using a modified adaboosting method. Planet. Space Sci. **99**, 112–117 (2014)
9. Kanan, C., Cottrell, G.: Color-to-grayscale: does the method matter in image recognition? PLOS ONE **7**(1), e29740 (2012)
10. Kasabov, N.: Foundations of Neural Networks, Fuzzy Systems, and Knowledge Engineering, pp. 257–340. The MIT Press, Cambridge (1996)
11. Kim, J.R., Muller, J.P., van Gasselt, S., Morley, J.G., Neukum, G.: Automated crater detection, a new tool for Mars cartography and chronology. Photogram. Eng. Remote Sens. **71**(10), 1205–1217 (2005)
12. Malin, M., Bell, J., Cantor, B., Caplinger, M., Calvin, W., Clancy, R.T., Edgett, K., Edwards, L., Haberle, R., James, F., Lee, S., Ravine, M., Thomas, P., Wolff, M.: Context camera investigation on board the Mars reconnaissance orbiter. J. Geophys. Res. E Planets **112**, E05S04 (2007)

13. Neukum, G., Konig, B., Fechtig, H., Storzer, D.: Cratering in the earth-moon system-consequences for age determination by crater counting. In: Proceedings Lunar Science Conference, 6th, Houston, vol. 3, pp. 2597–2620 (1975)
14. Meng, D., Yunfeng, C., Qingxian, W.: Novel approach of crater detection by crater candidate region selection and matrix-pattern-oriented least squares support vector machine. Chin. J. Aeronaut. **26**(2), 385–393 (2013)
15. Moller, M.F.: A scaled conjugate gradient algorithm for fast supervised learning. Neural Netw. **6**(4), 525–533 (1993)
16. Pedersen, S. J. K.: Circular Hough Transform. In: Aalborg University, Vision, Graphics, and Interactive Systems (2007)
17. Ponti, M., Nazaré, T., Thumé, G.: Image quantization as a dimensionality reduction procedure in color and texture feature extraction. Neurocomputing **173**(2), 385–396 (2016)
18. Rodionova, J.F., Dekchtyareva, K.I., Khramchikhin, A.A., Michael, G.G., Ajukov, S.V., Pugacheva, S.G., Shevchenko, V.V.: Morphological Catalogue of the Craters of Mars (2000). Shevchenko, V.V., Chicarro, A.F. (eds.)
19. Rees, D.G.: Foundations of Statistics, pp. 244–249. CRC Press, Boca Raton (1987)
20. Robbins, S., Hynek, B.: A new global database of Mars impact craters *geq* 1 km: Database creation, properties, and parameters. J. Geophys. Res. **117**(E6) (2012)
21. Salamunićcar, G., Lončarić, S.: Open framework for objective evaluation of crater detectionalgorithms with first test-field subsystem based on MOLA data. Adv. Space Res. **42**(2008), 6–19 (2008)
22. Salamunićcar, G., Lončarić, S.: Application of machine learning using support vector machines for crater detection from Martian digital topography data. In: 38th COSPAR Scientific Assembly, 18–15 July 2010, in Bremen, Germany, p. 3 (2010)
23. Salamunićcar, G., Lončarić, S., Mazarico, E.: LU60645GT and MA132843GT catalogues of Lunar and Martian impact craters developed using a crater shape-based interpolation crater detection algorithm for topography data. Planet. Space Sci. **60**(1), 236–247 (2012)
24. Schmidt, M.P., Muscato, J., Viseur, S., Jorda, L., Bouley, S., Mari, J.-L.: Robust detection of round shaped pits lying on 3D meshes application to impact crater recognition. In: EGU General Assembly 2015, vol. 17 (EGU2015), p. 7628 (2015)
25. Shufelt, J.A.: Performance evaluation and analysis of monocular building extraction from aerial imagery. IEEE Trans. Pattern Anal. Mach. Intell. **21**(4), 311–326 (1999)
26. Stepinski, T.F., Ding, W., Vilalta, R.: Detecting impact craters in planetary images using machine learning. In: Intelligent Data Analysis for Real-Life Applications: Theory and Practice, pp. 146–159. IGI Global (2012)
27. Szabo, T., Domokos, G., Grotzinger, J.P., Jerolmack, D.J.: Reconstructing the transport history of pebbles on Mars. In: Nature Communications, vol. 6, p. 8366 (2015)
28. Urbach, E.R., Stepinski, T.F.: Automatic detection of sub-km craters in high resolution planetary images. Planet. Space Sci. **57**(7), 880–887 (2009)
29. Wang, Y., Yang, G., Guo, L.: A novel sparse boosting method for crater detection in the high resolution planetary image. Adv. Space Res. **56**(5), 982–991 (2015)
30. Zuber, M.T., Smith, D.E., Solomon, S.C., Muhleman, D.O., Head, J.W., Garvin, J.B., Abshire, J.B., Bufton, J.L.: The Mars observer laser altimeter investigation. J. Geophys. Res. Planets **97**(E5), 7781–7797 (1992)

A System for Automatic Town Sign Recognition for Driver Assistance Systems

Dariusz Frejlichowski[(✉)] and Piotr Mikołajczak

Faculty of Computer Science and Information Technology,
West Pomeranian University of Technology, Szczecin,
Żolnierska 52, 71-210 Szczecin, Poland
dfrejlichowski@wi.zut.edu.pl, mikolajczak.priv@gmail.com

Abstract. The paper describes two different ways of recognizing the road signs that can be applied to the autonomous driver assistance systems. It provides the road sign content and analysis of implemented algorithms, in order to apply them in such systems, resulting in the extension of their functionalities. The mobile application implemented as part of performed experiments, works using the real–time data. The application has been tested practically—the smartphone placed in a car was registering and analyzing the road signs. The paper describes the possibilities of practical use of a mobile device in combination with a real–time data processing program for the detection and recognition of selected road signs. The theoretical part discusses some important automotive topics and selected methods for road signs analysis. As part of practical section, two different methods of road sign recognition, have been implemented and analyzed. The application has been studied and made for iOS system. The OpenCV library has been additionally used. Also, the possibilities of development and optimization of selected algorithms have been shown.

1 Introduction

Nowadays, one can observe fast technological progress in many fields, e.g. computer science, robotics, electronics, mechatronics. The development of robotics can result in replacing humans by machines in many areas of their activities. The last stage of this process concerns the systems operating without human interference. Currently, new technology in the automotive world is dynamically developed. This new technology aims to make vehicles able to move independently, without human actions.

Implementing the idea of a vehicle without a driver is a complex challenge. Appropriate algorithms and applications should be developed to replace the human's actions while driving. This is a complicated task because the driver's reactions to visual and auditory signals should be taken into account. The driver's experience and possibly his instinctive actions should also be taken

© Springer Nature Switzerland AG 2018
L. J. Chmielewski et al. (Eds.): ICCVG 2018, LNCS 11114, pp. 115–124, 2018.
https://doi.org/10.1007/978-3-030-00692-1_11

into consideration. Currently, many automotive companies present prototypes of self–moving vehicles, even racing cars, working without a driver.

The basic task of intelligent vehicles is to detect incidents and to analyze the environment, which enables efficient functioning. The purpose of one of these systems is the detection of road signs, what already had its beginnings in 2008 in the BMW 7 Series, Mercedes–Benz S–Class and Opel Insignia vehicles [4,11].

Recently, one can notice the development of driver assistance systems that consist of many independent units. Each component creates new visions, new opportunities, and new goals. As of today, technologies and solutions are being implemented, which in the near future will result in autonomous units [21]. It can be assumed that currently manufactured vehicles on the public market are already partially automated. Usually, these are already "standard" systems for us, which can significantly help us the driving. Such units include, among others: parking assistant, lane assistant, traffic light assistant, blind spot assistant, economic driving assistant, active cruise control, fatigue detection system, car preparation system for an accident, collision avoidance system in urban driving or automatic driving in a column of vehicles [3,7,20]. These are just exemplary functions that, over time, are more popular in everyday vehicles. All technologies joined together can create a completely independent unit, able to self–navigate. All activities related to driving cars such as twisting, accelerating, pedestrian attention, etc. will be performed by driver assistance systems for us. However, before this happens, all necessary units must be implemented that could reflect the work of our senses.

Many companies introduce the latest technologies striving to build a self–moving vehicle. One example is the Volvo sc90 car [10], which is one of the cars that is close to the implementation of a fully autonomous system. It is a car that moves, brakes itself, but also drives us. Unfortunately, the vehicle is still limited in some way, because it works on GPS signals, appropriate maps and radars. The question arises—what will happen when the car loses coverage or signal? This is the reason why one should create systems that operate in real–time and apply the artificial intelligence algorithms. In addition to these devices, the vehicle applies cameras and laser sensors that allow receiving data from the environment. Received data is analyzed and then processed, so that the vehicle will move by itself.

Fully autonomous vehicles are the closest vision of motoring, which, contrary to appearances, is not so easy to achieve. Many systems are still being tested and undergo a number of modifications. The automotive company that specializes in this type of car is Tesla [21]. The corporation deals with the study of psychological characteristics of drivers and cognitive processes while using the latest technologies [2]. The user is provided with the latest technological solutions with continuous updates. Analysis of the interaction between the driver and the vehicle enables constant development of systems, thanks to which in the near future, fully automated units may be developed.

The goal is to create a personal vehicle that will take care of the driver, providing him with comfort while driving, and will replace him in the activities performed while driving. Nevertheless, the most important assumption is the safety of a human. The systems are to be safe enough in order to not to kill people or cause an accident [23]. It is initially anticipated that in critical situations a driver will always be the person who has to take control of the vehicle. This can avoid an accident or a negative traffic incident. In order to achieve these goals, the car, thanks to driver assistance systems, must be able to predict virtually any road situation. The implemented algorithms must work quickly, efficiently and in real time. A variety of sensors, receivers, transmitters and other devices are necessary for this, transferring information to a computing unit—a computer that makes decisions and takes appropriate actions [16].

2 Related Works

When detecting road signs (Fig. 1), many methods of image processing and analysis can be applied. The most commonly used solutions for detection are based mainly on the recognition of geometric figures and colors. An exemplary method is the thresholding process, which consists in converting the image to a binary form (pixel value 0 or 1), thus reducing the information contained in the image [12]. From the input image we are able to extract important data much easier. Another method is the segmentation, which allows us to determine the approximate location of the selected area. We can search for interesting clusters of a given color in the image, thanks to which we get the required region. In order to determine the exact shapes of the characters, we can use various methods of

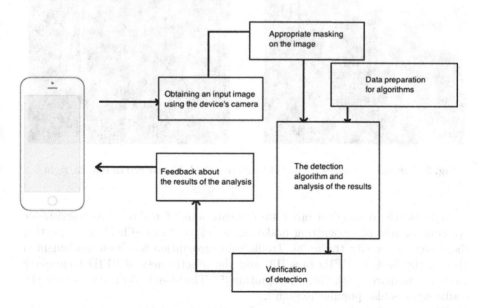

Fig. 1. Simplified operation model of the designed application for the town signs recognition.

finding figures and edges, which in the case of road signs is very effective, because each character has the appropriate shape and color that inform us about its function. The designation of a color or shape allows us to assign it to a given group of road signs.

The data considered when designing the application described in this paper is placed on E–17a and D–42 signs (see examples on Fig. 2). In the built–up area in Poland there is a speed limit of 50 km/h. By detecting the D–42 sign, the system is able to inform the driver about the restriction. Signs of this type are located on the right side of the road and are in white and black colors.

The city names for the E–17a sign are on a single–color green background and are written in white. These characteristics facilitate character analysis and allow the use of different detection methods. The system developed as part of the work described in the paper has the ability to detect and process the above–mentioned signs and to inform the driver about their content.

Fig. 2. Exemplary images with D–42 sign (on the left) and E–17a (on the right).

It is worth to mention other implementations of mobile driver assistance systems, in area of recognizing brake lights [14] and in the field of supporting the driver in the city traffic [8]. Traffic sign recognition has been implemented also on the basis of RFID tags [13] and the effectiveness of RFID technology has been compared with visual recognition [5]. The visual information about the traffic signs is also popular (e.g. [6]).

The first approach concerning the detection, described here, was provided in [15]. The proposed method is based on image segmentation in the RGB color space, and a corner detection for detecting characters. It was implemented in the Matlab environment and detects warning and prohibition signs. The program returns the result in a form of a detected character and the number of common features between the detected pattern and the sign. The presented solution provides satisfactory results. However, based on the tests performed, the algorithm appears to be inefficient for real–time analysis. Variable weather conditions and exposure are problematic during image analysis as well.

Another solution was presented in [24]. The author points out that the analysis of images obtained from the camera during the movement of a vehicle needs very high computing power due to large number of pixels in the image. The solution was presented for round signs that are speed limits in Australia. The goal was achieved by a fast radial symmetry detector that took the image from the camera mounted in the car. To classify the road sign a normalized cross–correlation was applied. The classification stage assumes that the characters are ideal and identically set. Under real conditions the signs are usually arranged differently. They are in various places, at different angles. This is an important restriction that probably will not work for Polish roads.

Another solution was developed in the Image Recognition Laboratory in Koblenz, Germany [18]. The system is designed for German and French road signs. It was based on color segmentation. In most cases signs in Europe are identified using ideograms. For this reason, four character detection methods were developed. The first involved detecting the arrows, which identifies a group of directional or warrant signs. The next module concerned the detection of speed limits and the analysis of the number of characters. Nearest neighbor module was applied to three classes of ideograms: prohibition signs, speed limitations and arrows, command signs. The fourth was based on neural networks and worked for ideograms of prohibition signs and speed limits. The described work presents an interesting approach to the problem of character detection. Different ways to detect a set of characters were presented. The algorithms were sophisticated, what can be a computational problem, because arrow analysis is a very slow process, what would prevent the work in real–time. In this case, the neural network and classifier are not very accurate, they only identify high resolution images, while low resolution images generate errors.

3   Description of the Program

The application is intended to work on a mobile device. The program performs image analysis in real time. The data is taken via the camera installed in the phone. When moving a passenger vehicle the device (e.g. smartphone with installed application) finds selected road signs. Thanks to the used algorithms the application, after detecting the mark, performs the appropriate analysis in order to provide the user the detailed information. The application consists of three basic modules. All gathered together will create a coherent system. MODULE1 is a module that searches for the D–42 sign using the cascade classifier. The image taken from the camera of the device is prepared for analysis. The area of interest is determined and the color image is changed to greyscale. Later, the character is detected. If successful, the information is sent to the user interface which informs about the event. MODULE2 is responsible for finding the E–17a sign. The whole process consists of a few stages that verify the correctness of the detection. The input image, which comes from the phone's camera, is prepared for analysis. The color space and the limited space on which the detection is carried out is changed. The first step is the search for rectangles in the image. If the assumptions regarding the size and shapes are fulfilled, a subsequent verification stage takes place, consisting in a thorough analysis of the found sub–frame.

When typical characteristics for analyzed character are recognized, the information about the found character goes to the user interface. MODULE3 is closely related to MODULE2. It processes a portion of the image from the camera that was previously prepared by MODULE2. The obtained fragment is analyzed by the algorithm of letter detection, which is to read the name of the town from the found character. However, before this operation, the Tesseract configuration is performed. A set of letters is established, which may consist of a text, a language of the text and the exact working time of the algorithm. The result is sent directly to the output image and annotation panel.

Two independent methods of road sign detection have been developed. The algorithms are based on a detailed analysis of the image, thanks to which the application is able to find the sign in real time.

The E–17a sign is characterized by a square shape and solid colors. The letters are white on a green background. This fact was used during the analysis. Before attempting image analysis, the color space is limited. After receiving only the green color due to the appropriate transformation of RGB colors to HSV, the image should be presented in black and white, what will greatly facilitate the process of its processing. This effect is obtained by binarizing the image. In result, the area of interest is defined as follows—the green color is white and the rest of the image is black. The next step is the search for the squares. For optimization, it was assumed that the width of the rectangle can not exceed the length of the area of interest (in this case half of the width of the input image—240 pixels) and the height will not be higher than 60% of the width. It will maintain the proportions of the road sign.

The obtained results have to be analyzed in order to verify if found figures are actually characters. For this purpose, it is verified if the detected image contains white pixels that are the names of the city. In the last step, the letter recognition system (OCR) was used for the obtained image. In order to optimize the results, a list of possible letters was pre–assumed.

The second detection method was used for the D–42 sign. It is characterized by a constant pattern and colors. In order to find it the Haar's cascade classifier was used to detect objects [3]. The algorithm is based on analyzing each part of the image in order to find previously implemented pattern. It has many features that combined into one give effective results. The algorithm is mainly based on finding rectangular shapes (Haar). The feature used in the classifier is determined by the shape, location in the area of interest and scale.

An image database has to be prepared in order to create a cascade classifier file. It consists of positive and negative samples. Positive samples contain examples of the subject of the search. In this case it is a D–42 sign. About 50 images have been used for this purpose. Negative samples contain images with the environment in which the object can be sought. Our subject of search could not appear on these samples.

For the optimization and acceleration of the algorithms only the right center part of the device's display was used, because it is a region of interest in which signs can be found. The built–in speech synthesizer implemented in the iPhone was used to inform the driver about the events.

The Apple Development programming environment was used to achieve the goal of the work and Xcode, which is used to create software. It is available free of charge and provided with Mac OS version 9.1. The high–level language used was the Objective C. The C++ OpenCV library was also applied [9,17,19] as well as the tools such as Tesseract OCR and Cascade Classifier [1,22].

Fig. 3. Exemplary test images with road signs in bad weather conditions.

4   Obtained Experimental Results

All tests were carried out using the Apple iPhone 6 device on which the developed program was installed. The only input source was the image captured via the mobile device using the built–in camera. The program worked in real–time. The tests consisted of three stages. Firstly, the program was analyzed at home. The phone was placed in front of the computer display, on which 111 previously prepared test images containing traffic signs were provided. The images were taken from different perspectives and in various weather conditions. The goal was to recognize selected road signs. For this stage, an efficiency of 96.5% was obtained for the D–42 sign and 93.9% for the E–17a sign.

The second test was similar to the previous one. However, instead of a series of photos, several video sequences that were recorded while driving the car, were displayed in front of the device. For the 43 test sequences, 96% efficiency was obtained for the D–42 sign and 93.7% for the E–17a sign.

The last test can be considered the best verification of the efficiency of the program, because it took place in the target environment in which the software should work. The phone was placed in a tripod in the vehicle's split board. The application has been tested while moving the car on public roads in Poland on a section about 500 km. In this case, the efficiency was 94.9% for the D–42 sign and 90.3% for the E–17a sign.

After analyzing the test results we can see that the program is able to positively recognize selected road signs and process them in real time. The effectiveness obtained during the tests was 94.2%. Few errors were caused by factors such as bad weather, inadequate focusing on the phone, insufficient computing power, wrong setting of the device's sensitivity to green, too low resolution of the input image, too small number of samples. The nature of the images in real conditions was the most important problem during test—see Fig. 3 for some examples.

5   Conclusions

The developed application uses two approaches to detect road signs. It can give the information about the environment in a simple way using image analysis. The tests show how simple algorithms deal with the detection of road signs. The combination of several components made it possible to create a functional system operating in real time. The application is one of the elements of driver assistance system that shows another approach to the problem of road signs detection. The field is constantly improved, many large corporations are betting on the development of such systems. The work presents an idea that has been implemented in a simple way, yielding decent results. The estimated error is only 5–9%. An algorithm for recognizing selected road sings has been created and implemented.

The whole system can be expanded by a larger number of signs. The program itself could be implemented on a more efficient device than would have better computing power, what would increase the speed of work and would give better results. An example of such device is the Raspberry Pi.

The system could be an element of offline navigation system that could work in real time, regardless of network coverage. After increasing the detection range the program could be implemented in autonomous vehicles. In addition, it is an interesting alternative for people who value security, but do not intend to purchase vehicles with the latest technologies. Almost everyone has now a mobile device. Thanks to such an application, the system would inform about road signs and dangers that the driver might not notice. However, it should be remembered that no device can fully replace a human being. These are only driver assistance systems that ensure greater safety and comfort while driving the vehicle. The final decision will always be made by the driver.

References

1. Cascade Classification. https://docs.opencv.org/2.4/modules/objdetect/doc/cascade_classification.html. Accessed 20 Oct 2017
2. Dikmen, M., Burns, C.: Trust in autonomous vehicles—the case of tesla autopilot and summons. In: Proceedings of the 2017 IEEE International Conference on Systems, Man, and Cybernetics (SMC), Banff, AB, pp. 1093–1098 (2017)
3. Fint, P., Nikolaus, R., Zimmermann, M.: Efficiently safeguarding driver assistance systems. ATZelektronik Worldwide **12**(1), 64–69 (2017)
4. Forczmanski, P.: Recognition of occluded traffic signs based on two–dimensional linear discriminant analysis. Arch. Transp. Syst. Telemat. **6**(3), 10–13 (2013)
5. Forczmański, P., Małecki, K.: Selected aspects of traffic signs recognition: visual versus RFID approach. In: Mikulski, J. (ed.) TST 2013. CCIS, vol. 395, pp. 268–274. Springer, Heidelberg (2013). https://doi.org/10.1007/978-3-642-41647-7_33
6. Frejlichowski, D.: Application of the polar–fourier greyscale descriptor to the automatic traffic sign recognition. In: Kamel, M., Campilho, A. (eds.) ICIAR 2015. LNCS, vol. 9164, pp. 506–513. Springer, Cham (2015). https://doi.org/10.1007/978-3-319-20801-5_56
7. Ippen, H.: Multimedia Highlights. Auto Zeitung **4**, 100–101 (2013)
8. Iwan, S., Małecki, K., Stalmach, D.: Utilization of mobile applications for the improvement of traffic management systems. In: Mikulski, J. (ed.) TST 2014. CCIS, vol. 471, pp. 48–58. Springer, Heidelberg (2014). https://doi.org/10.1007/978-3-662-45317-9_6
9. Kaehler, A., Bradski, G.R.: OpenCV 3 Computer image recognition in C++ using the OpenCV library, Helion S.A. (2018). (in Polish)
10. Kumar, S.: The innovation centre brings value engineering for low–cost solutions. Autotechreview **5**(11), 18–20 (2016)
11. Liang, M., Yuan, M., Hu, X., Li J., Liu, H.: Traffic sign detection by ROI extraction and histogram features–based recognition. In: Proceedings of the 2013 International Joint Conference on Neural Networks (IJCNN), pp. 739–746 (2013)
12. Mahatme, M.B., Kuwelkar, S.: Detection and recognition of traffic signs based on RGB to RED conversion. In: Proceedings of the International Conference on Computing Methodologies and Communication (ICCMC), pp. 447–451 (2017)
13. Małecki, K., Kopaczyk, K.: RFID-based traffic signs recognition system. In: Mikulski, J. (ed.) TST 2013. CCIS, vol. 395, pp. 115–122. Springer, Heidelberg (2013). https://doi.org/10.1007/978-3-642-41647-7_15
14. Małecki, K., Watróbski, J.: Mobile system of decision–making on road threats. Procedia Comput. Sci. **112**, 1737–1746 (2017)
15. Matuszewski, J.: Intelligent road sing recognition system. Przeglad Elektrotechniczny **92**(1), 41–44 (2016). (in Polish)
16. Muehlenberg, M., Seubert, T.: Driver assistance systems based on image sensors. ATZ Worldwide **104**(7–8), 10–12 (2002)
17. OpenCV. https://opencv.org. Accessed 12 Sep 2017
18. Priese, L., Lakmann, R., Rehrmann, V.: Ideogram identification in realtime traffic sign recognition system. In: Proceedings of the Intelligent Vehicles '95 Symposium, Detroit, MI, pp. 310–314 (1995)

19. Rafajłowicz, E., Rafajłowicz, W., Rusiecki, A.: Image processing algorithms and introduction to work with the OpenCV library, Wrocław (2009). (in Polish)
20. Electronic systems ABS, ESP, ASR: Discover the security alphabet. http:// akademia.autoswiat.pl/baza-wiedzy/systemy-elektroniczne-abs-esp-asr-poznaj-alfabet-bezpieczenstwa. Accessed 1 Oct 2017. (in Polish)
21. Tesla. https://www.tesla.com/de_DE. Accessed 30 Dec 2017
22. Tesseract ORC. https://github.com/tesseract-ocr/tesseract/wiki. Accessed 2 Nov 2017
23. Wicher, J.: Car and traffic safety, Warszawa (2012). (in Polish)
24. Barnes, N., Zelinsky, A.: Real-time radial symmetry for speed sign detection. In: Proceedings of the IEEE Intelligent Vehicles Symposium, pp. 566–571 (2004)

Selective and Simple Graph Structures for Better Description of Local Point-Based Image Features

Grzegorz Kurzejamski$^{(\boxtimes)}$ and Marcin Iwanowski

Institute of Control and Industrial Electronics, Warsaw University of Technology,
ul.Koszykowa 75, 00-662 Warsaw, Poland
{grzegorz.kurzejamski,marcin.iwanowski}@ee.pw.edu.pl

Abstract. The paper presents simple graph features based on a well-known image keypoints. We discuss the extraction method and geometrical properties that can be used. Chosen methods are tested in KNN tasks for almost 1000 object classes. The approach addresses problems in applications that cannot use learning methods explicitly, as real-time tracking, chosen object detection scenarios and structure from motion. Results imply that the idea is worth further research for chosen systems.

1 Introduction

A broad classification of image features consists of global and local approaches. Global term is self explanatory, but a locality aspect of a local feature may vary. This work tries to argue that for some applications one should use more features with richer (as more global) description. Big number of features of big size usually implies a huge computational cost. Current hashing, parallel computing and feature ranking methods deal with these problems well. On the other hand doubling number of local features in the image is not trivial, as added keypoints may be highly unstable. Doubling feature space is not trivial neither, as new features might not describe more of an information variance. Thus we propose a simple and fast method of generating a lot of new features (further called graphlets) with higher and usable feature space. Each graphlet may contain geometrical correlation data and consists of three independent local features. Its creation cost is low and after using very simple filtering methods system can operate on a bigger number of features with higher matching capabilities. This approach may be considered as a brutal one, but applied correctly can lead to increase in matching accuracy and a substantial increase in unique true positive matches in local feature domain. Overabundance of data is computationally demanding and may be applied only to chosen systems. Efficiency in this respect is widely discussed in further sections.

The aim of this new graph-like features is to be easily hashable and organized based on a numeric features values and to maintain high matching accuracy. The structure of the hashing mechanism can further be tested with machine learning

L. J. Chmielewski et al. (Eds.): ICCVG 2018, LNCS 11114, pp. 125–136, 2018.
https://doi.org/10.1007/978-3-030-00692-1_12

methods. If the features match accuracy is very high it is possible to use the graphlets in a sequential manner without full feature pool analysis, as with using decision trees on partial bag-of-words approach.

In case of a structure from motion we want to include more keypoints matches per single matching process. The real application of structure from motion is not tested in this paper though, as the first tests are created to isolate the matching problem.

Local features and its correlations can be seen as a graph with edges being correlations, and vertices being local features. Comparing two graphs is considered an NP-hard problem. The methods of harnessing the local features correlations in the global domain may be not trivial. A lot of attention is still needed here.

Through the years the object detection research has been carried for various applications. Last decade was a time for a substantial headway for local features and descriptors. Current trends favour the use of deep convolutional neural networks to do the hard work. Crushing older approaches to common classification problems in matters of both precision and detection resolving time, modern learning mechanisms continue to push the computer vision frontiers. However a learning step is not possible in many real situations, as the prior data may be unobtainable or prone to sudden changes. To present but a few, product casing detection problem consists of hundreds of thousands of object classes, which may contain common graphical elements. Because of the sheer volume of data and constant redesigning work done by a companies around the world the learning procedure is not applicable to this scenario. As the product casings can be richly and discriminatively described by local feature descriptors, using bag of words based methods is vastly exploited. These are the applications where the description generalization mechanism is not needed. Rather the filtering of false matches and handling of partial data is important.

Local features are inherently used in flow tracking scenarios and Structure from Motion applications. The estimation of a 3D point or, alternatively, an estimation of a swarm trajectory is very impervious to false match assignment or low matches pool. Here, an absolute number of true assignments can even have much more leverage than a precision, as false matches can be discarded in a longer run. This can lead to a need for a bigger features pool, that cannot be always done with simple multiplying the number of probing points. A lot of scale and rotation invariant keypoint detectors are made so it will utilize most of the visually salient regions, exhausting the potential capacity of the algorithm for a given image. This task can be done though with augmenting existing keypoint pool with additional correlation data.

2   Related Work

There are many different feature points extraction and description methods. One of the most popular are: [1, 4, 17, 20, 23]. All of them contain rich feature description and often additional information about scale and rotation. Lowe in

[19] proposes generalized Hough Transform for clustering the vote space, giving good results for multi-object detection. Authors of [2] create a 4D voting space and use combination of Hough, RANSAC and Least Squares Homography Estimation in order to detect and accept potential objects' instances. Zickler in *et al.* [31] use angle differences criterion in addition to RANSAC mechanism and a vote number threshold. This single criterion gave better results, incorporating features' geometrical correlations that couldn't be used in RANSAC explicitly. Authors of [14,15] showed that using features' correlation tests for vote space is crucial for achieving high precision.

Many multi-detection systems use Histogram of Oriented Gradients [7] and Deformable Part Models [11]. Interesting use of DPM and LSH can be also found in the work of Dean *et al.* [8]. The biggest drawback of the Deformable Part Models and Histogram of Oriented Gradients is that they usually need a learning stage.

There are many algorithms based on graph structures. Most of them deal with high order graphs and correspondences optimization. Authors of [3] used graph kernels for categorization of big graphs. Paper [5] presents using machine learning for parameter estimation for graph matching algorithm. There are some approaches to object detection and categorization with use of trees as in [6]. There is a lot to be told about global feature points correspondences estimation in work [9,30]. Authors of [10] presented an algorithm designed for high order graphs. Common approach to graph comparison is using hyper graphs, as presented in [16] Here they used a random walks on hyper graphs to estimate the level of isomorphism. Some researches used Markov Random Fields for graph structures as in [22]. This unfortunately can be used only for scenes of strictly defined type. A lot of graph algorithms uses notion of partial or full isomorphism of graphs. It is not trivial to create a approximation of the isomorphism criterion. This problem has been discussed in [24]. There are some algorithms optimized for graphs with more than a 100 thousands nodes, as in [26]. Graph structures has been successfully used in deformed models comparison. The example can be Deformable Part Models and the work presented in [27]. A lot of information about graph matching can be found in a review [28]. There are some non-graph meta structures used to incorporate geometrical data on feature points. Authors of [21] used simple shape context for feature points, but still the context itself is not using scale and rotation distribution.

Deep neural networks have also been used to train feature descriptors [25,29]. LIFT [29] uses a neural network for detection and description. MatchNet [13] uses Siamese neural network for that purpose. Work [18] presents training context-augmented descriptors based on FREAK.

3 Graphlets

A graphlet is build upon three feature points, as shown in Fig. 1. V1 is a root of the graphlet, and has two connected vertices, referenced later as children V2 and V3. Each feature point consists of a base descriptor, size and a rotation.

Each graphlet's data could be augumented by additional information calculated from the structural characteristics of a graphlet. For testing purposes we chose:

- The angle between the children calculated clockwise from V2 to V3.
- Quotient of lengths of <V1, V2> and <V1, V3> edges.
- Quotient of lengths of <V1, V2> and root size.
- Quotient of child V2's size and root size.
- Quotient of child V3's size and root size.
- Difference between V1 and V2 rotation angles.
- Difference between V1 and V3 rotation angles.
- Difference between root rotation and <V1, V2> direction.
- Difference between root rotation and <V1, V3> direction.

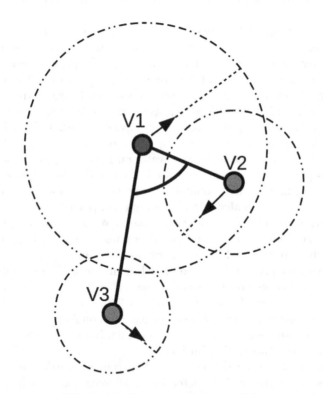

Fig. 1. A basic structure of a graphlet.

The features above are a basic ones and a list of another possibilities could be long. They can be calculated during matching or voting process, but usually they can be calculated very quickly if there is no storage requirements. Graphlets may be generated easily from a set of feature points. However this can lead to generation of overabundance of data. We are operating on a $O(N^3)$ number of graphlet instances. Leaving out the restrictions, the graphlet generator may produce too much data to process. Thus we created a set of rules: the maximum difference in keypoint sizes inside single graphlet and a maximum edge length proportional to root size. We used SIFT for tests and we used a factor threshold of a 2.0. The sizes of V1, V2 and V3 should not differ very much, as keypoints at different scales may have different stability. Because of the keypoints instability the features shouldn't be close together in the image space domain. We checked if all the edges in the graphlet are longer than a 1/4th of a root size. This method can still produce too much data for dense keypoint areas. During the processing we put a constraint on a number of neighbours around the root that could produce graphlets. We chose 20 for this limitation. Preliminary tests showed that this limitation has little impact on the outcome of the main ones. This is probably because we are dealing with surfeit of data.

4   Experimental Setup

The experiment consists of multiple tests, with the first one being the baseline. The baseline test does not use graphlets and is computed for the reference. We used SIFT detector and descriptor for all computations.

4.1   Image Database

The image database used was the ALOI [12] color image collection of one thousand small objects. Objects have been photographed on a black background imposing different illumination conditions, framing and color alterations. For our tests we used grayscale images with illumination shifts. Each image presents the object in its default position. There is only one light source used during the shots so changes in the appearance of the same object may differ substantially. This changes are presented in Fig. 2. Illumination direction changes are the most erroneous transformations of the object's appearance right beside viewing angle change. Still framing lets us generate a ground truth for the matching process, giving a small space for error, as location of the same keypoint may change slightly for different images. This is important to emphasize, that for the most different shots in class there is less than 30% of the common keypoints present in the image (more in Sect. 4.2). This is a very hard task for a matching algorithm, as data is very noisy. If we couldn't obtain at least 50 feature points per image in the class, we discarded it. We achieved an average of 314 feature points per image afterwards.

4.2   Preliminary Research: Feature Points Stability

We assessed feature points stability for ALOI database. Having the objects in the same pose, can we assume that each of the characteristic point should appear in the same place in image domain for every image in the same class. That said, because of the changes in the light position, the keypoint detector may show some positions' fluctuations for properly matched points. Thus we set a global

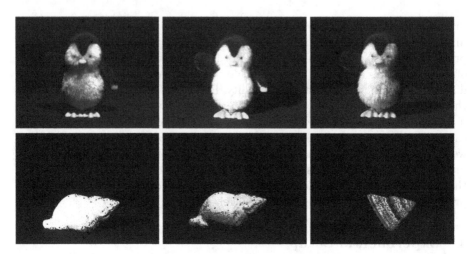

Fig. 2. Example of the change in objects' appearance for different illumination angle. Taken from ALOI database. Second row presents keypoints' locations extracted by SIFT.

threshold for correct match assumption on a level of 6 px as 1/128th of the image's width.

The stability of the points in our test is very low and may create substantial challenge for detection systems of various sort. In Table 1 we present the accuracy calculated using SIFT KNN in regards to different distance thresholds without use of any filtering mechanism. Results show that single KNN on SIFT generates bad matches most of the time.

On the other hand we've got a static test with keypoint detection repetitiveness. We checked if any of the feature points is present position-wise in every other image of the same class. We can see that, depending on the acceptance threshold, it oscillates around 55% on average. It may be enough for feature point matches, but when we are dealing with graphlets we have to put the probability to proper exponentiation. In our case it is roughly 24%. It means that more than 75% of the generated graphlets has no proper match and must be filtered out. This is basically the biggest risk of the approach.

Table 1. Accuracy of feature points L2 KNN without filtering for different thresholds.

Threshold (in px)	3	6	9
Match accuracy	23.3%	25.5%	27.1%
Keypoint detection repetitiveness	42.6%	62.2%	72.78%

4.3 In-Class Nearest Neighbours Search:

We've done set of in-class matching tests of the feature points and graphlets. Each test tries to measure different aspect of the graphlet usability. For each matching process we used a selection of filtering methods and a voting schemas. The distance filtering is discarding the matches with distance higher than a threshold. A threshold is calculated as a the fraction of the difference between minimal and maximal distance present in single image-to-image matching. We did not research deeply the thresholding mechanism but chose the thresholding factor for the best results in a basic matching scenario. Filtering for graphlets has additional simple tests based on its augmented, geometrical properties. Properties with scalar values are tested if its division lays in $< 1.2, 0.8 >$ interval. Rotational values are subtracted and tested against absolute maximum value of 20 degrees. Voting scheme consists of testing graphlet versus graphlet with its geometrical data. If passed, we vote for each feature point match. After full graphlet KNN we have pools of match propositions per each keypoint in the query image.

T1 - SIFT Nearest Neighbour Test: We calculate full nearest neighbours search between images from the same class. The nearest search uses L2 distance and basic keypoint features (SIFT). The matches are filtered by distance threshold.

T2 - Graphlets Nearest Neighbour Search: Each graphlet is considered as an independent feature. The distance is obtained by adding corresponding distances between V1s, V2s and V3s calculated from L2 SIFT distances. We are passing on the computation of the square in L2 metric, so adding the distance values is equal to calculating the distance between concatenated SIFT vectors in each graphlet. After matching process the geometrical filtering occurs. Because of the computational cost (roughly $O(n^6)$ for $n =$ feature points) this test is only for research purposes. If the accuracy for graphlet matching is lower than normal features it may be a signal that overabundance of data is making additional geometrical constraints not adequate for the problem.

T3 - SIFT Nearest Neighbour with Graphlets Filtering: In this test we incorporate graphlets geometrical tests for filtering matches obtained in SIFT nearest neighbours search with distance filtering. We've got information about all graphlets from a given keypoint. We check if there is at least one common graphlet in the set on both sides of the match, rooted in according keypoint. We do not do this operation if any of the matched keypoints has less than three graphlets present. Thus graphlets add here a second layer of filtering only.

T4 - Nearest Neighbour Search with Graphlet Voting: This test considers using graphlet matching first, incorporating only geometrical consistency test. After accepting match proposition (between any graphlets pair) the votes for corresponding keypoints matches are saved with singular weight. After that we have votes pool per each keypoint in a query image with different weights, which can be used for normal L2 distance computation between feature points. The threshold can be chosen as a minimal vote weight to consider point for computation. This test, the same as in previous one, has to be considered as a benchmark for graphlets mathematical properties. Even if we used hashing optimization for votes generation, it is still highly exponential computational burden for real application.

4.4   Feature Points and Software Considerations

We used OpenCV library for SIFT implementation. The testing platform is an application written in C++. Many computational modules have an overhead coming from usage of slow containers and a lot of additional statistics-related computations. Graphlet creation is fast as presented in the Table 2 and scales linearly with the keypoints number. If any more advanced geometrical features will be used, the computational cost may rise. We did not test the memory management as the implementation uses a lot of additional data containers implemented solely for easier tests redesigning.

Table 2. Average description times per image.

SIFT detect and compute	Graphlets generation (ms)
272.9	6.7

5   Results

We saw improvements in matching quality in each procedure incorporating graphlets. The highest accuracy for single SIFT L2 nearest neighbour test we achieved were **56.5%** per image pair and **41.5%** globally. Graphlets match in T2 test achieved **66.3%** and **62.2%** respectively. As the procedure is not feasible in real application, this only gives the information, that graphlets may be more stable than feature points despite exponentially bigger features pool.

Figure 3 presents results for T1 and T3 with different threshold ratio used for L2 distance filtering. We can see that graphlet filtering has small, positive impact on overall accuracy per image pair, and substantial impact for global accuracy. The reason for that is its ability to diminish the dispersion in filtering metrics, which can be observed with blue dots representing single image pair matching operation.

Figure 4 presents results for T4 test for two thresholds. Threshold is the minimal vote's weight to accept a keypoint for L2 SIFT matching. This gives very good result, achieving high accuracy for higher thresholds (many match

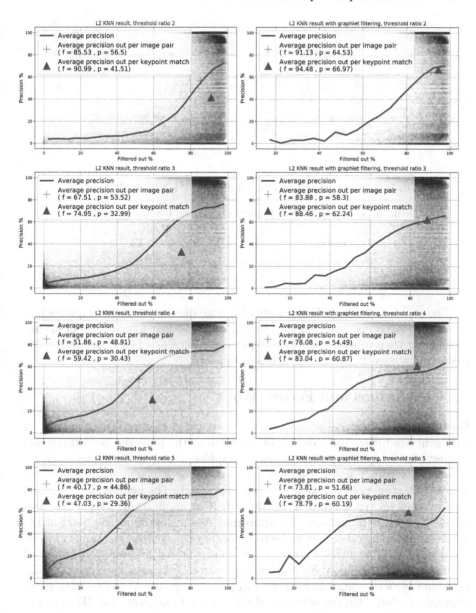

Fig. 3. Results for distance filtering and distance + graphlet geometrical filtering.

candidates are filtered out). However the most important aspect here is much higher consistency in high accuracy matches through whole spectrum of filtered out metric. The average filtered out amount is much lower than in previous tests, which gives much more useful matches in practise. This can be crucial for many real applications, where match set should be dense.

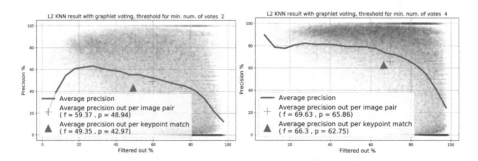

Fig. 4. Results for graphlets voting and then L2 KNN for filtered pools.

Table 3. Matching times for single image pair KNN computation.

Test number	T1	T2	T3	T4
Processing time in ms (ms)	36	2452	57	1968

The processing times (Table 3) are at a huge disadvantage for graphlets in a brute-force KNN computation with tests T2 and T4 being two orders of magnitude slower than other approaches. Implementation was a brutal one thus using hashing may greatly decrease processing times.

6   Conclusions and Future Work

Results for graphlets are promising. We were afraid that the sheer amount of data generated from unstable keypoints will limit the potential descriptive gain coming from additional geometric data. Graphlets stood up during tests, giving very good accuracy and substantial gain in unique keypoint correspondences. This is a starting point for more specialized research. The number of augmented features and its types are to be evaluated. Real applications do not use brutal KNN, with approximate algorithms and hashing in mind. Big part of the graphlets' geometrical data is prone to significant changes due to change in viewing directions. The filtering stage is thus much altered by level of bias needed to maximize the accuracy for a given application. For instance, if we are talking about structure from motion, we can have a sequence of images with slight appearance shifts. On the other hand we can try to generate the 3D model of the city from thousands of hand-made photos from the Internet, that will vary a lot. In this case using graphlets should be evaluated with proper tests. Hashing with segmentation of the data based on a geometrical features is another way of filtering out false matches. In such systems matching graphlets may be feasible computational wise.

Beside testing out production-type approaches on real scenarios, there are many new description ideas that could be implemented, as using line descriptors. Normalized descriptor over the line theoretically should not be altered by geometrical transformations.

As for the object detection in multi-object and multi-detection scheme, graphlets may have much more geometrical stability than single keypoint. In this scenario the object localization step is crucial. Graphlet has more geometrical constraints and thus may be better vote candidate for the task.

References

1. Alahi, A., Ortiz, R., Vandergheynst, P.: FREAK: fast retina keypoint. In: IEEE Conference on Computer Vision and Pattern Recognition (CVPR) 2012, pp. 510–517, June 2012
2. Azad, P., Asfour, T., Dillmann, R.: Combining harris interest points and the SIFT descriptor for fast scale-invariant object recognition. In: IEEE/RSJ International Conference on Intelligent Robots and Systems 2009. IROS 2009, pp. 4275–4280, October 2009
3. Bai, L., Hancock, E.R.: Fast depth-based subgraph kernels for unattributed graphs. Pattern Recogn. **50**, 233–245 (2016). https://doi.org/10.1016/j.patcog.2015.08.006
4. Bay, H., Ess, A., Tuytelaars, T., Gool, L.V.: Speeded-up robust features (SURF). Comput. Vis. Image Underst. **110**(3), 346–359 (2008). Similarity Matching in Computer Vision and Multimedia
5. Caetano, T.S., McAuley, J.J., Cheng, L., Le, Q.V., Smola, A.J.: Learning graph matching. IEEE Trans. Pattern Anal. Mach. Intell. **31**(6), 1048–1058 (2009). https://doi.org/10.1109/Ftpami.2009.28
6. Cantoni, V., Cinque, L., Guerra, C., Levialdi, S., Lombardi, L.: 2-D object recognition by multiscale tree matching. Pattern Recognit. **31**(10), 1443–1454 (1998)
7. Dalal, N., Triggs, B.: Histograms of oriented gradients for human detection. In: IEEE Computer Society Conference on Computer Vision and Pattern Recognition 2005, CVPR 2005, vol. 1, pp. 886–893, June 2005
8. Dean, T., Ruzon, M., Segal, M., Shlens, J., Vijayanarasimhan, S., Yagnik, J.: Fast, accurate detection of 100,000 object classes on a single machine. In: Proceedings of IEEE Conference on Computer Vision and Pattern Recognition, Washington, DC, USA (2013)
9. Demirci, M.F., Shokoufandeh, A., Keselman, Y., Bretzner, L., Dickinson, S.: Object recognition as many-to-many feature matching. Int. J. Comput. Vis. **69**(2), 203–222 (2006). https://doi.org/10.1007/Fs11263-006-6993-y
10. Duchenne, O., Bach, F., Kweon, I.S., Ponce, J.: A tensor-based algorithm for high-order graph matching. IEEE Trans. Pattern Anal. Mach. Intell. **33**(12), 2383–2395 (2011). https://doi.org/10.1109/Ftpami.2011.110
11. Felzenszwalb, P., Girshick, R., McAllester, D., Ramanan, D.: Object detection with discriminatively trained part-based models. IEEE Trans. Pattern Anal. Mach. Intell. **32**(9), 1627–1645 (2010)
12. Geusebroek, J.M., Burghouts, G.J., Smeulders, A.W.: The amsterdam library of object images, January 2005. https://doi.org/10.1023/B:VISI.0000042993.50813.60
13. Han, X., Leung, T., Jia, Y., Sukthankar, R., Berg, A.C.: Matchnet: unifying feature and metric learning for patch-based matching. In: CVPR (2015)
14. Kurzejamski, G., Zawistowski, J., Sarwas, G.: A framework for robust object multi-detection with a vote aggregation and a cascade filtering. CoRR abs/1512.08648 (2015). http://arxiv.org/abs/1512.08648

15. Kurzejamski, G., Zawistowski, J., Sarwas, G.: Robust method of vote aggregation and proposition verification for invariant local features. In: VISAPP 2015 - Proceedings of the International Conference on Computer Vision Theory and Applications, pp. 593–600, March 2015

16. Lee, J., Cho, M., Lee, K.M.: Hyper-graph matching via reweighted random walks. In: 2011 IEEE Conference on Computer Vision and Pattern Recognition (CVPR), pp. 1633–1640. IEEE, June 2011. https://doi.org/10.1109/Fcvpr.2011.5995387

17. Leutenegger, S., Chli, M., Siegwart, R.: BRISK: binary robust invariant scalable keypoints. In: IEEE International Conference on Computer Vision (ICCV) 2011, pp. 2548–2555, November 2011

18. Loquercio, A., Dymczyk, M., Zeisl, B., Lynen, S., Gilitschenski, I., Siegwart, R.: Efficient descriptor learning for large scale localization. In: ICRA (2017)

19. Lowe, D.: Distinctive Image Features From Scale-invariant Keypoints, vol. 60, pp. 91–110. Kluwer Academic Publishers, Hingham (2004)

20. Lowe, D.: Object recognition from local scale-invariant features. In: The Proceedings of the Seventh IEEE International Conference on Computer Vision 1999, vol. 2, pp. 1150–1157 (1999)

21. Lv, X., Wang, Z.J.: Perceptual image hashing based on shape contexts and local feature points. IEEE Trans. Inf. Forensics Secur. **7**(3), 1081–1093 (2012). https://doi.org/10.1109/Ftifs.2012.2190594

22. Myeong, H., Chang, J.Y., Lee, K.M.: Learning object relationships via graph-based context model. In: 2012 IEEE Conference on Computer Vision and Pattern Recognition (CVPR), pp. 2727–2734. IEEE, June 2012. https://doi.org/10.1109/Fcvpr.2012.6247995

23. Rublee, E., Rabaud, V., Konolige, K., Bradski, G.: ORB: An efficient alternative to SIFT or SURF. In: IEEE International Conference on Computer Vision (ICCV) 2011, pp. 2564–2571, November 2011

24. Shervashidze, N., Schweitzer, P., van Leeuwen, E.J., Mehlhorn, K., Borgwardt, K.M.: Weisfeiler-lehman graph kernels. J. Mach. Learn. Res. **12**, 2539–2561 (2011). http://dl.acm.org/citation.cfm?id=1953048.2078187

25. Simo-Serra, E., Trulls, E., Ferraz, L., Kokkinos, I., Fua, P., Moreno-Noguer, F.: Discriminative learning of deep convolutional feature point descriptors. In: ICCV (2015)

26. Tian, Y., Patel, J.M.: Tale: a tool for approximate large graph matching. In: 2008 IEEE 24th International Conference on Data Engineering (ICDE 2008), pp. 963–972. IEEE, April 2008. https://doi.org/10.1109/Ficde.2008.4497505

27. Torresani, L., Kolmogorov, V., Rother, C.: Feature correspondence via graph matching: models and global optimization. In: Forsyth, D., Torr, P., Zisserman, A. (eds.) ECCV 2008. LNCS, vol. 5303, pp. 596–609. Springer, Heidelberg (2008). https://doi.org/10.1007/978-3-540-88688-4_44

28. Vento, M.: A long trip in the charming world of graphs for pattern recognition. Pattern Recogn. **48**(2), 291–301, February 2015. https://doi.org/10.1016/Fj.patcog.2014.01.002

29. Yi, K.M., Trulls, E., Lepetit, V., Fua, P.: Lift: Learned invariant feature transform. In: ECCV (2016)

30. Zass, R., Shashua, A.: Probabilistic graph and hypergraph matching. In: 2008 IEEE Conference on Computer Vision and Pattern Recognition (CVPR), pp. 1–8. IEEE, June 2008. https://doi.org/10.1109/Fcvpr.2008.4587500

31. Zickler, S., Efros, A.: Detection of multiple deformable objects using PCA-SIFT. In: Proceedings of the 22nd National Conference on Artificial Intelligence, AAAI 2007, vol. 2, pp. 1127–1132. AAAI Press (2007)

Scene Recognition for Indoor Localization of Mobile Robots Using Deep CNN

Piotr Wozniak[4], Hadha Afrisal[2], Rigel Galindo Esparza[3],
and Bogdan Kwolek[1(✉)]

[1] AGH University of Science and Technology, 30 Mickiewicza, 30-059 Kraków, Poland
bkw@agh.edu.pl
[2] Universitas Gadjah Mada, Bulaksumur, Yogyakarta 55281, Indonesia
[3] Monterrey Institute of Technology and Higher Education,
Av. E. G. Sada 2501 Sur, Tecnológico, 64849 Monterrey, Mexico
[4] Rzeszów University of Technology,
Al. Powstańców Warszawy 12, 35-959 Rzeszów, Poland
http://home.agh.edu.pl/~bkw/contact.html

Abstract. In this paper we propose a deep neural network based algorithm for indoor place recognition. It uses transfer learning to retrain VGG-F, a pretrained convolutional neural network to classify places on images acquired by a humanoid robot. The network has been trained as well as evaluated on a dataset consisting of 8000 images, which were recorded in sixteen rooms. The dataset is freely accessed from our website. We demonstrated experimentally that the proposed algorithm considerably outperforms BoW algorithms, which are frequently used in loop-closure. It also outperforms an algorithm in which features extracted by FC-6 layer of the VGG-F are classified by a linear SVM.

1 Introduction

In recent years, development of mobile robots has reached a promising milestone in terms of low-energy and effective locomotion [11,20]. With these achievements, it is expected that in a near future, service robots will be ready to be employed in a massive scale. In many home, office or hospital settings a humanoid robot needs to navigate from one place to other places autonomously, for instance while transporting and collecting items from one room to other rooms, and so on. Any service humanoid robot is expected to work autonomously or semi-autonomously in those settings, therefore there are still many open-problems especially related to robot localization and mapping, which need to be investigated further [19].

Long-term localization and navigation in unknown environments is becoming increasingly important task for service robots. Such robots should cope with observation errors and the localization should work even in unexpected and dynamic situations, and possibly self-similar environments. The aim of Simultaneous Localization and Mapping (SLAM) is constructing or updating a map of an unknown environment while simultaneously keeping the track of the robot's location within it. Noisy measurements of the robot's odometry as well as noisy

© Springer Nature Switzerland AG 2018
L. J. Chmielewski et al. (Eds.): ICCVG 2018, LNCS 11114, pp. 137–147, 2018.
https://doi.org/10.1007/978-3-030-00692-1_13

observations of the environment lead to errors that accumulate over time, growing uncertainty of each subsequent pose and map estimation. In consequence, errors in the map estimation lead to errors in the pose estimation, and errors in pose estimation analogously lead to further errors in the map estimation [3]. In order to reliably maintain error bounds on robot's position during SLAM over long trajectories, so-called loop-closures need to be recognized, which can be achieved by collecting data associations between map and map, image and image, or images and map. Without loop-closure, the position estimated on the basis of (visual) odometry diverges from the true state since the errors accumulate over time [17]. Reliable detecting loop-closures is an important issue since any incorrect recognition of revisited places may lead to substantial mapping errors in indoor localization. Motion blur and object occlusions are among the factors that most deteriorate localization performance. Place recognition is perceived as important component towards semantic mapping and scene understanding.

The problem of qualitative robot localization refers to determining the place where the robot is present [13]. For instance, in an indoor environment a service robot should be able to determine that it is in a particular room, which may be a seminar room, lab, conference room, etc. During navigation the robot learns from experience and then recognizes previously observed places in known environment(s) and eventually categorizes previously unseen places in new rooms. This task is closely related to semantic localization, which consists in determining by a robot its location semantically with respect to objects or regions in the scene rather than reporting 6-DOF pose or position coordinates [3].

Visual place recognition algorithm is one of many solutions to provide a mobile robot with a localization ability, particularly for navigating in an indoor environment in which the robot's localization and navigation cannot only rely on the Ground Positioning System (GPS) [16]. Vision cameras are a natural choice for appearance-based SLAM, where the environment is modeled in a topological way by means of a graph. In such an approach, each graph node represents a distinctive visual location that was visited by the robot, while the edges indicate paths between places. On the basis of such a representation, the loop closure can be detected by direct image comparison, which allows us to avoid the need for maintenance and estimation of the position of the feature landmarks determined in the environment [8]. In recently proposed OpenABLE [1], the loop closure is detected on the basis of fast LDB global descriptor, which is based on idea of random comparisons between intensities of pixels in the neighborhood of the center. The main drawback of the OpenABLE is its poor scaling with the number of frames stored in the image database. Since the matching times increase linearly with the growing size of the database, the OpenABLE can only be employed in environments of limited size. Reliable recognition of the indoor place can therefore be used to constrain the searching for images only to image subset representing the currently visited room or place.

In this paper, we consider place recognition on the basis of images from a RGB camera mounted on a humanoid robot. We compare the performance of algorithms for visual recognition of the place on the basis of handcrafted features and deep learned-features. For the handcrafted features, we investigate the performance of widely used Bag-of-Words algorithm and Histogram of Uniform Pattern (HOUP) algorithm. For the learned-features, we demonstrate the performance of transfer-learning method for VGG [26] deep neural network. We introduce a dataset for visual recognition of the indoor places, which has been recorded using Nao humanoid robot in sixteen different rooms.

2 Relevant Work

There are two main approaches to achieve indoor localization of a mobile robot: SLAM and appearance-based. Visual SLAM can be computationally expensive due to the complexity connected with 3D reconstructions. Methods based on appearance can achieve good performance in coarse determining the camera location on the basis of predefined, limited set of place labels. FAB-MAP [6] is a probabilistic approach to recognize places on the basis of appearance information. The algorithm learns a generative model of the visual words using a Chow-Liu tree to model the co-occurrence probability. It performs matching the appearance of current scene to the same (similar) previously visited place through converting the images into Bag-of-Words representations built on local features such as SIFT or SURF.

Visual place description techniques can be divided into two broad categories: those that are based on local features; and those that describe the whole scene. Several local handcrafted features for visual place recognition have been investigated, such as SIFT [15] or SURF [2], binary-based local features such as BRISK [12] or ORB [21], and other feature descriptors such as lines [32], corner and edges [9], and HOUP [23]. Global or whole-image descriptors of the images, called also image signatures, such as Gist [18] process the whole image regardless of its content, and were investigated in place recognition as well [28].

One method which is commonly used in visual place recognition is Bag-of-Words (BoW) or Bag-of-Features (BoF), which usually follows three main steps: (1) extraction of local image features, (2) encoding of the local features in an image descriptor, and (3) classification of the image descriptor [4]. Sivic et al. [27] proposed an effective BoW method for object retrieval. Their method searches for and localizes all the occurrences of an object in a video, given a query image of the object. Local viewpoint invariant SIFT features are quantized on the basis of a pretrained visual word vocabulary and aggregated into a term frequency-inverse document frequency (tf-idf) vector. A benefit of the tf-idf representation is that it can be stored in the inverted file structure that yields an immediate ranking of the video frames containing the object. A successful visual place recognition technique has been achieved by Dorian's algorithm [7], which utilizes binary encoding to describe features in a very effective and efficient BoW algorithm. However, its main limitation is the use of features that lack of rotation and scale invariance. Another significant challenge in developing robust BoW-based visual place recognition algorithm is the existence of many similar and repetitive structures in man-made indoor settings, such as tiles, ceilings, windows, doors, and many more [31]. In addition, many of those methods are not robust to viewpoint and illumination changes [29].

Recent advancement in machine learning and deep learning has shed the light on a novel approach of utilizing Convolutional Neural Network (CNN) for many applications in vision-based recognition [24]. CNNs offer a new way of employing learned features for solving image retrieval problems as demonstrated in visual place recognition and categorization [5,14]. However, implementing deep learning for mobile robots is not quite straightforward, especially to carry out complex problems such as place recognition, SLAM and pose estimation, in which a high uncertainty is a considerable challenge [30]. Another challenge is that limited battery life makes it not easy to implement and execute in real-time algorithms that are based on deep models. Additionally, there is also need to cope with blurring and rotation of images around the optical axis, which arise during locomotion of the humanoid robot.

3   Image Descriptors

Below we outline descriptors that were used in our algorithm and experiments.

3.1   Handcrafted Descriptors

SIFT. SIFT feature [15], called SIFT keypoint is a selected image region with an associated descriptor. The keypoints can be extracted by the SIFT detector, whereas their descriptors can be expressed by the SIFT descriptor. By searching for image blobs at multiple positions and scales, the SIFT detector provides invariance to translation, rotations, and re-scaling of the image. The SIFT descriptor is a 3D spatial histogram of the image gradients describing the content of the keypoint region. It is calculated with respect to gradient locations and orientations, which are weighted by the gradient magnitude and a Gaussian window superimposed over the region.

HOUP. Histogram of Oriented Uniform Patters is a descriptor that is calculated by filtering the image sub-block by a Gabor Filter with different orientations. The output of the Gabor filter is then used to calculate Local Binary Patterns (LBP). The Principal Component Analysis (PCA) is then executed to reduce the dimensionality of such patterns of textural features. In [23] the input image is divided into 3×3 blocks. Each block undergoes Gabor filtering, and then LBPs are computed for each block. The block has 58 uniform + 1 non uniform patterns for each orientation, and it is represented by a vector of size $59 \times 6 = 354$. The PCA reduces the dimension of each block representation from 354 to 70. The descriptor of the whole image has size equal to $70 \times 9 = 630$. Finally, Support Vector Machines (SVM) and K-nearest neighbors (k-NN) classifiers were executed to achieve place recognition.

3.2   Learned Descriptors

Transfer learning is a machine learning approach in which a model developed and then learned for a certain task is reused as the starting point for a model on another setting. It allows to reuse knowledge learned from tasks for which a lot of labeled data is available to settings, where only little labeled data is in disposal. The utilization of a pretrained models is now a common approach, particularly when patterns extracted in the original dataset are useful in the context of another setting. This is due to the reason that enormous resources are required to train deep learning models, and/or large and challenging datasets on which deep learning models can be trained. For example, the Alex-Net required about 2–3 weeks to train using GPU and utilized approximately 1.2 million images. It was trained on a subset of the ImageNet database, which has been utilized in ImageNet Large-Scale Visual Recognition Challenge (ILSVRC-2012) [22]. The model can classify images into 1000 object categories. It has learned rich feature representations for a wide range of images.

The pretrained deep neural networks demonstrated its usefulness in many classification tasks, including visual place recognition. However, more often in practice a technique called fine-tuning is employed. In such an approach the chosen deep model that was trained on a large dataset like the ImageNet is utilized to continue training it (i.e. running back-propagation) on the smaller dataset we have. The networks trained on a large and diverse datasets like the ImageNet capture well universal features like curves and edges in their early layers, that are useful in most of the classification tasks. Another fine-tuning technique, which can be useful if the training dataset is really small, consists in taking the output of the intermediate layer prior to the fully connected layers as the features (bottleneck features) and then learning a linear classifier (e.g. SVM) on top of it. The reason for this is that the SVMs are particularly good at determining decision boundaries on small amounts of data.

The VGG-F network is an eight layer deep convolutional neural network (DCNN), see Fig. 1, which has been originally designed and trained for image classification. Its architecture is similar to the one used by Krizhevsky et al. [10]. The input image size is $224 \times 224 \times 3$. Fast processing is ensured by the four pixel stride in the first convolutional layer. The network has been trained on ILSVRC data using gradient descent with momentum. The hyper-parameters are the same as used by Krizhevsky. Data augmentation in the form of horizontal flips, random crops, and RGB color jittering has been applied in the learning process.

The deep features can be extracted after removing the last classification layer consisting of 1000 neurons. The only image pre-processing is to resize the input images to the network input size and to subtract the average image, which is provided together with the network parameters.

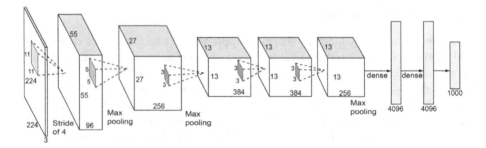

Fig. 1. Architecture of VGG-F.

4   CNN-Based Indoor Place Recognition

We investigated the features extracted by both 6th and 7th layers of VGG-F network. We compared the accuracies of place recognition using the features extracted by the layers mentioned above. The classification has been done using a linear SVM. As it turned out that far better results can be obtained on the basis of FC-6 features, the FC-6 features were used in evaluations described below. Afterwards, we removed the last layer from VGG-F and added three new layers to the layer graph: a fully connected layer, a softmax layer, and a classification output layer. The fully connected layer has been set to have the same size as the number of classes in the place recognition dataset. In order to achieve faster learning in the added layers than in the transferred layers, the learning rate factors of the fully connected layer have been increased. Such a deep neural network has been fine-tuned on place recognition datasets investigated in this work. The learning has been conducted using stochastic gradient descent with momentum (SGDM) optimizer with initial learning rate set to 0.0001, momentum set to 0.9 and L2 regularization set to 0.0001. The batch size has been set to ten samples.

The images acquired by Nao robot during walking are usually rotated around the optical axis. In general, for the CNN networks two approaches can be incorporated to encode rotation invariance: (1) employing rotations to the feature maps or alternatively to the input image, or (2) applying rotations to the convolution filters. The first approach comes down to a common practice of augmenting the training set with several rotated instances of the training images. Such a method permits the model to incorporate the rotation invariance [25]. We coped with the problem of rotated images around the optical axis, as well as scale variations through augmenting the data by image rotations in range $-10,\ldots,10$ deg, and shifting them horizontally and vertically in range $-20,\ldots,20$ pixels.

5   Experimental Results

At the beginning of the experiments we conducted experimental evaluations on York Univ. Dataset [14]. The dataset has been recorded using a color camera (Point Grey Bumblebee) mounted on Pioneer and Virtual Me mobile robots in two different lighting conditions (daylight and night time). On the Pioneer robot the camera was 88 cm above the ground level, whereas on Virtual Me robot it was mounted 117 cm above the floor. The dataset consists of 29 917 images for 11 places, with 100–500 images belonging to each place. All images have been acquired with a resolution of 640×480 pixels, with the camera fixed at an upright location. During data recording the robots were manually driven at the speed of approximately 0.5 meters per second through all the eleven places. The images were acquired at the rate of approximately three frames per second.

As in [14], we determined the accuracies of place recognition in four scenarios:

- Same Robot, Same Lighting Conditions
  Pioneer 1 – Pioneer 2 (Day - day or night - night) and Virtual Me 1 - Virtual Me
- Same Robot, Different Lighting Conditions
  Pioneer 1 – Pioneer 2 (Day - night or night - day) and Virtual Me 1 - Virtual Me 2 (Day - night or night - day)
- Different Robot, Same Lighting Conditions
  Pioneer – Virtual Me (Day - day or night - night) and Virtual Me - Pioneer (Day - day or night - night)
- Different Robot, Different Lighting Conditions
  Pioneer – Virtual Me (Day - night or night - day) and Virtual Me - Pioneer (Day - night or night - day)

The accuracy of place recognition in each scenario has been determined as the average of diagonal values in the confusion matrix.

We compared the recognition accuracies of algorithms operating both on handcrafted features and learned features. At the beginning we evaluated BoW algorithm operating on SIFT features. The classification has been performed using a k-NN as well as a linear SVM. The next algorithm was based on HOUP descriptor and a linear SVM. In the third algorithm the features extracted by a pretrained VGG-F deep neural network were classified by a linear SVM. Table 1 presents experimental results that were achieved on York Univ. Dataset [14] by mentioned above algorithms.

As can be seen in Table 1, the algorithm based on VGG-F and the linear SVM achieves far better accuracies in comparison to results obtained in [14]. As we can observe, in experiment #7 and #8 the accuracy of VGG-F+SVM algorithm is relatively low compared to other experiments (only 86% and 89%), i.e. when using different camera and different lighting condition for training and testing subset of images.

In the next stage of the experiments the evaluations were performed on our dataset for visual recognition of the place, which has been recorded with the Nao humanoid robot. During walking the robot acquired the images from the onboard camera. The dataset has been recorded in rooms, offices and laboratories

Table 1. Place recognition accuracy [%] on York Univ. Dataset [14], [A]BoW using SIFT with k-NN classifier, [B]BoW using SIFT with SVM classifier, [C]HOUP with SVM classifier, [D]VGG-F features classified by SVM.

Experiment	Training set	Testing set	Lighting conditions	Accuracy [%]			
				BoW+SIFT		HOUP	VGG-F, FC-6
				k-NN[A]	SVM[B]	SVM[C]	SVM[D]
1	Pioneer	Pioneer	same	68	75	98	99
2	Virtual Me	Virtual Me	same	66	77	98	98
3	Pioneer	Pioneer	different	60	72	93	94
4	Virtual Me	Virtual Me	different	62	73	93	92
5	Pioneer	Virtual Me	same	58	69	92	92
6	Virtual Me	Pioneer	same	58	68	92	95
7	Pioneer	Virtual Me	different	55	64	82	86
8	Virtual Me	Pioneer	different	58	66	85	89

of our department. In each of the sixteen rooms we recorded from 309 to 627 color images of size 640 × 480. The total number of images is equal to 8000. The dataset is available for download at http://pwozniak.kia.prz.edu.pl/ICCVG2018.html.

Table 2 presents experimental results that were achieved by the investigated algorithms. As we can observe, the SVM classifier operating on SURF features quantized by BoW achieves the lowest recognition performance. In the discussed algorithm the dataset was split in proportions 0.6, 0.2 and 0.2 for training, validation and testing parts, respectively. The C parameter of the SVM classifier has been determined experimentally in a grid search. As can been seen, the SVM operating on features extracted by FC-6 layer of the pretrained VGG-F achieves far better results. The discussed results were achieved in 10-fold cross-validation. The next row contains results that were achieved using testing data with no

Table 2. Place recognition performance on our dataset. [A] SURF, BoW, SVM classifier, [B] Features extracted by VGG-G, SVM classifier, [C] Features extracted by VGG-G, SVM classifier, no-blur, [D] VGG-F fine-tuned, [E] VGG-F fine-tuned, data augmentation.

	Accuracy	Precision	Recall	F1-score
[A]BoW, SURF, SVM	0.7307	0.7307	0.7312	0.7310
[B]VGG-F, SVM	0.9513	0.9510	0.9483	0.9488
[C]VGG-F, SVM, no-blur	0.9544	0.9544	0.9549	0.9536
[D]VGG-F fine-tuned	0.9719	0.9712	0.9720	0.9716
[E]VGG-F fine-tuned, aug.	0.9669	0.9657	0.9676	0.9666

motion blur. The blurred images were removed from the test subset of dataset manually. We can notice, after suppression of blur noise from the test data the improvement in the recognition performance is insignificant. The best results were achieved by the fine-tuned VGG-F. The discussed results were achieved by the deep neural network that has been trained in four epochs. Having on regard that considerable part of the images is contaminated by motion blur as well as bearing in mind that many of them are rotated, we fine-tuned the VGG-F neural network on the augmented data. As can been seen in the last row of Table 2, the data augmentation does not improve the recognition performance.

The experiments were conducted using scripts prepared in Matlab and Python. They were performed on a PC computer equipped in i7, 3GHz CPU with 16 GB RAM and NVidia Quadro K2100M with 2 GB RAM. On the GPU the classification time of single image by fine-tuned VGG-F is 0.0873 s.

6 Conclusions

In this paper we proposed an algorithm for visual place recognition on images acquired by a humanoid robot. During robot locomotion the images undergo rotations as well contamination by the motion blur. We recorded a dataset for indoor place recognition and made it publicly available. We demonstrated experimentally that a deep neural network, which has been built on the basis of pretrained VGG-F through removing the last layer and then adding a fully connected layer, softmax layer and the output one achieves the best classification performance. We demonstrated that the learned model deals well with motion blur as well as rotations that arise during robot locomotion.

Acknowledgment. This work was supported by Polish National Science Center (NCN) under a research grant 2014/15/B/ST6/02808.

References

1. Arroyo, R., Alcantarilla, P., Bergasa, L., Romera, E.: OpenABLE: an open-source toolbox for application in life-long visual localization of autonomous vehicles. In: IEEE International Conference on Intelligent Transportation Systems, pp. 965–970 (2016)
2. Bay, H., Tuytelaars, T., Van Gool, L.: SURF: Speeded up robust features. Eur. Conf. Comput. Vis. **3951**, 404–417 (2006)
3. Cadena, C., et al.: Past, present, and future of simultaneous localization and mapping: toward the robust-perception age. IEEE Trans. Robot. **32**(6), 1309–1332 (2016)
4. Chatfield, K., Lempitsky, V.S., Vedaldi, A., Zisserman, A.: The devil is in the details: an evaluation of recent feature encoding methods. In: British Machine Vision Conference (BMVC) (2011)
5. Chen, Z., Lam, O., Jacobson, A., Milford, M.: Convolutional neural network-based place recognition. In: Australasian Conference on Robotics and Automation (2014). https://eprints.qut.edu.au/79662/

6. Cummins, M., Newman, P.: FAB-MAP: probabilistic localization and mapping in the space of appearance. Int. J. Rob. Res. **27**(6), 647–665 (2008)
7. Galvez-Lopez, D., Tardos, T.: Bags of binary words for fast place recognition in image sequences. IEEE Trans. Robot. **28**, 1188–1197 (2012)
8. Garcia-Fidalgo, E., Ortiz, A.: Vision-based topological mapping and localization by means of local invariant features and map refinement. Robotica **33**, 1446–1470 (2014)
9. Harris, C., Stephens, M.: A combined corner and edge detector. Alvey Vis. Conf. **15**, 10–5244 (1988)
10. Krizhevsky, A., Sutskever, I., Hinton, G.: ImageNet classification with deep convolutional neural networks. In: Advances in Neural Processing Systems, pp. 1097–1105 (2012)
11. Kuindersma, S., et al.: Optimization-based locomotion planning, estimation, and control design for the atlas humanoid robot. Adv. Neural Proc. Syst. **40**, 429–455 (2016)
12. Leutenegger, S., Chli, M., Siegwart, R.: BRISK: binary robust invariant scalable keypoints. In: International Conference on Computer Vision (ICCV) (2011)
13. Levitt, T., Lawton, D.: Qualitative navigation for mobile robots. Artif. Intell. **44**(3), 305–360 (1990)
14. Li, Q., Li, K., You, X., Bu, S., Liu, Z.: Place recognition based on deep feature and adaptive weighting of similarity matrix. Neurocomputing **199**, 114–127 (2016)
15. Lowe, D.: Distinctive image features from scale-invariant keypoints. Int. J. Comput. Vis. **60**(2), 91–110 (2004)
16. Lowry, S., et al.: Visual place recognition: a survey. IEEE Trans. Robot. **32**, 1–19 (2016)
17. Newman, P., Ho, K.: SLAM-loop closing with visually salient features. In: Proceedings of IEEE International Conference on Robotics and Automation, pp. 635–642 (2005)
18. Oliva, A., Torralba, A.: Building the gist of a scene: the role of global image features in recognition. In: Visual Perception, Progress in Brain Research, vol. 155, pp. 23–36. Elsevier (2006)
19. Oriolo, G., Paolillo, A., Rosa, L., Vendittelli, M.: Humanoid odometric localization integrating kinematic, inertial and visual information. Auton. Robots **40**, 867–879 (2016)
20. Radford, N., et al.: Valkryrie: NASA's first bipedal humanoid robot. J. Field Robot. **32**, 397–419 (2015)
21. Rublee, E., Rabaud, V., Konolige, K., Bradski, G.: ORB: an efficient alternative to SIFT or SURF. In: International Conference on Computer Vision (ICCV), vol. 32 (2011)
22. Russakovsky, O., et al.: ImageNet large scale visual recognition challenge. Int. J. Comput. Vis. **115**(3), 211–252 (2015)
23. Sahdev, R., Tsotsos, J.: Indoor place recognition system for localization of mobile robots. In: IEEE Conference on Computer and Robot Vision, pp. 53–60 (2016)
24. Schönberger, J., Hardmeier, H., Sattler, T., Pollefeys, M.: Comparative evaluation of hand-crafted and learned local features. In: IEEE Conference on Computer Vision and Pattern Recognition, pp. 6959–6968 (2017)
25. Simard, P., Steinkraus, D., Platt, J.: Best practices for convolutional neural networks applied to visual document analysis. In: International Conference on Document Analysis and Recognition, pp. 958–963 (2003)
26. Simonyan, K., Zisserman, A.: Very deep convolutional networks for large-scale image recognition. CoRR abs/1409.1556 (2014)

27. Sivic, J., Russell, B., Efros, A., Zisserman, A., Freeman, W.: Discovering objects and their location in images. In: IEEE International Conference on Computer Vision, vol. 1, pp. 370–377 (2005)
28. Sünderhauf, N., Protzel, P.: BRIEF-Gist - closing the loop by simple means. In: IEEE/RSJ International Conference on Intelligent Robots and Systems, pp. 1234–1241 (2011)
29. Sünderhauf, N., et al.: Place recognition with convNet landmarks: viewpoint-robust, condition-robust, training-free. In: Proceedings of Robotics: Science and Systems XII (2015)
30. Tai, L., Liu, M.: Deep-learning in mobile robotics - from perception to control systems: a survey on why and why not. arXiv (2016)
31. Torii, A., Sivic, J., Pajdla, T., Okutomi, M.: Visual place recognition with repetitive structures. In: Proceedings of the IEEE Conference on Computer, Vision and Pattern Recognition (2013)
32. Wang, Z., Wu, F., Hu, Z.: MSLD: a robust descriptor for line matching. Pattern Recogn. **42**, 941–953 (2009)

Character Recognition Based
on Skeleton Analysis

Kacper Sarnacki[1(✉)] and Khalid Saeed[2]

[1] Warsaw University of Technology, plac Politechniki 1, 00-661 Warsaw, Poland
`k.sarnacki@mini.pw.edu.pl`
[2] Bialystok University of Technology, Wiejska 45A, 15-001 Białystok, Poland
`k.saeed@pb.edu.pl`

Abstract. Character Recognition is a prominent field of research in pattern recognition. Low error rate of methods presented in other papers indicates that the problem of recognizing typewritten fonts is solved, using mainly deep learning methods. However, those algorithms do not work as well for recognizing handwritten characters, since learning discriminative features is much more complex for this problem so it still remains an interesting issue from research point of view. This document presents a proposal to solve handwritten characters recognition problem using k3m skeletonization algorithm. The idea has been designed to work correctly regardless of the width of the characters, their thickness or shape. This is an innovative method not considered in previous papers, which yields results comparable to the best ones achieved so far, what is proven in tests. The method can be also easily extended to signs other than glyphs in Latin alphabet.

1 Introduction

Optical Character Recognition (OCR) methods can be divided by nature of the problem, i.e. type of the analyzed characters and method of its acquisition. The classical taxonomy of ORC problems is presented in Fig. 1.

OCR online assumes recognition of the characters in real time, including writing pressure, azimuth or speed. Special devices such as electronic pads and pens are used for this purpose.

In turn, OCR offline focuses on ready, static text - these are often photos or scans of documents. Without access to other data (as writing pressure), the only way to recognize glyphs is to analyze their shapes. Handwritten fonts are characterized by style specific to the writer. It is much more difficult to segment individual glyphs from the word, compared to typewritten glyphs that are separated. These types of characters are often difficult to predict and handwriting glyphs recognition still remains an open problem. This OCR species is often referred to as ICR (Intelligent Character Recognition). The typewritten glyphs can be divided into calligraphic and decorative. The first type is a much easier problem. It contains typical formal fonts, used in documents. It is characterized

© Springer Nature Switzerland AG 2018
L. J. Chmielewski et al. (Eds.): ICCVG 2018, LNCS 11114, pp. 148–159, 2018.
https://doi.org/10.1007/978-3-030-00692-1_14

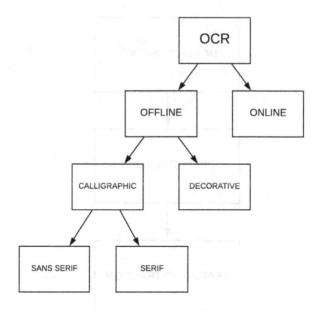

Fig. 1. Taxonomy of OCR systems

by readability, which makes algorithms achieve recognition efficiency up to 99%. On the other hand, decorative fonts are an interesting theme - these fonts are supposed to imitate those written by hand. They often include roundings and loops that give them unique style and make this problem similar to the problem of handwritten characters recognition.

Literature focuses on recognizing the letters of the Latin alphabet, not including glyphs specific to a given language. For Polish, an interesting problem is to distinguish letters such as z, ż and ź or o and ó. This work presents an universal algorithm that can be used to recognize all these letters.

2   Previous Attempts

There are many approaches to recognize characters. The general diagram of OCR system is shown in Fig. 2.

First step of the algorithm is to acquire data. This can be done by scanning or taking photo of the document or by extracting glyphs from font file. Next step is preprocessing. The most common approach involves manipulating the histogram, resampling and noise reduction. The purpose of these operations is to improve image quality. The final step at this stage is usually binarization.

Feature extraction determines how a glyph will be represented during classification process. Various approaches to problems can be found in the literature [1–4]. The geometrical approach analyzes shape of the glyph in the image basing on distribution of its pixels in the image. Methods such as Zoning [7], Crossings [5] or Projection histograms [6] can give over 90% efficiency in recognizing

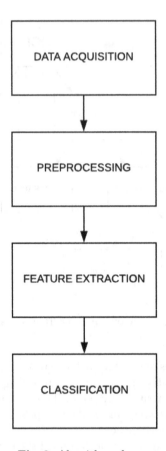

Fig. 2. Algorithm phases

characters in an image. Time based invariants, such as Central moments or Hu moments [10], allow to get results within 85%. Another approach is based on unitary transforms [11–13]. Methods that use some transformations such as Fourier transform, Cosine transform or Hadamard transform offer results of around 88%.

The most popular approaches to classification in the field of character recognition are neural networks and statistical approaches. The best results can be obtained by analyzing the character not only locally, but globally: including all characters within full word and sentence. This allows to eliminate errors based on fact that a single glyph has been identified incorrectly. However, this approach assumes using a dictionary of accepted words, which is not always possible.

3   Algorithm Description

The algorithm presented in this document has been visualized on the Fig. 3.

The diagram describes process of finding probability P that two glyphs belong to one class. d is a coefficient that specifies significance of a condition

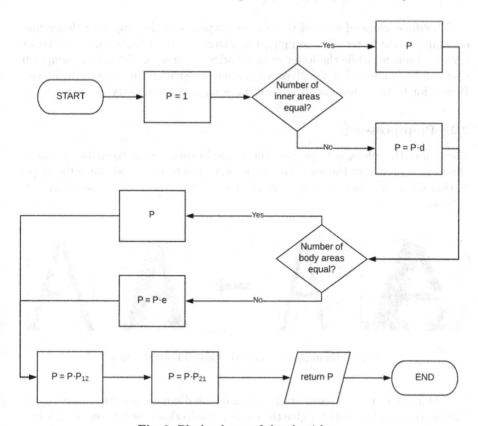

Fig. 3. Block scheme of the algorithm

that numbers of inner areas of glyphs must be equal. In turn, e is a coefficient defining the significance of a condition, that numbers of parts that make up the glyph must be equal. P_{12} describes probability that glyph 1 is similar to glyph 2, and P_{21} describes probability that glyph 2 is similar to glyph 1.

The algorithms for calculating introduced probabilities are described in detail in the paragraphs below.

3.1 Data Acquisition

The glyph database was created by extracting characters from font files with extension *.ttf*. Eleven fonts were selected, from each there were extracted alphanumeric characters: 0–9, *a–z* and *A–Z*, including characters specific to the Polish language: ą, ć, ę, ł, ń, ó, ś, ź, ż. Fonts of different weight were selected, as well as italic. The conversion consisted of retrieving each of characters in size 60*pt* and converting them into bitmap - guaranteeing a lossless conversion. The interior color of the digit was set to black, while the background color was given white.

The dimensions of each of the images prepared in this way vary depending on shape of the letter. For example, the letter I in most fonts will be saved as a vertical image, while the letter w as a horizontal image. The only assumption that can be made is that the glyph will adhere to each of the edges of the image. Hence, for further analysis normalization of images is necessary.

3.2 Preprocessing

The aim of this phase is to prepare the image in such way as to enable the most efficient extraction of features. The key operation is to modify shape of the glyph so that shapes of the same types are similar to each other, regardless of the font (Fig. 4):

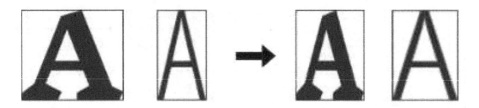

Fig. 4. Example of expected A glyph normalization

Unfortunately, a simple operation of changing dimensions of the image to certain universal values will not give the correct results, because for some characters it will deform them, as shown in Fig. 5.

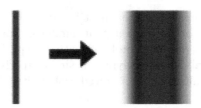

Fig. 5. Example of invalid 'I' glyph normalization

In addition, the expected results of the standardization are glyphs of similar weight. This is not guaranteed by the image stretching operation.

The applied standardization technique is based on skeletonization algorithm. The first step is to change the image size to 64×32 pixels. Then, on the modified image, a thinning algorithm is carried out using k3m algorithm [8]. Then on the thinned image dilatation is applied. This operation means that each glyph, regardless of the font and its weight, will have the same thickness. The results of normalization are shown in Fig. 6.

ŹMkPXł

Fig. 6. Example glyphs after normalization

This standardization ensures that each glyph meets the following conditions:

- It is saved as a *.bmp* image with resolution 64 × 32 pixels
- Despite change of dimensions, the glyph retains characteristical features of its original shape
- Each glyph has a constant thickness regardless of font
- It is binarized - it has exactly 2 color values. There are no other values that could arise, contrary to results of resizing

3.3 Feature Extraction

In order to determine features of the glyph, it is necessary to determine what is body and skeleton of a character.

Body of glyph is a set of pixels that describes this character. In case of the standardized database, these are black pixels. Body of each character consists of at least one part. Body of glyph g will be denoted as $body(g)$.

Skeleton of glyph is a set of pixels that was created by skeletonization of the glyph body. Skeleton of glyph g will be denoted as $skel(g)$.

Function $parts(g)$ will be used to specify number of body parts of the glyph. Function $inner(g)$ will be used to describe number of inner areas of the glyph.

Fig. 7. Body of character d together with the skeleton inside its body

The glyph d introduced in the Fig. 7 has got one body part and one inner area. Therefore $parts(d) = 1$ and $inner(d) = 1$.

It is worth noting that for a given glyph g the relation is true:

$$\forall_p p \in skel(g) \Rightarrow p \in body(g) \tag{1}$$

where:

p - pixel of the image representing g.

Skeleton of a character has a shape similar to the shape of its body. It is also possible to represent pixels of the skeleton as a sequence by creating at least one coherent path and that the number of these paths is minimal.

Fig. 8. Paths creating skeleton of glyph d

A sequence describing the glyph shown in the image has the following form: $[A, B, C, D]$. Since all points are not needed to properly describe the character, resulting vector is subjected to a sampling process. As a result, a shorter vector will be created that still describes the shape of the glyph (Fig. 8).

It is worth noting that glyphs may differ in length of the feature vector. However, for the used classifier this is not a problem and normalization of the vector is not necessary.

Two additional parameters will be used to describe the glyph: the number of elements that make up body of the glyph and number of areas inside the glyph. The first parameter specifies number of black areas that are completely separated by white area. The second parameter is number of white areas, limited entirely by black area and not adjacent to any edge of the image.

To determine both parameters, there can be used flood fill algorithm with 8-connectivity of each pixel.

3.4   Classification

In classification process, it is needed to use Eq. (1) and follow [9]. If a glyph g_1 is of the same type as glyph g_2, then their skeletons are similar. If their skeletons are similar, according to (1), probability that skeleton of g_1 is inside body of g_2 is approximately equal 1, and probability that skeleton of g_2 is inside body of g_1 is approximately equal 1. Given that g_1 and g_2 are normalized, these are valid dependencies:

$$P_{12} = \frac{|skel(g_1) \cap body(g_2)|}{|skel(g_1)|} \approx 1 \tag{2}$$

$$P_{21} = \frac{|skel(g_2) \cap body(g_1)|}{|skel(g_2)|} \approx 1 \tag{3}$$

Let $f : G^2 \to [0,1]$ be a function that specifies similarity of types of two glyphs. Value 1 means that the characters are of the same type. The f function can be defined as follows:

$$f(g_1, g_2) = P_{12} \cdot P_{21} = \frac{|skel(g_1) \cap body(g_2)| \cdot |skel(g_2) \cap body(g_1)|}{|skel(g_1)| \cdot |skel(g_2)|} \qquad (4)$$

Then the analysis should take into account number of internal areas and number of body parts that make up the glyph. Let $d \in [0; 1]$ be a parameter denoting percentage to which the probability will be reduced if numbers of inner areas are not equal:

$$c_1(g_1, g_2) = 1 - (1 - d) \cdot sgn(|inner(g_1) - inner(g_2)|) \qquad (5)$$

Let $e \in [0; 1]$ be a parameter denoting percentage to which the probability will be reduced if numbers of body parts are not equal:

$$c_2(g_1, g_2) = 1 - (1 - e) \cdot sgn(|parts(g_1) - parts(g_2)|) \qquad (6)$$

Then similarity function f' can be written as follows:

$$f'(g_1, g_2) = f(g_1, g_2) \cdot c_1(g_1, g_2) \cdot c_2(g_1, g_2) \qquad (7)$$

As for the classification process a function of distance between two glyphs is needed, it can be defined using f similarity function as follows:

$$dist(g_1, g_2) = 1 - f'(g_1, g_2) \qquad (8)$$

The $dist : G^2 \to [0,1]$ function returns 0 if distance between two glyphs equals 0, that is the glyphs are of the same type.

Classification process is based on roulette method used in genetic algorithms. Assuming g_t is a tested glyph, it is compared to every character in the database. Then the results are sorted in ascending order by distance and analyzed sequentially. The probability that the some g_i will be selected equals $f'(g_t, g_i)$. Type of selected glyph is the type that is assigned to the tested glyph.

Since in a pessimistic case none of the glyphs may be selected, there should be set a boundary such that some i-th glyph in the sequence will always be selected if previous $i - 1$ glyphs haven't been selected.

3.5   Testing Method

The classifier has been tested on eleven fonts of different shape, weight, type (handwritten, serif, sans-serif, monospace), including italic fonts. There was tested effectiveness of recognizing Latin letters, Polish letters and digits. The solution was tested using cross-validation with division of the set into 5 parts, as it is one of the most commonly used method for testing [14].

4   Results

4.1   Digits Test

Tested entities: digits 0–9
Effectiveness: 99.09%. (See Table 1)

Table 1. Results of digits recognition

	0	1	2	3	4	5	6	7	8	9
0	11	0	0	0	0	0	0	0	0	0
1	0	10	0	0	1	0	0	0	0	0
2	0	0	11	0	0	0	0	0	0	0
3	0	0	0	11	0	0	0	0	0	0
4	0	0	0	0	11	0	0	0	0	0
5	0	0	0	0	0	11	0	0	0	0
6	0	0	0	0	0	0	11	0	0	0
7	0	0	0	0	0	0	0	11	0	0
8	0	0	0	0	0	0	0	0	11	0
9	0	0	0	0	0	0	0	0	0	11

4.2   Polish Alphabet Test

Tested entities: characters a–z with polish letters
Effectiveness: 94.03% (See Table 2)

4.3   Test Analysis

The presented tests show that the algorithm is almost flawless for the problem of recognizing numbers, achieving efficiency at the level of 99%. For letters, the algorithm also performed very well, achieving results of 94.76% for Latin alphabet and 94.03% for Polish alphabet. It is worth noting that the addition of Polish letters did not significantly reduce the effectiveness of the algorithm. The method usually distinguished letters that might seem similar, like ó and o or as ć and c. The biggest problem when analyzing Polish letters was a problem with distinguishing letters ż and ź.

Nevertheless, for both alphabets, the algorithm gives very good results. The biggest problem of the presented solution are frequent mistakes of the letters i and l, which can be explained by the similar shape of both glyphs - both are usually represented as vertical lines. It is worth paying attention to the fact that the presented algorithm does not differ significantly in efficiency compared to other OCR systems using geometric approach. Detailed results are shown in Table 3.

Table 2. Results of Polish alphabet recognition

	a	ą	b	c	ć	d	e	ę	f	g	h	i	j	k	l	ł	m	n	ń	o	ó	p	q	r	s	ś	t	u	v	w	x	y	z	ź	ż
a	21	0	1	0	0	0	0	0	0	0	0	0	0	0	0	0	0	0	0	0	0	0	0	0	0	0	0	0	0	0	0	0	0	0	0
ą	0	22	0	0	0	0	0	0	0	0	0	0	0	0	0	0	0	0	0	0	0	0	0	0	0	0	0	0	0	0	0	0	0	0	0
b	0	0	21	0	0	0	0	0	0	0	0	1	0	0	0	0	0	0	0	0	0	0	0	0	0	0	0	0	0	0	0	0	0	0	0
c	0	0	0	18	0	0	0	0	0	0	0	0	0	0	0	0	0	0	0	0	0	0	4	0	0	0	0	0	0	0	0	0	0	0	0
ć	0	0	0	0	19	0	0	0	0	0	0	0	0	0	0	0	0	0	0	0	0	0	3	0	0	0	0	0	0	0	0	0	0	0	0
d	0	0	0	0	0	21	0	0	0	0	0	0	0	0	0	0	0	0	0	1	0	0	0	0	0	0	0	0	0	0	0	0	0	0	0
e	0	0	0	1	0	0	19	0	0	0	1	0	0	0	0	1	0	0	0	0	0	0	0	0	0	0	0	0	0	0	0	0	0	0	0
ę	0	0	0	0	0	0	0	20	0	0	0	0	0	0	0	0	0	0	0	1	0	0	0	0	1	0	0	0	0	0	0	0	0	0	0
f	0	0	0	0	0	0	0	0	20	0	0	0	0	0	0	0	0	0	0	0	0	1	0	0	0	0	0	0	0	0	1	0	0	0	0
g	0	0	0	0	0	0	0	0	0	22	0	0	0	0	0	0	0	0	0	0	0	0	0	0	0	0	0	0	0	0	0	0	0	0	0
h	0	0	1	0	0	0	0	0	0	0	21	0	0	0	0	0	0	0	0	0	0	0	0	0	0	0	0	0	0	0	0	0	0	0	0
i	0	0	0	0	0	0	0	0	1	0	0	16	0	0	5	0	0	0	0	0	0	0	0	0	0	0	0	0	0	0	0	0	0	0	0
j	0	0	0	0	0	0	0	0	0	0	0	1	21	0	0	0	0	0	0	0	0	0	0	0	0	0	0	0	0	0	0	0	0	0	0
k	0	0	0	0	0	0	0	0	0	0	0	0	0	22	0	0	0	0	0	0	0	0	0	0	0	0	0	0	0	0	0	0	0	0	0
l	0	0	0	0	0	0	0	0	0	0	0	3	0	0	19	0	0	0	0	0	0	0	0	0	0	0	0	0	0	0	0	0	0	0	0
ł	0	0	0	0	0	0	0	0	0	0	0	0	0	0	0	22	0	0	0	0	0	0	0	0	0	0	0	0	0	0	0	0	0	0	0
m	0	0	0	0	0	0	0	0	0	0	0	0	0	0	0	0	22	0	0	0	0	0	0	0	0	0	0	0	0	0	0	0	0	0	0
n	0	0	0	0	0	0	0	0	0	0	0	0	0	0	0	0	0	22	0	0	0	0	0	0	0	0	0	0	0	0	0	0	0	0	0
ń	0	0	0	0	0	0	0	0	0	0	0	0	0	0	0	0	0	1	19	0	1	0	0	0	0	0	0	0	1	0	0	0	0	0	0
o	0	0	0	0	0	0	0	0	0	0	0	0	0	0	0	0	0	0	0	22	0	0	0	0	0	0	0	0	0	0	0	0	0	0	0
ó	0	0	0	0	0	0	0	0	0	0	0	0	0	0	0	0	0	0	0	0	22	0	0	0	0	0	0	0	0	0	0	0	0	0	0
p	0	0	0	0	0	0	0	0	0	0	0	0	0	0	0	0	0	0	0	0	0	22	0	0	0	0	0	0	0	0	0	0	0	0	0
q	0	0	0	0	0	0	0	0	0	0	0	0	0	0	0	0	0	0	0	1	0	0	21	0	0	0	0	0	0	0	0	0	0	0	0
r	0	0	0	0	0	0	0	1	0	0	0	0	0	0	0	0	0	0	0	0	0	0	0	21	0	0	0	0	0	0	0	0	0	0	0
s	0	0	0	0	0	0	0	0	0	0	0	0	0	0	0	0	0	0	0	0	0	0	0	0	22	0	0	0	0	0	0	0	0	0	0
ś	0	0	0	0	0	0	0	0	0	0	0	0	0	0	0	0	0	0	0	0	0	0	0	0	0	22	0	0	0	0	0	0	0	0	0
t	0	0	0	0	0	0	0	0	0	0	0	2	0	0	0	0	0	0	0	0	0	0	0	0	0	0	20	0	0	0	0	0	0	0	0
u	0	0	0	0	0	0	0	0	0	0	0	0	0	0	0	0	0	0	0	2	0	0	0	0	0	0	0	20	0	0	0	0	0	0	0
v	0	0	0	0	0	0	0	0	0	0	0	0	0	0	0	0	0	0	0	0	0	0	0	0	0	0	0	0	21	0	0	0	1	0	0
w	0	0	0	0	0	0	0	0	0	0	0	0	0	0	0	0	0	0	0	0	0	0	0	0	0	0	0	0	0	22	0	0	0	0	0
x	0	0	0	0	0	0	0	0	0	0	0	0	0	0	0	0	0	0	0	0	0	0	0	0	0	0	0	0	0	0	22	0	0	0	0
y	0	0	0	0	0	0	0	0	0	0	0	0	0	0	0	0	0	0	0	0	0	0	0	0	0	0	0	0	0	0	0	22	0	0	0
z	0	0	0	0	0	0	0	0	0	0	0	0	0	0	0	0	0	0	0	0	0	0	0	0	0	0	0	0	0	0	0	0	22	0	0
ź	0	0	0	0	0	0	0	0	0	0	0	0	0	0	0	0	0	0	0	0	0	0	0	0	0	0	0	0	0	0	0	0	0	18	4
ż	0	0	0	0	0	0	0	0	0	0	0	0	0	0	0	0	0	0	0	0	0	0	0	0	0	0	0	0	0	0	0	0	0	4	18

Table 3. Comparing classification results

Technique	Latin letters	Digits
Authors Method	94.8%	99.1%
Zoning	91.9%	97.0%
Crossings	93.5%	95.8%
Projection Histograms	93.1%	93.6%
Central Moments	84.5%	91.8%
Fourier Transform	79.5%	81.8%
cre Hadamard Transform	79.7%	90.3%
Cosine Transform	88.8%	95.8%

5   Conclusions

Tests conducted in the user work prove that the presented algorithm can successfully compete with the best known algorithms. Its efficiency of around 95% makes it suitable as an OCR tool. The algorithm shows features of being resistant to glyph thickness, italics and small shape changes. This makes it suitable also for handwritten characters. Versatility and intuitiveness of the algorithm make it a promising proposition to work with not only Latin or Polish, but also Arabic or Chinese alphabet, to which other methods may be unadjusted.

The applied classification method based on probability theory makes that if in case of a priori knowledge the best suited glyph is incorrect, it is possible to match the glyph with the next highest probability. This is a big advantage over for example neural networks that return information about the best class only, not including probability of belonging to other classes. The knowledge about successive probabilities of classes may turn out to be crucial while working with full words.

The biggest advantage of the algorithm is intuitiveness and ease of interpretation of the results. Another positive aspect is time complexity - when analyzing a single character, the most complex operation is the use of a skeletonization algorithm. This makes the algorithm a good candidate for further development and adaptation to a specific problem.

References

1. Sazaklis, G.N.: Geometric Methods for Optical Character Recognition, Ph.D. dissertation, State University of New York at Stony Brook (1997)
2. Devijver, P.A., Kittler, J.: Pattern Recognition: A Statistical Approach. Prentice-Hall, London (1982)
3. Lorigo, L.M., Govindaraju, V.: Ofine Arabic handwriting recognition: a survey. IEEE Trans. Pattern Anal. Mach. Intell. **28**(5), 712–724 (2006)
4. Jayadevan, R., Kolhe, S.R., Patil, P.M., Pal, U.: Offline recognition of devanagari script: a survey. IEEE Tran. Syst. Man Cybern. Part C Appl. Rev. **41**(6), 782–796 (2011)
5. Saeed, K., Homenda, W. (eds.): CISIM 2015. LNCS, vol. 9339. Springer, Cham (2015). https://doi.org/10.1007/978-3-319-24369-6
6. Trier, O.D., Jain, A.K., Taxt, T.: Feature extraction methods for character recognition - a survey. Pattern Recogn. **29**(4), 641–662 (1996)
7. Pradeep, J., Srinivasan, E., Himavathi, S.: Diagonal based feature extraction for handwritten alphabets recognition system using neural network. Int. J. Comput. Sci. Inf. Technol. **3**(1), 27–38 (2011)
8. Saeed, K., Tabedzki, M., Rybnik, M., Adamski, M.: K3M: a universal algorithm for image skeletonization and a review of thinning techniques. AMCS **20**(2), 317–335 (2010)
9. Mittendorf, E., Schäuble, P., Sheridan, P.: Applying probabilistic term weighting to OCR text in the case of a large alphabetic library catalogue. In: Proceedings of the 18th Annual International ACM SIGIR Conference on Research and Development in Information Retrieval, 01 July 1995, pp. 328–335 (1995)

10. Hu, M.-K.: Visual pattern recognition by moment invariants. IRE Trans. Inf. Theory **IT–8**, 179–187 (1962)
11. Pratt, W.K., Andrews, H.C.: Transform image coding. University of Southern California, Report No. 387 (1970)
12. Ahmed, N., Natarajan, T., Rao, K.R.: Discrete cosine transform. IEEE Trans. Comput. **C–23**(1), 90–93 (1974)
13. Ramakrishnan, A.G., Bhargava Urala, K.: Global and local features for recognition of online handwritten numerals and tamil characters. In: MOCR 2013, Proceedings of the 4th International Workshop on Multilingual OCR (2013)
14. Xu, L., et al.: Stochastic cross validation. Chemom. Intell. Lab. Syst. **175**, 74–81 (2018)

Weather Characterization from Outdoor Scene Images

Jenade Moodley and Serestina Viriri$^{(\boxtimes)}$

School of Mathematics, Statistics and Computer Science,
University of KwaZulu-Natal, Durban, South Africa
{214520141,viriris}@ukzn.ac.za

Abstract. This paper presents a variety of techniques to characterize outdoor scene images into their respective weather components; the sky condition (sunny or cloudy), the presence of rain, and the visibility. Weather characterization is not an easy task due to a large variety of outdoor scene images. Each weather component is characterized individually. The results obtained are promising. The accuracy rates for the weather components achieved are; the sky condition attained 80%, the presence of rain attained 60%, and visibility achieved a mean squared error (MSE) of 1.41.

Keywords: Weather components · Sky condition · Rain presence Visibility

1 Introduction

Weather can be defined as the state of the atmosphere at a given time. This state is made up of factors such as wind speed, temperature, humidity, cloudiness, moisture, pressure, visibility, etc. [1]. Some of these factors, such as cloudiness and visibility, can be determined by the naked eye, and hence can be determined by an image. Due to global warming and natural phenomena, weather conditions are becoming steadily more erratic around the globe. The need for robust weather characterization algorithms have steadily been on the rise as there has been an increase in extreme weather, most of which are difficult to evaluate on-site by humans, for example, The European Heat Wave in 2003 [2].

As technology has advanced, there has been a significant increase in information gathering. The amount of information is usually too large for even a team of individuals to process, and there is still the matter of human error. By determining the weather through an image, we save cost as well as time [3], thus allowing us to gather sufficient information on the state of the weather, which can be processed electronically and easily as opposed to using expensive weather detection equipment.

This paper makes an attempt to characterize the weather from outdoor scene images using computer vision and image processing. As humans, this is a relatively easy task to accomplish with the naked eye. However, when applied to computer vision, the task becomes substantially more complex.

© Springer Nature Switzerland AG 2018
L. J. Chmielewski et al. (Eds.): ICCVG 2018, LNCS 11114, pp. 160–170, 2018.
https://doi.org/10.1007/978-3-030-00692-1_15

Outdoor scene images can be captured at different times of the day using different equipment. The resulting images of the same weather condition are sometimes worlds apart in terms of the features captured. In an image, rain is depicted as streaks dispersed throughout the entire, or part of the image. These streaks can be interpreted as merely noise by a computer vision application. Visibility is measured at the scene of the image using expensive weather detection equipment and even humans can have difficulty in correctly determining the range of visibility in an area much less an outdoor scene image.

2   Literature Review and Related Work

A large variety of literature, which consist of a mixture of academic papers and theses, was analyzed as research in weather characterization using image processing. Some of said papers discuss analyzing the depicted weather pattern in the image whilst others focused on removing or adding certain weather aspects to enhance the image.

Stated and proven by the work of Islam et al. [4], the time and location in which image is captured indirectly defines the appearance of the scene. Scene structure, local weather conditions, and the position of the sun are directly relevant variables that effect the appearance of an outdoor scene image. Islam et al. [4] presented a large dataset of archived time-lapse imagery with associated geo-location and weather annotations collected from multiple sources. Through validation via crowdsourcing, the reliability of this automatically gathered data is estimated. This dataset is used to investigate the value of direct geo-temporal context for the problem of predicting the scene appearance and show that explicitly incorporating the sun position and weather variables significantly reduces reconstruction error.

The work of Lagorio et al. [5] concentrates on the analysis of outdoor scenes for vehicle traffic control. In this scenario, the analysis of weather conditions is considered to signal specific and potentially dangerous situations such as the presence of snow, fog, or heavy rain. Their system uses a statistical framework based on the mixture of Gaussian models to identify changes both in the spatial and temporal frequencies which characterize specific meteorological events.

Bossu et al. [6] created a system based on computer vision is presented which detects the presence of rain or snow. A classical Gaussian Mixture Model is used to separate the foreground from the background in an image. The foreground model serves to detect rain and snow, since these are dynamic weather phenomena. Selection rules are set in place to select the potential rain streaks. These rules are based on photometry and size. A Histogram of Orientations of rain or snow Streaks (HOS), is computed, which is assumed to follow a model of Gaussian uniform mixture. The Gaussian distribution represents the orientation of the rain or the snow whereas the uniform distribution represents the orientation of the noise. An algorithm of expectation maximization is used to separate these two distributions. Following a goodness-of-fit test, the Gaussian distribution is temporally smoothed and its amplitude allows deciding the presence of rain or snow. When the presence of rain or of snow is detected, the HOS makes it possible to detect the pixels of rain or of snow in the foreground images, and to estimate the intensity of the precipitation of rain or of snow.

Lu et al. [7] proposed a collaborative learning approach for labelling an image as either sunny or cloudy. Their weather feature combines special cues after properly encoding them into feature vectors. They then work collaboratively in synergy under a unified optimization framework that is aware of the presence (or absence) of a given weather cue during learning and classification.

Caraffa et al. [8] proposed an original algorithm, based on entropy minimization, to detect the fog and estimate its extinction coefficient by the processing of stereo pairs. This algorithm is fast, provides accurate results using low cost stereo cameras sensor which can work when the cameras are moving.

Htay et al. [9] proposed a combination of 3 algorithms to classify an image into semantic concepts such as tree, sky, road, etc. The modified Marker-Controlled Watershed algorithm (MCWS) is used to segment the input image, texture feature vectors are extracted from segmented regions by Gray- Level Co-occurrence Matrix (GLCM). Finally, classification is performed by 3-layer Artificial Neural Network (ANN).

3   Methods and Techniques

The sky condition is characterized using a similar method to the method presented by Lu et al. [7]. A weather feature based on the sky intensity, shadow percentage and haze presence is calculated for the outdoor scene image. These features are then compared to the pre-calculated features of other images of known sky conditions using a number of classifiers namely SVM, ANN and KNN.

The presence of rain is computed based on an extended variant of the method proposed by Bossu et al. [6]. The foreground is first seperated from the background as rain presence is determined in the foreground of the image. All contours present in the foreground are detected and a size selection rule is applied to choose the relevant contours. A histogram of orientations of streaks is then computed based on the distribution of the contour data. The histogram data is then compared to the data of images with and without rain-streaks using a number of classifiers namely SVM, ANN and KNN.

Visibility is heavily influenced by the amount and density of fog in the area. To calculate visibility, a method based on the method presented by Caraffa et al. [8] is proposed. A fog extinction co-efficient β is calculated based on entropy minimization. The value of β as well as the minimized entropy is compared with the data calculated from images with known visibility measures using a number of classifiers namely SVM, ANN and KNN.

4   The Sky Condition

To calculate the sky condition, the first task is to segment the sky from the rest of the image. The weather feature is then formed by calculating the percentage of RGB values present in the segmented sky region, the percentage of shadows in the image and finally the median value of the darkchannel of the image to denote the haze. These values are then used to classify the image.

4.1 Pre-processing

Histogram Equalization. Histogram equalization [10] adjusts the contrast of the image using the image's histogram of pixel intensities. This method is used to increase the global contrast of an image. Histogram equalization allows for areas of lower local contrast to gain a higher contrast. This is done by spreading out the most frequent intensity values. This makes histogram equalization a useful method for images in which both the foreground and background of the image are both bright or both dark.

4.2 Sky Segmentation

Gaussian Blurring. Gaussian smoothing [11] is used to blur or smoothen an image. The degree of smoothing is determined by the standard deviation of the Gaussian distribution of the data. Gaussian blur is applied to an image by convolving the image with a Gaussian function. This is known as a two-dimensional Weierstrass transform.

The Gaussian function in two-dimensions (a digital image is a 2-D matrix) is given by:

$$G(x, y) = \frac{1}{2\pi\sigma^2} e^{-\frac{x^2+y^2}{2\sigma^2}} \tag{1}$$

The Gaussian outputs a weighted average of each pixel's neighborhood, with the average weighted more towards the value of the central pixels.

One of the principle justifications for using the Gaussian as a smoothing filter is due to its frequency response. Most convolution-based smoothing filters act as lowpass frequency filters. This means that the Gaussian filter removes high spatial frequency components from an image. The frequency response of a convolution filter, i.e. its effect on different spatial frequencies, can be seen by taking the Fourier transform of the filter.

Erosion. Erosion [12] is used to "erode away" the boundaries of regions of foreground pixels. This causes areas of foreground pixels to shrink in size, enabling holes within those areas to become larger. The erosion operator requires two pieces of input data: the image to be eroded, and a small set of coordinate points called a structuring element or kernel. It is the kernel that determines the precise effect of erosion on the input image. The erosion operator is defined by:

$$A \ominus B = \{z | (B)_z \subseteq A\} \tag{2}$$

This means that erosion of image A by kernel B is the set of all points z such that B, translated by z, is contained in A.

Dilation. Dilation [12] is used to gradually enlarge the boundaries of regions of foreground pixels. This causes areas of foreground pixels to grow in size, enabling holes within those areas to become smaller. The dilation operator requires two pieces of input data: the image to be dilated, and a small set of coordinate points called a structuring element or kernel. It is the kernel that determines the precise effect of dilation on the input image. The dilation operator is defined by:

$$A \oplus B = \{z | (\hat{B})_z \cap A \neq \emptyset\} \tag{3}$$

This means that dilation of image A by kernel B is the set of all displacements z such that B and A overlap by at least one element.

4.3   Shadow Detection

To detect shadows in the image, this paper presents a method based on the method of shadow detection presented by Chung et al. [13] which is based on Successive Thresholding Scheme (STS). In the STS proposed by Chung et al., a modified ratio map is presented to increase the gap between the ratio values of nonshadow and shadow pixels. By applying global thresholding on this ratio map, a coarse-shadow map is constructed to classify the image into candidate shadow pixels and nonshadow pixels. In order to detect true shadow pixels from the range of candidate shadow pixels, the connected component process is applied to the candidate shadow pixels in order to group the candidate shadow regions. For each candidate shadow region, local thresholding is applied iteratively to segment the true shadow pixels from the candidate shadow region. Finally, for the remaining candidate shadow regions, a fine-shadow determination process is applied to identify if each remaining candidate shadow pixel is a true shadow pixel.

Ratio Map. Based on the HSI colour model, the hue-equivalent image H_e and the intensity-equivalent image I_e used in the ratio map is given by:

$$H_e = \left(\tan^{-1} \left(\frac{V_2}{V_1} \right) + \pi \right) \times \frac{255}{2\pi} \tag{4}$$

$$I_e = \frac{1}{3}R + \frac{1}{3}B + \frac{1}{3}G \tag{5}$$

The ratio value argument used by the ratio map is given by

$$r(x, y) = round\left(\frac{H_e(x, y)}{I_e(x, y) + 1} \right) \tag{6}$$

The value of T_s is determined when condition $\sum_{i=0}^{T_s} P(i) = P_s$ holds. $P(i)$ is the probability of ratio value i in $\{r(x, y)\}$ and σ is calculated by $\sqrt{\sum_{i=0}^{T_s} P(i)(i - T_s)^2}$ and P_s is set to 0.95.

4.4   Weather Feature

Sky. The percentage of each pixel value present in the sky region across all 3 channels is then calculated. This forms 3 vectors, each of size 256. The method of principal component analysis is used to reduce each of these vectors to a single value, forming 3 values for the sky feature.

Shadow. To determine the shadow regions, this paper proposes a method based on the method presented by Chung et al. [13] denoted in Sect. 4.3. The final step of forming the shadow feature is to calculate the percentage of the image taken up by these shadow regions.

Haze. The dark channel prior approach [14] has been found to work well when dealing with haze in an image. The dark channel of an image is given by

$$J^k(x) = min\left\{min\left\{J^c(y)\right\}\right\} \qquad y \in \Omega(x) \tag{7}$$

where J^c is a colour channel and $\Omega(x)$ is a local patch centered at x. The median pixel value of this dark channel image is taken to form the haze feature.

5   Rain Presence

To determine the presence of rain, this paper proposes a method based on the Histogram of Orientation of Streaks method proposed by Bossu et al. [6] to determine possible rain streaks in the image. The image is then classified based on these histogram values.

5.1   Pre-processing

5.1.1   Background Subtraction

Rain streaks are present in the foreground of the image, hence the image's background needs to be removed.

Sobel Operator. The Sobel operator [12] performs a 2-D spatial gradient measurement on an image which emphasizes regions of high spatial frequencies which correspond to edges. It is used to find the approximate absolute gradient magnitude at each point in a grayscale image.

These kernels are designed to respond to edges running vertically and horizontally relative to the pixel grid, one kernel for each of the two perpendicular orientations. The kernels can be applied separately to the input image, to produce separate measurements of the gradient component in each orientation. These can be combined together to find the absolute magnitude of the gradient at each point and the orientation of that gradient.

5.2   Segmentation of Potential Rain Streaks

Contour Detection. The first task is to find all contours present in the foreground of the image. A size selection rule is then applied to choose streaks of a certain size. After extensive testing, contours with a minimum area of 5 pixels and a maximum area of 12 pixels are chosen.

5.3 Construction of Histogram of Orientations Streaks

To construct the Histogram of Orientations of rain or snow Streaks (HOS), the geometric moments of each blob (detected with the size-selection rule) are used to determine the orientation of each blob.

Geometric Moments. Each segmented blob $B_i, 1 \leq i \leq P$ can be depicted as an elliptic disk characterized by its 5 parameters: tilt angle θ, gravity centre (x_0, y_0), major semi-axis a and short semi-axis b. Given the nature of the ellipse, the HOS will have 180 values with $\theta \in [0, \pi]$. The method of geometric moments is used to compute the geometric parameters of the associated ellipse [6]. The central second order moments are given by:

$$m_i^{20} = \frac{1}{m_i^{00}} \sum_{(x,y) \in B_i} (x - x_0)^2 \tag{8}$$

$$m_i^{11} = \frac{1}{m_i^{00}} \sum_{(x,y) \in B_i} (x - x_0)(y - y_0) \tag{9}$$

$$m_i^{02} = \frac{1}{m_i^{00}} \sum_{(x,y) \in B_i} (y - y_0)^2 \tag{10}$$

The short semiaxis and major semiaxis of the ellipse is denoted by:

$$a_i = \sqrt{\lambda_i^1} \tag{11}$$

$$b_i = \sqrt{\lambda_i^2} \tag{12}$$

where λ_i^1 and λ_i^2 are the eigenvalues of the matrix.

The tilt angle or orientation θ_i of the blob B_i is given by:

$$\theta_i = \frac{1}{2} \tan^{-1} \left(\frac{2m_i^{11}}{m_i^{02} - m_i^{20}} \right) \tag{13}$$

Finally, the HOS is denoted as:

$$h(\theta) = \sum_{i=1}^{P} \frac{a_i}{d\theta_i \sqrt{2\pi}} e^{-\frac{1}{2}\left(\frac{\theta - \theta_i}{d\theta_i}\right)^2} \tag{14}$$

where $d\theta_i$ is denoted by:

$$d\theta_i = \frac{\sqrt{(m_i^{02} - m_i^{20})^2 + 2(m_i^{11})^2}}{(m_i^{02} - m_i^{20})^2 + 4(m_i^{11})^2} dm \tag{15}$$

where the value of dm is chosen empirically by performing simulation tests. After extensive testing, the value for dm is chosen to be 1000.

6 Visibility

To determine the visibility depicted in the image, this paper proposes a method based on the original method proposed by Caraffa et al. [8] which estimates the density of fog in the image as well as the fog extinction co-efficient β based on entropy minimization. As visibility is dependant on fog, the visibility of the image is classified using the value for β as well as the minimized entropy.

6.1 Pre-processing

6.1.1 Estimation of Fog

The first task is to calculate the sky intensity I_s. Using this value, as well as variable values for the fog extinction co-efficient β, a restored image without fog is created. The entropy of these restored images is then calculated and the value of β is chosen from the image with the lowest entropy.

Calculation of Sky Intensity. The sky region needs to first be segmented from the image. The highest pixel value from this region of pixels is chosen to be the value of I_s.

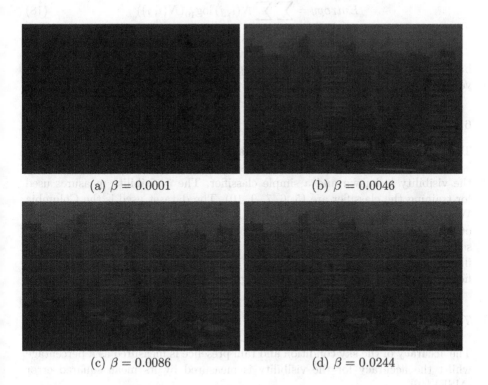

(a) $\beta = 0.0001$　　　　　　(b) $\beta = 0.0046$

(c) $\beta = 0.0086$　　　　　　(d) $\beta = 0.0244$

Fig. 1. Image restoration with different values of β

Entropy Minimization. Using the value of I_s from Sect. 6.1, the restored image $I_0(x)$ is calculated using:

$$I_0(x) = I(x)e^{\beta D(x)} - I_s(e^{\beta D(x)} - 1) \tag{16}$$

for variable values of β where $D(x)$ represents the depth map of the image. In cases where the depth map is unknown, $D(x)$ is set to 1.

The entropy of image $I_0(x)$ is then calculated. Entropy is defined as the average amount of information produced by a probabilistic stochastic source of data [15]. The formula for entropy, as described by [12] is given as follows:

The first step is to calculate the normalized matrix $N(i, j)$

$$N(i,j) = \frac{P(i,j)}{\sum_{i=0}^{M} \sum_{j=0}^{N} P(i,j)} \tag{17}$$

where P(i, j) represents the pixel value at point (i, j), M is the number of rows in the image matrix and N is the number of columns of the image matrix.

Entropy can then be calculated using:

$$Entropy = \sum_{i=0}^{M} \sum_{j=0}^{N} N(i,j) \log_{10}(N(i,j)) \tag{18}$$

The chosen values for β are 0.0001, 0.0046, 0.0086 and 0.0244 as these values have shown to be quite successful in entropy minimization. The effects of different values of β in image restoration are shown in Fig. 1.

6.2   Classification

The vector consisting of the chosen β value as well as the minimized entropy, is used to classify the image using the same vector values of images in which the visibility is known and a simple classifier. The 5 visibility measures used for training the classifier are (5, 6, 7, 9, 10). The dataset used is the Columbia Weather and Illumination Database (WILD). WILD is an extensive database of high quality images of an outdoor urban scene, acquired every hour over all seasons. It includes images of the scene taken under a variety of weather and illumination conditions. Three classifiers, namely Support Vector Machine, Artificial Neural Network and K-Nearest Neighbour (with k = 3), were implemented.

7   Results

The accuracy of the sky condition and rain presence is measured as a percentage whilst the accuracy for the visibility is measured by its mean squared error (MSE) [16].

When calculating sky condition, the support vector machine was the best classifier as it produced an accuracy rate of 80%. When calculating the presence

	SVM	ANN	KNN
Sky condition	80%	60%	70%
Rain presence	50%	30%	60%
Visibility	2.0	9.2	4.9

of rain, the k-nearest neighbour algorithm, with k = 3, was the best classifier as it produced an accuracy rate of 60%. When calculating the visibility, the support vector machine was the best classifier as it produced a mean-squared error of 2.0. This means that the predicted visibility would be in the range of ±1.41 (RMSE) from the actual visibility.

8 Conclusion

This paper presented a variety of techniques that characterized outdoor scene images efficiently. The overall results achieved are very promising. The accuracy rates for the weather components achieved are; the sky condition attained 80%, the presence of rain attained 60%, and visibility achieved a mean squared error (MSE) of 1.41.

References

1. Dictionary.com unabridged, September 2017
2. Bhattacharya, S.: European heatwave caused 35000 deaths (2003)
3. Digital image processing, September 2017
4. Islam, M., Jacobs, N., Wu, H., Souvenir, R.: Images+ weather: collection, validation, and refinement. In: IEEE Conference on Computer Vision and Pattern Recognition Workshop on Ground Truth, vol. 6, p. 2 (2013)
5. Lagorio, A., Grosso, E., Tistarelli, M.: Automatic detection of adverse weather conditions in traffic scenes. In: IEEE Fifth International Conference on Advanced Video and Signal Based Surveillance, 2008, AVSS 2008, pp. 273–279. IEEE (2008)
6. Bossu, J., Hautière, N., Tarel, J.-P.: Rain or snow detection in image sequences through use of a histogram of orientation of streaks. Int. J. Comput. Vis. **93**(3), 348–367 (2011)
7. Lu, C., Lin, D., Jia, J., Tang, C.-K.: Two-class weather classification. In: Proceedings of the IEEE Conference on Computer Vision and Pattern Recognition, pp. 3718–3725 (2014)
8. Caraffa, L., Tarel, J.P.: Daytime fog detection and density estimation with entropy minimization. In: ISPRS Annals of the Photogrammetry, Remote Sensing and Spatial Information Sciences, vol. 2, no. 3, p. 25 (2014)
9. Htay, K.K., Aye, N.: Semantic concepts classification on outdoor scene images based on region-based approach. Int. J. Futur. Comput. Commun. **3**(6), 427 (2014)
10. Wikipedia: Histogram equalization – wikipedia, the free encyclopedia (2017). Accessed 24 Sept 2017
11. Wikipedia: Gaussian blur – wikipedia, the free encyclopedia (2017). Accessed 24 Sept 2017

12. Woods, R.E., Masters, B.R., Gonzalez, R.C.: Digital image processing, third edition. J. Biomed. Opt. **14**(2), 14 (2009)
13. Chung, K.-L., Lin, Y.-R., Huang, Y.-H.: Efficient shadow detection of color aerial images based on successive thresholding scheme. IEEE Trans. Geosci. Remote. Sens. **47**(2), 671–682 (2009)
14. He, K., Sun, J., Tang, X.: Single image haze removal using dark channel prior. IEEE Trans. Pattern Anal. Mach. Intell. **33**(12), 2341–2353 (2011)
15. Wikipedia: Entropy (information theory) – wikipedia, the free encyclopedia (2017). Accessed 25 Sept 2017
16. Deziel, C.: How to calculate MSE, June 2017

3D and Stereo Image Processing

Clustering Quality Measures for Point Cloud Segmentation Tasks

Jakub Walczak and Adam Wojciechowski[✉]

Institute of Information Technology, Łódź University of Technology, Łódź, Poland
adam.wojciechowski@p.lodz.pl

Abstract. This paper presents improved weighted measures for a point cloud segmentation quality evaluation. They provide more reliable and intuitive appraisal as well as more representative classification characteristics. The new measures are compared with the existing ones: based on classification, and based on information theory. The experiments and measures evaluation were performed for the recently outstanding fresh planes segmentation method. Experiments results showed that newly elaborated measures provide a researcher with distinguished information about segmentation output. This paper introduces recommendations for quality measures adjustment to a particular planar fragments detection problem, what implies contributions for effective development of such methods.

Keywords: Point cloud segmentation · Quality measures
Plane detection

1 Introduction

Point cloud segmentation, being usually a step preceding semantic analysis of a set, is a task of high interest of many researchers. Besides cases like recognizing structures within a point cloud [23], hand pose and face segmentation [10–12], big data visualisation [13] or urban and architectural reconstruction [14], segmentation may be successfully used for compression purposes [22] thanks to storing objects by means of mathematical formulas instead of thousands of 3D points. Certainly, these are just a few out of plenty of possibilities where 3D segmentation contributes.

Beyond any doubt, any algorithm, by definition, is meant to produce a good or expected results in the context of presumed characteristics. These characteristics, or rather measures, allowed us to clearly compare algorithms and understand their flaws. That is why a quality measure should be carefully chosen prior to actual problem and method definition.

In this paper, we introduced two novel measures for segmentation quality assessment: weighted classification statistics (WCS) - improved version of the ordinary classification statistics (OCS), and planarity statistics (PS) as an indicator of planes extraction quality. Additional contribution of this paper is evaluation of new and existing measures for selected model-based method of planes

© Springer Nature Switzerland AG 2018
L. J. Chmielewski et al. (Eds.): ICCVG 2018, LNCS 11114, pp. 173–186, 2018.
https://doi.org/10.1007/978-3-030-00692-1_16

detection (as a reference a recent Li et al. method [3] has been chosen) and proposal of recommendations concerning particular measures.

2   Related Works

2.1   Planes Segmentation Methods

Among all methods aiming at segmentation of point clouds, Nguyen and Le identified five main categories, namely: edge-based, region-based, attributes-based, graph-based, and model-based methods [15]. Current studies focus mainly on model-based group, especially on the approaches based on random sample consensus (RANSAC). Below, we review above groups briefly to emphasize the main differences and to justify why recently the most effective Normal Distribution Transform cell-based RANSAC method, by Li et al. [3], was opted for our experiments.

Edge-based methods are constituted by methods employing gradient- or line-fitting algorithms for locating interesting points. Bhanu et al. proposed range images processing for edges extraction [1]. On the other hand, Sappa and Devy [19] relied on binary edge map generation with scan-lines approximation in orthogonal directions. These methods are characterized by sensitivity both to existing noise and non-uniform point distribution.

Region-based algorithms use greedy approach to examine similarity or distinctiveness in a limited vicinity. Rabbani et al. [18] applied simple region growing approach taking into account surface normal and points' connectivity. On the other hand, Xiao et al. [24] proposed subregion based region growing, where each subregion is considered as a planar one or not, based on Principal Component Analysis (PCA) or KLT [25]. Region-based methods, suffer from dependence on seed point selection as well as from the fact, that decision is made locally, and it may be not correct from the global point of view.

Generally, segmentation methods based on attributes make use of clustering algorithms built onto extracted attributes. Mean-shift clustering [6], hierarchical clustering [7], contextual processing [8] or statistically supported clustering [9] are cases in point. Limitations of this group are clustering methods constraints themselves. For *k-means* clustering, number of clusters need to be known in advance. On the other hand, for other methods, high noise sensitivity or time complexity involved with multidimensionality may occur.

Among the algorithms based on graphs, one may find the method making use of colour information added to laser scans [21] or the method of vicinity graph presented in [2]. Clearly, graph-based methods may need a complex preprocessing phase, like training [15].

Most of methods employing a model makes use of RANSAC algorithm. Its main advantage is inherent robustness against outlying data, unlike the other methods. Currently, it appears in many variations. Schnabel et al. [20] used RANSAC for efficient detection of planes, cylinders and spheres. They evaluated their method by means of correctly detected regions. Oehler et al. [16] combined RANSAC with Hough transform [17] to increase quality of planes detection.

Here, the authors identified number of true positives (TP) with 80% overlap region in order to evaluate their algorithm. Xu et al. [5] evaluated usability of different functions for weighted RANSAC in terms of their completeness (Eq. 4), correctness (Eq. 3), and quality (Eq. 5). Calvo et al. [33] engaged k-means strategy together with RANSAC to search for predefined model (like cube or pyramid) in a point cloud. They evaluated this algorithm by comparing an average angular deviation between normal vectors detected in a cloud and those known from a reference set. Finally, Li et al. [3] introduced an improved RANSAC-based method for uniform space division, which, following authors, presents itself as the most efficient state-of-art solution. Thus it was selected as a point cloud reference segmentation method.

The algorithm proposed by Li et al. relies on space division into cells of fixed size, whose dimensions have to be tuned for point cloud specifically. Cells are then classified either as planar ones or not. The decision is made on the grounds of eigenvalues, being the output of PCA procedure. If the ratio of the two greatest eigenvalues is lower than assumed threshold te, a cell is said to be a planar one (Eq. 1). For the dataset Room-1 [31], the authors assumed $te = 0.01$, whereas for Room-2 dataset [31], they took $te = 0.02$. The formula for te was determined by the authors empirically, taking into account that it is influenced by the cell size s and the noise level ϵ (Eq. 2).

$$\frac{\lambda_1}{\lambda_2} < te. \tag{1}$$

where λ_1 and λ_2 are, respectively the greatest, and the middle eigenvalue.

$$(\frac{\epsilon}{s})^2 < te < 0.04. \tag{2}$$

Subsequently, the authors performed plane segmentation procedure, called NDT-RANSAC. In short, it consists of RANSAC- like examination of an individual planar cell. From each planar cell, the minimal set of three points is randomly taken to construct a hypothetical plane which may differ from that obtained with PCA. Having calculated a plane parameters, the rest of planar cells are compared to the current one, in terms of normal vector angular deviation and relative shift between objects. The plane, obtained by merging coherent patches is then refined taking into account its consensus set. The authors used verification measures based on confusion matrix analysis and they claim the quality of their segmentation procedure exceeds 88.5% of correctness (Eq. 3) and 85% of completeness (Eq. 4).

2.2 Current Quality Measures

Classification-Based Measures. Many current researchers, appraise their methods with confusion matrix analysis, treating the segmentation task as a kind of classification problem [3–5]. This kind of assessment relies on calculation of three basic measures using for classification evaluation:

correctness (also referred to as precision, Eq. 3), completeness (known also as recall or sensitivity, Eq. 4), and quality (Eq. 5) according to maximum overlapping technique introduced by Awrangjeb and Fraser [32].

$$correctness = \frac{||TP||}{||TP|| + ||FP||} \tag{3}$$

$$completeness = \frac{||TP||}{||TP|| + ||FN||} \tag{4}$$

$$quality = \frac{||TP||}{||TP|| + ||FN|| + ||FP||} \tag{5}$$

where $|| \cdot ||$ states for a cardinality of a set; TP, FP, FN states, respectively, for: true positives, false positives, and false negatives.

These measures do require unambiguous correspondence finding among groups of reference clustering $\mathcal{R}_i$, such that $\mathcal{R} = \{\mathcal{R}_1, \mathcal{R}_2, \mathcal{R}_3, ..., \mathcal{R}_n\}$ ($\bigcup_{i=1}^{n} \mathcal{R}_i = D$) and clustering being apprised $\mathcal{O}_j$, where $\mathcal{O} = \{\mathcal{O}_1, \mathcal{O}_2, \mathcal{O}_3, ..., \mathcal{O}_m\}$ ($\bigcup_{j=1}^{m} \mathcal{O}_j = D$). Both clusterings are built over the dataset D. This correspondence is usually determined by searching patches that overlap the most [32], namely we look for the corresponding clusters $\mathcal{O}_j$ and $\mathcal{R}_i$ where:

$$\arg\max_j \frac{||\mathcal{O}_j \cap \mathcal{R}_i||}{||\mathcal{O}_j||} = \arg\max_i \frac{||\mathcal{O}_j \cap \mathcal{R}_i||}{||\mathcal{R}_i||}.$$

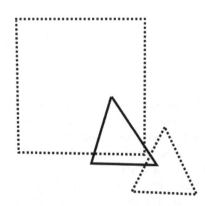

Fig. 1. A case of improper correspondence finding with maximum- overlapping method

Nevertheless these metrics consider solely number of clusters classified as TP, FP or FN. They do not take into account cardinality of overlapping regions, hence these statistics may be easily far-fetched and results might not be reliable. Depending on the presumed overlapping threshold (if any), these measures fail in case of high ratio of FP or FN, or highly unexpected output (see Fig. 1). In Fig. 1, we may clearly see that, using maximum overlapping strategy, a solid-line triangle will be associated with a dashed rectangle rather than its actual counterpart.

Micro- and Macro- averaging. The other approach for clustering quality assessment, or its variation applicable for any measures, are techniques being widely used in machine learning domain for multi-label classification, called micro- and macro- averaging. They aggregate intermediate results into global information. Manning et al. [29] defined macro-averaging as arithmetical average across classes and micro- averaging as weighted mean of multi-label classification measures. Hence, we may formally define macro-averaging as the arithmetic mean of the values and micro-averaged completeness, correctness and quality as in the Eqs. 7 and 8 [30].

$$correctness = \frac{\sum ||TP||}{\sum (||TP|| + ||FP||)} \tag{6}$$

$$completeness = \frac{\sum ||TP||}{\sum (||TP|| + ||FN||)} \tag{7}$$

$$quality = \frac{\sum ||TP||}{\sum (||TP|| + ||FP|| + ||FN||)} \tag{8}$$

where TP,FN,FP states respectively for true positives, false negatives, and false positives.

Variation of Information. Besides correctness, completeness, and quality relying solely on the binary decision: does cluster correspond or not, there is another group of methods for clustering comparison [34] making use of fuzzy correspondences, defined by information theory and information entropy of Shannon [26] (Eq. 9).

$$H(\mathcal{R}) = -\sum_{i=1}^{n} \frac{||\mathcal{R}_i||}{||\mathcal{D}||} \log_2 \left(\frac{||\mathcal{R}_i||}{||\mathcal{D}||} \right) \tag{9}$$

where $\mathcal{R}_i$ is the cluster being considered and $||\mathcal{R}_i||$ stands for its cardinality.

One of measures constructed on the notion of information entropy, is mutual information $I(\cdot, \cdot)$. Mutual Information of two random variables $\mathcal{O}$ and $\mathcal{R}$ ($I(\mathcal{O}, \mathcal{R})$), as Gelfand and Yaglom [27] defined, is the amount of information of $\mathcal{O}$ contained within the variable $\mathcal{R}$ and may be represented with Eq. 10.

$$I(\mathcal{O}, \mathcal{R}) = \sum_{j \leq m} \sum_{i \leq n} \frac{||\mathcal{R}_i \cap \mathcal{O}_j||}{||\mathcal{D}||} \log \frac{||\mathcal{R}_i \cap \mathcal{O}_j|| \cdot ||\mathcal{D}||}{||\mathcal{O}_j|| \cdot ||\mathcal{R}_i||} \tag{10}$$

Mutual Information evaluates many-to-many relations, unlike classification-based measures relying on one-to-one correspondences. Hence Mutual Information provides insight into segmentation result by means of many-to-many relations. Another method, inspired by information entropy was introduced by Meilă. She derived measure of Variation of Information (VoI) dedicated for comparing clusterings. Meilă [28] defined VoI as loss and gain of information while switching from clustering $\mathcal{O}$ to the clustering $\mathcal{R}$.

$$VoI(\mathcal{O}, \mathcal{R}) = H(\mathcal{O}) + H(\mathcal{R}) - 2I(\mathcal{O}, \mathcal{R}) \tag{11}$$

where $H(\cdot)$ is an information entropy (Eq. 9) and $I(\cdot, \cdot)$ is Mutual Information (Eq. 10).

Although, VoI is not directly dependent on the number of points $||\mathcal{D}||$, value of Variation of Information is constrained with upper bounds according to (12). The best possible value of VoI, for the perfect clustering ($\mathcal{O} = \mathcal{R}$) is zero. Moreover, it is true metric, unlike Mutual Information.

$$VoI_{max}(\mathcal{O}, \mathcal{C}) \leq \log ||\mathcal{D}|| \tag{12}$$

Superiority of VoI over classification- based measures is the fact that no one-to-one correspondence has to be found a priori. It produces reliable results even in case of significant clusters' granulation and partial overlapping. Hence it may be thought of as fuzzy decision about clusters correspondences rather than binary: *yes* or *no*.

3 New Quality Measures

Since we focus on evaluation of planarity detection methods, by example of Li et al. [3] approach, four distinguished measures were used.

1. Variation of Information - (VoI)
2. ordinary classification statistics (used in [3]) - (OCS)
3. micro- and macro- weighted classification statistics in terms of overlapping size (see Subsect. 3.1) - (WCS)
4. micro- and macro- averaged planarity statistics (see Subsect. 3.2) - (PS)

Two last of them, weighted classification statistics (WCS) and planarity statistics (PS), are newly derived ones as none of the reviewed authors exploited them and it became the contribution of this paper.

3.1 Weighted Classification Statistics

Weighted classification statistics (WCS) measure is influenced by the number of common part between a reference cluster and the best fitting resulting cluster not being associated yet. In the Fig. 2 we may see correspondence found between a reference cluster (dashed border) and an output cluster (solid line rectangle). The correspondence is found with maximum common-part strategy. In that image (Fig. 2), TP is the cardinality of the inner white region, strips signify region whose cardinality is said to be FP, and the number of points belonging to grey region pose the number of FN.

To clearly state it, for each reference cluster $R_i \in \mathcal{R}$ the set of remaining output clusters is searched to identify the cluster $\mathcal{O}_j \in \mathcal{O}$ whose the largest number of points lies within $\mathcal{R}_i$. Having found one-to-one correspondence between the reference $\mathcal{R}_i$ and the output cluster $\mathcal{O}_j$, TP, FP, and FN are calculated. True positives are thought of as the common part between corresponding clusters. The number of false positives (Eq. 13) is calculated as a difference between sum

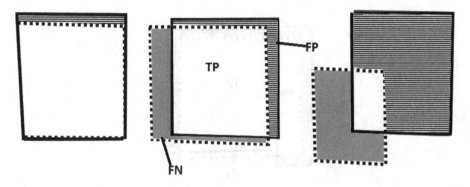

Fig. 2. Idea of WCS measure. The dashed lines state for a reference cluster, solid line borders identify output cluster. White region is said to be TP, grey area- FN, and stripped region- FP

of cardinalities of the output clustering $\mathcal{O}_j \in \mathcal{O}'$ (assuming some clusters of $\mathcal{O}$ may be rejected $\mathcal{O}' \subset \mathcal{O}$) and the number of TP. False negatives (Eq. 14) are calculated as a difference of the whole set cardinality $||\mathcal{D}||$ and the number of TP. This way of calculating local clustering characteristics gives us appraisal of an individual result influenced by overlapping size.

Contrary to the OCS, a significance of correspondence in the case presented in the Fig. 1 will be properly diminished with respect to the size of overlapping part. In the Fig. 2 one may see, that value of WCS will vary much whereas OCS may still indicate the same values.

$$||FP|| = \bigcup_{\mathcal{O}_j \in \mathcal{O}'} ||\mathcal{O}_j|| - ||TP|| \text{ where } \mathcal{O}' \subset \mathcal{O} \tag{13}$$

$$||FN|| = ||\mathcal{D}|| - ||TP|| \tag{14}$$

3.2 Planarity Statistics

Planarity statistics (PS) measure supplies the estimation of actual planar fragments detection without penalty for division of fragments which constitute the one actual plane (Fig. 3). Penalty is put only for those points of an output cluster which exceed a reference plane and those of an output cluster which do not have their counterpart in a reference one. It identifies TP, FP, and FN as in the Fig. 3, where inner white region describes TP, strips signify FP, and gray region- FN. Everything under the condition that overlapping part of a single output cluster has to be at the level of, at least, 50% to consider a part of a cluster as TP.

4 Results and Discussion

Experiments were carried out for the dataset Room-1 [31] down-sampled to the size of 121,988 points, and for Room-2 [31] built of 292,997 points.

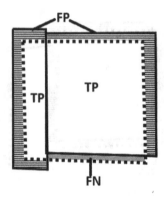

Fig. 3. Idea of planarity statistics (PS) appraisal. The dashed lines state for a reference cluster, solid line borders identify output clusters

Two reference clusterings, for each room dataset, were manually labelled. The detailed clusterings identified as much planar fragments as it was perceptually justified, whereas general clusterings, resembled the reference clusterings of Li et al. [3].

For Room-1, the first, more exact and detailed clustering, including significantly more planar clusters, contained 73 groups of points, whereas the second one - general, only 10 clusters. For Room-2, detailed clustering had 32 groups of points, and general included only 7 clusters. Experiment configuration was like that used in the Li's method [3] (see Table 1) and reflected semantic characteristics of considered rooms. Detailed clusterings reflected all perceptually perceived planar fragments, whereas general, less detailed, clusterings reflected mainly the largest planar fragments. Different number of clusters, though possible, were not considered.

Table 1. Values of parameters of the method by Li et al. [3] used during experiments

Parameter	Value for Room-1	Value for Room-2
Cell size	0.5	0.5
te	0.01	0.02
max. plane shift	0.08	0.076
max. angle deviation between normals	15°	15°

Analysing quality measures, applied for classification tests performed for the planarity detection procedure introduced in [3], we may notice how considered measures reflected selected aspects of the datasets classification procedure. As the output of our experiments, we have examined four classification quality measures: Variation of Information (VoI), ordinary classification statistics (OCS), and those introduced in this paper: weighted classification statistics (WCS), and planarity statistics (PS). Experiments were conducted for the general clustering of the reference sets (see Table 2) - similar to that used by Li et al., and for the detailed clustering of the reference sets (see Table 4). We have also compared values of OCS and WCS for general clusterings with switched values of te - clustering method parameter, as to evaluate usability of the proposed measures (Table 3).

Table 2. Values of measures for Room-1 and Room-2 datasets for Li's method [3] obtained by applying general clustering and suggested values of te ($te = 0.01$ for Room-1 and $te = 0.02$ for Room-2)

Measure			Value for Room-1	Value for Room-2
VoI			1.01	0.70
OCS	Correctness		90.00%	44.44%
	Completeness		75.00%	57.14%
	Quality		69.23%	33.33%
WCS	Correctness	Micro-averaged	85.68%	75.12%
		Macro-averaged	74.50%	74.73%
	Completeness	Micro-averaged	95.61%	81.36%
		Macro-averaged	89.03%	80.12%
	Quality	Micro-averaged	82.44%	64.10%
		Macro-averaged	72.21%	71.49%
PS	Correctness	Micro-averaged	92.02%	91.96%
		Macro-averaged	86.69%	91.43%
	Completeness	Micro-averaged	82.95%	59.56%
		Macro-averaged	98.25%	99.97%
	Quality	Micro-averaged	77.39%	56.62%
		Macro-averaged	85.18%	91.42%

Values of OCS for general clustering of reference sets are close to these, presented by Li et al. [3]. On the other hand, the OCS values for detailed clustering of reference sets (see Table 4) differ much, but it is clear, since we provide much more detailed clustering. We may think that all output clusters have found their reference counterpart. But there are many planar fragments skipped by the algorithm [3], like a chair or a suitcase. Hence some reference clusters do not have their corresponding clusters in the output, what obviously leads to low completeness indicator. On the other hand, WCS values seems to vary a lot from OCS (Table 4). Correctness values of WCS, lower than that of OCS, point out that corresponding reference and output clusters do not overlap perfectly and may be shifted with respect to each other. On the other hand, very high completeness values inform us about low number of FN. This might be interpreted in such a way that larger planes found proper counterpart and smaller reference clusters were not associated.

Table 3. Values of measures for Room-1 and Room-2 datasets for Li's method [3] obtained by applying general clustering and switched values of te ($te = 0.02$ for Room-1 and $te = 0.01$ for Room-2)

Measure			Value for Room-1	Value for Room-2
VoI			1.34	2.16
OCS	Correctness		100.0%	66.67%
	Completeness		66.67%	57.14%
	Quality		66.67%	44.44%
WCS	Correctness	Micro-averaged	84.90%	62.69%
		Macro- averaged	74.68%	62.40%
	Completeness	Micro-averaged	86.80%	48.29%
		Macro-averaged	84.58%	54.06%
	Quality	Micro-averaged	75.19%	37.51%
		Macro-averaged	69.42%	46.69%
PS	Correctness	Micro-averaged	92.17%	82.00%
		Macro-averaged	89.12%	84.02%
	Completeness	Micro-averaged	72.61%	42.14%
		Macro-averaged	93.81%	84.66%
	Quality	Micro-averaged	68.40%	38.57%
		Macro-averaged	83.67%	69.92%

Table 4. Values of measures for Room-1 and Room-2 datasets for Li's method [3] obtained by applying detailed reference clustering

Measure			Value for Room-1	Value for Room-2
VoI			1.69	2.78
OCS	Correctness		80.00%	55.55%
	Completeness		10.96%	15.62%
	Quality		10.67%	13.88%
WCS	Correctness	Micro-averaged	70.85%	45.33%
		Macro-averaged	67.24%	43.03%
	Completeness	Micro-averaged	99.69%	79.99%
		Macro- averaged	99.02%	78.08%
	Quality	Micro-averaged	70.70%	40.71%
		Macro-averaged	67.13%	38.13%
PS	Correctness	Micro-averaged	83.78%	75.38%
		Macro-averaged	81.46%	77.43%
	Completeness	Micro-averaged	71.62%	32.62%
		Macro-averaged	99.94%	92.27%
	Quality	Micro-averaged	62.91%	29.48%
		Macro-averaged	81.43%	71.97%

High values of PS for Room-1, both micro- and macro- averaged, suggest that planar fragments, mainly, do not contain many disturbing points from other planar patches. For Room-2 we may see poorer values of micro-averaged completeness and quality of PS. From this, we may suspect that the Li's method [3] finds only basic planes in Room-2 like a wall, a ceiling, or a floor.

Let us compare values of measures between Tables 2 and 3, where values of te were switched. Values of OCS indicate increase of correctness and fall of completeness and quality. These values indicate that, approximately, one more correct correspondence was found (TP) but number of undetected reference clusters (FN) grew. WCS values give us more information. For Room-1, micro- and macro- averaged correctness remain virtually equal, what suggests that actually numbers of TP and FP have not changed much- the same correspondences were found. On the other hand, fluctuations in WCS completeness and quality tell us that number of FN increased for larger fragments (clusters of more points). For Room-2 we may see slightly different tendency. Values of correctness and quality increased and the completeness remained the same. This would suggest that $te = 0.01$ for Room-2 suits better than $te = 0.02$. However, values of OCS and PS indicate something opposite. Actually, fewer points from larger and smaller clusters were grouped correctly.

Having analysed results presented in the Tables 2 and 4, several conclusions may be withdrawn. First of all, ordinary classification statistics might be useful for tasks of clusters counting, for instance, how many roofs terrestrial laser scan contains or how many potential walls we have in our indoor scan. OCS provides quantitative evaluation of an output clustering. On the other hand, if we would like to know how well our resulting clusters fit a reference set, we need a qualitative measure, supported by WCS. This measure allows a researcher to construct a method that focuses on maximizing overlapping parts for major clusters, whereas penalty put onto undetected small regions is accordingly smaller. This measure may be valuable for compression purposes, where we expect an algorithm to reduce size, most of all of the greatest regions, preserving at the same time the highest possible quality. Measuring PS, in turn, gives us insight into the process of space division. Regardless to the approach we use for space division, either hierarchical or uniform, it has to supply sufficiently small patches that only one plane is contained therein. Planarity statistics let us appraise whether space was divided enough to enable then the proper segments aggregation.

Comparing values of both - general and detailed clusterings (respectively, Tables 2 and 4), one may noticed that values of OCS differ a lot, when number of reference clusters has changed. The opposite tendency we may see for our measures: WCS and PS, which indicate quantitative evaluation, which regardless to the reasonable changes of number of reference clusters, point out similar assessment of the method.

5   Conclusions

In this paper, we presented two new measures used for sophisticated assessment of planes detection methods, namely: weighted classification statistics and planarity statistics. These measures were compared with two, the most popular ones. The results of the performed experiments indicate benefits of the introduced measures, because they focus on different aspects of segmentation and supplement classical approach. Whereas OCS may sometimes indicate better results, WCS clearly suggest deterioration of clustering. Planarity statistics show how good planes we found, regardless to the fact how many of them were considered. Thanks to that, we may estimate if partition is sufficient to cover each plane. On the other hand, weighted classification statistics provide us with the information how big regions were found correctly. Since each measure has its own application, we provided also recommendations concerning using particular measures for dedicated purposes.

References

1. Bhanu, B., Lee, S., Ho, C., Henderson, T.: Range data processing: representation of surfaces by edges. In: Proceedings - International Conference on Pattern Recognition, pp. 236–238. IEEE Press, New York (1986)
2. Golovinskiy, A., Funkhouser, T.: Min-cut based segmentation of point clouds. In: 2009 IEEE 12th ICCV Workshops, Kyoto, pp. 39–46 (2009)
3. Li, L., Yang, F., Zhu, H., Li, D., Li, Y., Tang, L.: An improved RANSAC for 3D point cloud plane segmentation based on normal distribution transformation cells. Remote Sens. **9**(5), 433 (2017)
4. Wang, Y., et al.: Three-dimensional reconstruction of building roofs from airborne LiDAR data based on a layer connection and smoothness strategy. Remote Sens. **8**(5), 415 (2016)
5. Xu, B., Jiang, W., Shan, J., Zhang, J., Li, L.: Investigation on the weighted RANSAC approaches for building roof plane segmentation from LiDAR point clouds. Remote Sens. **8**(1), 5 (2015)
6. Liu, Y., Xiong, Y.: Automatic segmentation of unorganized noisy point clouds based on the Gaussian map. Comput. Aided Des. **40**(5), 576–594 (2008)
7. Lu, X., Yao, J., Tu, J., Li, K., Li, L., Liu, Y.: Pairwise linkage for point cloud segmentation. ISPRS Ann. Photogrammetry Rem. Sens. Spat. Inf. Sci. **3**(3), 201–208 (2016)
8. Romanowski, A., Grudzien, K., Chaniecki, Z., Wozniak, P.: Contextual processing of ECT measurement information towards detection of process emergency states. In: 13th International Conference on Hybrid Intelligent Systems (HIS 2013), pp. 291–297. IEEE (2013)
9. Wosiak, A., Zakrzewska, D.: On integrating clustering and statistical analysis for supporting cardiovascular disease diagnosis. In: Annals of Computer Science and Information Systems, pp. 303–310. IEEE Press, Lodz (2015)
10. Pólrola, M., Wojciechowski, A.: Real-time hand pose estimation using classifiers. In: Bolc, L., Tadeusiewicz, R., Chmielewski, L.J., Wojciechowski, K. (eds.) ICCVG 2012. LNCS, vol. 7594, pp. 573–580. Springer, Heidelberg (2012). https://doi.org/10.1007/978-3-642-33564-8_69

11. Staniucha, R., Wojciechowski, A.: Mouth features extraction for emotion classification. In: 2016 Federated Conference on Computer Science and Information Systems, pp. 1685–1692. IEEE Press, Gdansk (2016)
12. Forczmanski P., Kukharev G.: Comparative analysis of simple facial features extractors. J. Real-Time Image Process. 1(4), 239–255 (2007)
13. Skuza, M., Romanowski, A.: Sentiment analysis of Twitter data within big data distributed environment for stock prediction. In: Federated Conference on Computer Science and Information Systems, pp. 1349–1354. IEEE (2015)
14. Martinović, A., Knopp, J., Riemenschneider, H., Gool, L.V.: 3D all the way: semantic segmentation of urban scenes from start to end in 3D. In: 2015 IEEE Conference on Computer Vision and Pattern Recognition (CVPR), pp. 4456–4465. IEEE Press, Boston (2015)
15. Nguyen, A., Le, B.: 3D point cloud segmentation: a survey. In: 013 6th IEEE Conference on Robotics, Automation and Mechatronics (RAM), pp. 225-230. IEEE Press, Manila (2013)
16. Oehler, B., Stueckler, J., Welle, J., Schulz, D., Behnke, S.: Efficient multi-resolution plane segmentation of 3D point clouds. In: Jeschke, S., Liu, H., Schilberg, D. (eds.) ICIRA 2011. LNCS (LNAI), vol. 7102, pp. 145–156. Springer, Heidelberg (2011). https://doi.org/10.1007/978-3-642-25489-5_15
17. Chmielewski, L.J., Orłowski, A.: Hough transform for lines with slope defined by a pair of co-primes. Mach. Graph. Vis. 22(1/4), 17–25 (2013)
18. Rabbani, T., van den Heuvel, F.A., Vosselman, G.: Segmentation of point clouds using smoothness constraint. Int. Arch. Photogrammetry Remote Sens. Spatial Inf. Sci. 36, 248–253 (2006)
19. Sappa, A.D., Devy, M.: Fast range image segmentation by an edge detection strategy. In: 3-D Digital Imaging and Modeling, pp. 292–299. IEEE Press, Quebec (2001)
20. Schnabel, R., Wahl, R., Klein, R.: Efficient RANSAC for point-cloud shape detection. Comput. Graph. Forum 26(2), 214–226 (2007)
21. Strom, J., Richardson, A., Olson, E.: Graph-based segmentation for colored 3D laser point clouds. In: 2010 IEEE/RSJ International Conference on Intelligent Robots and Systems, pp. 2131–2136. IEEE Press, Taipei (2010)
22. Vaskevicius, N., Birk, A., Pathak, K., Schwertfeger, S.: Efficient representation in 3D environment modeling for planetary robotic exploration. Adv. Robot. 24(8–9), 1169–1197 (2010)
23. Vosselman, G., Gorte, G.H., Sithole, G., Rabbani, T.: Recognizing structures in laser scanner point cloud. Int. Arch. Photogrammetry Remote Sens. Spatial Inf. Sci. 36(8), 33–38 (2003)
24. Xiao, J., Zhang, J., Adler, B., Zhang, H., Zhang, J.: Three-dimensional point cloud plane segmentation in both structured and unstructured environments. Robot. Auton. Syst. 61(12), 1641–1652 (2013)
25. Puchała, D.: Approximating the KLT by maximizing the sum of fourth-order moments. IEEE Sig. Process. Lett. 20(3), 193–196 (2013)
26. Shannon, C.: A mathematical theory of communication. Bell Syst. Tech. J. 27, 379–423 (1948)
27. Gelfand, I.M., Yaglom, A.M.: Calculation of the Amount of Information about a Random Function Contained in Another Such Function. American Mathematical Society, Washington (1959)
28. Meilă, M.: Comparing clusterings by the variation of information. In: Schölkopf, B., Warmuth, M.K. (eds.) COLT-Kernel 2003. LNCS (LNAI), vol. 2777, pp. 173–187. Springer, Heidelberg (2003). https://doi.org/10.1007/978-3-540-45167-9_14

29. Manning, C.D., Raghavan, P., Schütze, H.: Introduction to Information Retrieval. Cambridge University Press, Cambridge (2008)
30. Sebastiani, F.: Machine learning in automated text categorization. ACM Comput. Surv. **34**(1), 1–47 (2002)
31. Rooms UZH Irchel Dataset. http://www.ifi.uzh.ch/en/vmml/research/datasets. html
32. Awrangjeb, M., Fraser, C.S.: An automatic and threshold-free performance evaluation system for building extraction techniques from airborne LIDAR data. IEEE J. Sel. Topics App. Earth Observ. Remote Sens. **7**(10), 4184–4198 (2014)
33. Saval-Calvo, M., Azorin-Lopez, J., Fuster-Guillo, A., Garcia-Rodriguez, J.: Three-dimensional planar model estimation using multi-constraint knowledge based on k-means and RANSAC. Appl. Soft Comput. **34**, 572–586 (2015)
34. Wagner, S., Wagner, D.: Comparing Clusterings - An Overview. Universität Karlsruhe (TH), Karlsruhe (2007)

Multi-camera Photometric Simulation for Creation of 3D Object Reconstruction System

Dawid Sobel[1], Karol Jedrasiak[2(✉)], and Aleksander Nawrat[1]

[1] Silesian University of Technology, Gliwice, Poland
dawid.sobel@polsl.pl
[2] The University of Dabrowa Gornicza, Dabrowa Gornicza, Poland
kjedrasiak@wsb.edu.pl

Abstract. Photogrammetry allows a three-dimensional reconstruction of the object based on its multiple photographies. The quality of the reconstruction result depends mostly on the gloss, the diversity of the texture, the lighting conditions, the quality of the camera calibration and the shape of the object. The article presents the results of a simulation of a multi-camera reconstruction system, for the needs of developing a 3D objects reconstruction system (3D scanner). The 3D reconstruction system works by simultaneously taking photographs of cameras located around the object. The simulation was created to investigate the optimal distribution of cameras and projectors casting a pattern that increases the number of characteristic points on the surface of the object. The impact of background removal in images on the reconstruction result as well as the texture quality of the object depending on the resolution and distance of the cameras from the object were also investigated. The graphic engine used to create the simulation also allows testing of various types of object lighting. The presented results prove that the parameters of the system structure, such as the placement of cameras, projectors, the selection of patterns projected by the projectors are important and their values can be determined at the stage of system simulation. Conceptual errors at the simulation stage can be removed with minimal cost and the actual system can be created on the basis of tested assumptions. The conducted research in real-world conditions of the designed 3D object reconstruction system based on simulated parameters confirms the validity of the use of simulation.

Keywords: Reconstruction 3D · Photogrammetry · 3D scanner

1 Introduction

As part of publication work, we investigated the possibility of simulating the 3D reconstruction system in the game engine. The demand for this type of research results from the intention to physical implement such a scanner. The simulation

© Springer Nature Switzerland AG 2018
L. J. Chmielewski et al. (Eds.): ICCVG 2018, LNCS 11114, pp. 187–198, 2018.
https://doi.org/10.1007/978-3-030-00692-1_17

was to show whether it is possible to determine the specifications of the scanner, its structure, the components used, their arrangement based on tests carried out in a virtual environment. The identification of technical parameters and problems at the simulation stage of scanner may speed up the process of its construction and commissioning. The tests carried out in the simulation environment were repeated in the corresponding to them real conditions in order to verify the results obtained earlier.

The created scanner consists of cameras, projectors, lighting and a construction frame. Game engine allows you to create threedimensional scene on which we can arrange elements of the reconstruction system and models of objects, whose shape and texture are to be recreated. Then the cameras spread around the object render the images, which serve as the entry point in the reconstruction software. In the next chapter, we presented an overview of current research on reconstruction. Along with the research, we also described the application of these results in practice.

The next section contains a detailed description of the reconstruction system and its elements, which are implemented in a virtual environment. Then we described the reconstruction from data collected only from pictures, reconstruction with using the pattern projected by the projector, reconstruction with background of the object subtraction and reconstruction of the glossy element which strongly reflects light. We have presented both methods used in virtual and real implementation. At the end of the chapter, we presented the criterion on the basis of which the assessment and comparison of results were made. Sect. 4 contains the results of currently completed tests. In the last chapter, we summarized the results of the research and made conclusions about the validity of the reconstruction system simulation.

2   Application of 3D Reconstruction

Various methods are used to capture the object or scenery for 3D reconstruction. Recently, there is an increase number of 3D models built based on data acquired from combination of terrestrial surveying and unmanned aerial vehicles (UAVs) in order to close possible 3D modelling gaps and create orthoimages [1–3]. For example, UAV and terrestrial image acquisition platforms are used in [4] to study gullies with their complex morphologies. It has been shown that using both techniques allow for comprehensive gully models with high spatial resolution at frequent intervals. More and more often, scans are also being execute by robots, like e.g. in cooperative scanning performed by two industrial robot arms [5].

Cooperation between different approaches to acquire the data for 3D model are involved mostly in reconstruction of sceneries and vast spaces. UAVs are used e.g. for road mapping [6] and thermal analyses [7]. High resolution surface scanning, radiological MRI and real data based animation are used to reconstruct and analyze traffic accidents [8].

Whole sceneries and localizations are scanned using approaches like CHISEL – a system for a house scale 3D reconstruction [9]. This particular reconstruction method can be used with high resolution in real time on a mobile device. 3D scanning is commonly used for surveying and mapping of man-made structures and sites [13–15]. Usually, high quality 3D models of objects are constructed using different viewpoints, like it is shown when scanning the monument by [10]. It is especially useful to reconstruct a 3D digital model of objects with complex surfaces and sub millimeter-sized features [11]. Reconstruction of complex microstructures are used for construction work, as well as damage detections of large-surface objects. For example, [12] collects 3D micro-texture of asphalt pavement and reconstructs using binocular vision method for rapid extraction of the 3D image.

3D scanning was used e.g. for damage detection of wind turbine blades to maintain efficient and safe energy generation [16]. Building damage assessment was also used in [17] study, when the researchers reported the use of 3D scanning of residential buildings damaged during Hurricane Sandy. The researchers suggest that using 3D scanning can support post-disaster damage assessment needs for buildings, bridges or other man-made structures [18].

Archeology research is another example where 3D reconstruction is widely used and not only above the ground, but also underwater [19]. In archeology image-based 3D modeling is used to record entire excavations [20]. This approach increase the quality of obtained pictures and data and allows documentation and visualization of the archeological heritage.

Landscapes and their fragments can be reconstructed using 3D scanning approaches, like in [21]. In this study, the researchers scanned the rock slopes for obtaining the orientation of slope and possibility to monitor the slope for quantification of rock fall rates across wide areas. 3D reconstruction of the slopes allowed also to model detailed future deformations and possible rock damage. Therefore, 3D scanning may be used to alert residents about possible natural failure [22].

3D reconstruction of natural environments has been used extensively in agriculture, geology and botany studies. 3D models representing the shape and size of single plants and whole areas of fields and forests, can provide critical information for plant breeding and cultivation [23]. 3D representation of trees has been described e.g. in [24,25]. 3D scanning can help to predict phenotyping features, like size and number of leaves [26], what helps the producers in precision farming. 3D approaches are used also in forestry for the vegetation monitoring or fires surveillance [27].

Living objects, like plants, animals and human's body can be reconstructed in 3D [28]. 3D reconstruction is used to measure body parts, like e.g. feet in order to personalize 3D printed shoes [29]. Companies develop applications, like VisuaLook, that allow the measurement-based 3D reconstruction of the body and provide a service for the visualization of virtual looks at online shops [30]. Moreover, efficient 3D reconstruction is often use for face recognition [31].

3D scanners are used also on microlevel, e.g. to monitor the pulse in realtime [47] and reconstruct in 3D blood vessels from a limited number of projections [48]. 3D scanning techniques are used in biomedicine and science extensively, e.g. in super resolution fluorescence microscopy for reconstruction of thick tissue blocks [49,50]. By using it in research, like in ultramicroscopy for reconstruction of e.g. mouse embryos [51], it is possible to obtain high-level detailed insight into the anatomy of organisms and to screen for disease models.

Nowadays, not only body parts, but also full body scans are being designed. Full body shape scans are used for anthropometric surveying, clothing design or entertainment. For example, [32] developed a scanning environment based on multiple depth cameras for full-body scans, free of template markers and fully automatic. [33] Constructed a system that captures the human skeleton through a wall by tracing the 3D positions of the limbs and body parts. 3D scans can not only reconstruct the stationary objects and figures, but also the movements. [34] Used 3D reconstruction to model a moving person for longterm person reidentification based on difference in poses or walking. This approach is used also in sport training. 3D reconstruction of body postures can help athletes to master the techniques and improve the training program. 3D scans allow tracking of body movement and its parts, including the translational and rotational degrees of freedom [35]. 3D scanning can be used to characterize the golf swing [36] or underwater swimming [37].

Three dimensional reconstruction use increases in field of medicine and biology research. 3D scanning is involved in surgery and preoperative clinical practice planning, prosthetic design and education tool for teaching and doctor-patient interaction [41–43]. 3D whole body scanners are commonly used for healthcare applications, like in rehabilitation engineering [38]. An example is described in [39] where photogrammetry is used for the data acquisition and processing of human body models for design of prostheses and orthoses. Preoperative 3D reconstruction and rapid prototyping was applied for treatment of complex severe spinal deformity in [40]. Rehabilitation and surgeries acquire advantages by suing 3D reconstruction methods. An example is neuronavigation using endoscopy by reconstructing patient specific anatomy in three dimensions [44]. Another example is use of 3D scanning techniques for corrective surgery for Lenke 1 AIS patients [45]. [46] Used 3D techniques for heart modeling and 3D printing for individualized planning for percutaneous structural intervention. An alternative application to the above is the 3D reconstruction of objects, in particular people, for the needs of professional simulation systems. Training of officers of uniformed services in the field of conducting antiterrorist activities at the intervention level requires preparation of an officer for each possible situation. We believe that using photorealistic avatars animated using Motion Capture will contribute to improving the realism of the training.

3   Simulation of Reconstruction System

In a virtual environment, we have designed and constructed a 3D scanner. This scanner consists of 145 virtual cameras arranged on rings around the central point. Rings there are arranged at different heights (Fig. 1). The cameras are directed towards the inside of the circles. The position and orientation of cameras

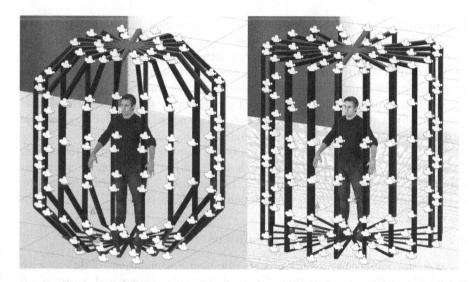

Fig. 1. Visualization of two different configurations of virtual cameras and projectors placement in the scanner.

and the number of rings are controlled by the created script and controlled by the user's panel. Apart from cameras, it is also possible to determine the position and number of projectors placed around the scanner. Projectors throw a pattern which increases the texture diversity. This allows to find corresponding image points in neighboring cameras. An additional element is the lighting control system enabling testing of reconstruction of glossy objects and tests of uniform illumination of objects, eliminating shadows.

The result of the simulation are images from cameras located in the scanner, which are next processed in software for 3D reconstruction based on photographs. The result of the reconstruction depends on the placement of cameras, their number, resolution, lighting, optical properties of the material and texture characteristics. By changing individual parameters of the system, it is possible to determine the best configuration for obtaining the best results.

3.1   Reconstruction in Virtual Environment

During the simulation, we examined the quality of the reconstitution result depending on the applied elements and system parameters. The results of the various reconstruction processes are presented in the next chapter.

As a test object, we chose the 3D model of a person with a high-resolution texture. We placed the object at the central point of the scanner. The reconstruction consisted of processing photographs from virtual cameras placed around the object. We set up a uniform lighting of the stage, simulating LED strips arranged on the vertical elements of the scanner structure. As part of the test, we modified the position and orientation of the cameras to find the optimal configuration for human scaling. The number of cameras was also changed. In addition, we tested the configuration with cameras with closeups on the hands and face in order to find more characteristic punts and a more accurate representation of the shape.

We tried to improve the result of the reconstruction by subtracting the background from the acquired images. Because the scene was static, it was possible to take two shots. The first one where the scanner was empty and the second with the object inside. On the basis of the difference of images, it was possible to determine the mask of reconstruction.

In this case, we added four projectors to the scanner to illuminate the object. As a result, the uniform texture surfaces on the object became more characteristic. The tests consisted in determining the resolution and pattern projected by the projector, for which the reconstruction gives the best result.

3.2   Reconstruction in Real Conditions

In order to compare the results of tests obtained in simulation conditions with the results of the reconstruction of real photographs, we created a test stand consisting of two test objects and a camera. The first object was a rocker, covered with metallic varnish and the other a semi-transparent coolant tank. The type of objects guaranteed the lack of good results of reconstruction in the absence of any modifications. This is due to the optical properties of reflecting or transmitting materials and the uniformity of their texture.

Reconstruction based on photographs of unmodified objects ended in failure due to lack of detected characteristic points on the surface of the objects. Therefore, we introduced the first modification of the reconstruction process which consisted in increasing the texture characteristics of the object by covering its surface with matting agent (Fig. 2). We chose this measure due to the ease of its application and the possibility of later washing. Images recorded with the camera have been processed using the same software as images rendered from virtual cameras.

As in the previous method, we covered the objects with a matting agent. Then, we placed projectors with a resolution of 1920×1080 on two sides of

Fig. 2. Photographs of scanned objects. On the left, a translucent coolant tank and a rocker arm covered with a matting substance. On the right, the same objects with matting agent and additionally illuminated patterns from the projector.

scanned objects. High image resolution guaranteed a high specificity of texture on the object. Then we made a series of 50 photos. We have repeated this process once again using another type of matting agent, with a smaller size of individual particles covering the entire surface once more.

4   Results

We underwent a visual evaluation of the results of our tests due to the lack of other quality indicators for reconstitution. First of all, we paid attention to the shape of the mesh of the reconstructed objects. We asked ourselves whether the shape of the obtained object resemble the original object. Is it possible to observe inequalities of the surface or holes in the model. We also compared the input and output texture of the object and paid attention to the areas where the cardboard is missing or badly mapped.

Below we present the results of the reconstruction for the data collected in the scanner simulation and for the data recorded on the objects by the camera.

4.1   Reconstruction on Simulated Data

The main purpose of creating the simulation was to determine the proper configuration of the camera layout, which would ensure correct human reconstruction. We have carried out several reconstructions, changing the number of cameras and their location, step by step increasing the quality of reconstitution. In the last simulation 145 cameras were deployed on the surface of the cylinder and directed towards the center of the scanner. Attempts to use additional cameras, closer to hands, failed because the reconstruction software could not find characteristic points that would connect points to a similar image with points that were indexed to them on other cameras. As an example of the object we chose the hand due to its complex shape and the fact that we could easily assess the quality of the resulting reconstruction.

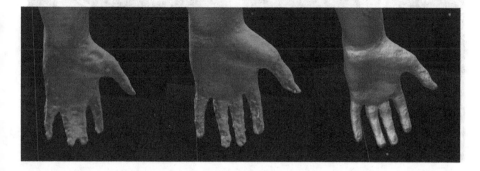

Fig. 3. Results of human hand reconstruction in three simulated scanner configurations. From left to right there are results acquired using configuration: I, II, III.

Below we present the test result for the scanner in three configurations (Fig. 3). In the first configuration the cameras are placed only on the vertical elements of the scanner's structure and are directed in front of each other. In the second configuration the cameras are also placed on the floor and ceiling of the scanner. In addition, the cameras located on the circumference of the ring look alternately 5° down and 5° up. The last configuration also contains 4 projectors illuminating the model from 4 sides.

We obtained the best result using cameras in the second configuration and using projectors with a resolution of 1920 × 1080 (Fig. 3, right).

The tests of reconstructing objects strongly reflecting the light ended in failure because no configuration of cameras, settings of projectors and the type of pattern did not allow to obtain data from which reconstruction would be possible. Improvement in quality tests by removing the background also did not produce better results than the solution obtained in the third scanner configuration described above.

4.2   Verification of Simulation Test Results

Studies of the reconstruction process on real objects have allowed us to refer to problems encountered in simulation tests and verify the quality of the approximation of real phenomena by simulation. Selected objects (Fig. 2), subjected to modifications described in Sect. 3.2, were photographed and the collected data served as input information in the reconstruction process carried out in the ready software. Below we present only the test results for three different process modifications carried out (Fig. 4).

In the first of them, the object was covered only with matting agent and increasing the number of characteristic points on its surface. In the second case, the object was additionally illuminated by a pattern from the projector. In the

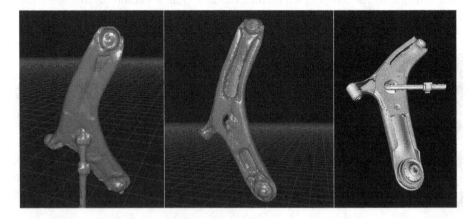

Fig. 4. Comparison of the results of reconstruction of the actual object for various modifications of the data collection process, on the example of the rocker.

last case, the matting agent has been changed to one that covers the entire surface of the item being scanned. Reconstructions on data collected from non-modified objects ended in failure.

In the case of the rocker the best result was obtained using a matting agent, covering the entire surface of the object and illuminating the object with the pattern from the projector.

We have also tested the effect of the matting agent and pattern lighting on the outcome of reconstruction of the coolant tank (Fig. 5). With the use of the matting agent alone, reconstruction is not possible because the object in the sequence of the sequence has a homogeneous texture, consisting of points that are difficult to explicitly characterize. The illumination of the object with the pattern from the projector made it possible to reconstruct the object.

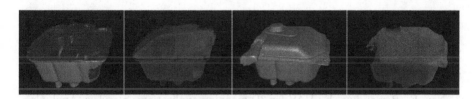

Fig. 5. The result of reservoir recollection based on a series of photos from the camera. On the left, the result of the coolant tank reconstruction covered only with artificial snow. On the right the result of the reconstruction of the tank covered with a matting agent and a patterned projector.

5   Summary of Results

Performing tests of the scanner's operation in a virtual environment has many advantages. The first of these is the cost associated with changes in the project. The change involving the camera relocation in a virtual environment involves a much lower cost than changing the position or orientation of the camera in a physical construction.

Another advantage of the simulation is the possibility to test the scanner on objects with different shapes, different textures and different optical properties. The object can be placed in any position inside the scanner, so you can check which parts of the object's surface are not visible for several cameras at the same time. Simulation results provide information on what types of surfaces or textures consist of a sufficient number of characteristic points or prevent the correct pairing of points on images from neighboring cameras.

The simulation also serves to determine the size and construction of the supporting structure for cameras and projectors, designing diagrams and length of electrical and transmission connections between system components.

We realize that the virtual environment can to some extent only approximate conditions in reality, which is why all tests carried out in a virtual environment have been also confirmed in the real environment.

The results of tests carried out in a real environment have proven that the results obtained from simulation tests can serve as a guide at the design and construction stage of the scanner. The problems observed in the simulated reconstruction system are reflected in those we observed during real tests.

Data obtained from the simulated scanner and from photos in real tests can be processed using the same methods and used for the purpose of professional simulation systems [52].

Acknowledgment. This work has been supported by National Centre for Research and Development as a project ID: DOB-BIO6/11/90/2014, Virtual Simulator of Protective Measures of Government Protection Bureau.

References

1. Pueschel, H., Sauerbier, M., Eisenbeiss, H.: A 3D model of Castle Landenberg (CH) from combined photogrammetric processing of terrestrial and UAV-based images. Int. Arch. Photogramm. Remote. Sens. Spat. Inf. Sci. **37**(B6b), 93–98 (2008)
2. Remondino, F., et al.: Multi-sensor 3D documentation of the Maya site of Copan. In: Proceedings of 22nd CIPA Symposium, Kyoto, Japan (2009)
3. Nex, F., Remondino, F.: UAV for 3D mapping applications: a review. Appl. Geomatics **6**(1), 1–15 (2014)
4. Stoecker, C., Eltner, A., Karrasch, P.: Measuring gullies by synergetic application of UAV and close range photogrammetry-a case study from Andalusia, Spain. Catena **132**, 1–11 (2015)
5. Wagner, M., et al.: 3D scanning of workpieces with cooperative industrial robot arms. In: Proceedings of ISR 2016: 47st International Symposium on Robotics; VDE (2016)
6. Zhang, C.: An UAV-based photogrammetric mapping system for road condition assessment. Int. Arch. Photogramm. Remote Sens. Spatial Inf. Sci **37**, 627–632 (2008)
7. Hartmann, W., et al.: Determination of the UAV position by automatic processing of thermal images. Int. Arch. Photogramm. Remote. Sens. Spat. Inf. Sci. **39**, B6 (2012)
8. Buck, U., et al.: Application of 3D documentation and geometric reconstruction methods in traffic accident analysis: with high resolution surface scanning, radiological MSCT/MRI scanning and real data based animation. Forensic Sci. Int. **170**(1), 20–28 (2007)
9. Klingensmith, M., et al.: Chisel: real time large scale 3D reconstruction onboard a mobile device using spatially hashed signed distance fields. Robot. Sci. Syst. **4** (2015)
10. Koutsoudis, A., et al.: Multi-image 3D reconstruction data evaluation. J. Cult. Herit. **15**(1), 73–79 (2014)
11. Galantucci, L.M., Pesce, M., Lavecchia, F.: A powerful scanning methodology for 3D measurements of small parts with complex surfaces and sub millimeter-sized features, based on close range photogrammetry. Precis. Eng. **43**, 211–219 (2016)
12. Ran, M., et al.: Asphalt pavement texture 3D reconstruction based on binocular vision system with SIFT algorithm. In: 2017 International Conference on Smart Grid and Electrical Automation (ICSGEA). IEEE (2017)

13. Cabuk, A., Deveci, A., Ergincan, F.: Improving heritage documentation. In: GIM International, vol. 21 (2007)
14. Oczipka, M., et al.: Small drones for geo-archaeology in the steppe: locating and documenting the archaeological heritage of the Orkhon Valley in Mongolia. In: Remote Sensing for Environmental Monitoring, GIS Applications, and Geology IX, vol. 7478. International Society for Optics and Photonics (2009)
15. Chiabrando, F., et al.: UAV and RPV systems for photogrammetric surveys in archaelogical areas: two tests in the Piedmont region (Italy). J. Archaeol. Sci. **38**(3), 697–710 (2011)
16. Marks, R., et al.: Damage detection in a composite wind turbine blade using 3D scanning laser vibrometry. Proc. Inst. Mech. Eng. Part C J. Mech. Eng. Sci. **231**(16), 3024–3041 (2017)
17. Zhou, Z., Gong, J., Guo, M.: Image-based 3D reconstruction for posthur-ricane residential building damage assessment. J. Comput. Civ. Eng. **30**(2), 04015015 (2015)
18. Pollefeys, M., et al.: Automated reconstruction of 3D scenes from sequences of images. ISPRS J. Photogramm. Remote. Sens. **55**(4), 251–267 (2000)
19. Capra, A.: 3D reconstruction of an underwater archaelogical site: comparison between low cost cameras. Int. Arch. Photogramm. Remote. Sens. Spat. Inf. Sci. **40**(5), 67 (2015)
20. De Jeroen, R.: On introducing an image-based 3D reconstruction method in archaeo-logical excavation practice. J. Archaeol. Sci. **41**, 251–262 (2014)
21. Abellan, A., et al.: Terrestrial laser scanning of rock slope instabilities. Earth Surf. Process. Landforms **39**(1), 80–97 (2014)
22. Shen, Y.-L., et al.: Reconstruction of disaster scene from UAV images and flight-control data. Geogr. Geo-Inf. Sci. **27**(6), 13–17 (2011)
23. Diaz-Varela, R.A., et al.: High-resolution airborne UAV imagery to assess olive tree crown parameters using 3D photo reconstruction: application in breeding trials. Remote Sens. **7**(4), 4213–4232 (2015)
24. Nock, C., et al.: Assessing the potential of low-cost 3D cameras for the rapid measurement of plant woody structure. Sensors **13**(12), 16216–16233 (2013)
25. Newcombe, L.: Green fingered UAVs. Unmanned Vehicle 20 (2007)
26. Nguyen, T.T., et al.: Structured light-based 3D reconstruction system for plants. Sensors **15**(8), 18587–18612 (2015)
27. Grenzdoerffer, G.J., Engel, A., Teichert, B.: The photogrammetric potential of low-cost UAVs in forestry and agriculture. Int. Arch. Photogramm. Remote Sens. Spat. Inf. Sci. **31**(B3), 1207–1214 (2008)
28. Ballester, A., et al.: Low-cost data-driven 3D reconstruction and its applications. In: Proceedings of 6th International Conference on 3D Body Scanning Technologies, vol. 10, no. 15.184 (2015)
29. Rout, N., et al.: 3D foot scan to custom shoe last. Spec. Issue Int. J. Comput. Commun. Technol. **1**(2-4), 14–18 (2010)
30. VisuaLook, H2020-SMEINST-1-2014 -662847: Novel clothing e-commerce application for reliable size assignment and realistic fitting visualization (VisuaLook), H2020, European Commission
31. Jiang, D., et al.: Efficient 3D reconstruction for face recognition. Pattern Recogn. **38**(6), 787–798 (2005)
32. Liu, Z., et al.: Template deformation-based 3-D reconstruction of full human body scans from low-cost depth cameras. IEEE Trans. Cybern. **47**(3), 695–708 (2017)
33. Adib, F., et al.: Capturing the human figure through a wall. ACM Trans. Graph. (TOG) **34**(6), p. 219 (2015)

34. Munaro, M., et al.: 3D reconstruction of freely moving persons for re-identification with a depth sensor. In: 2014 IEEE International Conference on Robotics and Automation (ICRA). IEEE (2014)
35. Zhang, N.: Study on the movement posture and sports characteristics based on the 3D reconstruction of human body. J. Comput. Theoret. Nanosci. **13**(12), 10342–10346 (2016)
36. Friel, K., et al.: The use of 3D scanning for sporting applications. In: Three-Dimensional Imaging, Visualization, and Display 2015, vol. 9495. International Society for Optics and Photonics (2015)
37. Bernardina, G.R.D., et al.: Action sport cameras as an instrument to perform a 3D underwater motion analysis. PloS one **11**(8), e0160490 (2016)
38. Mikołajewska, E., et al.: 3D printing technologies in rehabilitation engineering (2014)
39. Grazioso, S., Selvaggio, M., Di Gironimo, G.: Design and development of a novel body scanning system for healthcare applications. Int. J. Interact. Design Manuf. (IJIDeM), 1–10 (2017)
40. Mao, K., et al.: Clinical application of computer-designed polystyrene models in complex severe spinal deformities: a pilot study. Eur. Spine J. **19**(5), 797–802 (2010)
41. McGurk, M.: Rapid prototyping techniques for anatomical modelling in medicine. Ann. R. Coll. Surg. Engl. **79**(3), 169 (1997)
42. Hurson, C., et al.: Rapid prototyping in the assessment, classification and preoperative plan-ning of acetabular fractures. Injury **38**(10), 1158–1162 (2007)
43. Bustamante, S., et al.: Novel application of rapid prototyping for simulation of bronchoscopic anatomy. J. Cardiothorac. Vasc. Anesth. **28**(4), 1122–1125 (2014)
44. Iloreta, A., et al.: The novel use of 3D reconstruction and immersive neuronavigation for resection of skull base lesions in endoscopic endonasal skull base surgery. J. Neurol. Surg. Part B Skull Base **78**(S 01), A156 (2017)
45. Yang, M., et al.: Application of 3D rapid prototyping technology in posterior corrective surgery for Lenke 1 adolescent idiopathic scoliosis patients. Medicine **94**(8) (2015)
46. Dankowski, R., et al.: 3D heart model printing for preparation of percutaneous structural interventions: description of the technology and case report. Kardiologia Polska (Polish Heart Journal) **72**(6), 546–551 (2014)
47. Shao, X., et al.: Real-time 3D digital image correlation method and its application in human pulse monitoring. Appl. Optics **55**(4), 696–704 (2016)
48. Li, M., Yang, H., Kudo, H.: An accurate iterative reconstruction algorithm for sparse objects: application to 3D blood vessel reconstruction from a limited number of projections. Phys. Med. Biol. **47**(15), 2599 (2002)
49. Arganda-Carreras, I., et al.: 3D reconstruction of histological sections: application to mammary gland tissue. Microsc. Res. Tech. **73**(11), 1019–1029 (2010)
50. Park, S., et al.: Superresolution fluorescence microscopy for 3D reconstruction of thick samples. Mol. Brain **11**(1), 17 (2018)
51. Becker, K., et al.: Ultramicroscopy: 3D reconstruction of large microscopical specimens. J. Biophotonics **1**(1), 36–42 (2008)
52. Nawrat, A., Jedrasiak, K., Ryt, A., Sobel, D.: Multimedia firearms training system. World Acad. Sci. Eng. Technol., Int. J. Comput. Electr. Autom. Control. Inf. Eng. **10**(11), 1988–1997 (2016)

Quality Evaluation of 3D Printed Surfaces Based on HOG Features

Piotr Lech, Jarosław Fastowicz, and Krzysztof Okarma(✉)

Department of Signal Processing and Multimedia Engineering,
Faculty of Electrical Engineering,
West Pomeranian University of Technology, Szczecin,
26 Kwietnia 10, 71-126 Szczecin, Poland
{piotr.lech,jfastowicz,okarma}@zut.edu.pl

Abstract. The main purpose of the visual quality assessment of 3D prints is the detection of surface distortions which can be made using various approaches. Nevertheless, a reliable classification of 3D printed samples into low and high quality ones can be troublesome, especially assuming the unknown color of the filament. Such a classification can be efficiently conducted using the approach based on the Histogram of Oriented Gradients (HOG) proposed in this paper. Obtained results are very promising and allow proper classification for the most of the tested samples, especially for some of the most typical distortions.

Keywords: 3D prints · Quality assessment · HOG features

1 Introduction

Visual quality assessment of 3D printed surfaces is one of the up-to-date challenges for image analysis applications for Industry 4.0 purposes. Due to the availability of relatively cheap 3D printers for home use and rapid growth of their popularity the quality of final 3D prints obtained using such low-cost devices, especially constructed partially in an experimental way, is not always perfect. Therefore the visual on-line monitoring of the 3D objects during the printing process is highly demanded, especially considering the possible use of quite cheap web cameras.

The main goal of this paper is related to the automatic visual classification of the 3D printed surfaces in view of their quality. Assuming high universality of the proposed method, the color of the filament should remain unknown and therefore the perfect solution should be fully color independent. To face this challenge the analysis of some regular linear patterns representing the consecutive layers of the filament has been assumed with the use of the Histogram of Oriented Gradients (HOG).

Assuming the possibility of detection of some typical distortions of the printed surfaces during printing, their immediate correction could be possible as well as the emergency stop for more serious quality issues, allowing saving the filament and time.

© Springer Nature Switzerland AG 2018
L. J. Chmielewski et al. (Eds.): ICCVG 2018, LNCS 11114, pp. 199–208, 2018.
https://doi.org/10.1007/978-3-030-00692-1_18

The main sources of problems influencing the quality of the 3D prints are:

- poor quality of the filament,
- presence of distortions during the printing process,
- poor quality materials used for the construction of the printing device,
- wrong setup for printing parameters (temperature, movement speed, rotation of stepper motors, etc.).

Nevertheless, the quality evaluation of 3D printed surfaces is not an easy task. As far as we know currently there is no reliable method which can be efficiently applied for this purpose. One of the first visual approaches to the on-line monitoring of the 3D printing process has been presented by Fang [5], allowing detection of defects during fused deposition of ceramic materials. Another approach for monitoring the top surface of the printed object has been described by Cheng [3] comparing the consecutive layers using the fuzzy model for detection of under- or over-filling. Some other methods for visual fault detection have been proposed by Chauhan [1, 2] whereas some other researchers have tried to utilize neural networks [19] or have proposed the detection of feeder jams implemented in LabVIEW [18].

Probably the most interesting solution based on using five cameras and Raspberry Pi modules has been presented in Straub's paper [13]. Nevertheless, the proper detection of "dry printing" in this system requires very precise calibration and its additional disadvantage is high sensitivity to motions of cameras and varying lighting conditions.

In some recent papers the use of optical coherence tomography for *in situ* monitoring of additive manufacturing process using selective laser sintering has been proposed [8] as well as the application of thermal imaging [9]. Some ideas of detection of attacks against 3D printed objects and other cybersecurity issues have been discussed in the recent Straub's paper [16] whereas some special cases have been discussed in the other papers i.e. changing fill level [14], the presence of micro-defects [15] or the use of incorrect filament [17].

Since the use of cameras may introduce some additional problems caused by uneven lighting, necessity of color calibration etc., the initial research should be conducted assuming more predictable lighting conditions. Therefore we have decided to prepare a database of 3D printed flat plates obtained using Prusa i3 and Ormerod RepRap Pro 3D printers for various colors of PLA and ABS filaments. Such samples have been scanned using a flatbed scanner. To minimize the influence of light distribution on the scanning results all the samples have been placed such that the consecutive filament layers have been located perpendicularly to the scanning direction. For such prepared set of images obtained for low and high quality 3D prints various image analysis method can be applied to achieve proper classification of samples.

During previous experiments we have investigated the possible use of the texture analysis based on the GLCM [6, 10] as well as image quality assessment inspired approach [11, 12] and the application of entropy [7]. The most of the previously proposed metrics have been verified using the limited number of PLA samples being the first part of the dataset used in this paper (samples no. 1–18).

The quality evaluation of those samples based on the GLCM features presented in the paper [10] leads to proper results using the combination of two Haralick features (correlation and homogeneity) calculated for the vertical GLCM assuming the presence of horizontal patterns representing individual layers. Nevertheless, this method requires the analysis of their change depending on the offset used during the calculation of the GLCM so its real-time application would be troublesome. Results presented in the paper [6] have been achieved analyzing the peak to peak homogeneity for the offsets greater than 15 pixels and therefore the time consuming calculation of several GLCMs is required as well.

The application of some image quality metrics requires presented in our earlier papers requires their local calculations and comparison of their values obtained for several fragments of captured images. Such necessity is caused by the use of the full-reference image quality metrics which are usually much more universal than the state-of-the-art no-reference ("blind") metrics. Such an application of the popular SSIM and CW-SSIM metrics presented in the paper [12] does not lead to satisfactory results and the correct classification has been obtained only for the Structural Texture Similarity (STSIM) metric applied for the image divided into 16 blocks. However, the necessity of mutual comparisons between all image fragments decreases the computational efficiency significantly.

A proper classification has been obtained utilizing the local entropy [7], although such approach leads to different values for various colors and the use of different thresholds is necessary. Therefore the application of such a method would require the prior knowledge of the filament's color.

To investigate a new approach based on the Histogram of Oriented Gradients (HOG) and reliably evaluate its advantages some additional samples have been printed using not only the plastic PLA filaments but also ABS materials introducing some different colors of filaments. However, due to relatively poor quality of those materials, the overall quality of the obtained ABS samples is worse and the presence of some additional cracks can be easily noticed in some of the printed objects.

Nevertheless, during experiments discussed in this paper we have not focused on the detection of cracks and therefore our main task is the overall quality evaluation of the scanned surfaces of the 3D prints. It has been assumed that the most troublesome samples containing small local distortions and cracks should be then additionally analyzed. However, it should be noted that in most applications the samples containing cracks are just rejected and classified as poor quality 3D prints.

2 Description of the Method and Experimental Results

Analyzing the structure of layers for high and low quality prints (some of the samples used in our experiments are illustrated in Figs. 1 and 2), it can be observed that the changes of the luminance are much more regular for high quality prints

Fig. 1. Selected high quality 3D prints obtained using three PLA (top images from left) and five ABS filaments. (Color figure online)

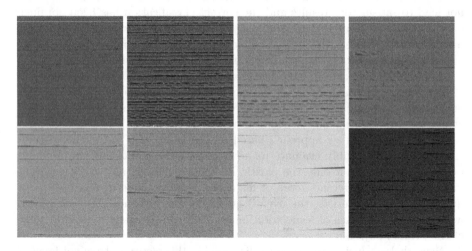

Fig. 2. Selected low quality 3D prints obtained using three PLA (top images from left) and five ABS filaments. (Color figure online)

and their orientation is quite well predictable and similar for the whole surface of the sample. The highest gradient values should be then horizontal or vertical dependently on the direction of scanning. Therefore it should be possible to determine the quality of the sample by the analysis of the gradients for selected orientations. Such operation can be made using the Histogram of Oriented Gradients (HOG) which is one of the most popular feature descriptors used e.g. for text recognition purposes or human detection [4].

Since the HOG descriptors should be calculated locally and the cell size as well as the block size should be chosen appropriately for the specified resolution of images, some initial experiments have been made and the parameters for 1700×1700 pixels scans have been set as 32×32 for the cell size and 4×4 for the block size. The choice of smaller cells results in much worse classification into high and low quality samples due to the strong influence of small details.

Due to the use of the signed orientation and the overlap of half the block size the obtained vector consists of 40000 features for each image (10000 features for each orientation). As in the ideal case the local features should be similar for high quality samples, one may expect low standard deviation of HOG features in comparison to low quality samples. We have assumed that such measure is more useful for classification and quality evaluation of 3D printed surfaces than the average or median values of HOG features and the obtained experimental results have confirmed its validity. Therefore it is proposed to apply the standard deviation of the HOG features as the overall quality metric.

It should also be noted that the quality evaluation of the 3D printed surfaces with the use of the HOG features calculated for unsigned orientation for the whole image, also using their standard deviation, does not lead to satisfactory results as shown in Fig. 3. All the results presented for the samples (in all plots in the paper) are shown in the following manner: the first 14 samples have been printed using PLA filaments and assessed as high or low quality samples only (high quality orange samples have not been produced) whereas the next samples obtained using ABS filaments, have been assessed as high, moderately high, moderately low and low quality ones.

The colors of the samples are reproduced in plots and the filled markers denote the samples without any cracks whereas the 3D prints with cracks are marked with empty shapes. Higher quality samples are represented by round shapes (circles for high quality prints and stars for moderately high quality

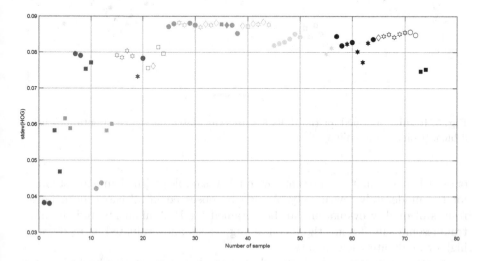

Fig. 3. Results obtained for the HOG features calculated for unsigned orientations using 4 bins. (Color figure online)

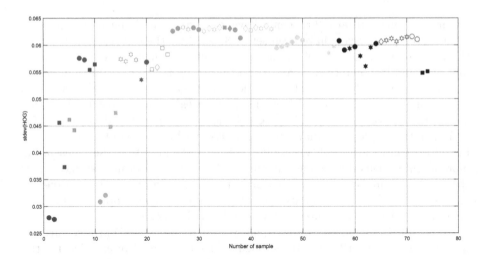

Fig. 4. Results obtained for the HOG features calculated for signed orientations using 8 bins. (Color figure online)

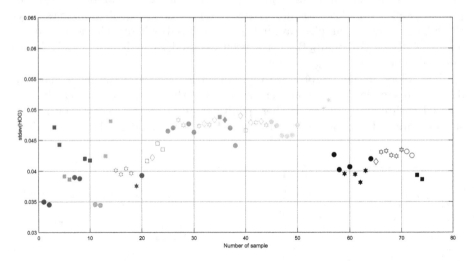

Fig. 5. Results obtained for the HOG features calculated for signed orientations using 3 bins. (Color figure online)

ones) whereas squares represent low quality samples with diamonds standing for the moderately low quality. As can be observed in all cases much better results of quality evaluation can be obtained for PLA filaments and the most troublesome samples are those containing cracks and evaluated as moderately high or moderately low quality.

Another important issue is the selected number of orientation bins which can significantly influence the obtained results as shown in Figs. 4 and 5 where the

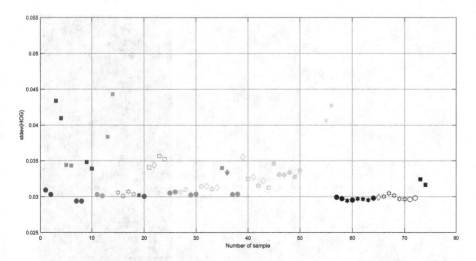

Fig. 6. Results obtained using proposed method based on the standard deviation of the HOG features calculated for signed orientations using 4 bins. (Color figure online)

results obtained for 8 and 3 orientation bins have been illustrated assuming the use of signed orientation. As it can be easily noticed, results obtained for 8 bins are quite similar to the use of 4 bins with unsigned orientation, although some changes can be observed e.g. for low quality green PLA samples (no. 13 and 14). Calculations conducted for three HOG bins have led to poor results as very similar values can be obtained for the samples with the same color and different quality (e.g. pink ABS or dark green ABS where low values obtained for low quality prints are surprising, similarly as in the other two cases).

Analyzing the results presented in Fig. 6 for the proposed method based on the standard deviation of the HOG features, calculated for signed orientations using 4 bins, a proper classification of the PLA prints, as well as the most of the ABS samples, can be made setting the threshold value at 0.032. The standard deviations of the HOG features obtained for high quality samples marked by solid circles for all colors of PLA filaments, as well as for all ABS materials except yellow, are smaller whereas the values obtained for all low quality samples are higher.

Considering the moderate high and moderate low quality samples as high and low respectively, the most of them can also be classified correctly even if they contain some small cracks (treated as not influencing the overall quality). Some problems occur only for two "salmon" color samples (no. 32 and 34) and the dark green sample no. 65. It should also be noted that the classification of the yellow samples is generally correct but due to the high brightness of the filament the threshold value should be adjusted. Nevertheless, the color calibration towards full independence on filament's color will be one of the directions of our future research.

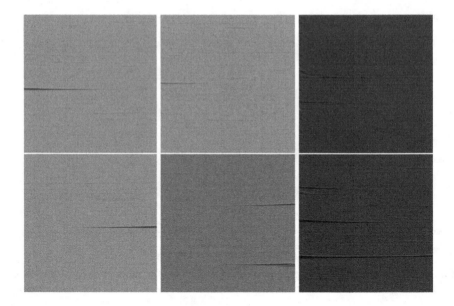

Fig. 7. Troublesome moderately low quality samples no. 23, 34 and 65 containing cracks which have been incorrectly classified (top row) in comparison to some moderately high quality samples no. 31, 42 and 67 (bottom row). (Color figure online)

Three mentioned moderately low quality samples with cracks, being troublesome for the proposed method are shown in the top row of Fig. 7. Nevertheless, their assessment as moderately low quality ones seems to be quite doubtful especially in comparison with the exemplary moderately high quality 3D prints illustrated in the bottom row of Fig. 7. In fact, two "salmon" color images shown in the left column of Fig. 7 are the illustrations of both sides of the same 3D print and some minor distortions which can be noticed in the upper images can hardly influence the overall results due to the assumed relatively large cell size.

3   Concluding Remarks and Future Challenges

The method of quality evaluation of the 3D printed surfaces proposed in the paper allows to determine the expected quality for almost all of the tested samples. Presented approach can be efficiently used for the classification of high and low quality surfaces and some minor issues are related to the proper classification of moderate quality samples. Since the proposed method is not fully color independent and is quite sensitive to the presence of cracks, it can be considered as the work being still in progress. Nevertheless, the results reported in the paper are promising and the proposed HOG based approach can be further examined.

Nevertheless, it should be noted that one of the most relevant issues influencing the results is the proper choice of the number of orientation bins. Considering the assumptions related to the expected presence of regular horizontal or vertical patterns representing individual filament's layers, after experimental verification, the best classification results have been obtained for 4 signed orientation bins using the standard deviation of the HOG features as the quality metric. The proposed approach allows to determine properly the quality of almost all samples used in our experiments in most cases independently on their color.

Our future work will be concentrated on the development of some crack detection algorithms as well as the incorporation of the additional color calibration in the proposed algorithm. Such a calibration should also consider some filament's physical properties such as e.g. its semi-transparency. The use of the combination of color information from different RGB channels or some other color spaces will be considered as well.

Another direction of our further research may be the combination of the presented algorithm with some of the previously developed methods based on entropy and texture analysis. The developed solution will also be verified using the images captured by cameras with additional automatic tuning of the HOG parameters dependent on the resolution of the captured images.

References

1. Chauhan, V., Surgenor, B.: A comparative study of machine vision based methods for fault detection in an automated assembly machine. Procedia Manuf. **1**, 416–428 (2015). https://doi.org/10.1016/j.promfg.2015.09.051
2. Chauhan, V., Surgenor, B.: Fault detection and classification in automated assembly machines using machine vision. Int. J. Adv. Manuf. Technol. **90**(9), 2491–2512 (2017). https://doi.org/10.1007/s00170-016-9581-5
3. Cheng, Y., Jafari, M.A.: Vision-based online process control in manufacturing applications. IEEE Transa. Autom. Sci. Eng. **5**(1), 140–153 (2008). https://doi.org/10.1109/TASE.2007.912058
4. Dalal, N., Triggs, B.: Histograms of oriented gradients for human detection. In: 2005 IEEE Computer Society Conference on Computer Vision and Pattern Recognition (CVPR 2005), vol. 1, pp. 886–893, June 2005. https://doi.org/10.1109/CVPR.2005.177
5. Fang, T., Jafari, M.A., Bakhadyrov, I., Safari, A., Danforth, S., Langrana, N.: Online defect detection in layered manufacturing using process signature. In: Proceedings of IEEE International Conference on Systems, Man and Cybernetics, San Diego, California, USA, vol. 5, pp. 4373–4378, October 1998. https://doi.org/10.1109/ICSMC.1998.727536
6. Fastowicz, J., Okarma, K.: Texture based quality assessment of 3D prints for different lighting conditions. In: Chmielewski, L.J., Datta, A., Kozera, R., Wojciechowski, K. (eds.) ICCVG 2016. LNCS, vol. 9972, pp. 17–28. Springer, Cham (2016). https://doi.org/10.1007/978-3-319-46418-3_2
7. Fastowicz, J., Okarma, K.: Entropy based surface quality assessment of 3D prints. In: Silhavy, R., Senkerik, R., Kominkova Oplatkova, Z., Prokopova, Z., Silhavy, P. (eds.) CSOC 2017. AISC, vol. 573, pp. 404–413. Springer, Cham (2017). https://doi.org/10.1007/978-3-319-57261-1_40
8. Gardner, M.R., et al.: In situ process monitoring in selective laser sintering using optical coherence tomography. Optical Engineering **57**, 1–5 (2018). https://doi.org/10.1117/1.OE.57.4.041407

9. Lane, B., Moylan, S., Whitenton, E.P., Ma, L.: Thermographic measurements of the commercial laser powder bed fusion process at NIST. Rapid Prototyp. J. **22**(5), 778–787 (2016). https://doi.org/10.1108/RPJ-11-2015-0161

10. Okarma, K., Fastowicz, J.: No-reference quality assessment of 3D prints based on the GLCM analysis. In: Proceedings of the 2016 21st International Conference on Methods and Models in Automation and Robotics (MMAR), pp. 788–793 (2016). https://doi.org/10.1109/MMAR.2016.7575237

11. Okarma, K., Fastowicz, J.: Quality assessment of 3D prints based on feature similarity metrics. In: Choraś, R.S. (ed.) IP&C 2016. AISC, vol. 525, pp. 104–111. Springer, Cham (2017). https://doi.org/10.1007/978-3-319-47274-4_12

12. Okarma, K., Fastowicz, J., Tecław, M.: Application of structural similarity based metrics for quality assessment of 3D prints. In: Chmielewski, L.J., Datta, A., Kozera, R., Wojciechowski, K. (eds.) ICCVG 2016. LNCS, vol. 9972, pp. 244–252. Springer, Cham (2016). https://doi.org/10.1007/978-3-319-46418-3_22

13. Straub, J.: Initial work on the characterization of additive manufacturing (3D printing) using software image analysis. Machines **3**(2), 55–71 (2015). https://doi.org/10.3390/machines3020055

14. Straub, J.: 3D printing cybersecurity: detecting and preventing attacks that seek to weaken a printed object by changing fill level. In: Proceedings of SPIE – Dimensional Optical Metrology and Inspection for Practical Applications VI, Anaheim, California, USA, vol. 10220, pp. 102200O-1–102200O-15, June 2017. https://doi.org/10.1117/12.2264575

15. Straub, J.: An approach to detecting deliberately introduced defects and microdefects in 3D printed objects. In: Proceedings of SPIE - Pattern Recognition and Tracking XXVII, Anaheim, California, USA, vol. 10203, pp. 102030L-1–102030L-14, June 2017. https://doi.org/10.1117/12.2264588

16. Straub, J.: Identifying positioning-based attacks against 3D printed objects and the 3D printing process. In: Proceedings of SPIE - Pattern Recognition and Tracking XXVII, Anaheim, California, USA, vol. 10203, pp. 1020304-1–1020304-13, June 2017. https://doi.org/10.1117/12.2264671

17. Straub, J.: Physical security and cyber security issues and human error prevention for 3D printed objects: detecting the use of an incorrect printing material. In: Proceedings of SPIE - Dimensional Optical Metrology and Inspection for Practical Applications VI, Anaheim, California, USA, vol. 10220, pp. 102200K-1–102200K-16, June 2017. https://doi.org/10.1117/12.2264578

18. Szkilnyk, G., Hughes, K., Surgenor, B.: Vision based fault detection of automated assembly equipment. In: Proceedings of the ASME/IEEE International Conference on Mechatronic and Embedded Systems and Applications, Parts A and B, Washington, DC, USA, vol. 3, pp. 691–697, August 2011. https://doi.org/10.1115/DETC2011-48493

19. Tourloukis, G., Stoyanov, S., Tilford, T., Bailey, C.: Data driven approach to quality assessment of 3D printed electronic products. In: Proceedings of the 38th International Spring Seminar on Electronics Technology (ISSE), Eger, Hungary, pp. 300–305, May 2015. https://doi.org/10.1109/ISSE.2015.7248010

Convolutional Neural Network-Based Action Recognition on Depth Maps

Jacek Trelinski and Bogdan Kwolek[✉]

AGH University of Science and Technology,
30 Mickiewicza, 30-059 Kraków, Poland
bkw@agh.edu.pl
http://home.agh.edu.pl/~bkw/contact.html

Abstract. In this paper, we present an algorithm for action recognition that uses only depth maps. We propose a set of handcrafted features to describe person's shape in noisy depth maps. We extract features by a convolutional neural network (CNN), which has been trained on multi-channel input sequences consisting of two consecutive depth maps and depth map projected onto an orthogonal Cartesian plane. We show experimentally that combining features extracted by the CNN and proposed features leads to better classification performance. We demonstrate that an LSTM trained on such aggregated features achieves state-of-the-art classification performance on UTKinect dataset. We propose a global statistical descriptor of temporal features. We show experimentally that such a descriptor has high discriminative power on time-series of concatenated CNN features with handcrafted features.

1 Introduction

Action recognition is an active research topic with plenty of potential applications [1,2]. Research has focused on extracting conventional RGB image sequences and handcrafted features. Compared to traditional RGB image sequences the depth maps offer range information and are less sensitive to illumination changes. However, most current approaches to action recognition on depth maps are based on handcrafted features [3], which in many scenarios can provide insufficient discriminative power. Typically, human actions are recognized by extracting spatio-temporal features that are classified by multi-class discriminative classifiers and/or extracting time-series that are classified by Dynamic Time Warping (DTW) algorithms or algorithms relying on generative statistical models such as Hidden Markov Models (HMMs). However, in case of use of DTW the classification time of image/depth map sequences can be significant, whereas HMMs require considerable amount of training data.

Typical activity recognition algorithm involves three main steps: feature extraction, quantization/dimension reduction and classification. Approaches based on depth maps perform recognition using features extracted from depth maps and/or skeleton features, which are provided by Kinect motion sensors.

© Springer Nature Switzerland AG 2018
L. J. Chmielewski et al. (Eds.): ICCVG 2018, LNCS 11114, pp. 209–221, 2018.
https://doi.org/10.1007/978-3-030-00692-1_19

Designing both effective and efficient features of depth sequence representations for action recognition is not an easy task due to several reasons [4]. The main reason is that in contrast to typical color features, the depth maps do not have as much texture. Typically, they are too noisy both spatially and temporally to apply gradient operators both in space and time or to compute the optical flow, which is very useful motion descriptor and has proven to be useful in action recognition on RGB image sequences [1]. Last but not least, action recognition is typically performed on depth maps acquired by a single depth sensor. Thus, body parts are typically occluded, which in general leads to poor robustness of global features [4]. In order to cope with the challenges mentioned above, the researches developed several features that are semi-local, highly discriminative and robust to occlusion [5].

Due to noisy character of depth maps that prevent applying local differential operators, the number of depth maps-based sequential approaches, which achieved competitive results in comparison to depth-maps or depth-maps space-time volume approaches is quite limited [6]. Since the skeleton data is one of the most natural features for modeling action dynamics from depth maps, the most successful approaches use skeleton information [7]. In [8] a feature called Histogram of 3D Joint Locations (HOJ3D) that encodes spatial occupancy information with regard to the skeleton root was proposed. The HOJ3D features are computed on action depth sequences, projected using LDA and then clustered into k posture visual words, which represent the prototypical poses of actions. The temporal evolutions of such visual words are modeled by discrete HMMs.

In this work, we present an algorithm for action recognition that uses only depth maps. We propose a set of handcrafted features to describe person's shape in noisy depth maps. We show experimentally that combining features extracted by a convolutional neural network (CNN) and proposed features leads to better classification performance. We show experimentally that LSTM trained on such aggregated features achieves state-of-the-art classification performance on UTKinect dataset. We propose a global statistical descriptor of temporal features. We show experimentally that such a descriptor has high discriminative power on time-series of concatenated CNN features with handcrafted features.

2   Datasets and Relevant Work

Introduction of low-cost 3D depth cameras such as MS Kinect have created many opportunities for human motion analysis and activity recognition. Li et al. [9] introduced a method for recognition of human actions from depth map sequences. It uses 3D contour points and does not require joint tracking. At the beginning, depth maps are projected onto three orthogonal Cartesian planes, and then a number of points along the contours of such projections are sampled for each frame. The motion dynamics is modeled by means of an action graph, whereas a Gaussian Mixture Model is used to robustly capture the statistical distribution of the points. The evaluation of the method has been performed on an introduced dataset, which later became known as the Microsoft Research (MSR) Action3D dataset. Experimental results have shown that high recognition accuracy can be achieved by sampling only about 1% of 3D points from the depth maps.

The MSR Action3D dataset [9] consists of twenty different actions, performed by ten different performers with up to three different repetitions. This makes in total 567 depth map sequences and each one contains depth maps and skeleton joint positions. As explained by the authors, ten sequences are not valid since the skeletons were either missing or wrong. The different actions are high arm wave, horizontal arm wave, hand catch, hammer, high throw, forward punch, draw X, draw tick, draw circle, two hand wave, hand clap, side-boxing, bend, side kick, forward kick, jogging, tennis swing, golf swing, tennis serve, pick up & throw. These gaming actions cover different variations of the motion of torso, arms and legs. The mentioned above actions are performed without any interaction with objects. Each subject is facing the Kinect and is positioned in the center of the scene. Two main challenges in action recognition arise due to the high similarity between different groups of actions and changes of the execution speed of actions.

The dataset is divided into three subsets of eight actions each, which are called AS1, AS2 and AS3. The AS1 and AS2 subsets group actions with similar movement, while AS3 subset groups more complex actions together. For each subset, there are three different tests, i.e., Test One (T1), Test Two (T2), and Cross Subject Test (CST). In the test T1, 1/3 of the subset is utilized as training and the rest as testing, whereas in the test T2, 2/3 of subjects are utilized as training and the rest ones are used as testing. In the CST test, half of the subset is employed as training and the rest as testing.

UTKinect dataset [10] contains actions of ten different people performing one of 10 actions (walk, sit down, stand up, pick up, carry, throw, push, pull, wave hands and clap hands) in an office setting. Each subject performs each action twice. The dataset contains 200 data sequences with depth information, RGB data and skeleton joint locations, which were recorded at 15 fps. The actions included in the discussed dataset are similar to those from MSR Action3D, but they present some additional challenges: the actions were registered from different views. What is more, there are occlusions caused by human-object interactions or by lack of some body parts in the camera's field of view. Thus, the discussed dataset is more challenging than MSR Action3D dataset due to viewpoint variation and absence of body parts in the camera's field of view.

As noticed in a recently published survey [3], among datasets utilized in evaluation of action recognition algorithms, MSR dataset and UTKinect dataset are the most popular and widely used. For MSR Action3D dataset, most of the studies follow the evaluation setting of Li et al. [9], such they first divide the twenty actions into three subsets AS1, AS2, AS3, each having eight actions. For each subset, the tests T1, T2 and CST are typically performed. Most papers report classification accuracy better than 90% in the first two tests. In the third test, however, the recognition performance is usually far lower. This means that many of these methods do not have good generalization ability when different performer is performing the action, even in the same environmental conditions. For instance, the method of Li et al. achieves 74.7% classification accuracy in the CST test, whereas 91.6% and 94.2% accuracies were achieved in tests T1 and T2, respectively.

As mentioned in Introduction, methods based on locations of the joints achieve far better classification performance than methods relying on depth maps or points clouds [7]. However, as noted in [11], skeleton-based methods are not applicable for applications, where skeleton data is not accessible. Since our method uses depth data only, below we discuss only depth-based methods.

In [12], depth images were projected onto three orthogonal planes and then accumulated to generate Depth Motion Maps (DMMs). Afterwards, the histograms of the oriented gradients (HOGs) computed from DMMs were utilized as feature descriptors. In [13] another method with no dependence on the skeletal joints information has been proposed. In the discussed method, random occupancy pattern (ROP) features were extracted from depth map sequences and a sparse coding was employed to encode these features. In [14], the depth map sequence is divided into a spatiotemporal grid. Afterwards, a simple feature called global occupancy pattern is extracted, where the number of the occupied pixels is stored for each grid cell. In [15] depth cuboid similarity features (DCSF) are built around the local spatio-temporal interest points (STIPs), which are extracted from depth map sequences. A method proposed in [16] does not require a skeleton tracker and calculates a histogram of oriented 4D surface normals (HON4D) in order to capture complex joint shape-motion cues at pixel-level. Unlike in [12], the temporal order of the events in the action sequences is encoded and not ignored. A recently proposed method [11] utilizes the from three projection views to capture motion cues and then employs LBPs for compact feature representation. In a more recent method [17], recognition of human action from depth maps is done using weighted hierarchical depth motion maps (WHDMM) and three-channel deep convolutional neural networks (3ConvNets).

3   Shape Features for Action Recognition

In our work we employ both handcrafted features and features extracted by convolutional neural networks (CNNs). In this Section we explain how we have extracted handcrafted and CNN features on the depth maps from datasets utilized in this work. The action performers are extracted from the background in the utilized datasets so no preprocessing step was needed to delineate the person.

3.1   Handcrafted Features

Given that pixels with non-zero values represent the performer on depth maps, only pixels with non-zero values were utilized in calculation of handcrafted features. The first feature is the ratio of the area occupied by the performer to the size of the whole depth map. The next nine features are calculated on the basis of the coordinates of pixels with non-zero depth values for axis x, y and z, i.e. coordinates of pixels belonging to the performer. Based on such pixel coordinates we calculated the following features: (i) standard deviation of the non-zero pixel coordinates for axis x, y and z, respectively, (ii) skewness of the non-zero pixel coordinates for axis x, y and z, and (iii) correlation between the non-zero pixel coordinates for axes xy, xz and yz. The handcrafted features were determined on depth maps scaled-down to sizes 60×60. For each depth map all features were normalized to zero mean and unit variance within the whole map.

3.2   Learning Convolutional Neural Network-Based Features

Convolutional Neural Network. Convolutional neural networks are a category of neural networks that have proven to be very effective in areas such as image recognition and classification [18]. A CNN consist of one or more convolutional layers, very often with a subsampling step, followed by one or more fully connected layers as in typical multilayer neural networks [19]. They are neural architectures that integrate feature extraction and classification in a single framework. The main advantage of CNNs is that they are easier to train and have fewer parameters than fully connected networks with the same number of hidden units. Like classical neural networks they can be trained with a version of the back-propagation algorithm.

In the proposed algorithms the input depth maps have size 60×60 pixels. The convolutional layer C1 consists of sixteen 5×5 convolutional filters that are followed by a subsampling layer. The next convolutional layer C2 operates on sixteen feature maps of size 28×28. It consists of sixteen 5×5 convolutional filters that are followed by a subsampling layer. It outputs sixteen feature maps of size 12×12. The next fully connected layer FC consists of 100 neurons. At the learning stage, the output of the CNN is a softmax layer with number of neurons equal to the number of actions to be recognized. Such a network has been learned on depth maps from training parts of depth map sequences. After the training, the layer before the softmax has been used to extract shape features. The shape features were then stored in feature vectors. Having on regard that a typical action sequence consists of a number of depth maps, which are represented by multidimensional vectors, the actions are represented as multidimensional, i.e. multivariate time-series, where on every time stamp (for single depth map) we have more than just one variable. Such multidimensional time-series are classified by algorithms, which are described in Sect. 4.

Learning Convolutional Neural Networks. The neural networks have been trained on depth maps of size 60×60. Initially we trained a CNN with single channel input map on all depth maps from training parts of datasets. As it turned out, better results can be achieved by CNNs that are trained on multi-channel depth maps. In the discussed representation of the action data, we determined pairs of depth images in such a way that first element of the pair is the current depth map and the second element is the next depth map. In other words, a single par consists of two consecutive depth maps from a given depth map sequence. The images from the pair were then stored in two channels of a three-channel data representation. The third channel contains the projected depth map onto an orthogonal Cartesian plane. This means that we generated a side-view of the depth map, which has then been scaled to size 60×60. In such a data representation the CNN network operates on 3-channel depth maps, where two maps are taken from the pair, whereas the third component is the projected depth map onto the orthogonal Cartesian plane. The size of the feature vector extracted by the CNN is equal to 100.

4   Action Classification

In this Section we explain how the actions are classified using the proposed shape features. In Subsect. 4.1 we present action classification with logistic regression. Afterwards, in Subsect. 4.2 we outline dynamic time warping, which has been used to classify actions represented as time-series of features extracted by the CNN. In last Subsection we outline the LSTM network, which has been used to classify actions on the basis of vectors of CNN features as well as vectors consisting of concatenated CNN features and handcrafted features.

4.1   Action Classification Using Global Statistical Description of Temporal Features

The handcrafted features, which describe person's shape in a single frame were stored in multidimensional vectors to represent actions. Given such a multidimensional vector, i.e. multivariate time-series, a global statistical description of temporal features has been calculated. For each time-series we calculated the mean, standard deviation and skewness. This means that a single action is represented by a vector of size thirty. Alternatively, at the frame-level we concatenated the handcrafted features with CNN features. Having on regard that the size of feature vector extracted by the CNN is 100, the size of the vector with concatenated handcrafted and CNN features has size 110. Thus, the size of the vector representing the action sequence is equal to 330. The recognition of actions has been achieved using classical logistic regression classifier [20].

4.2   DTW-based Action Classification

In time-series classification problem one of the most effective methods is the 1-NN-DTW, which is a special k-nearest neighbor classifier with $k = 1$ and a dynamic time warping for distance measurement. DTW is a method that calculates an optimal match between two given sequences [21]. The sequences are warped non-linearly in the time dimension to find the best match between two samples such that when the same pattern exists in both sequences, the distance is smaller. Denote $D(i, j)$ as the DTW distance between sub-sequences $x[1 : j]$ and $y[1 : j]$. Then the DTW distance between x and y can be computed by the dynamic programming algorithm using the following iterative equation:

$$D(i, j) = \min\{D(i - 1, j - 1), D(i - 1, j), D(i, j - 1)\} + |x_i, y_j| \qquad (1)$$

The time complexity of calculation of DTW distance is $O(nm)$, where n and m are the length of x and y, respectively.

4.3   LSTM-Based Action Classification

In this Subsection we describe action recognition algorithm that is composed of LSTM recurrent layers, which are capable of automatically learning and modeling temporal dependencies. Recently, such architectures demonstrated state-of-the-art recognition performance in speech recognition [22].

Long Short-Term Memory Units. Unlike traditional neural networks, recurrent neural networks (RNNs), take as their input not just the current input example, but also what they perceived one step back in time. RNNs allow cycles in the network graph such that the output from neuron n in layer l at time step t is fed via weighted connections to each neuron in the layer l (including the neuron i) at time step $t + 1$. One of the main issues in RNN training is the vanishing gradient. In order to cope with this undesirable effect a variation of recurrent net with so-called Long Short-Term Memory units, or LSTMs [23], were proposed by the Hochreiter & Schmidhuber as a solution to the vanishing gradient problem. LSTMs are recurrent neural networks that contain a memory to model temporal dependencies in time-series. An LSTM uses a memory cell with a gated input, gated output and gated feedback loop. In such a cell, information can be stored in, written to, or read from a cell, like data in a computers memory. An additional enhancement is the use of bidirectional layers. In a bidirectional RNN, there are two parallel RNNs, where one of them reads the input sequence forwards and the other reads the input sequence backwards.

It is worth noting that an LSTM network can be discriminative or generative. This means that LSTM can be used for classification tasks or to generate similar sequences like the training samples. In this paper, we utilize the discriminative ability of the LSTM for classification of series of action features.

Learning LSTMs. The actions are classified by a neural network with one hidden layer of LSTM cells. The input layer of the neural network operates on a given number of the features per time step. This means that descriptors extracted by the CNN (or CNN features concatenated with the handcrafted features of person's shape) are provided to the LSTM network one at a time. Depending on the variant of the algorithm, there are 100 (CNN operating on single channel depth maps), or 110 (handcrafted shape features concatenated with CNN features) input neurons (one for each element in the descriptor), 50 memory blocks (each with a memory cell and an input, forget and output gate), and 10 or 20 output neurons (one for each action class). The output layer contains neurons that are connected to LSTM outputs at each time step. In a single time step the input neurons are activated with descriptor values. Afterwards, the memory cells and the gates determine activation values based on the input values and on previous memory cell states. Then, the activations computed in such a way propagate to the output layer, and the process described above is repeated for the next descriptor from the action sequence. Finally, the softmax activation function is applied for each output neuron. Owing to the softmax the sum of all outputs is equal to one.

5 Results and Discussion

The proposed framework has been evaluated on two publicly available bench-mark datasets: MSR Action3D dataset and UTKinect dataset. The datasets were chosen due to their popularities in action recognition community. In the evaluations and all experiments, we used 557 sequences of MSR Action3D dataset. Half of the subjects were used as training data and the rest of the subjects as test data. It is worth noting that the classification setting employs half of the subjects as the training data and the rest of them as test data, which is different in comparison to evaluations based on AS1, AS2 and AS3 data splits and averaging the classification accuracies over such data splits. The classification performances obtained in the discussed setting are lower in comparison to classification performances achieved in AS1, AS2, AS3 setting due to larger variations across the same actions performed by different subjects. The cross-subject evaluation scheme that was utilized in [15,17] has been adopted in all experiments. It is worth noting that this scheme is different from the scheme employed in [8], where more subjects have been utilized for the training.

Table 1 shows recognition performance on challenging UTKinect dataset that has been achieved by logistic regression classifier using shape features and global statistical descriptors of temporal features. As we can observe, the concatenation of CNN and handcrafted features at frame-level leads to better classification performance in comparison to algorithm using only CNN features.

Table 1. Recognition performance on UTKinect achieved by logistic regression classifier using frame-features and global statistical descriptors of temporal features.

	Accuracy	Precision	Recall	F1-score
CNN	0.8804	0.8999	0.8804	0.8723
CNN + handcrafted	0.9130	0.9172	0.9130	0.9094

Table 2 shows recognition performance that has been obtained by 1-NN-DTW and LSTM classifiers using time-series of shape features. The first row in discussed table presents results that have been achieved by DTW calculating Euclidean distance on CNN features. The second row in Table 2 shows the recognition performance that has been obtained using the CNN features and the

Table 2. Recognition performance on UTKinect dataset using CNN features, achieved by 1-NN-DTW and LSTM classifiers.

Features	Classifier	Accuracy	Precision	Recall	F1-score
CNN	DTW	0.8804	0.9127	0.8804	0.8824
CNN	LSTM	0.9457	0.9532	0.9457	0.9455
CNN + handcrafted	LSTM	0.9565	0.9584	0.9565	0.9551

LSTM classifier. As we can notice, the LSTM classifier operating on CNN features achieves considerably better results in comparison to 1-NN-DTW classifier using CNN features. The best results on UTKinect dataset were achieved by the LSTM operating on concatenated.

CNN features and handcrafted features at frame-level. The classification accuracy of the proposed LSTM-based algorithm for action recognition on depth maps is better in comparison to classification accuracy achieved by the state-of-the-art algorithm [17], which is also based on a CNN.

Table 3 presents the recognition performance of the proposed method compared with the previous depth-based methods on the UTKinect dataset. As we can notice, the proposed method outperforms both methods based on handcrafted features [15, 24, 25] as well as recently proposed methods that are based on deep convolutional neural networks. Our method algorithm considerably from the WHDMM + 3DConvNets method that employs weighted hierarchical depth motion maps (WHDMMs) and three 3D ConvNets. The WHDMMs are employed at several temporal scales to encode spatiotemporal motion patterns of actions into 2D spatial structures. In order to provide sufficient amount of training data, the 3D points are rotated and then used to synthesize new exemplars. In contrast, we recognize actions using LSTM or DTW, which operate on CNN features, concatenated with handcrafted features. The improved performance of our method may suggest that the proposed method has better viewpoint tolerance than other depth-based algorithms, including [17].

Table 3. Comparative recognition performance of the proposed method and previous depth-based methods on the UTKinect dataset.

Method	Accuracy [%]
DSTP + DSF [15]	78.78
Random Forests [24]	87.90
SNV [25]	88.89
WHDMM + 3DConvNets [17]	90.91
Proposed Method	**95.65**

Table 4 presents results that were achieved on MSR Action3D dataset. As we can observe, the best results were achieved by logistic regression classifier trained on the global statistical descriptor of time-series, consisting of vectors of concatenated CNN and handcrafted features.

Table 5 shows the recognition performance of the proposed method compared with the previous depth-based methods on the MSR-Action3D dataset. The recognition performance of the proposed framework has been determined using the same experimental cross-subject setting as that in [26], where subjects 1, 3, 5, 7, and 9 were utilized for training and subjects 2, 4, 6, 8, and 10 were utilized for testing. As we can notice, the proposed method achieves better

Table 4. Recognition performance on MSR Action3D dataset using CNN features, CNN features concatenated with handcrafted features, which has been achieved by 1-NN-DTW, LSTM and logistic regression classifiers, respectively.

Features	Classifier	Accuracy	Precision	Recall	F1-score
CNN	DTW	0.8109	0.8292	0.8109	0.8082
CNN	LSTM	0.7091	0.7106	0.7091	0.6978
CNN + handcrafted	LSTM	0.7309	0.7234	0.7273	0.7082
CNN	logistic regression	0.8254	0.8361	0.8255	0.8167
CNN + handcrafted	Logistic regression	0.8472	0.8598	0.8473	0.8440

classification accuracy in comparison to methods proposed in [9,26], and it has worse performance in comparison to recently proposed methods relying both on handcrafted features [12,27] and features extracted by deep learning methods [17]. One of the main reasons for this is insufficient amount of training data. It is worth noting that method [17] uses synthesized training samples on the basis of 3D points. As shown in Table 5, on more challenging UTKinect dataset the discussed method [17] achieved worse results in comparison to results obtained by our algorithm.

Table 5. Comparative recognition accuracy of the proposed method and previous depth-based methods on the MSR-Action3D dataset.

Method	Accuracy [%]
Bag of 3D Points [28]	74.70
Actionlet Ensemble [26]	82.22
Our Method	84.72
Depth Motion Maps [12]	88.73
Range Sample [27]	95.62
WHDMM + 3DConvNets [17]	100

The results presented above were achieved using CNNs trained on pairs of consecutive depth maps as well as depth map projections. Without the depth map projections the recognition accuracy of the algorithm is almost two percent smaller in comparison to algorithms not using depth map projections. The recognition accuracy of the algorithm using CNNs trained on single depth maps instead of pairs of consecutive depth maps is smaller more than seven percent.

The proposed method has been implemented in Python using Theano and Lasagne deep learning frameworks. The Lasagne library is built on top of Theano. The values of the initial weights in CNNs and LSTM networks were drawn randomly from uniform distributions. The cross-entropy loss function has been used in the minimization. The CNN networks were trained using SGD with momentum.

The LSTM has been trained using backpropagation through time (BPTT) [29]. Much computations were performed on a PC computer equipped with an NVIDIA GPU card. The source code of the proposed algorithms is freely available[1].

6   Conclusions

In this work a method for action recognition on depth map sequences using concatenated CNN features with handcrafted ones has been proposed. Due to considerable amount of noise in depth maps that prevent applying local differential operators, the number of depth maps-based sequential approaches is quite limited. We demonstrated experimentally that a sequential algorithm, in which an LSTM or a DTW operates on time-series of CNN features can achieve superior results in comparison to results achieved by state-of-the-art algorithms, including recently proposed deep learning algorithms. The method has been evaluated on two widely employed benchmark datasets and compared with state-of-the-art methods. We demonstrated experimentally that on challenging UTKinect dataset the proposed method achieves superior results in comparison to results achieved by recent methods. In comparison to recently proposed WHDMM+ 3DConvNets method [17] it achieves about 5% improvement in the recognition accuracy in the cross-subject evaluation scheme. In our experiments, data of subjects with even numbers was used for learning of the models, whereas data of subjects with odd numbers were utilized for testing the classifiers.

Acknowledgments. This work was supported by Polish National Science Center (NCN) under a research grant 2014/15/B/ST6/02808.

References

1. Aggarwal, J., Ryoo, M.: Human activity analysis: a review. ACM Comput. Surv. **43**(3), 16:1–16:43 (2011)
2. Malawski, F., Kwolek, B.: Real-time action detection and analysis in fencing footwork. In: 40th International Conference on Telecommunications and Signal Processing (TSP), pp. 520–523 (2017)
3. Liang, B., Zheng, L.: A survey on human action recognition using depth sensors. In: International Conference on Digital Image Computing: Techniques and Applications, pp. 1–8 (2015)
4. Aggarwal, J., Xia, L.: Human activity recognition from 3D data: a review. Pattern Recogn. Lett. **48**, 70–80 (2014)
5. Chen, L., Wei, H., Ferryman, J.: A survey of human motion analysis using depth imagery. Pattern Recogn. Lett. **34**(15), 1995–2006 (2013)
6. Ye, M., Zhang, Q., Wang, L., Zhu, J., Yang, R., Gall, J.: A survey on human motion analysis from depth data. In: Grzegorzek, M., Theobalt, C., Koch, R., Kolb, A. (eds.) Time-of-Flight and Depth Imaging. Sensors, Algorithms, and Applications. LNCS, vol. 8200, pp. 149–187. Springer, Heidelberg (2013). https://doi.org/10.1007/978-3-642-44964-2_8

---

[1] https://github.com/tjacek/DeepActionLearning.

7. Lo Presti, L., La Cascia, M.: 3D skeleton-based human action classification. Pattern Recogn. **53**(C), 130–147 (2016)
8. Xia, L., Chen, C.C., Aggarwal, J.: View invariant human action recognition using histograms of 3D joints. In: CVPR Workshops, pp. 20–27 (2012)
9. Li, W., Zhang, Z., Liu, Z.: Action recognition based on a bag of 3D points. In: IEEE International Conference on Computer Vision and Pattern Recognition - Workshops, pp. 9–14 (2010)
10. Xia, L., Chen, C., Aggarwal, J.: Human detection using depth information by Kinect. In: CVPR 2011 Workshops, pp. 15–22 (2011)
11. Chen, C., Jafari, R., Kehtarnavaz, N.: Action recognition from depth sequences using depth motion maps-based local binary patterns. In: 2015 IEEE Winter Conference on Applications of Computer Vision, pp.1092–1099 (2015)
12. Yang, X., Zhang, C., Tian, Y.L.: Recognizing actions using depth motion maps-based histograms of oriented gradients. In: Proceedings of the 20th ACM International Conference on Multimedia, pp. 1057–1060. ACM (2012)
13. Wang, J., Liu, Z., Chorowski, J., Chen, Z., Wu, Y.: Robust 3D action recognition with random occupancy patterns. In: Fitzgibbon, A., Lazebnik, S., Perona, P., Sato, Y., Schmid, C. (eds.) ECCV 2012. LNCS, pp. 872–885. Springer, Heidelberg (2012). https://doi.org/10.1007/978-3-642-33709-3_62
14. Vieira, A.W., Nascimento, E.R., Oliveira, G.L., Liu, Z., Campos, M.F.M.: STOP: space-time occupancy patterns for 3D action recognition from depth map sequences. In: Alvarez, L., Mejail, M., Gomez, L., Jacobo, J. (eds.) CIARP 2012. LNCS, vol. 7441, pp. 252–259. Springer, Heidelberg (2012). https://doi.org/10.1007/978-3-642-33275-3_31
15. Xia, L., Aggarwal, J.: Spatio-temporal depth cuboid similarity feature for activity recognition using depth camera. In: IEEE International Conference on Computer Vision and Pattern Recognition, pp. 2834–2841 (2013)
16. Oreifej, O., Liu, Z.: HON4D: histogram of oriented 4D normals for activity recognition from depth sequences. In: IEEE Internatiponal Conference on Computer Vision and Pattern Recognition, pp. 716–723 (2013)
17. Wang, P., Li, W., Gao, Z., Zhang, J., Tang, C., Ogunbona, P.: Action recognition from depth maps using deep convolutional neural networks. IEEE Trans. Hum. Mach. Syst. **46**(4), 498–509 (2016)
18. Schmidhuber, J.: Deep learning in neural networks: an overview. Neural Netw. **61**, 85–117 (2015)
19. LeCun, Y., Haffner, P., Bottou, L., Bengio, Y.: Object recognition with gradient-based learning. Shape, Contour and Grouping in Computer Vision. LNCS, vol. 1681, pp. 319–345. Springer, Heidelberg (1999). https://doi.org/10.1007/3-540-46805-6_19
20. Bishop, C.M.: Pattern Recognition and Machine Learning. Information Science and Statistics. Springer, New York (2006)
21. Paliwal, K., Agarwal, A., Sinha, S.: A modification over Sakoe and Chiba's dynamic time warping algorithm for isolated word recognition. Signal Process. **4**(4), 329–333 (1982)
22. Sainath, T., Vinyals, O., Senior, A., Sak, H.: Convolutional, long short-term memory, fully connected deep neural networks. In: IEEE International Conference on Acoustics, Speech and Signal Processing, pp. 4580–4584 (2015)
23. Hochreiter, S., Schmidhuber, J.: Long short-term memory. Neural Comput. **9**(8), 1735–1780 (1997)
24. Zhu, Y., Chen, W., Guo, G.: Fusing multiple features for depth-based action recognition. ACM Trans. Intell. Syst. Technol. **6**(2), 18:1–18:20 (2015)

25. Yang, X., Tian, Y.L.: Super normal vector for activity recognition using depth sequences. In: IEEE International Conference on Computer Vision and Pattern Recognition, pp. 804–811 (2014)
26. Wu, Y.: Mining actionlet ensemble for action recognition with depth cameras. In: IEEE International Conference on Computer Vision and Pattern Recognition, pp. 1290–1297 (2012)
27. Lu, C., Jia, J., Tang, C.: Range-sample depth feature for action recognition. In: IEEE International Conference on Computer Vision and Pattern Recognition, pp. 772–779 (2014)
28. Ji, X., Liu, H.: Advances in view-invariant human motion analysis: a review. IEEE Trans. Syst. Man Cybern. Part C **40**(1), 13–24 (2010)
29. Werbos, P.: Backpropagation through time: what it does and how to do it. Proceedings of the IEEE **78**(10), 1550–1560 (1990)

An Integrated Procedure for Calibrating and Distortion Correction of the Structure Sensor and Stereo-Vision Depth Sensors

Dariusz Rzeszotarski$^{(\boxtimes)}$ and Pawel Strumillo

Institute of Electronics, Łódź University of Technology, 90-924 Łódź, Poland
{dariusz.rzeszotarski,pawel.strumillo}@p.lodz.pl

Abstract. The paper presents a calibration procedure of a 3D scene reconstruction system consisting of an active depth sensor (Structure Sensor) and a stereo camera with a wide view angle lenses. The wide angle lenses with large radial distortions used in the stereoscopic part of the system require application of a fish-eye model for correcting geometric distortions while for the infrared camera of the Structure Sensor a traditional pinhole model is sufficient. Calibration of the system comprises also a procedure for correcting depth distortions introduced by the Structure Sensor device. A simple yet efficient method for calibrating the cameras using functions provided by OpenCV library is proposed. The system is a part of a device helping visually impaired people to navigate in the environment.

1 Introduction

Nowadays 3D computer vision finds wider and wider applications. In case of mobile and autonomous systems the 3D data about the environment geometry is usually provided either by passive sensors - stereo cameras or active depth sensors like the Structure Sensor (SS) or Kinect devices [2,12]. Both approaches have their advantages and shortcomings.

Active depth sensors are based mainly on infrared structured-light or Time-of-Flight (ToF) technologies [2,4,12]. An example of a ToF camera is Kinect 2 device while the first versions of the Kinect and the Structure Sensor use infrared structured light pattern projector and a low range infrared CMOS camera. The main constraint of active infrared depth sensors is that their applications are limited to indoors spaces or at least to lighting conditions in which CMOS camera is not blinded and is able to recognize infrared pattern reflected by an object being observed. In case of the SS device the range of depth reconstruction is 400–4000 mm. The 3D depth map is delivered by the SS device with 30 fps rate with 640×480 spatial resolution and with high depth accuracy of 0.12–1% depending on the distance to an object (the higher the distance the lower the accuracy).

On the other hand stereo-vision systems are more customizable. There are many stereo-vision camera manufactures providing ready to use cameras with

© Springer Nature Switzerland AG 2018
L. J. Chmielewski et al. (Eds.): ICCVG 2018, LNCS 11114, pp. 222–233, 2018.
https://doi.org/10.1007/978-3-030-00692-1_20

different base length and distance range. There are also stereo-vision kits available with two synchronized cameras that can be mounted with the customizable base length and optics. However, stereo-vision systems contrary to active depth sensor perform poorly in low lighting conditions. Therefore the two depth sensor types are complementary regarding lighting conditions.

A 3D reconstruction module presented in this paper is a part of the device helping visually impaired people to navigate [1]. It should reconstruct the 3D scene in front of the user in different lighting conditions in indoor and outdoor environments. Therefore the two passive and active types of sensors are being used.

To take advantage of complementary features of the two sensors and to reconstruct 3D structure of a scene regardless of lighting conditions a fusion of the depth maps from both types of the sensors is applied. To that end calibration of the system is necessary. Calibration of the system includes evaluation of optical parameters of the sensors and relative positions of reference frames associated with each sensor and also evaluation and correction of distortions of depth data provided by the SS device.

2 Literature Review

Calibration of a 3D reconstruction system refers to estimation of the optical parameters of the cameras and their relative positions [11]. Calibration of an active depth sensor also includes establishing a relation between the depth data provided by the sensor and their true values. Recent literature is abundant with articles describing various methods of calibration between the depth sensor and single RGB camera. Smisek [7] et al. calibrate the Kinect device in three steps: (1) they estimate cameras intrinsic parameters (focal length in pixels, principal point coordinates, geometrical distortion coefficients) and the relative position of RGB and IR cameras, (2) they introduce the depth camera model describing a relation between the disparity value provided by the Kinect and the depth value, (3) depth model coefficients are computed by optimizing their values to best fit the model using the calibration points and their projections onto the best plane.

Herrera et al. [6] propose a calibration method of the Kinect device from RGB images and depth images pairs. The main disadvantage of the method, however, is the requirement of manual marking of four corners of the calibration object in depth images. Zhang and Zhang [13] also propose the calibration method using only RGB and the depth images. They introduce linear depth model relating the depth values with the corrected ones. All the parameters are finally refined by non-linear optimization.

Darwish [3] calibrates the SS device along with RGB camera mounted in the iPad and introduces analytical spatial distortion model of disparity from the depth sensor assuming radial and tangential nature of the distortions.

The distortion models used in the reviewed literature use disparity values. As Karan [9,10] pointed out current active depth sensor devices use OpenNI API which provides only depth values, and taking this into account, he introduces the first nonlinear correction model in depth domain although omitting spatial distortions.

The system introduced in this article consists of stereo camera. The field of view (FoV) of this camera differs significantly from FoV of the SS depth sensor. Our method enables to build fused depth or disparity maps in real time. The calibration method described in this article addresses the following issues: (1) choosing an appropriate camera model describing optical properties of wide-angle lenses; (2) evaluation of relative position of sensors defined by different camera models (pinhole and fish-eye); (3) correction of spatial depth distortions of the SS device instead of just spatial disparity distortions (as the OpenNI library provides for the depth data).

3 Description of the System

The system consists of stereo camera LI-OV580-STEREO from Leopard Imagining and the Structure Sensor from Occipital Fig. 1a. The relative position of the cameras is shown in Fig. 1b. The figure shows top view of the coordinate frames associated with each camera. L, R denote left and right images of the stereo camera, IR - is the CMOS camera of the SS device that is sensitive to infrared radiation and thus is able to visualise the pattern being projected onto the scene by the infrared structure light projector (IR_P).

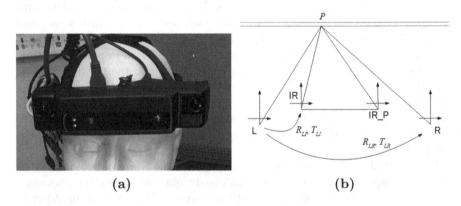

(a)   (b)

Fig. 1. The 3D reconstruction system: **a** The headgear with stereo and SS depth sensors. **b** Relative positions of the sensors and the parameters describing their relative positions.

3D coordinates of point P in the world reference frame are: $X = [X, Y, Z]^T$. Point P is visualised and its image coordinates are $x_L = [x_L, y_L]^T$, $x_R = [x_R, y_R]^T$ in the left and right camera respectively.

The input images of the stereo camera are rectified i.e. their horizontal lines are aligned, i.e. the projections of point P defined in a 3D scene onto the rectified images have the same vertical components of their image coordinates $x_L = [x_L, y_L]^T$, $x_R = [x_R, y_R]^T$, $y_L = y_R = y$. Knowing the rectified image coordinates x_L, x_R of a given point P its 3D coordinates in the left camera reference frame can be calculated using the following formula:

$$Z_L = f_x \frac{\|T_{LR}\|}{d}, \quad X_L = Z_L \frac{x_L - c_x}{f_x}, \quad Y_L = Z_L \frac{y_L - c_y}{f_y}, \tag{1}$$

where $d = x_L - x_R$ is called disparity, f_x, f_y, c_x, c_y are intrinsic parameters of the left and right rectified images which are the same for both (L and R) cameras; f_x, f_y are horizontal and vertical focal lengths expressed in pixels, c_x, c_y are image coordinates of the principal points (principal point is defined as intersection of Z axis with image plane), $\|T_{LR}\|$ is length of the translation vector between the left and right camera.

The same point P can be located with the use of the SS device: a specific infrared pattern is projected by IR_P onto point P and its image is visible in infrared camera IR. The IR image containing the infrared pattern is compared to the image of a plane placed at a given distance and containing the same infrared pattern. For each pixel p_I with coordinates $x_I = [x_I, y_I]^T$ represented by a surrounding area with a distinguishable infrared pattern a corresponding pixel x_I' with the same pattern is found in the saved image. The difference in horizontal components of coordinates of the matched pixels is a disparity value inversely proportional to the distance likewise as in a stereo vision system as given in Eq. (1). The matching algorithm is implemented in the SS device and the output is a depth map, i.e. a 2-D array with depth values of respective pixels.

R_{LR}, T_{LR} denote extrinsic parameters (the rotation matrix and the translation vector) relating X_L coordinates in the reference frame of the left camera to X_R coordinates in the reference frame of the right camera:

$$X_L = R_{LR} X_R + T_{LR} \tag{2}$$

R_{LI}, T_{LI} denote extrinsic parameters (the rotation matrix and the translation vector) relating X_L coordinates in the reference frame of the left camera to X_I coordinates in the reference frame of the infrared camera (IR) of the SS device:

$$X_L = R_{LI} X_I + T_{LI} \tag{3}$$

The relation between 3D coordinates $X_{L\|}$ in the rectified left camera reference frame and 3D coordinates X_I in the infrared camera reference frame is as follows:

$$X_{L\|} = R_L R_{LI} X_I + R_L T_{LI}, \tag{4}$$

where R_L is a rotation matrix relating 3D coordinates after and before rectification: $X_{L\|} = R_L X_L$.

It is assumed that the depth map refers to a 2-D array with Z components of 3D coordinates. The point cloud map term refers to 2-D array with X, Y and Z

3D coordinates. The depth map produced by the SS device is a 2-D array that associates each pixel $p(x_I, y_I)$ from the corresponding infrared image with a Z_I component of $\boldsymbol{X_I}$ coordinate of a point from the object being observed. The X_I and Y_I components of a given element from the depth map can be retrieved using the formula:

$$X_I = \frac{Z_I}{f_{Ix}}(x_I - c_{Ix}), \quad Y_I = \frac{Z_I}{f_{Iy}}(y_I - c_{Iy}), \tag{5}$$

where IR camera intrinsic parameters $f_{Ix}, f_{Iy}, c_{Ix}, c_{Iy}$ can be retrieved from the SS device using the OpenNI SDK or from the calibration procedure described in the next section. Using Eq. (1) the depth or a 3D point cloud map can be also computed from the disparity map based on the rectified images from the stereo camera.

4   Calibration

Calibration of the system requires evaluation of the following parameters: (1) intrinsic parameters of each single camera: the left and right camera of the stereo pair and an infrared CMOS camera from the SS device. (2) extrinsic parameters describing a relative position of the left and right camera of the stereo vision system and relative position of the left and infrared camera from the SS device; the extrinsic parameters are defined by Eqs. (2) and (3).

Calibration results of the three cameras (i.e. two cameras from the stereo vision system and one infrared camera of the SS device) with the use of a standard pinhole model with radial and tangential distortions are strongly vulnerable to positioning of the calibration board.

This is because we have used calibration procedures with fish-eye camera model for the left and right camera. The model was introduced in [8] and is available in fish-eye module of the OpenCV library.

The OpenCV library provides procedures for evaluating intrinsic parameters of a camera described with pinhole or fish-eye camera models. It also provides procedures for evaluation of relative position of two cameras described either by the pinhole or fish-eye camera models. The problem is that the left-infrared pair consists of cameras depicted by two different models: pinhole and fish-eye respectively. Therefore first intrinsic parameters of the left and right cameras and their relative position (R_{LR}, T_{LR}) was computed with the use of OpenCV calibration procedures for fish-eye model. Then using pairs of infrared images and rectified left images of the calibration board, intrinsic parameters of the infrared camera and its relative position (from Eq. (4)) against rectified left camera were computed by applying OpenCV calibration procedures for pinhole camera model.

The quality of the applied rectification procedure is evaluated as an average difference between $y-$components of corners found in the left and right rectified image in each position of the calibration board:

$$\Delta_{\|y} = \sum_{j=1}^{M}\sum_{i=1}^{N} \frac{|y_{Lji} - y_{Rji}|}{MN} \tag{6}$$

where j is the index of the calibration board position, M is the number of calibration board positions, i is the index of corners pair, N is the number of corners in the calibration board.

The quality of evaluation of the extrinsic parameters relating positions of the infrared camera from the SS device to the left RGB camera is measured by average difference between image coordinates x'_{Ii} of corners found in the infrared image and image coordinates x_{Ii} of corners reconstructed from the stereo camera and reprojected onto the infrared image:

$$\Delta_{LRI} = \sum_{j=1}^{M} \sum_{i=1}^{N} \frac{\|x'_{Iji} - x_{Iji}\|}{MN} \tag{7}$$

where j is index of calibration board position, M is the number of the calibration board positions, i is the index of corners, N is the number of corners in the calibration board.

Calibration Results

Table 1 shows average reprojection error in pixels for each calibration procedure used for estimation of extrinsic parameters $(R_{LR}, T_{LR}, R_{LI}, T_{LI})$. The values of the stereo camera reprojection errors Δ_{LR} are smaller for the fish-eye camera model than for the pinhole camera model.

Table 1. The average re-projection error in pixels of the calibration procedure: Δ_{LR}, Δ_{LI} - left-right, left-infrared relative position. Δ_{LRI} is the average reprojection error between stereo and IR camera. $\Delta_{\|y}$ is the average difference in y-components of corners image coordinates in the rectified left-right pair.

Camera model	$\Delta_{LR}[pix]$	$\Delta_{LI}[pix]$	$\Delta_{LRI}[pix]$	$\Delta_{\|y}[pix]$
pinhole	0.780	0.790	0.631	0.436
fish-eye	0.520	0.678	0.611	0.190

The reprojection error Δ_{LRI} calculated with use of Eq. (7) can be applied to evaluate the quality of R_{LI}, T_{LI} used for re-projecting of depth maps from the SS device onto the left rectified RGB image. Comparing the values of Δ_{LRI} from Table 1 shows that the reprojection error does not depend on choosing the model of the left RGB camera. This result is not surprising since the model of the infrared camera remains the same. On the other hand Table 1 shows that the quality of rectification evaluated as average difference between y-components of corners found in the left and right image is smaller if the fish-eye camera model is chosen for stereo cameras instead of the pinhole camera model.

5   Evaluation and Correction of Depth Distortions

In order to evaluate the quality of depth data provided by the SS device the following setup is proposed. As Smisek in [7] noticed in case of the Kinect device a misalignment can occur between the infrared image and the depth image. In case of the Kinect the misalignment was noticed both along the horizontal and vertical axis of the image.

In order to evaluate the misalignment between the infrared and depth images from the SS device a calibration board was used. First, corners from the calibration board were found in an left RGB image. Next, based on the image coordinates of the found corners and their known 3D position in the calibration board reference frame the calibration board position in the left RGB camera reference frame was evaluated. Knowing the dimensions of the calibration board additional reference points were added at the edges of the board (Fig. 2a). Since the system was calibrated the reference points were projected onto the depth image. As the Fig. 2b shows in case of the SS device only the horizontal misalignment can be noticed.

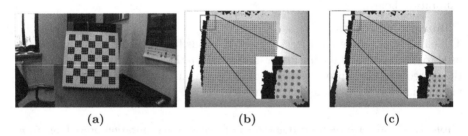

| (a) | (b) | (c) |

Fig. 2. (a) Reference points for misalignment evaluation. (b) Misaligned depth images. (c) Aligned depth images

In order to find the value of the misalignment the depth image was shifted by 0.1 pixel till the reprojected reference points were aligned with the edges of the calibration board. Figure 2c shows that the depth image shifted horizontally by 3 pixels can be regarded as aligned.

As noticed in [3,5,7] depth sensors based on a structure light introduce spatial nonlinear depth distortions. To evaluate the spatial depth distortions introduced by the SS device a sequence of depth images with plane object (plane wall) at distances in the range of 1000 to 3000 mm was taken. For each depth image from the sequence (using Eq. 5) a set of 3D coordinates $X_D = [X_D, Y_D, Z_D]$ evenly distributed with 5 pixel step along x and y axis was chosen. As the set of 3D coordinates X_D belongs to the wall plane object it was fitted to a plane equation. For each point X_D from the set a plane fit residual was calculated as:

$$\Delta Z = Z_D - Z_p, \tag{8}$$

where Z_p is the depth component of projection of X_D 3D coordinate onto the fitted plane.

Figures 3a, b show 3D images of spatial distribution of plane fit residuals of depth image (red dots) from the SS device.

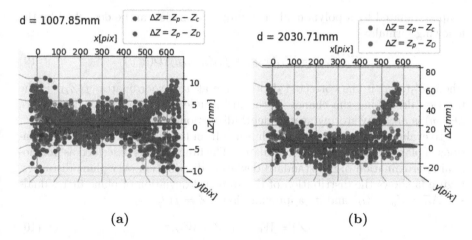

Fig. 3. 3D images of spatial distribution of the plane fit residuals: of distorted depth maps (red dots), of undistorted depth maps (green dots), along with the view of zero level at different distances **a** 1007.85 mm, **b** 2030.71 mm (Color figure online)

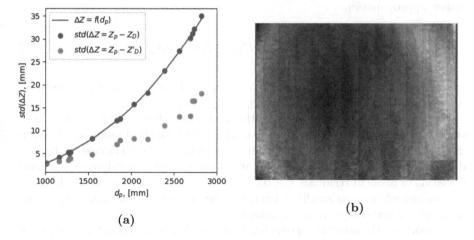

Fig. 4. a Standard deviation of difference between depth values and their projections onto the fitted plane. **b** The evaluated depth distortion pattern

Figure 4a show values of standard deviation of plane fit residuals $std(\Delta Z = Z_p - Z_D)$ for different plane distances d_p. By comparing the figures one can note that the shape of the spatial depth distortions does not change with the distance but the magnitude of the distortions increases as the distance of the plane increases. In order to correct the depth images captured by the SS device the following spatial depth distortion model is proposed. The model is similar to the one proposed by Herrera [5] but it is defined in the depth domain instead of disparity domain and the function depicting the change of distortions magnitude is approximated by a polynomial. The proposed model can be described by the following formula:

$$Z'_D(x, y) = Z_D(x, y) + f(Z_D(x, y))D(x, y) \tag{9}$$

where $Z'_D(x, y)$ is the corrected depth value at x, y coordinates, $f(Z_D)$ is the function describing the change of the magnitude of spatial depth distortions, $D(x, y)$ is an array storing spatial depth distortions pattern.

To evaluate $f(Z_D)$ for each depth frame from the sequence a standard deviations of plane fit residuals were calculated. The function was described as polynomial approximation of the standard deviation distribution over plane distances. Figure 4a shows the distribution of the standard deviation of plane fit residuals $std(\Delta Z = Z_p - Z_D)$ and its approximation $\Delta Z = f(d_p)$:

$$f(Z) = W_0 + W_1 Z + W_2 Z^2 \tag{10}$$

In order to evaluate depth distortion pattern $D(x, y)$ from the depth sequence four frames with distinctive plane distances were chosen. Each element of depth distortions pattern $D(x, y)$ at coordinates x, y was evaluated using a linear least square approximation:

$$\sum_{i=1}^{N} |\Delta Z_i(x, y) - D(x, y) f(Z_{Di}(x, y))|^2 \tag{11}$$

where i is the index of depth frame, $N = 4$ is the number of depth frames used for approximation, $\Delta Z_i(x, y) = Z_p(x, y) - Z_D(x, y)$

Figure 4b shows the evaluated depth distortions pattern image. Figures 3a, b show 3D images of spatial distribution of plane fit residuals of undistorted (green dots) and distorted (red dots) depth image recorded by the SS device at different distances from plane wall object. Figure 4a shows that the values of standard deviation of plane fit residuals $std(\Delta Z = Z_p - Z'_D)$ for the corrected depth values Z'_D are almost twice as smaller than the plane fit residuals $std(\Delta Z = Z_p - Z_D)$ obtained for raw distorted depth values Z_D.

To evaluate the accuracy of depth values provided by the SS device a sequence of RGB and depth images with calibration board at distances in the range of 500 to 2000 mm was taken. For each j-th RGB-depth frame pair the position of the calibration board was evaluated from the detected chessboard corners in the left RGB image using OpenCV function solvePnP. The j-th position is depicted by rotation matrix R_{Lj} and translation vector T_{Lj}. Knowing the position of the calibration board and the relative position of the left and IR cameras the known 3D coordinates of chessboard corners X_i were transformed into the reference frame of the depth image: $X_{Ii} = [X_{Ii}, Y_{Ii}, Z_{Ii}]^T$.

In order to retrieve for each i-th reference point a corresponding depth value Z_{Di} from the depth image, their image coordinates x_{Ii}, y_{Ii} were calculated by projecting the 3D coordinates X_{Ii} onto the depth image. After projecting the reference points onto the depth image I_D a set of depth values Z_{Di} belonging to the calibration board plane can be calculated. Using Eq. 5 a complete set of 3D coordinates $X_{Di} = [X_{Di}, Y_{Di}, Z_{Di}]^T$ of the reference points provided by the SS device can be obtained.

To evaluate the accuracy of the depth values provided by the SS device for each j-th depth-RGB frame depth components of two distance vectors were compared: (1) depth component Z_{Bj} of the vector connecting point $[0, 0, 0]$ in the depth reference frame and its projection onto the plane defined by the plane equation obtained from known 3D coordinates X_{Ii} of chessboard corners, (2) depth component Z_{Dj} of the vector connecting the point $[0, 0, 0]$ in the depth reference frame and its projection onto the plane defined by the plane equation obtained from 3D coordinates X_{Di} provided by the SS device.

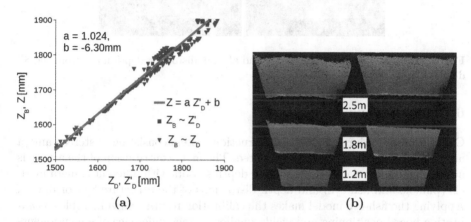

(a)   (b)

Fig. 5. a 3D view of a wall at different distances before and after undistorting depth maps from the SS device. **b** Depth components of plane distance obtained using calibration board position vs. depth components of plane distance obtained using depth values from the SS device along with linear approximation of the relation. (Color figure online)

Figure 5a shows depth components Z_B of the plane distance vector obtained from the calibration board position vs. plane distances Z_D, Z'_D obtained from the SS device distorted depth values (blue triangles) and corrected (red squares) ones. Figure 5a also shows the linear approximation (green line) of the relation between the expected depth components Z and corrected depth values Z'_D. As expected the distribution of expected depth components Z_B vs. Z'_D corrected depth components is less divergent from the linear approximation than the distribution Z_B vs. Z_D depth components before correction.

Figure 5b shows 3D visualizations of point clouds of wall object at different distances before correction (left column) of the depth components and after correction (right column) of the depth components. Figure 6 shows 3D visualizations of point clouds of staircase before (left image) and after (right image) the depth components correction.

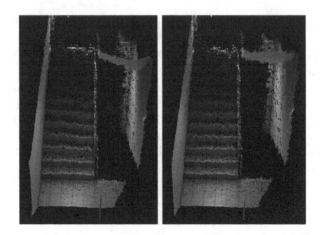

Fig. 6. 3D view of the staircase before and after undistorting depth maps from the SS device

6 Conclusions

Calibration procedure of a 3D reconstruction system consisting of stereo camera and an active depth sensor was presented. The main contribution of the article is addressing issues related to combining depth sensors with different camera models (pinhole and fish-eye) and depth distortions of the Structure Sensor device. Applying the fish-eye model makes the calibration results less vulnerable to calibration board positioning and yields smaller average difference of y components of image coordinates of corresponding points after rectification. The model of spatial depth distortions of the SS device is introduced as an alternative to popular in literature spatial disparity distortions model tested mostly for Kinect active depth sensors. Correction of depth maps from the SS device with the proposed model gives twice as smaller plane fit residuals as before correction.

References

1. Caraiman, S., et al.: Computer vision for the visually impaired: the sound of vision system. In: Proceedings of the IEEE Conference on Computer Vision and Pattern Recognition, pp. 1480–1489 (2017)
2. Dal Mutto, C., Zanuttigh, P., Cortelazzo, G.M.: Time-of-Flight Cameras and Microsoft Kinect^{TM}. Springer, New York (2012). https://doi.org/10.1007/978-1-4614-3807-6
3. Darwish, W., Tang, S., Li, W., Chen, W.: A new calibration method for commercial RGB-D sensors. Sensors **17**(6), 1204 (2017). Calibration
4. Hansard, M., Lee, S., Choi, O., Horaud, R.P.: Time-of-Flight Cameras: Principles, Methods and Applications. Springer, London (2013). https://doi.org/10.1007/978-1-4471-4658-2
5. Herrera, D., Kannala, J., Heikkilä, J.: Joint depth and color camera calibration with distortion correction. IEEE Trans. Pattern Anal. Mach. Intell. **34**(10), 2058–2064 (2012)

6. Herrera, C.D., Kannala, J., Heikkilä, J.: Accurate and practical calibration of a depth and color camera pair. In: Real, P., Diaz-Pernil, D., Molina-Abril, H., Berciano, A., Kropatsch, W. (eds.) CAIP 2011. LNCS, vol. 6855, pp. 437–445. Springer, Heidelberg (2011). https://doi.org/10.1007/978-3-642-23678-5_52

7. Smisek, J., Jancosek, M., Pajdla, T.: 3D with kinect. In: 2011 IEEE International Conference on Computer Vision Workshops (ICCV Workshops), pp. 1154–1160 (2011)

8. Kannala, J., Brandt, S.S.: A generic camera model and calibration method for conventional, wide-angle, and fish-eye lenses. IEEE Trans. Pattern Anal. Mach. Intell. **28**(8), 1335–1340 (2006)

9. Karan, B.: Calibration of depth measurement model for kinect-type 3D vision sensors (2013)

10. Karan, B.: Calibration of kinect-type RGB-D sensors for robotic applications. FME Trans. **43**(1), 47–54 (2015)

11. Rzeszotarski, D., Pełczyński, P.: Software application for calibration of stereoscopic camera setups. Metrol. Meas. Syst. **19**(4), 805–816 (2012)

12. Sell, J., O'Connor, P.: The xbox one system on a chip and kinect sensor. IEEE Micro **34**(2), 44–53 (2014)

13. Zhang, C., Zhang, Z.: Calibration between depth and color sensors for commodity depth cameras. In: Shao, L., Han, J., Kohli, P., Zhang, Z. (eds.) Computer Vision and Machine Learning with RGB-D Sensors. ACVPR, pp. 47–64. Springer, Cham (2014). https://doi.org/10.1007/978-3-319-08651-4_3

Second-Order Algebraic Surfaces
and Two Image Photometric Stereo

Ryszard Kozera[1,2]($\boxtimes$) and Alexander Prokopenya[1] ⬤

[1] Faculty of Applied Informatics and Mathematics, Warsaw University of Life
Sciences - SGGW, ul. Nowoursynowska 159, 02-776 Warsaw, Poland
ryszard.kozera@gmail.com, alexander_prokopenya@sggw.pl
[2] Department of Computer Science and Software Engineering, The University of
Western Australia, 35 Stirling Highway, Crawley, Perth, WA 6009, Australia

Abstract. This paper discusses the special case of reconstructing the
unknown Lambertian surface from two-image photometric stereo. Both
images are assumed here to be formed by a genuine second-order algebraic surface. The corresponding uniqueness issue is discussed for different pairs of image irradiance equations under various illumination settings. Illustrative examples supplement presented analysis and demonstrate its main gist.

Keywords: Photometric stereo · Uniqueness · Shape reconstruction

1 Introduction

A standard single image *shape-from-shading problem* [1,2] admits a distant point
illumination of $S = graph(u)$, along a given direction $p = (p_1, p_2, p_3)$ with $u \in C^2$
representing the unknown function defined over an image $\Omega = \{(x, y) \in \mathbb{R}^2 :
E(x, y) \geq 0\}$. Here $E : \Omega \to [0, 1]$ measures the intensity of the light reflected
from S and registered over Ω. For a given physical material coating the surface S
one may estimate either experimentally or theoretically the so-called *reflectance
map* R governing surface reflectance property usually depending on a normal
vector field $n(s) = (n_1(s), n_2(s), n_3(s)) \perp S$, where $s = (x, y, u(x, y)) \in S$. Such
setting reduces the shape-from-shading problem into a single *image irradiance
equation* (see [1]):

$$R(n_1(x, y, z), n_2(x, y, z), n_3(x, y, z)) = E(x, y), \qquad (1)$$

defined over an image Ω. Since for $S = graph(u)$ its normal, up to a scaling
factor, reads as $n(x, y, u(x, y)) = (u_x(x, y), u(x, y), -1)$, the Eq. (1) reformulates
into $R(x, y) = E(x, y)$ over Ω. In particular, the respective laws of optics (see
[1,2]) permit to determine the exact analytic formula governing the reflectance
map R for the family of *Lambertian surfaces*. The mapping R is here proportional
to the $\cos \alpha$, where α forms the angle between the unknown normal $n(s) \perp S$
and a given light-source direction p. This leads to a well-known variant of (1)

L. J. Chmielewski et al. (Eds.): ICCVG 2018, LNCS 11114, pp. 234–247, 2018.
https://doi.org/10.1007/978-3-030-00692-1_21

while illuminating the unknown Lambertian surface S by a parallel beam of light along the p direction (see [1]):

$$\frac{p_1 u_x(x,y) + p_2 u_y(x,y) - p_3}{\sqrt{p_1^2 + p_2^2 + p_3^2}\sqrt{u_x^2(x,y) + u_y^2(x,y) + 1}} = E(x,y). \tag{2}$$

The left-hand side of (2) results (with $s = (x, y, u(x,y)) \in S$) from $\cos(\alpha(s)) = \langle p|n(s)\rangle(\|p\|\|n(s)\|)^{-1}$, where $\langle \cdot|\cdot \rangle$ denotes a standard Euclidean dot product in $\mathbb{R}^3$ and $\| \cdot \|$ its respective induced norm. From now on, without loss of generality, the illumination direction p is assumed to be normalized i.e. $\|p\| = 1$. The uniqueness and existence analysis for (2) is complex and usually yields multiple solutions (see e.g. [3–9]).

To disambiguate generically *ill-posed* shape-from-shading problem, consecutive multiple illuminations of S from linearly independent directions can be applied. This technique called *photometric stereo* (see e.g. [1,10]) in principle disambiguates (2). More specifically, as demonstrated in [1,11] *three image photometric stereo* guarantees a unique solution (modulo a vertical shift) to the corresponding system of three image irradiance equations:

$$\frac{\langle p|n(s)\rangle}{\|n(s)\|} = E_p(x,y), \quad \frac{\langle q|n(s)\rangle}{\|n(s)\|} = E_q(x,y), \quad \frac{\langle r|n(s)\rangle}{\|n(s)\|} = E_r(x,y), \tag{3}$$

defined over the intersection of three images $\Omega = \Omega_p \cap \Omega_q \cap \Omega_r$. The entire process of reconstructing u (and thus of $S = graph(u)$) falls into two steps: first *(a) gradient computation* and then *(b) gradient integration* e.g. with the aid of the formula:

$$u(x,y) = u(x_0, y_0) + \int_\gamma u_x(x,y)dx + u_y(x,y)dy. \tag{4}$$

Here (x_0, y_0) is any but fixed point in a simply-connected Ω and $\gamma \subset \Omega$ forms an arbitrary piecewise smooth curve joining "frozen" (x_0, y_0) with varying $(x, y) \in \Omega$. The unknown value $u(x_0, y_0) = const$ stands for a free vertical shift in u.

In contrast, the case of *two-light source photometric stereo* with p and q linearly independent illumination directions is modelled (over $\Omega = \Omega_p \cap \Omega_q$) by the corresponding system of two-image irradiance equations:

$$\frac{p_1 u_x(x,y) + p_2 u_y(x,y) - p_3}{\sqrt{u_x^2(x,y) + u_y^2(x,y) + 1}} = E_p(x,y),$$

$$\frac{q_1 u_x(x,y) + q_2 u_y(x,y) - q_3}{\sqrt{u_x^2(x,y) + u_y^2(x,y) + 1}} = E_q(x,y). \tag{5}$$

It turns out that solving (5) constitutes much more intricate problem in comparison to (3) - see [11–13]. Indeed, as shown in the latter, solving (5) yields first possibly multiple formulas for the unknown vector field $v(x, y) = (v_1(x, y), v_2(x, y))$:

$$v_1(x, y) = \frac{E_p(x, y)(q_1 \langle p|q \rangle - p_1) + E_q(x, y)(p_1 \langle p|q \rangle - q_1) + a\varepsilon(x, y)\sqrt{\Lambda(x, y)}}{E_p(x, y)(p_3 - q_3 \langle p|q \rangle) + E_q(x, y)(q_3 - p_3 \langle p|q \rangle) + b\varepsilon(x, y)\sqrt{\Lambda(x, y)}},$$
(6)

$$v_2(x, y) = \frac{E_p(x, y)(q_2 \langle p|q \rangle - p_2) + E_q(x, y)(p_2 \langle p|q \rangle - q_2) + c\varepsilon(x, y)\sqrt{\Lambda(x, y)}}{E_p(x, y)(p_3 - q_3 \langle p|q \rangle) + E_q(x, y)(q_3 - p_3 \langle p|q \rangle) + b\varepsilon(x, y)\sqrt{\Lambda(x, y)}},$$

where $\varepsilon(x, y) = \pm 1$ so that $f(x, y) = \varepsilon(x, y)\sqrt{\Lambda(x, y)}$ is smooth for $u \in C^2$ and continuous for $u \in C^1$. The extra notation used in (6) resorts to:

$$a = p_3 q_2 - p_2 q_3, \quad b = p_1 q_2 - p_2 q_1, \quad c = p_1 q_3 - p_3 q_1,$$
$$\Lambda(x, y) = 1 - E_p^2(x, y) - E_q^2(x, y) - \langle p|q \rangle \left(\langle p|q \rangle - 2E_p(x, y)E_q(x, y) \right). \quad (7)$$

Noticeably the function Λ is non-negative over the whole image Ω (see [11–13]).

   (a) Evidently formulas (6) render a unique vector $v(x, y)$, wherever $\Lambda(x, y)$ vanishes. In such special case, the vector v is parallel to the plane spanned by both vectors p and q (see [11–13]). The latter follows from the fact that $p \times q = (-a, -c, b)$, $n(x, y, u(x, y)) = (u_x(x, y), u_y(x, y), -1)$ and

$$\Lambda(x, y) = \frac{(au_x(x, y) + cu_y(x, y) + b)^2}{1 + u_x^2(x, y) + u_y^2(x, y)} = \frac{(\langle p \times q | n(x, y, u(x, y)) \rangle)^2}{\|n(x, y, u(x, y))\|^2}. \quad (8)$$

Assuming that both E_p and E_q are formed upon illuminating a genuine Lambertian C^2 surface $S = graph(u)$ (i.e. with $u \in C^2$) the rare case of $\Lambda \equiv 0$ over Ω results in a unique *integrable* C^1 vector field v. This forces by default the satisfaction of the so-called *integrability condition*:

$$(v_1(x, y))_y = (v_2(x, y))_x, \quad (9)$$

holding over entire image Ω. It guarantees the existence of a unique $u \in C^2$ (modulo constant) satisfying (5) which gradient $\nabla u(x, y) = (u_x(x, y), u_y(x, y))$ coincides with $v(x, y)$ determined uniquely by (6) (as here $\Lambda \equiv 0$). Ultimately, the function u can be recovered from $\nabla u(x, y)$ e.g. with the aid of integration formula (4). More geometrical and analytic insight covering the case $\Lambda \equiv 0$ over Ω with arbitrary setting of p and q can be found in [11,12].

   (b) The case of $\Lambda > 0$ over the whole image Ω (or its sub-domains) yields in (6) two vector fields $v^+(x, y)$ and $v^-(x, y)$ with either $\varepsilon(x, y) \equiv 1$ or $\varepsilon(x, y) \equiv -1$, set respectively. Subject to the satisfaction of the integrability condition (9) here there exist either one or two C^2 solutions to (5), which if integrable can be found e.g. with (4). It can also be shown (see [11,12]) that if u forms a genuine solution to (5) then one vector fields in (6) coincides with $v = (u_x, u_y)$ and the second one (either integrable or not) can be re-expressed in terms of v according to:

$$\hat{v} = \left(\frac{(a^2 - b^2 - c^2)u_x + 2acu_y + 2ab}{2abu_x + 2bcu_y + b^2 - a^2 - c^2}, \frac{2acu_x + (c^2 - a^2 - b^2)u_y + 2bc}{2abu_x + 2bcu_y + b^2 - a^2 - c^2} \right). \quad (10)$$

Combining now (9) with (10) reformulates the integrability condition (over any domains where Λ is positive) into *the second-order non-linear PDE in two independent variables*:

$$a \left(bu_y(x, y) - c \right) u_{xx}(x, y) + \left(a^2 - c^2 - abu_x(x, y) + bcu_y(x, y) \right) u_{xy}(x, y)$$
$$+ c \left(a - bu_x(x, y) \right) u_{yy}(x, y) = 0, \quad (11)$$

for the arbitrary settings of p and q. Evidently, since (11) imposes a strong constraint on u, one can conclude that generically the Eq. (11) *disambiguates two-image photometric stereo* - see [11–13]. The rare cases of the existence of two C^2 solutions to (5) (over sub-domains, where $\Lambda > 0$) and extensive analysis for their geometrical and analytic interrelations are discussed for the special setting of illumination directions $p = (0, 0, -1)$ and q arbitrary in [11,12]. Some other illumination configurations are also addressed in [13]. Remarkably, by [11,12] there is another possible source of ambiguities in (6) as outlined below.

(c) For majority of $C^{1,2}$ Lambertian surfaces illuminated along two non-parallel directions p and q the topology of the pre-image of $\Lambda \geq 0$ results in $\Omega = \Omega^{(1)} \cup \Omega^{(2)} \cup \Gamma$ with both disjoint $\Omega^{(1)}$ and $\Omega^{(2)}$ simply connected (over which $\Lambda > 0$) and Γ forming a C^1 curve defined implicitly by the equation $\Lambda(x, y) = 0$. The global uniqueness analysis for (5) over $\Omega \supset \Gamma$ relies now partially on the discussion from *(a)* and *(b)*. Indeed, in the generic case of a unique C^2 solution to (5) over each $\Omega^{(1,2)}$ (see *(a)* and *(b)*) the unambiguous $S = graph(u)$ over Ω follows straightforwardly. In contrast, the non-generic case with dual solutions to (5) over each $\Omega^{(1,2)}$, requires an extra treatment. Indeed, here the issue of feasible gluing $u \in C^2(\Omega^{(1)})$ with $\hat{u} \in C^2(\Omega^{(2)})$ along *bifurcation curve* Γ to form a global $C^{1,2}(\Omega)$ solution to (5) should be investigated. Visibly, up two four C^2 solutions to (5) over Ω may eventuate. The global uniqueness and existence analysis for (5) (with $\Gamma \subset \Omega$) tackling the issue of *bifurcations* along Γ is performed in [11,12] for $p = (0, 0, 1)$ and $q = (q_1, q_2, q_3)$ arbitrary.

This work addresses the uniqueness problem to (5) for *the second-order algebraic Lambertian surface $S = graph(S)$* illuminated by two distant light-sources forming two linearly independent beams of lights. The discussion to follow (see also [13–15]) covers more general illumination configurations than $p = (0, 0, -1)$ and $q = (q_1, q_2, q_3)$ analyzed in [11,12]. Illustrative examples supplement the theoretical argument presented in this paper. The alternative models for photometric stereo admitting light-sources and camera situated close to S together with perspective projection camera model are discussed e.g. in [17–20].

2   Second-Order Algebraic Surfaces and Photometric Stereo

Assume that $S = graph(u)$ represents the genuine *second-order algebraic surface* given by a quadratic function $u : \Omega \to \mathbb{R}$ defined (up to a constant shift) as:

$$u(x,y) = u_{20}x^2 + u_{02}y^2 + u_{11}xy + u_{10}x + u_{01}y, \qquad (12)$$

where u_{ij} are constant coefficients with $u_{20}^2 + u_{02}^2 + u_{11}^2 \neq 0$. The latter excludes S to be of planar shape as already covered in [11]. Suppose that u from (12) is illuminated along p and q directions. The latter guarantees the existence of at least one C^2 solution to (5) over Ω which also forms a C^∞ quadratic function.

It is well-known that the expression $D = u_{11}^2 - 4u_{20}u_{02}$ determines the geometrical character of the second-order algebraic surface S - see [21]. Indeed, the expression (12) represents either *an elliptic paraboloid* (if $D < 0$) or *a hyperbolic paraboloid* (if $D > 0$) or lastly *a parabolic cylinder* (if $D = 0$).

The respective derivatives of u defined in (12) satisfy:

$$u_x(x,y) = 2u_{20}x + u_{11}y + u_{10}, \quad \text{and} \quad u_y(x,y) = u_{11}x + 2u_{02}y + u_{01}. \quad (13)$$

Both images Ω_p and Ω_q are registered over:

$$\Omega_p = \{(x,y) : (2u_{20}p_1 + u_{11}p_2)x + (u_{11}p_1 + 2u_{02}p_2)y + u_{10}p_1 + u_{01}p_2 - p_3 \geq 0\},$$
$$\Omega_q = \{(x,y) : (2u_{20}q_1 + u_{11}q_2)x + (u_{11}q_1 + 2u_{02}q_2)y + u_{10}q_1 + u_{01}q_2 - q_3 \geq 0\}.$$

Furthermore, by (8) and (13) the equation $\Lambda(x,y) = 0$ (along which (6) yields a unique normal $(u_x, u_y, -1)$) reformulates into:

$$(2u_{20}a + u_{11}c)x + (u_{11}a + 2u_{02}c)y + u_{10}a + u_{01}c + b = 0. \qquad (14)$$

1. If $(2u_{20}a + u_{11}c)^2 + (u_{11}a + 2u_{02}c)^2 > 0$ then (14) defines a straight line Γ (with normal $(2u_{20}a + u_{11}c, u_{11}a + 2u_{02}c)$ to Γ) as a bifurcation curve.

2. On the other hand if both $2u_{20}a + u_{11}c = 0$ and $u_{11}a + 2u_{02}c = 0$ then again by (14) we should also have:

$$u_{10}a + u_{01}c + b = 0. \qquad (15)$$

The latter implies that $\Lambda \equiv 0$ over Ω. In contrast if here (15) does not hold then $\Lambda > 0$ over Ω.

2a. If $a = c = 0$ then the latter would result in $b = 0$ which is impossible as $0 \neq p \times q = (-a, -c, b)$. Thus for $a = c = 0$ the $\Lambda > 0$ holds over the entire image Ω.

2b. On the other hand if $(a, c) \neq (0, 0)$ then

$$\begin{pmatrix} 2u_{20} & u_{11} \\ u_{11} & 2u_{02} \end{pmatrix} \circ \begin{pmatrix} a \\ c \end{pmatrix} = \begin{pmatrix} 0 \\ 0 \end{pmatrix}$$

is only possible if $D = 0$ which together with (15) results in Λ vanishing over entire Ω. If however $D = 0$ and (15) does not vanish then $\Lambda > 0$ over Ω.

In addition, over each $\Omega^{(1,2)}$ the formulas (6) yield two vector fields which if both integrable they force u from (12) to satisfy (11). Substituting (13) into (11) reformulates the necessary and sufficient condition for the integrability of both vector fields into:

$$b(u_{11}^2 - 4u_{20}u_{02})(cx - ay) + (a^2 - c^2 - abu_{10} + bcu_{01})u_{11} + 2ac(u_{02} - u_{20})$$
$$+ 2b(au_{20}u_{01} - cu_{02}u_{10}) = 0. \quad (16)$$

Note that the symmetric argument can be applied to $\hat{u}$ obtained upon integrating the dual vector field in (6). Thus for both (6) to be integrable (when $\Lambda > 0$ over any $\bar{\Omega} \subset \Omega$) the dual $\hat{u}$ needs also to obey (16) over $\bar{\Omega}$.

We discuss now the Eq. (11) (and also its special form (16) for u satisfying (12)) under various illumination configurations.

Case 1. Assume now that $a = c = 0$. Thus by (7) the cross product $p \times q = (-a, -c, b) = (0, 0, b)$ and therefore $b \neq 0$ with p and q are parallel to OXY-plane resulting in $p_3 = q_3 = 0$. Hence p and q are perpendicular to the OZ-axis. Noticeably there is no bifurcation line Γ passing through Ω. Indeed by (8) and $b \neq 0$ the function Λ is positive over Ω (see also the alternative explanation preceding the Case 1). Thus for any non-parallel $p = (p_1, p_2, 0)$ and $q = (q_1, q_2, 0)$ there exist exactly two vector fields $v^{\pm}$ determined in (6). A simple inspection shows that if $a = c = 0$ the Eq. (16) (and in fact its general counterpart (11)) is satisfied identically and hence both $v^{\pm}$ are integrable. Consequently there are exactly two C^2 solutions to (5) over Ω. Furthermore, by (10) the resulting two vector fields $v^{\pm}$ amount either to (u_x, u_y) or to $(-u_x, -u_y)$. The latter renders two mirror-like reflection surfaces $S_1 = graph(u)$ and $S_2 = -graph(u)$ with identical Gaussian curvatures:

$$K_u(x, y) = K_{-u}(x, y) = \frac{u_{xx}(x, y)u_{yy}(x, y) - u_{xy}^2(x, y)}{(1 + u_x^2(x, y) + u_y^2(x, y))^2}. \quad (17)$$

calculated either at $(x, y, u(x, y)) \in S_1$ or at $(x, y, -u(x, y)) \in S_2$, respectively. In fact (17) can also be re-expressed in terms of p, q, E_p, and E_q upon using (6) with $\varepsilon \equiv 1$ or $\varepsilon \equiv -1$ over Ω.

If now additionally u satisfies (12) then by (13) and (17), the respective Gaussian curvatures of S_1 and S_2 have constant signs (determined by $D = 4u_{20}u_{02} - u_{11}^2$) and are equal to:

$$K_{(u,-u)}(x, y) = \frac{4u_{20}u_{02} - u_{11}^2}{((2u_{20}x + u_{11}y + u_{10})^2 + (u_{11}x + 2u_{02}y + u_{01})^2 + 1)^2}. \quad (18)$$

Here both quadratics u and $-u$ over Ω form mirror-like reflected pairs of either two elliptic or two hyperbolic paraboloids or a single pair of parabolic cylinders.

The reconstruction of u (and thus of $-u$) can be found e.g. upon integrating one of the vector fields from (6) with the aid of (9). The alternative is to determine the unknown coefficients u_{20}, u_{02}, u_{11}, u_{10}, and u_{01} from (12) upon substituting (13) into (5) (or into (9)) over several (at least 6) image points. The topic of reconstructing u satisfying (12) is omitted in this paper.

Case 2. If p and q are positioned in the plane parallel to OZ-axis then $(p \times q) = (-a, -c, b) \perp$ to OZ-axis and therefore $b = 0$ and hence $a^2 + c^2 > 0$. The latter reduces the integrability condition (11) into (over each $\Lambda > 0$):

$$ac(u_{yy}(x, y) - u_{xx}(x, y)) + (a^2 - c^2)u_{xy}(x, y) = 0. \tag{19}$$

A similar equation is studied for $p = (0, 0, -1)$ and $q = (q_1, q_2, q_3)$ in [11,12] and also for other vertical configurations in [13]. Recently a general setting of p and q parallel to the OZ-axis is also discussed in [15,16]. We supplement now the above with some extra analytic insight in the context of $S = graph(u)$ for u satisfying the constraint (12). Indeed assume now u satisfies the integrability condition (19). Consider a new coordinate system $T(x, y) = (\xi(x, y), \eta(x, y))$ (recall that $a^2 + c^2 > 0$) defined according to:

$$\xi(x, y) = ax + cy, \quad \eta(x, y) = ay - cx. \tag{20}$$

Having introduced $\bar{u}(\xi, \eta) = u(T^{-1}(\xi, \eta) = u(x, y)$, the chain rule upon calculating $u_{xx}(x, y) = (\bar{u}(\xi, \eta))_{xx}$, $u_{yy}(x, y) = (\bar{u}(\xi, \eta))_{yy}$ and $u_{xy}(x, y) = (\bar{u}(\xi, \eta))_{xy}$ re-transforms PDE (19) into $\bar{u}(\xi, \eta) = 0$ which with the aid of simple integration leads to (up to a constant):

$$u(x, y) = \phi(ax + cy) + \psi(ay - cx), \tag{21}$$

for some $\phi, \psi \in C^2$. An inspection shows (see also [11,12]) that (modulo constant):

$$\phi(t) = u(\frac{a}{a^2 + c^2}t, \frac{c}{a^2 + c^2}t), \quad \psi(t) = u(-\frac{c}{a^2 + c^2}t, \frac{a}{a^2 + c^2}t). \tag{22}$$

Furthermore, $b = 0$ substituted in (10) yields the second integrable vector field:

$$\hat{v}(x, y) = \left(\frac{(c^2 - a^2)u_x(x, y) - 2acu_y(x, y)}{a^2 + c^2}, \frac{(a^2 - c^2)u_y(x, y) - 2acu_x(x, y)}{a^2 + c^2} \right).$$

By (21), upon substituting $u_x(x, y) = a\dot{\phi}(ax + cy) - c\dot{\psi}(ay - cx)$ and $u_y(x, y) = c\dot{\phi}(ax + cy) + a\dot{\psi}(ay - cx)$ into the latter we arrive at:

$$\hat{v}_1(x, y) = a\dot{\phi}(ax + cy) + c\dot{\psi}(ay - cx), \quad \hat{v}_2(x, y) = c\dot{\phi}(ax + cy) - a\dot{\psi}(ay - cx).$$

A simple verification shows that the second solution $\hat{u}$ to (5) satisfying $(\hat{u}_x, \hat{u}_y) = (\hat{v}_1, \hat{v}_2)$ coincides with:

$$\hat{u}(x, y) = \phi(ax + cy) - \psi(ay - cx). \tag{23}$$

Taking into account (21) and (23) the Gaussian curvatures of $S_1 = graph(u)$ and $S_2 = graph(\hat{u})$ at $(x, y, u(x, y))$ and at $(x, y, \hat{u}(x, y))$, respectively satisfy:

$$K_u(x, y) = -K_{\hat{u}}(x, y). \tag{24}$$

Assume now that u is a quadratic (12) which fulfills (5) over some simply connected $\bar{\Omega} \subset \Omega$ (with $\Lambda > 0$). Then the condition (19) for the dual vector field to be integrable simplifies into:

$$(a^2 - c^2)u_{11} + 2ac(u_{02} - u_{20}) = 0. \tag{25}$$

Recall that for $D \neq 0$ the set $\Lambda(x, y) = 0$ defines a bifurcation curve Γ. For $D = 0$ the level set $\Lambda = 0$ may either represent a curve Γ or possibly be identically satisfied over Ω (which occurs for normal $(u_x, u_y, -1)$ parallel to p, q-plane). We are ready now to collate the uniqueness analysis for Case 2.

(i) Suppose now that u from (12) satisfies (25) over simply connected $\bar{\Omega} \subset \Omega$ not containing Γ. The combination of (20), (22) and (23) guarantees $\hat{u}$ to form the second-order algebraic surface $S_v = graph(v)$ over $\bar{\Omega}$. If the *bifurcation straight line* does not pass through Ω then both u and $\hat{u}$ are the only two C^2 solutions to (5) over Ω. By (24) they represent the pairs of either elliptic and hyperbolic paraboloids or two parabolic cylinders.

(ii) In case when Γ passes through Ω and u defined in (12) satisfies (25) then two C^2 solutions to (5) exist over each $\Omega^{(1,2)}$ - see (b). Consequently, up to four $C^{1,2}$ global solutions over Ω can possibly be defined upon gluing along Γ the pairs of quadratics defined either over $\Omega^{(1)}$ or over $\Omega^{(2)}$. The analysis formulating the sufficient conditions to guarantee the successful $C^{1,2}$ bifurcations along Γ exceeds the scope of this paper. At this point it should be noted however, that out of four C^1 solutions to (5) at least two of them define C^2 functions along Γ. These two C^2 functions represent quadratics over Ω which are expressible with the homogeneous representation (12). The case of gluing quadratic surfaces with $D > 0$ and $D < 0$ (since both vector fields in (6) coincide along Γ) does not render C^2 bifurcations. The relevant clues can be found in [11,12].

(iii) The case when $(u_x, u_y, -1)$ is parallel to p, q-plane over entire image Ω results in $\Lambda \equiv 0$. As indicated above the latter amounts to $D = 0$ (i.e. $S = graph(u)$ represents a parabolic cylinder). Here a unique vector field in (6) renders (upon integration) a unique C^2 solution to (5) (a parabolic cylinder). Obviously the Gaussian curvature of $S = graph(u)$ vanishes everywhere since $D = 0$. Note that the latter is only possible if the p, q-plane (here parallel to OZ-axis) is also orthogonal to the symmetry line of the parabolic cylinder coinciding with the critical points $u_x(x, y) = 2u_{20}x + u_{11}y + u_{10}$ and $u_y = u_{11}x + 2u_{02}y + u_{01}$ which as $D = 0$ over Ω determines the straight line contained in the OXY-plane.

(iv) The generic case occurs when one of the computed vector fields (6) over $\Omega^{(1,2)}$ is not integrable. This is common as (25) (and also (19)) is rarely satisfied. The latter results in a unique solution $u \in C^2(\Omega)$ to (5), which if additionally satisfies (12) then $S = graph(u)$ represents the second order algebraic surface.

Note that in all sub-items (i)–(iv) the recovery of u can be performed as outlined in Case 1. However the non-generic case of two C^2 solutions to (6) yields another possible integration scheme. Indeed, once u is found the combination of (21) and (22) renders $\hat{u}$ from the "conjugated" form (23).

Case 3. We assume now that either $ab \neq 0$ or $cb \neq 0$. Recall that $b \neq 0$ excludes the p, q-plane to be orthogonal to OXY-plane.

(v) The case when $\Lambda \equiv 0$ over any sub-domain of Ω is impossible as otherwise the surface S coincides with parabolic cylinder illuminated by p and q orthogonal to OXY plane (see item *(iii)*). The latter leads to $b = 0$ which contradicts one of the Case 3 assumptions.

Assume now that $(2u_{20}a + u_{11}c)^2 + (u_{11}a + 2u_{02}c)^2 > 0$. The latter combined with (14) determines the pre-image of $\Lambda = 0$ forming a straight line as a bifurcation curve Γ for u in (12). Thus over each $\Omega^{(1,2)}$ we may have elliptic or hyperbolic paraboloid or the parabolic cylinder. In particular for the parabolic cylinder the plane perpendicular to the symmetry line of $graph(u)$ represented by $u_x(x,y) = 2u_{20}x + u_{11}y + u_{10} = 0$ and $u_y(x,y) = u_{11}x + 2u_{02}y + u_{01} = 0$ is parallel to $p \times q$.

The opposite case $2u_{20}a + u_{11}c = u_{11}a + 2u_{02}c = 0$ coupled with $(a, c) \neq (0, 0)$ by previous analysis leads to $D = 0$ (a parabolic cylinder). The sub-case when $u_{10}a + u_{01}c + b = 0$ is impossible as then $\Lambda \equiv 0$ over Ω, which has been just excluded. In contrast $u_{10}a + u_{01}c + b \neq 0$ yields $\Lambda > 0$ over Ω. Here for this parabolic cylinder the plane perpendicular to symmetry line of u represented by $u_x(x,y) = 2u_{20}x + u_{11}y + u_{10} = 0$ and $u_y(x,y) = u_{11}x + 2u_{02}y + u_{01} = 0$ is not parallel to $p \times q$.

(vi) Evidently for any sub-domain $\bar{\Omega} \subset \Omega$ where $\Lambda > 0$ two vector fields in (6) eventuate. In a generic case when (16) is not satisfied then there exists exactly one $u \in C^2$ solution to (5) over $\bar{\Omega}$. If additionally u fulfills (12) then its graph represents a second-order algebraic surface.

(vii) Assume now a non-generic situation in which (16) is satisfied over any open subset of $\bar{\Omega} \subset \Omega$ with $\Lambda > 0$. The latter is only possible to hold over entire $\bar{\Omega}$ if $D = u_{11}^2 - 4u_{20}u_{02} = 0$ which ultimately leads to:

$$(a^2 - c^2 - abu_{10} + bcu_{01})u_{11} + 2ac(u_{02} - u_{20}) + 2b(au_{20}u_{01} - cu_{02}u_{10}) = 0. \tag{26}$$

Thus only parabolic cylinders may lead in rare cases to potential ambiguities while solving (5) subject to $ab \neq 0$ or $cb \neq 0$.

3   Examples

The discussion presented in Sect. 2 is illustrated below with some examples.

Example 1. Let the Lambertian surface $S_1 = graph(u)$ be represented by the quadratic function:

$$u(x, y) = 2x^2 - 5xy - y^2 + 3y. \tag{27}$$

The resulting discriminant $D = u_{11}^2 - 4u_{20}u_{02} = 33 > 0$ and hence the graph of (27) forms a hyperbolic paraboloid. Assume that normalized illumination directions p and q read as:

$$p = (1, 0, 0), \qquad q = \left(\frac{1}{3}, \frac{2\sqrt{2}}{3}, 0 \right). \tag{28}$$

Since $p \times q = (0, 0, 2\sqrt{2}/3)$ the Case 1 from Sect. 2 is here dealt. The respective synthetically generated (in *Mathematica* [22]) image intensities:

$$E_p(x, y) = \frac{4x - 5y}{\sqrt{10 + 41x^2 - 20xy + 29y^2 - 30x - 12y}},$$

$$E_q(x, y) = \frac{6\sqrt{2} + (4 - 10\sqrt{2})x - (5 + 4\sqrt{2})y}{3\sqrt{10 + 41x^2 - 20xy + 29y^2 - 30x - 12y}}, \qquad (29)$$

are registered over and image $\Omega = \Omega_p \cap \Omega_q$ (see Fig. 1):

$$\Omega = \{(x, y) \in R^2 : y \leq \frac{6\sqrt{2} + (4 - 10\sqrt{2})x}{5 + 4\sqrt{2}} \wedge y \leq \frac{4x}{5}\}.$$

Cumbersome computations in *Mathematica* show that for each $(x, y) \in \Omega$ the function Λ defined in (8) satisfies $\Lambda(x, y) = (8/9)(10 + 41x^2 - 20xy + 29y^2 - 30x - 12y)^{-1} > 0$. The latter coupled with (6) yields two integrable vector fields:

$$(u_x^+, u_y^+) = (4x - 5y, -5x - 2y + 3), \quad (u_x^-, u_y^-) = (-4x + 5y, 5x + 2y - 3).$$

Evidently, the first vector field (u_x^+, u_y^+) coincides with the gradient of (27), whereas (u_x^-, u_y^-) corresponds to the $\nabla(-u)$ which represents the reflected hyperbolic paraboloid $S_2 = -graph(u)$. The latter agrees with the discussion from Case 1 of Sect. 2.

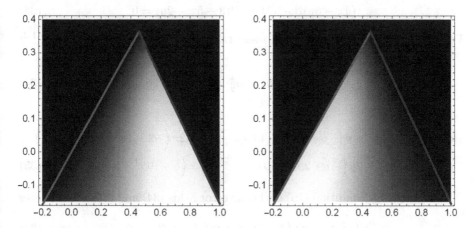

Fig. 1. Photometric stereo images E_p and E_q from (29) for surface (27) and with illumination directions (28).

Example 2. Assume that $S_1 = graph(u)$ (with u as in (27)) is illuminated along the unit directions:

$$p = \left(-\alpha\sqrt{1 - \beta^2}, -\alpha\beta, -\sqrt{1 - \alpha^2}\right),$$

$$q = \left(\alpha\sqrt{1 - \beta^2}, \alpha\beta, -\sqrt{1 - \alpha^2}\right), \qquad (30)$$

which depend on two parameters $0 < \alpha < 1$ and $0 \le \beta \le 1$. Visibly the vector:

$$p \times q = \left(2\alpha\beta\sqrt{1-\alpha^2}, -2\alpha\sqrt{(1-\alpha^2)(1-\beta^2)}, 0\right) \qquad (31)$$

is perpendicular to the OZ-axis with $pq - plane$ parallel to the OZ-axis. The latter falls into the category of Case 2 discussed in Sect. 2. The corresponding image intensities (generated here synthetically in $Mathematica$) read as:

$$E_p(x,y) = A(x,y)\left(\sqrt{1-\alpha^2} + \alpha\beta(-3+5x+2y) + \alpha\sqrt{1-\beta^2}(-4x+5y)\right),$$

$$E_q(x,y) = A(x,y)\left(\sqrt{1-\alpha^2} + \alpha\beta(3-5x-2y) + \alpha\sqrt{1-\beta^2}(4x-5y)\right), \quad (32)$$

where $A(x,y) = (10 + 41x^2 - 20xy + 29y^2 - 30x - 12y)^{-1/2}$. Figure 2 shows the corresponding photometric two images (32) for $\alpha = 1/10$ and $\beta = 0$.

Coupling together (7), (30) with (32) yields (upon $Mathematica$ calculations):

$$\Lambda(x,y) = 4A^2(x,y)\alpha^2(1-\alpha^2)\left((4x-5y)\beta - \sqrt{1-\beta^2}(3-5x-2y)\right)^2 \ge 0.$$

An inspection shows that over Ω (defined by $0 \le E_{p,q} \le 1$) the pre-image $\Lambda(x,y) = 0$ coincides with:

$$(4x-5y)\beta - \sqrt{1-\beta^2}(3-5x-2y) = 0. \qquad (33)$$

Two vector fields determined in (6) and taken over disjoint components $\Omega^{(1,2)}$ (where $\Lambda > 0$) are equal to:

$$u_x^+ = 4x - 5y, \qquad u_y^+ = 3 - 5x - 2y, \qquad (34)$$

$$u_x^- = 6\beta\sqrt{1-\beta^2} + y\left(-5 + 10\beta^2 - 4\beta\sqrt{1-\beta^2}\right) - 2x\left(-2 + 4\beta^2 + 5\beta\sqrt{1-\beta^2}\right),$$

$$u_y^- = -3 + 6\beta^2 - 2y\left(-1 + 2\beta^2 + 5\beta\sqrt{1-\beta^2}\right) + x\left(5 - 10\beta^2 + 8\beta\sqrt{1-\beta^2}\right). \quad (35)$$

The integrability condition (16) for both vector fields (34) and (35) reformulates into:

$$4\alpha^2(1-\alpha^2)\left(5 - 10\beta^2 + 6\beta\sqrt{1-\beta^2}\right) = 0. \qquad (36)$$

In particular if $\beta = 0$ the illumination vectors p and q are parallel to the OXZ-plane. Evidently since $0 < \alpha < 1$ for $\beta = 0$ the integrability condition (36) is not met and thus the second vector field (35) with $\beta = 0$:

$$u_x^- = 4x - 5y, \qquad u_y^- = -3 + 5x + 2y$$

is not $integrable$. Hence for u defined in (27) the corresponding $S_1 = graph(u)$ illuminated by (30) (for $\beta = 0$) can be uniquely reconstructed from its registered two image intensities (32) over Ω.

On the other hand for $\beta_1 = \sqrt{(3 + \sqrt{34})/(2\sqrt{34})}$ and $\alpha_1 = 1/10$ the integrability condition (36) (upon e.g. verification in *Mathematica*) is satisfied and the second vector field in (35) equal to:

$$u_x^- = \frac{1}{\sqrt{34}}(15 - 37x + 5y), \quad u_y^- = \frac{1}{\sqrt{34}}(9 + 5x - 31y)$$

is now *integrable*. The latter leads to the second $\hat{u}$ representing a quadratic:

$$\hat{u}(x,y) = -\frac{37x^2}{\sqrt{34}} - \frac{31y^2}{2\sqrt{34}} + \frac{5xy + 15x + 9y}{\sqrt{34}} - \frac{111}{22\sqrt{34}} + \frac{6}{11}. \tag{37}$$

The constant term in (37) is chosen so that function $\hat{u}(x, y)$ takes the same values as the function $u(x, y)$ along the straight line (33) reduced to (for β_1):

$$y = \frac{1}{55}\left(5 - 5\sqrt{34} + 11(3 + \sqrt{34})x\right). \tag{38}$$

Upon substituting (38) into (27) and (37), we obtain along Γ

$$u(x,y) = v(x,y) = \frac{1}{121}\left(-2 - 31\sqrt{34}\right) - \frac{1}{275}\left(68 + 31\sqrt{34}\right)x(-10 + 11x). \tag{39}$$

Consequently, there exist exactly two C^2 Lambertian surfaces $S_1 = graph(u)$ and $S_2 = graph(\hat{u})$ over $\Omega^{(1,2)}$ which can be reconstructed based on E_p and E_q in (32) for p and q as in (30) (with β_1 and α_1). Both u and $\hat{u}$ are quadratics from (12). However, if the entire image $\Omega \supset \Gamma$ is considered then upon gluing the respective pairs of functions along (38) four C^1 solutions prevail (see Figs. 3 and 4). Two of them represent quadratics $u, \hat{u} \in C^2(\Omega)$ (with $D > 0$ and $D < 0$). The remaining pair consists of the hyperbolic paraboloid glued along Γ with the elliptic paraboloid. The gluing preserves here merely C^1 continuity along Γ.

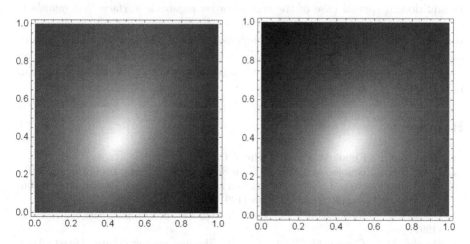

Fig. 2. Photometric stereo images E_p and E_q from (32) for surface (27) with illumination directions (30), where $\alpha = 1/10$ and $\beta = 0$.

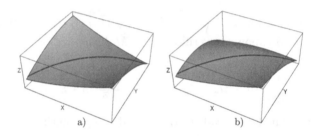

Fig. 3. Solutions to (32) over $\Omega \supset \Gamma$ glued along Γ from (38) (a) u as in (27), (b) u defined over $\Omega^{(1)}$ with $\hat{u}$ defined over $\Omega^{(2)}$. For p and q in (30) $\alpha = 1/10$ and $\beta = \beta_1$.

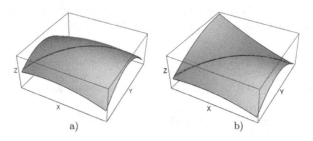

Fig. 4. Solutions to (32) over $\Omega \supset \Gamma$ glued along Γ from (38) (a) $\hat{u}$ as in (37), (b) $\hat{u}$ defined over $\Omega^{(1)}$ with u defined over $\Omega^{(2)}$. For p and q in (30) $\alpha = 1/10$ and $\beta = \beta_1$.

4 Conclusions

In this paper we analyze the uniqueness problem for reconstructing the Lambertian surface from two-image photometric stereo technique. The analysis extends first the results from [11–13] for a more general settings of illumination directions. In addition, a special case of the second-order algebraic surface $S = graph(u)$ (with u defined by (12)) illuminated from arbitrary two-light source directions is also studied in the context of ambiguous versus unambiguous pairs of photometric stereo images (see also [14,15]). A possible extension of this work may focus on reconstructing S from noisy images – relevant clues can be found e.g. in [23–27].

References

1. Horn, B.K.P.: Robot Vision. MIT Press, Cambridge (2001)
2. Horn, B.K.P., Brooks, M.J.: Shape from Shading. MIT Press, Cambridge (1989)
3. Deift, P., Sylvester, J.: Some remarks on shape-from-shading in computer vision. J. Math. Anal. Appl. 1(84), 235–248 (1991)
4. Oliensis, J.: Uniqueness in shape from shading. Int. J. Comput. Vis. 6(2), 75–104 (1991)
5. Brooks, M.J., Chojnacki, W., Kozera, R.: Shading without shape. Quart. Appl. Math. 50(1), 27–38 (1992)
6. Kozera, R.: Uniqueness in shape from shading revisited. Int. J. Math. Imaging Vision. 7, 123–138 (1997)

7. Kozera, R.: On complete integrals and uniqueness in shape from shading. Appl. Math. Comput. **73**(1), 1–37 (1995)
8. Bruss, A.: The eikonal equation: some results applicable to computer vision. J. Math. Phys. **5**(23), 890–896 (1982)
9. Brooks, M.J., Chojnacki, W., Kozera, R.: Circularly-symmetric eikonal equations and non-uniqueness in computer vision. J. Math. Anal. Appl. **165**(1), 192–215 (1992)
10. Woodham, R.J.: Photometric stereo: a reflectance map technique for determining surface orientation from multiple images. Opt. Eng. **19**(1), 139–144 (1980)
11. Kozera, R.: Existence and uniqueness in photometric stereo. Appl. Math. Comput. **44**(1), 1–104 (1991)
12. Kozera, R.: On shape recovery from two shading patterns. Int. J. Pattern Recognit. Artif. Intell. **6**(4), 673–698 (1992)
13. Onn, R., Bruckstein, A.M.: Integrability disambiguates surface recovery in two-image photometric stereo. Int. J. Comput. Vis. **5**(1), 105–113 (1990)
14. Kozera, R., Prokopenya, A.: Application of computer algebra for the reconstruction of surfaces from their photometric stereo images. Program. Comput. Softw. **43**(2), 98–104 (2017)
15. Kozera, R., Prokopenya, A.: Application of computer algebra to photometric stereo with two light sources. Program. Comput. Softw. **44**(2), 112–119 (2018)
16. Kozera, R., Prokopenya, A.: Orthogonal illuminations in two light-source photometric stereo. In: Saeed, K., Homenda, W. (eds.) CISIM 2016. LNCS, vol. 9842, pp. 402–415. Springer, Cham (2016). https://doi.org/10.1007/978-3-319-45378-1_36
17. Mecca, R., Wetzler, A., Bruckstein, A.M., Kimmel, R.: Near field photometric stereo with point light sources. SIAM J. Imaging Sci. **7**(4), 2732–2770 (2014)
18. Mecca, R., Falcone, M.: Uniqueness and approximation of photometric shape-from-shading model. SIAM J. Imaging Sci. **6**(1), 616–659 (2013)
19. Papadhimitri, T., Favaro, P.: A new perspective on uncalibrated photometric stereo. In: 26th IEEE Conference on Computer Vision and Pattern Recognition, pp. 1474–1481. IEEE Press, New York (2013). https://doi.org/10.1109/CVPR.2013.194
20. Tankus, A., Sochen, N., Yeshurun, Y.: Shape-from-shading under perspective projection. Int. J. Comput. Vis. **63**(1), 21–43 (2005)
21. Do Carmo, M.P.: Differential Geometry of Curves and Surfaces. Prentice-Hall, Englewood Cliffs (1976)
22. Wolfram, S.: The Mathematica Book. 5th Ed. Wolfram Media Inc. (2003)
23. Noakes, L., Kozera, R.: Nonlinearities and noise reduction in 3-source photometric stereo. J. Math. Imaging Vision **18**(2), 119–127 (2003)
24. Noakes, L., Kozera, R.: Denoising images: non-linear leap-frog for shape and light-source recovery. In: Asano, T., Klette, R., Ronse, C. (eds.) Geometry, Morphology, and Computational Imaging. LNCS, vol. 2616, pp. 419–436. Springer, Heidelberg (2003). https://doi.org/10.1007/3-540-36586-9_27
25. Noakes, L., Kozera, R.: The 2D leap-frog: integrability, noise and digitization. In: Bertrand, G., Imiya, A., Klette, R. (eds.) Digital and Image Geometry. LNCS, vol. 2243, pp. 352–364. Springer, Heidelberg (2001)
26. Shebanin, V., Atamanyuk, I., Kondratenko, Y.: Solution of vector random sequences based on polynomial degree canonical decomposition. East. Eur. J. Enterprise Techn. **5**(4–84), 4–12 (2016)
27. Karaçali, B., Snyder, W.: Noise reduction in surface reconstruction from given gradient vector field. Int. J. Comput. Vis. **6**(1), 25–44 (2004)

Low-Level and Middle-Level Image Processing

Improving RGB Descriptors
Using Depth Cues

Maciej Stefańczyk$^{(\boxtimes)}$ (iD)

Institute of Control and Computation Engineering,
Warsaw University of Technology,
Nowowiejska 15/19, 00-665 Warsaw, Poland
M.Stefanczyk@elka.pw.edu.pl
http://www.robotyka.ia.pw.edu.pl

Abstract. Geometrical distortions are tackled in different way in multiple keypoint detection and feature extraction algorithms. However, those are implemented as an integral part of the solution, making it impossible to use the same distortion removal method in other solutions. To the best of authors knowledge, there are no universal methods of distortion removal, that can be used as an intermediate step, between keypoint detection and feature extraction. Creating that kind of algorithm, instead of development of yet another 'robust descriptor', will enable seamless integration in existing applications, and, possibly, will increase object recognition success rate, independent of the selected keypoint detector/descriptor pair.

Keywords: RGB-D · Descriptors · Matching · Data fusion

1 Introduction

Service robotics, being one of the main research topics in the field around the world, aims at creation of robots able to cooperate with people or substitute them in tedious tasks out of the factories – either in dangerous environments (e.g. post-disaster areas), or at home. There is an aspiration to create robots able to help people in everyday chores, like cleaning or mowing. There is also a constantly growing market for associate and care robots, especially for elders or handicapped people.

In almost every service task, that requires cooperating with people or working in human environment, one of the key aspects is object recognition. In contrast to the structured factory environments, where objects are placed in specific places (e.g. on conveyors) objects in house may be placed virtually anywhere. They can be also occluded (by other objects), distorted (e.g. creased box or bag) or deformed in any way. Thus, robust object recognition methods are required.

A lot of objects, that people cope with every day, contain distinct texture. Packages have printed names, logos and article pictures, books have printed titles

© Springer Nature Switzerland AG 2018
L. J. Chmielewski et al. (Eds.): ICCVG 2018, LNCS 11114, pp. 251–262, 2018.
https://doi.org/10.1007/978-3-030-00692-1_22

and, in many cases, illustrations on the cover, even objects like cellphone can be treated as a textured from the algorithmic point of view.

For textured objects the state-of-the-art recognition and localization methods rely on matching feature point sets of object's model to the points extracted from current scene. There is, however, crucial problem in this approach – measurement distortions (scaling, rotation, perspective). Keypoint detection algorithms are quite invariant to those, as, for example, corner on the texture will keep its distinct nature even under distortion, but feature description for those keypoints can be quiet sensitive to those.

To cope with the scaling problem, a pyramid of pictures with different scales is used when descriptor is computed. Rotation invariance is achieved by calculating corner orientation (e.g. by average gradient in SIFT or geometric moments in FAST). The biggest problem is, undoubtedly, perspective distortion. In case, when measurements are supplemented with depth maps (aligned with the color image) it is possible to calculate surface characteristics of the object around the keypoint. This information can then be used to apply perspective correction either to the image itself or, if possible, inside feature descriptor algorithm. This additional step, in general, can be applied to any RGB descriptor, making them robust against perspective distortions and, as a result, making object detection and localization algorithms work better.

2   Related Work

2.1   Keypoint Detection

2D Detectors. Keypoint, in a computer vision, is a point of interest in the image, having some properties making it stand out in its surrounding (i.e. corners). One of the first developed corner detectors were Moravec operator and Harris detector (based on Moravec) [5]. Corner response function is calculated based on luminosity gradients in both directions. Shi and Tomasi proposed another improvement and simplification of corner response function calculation, which made detector faster [17].

In recent years researchers still work on this field, and new detectors are developed, like FAST [12]. Algorithm is quite efficient and works directly on luminosity image, without the need for intermediate gradient images calculation. For a given point, circle with 16 points circumference is analyzed, and point is marked as a corner if continuous segment of at least 12 points brighter or darker than the center is found.

Using Depth. It is worth noting, that keypoint detection itself is invariant to all geometrical distortions. In general, corner remains a corner even after rotation, scaling or any affine transform. There are, however, methods of filtering keypoints based on the depth data. Usage of 3D information allows for detection of unstable keypoints, lying on the edge of the object. Those points are not advisable for further processing, as the feature descriptor depends highly on the content of the background, and not of the object texture itself. Research on this field resulted, amongst others, in FAST-D detector [6], returning only stable points, lying inside the object and away from any edges.

There are also alternative methods for keypoint detection, based solely on depth/3D data. Three-dimensional version of Harris detector [18], instead of intensity, works on normal vectors computed for points in space. There are also algorithms using depth map directly, like NARF [19]. It detects edges in the depth map (surface discontinuity), and for other points gradients are calculated and then, based on them, keypoint response function is calculated. It is worth noting, that in NARF window size for calculations is in world units (e.g. centimeters), and not image units (i.e. pixels).

2.2 Feature Descriptors

Intensity Based Algorithms. Feature descriptor is a vector encoding interesting information around the keypoint. In many cases algorithms take into account only intensity of the keypoint surrounding, ignoring the color.

One of the most popular feature descriptors is SIFT [9]. It is invariant to scaling (works with image pyramids with different scales), rotation (for each point dominating gradient is calculated) and, to some extent, other geometric distortions. Final descriptor value is computed as a histogram of gradients in multiple subwindows. Main drawback of a SIFT is speed – it is rather slow to compute. SURF [3] is a speeded up feature, partly inspired by SIFT, but a lot faster to compute.

Speed of the aforementioned descriptors is unfortunately a problem – both are quite slow in computation, and also in matching (euclidean distance between two 256-element vectors must be calculated). Alternative approach relies on a binary descriptors, where each bit contains information about pair of points from keypoint surrounding. Those are both easy to compute (simple comparison of pixel brightness) and also very quick to compare with each other – Hamming distance is used.

One of the first binary descriptors was BRIEF [4]. It is based on uniform sampling grid, and actual sampling pattern was selected using machine learning approach. ORB [13] builds on BRIEF, adding rotation invariance (keypoint orientation computed based on geometrical moments) and improving sampling pattern to achieve better results.

Sampling pattern can be also more complicated. It could be built as a set of concentric circles (like in BRISK [7]), where comparison is both short-range (points close to each other) and long-range (points from greater distances), which, in theory, should capture local and global characteristics of the texture. FREAK [1] mimics human vision and retina construction, where more small areas are sampled near the keypoint, and peripheral areas from the outside are much bigger. This field is still under research, and one of the newest results are KAZE [2] and LATCH [8].

Pointcloud Descriptors. Different kinds of algorithms are used to describe pointcloud features. In Point Feature Histograms algorithm (PFH, [16]), for each keypoint its k-neighborhood is selected, and the histogram of differences between normal vectors is built. In Fast PFH [14], apart from speed optimization, invariance to viewpoint changes was added by normalizing coordinate systems with keypoint normal. Unfortunately, resulting feature vector relies on pointcloud density around the keypoint – if learning samples are dense (or close to the sensor) and testing is done on sparse clouds (or objects are far from the sensor) matching results can be worse.

PFH is a local descriptor – it describes only a keypoint surrounding. To recognize objects, many feature points must be used and matched between model and scene (just like in local RGB descriptors). Extension of the PFH to global object description (having one descriptor for the whole object) is Viewpoint Feature Histogram (VFH, [15]). Model of the object is made based on single view from RGB-D sensor, thus normal vectors of all visible points are pointed towards the sensor. Similarly to PFH, final descriptor is built as a histogram of differences in normal vector orientation. In this case, however, the reference direction is calculated as a vector from the camera center to the centroid of the object.

Radius-based Surface Descriptor (RSD, [10]) estimates surface radius in every point (for corners this radius is close to zero, for planes goes to infinity). Object is recognized based on the distribution of those radii. It is also possible to segment object into simple surfaces or approximate complex object, thus making it possible to grab unknown objects.

In SHOT (Signature of Histograms of OrienTations [20]) authors proposed two working modes. In general, algorithm is a combination of histogram and signature. For a given keypoint local reference frame is calculated, and in this frame histogram of normal vector directions is calculated. Points from the keypoint surrounding are also grouped by azimuth, elevation and distance, creating signature for the given part of the surface.

2.3 Existing Hybrid Approaches

Apart from the algorithms mentioned earlier, there are also hybrid approaches, using RGB and depth data directly. One of them is Binary Robust Appearance and Normals Descriptor (BRAND, [11]). As the name suggests – it is a binary descriptor, so its extraction and comparison is very fast. Part connected with color information works in a manner similar to BRIEF. Depth data (normal vectors to be precise) is also compared using the same sampling pattern, and final result depends on convexity of selected pair of vectors. Invariance to orientation is achieved by rotating the sampling pattern according to main direction of the color patch. Scaling invariance is achieved by using depth data – sampling pattern is scaled in range between 9 and 48 pixels, depending on the distance from the sensor to the keypoint. Final feature vector is constructed as a logical sum of the color and shape vectors. Authors didn't consider perspective distortions in their works, which can have big influence on final descriptor value under larger viewpoint changes.

Image Gradient and Normal Depth (iGRaND [21]) works in similar manner. Authors focused on robust method of local reference frame calculation for keypoints in RGB-D image. Keypoints, detected with FAST algorithm, are sorted based on surface diversity around – the bigger the diversity the bigger is the keypoint score. Final reference frame is calculated based on vector normal to the surface in keypoint and gradient direction in color image. Authors also proposed new variation of ORB descriptor based on this new reference frame. Part of the descriptor connected with intensity is calculated in classical way. Depth data is transformed to the new reference frame and then, in contrary to normal vectors in BRAND, z coordinate of points is compared. Final feature vector is a concatenation of color and depth ones.

2.4   Problem Formulation

Scaling. In feature extraction there are many possible geometrical distortions. Some of them are easy to cope with and existing algorithms do it rather well. One of such distortions is rotation, where just by calculating dominant orientation of the texture patch virtually any descriptor can be made rotation-invariant. Scaling invariance is achieved by using pyramids and computing descriptors for different scales. If depth information is available, it could be used to normalize distance and patch size. Although it is already done in some descriptors (e.g. BRAND), it could be used as a intermediate, data normalization step, enabling its usage for all existing algorithms.

Keypoint Filtering. Another research area, that can be beneficial when depth data is available, is keypoint filtering. Apart from simple rejection of unstable points lying near the edge of the object, points lying on creased or teared parts of the object can be also filtered out. For points lying near the edge of the object all pixels from the background can be rejected and only points from the object itself could be used to compute descriptor value.

Perspective Correction. The biggest possible quality improvement is connected with perspective correction. If detected keypoint lies on a surface, that is not perpendicular to sensors imaging axis, then surrounding of this point, projected to imaging plane, will change its shape depending on the viewing angle (for the simplest case of planar surface rectangular neighborhood will be skewed). For this reason, calculation of the descriptor will be flawed by taking into consideration points from the wrong surrounding, resulting in worse matching results in subsequent processing steps. Depth data can be used to calculate local reference frame in keypoint, which can be then used to calculate transformation of texture patch from the distorted view to the *en face* representation (perpendicular to sensor optical axis). When used on both, model and scene data, matching results should be much better, as descriptors would be calculated on normalized data.

3   Solution Details

3.1   Algorithm Characteristics

Algorithm, presented in following sections, is prepared mainly to correct perspective distortion and, to some extent, normalize scale. It is divided into few steps. In data preparation, XYZ-RGB pointcloud along with normal vectors is calculated, and set of keypoints is selected from the image. Then the local reference frame is calculated for each keypoint and point neighborhood is reprojected in a way, that mimics camera looking straight at the point along the normal vector.

3.2   Data Preprocessing

Pointcloud Calculation. As an input to the algorithm an RGB-D image is supplied, which is composed of a color image I_C along with a depth-map I_D aligned with it (without loss of generality we can assume that the depth map is represented in world units – meters). In first step depth map is converted to full XYZ pointcloud, represented in camera frame. Relation between the camera and object frames is shown on Fig. 1.

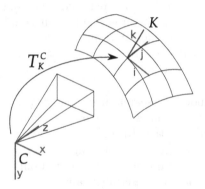

Fig. 1. Camera and object reference frames

To calculate XYZ from depth only, it is required to know intrinsic camera parameters, i.e. f_x and f_y, being camera focal length along horizontal and vertical axis, and (c_x, c_y) describing a point, where optical axis crosses imaging plane. For a given image point (u, v) its position in camera frame is calculated as follows:

$$p_z = I_D(u, v); \quad p_x = \frac{u - c_x}{f_x} p_z; \quad p_y = \frac{v - c_y}{f_y} p_z$$

Calculating this for each point with valid depth reading resultant pointcloud I_W is produced.

For every computed point, that has at least few close neighbors, normal vector is calculated. It is done by fitting a plane to those points and using its normal vector as a result. Set of all computed normal vectors is then used to produce normal map I_N.

Keypoint Detection. Keypoints are base for all other processing steps. Keypoint surrounding is used to calculate surface characteristics, and image from this surrounding is then recovered. Keypoint detection is a well studied problem, and in proposed solution two characteristics are important – point has to have defined position (as all points have) and size of its relevant surrounding r. Other keypoint properties (like pyramid level or direction) are not used at the moment.

3.3 Perspective Correction

Local Reference Frame. First step in image restoration process is calculation of local reference frame with origin in selected keypoint p_k. This frame is oriented in a way, that its z axis is identical with normal vector assigned to p_k, and x axis constructed as such that it points in the same direction as x axis of camera frame. Calculation of unit vectors of this frame in camera frame is enough to construct rotation part of transform matrix, and using keypoint position as a translation vector completes transform calculation. Normal vector, identical with unit vector k of z axis is read directly from I_N:

$$k = n = I_N(p_k)$$

and remaining two vectors are calculated as:

$$j = k \times [1, 0, 0] \quad and \quad i = j \times k$$

Position of keypoint is read directly from the pointcloud image I_R:

$$p_c = I_R(p_k)$$

This information is enough to construct full transformation matrix between camera and object reference frame:

$$T_K^C = \begin{bmatrix} i\ j\ k\ p_c \\ 0\ 0\ 0\ 1 \end{bmatrix}$$

Point p_c along with normal vector n are used to calculate equation of a plane P, that is tangential to the surface of the object in this point. It is assumed in this solution, that surrounding of the keypoint can be approximated by plane (Fig. 2).

Neighborhood Projection onto Image Plane. From the keypoint detection algorithm the size of the surrounding (in pixels) is known. The goal is to extract part of the image, which corresponds to square surrounding of size r, but aligned with local reference frame (lying flat on plane P, Fig. 3). In first step, the surrounding size must be converted from image units (pixels) to world units (meters) using camera intrinsic parameters. Distance t_z from the camera to the keypoint is known, but can also be altered if distance normalization is required. Size of this surrounding in world coordinates is then calculated as:

$$r' = \frac{r}{f} \cdot t_z$$

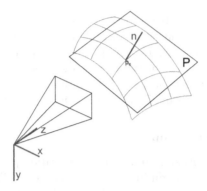

Fig. 2. Approximating keypoint surrounding with a plane

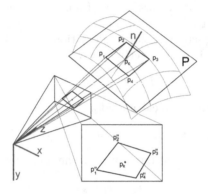

Fig. 3. Defining keypoint surrounding in a local reference frame and projecting ROI onto an image plane

and final ROI in local reference frame is defined by:

$$p_i = (\pm r', \pm r', 0)$$

In next step points p_i are transformed to the camera frame using T_K^C matrix:

$$p_i' = T_K^C \cdot p_i$$

Camera intrinsic parameters can be now used to calculate projection of points p_i onto image plane (represented in image coordinates, Fig. 3):

$$p_i'' = \left(f \cdot \frac{p_i'.x}{p_i'.z} + c_x, \quad f \cdot \frac{p_i'.y}{p_i'.z} + c_y \right)$$

Image Retrieval. When points p'' representing distorted point surrounding are calculated, last step is to use perspective transform, transforming those points into square with side of $2r$. This transformed region is then passed to the feature extraction algorithm, along with the modified keypoint parameters (as only part of the image is passed).

4   Tests and Evaluation

Presented solution was tested using simple simulator with planar, textured object. The texture comes from the real object (tea box), and is used to generate pair of images (RGB and depth) of distorted view. Distortion is composed of translation along camera z axis and rotation around x (tilt). Some example images are presented on Fig. 5.

4.1   Test Procedure

The goal of conducted tests was to check, whether proposed approach can be used for specified task. For reference, undistorted image and for a given tilt angle α and distance d:

1. set of keypoints is found in both images,
2. for each keypoint in reference image calculate descriptor D_r
3. for each keypoint in distorted image:
   (a) extract descriptor D_d from distorted image,
   (b) correct perspective and extract descriptor D_c,
   (c) correct perspective, normalize distance and calculate descriptor D_n
4. match sets of descriptors in pairs: D_r-D_d, D_r-D_c, D_r-D_n.

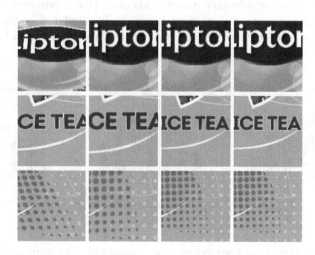

Fig. 4. Selected regions for 45° tilt.

During the tests, ORB was used as a both keypoint detector and feature extractor. To better visualize difference between distorted, corrected and normalized surrounding, three representative regions were chosen from the image. The central part of the image is prone only to straight perspective distortion, without skew. It is used to demonstrate perspective correction. Fragment with the "Ice tea" text has different distance from the camera, depending on the tilt angle, and is used to present distance normalization. Corner with dots is used to present skew distortion produced by tilting picture fragments that are away from image center. Results for different tilt angles are presented on Fig. 4. Pictures present, from the left: distorted image, image after perspective correction, image with additional distance normalization and reference image.

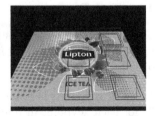

Fig. 5. Sample ROIs for 15, 30 and 45° tilt. Blue – Square in image space, red – square in local reference frame, no normalization, green – square in local reference frame with distance normalization. (Color figure online)

It can be seen, that for larger tilt angles first sample (with Lipton logo) differs greatly from the reference image. This distortion is removed successfully, and after applying presented method image looks similar to reference. Scale normalization can be clearly visible on 45° tilt, where only part of the text is visible without it.

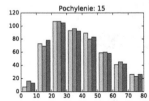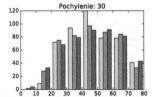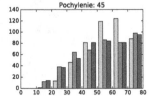

Fig. 6. Matching statistics for different tilt angles

Apart from the visual inspection, some numerical tests were conducted. For each resulting set of descriptors it was matched against reference set, and resulting distances were grouped into bins with step of 10. In perfect case, where descriptors are the same, all distances are 0, and in real world applications it is assumed, that the lower is the distance the better the matching is. To show impact of the distortion, histograms of the distances are presented on Fig. 6. First column of each bin (the light one) presents matching accuracy without any distortion removal. Middle column shows number of matches with given distance with perspective correction and the darkest one with additional distance normalization.

Even for the 15° it can be seen, that perspective correction gives more results with small distances, which maps to better matching performance. For bigger angles the disproportion gets bigger, and for 45° undistorted features outperforms the original ones many times. Distance normalization presents only slight performance change, but, if the reference distance is known, it is a viable option to use.

5 Summary

The article presented a method to improve matching performance of RGB descriptors in situations, where additional depth data is available. Presented approach is generalized – can be used for virtually any detector/descriptor pair as an plug-in, put between detection and extraction steps. Initial results confirmed the correctness of the approach.

Current solution uses planar approximation of the objects surface. Using more sophisticated surface reconstruction can be beneficial for more complex objects. Other improvement can be achieved by skipping image reprojection. Instead, modification of the descriptor pattern can be made, taking into consideration local properties of the surface. This approach, however, can work only for some algorithms, and is not as versatile as presented solution.

Acknowledgements. This work is funded by the National Science Centre, Preludium grant no. UMO-2017/25/N/ST6/02358.

References

1. Alahi, A., Ortiz, R., Vandergheynst, P.: Freak: fast retina keypoint. In: 2012 IEEE Conference on Computer Vision and Pattern Recognition (CVPR), pp. 510–517. IEEE (2012)
2. Alcantarilla, P.F., Bartoli, A., Davison, A.J.: KAZE features. In: Fitzgibbon, A., Lazebnik, S., Perona, P., Sato, Y., Schmid, C. (eds.) ECCV 2012. LNCS, vol. 7577, pp. 214–227. Springer, Heidelberg (2012). https://doi.org/10.1007/978-3-642-33783-3_16
3. Bay, H., Ess, A., Tuytelaars, T., Van Gool, L.: Speeded-up robust features (SURF). Comput. Vis. Image Underst. **110**(3), 346–359 (2008)
4. Calonder, M., Lepetit, V., Strecha, C., Fua, P.: BRIEF: binary robust independent elementary features. In: Daniilidis, K., Maragos, P., Paragios, N. (eds.) ECCV 2010. LNCS, vol. 6314, pp. 778–792. Springer, Heidelberg (2010). https://doi.org/10.1007/978-3-642-15561-1_56
5. Harris, C., Stephens, M.: A combined corner and edge detector. In: Alvey Vision Conference, vol. 15, p. 50. Citeseer (1988)
6. Kraft, M., Nowicki, M., Penne, R., Schmidt, A., Skrzypczyński, P.: Efficient RGB-D data processing for feature-based self-localization of mobile robots. Int. J. Appl. Math. Comput. Sci. **26**(1), 63–79 (2016)

7. Leutenegger, S., Chli, M., Siegwart, R.Y.: BRISK: binary robust invariant scalable keypoints. In: 2011 IEEE International Conference on Computer Vision (ICCV), pp. 2548–2555. IEEE (2011)
8. Levi, G., Hassner, T.: LATCH: learned arrangements of three patch codes. In: Winter Conference on Applications of Computer Vision (WACV). IEEE (2016)
9. Lowe, D.G.: Distinctive image features from scale-invariant keypoints. Int. J. Comput. Vis. **60**(2), 91–110 (2004)
10. Marton, Z.c., Pangercic, D., Blodow, N., Kleinehellefort, J., Beetz, M.: General 3D modelling of novel objects from a single view. In: 2010 IEEE/RSJ International Conference on Intelligent Robots and Systems (IROS), pp. 3700–3705. IEEE (2010)
11. Nascimento, E.R., Oliveira, G.L., Campos, M.F., Vieira, A.W., Schwartz, W.R.: BRAND: A robust appearance and depth descriptor for RGB-D images. In: 2012 IEEE/RSJ International Conference on Intelligent Robots and Systems, pp. 1720–1726. IEEE (2012)
12. Rosten, E., Drummond, T.: Machine learning for high-speed corner detection. In: Leonardis, A., Bischof, H., Pinz, A. (eds.) ECCV 2006. LNCS, vol. 3951, pp. 430–443. Springer, Heidelberg (2006). https://doi.org/10.1007/11744023_34
13. Rublee, E., Rabaud, V., Konolige, K., Bradski, G.: ORB: an efficient alternative to sift or surf. In: 2011 IEEE International Conference on Computer Vision (ICCV), pp. 2564–2571. IEEE (2011)
14. Rusu, R.B., Blodow, N., Beetz, M.: Fast point feature histograms (FPFH) for 3D registration. In: IEEE International Conference on Robotics and Automation, ICRA 2009, pp. 3212–3217. IEEE (2009)
15. Rusu, R.B., Bradski, G., Thibaux, R., Hsu, J.: Fast 3D recognition and pose using the viewpoint feature histogram. In: 2010 IEEE/RSJ International Conference on Intelligent Robots and Systems (IROS), pp. 2155–2162. IEEE (2010)
16. Rusu, R.B., Marton, Z.C., Blodow, N., Beetz, M.: Persistent point feature histograms for 3D point clouds. In: Proceedings of 10th International Conference on Intelligent Autonomous Systems (IAS-2010), Baden-Baden, Germany, pp. 119–128 (2008)
17. Shi, J., Tomasi, C.: Good features to track. In: 1994 IEEE Computer Society Conference on Computer Vision and Pattern Recognition, Proceedings CVPR 1994, pp. 593–600. IEEE (1994)
18. Sipiran, I., Bustos, B.: Harris 3D: a robust extension of the Harris operator for interest point detection on 3D meshes. Vis. Comput. **27**(11), 963–976 (2011)
19. Steder, B., Rusu, R.B., Konolige, K., Burgard, W.: NARF: 3D range image features for object recognition. In: Workshop on Defining and Solving Realistic Perception Problems in Personal Robotics at the IEEE/RSJ International Conference on Intelligent Robots and Systems (IROS), vol. 44 (2010)
20. Tombari, F., Salti, S., Di Stefano, L.: Unique signatures of histograms for local surface description. In: Daniilidis, K., Maragos, P., Paragios, N. (eds.) ECCV 2010. LNCS, vol. 6313, pp. 356–369. Springer, Heidelberg (2010). https://doi.org/10.1007/978-3-642-15558-1_26
21. Willis, A.R., Brink, K.M.: iGRaND: an invariant frame for RGBD sensor feature detection and descriptor extraction with applications. In: SPIE Commercial + Scientific Sensing and Imaging, International Society for Optics and Photonics, p. 98670P (2016)

Embedding Spatial Context into Spectral Angle Based Nonlinear Mapping for Hyperspectral Image Analysis

Evgeny Myasnikov$^{(\boxtimes)}$ (iD)

Samara University, Moskovskoe Shosse 34A, Samara 443086, Russia
mevg@geosamara.ru
http://ssau.ru

Abstract. Due to the high dimensionality and redundancy of hyperspectral images, an important step in analyzing such images is to reduce the dimensionality. In this paper, we propose and study the dimensionality reduction technique, which is based on the approximation of spectral angle mapper (SAM) measures by Euclidean distances. The key feature of the proposed method is the integration of spatial information into the dissimilarity measure. The experiments performed on the open hyperspectral datasets showed that the developed method can be used in the analysis of hyperspectral images.

Keywords: Hyperspectral image · Dimensionality reduction
Classification · Nonlinear mapping · Spectral angle
SAM · Spatial context

1 Introduction

Nowadays hyperspectral images are widely used in many different areas. On the one hand, the use of hyperspectral images opens new possibilities as it allows to extract information about materials (components) contained in an image. On the other hand, the use of hyperspectral images is associated with difficulties in storage, transmission, processing, and recognition. These difficulties are caused by high spectral dimensionality of such images. Thus, the important step of hyperspectral image processing techniques is the elimination of redundancy of such images while preservation of important spectral information.

Due to the above reasons, researchers' attention was given both to supervised feature selection techniques and to unsupervised dimensionality reduction techniques. Nevertheless due to the objective reasons such as valuable computational costs, less stability to changes in an image scene, necessity to the presence of ground truth information, feature selection techniques became less popular then dimensionality reduction techniques [1].

The reported study was funded by RFBR according to the research project no. 18-07-01312-a.

L. J. Chmielewski et al. (Eds.): ICCVG 2018, LNCS 11114, pp. 263–274, 2018.
https://doi.org/10.1007/978-3-030-00692-1_23

Both linear and nonlinear dimensionality reduction techniques are used with hyperspectral images. Linear techniques are used more often, and the most popular one is the principal component analysis technique (PCA) [2]. This technique searches the projection of data in the lower dimensional linear subspace, which minimizes the variance of data. Other examples of linear techniques are independent component analysis (ICA) [3], projection pursuit and some others.

The examples of nonlinear dimensionality reduction techniques used in hyperspectral image analysis are Locally-linear embedding (LLE) [4], Laplacian eigenmaps (LE) [5], Local Tangent Space Alignment (LTSA) [6], isometric embedding (ISOMAP) [7], Curvilinear component analysis (CCA), Curvilinear distance analysis (CDA) [8], and Nonlinear Mapping (NLM) [9]. These techniques are used in hyperspectral image processing less often, but it is known [10] that hyperspectral remote sensing images are affected by nonlinear mixing effects due to multipath light scattering and other reasons.

Nevertheless there is a considerable growth of popularity of such techniques in the field of hyperspectral image processing. It was shown that being compared to linear techniques, nonlinear methods allow, for example, to improve the accuracy of land cover classification and object detection. In the task of hyperspectral image visualization nonlinear techniques allow to generate false- (pseudo-) color representations of hyperspectral images with desirable features.

Nowadays we can indicate a number of works in which nonlinear dimensionality reduction techniques have been successfully applied to the processing of multi- and hyperspectral images. For example, CCA and CDA techniques have been applied to reduce the dimensionality of multispectral images in [11,12]. The LLE technique was used in [13], and the same technique was used in [14] together with LE technique. Later examples of the application of LLE, LE and LTSA techniques in hyperspectral image analysis can be found in papers [15–17]. The NLM technique has been applied in [18,22,26]. The citation list, with no doubts, can be expanded.

In all these nonlinear techniques, it is required to measure the dissimilarity between pixels of a hyperspectral image. The most commonly used measure for this purpose is the Euclidean distance. However, there are several other dissimilarity measures that have been used successfully in hyperspectral image analysis. The most widely used among them is the spectral angle (SAM) [19].

It was shown that this measure has advantages over the Euclidean distance in the field of hyperspectral image analysis; however, it has rarely been used in the field of nonlinear dimensionality reduction.

In particular, we can indicate only a few papers (for example, [15,20–22]), in which the SAM measure was used with nonlinear dimensionality reduction techniques. In [20], the SAM measure was used together with the Euclidean distance in the first stage of the ISOMAP method to determine neighbor pixels in the hyperspectral space. In [21], the authors study the effectiveness of the SAM measure and the Euclidean distance to reduce dimensionality using Laplacian eigenmaps. In [15], the SAM measure was used to improve the Laplacian eigenmaps method to reduce the sensitivity to data skips in temporal sequences of multispectral satellite images. The paper [22] proposed several nonlinear mapping methods based on the principle of preservation of spectral angles.

An important fact is that the above dimensionality reduction techniques act in the spectral space. However, hyperspectral images contain both spectral and spatial information. And the last type of information remains unused in traditional dimensionality reduction techniques [26]. In spite of the fact that we can indicate a lot of papers in which spatial information is used in image analysis, in particular, in the analysis of hyperspectral images (a recent review on this topic can be found in [23]), the number of papers devoted to the problem of using spatial information of hyperspectral images in nonlinear dimensionality reduction techniques, is rather small (see, for example, [24–26]).

In general, most of the methods used for this purpose can be attributed to one of two ways of taking into account spatial information: the use of kernel functions determined in the spatial-spectral domain and the use of extended dissimilarity measures that take into account the spectral characteristics of the local neighborhood of image pixels.

Thus, the use of non-Euclidean dissimilarity measures, together with exploiting the spatial context in nonlinear dimensionality reduction of hyperspectral image data, is currently insufficiently investigated.

In this paper we propose and study the nonlinear dimensionality reduction method based both on the principle of preserving the spectral angles, and also taking into account the spatial context of pixels in hyperspectral images. The paper is organized as follows. Section 2 briefly describes the basics of the nonlinear mapping technique. Then an approach based on the approximation of spectral angles by Euclidean distances is presented, and the description of the method used to take into account the spatial context is given. Besides a numerical optimization procedure is developed based on the stochastic gradient descent. Section 3 describes experimental studies. In this section, using hyperspectral images that are publicly available, the proposed method is compared with the principal component analysis technique (linear method) and some nonlinear dimensionality reduction methods. The effectiveness of the proposed approach is shown in terms of the accuracy of the classification. The paper ends up with the conclusion in Sect. 4.

2   Methods

Let us present the basics of the nonlinear mapping method before we start the description of the approach proposed in this paper. The description of the method in the following subsection is given according to [22].

2.1   Nonlinear Mapping Method

The nonlinear mapping method refers to the class of nonlinear dimensionality reduction techniques, based on the principle of preserving pairwise distances between points (vectors). It minimizes the following data mapping error:

$$\varepsilon_{ED} = \mu \cdot \sum_{i,j=1,i<j}^{N} \rho_{ij}(d(x_i, x_j) - d(y_i, y_j))^2. \tag{1}$$

Here N – is the number of data points, x_i are coordinates of data points in a multidimensional space R^M, y_i are coordinates of corresponding points in a lower dimensional space R^m, $d()$ is a distance function, μ and ρ_{ij} are constants, which define a specific error function. In this paper we used

$$\mu = 1/\sum_{i<j} d^2(x_i, x_j), \rho_{i,j} = 1. \tag{2}$$

The distance function $d()$ in expression (1) is usually the Euclidean distance.

To minimize the error (1), a number of numerical optimization methods can be used, but the methods based on the gradient descent algorithm are most often used [18]. In this paper we will also use the methods of this class.

Let us consider a simple gradient descent algorithm. Taking coordinates $Y = (y_1, y_2, ...y_N)$ in low-dimensional space as optimized parameters, the basic version of the algorithm makes a sequential refinement of the initial configuration of points $Y(0)$ in the output space using the following expression:

$$Y(t+1) = Y(t) - \alpha \nabla \varepsilon. \tag{3}$$

Here t is the number of an iteration, $\nabla \varepsilon$ is the gradient of the objective function, α is the coefficient (step size) of the gradient descent.

Thus, the iterative optimization process is defined by the following recurrence relation for the coordinates of data points in the output space:

$$y_{ik}(t+1) = y_{ik}(t) + 2\alpha\mu \sum_{j=1(j\neq i)}^{N} \rho_{i,j} \cdot \frac{d(x_i, x_j) - d(y_i, y_j)}{d(y_i, y_j)} \cdot (y_{ik}(t) - y_{jk}(t)). \tag{4}$$

This expression allows us to find some suboptimal solution of the problem $\varepsilon \to_Y min$ by initializing the output coordinates $y_i(0)$, followed by the iterative optimization using expression (4) until the coordinates $y_i(t)$ become stable.

Nonlinear Mapping Based on the Approximation of Spectral Angles by Euclidean Distances. As indicated in the introduction, the spectral angle mapper measure (SAM) [19]

$$\theta(x_i, x_j) = arccos\left(\frac{x_i \cdot x_j}{||x_i||||x_j||}\right) \tag{5}$$

is often used to measure the dissimilarity between image pixels in a hyperspectral space. The most natural approach to construct a nonlinear mapping method based on the principle of preserving pairwise spectral angles, is the introduction of the spectral angle mapping error in the following form [22]:

$$\varepsilon_{SAM} = \mu \sum_{i,j=1(i<j)}^{N} \left(\rho_{i,j} \left(\theta(x_i, x_j) - \theta(y_i, y_j)\right)^2\right). \tag{6}$$

In this case, the gradient descent approach can be applied to find the suboptimal solution. Some implementations of this approach for constructing the nonlinear mapping method are studied in [22]. It was also shown in [22] that good results in the dimensionality reduction of hyperspectral remote sensing images were obtained by approximating the original SAM measures by Euclidean distances in an output space.

This observation is in a good agreement with the fact that the distance between two points on a unit hypersphere is equal to the angle between the corresponding vectors. In addition, such a scheme is consistent with the approach adopted in multidimensional scaling. In accordance with this approach, we simply treat the SAM values as some dissimilarity measures that take values from the range $[0; \pi]$. In this case, expression (1) takes the form

$$\varepsilon_{SAM \to ED} = \mu \cdot \sum_{i,j=1(i<j)}^{N} \left(\rho_{ij} (\theta(x_i, x_j) - d(y_i, y_j))^2 \right) \tag{7}$$

and the corresponding optimization method can be directly obtained from expression (4) [22]:

$$y_i(t+1) = y_i(t) + 2\alpha\mu \sum_{j=1(i \neq j)}^{N} \rho_{i,j} \cdot \frac{\theta(x_i, x_j) - d(y_i, y_j)}{d(y_i, y_j)} \cdot (y_i(t) - y_j(t)). \tag{8}$$

Exploiting the Spatial Context in Dimensionality Reduction. As it was said in the introduction, the spatial context can be exploited in dimensionality reduction of hyperspectral images in several ways. In paper [26] two ways of exploiting the spatial context were proposed: the use of window functions and the use of order statistics. The best results in terms of the quality of a subsequent classification were obtained using order statistics. Therefore, in this paper it is proposed to use a similar approach for the SAM measure. We give a brief description of this approach below.

To embed the contextual information, for each pixel x_i of an image, we consider the spatial neighborhood of the radius R containing the pixels $x_1^i, x_2^i, ...x_K^i$. We order the pixels in the neighborhood so as the spectral dissimilarity with the pixel x_i increases in a spectral space:

$$\theta(x_i, x_{(1)}^i) \leq \theta(x_i, x_{(2)}^i) \leq ... \leq \theta(x_i, x_{(K)}^i). \tag{9}$$

Thus, for each pixel x_i, we obtain the set of order statistics: $\{x_{(1)}^i, x_{(2)}^i, ...x_{(K)}^i\}$. Then the feature space is extended by the first S order statistics (x_i is denoted here as $x_{(0)}^i$):

$$x_i^* = \left(x_{(0)}^i, x_{(1)}^i, .., x_{(S)}^i \right). \tag{10}$$

Further, in the dimensionality reduction stage we use the following modified dissimilarity measure in expressions (7) and (8):

$$\Delta(x_i^*, x_j^*) = \frac{\sum_{s=0}^{S} w_s \theta(x_{(s)}^i, x_{(s)}^j)}{\sum_{s=0}^{S} w_s}. \tag{11}$$

Here we use the inverse weighting $w_s = 1/(1+s)$, and S is the number of order statistics used as the spatial context.

Numerical Optimization Based on a Stochastic Gradient Descent. Unfortunately, the methods based on the simple gradient descent approach described above can not be directly applied to hyperspectral remote sensing imagery due to the high computational complexity and memory limitations of the base method [18]. All these methods require $O(N^2)$ operations to be performed at one iteration of the optimization process. For this reason, in this paper (as in [18, 22, 26]) we apply the stochastic gradient descent algorithm, based on mini-batches.

For this algorithm, the gradient value $\nabla\varepsilon$ in expression (3) is estimated using a random sample:

$$\tilde{\nabla}\varepsilon = \sum_{j=1}^{R} \nabla\varepsilon_{r_j}. \tag{12}$$

Here r is the random sample (mini-batch), used to approximate the gradient at the iteration t of the optimization process, r_j is the j-th element of this sample, R is the cardinality of the subset r. Using this approach, the cardinality of the batch determines the computational complexity of the algorithm for one iteration. Thus, for the subset of cardinality R, the computational complexity is reduced to $O(RNMmS)$.

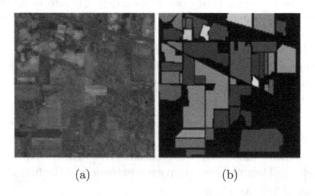

(a)   (b)

Fig. 1. Indian Pines scene: (a) representation of the scene in pseudo- (false-) colors, obtained using nonlinear mapping; (b) ground truth classification of the scene (classified pixels are shown in color) (Color figure online).

3   Experiments

In the experimental study, open and well-known hyperspectral remote sensing scenes were used [27]. The results of the experiments for the Indian Pines scene are given below. This scene (Fig. 1(a)) contains 145×145 pixels, and 224 spectral components obtained using the AVIRIS sensor. In the experiments we used the version containing only 200 components (some channels were removed due to a high noise level and water absorption). This hyperspectral scene is provided along with a ground truth classification mask (Fig. 1(b)), which was used to assess the classification quality.

In the first experiment, we evaluated the correctness of the proposed dimensionality reduction method. To estimate the quality, the hyperspectral data mapping error (7) was used, and the modified measure (11) was used as a dissimilarity measure in a hyperspectral space. The dependence of the error (7) on the iteration number for the first 50 iterations is shown in Fig. 2(a). As it can be seen from this figure, for the first few dozen iterations the error decreased by several orders of magnitude.

Figure 2(b) shows the dependence of the time of an iteration on the number S of order statistics. As it can be seen from the figure, the graph is linear, which agrees with the theoretical complexity estimate given in Sect. 2.

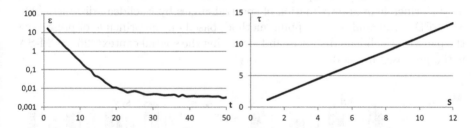

Fig. 2. Evaluation of the proposed method: the dependence of the error ε on the number of an iteration t for the dimensionality of the output space $m = 5$ and the number of order statistics $S = 5$ (a); the dependence of the time of an iteration on the number S of order statistics used as a spatial context (b).

In this section, the evaluation of the proposed approach is performed in terms of the classification quality. In particular, two well-known classifiers were used for the features obtained using the proposed dimensionality reduction method: the k-nearest neighbor (NN) classifier, and the support vector machine (SVM). To perform the experiments, the entire set of classified pixels (with a known ground truth classification) was divided into a training set containing 60% of the sample, and a test subset containing 40% of the sample. To assess the classification quality, the classification accuracy was used, defined as the fraction of correctly classified pixels in the total number of pixels classified.

In the second experiment, we evaluated the influence of the number S of order statistics used as a spatial context on the classification quality. Some results of

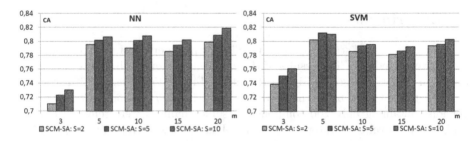

Fig. 3. Indian pines: Dependence of the classification accuracy CA on the dimensionality m of the output space ($m = 3, 5, 10, 15, 20$) for the different number of order statistics ($S = 2, 5, 10$).

the experiment are shown in Fig. 3. As it can be seen, in almost all the considered cases, the more order statistics were used, the higher was the classification quality.

In the third experiment, the proposed method was compared with base nonlinear dimensionality reduction methods, and the most widely used principal component analysis technique. Some results of the experiment are shown in Fig. 4. In this figure, the following notation is introduced: PCA is the principal component analysis technique, SAED is the nonlinear mapping method, based on the principle of approximation of spectral angles by Euclidean distances [22], SCM-ED is the nonlinear mapping method, based on the principle of preserving the pairwise Euclidean distances and exploiting the spatial context [26], SCM-SA is the proposed method.

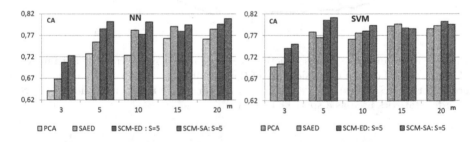

Fig. 4. Indian pines: Dependence of the classification accuracy CA on the dimensionality m of the output space ($m = 3, 5, 10, 15, 20$) for various dimensionality reduction methods.

As can be seen from the Fig. 4, the use of the method proposed in this paper has made it possible to achieve the best quality of classification in most of the considered cases. A more noticeable effect was achieved when using the nearest neighbor classifier. This can be explained by the fact that the reduced space is formed based on the principle of approximating pairwise dissimilarities between the pixels in the hyperspectral space by Euclidean distances in the reduced space.

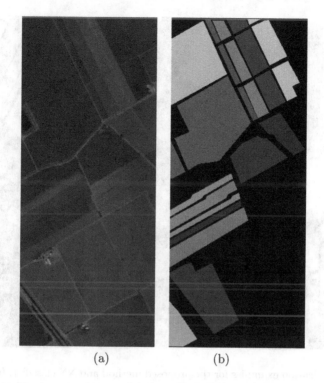

(a)   (b)

Fig. 5. Salinas hyperspectral scene: (a) representation of the scene in pseudo- (false-) colors, obtained using nonlinear mapping; (b) ground truth classification of the scene (classified pixels are shown in color) (Color figure online).

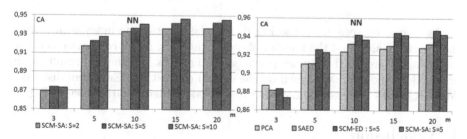

Fig. 6. Salinas: Dependence of the classification accuracy CA on the dimensionality m of the output space ($m = 3, 5, 10, 15, 20$) for the different number of order statistics ($S = 2, 5, 10$) (left) and various dimensionality reduction methods (right).

The results of experiments for another well known test hyperspectral scene Salinas (see Fig. 5) are shown in the Fig. 6. This image contains 512×217 pixels in 224 spectral components obtained using the AVIRIS sensor. As in the previous case, a version containing only 204 components was used.

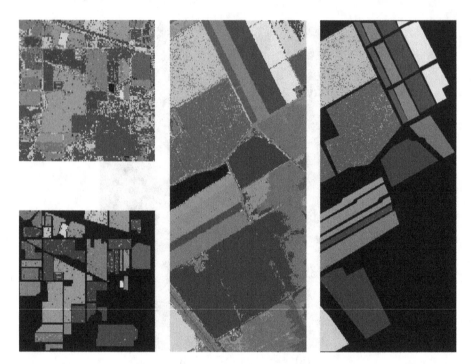

Fig. 7. Classification examples for the proposed method and NN classifier: Indian pines scene ($S = 10, m = 20, CA = 0.819$) (left), Salinas scene ($S = 10, m = 15, CA = 0,947$) (right). Classified pixels are shown in color with and without groundtruth mask (Color figure online).

As it can be seen from the Fig. 6, the classification accuracy grows with the dimensionality and the number of order statistics. Being compared to other methods, the proposed approach provided good results. But the best results were provided by the approach based on the spatial context and Euclidean distance. Some examples of classification using the proposed method are shown in Fig. 7.

4 Conclusion

In this paper we proposed and studied the unsupervised nonlinear mapping method, based on the approximation of spectral angles with Euclidean distances and exploiting the spatial context of hyperspectral images. Experimental research has shown that the use of the proposed method makes it possible to significantly improve the classification accuracy for the Indian Pines hyperspectral image, and provide good results for the Salinas image. Therefore the proposed method extends current dimensionality reduction toolkit, aimed to hyperspectral image processing.

The drawbacks of the proposed method include its long operating time, linearly increasing with the number of order statistics used as a spatial context.

In connection with this, a promising line of research is speeding up this method with the use of modern parallel computing hardware.

References

1. Lunga, D., Prasad, S., Crawford, M., Ersoy, O.: Manifold-learning-based feature extraction for classification of hyperspectral data. IEEE Sig. Process. Mag. **31**(1), 55–66 (2014)
2. Richards, J.A., Jia, X., Ricken, D.E., Gessner, W.: Remote Sensing Digital Image Analysis: An Introduction. Springer, Heidelberg (1999)
3. Wang, J., Chang, C.-I.: Independent component analysis-based dimensionality reduction with applications in hyperspectral image analysis. IEEE Trans. Geosci. Remote Sens. **44**(6), 1586–1600 (2006)
4. Roweis, S.T., Saul, L.K.: Nonlinear dimensionality reduction by locally linear embedding. Science **290**, 2323–2326 (2000)
5. Belkin, M., Niyogi, P.: Laplacian eigenmaps and spectral techniques for embedding and clustering. Adv. Neural Inf. Process. Syst. **14**, 586–691 (2001)
6. Zhang, Z., Zha, H.: Principal manifolds and nonlinear dimension reduction via local tangent space alignment. SIAM J. Sci. Comput. **26**(1), 313–338 (2005)
7. Tenenbaum, J.B., de Silva, V., Langford, J.C.: A global geometric framework for nonlinear dimensionality reduction. Science **290**, 2319–2323 (2000)
8. Demartines, P., Hérault, J.: Curvilinear component analysis: a self-organizing neural network for nonlinear mapping of data sets. IEEE Trans. Neural Netw. **8**(1), 148–154 (1997)
9. Sammon Jr., J.W.: A nonlinear mapping for data structure analysis. IEEE Trans. Comput. **C−18**(5), 401–409 (1969)
10. Bachmann, C.M., Ainsworth, T.L., Fusina, R.A.: Improved manifold coordinate representations of large-scale hyperspectral scenes. IEEE Trans. Geosci. Remote Sens. **44**(10), 2786–2803 (2006)
11. Journaux, L., Foucherot, I., Gouton, P.: Nonlinear reduction of multispectral images by curvilinear component analysis: application and optimization. In: International Conference on CSIMTA 2004 (2004)
12. Lennon, M., Mercier, G., Mouchot, M., Hubert-Moy, L.: Curvilinear component analysis for nonlinear dimensionality reduction of hyperspectral images. Proc. SPIE **4541**, 157–168 (2002)
13. Kim, D.H., Finkel, L.H.: Hyperspectral image processing using locally linear embedding. In: First International IEEE EMBS Conference on Neural Engineering, pp. 316–319 (2003)
14. Shen-En, Q., Guangyi, C.: A new nonlinear dimensionality reduction method with application to hyperspectral image analysis. In: IEEE International Geoscience and Remote Sensing Symposium, pp. 270–273 (2007)
15. Yan, L., Roy, D.P.: Improved time series land cover classification by missing observation- adaptive nonlinear dimensionality reduction. Remote Sens. Environ. **158**, 478–491 (2015)
16. Sun, W., et al.: Nonlinear dimensionality reduction via the ENH-LTSA method for hyperspectral image classification. IEEE J. Sel. Top. Appl. Earth Obs. Remote Sens. **7**(2), 375–388 (2014). Artcle No. 6419851

17. Hong, D.F., Yokoya, N., Zhu, X.X.: Local manifold learning with robust neighbors selection for hyperspectral dimensionality reduction. In: International Geoscience and Remote Sensing Symposium (IGARSS), pp. 40–43, November 2016. Article No. 7729001

18. Myasnikov, E.: Evaluation of stochastic gradient descent methods for nonlinear mapping of hyperspectral data. In: Campilho, A., Karray, F. (eds.) ICIAR 2016. LNCS, vol. 9730, pp. 276–283. Springer, Cham (2016). https://doi.org/10.1007/978-3-319-41501-7_31

19. Kruse, F.A., et al.: The Spectral Image Processing System (SIPS) interactive visualization and analysis of imaging spectrometer data. Remote Sens. Environ. **44**, 145–163 (1993)

20. Bachmann, C.M., Ainsworth, T.L., Fusina, R.A.: Exploiting manifold geometry in hyperspectral imagery. IEEE Trans. Geosci. Remote Sens. **43**(3), 441–454 (2005)

21. Yan, L., Niu, X.: Spectral-angle-based Laplacian Eigenmaps for nonlinear dimensionality reduction of hyperspectral imagery. Photogramm. Eng. Remote Sens. **80**(9), 849–861 (2014)

22. Myasnikov, E.: Nonlinear mapping based on spectral angle preserving principle for hyperspectral image analysis. In: Felsberg, M., Heyden, A., Krüger, N. (eds.) CAIP 2017. LNCS, vol. 10425, pp. 416–427. Springer, Cham (2017). https://doi.org/10.1007/978-3-319-64698-5_35

23. Wang, L., Shi, C., Diao, C., Ji, W., Yin, D.: A survey of methods incorporating spatial information in image classification and spectral unmixing. Int. J. Remote Sens. **37**(16), 3870–3910 (2016)

24. Borhani, M., Ghassemian, H.: Kernel multivariate spectral-spatial analysis of hyperspectral data. IEEE J. Sel. Top. Appl. Earth Obs. Remote Sens. **8**(6), 2418–2426 (2015). Article No. 7056457

25. Sun, W., Liu, C., Li, W.: Hyperspectral imagery classification using the combination of improved Laplacian eigenmaps and improved k-nearest neighbor classifier. Wuhan Daxue Xuebao (Xinxi Kexue Ban)/Geomatics Inf. Sci. Wuhan Univ. **40**(9), 1151–1156 (2015)

26. Myasnikov, E.: Exploiting spatial context in nonlinear mapping of hyperspectral image data. In: Battiato, S., Gallo, G., Schettini, R., Stanco, F. (eds.) ICIAP 2017. LNCS, vol. 10485, pp. 180–190. Springer, Cham (2017). https://doi.org/10.1007/978-3-319-68548-9_17

27. Hyperspectral Remote Sensing Scenes. http://www.ehu.eus/ccwintco/index.php?title=HyperspectralRemoteSensingScenes

Color Object Retrieval
Using Local Features Based
on Opponent-Process Theory

Paula Budzakova[1] , Elena Sikudova[2] , and Zuzana Berger Haladova[1]([⊠])

[1] Faculty of Mathematics, Physics and Informatics,
Comenius University in Bratislava, Bratislava, Slovakia
budzakova9@uniba.sk, zhaladova@gmail.com
[2] Faculty of Mathematics and Physics, Charles University, Prague, Czech Republic
sikudova@fmph.uniba.sk

Abstract. Although the color is perceived as an irreplaceable element describing the world around us, the techniques for extracting of the local features are mostly based on the description of the intensities - while the color information is being fully ignored. This paper proposes a method for extracting of the local features of the color image. As a basic model we have chosen the approach to the human visual system using chromatic opponent channels and the SIFT (Scalable Invariant Feature Transform) method. The idea of this solution is the incorporation of the opponent chromatic channels by replacing the grayscale information in the SIFT method, so that the key points are detected on two separate opponent channels. For the interesting points found in the two channels, the descriptors are formed which are then united into one set. We also propose the new methods for the validation of the keypoint pairing utilizing the keypoint orientation consistency check. The algorithm was tested in an object retrieval experiment.

1 Introduction

Among the most used descriptions of color images are global features like color histograms of particular color channels or quantized color palettes. Although easy to compute, global histograms are not suitable for object retrieval applications. In order to use the histogram features in such applications, object segmentation should be performed as a first step. Even then the matching of similar objects is not very successful.

On the other hand, using local features we can describe the image by as many features as we wish. Local features describe a narrow neighborhood of a given pixel. Basically we want to describe the parts of the image where something "interesting" happens. In these interesting points (IPs) usually a big variation of intensity is found. A homogeneous patch of image does not contain interesting points. The interestingness of a point varies in individual detector methods.

Extraction of local features in images consists of two steps. In the first step a chosen detector is applied to the image to identify the interesting points and

L. J. Chmielewski et al. (Eds.): ICCVG 2018, LNCS 11114, pp. 275–286, 2018.
https://doi.org/10.1007/978-3-030-00692-1_24

in the second step the neighborhood of these point is described by a chosen descriptor.

Most of the local feature extraction methods detect points and build descriptors, such that the points and descriptors are affine invariant. It means, they stay the same, even if the object is rotated, translated or scaled. The photometric invariance is usually not considered.

For grayscale images, the well known approaches of detection and description of interesting point are SIFT (Lowe 2004), SURF (Bay et al. 2008) and ORB (Rublee et al. 2011).

We propose a new SIFT-based method modification to extract local features from color image using human visual system.

In this paper we describe the existing color modification of the SIFT method and propose a new approach based on opponent process theory. We evaluate the method on an object retrieval task and compare it with several well known approaches.

2   Existing Methods

Initially, local features were designed to work on grayscale images. In the past couple of years several modification that include color information appeared.

An extensive overview by Mikolajczyk and Schmid (2005) evaluated the SIFT among the best performing descriptors for intensity images. In many modifications of the SIFT methodology, color information is added after detecting the interest points in the intensity image. The SIFT descriptor is then computed on each color channel. That is the case of RGB-SIFT, HSV-SIFT, YCbCr-SIFT and rg-SIFT evaluated in (Li et al. 2014).

In this work the YCbCr-SIFT was found to have the best performance. Li et al. (2014) employed the grayscale SIFT detector and descriptor combined with local color kernel histogram description.

The authors of C-SIFT (Abdel-Hakim and Farag 2006) compute the interesting points from the reflectance property invariant H and show that their approach gives better results that the grayscale SIFT method. In their work the color invariants (based on the Kubelka-Munk theory) are the ratios of partial derivatives of the photometric reflectance $E(\lambda, \mathbf{x})$.

Cui et al. (2010) used the SIFT methodology at each channel of a perception-based color space.

Nowadays, there is an strong ongoing research in the area of Convolutional neural networks. However as extensively reviewed in (Zheng et al. 2017) there are still scenarios (e.g. when no prior knowledge about the datasets is available) when they are outperformed by standard local features.

3   Algorithm

The pipeline of the proposed NOpp-SIFT algorithm is illustrated in Fig. 1. The first step is to convert RGB values to an opponent color space. Then we apply

SIFT detector on the chromatic channels, compute the descriptors and match the descriptor in order to retrieve similar objects. Individual steps of the algorithm are described in detail in the following subsections.

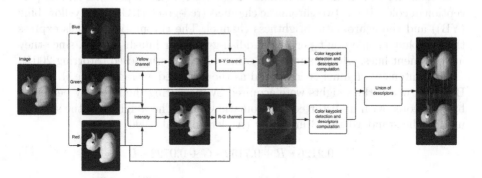

Fig. 1. The pipeline of the proposed algorithm.

Fig. 2. Sample images from the ALOI database

3.1   Dataset

Our method was designed to retrieve objects with very dark or black background from the ALOI (Geusebroek et al. 2005) database of objects. This database contains different objects which undergone different transformations such as change of the light source position, change of illumination intensity, change of illumination color temperature and object rotation. Our dataset was selected to contain objects of varying colors. Sample images from the database can be seen in Fig. 2.

3.2   Preprocessing

We decided to use the color space based on human visual system Jost et al. (2005), which is used for detecting visually salient features in images. The opponent color model is a model of human visual system that represents human perception of color. It has two chromatic channels (red-green (RG) and a yellow-blue (YB)) and the achromatic brightness channel. The chromatic channels express the fact that people don't perceive reddish-greens, or bluish-yellows, since they are opponent hues, which cancel each other when superimposed (Storring 2004).

The intensity channel is computed as the weighted average of the R, G and B values, where the weights were acquired by measuring the intensity perceived by the people with undistorted trichromatic vision. The weights are the same as used in the standard sRGB model by (Anderson et al. 1996)

$$I = 0.2126 * R + 0.7152 * G + 0.0722 * B. \tag{1}$$

In this color space the two chromatic channels (RG and YB) proposed in Swain and Ballard (1991) are normalized by the intensity channel, which removes the effect of intensity variations. The channels are defined as follows

$$RG = \frac{(R - G)}{I} \tag{2}$$

and

$$YB = \frac{(B - Y)}{I}, \tag{3}$$

where

$$Y = \frac{(R + G)}{2}. \tag{4}$$

Now we proceed with the detection of the interesting points in the chromatic channels.

3.3   Interesting Point Detection

SIFT algorithm introduced by Lowe (2004) consists of a scale and rotation invariant detector and a HOG (histogram of oriented gradients) descriptor. SIFT detector uses a Gaussian scale pyramid. The image is scaled to K sizes – octaves. Each octave is then recurrently filtered by a 2D Gaussian.

Two consecutive images in each octave are then subtracted and the resulting $N - 1$ DoG (difference of Gaussians) images are approximations of LoG (Laplacian of Gaussians) images. The points of interest are identified in $3 \times 3 \times 3$ neighborhood in the DoG space. The octave in which the IP was found represents the "scale" of the IP and determines the size of the neighborhood for descriptor extraction of that point.

In our method the SIFT IP detection is applied directly on each opponent chromatic channel. Figure 3 illustrates, that different IPs are found in the chromatic channels, which increases the total number detected IPs.

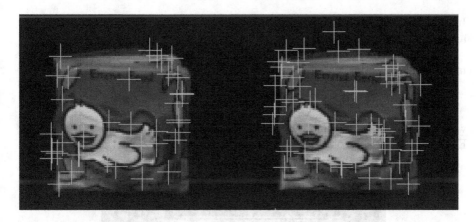

Fig. 3. Interesting points detected by SIFT method in red-green (left) and a yellow-blue (right) channels (color figure online)

3.4 Descriptor

SIFT uses a descriptor based on histogram of oriented gradients (HOG). For each detected interesting point, its neighborhood is divided into 16 (4×4) subregions. The size of the neighborhood is determined by the scale of the IP and one of its axes is aligned to the orientation of the IP. Each subregion is sampled to 16 points (4×4) and the gradients are computed in each of them. The magnitude of the gradients is weighted by a Gaussian with the mean in the IP. The magnitudes and orientations are described by 8 bin histograms. The resulting descriptor is a 128 bin histogram consisting of concatenated histograms of the 16 subregions.

Many color enhanced SIFT algorithms suggest to concatenate the color information from different channels into one descriptor. In our algorithm we apply the SIFT description on the chromatic channels and keep this information separated. That means IPs detected in RG channel are described only by its neighborhood in the RG channel. The final set of object descriptors is the union of descriptors of IPs found in both chromatic channels.

3.5 Descriptor Matching

Descriptor matching is an important step in using local features for object detection, image aligning and in other computer vision applications. There are several matching strategies.

Vector descriptors can be matched according to their distance in the vector space. If the distance is below a threshold, the two descriptor are pronounced a match. Then a descriptor can have several matches. In the nearest neighbor strategy, two descriptors match, if they are the closest and their distance is below the threshold. With this strategy, there is at most one match but it might not be correct, especially when there are few similar interesting points in the image.

In this case the distances from the nearest and the second nearest descriptors are similar.

This property is exploited in the nearest neighbor distance ratio (NNDR) matching, where the descriptors are matched if

$$||D_A - D_B||/||D_A - D_C|| < t, \tag{5}$$

where D_B is the first and D_C is the second nearest neighbor to D_A. The Euclidean distance is used to find the nearest neighbors (Fig. 4).

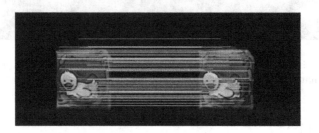

Fig. 4. NNDR descriptor matching for objects with the change of color temperature

3.6 Object Matching

We propose 3 object matching strategies. The first one uses NNDR IP matching and two objects are pronounced to be similar (or copies of the same object), if the number of matched IPs exceeds a threshold. The threshold is determined empirically as explained in the following section. The second strategy uses the nearest neighbor IP matching and the keypoint orientation as a consistency check. The keypoint orientation is extracted in the process of keypoint detection

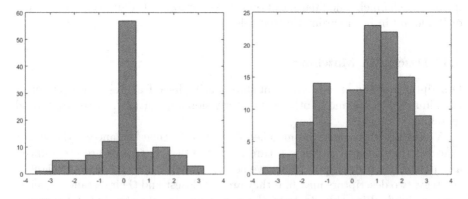

Fig. 5. Histogram of keypoint orientation differences of two images of the same (left) and different (right) objects.

Fig. 6. Matches with correct (yellow) and incorrect (green) orientation filtered by NOpp-Sift+NNDR+Orientation (Color figure online)

in the SIFT method. It is the dominant orientation of the gradient extracted from the the neighborhood of the keypoints. In our method we compute the histogram of the orientation differences of all matched pairs of keypoints. The highest peak in the histogram represents the dominant consistent orientation difference between the compared objects. When two objects are the same, the highest peak of the histogram represent their orientation difference (see Fig. 5 left). The histogram of orientation differences of two dissimilar objects can be seen on Fig. 5 right. The third method combines both strategies. It uses NNDR IP matching followed by orientation consistency check. In the orientation check process we compute the median of the orientation difference of matched IPs and we filter all the pairs with distance from median higher than 0.5. The matches preserved and filtered by this method can be seen on Fig. 6.

4   Experiments and Results

We conducted two experiments to show the performance of our method. The first experiment showed that our method satisfied the photometric invariance property. The second one showed that our method has a high performance in object retrieval application.

4.1   Photometric Invariance

Our first hypothesis, that the photometric invariance of our approach was higher than the one of original grayscale SIFT was validated by computing the number of IPs found in grayscale image and in the chromatic channels and comparing the number of matched IPs. High number of matched IPs means that these IPs are photometrically invariant, i.e. stable under varying lighting conditions. Table 1 shows the mean numbers of detected and matched IPs.

Table 1. Mean numbers of detected and matched IPs

Method/mean number of	Detected IPs	Matched IPs
SIFT	13	2
NOpp-SIFT	53	21

Applying the SIFT detector on the chromatic channels increases the number of found IPs, so the probability of correct IP match increases. This situation is illustrated in Fig. 7, where significantly less IPs were found using only the grayscale image.

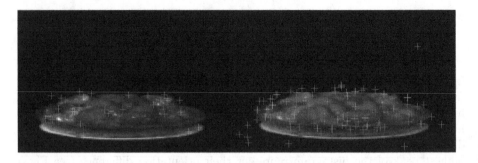

Fig. 7. IPs detected by grayscale SIFT (left) and the NOpp-SIFT (right).

The small number of matched IPs results in poor identification of objects in the database. In many cases there was no match found on objects with different light source position as illustrated in Fig. 8.

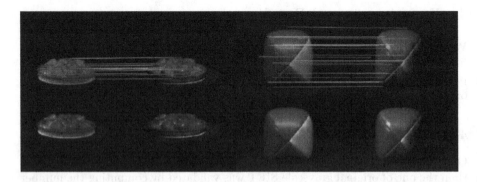

Fig. 8. Objects with different light source position and their matched IPs. Colored images were processed with NOpp-SIFT, grayscale images with SIFT.

4.2 Object Retrieval

The previous experiment showed that the color information in our NOpp-SIFT approach can be beneficial in the task of retrieval of objects illuminated by changing light.

We compared the performance of our NOpp-SIFT, NOpp-SIFT+orientation and NOpp-SIFT+NNDR+orientation with the original grayscale SIFT and the following color enhanced SIFT methods. YCbCr-SIFT, which was evaluated as the best by Li et al. (2014), CSIFT proposed by Abdel-Hakim and Farag (2006) and Opponent-SIFT (van de Sande et al. 2010), where the opponent channels are not normalized by the intensity.

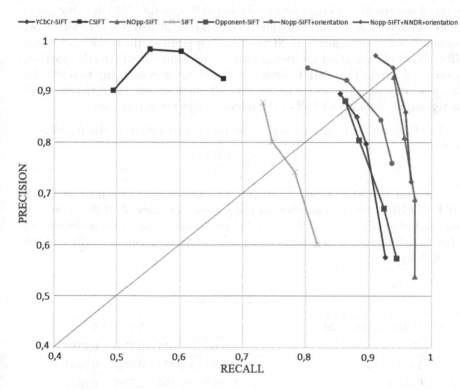

Fig. 9. Precision/recall curve for SIFT, YCbCr-SIFT, CSIFT, Opponent-SIFT, NOpp-SIFT (our approach), NOpp-SIFT+orientation (our approach) and NOpp-SIFT+NNDR+orientation (our approach)

We tested the methods on 303 images of different objects. The database contained up to 35 modification of each object. The results are presented as Precision-Recall graph in Fig. 9, where precision (P) is defined as

$$P = \frac{\text{number of retrieved relevant images}}{\text{number of retrieved images}} \tag{6}$$

and recall (R) as

$$R = \frac{\text{number of retrieved relevant images}}{\text{number of relevant images}}. \tag{7}$$

The objects were retrieved when the numbers of matched IPs was higher or equal to 3, 4, 5 and 6 for the methods using NNDR matching. For our orientation consistency check we use the ratio between the number of keypoints found on the query image and the height of the peak of the orientation difference histogram. Ratios were set to 2.5, 2.75, 3 and 3.25. The PR graph was constructed from (precision, recall) values for these thresholds (and ratio) of matched IPs. The top right point, where precision and recall equals one is the ideal performance of a retrieval system. We can see that our algorithm NOpp-Sift+NNDR+Orientation achieved the best performance for all thresholds on matched IPs. Overall the performance of all our algorithms NOpp-Sift, NOpp-Sift+Orientation and NOpp-Sift+NNDR+Orientation was better that the performance of the other methods in terms of recall. The CSIFT algorithm has higher precision (up to 0.980) but the recall was very low, which means that although almost all retrieved objects were relevant, only about half of the relevant object was retrieved.

The F_1 score defining accuracy or the trade-off between precision and recall defined as

$$F_1 = \frac{2PR}{P + R} \tag{8}$$

can be seen in Tables 2 and 3. Again, we can see that our method NOpp-SIFT+NNDR+Orientation achieved the highest accuracy of 94,2%. The other proposed algorithms NOpp-Sift and NOpp-Sift+orientation outperformed the other tested algorithms in therms of F1 score (highest accuracy 93,3% and 89% respectively).

Table 2. F1 score

Methods/threshold	3	4	5	6
SIFT	0,6933	0,7614	0,7731	0,7980
YCbCr-SIFT	0,7079	0,8433	0,6035	0,8742
CSIFT	0,7760	0,7455	0,7069	0,6385
Opponent-SIFT	0,7135	0,7776	0,8418	0,8716
NOpp-SIFT	0,6937	0,8067	0,8770	0,9330
NOpp-SIFT+NNDR+Orientation	**0,8273**	**0,9057**	**0,9415**	**0,9384**

Table 3. F1 score

Method/ratio	2.5	2.75	3	3.25
NOpp-SIFT+orientation	0.8687	0.8920	0.8797	0.8386

5   Conclusions

In this paper we presented a method suitable for colored object retrieval using a SIFT modification based on opponent process theory. Our algorithm applies the detector on the two chromatic channels and describe the interesting point found in these channels separately. The final set of object descriptors is the union of descriptors.

We showed that our approach exhibits a photometric invariance by successful matching of objects modified by change of the light source position, change of illumination intensity and change of illumination color temperature. We also proposed and evaluate three match selection strategies, one using standard second nearest neighbor approach second using the orientation consistency check and third combining both. In the future we would like to focus on speeding-up the algorithm by parallelization of the detection process in the chromatic channels. We would also run experiments on databases of objects with cluttered backgrounds and images with more that one object.

Acknowledgement. This work was supported by the VEGA 1/0796/18 grant.

References

Abdel-Hakim, A.E., Farag, A.A.: CSIFT: a SIFT descriptor with color invariant characteristics. In: 2006 IEEE Computer Society Conference on Computer Vision and Pattern Recognition, vol. 2, pp. 1978–1983. IEEE (2006)

Anderson, M., Motta, R., Chandrasekar, S., Stokes, M.: Proposal for a standard default color space for the internet's RGB. In: Color and Imaging Conference, vol. 1996, pp. 238–245. Society for Imaging, Science and Technology (1996)

Bay, H., Ess, A., Tuytelaars, T., Van Gool, L.: Speeded-up robust features (SURF). Comput. Vis. Image Underst. **110**(3), 346–359 (2008)

Cui, Y., Pagani, A., Stricker, D.: Sift in perception-based color space. In: 2010 17th IEEE International Conference on Image Processing (ICIP), pp. 3909–3912. IEEE (2010)

Geusebroek, J.-M., Burghouts, G.J., Smeulders, A.W.: The Amsterdam library of object images. Int. J. Comput. Vis. **61**(1), 103–112 (2005)

Jost, T., Ouerhani, N., Von Wartburg, R., Müri, R., Hügli, H.: Assessing the contribution of color in visual attention. Comput. Vis. Image Underst. **100**(1), 107–123 (2005)

Li, D., Ke, Y., Zhang, G.: A SIFT descriptor with local kernel color histograms. In: 2011 Second International Conference on Mechanic Automation and Control Engineering (MACE), pp. 992–995. IEEE (2011)

Li, Q., Chen, J., Peng, Q., Wu, X.: Application of localized soft-assignment coding and CSIFT in image classification. In: Proceedings of International Conference on Internet Multimedia Computing and Service, p. 246. ACM (2014)

Lowe, D.G.: Distinctive image features from scale-invariant keypoints. Int. J. Comput. Vis. **60**(2), 91–110 (2004)

Mikolajczyk, K., Schmid, C.: A performance evaluation of local descriptors. IEEE Trans. Pattern Anal. Mach. Intell. **27**(10), 1615–1630 (2005)

Rublee, E., Rabaud, V., Konolige, K., Bradski, G.: ORB: an efficient alternative to sift or surf. In Proceedings of the 2011 International Conference on Computer Vision, ICCV 2011, pp. 2564–2571. IEEE Computer Society, Washington, DC (2011)

Storring, M. computer vision and human skin colour. Ph.D. thesis, Faculty of Engineering and Science Aalborg University, Denmark (2004)

Swain, M., Ballard, D.: Color indexing. Int. J. Comput. Vis. **7**(1), 11–32 (1991)

van de Sande, K., Gevers, T., Snoek, C.: Evaluating color descriptors for object and scene recognition. IEEE Trans. Pattern Anal. Mach. Intell. **32**(9), 1582–1596 (2010)

Zheng, L., Yang, Y., Tian, Q.: SIFT meets CNN: a decade survey of instance retrieval. IEEE Trans. Pattern Anal. Mach. Intell. **40**(5), 1224–1244 (2017)

Extracting Textual Overlays from Social Media Videos Using Neural Networks

Adam Słucki[1,3]($\boxtimes$), Tomasz Trzciński[2,3], Adam Bielski[3], and Paweł Cyrta[3]

[1] Polish-Japanese Academy of Information Technology, Warsaw, Poland
[2] Warsaw University of Technology, Warsaw, Poland
[3] Tooploox, Wrocław, Poland
{adam.slucki,tomasz.trzcinski,adam.bielski,pawel.cyrta}@tooploox.com

Abstract. Textual overlays are often used in social media videos as people who watch them without the sound would otherwise miss essential information conveyed in the audio stream. This is why extraction of those overlays can serve as an important meta-data source, e.g. for content classification or retrieval tasks. In this work, we present a robust method for extracting textual overlays from videos that builds up on multiple neural network architectures. The proposed solution relies on several processing steps: keyframe extraction, text detection and text recognition. The main component of our system, i.e. the text recognition module, is inspired by a convolutional recurrent neural network architecture and we improve its performance using synthetically generated dataset of over 600,000 images with text prepared by authors specifically for this task. We also develop a filtering method that reduces the amount of overlapping text phrases using Levenshtein distance and further boosts system's performance. The final accuracy of our solution reaches over 80% and is au pair with state-of-the-art methods.

1 Introduction

Videos published on social media are commonly described only with their title, short summary and unstructured keywords. Extracting additional information from textual overlays such as captions, key ideas or scene level summaries can be a crucial component of a content retrieval system, video classifier or intelligent advertisement targeting. The problem of extracting this information is twofold. First part of the problem is choosing frames on which OCR will be performed and the second is text detection and recognition on those frames. There are many domain-specific difficulties related to the detection and recognition in social media videos. Backgrounds of textual overlays in those videos are rarely solid and contrastive. They are often displayed as part of a background and have various font sizes, colors and combinations. We present examples of frames with text appearing in social media videos in Fig. 1.

In this paper, we present an entire working pipeline for text extraction tailored specifically for social media videos. We propose a multi-component system that consists of frame extraction, text detection, text recognition and

© Springer Nature Switzerland AG 2018
L. J. Chmielewski et al. (Eds.): ICCVG 2018, LNCS 11114, pp. 287–299, 2018.
https://doi.org/10.1007/978-3-030-00692-1_25

post-processing by text merging and rectification. Figure 2 shows an overview of our system. We also propose a method for generating synthetic training data designed for textual overlays commonly appearing in social media videos. Extending our training dataset with the synthetically generated data allows our text recognition model to reduce a word level recognition error by 20% compared to a general, pre-trained CRNN [12] model for text recognition. The main contribution of this work is a complete system that allows its user to extract video overlays with minimal amount of textual overlap and state-of-the-art text detection and recognition results. We also describe the details of a training data generation algorithm that takes into account visual characteristics of overlays in online videos and we show how using this algorithm improves the accuracy of our system. Finally, we propose a new method based on the Levenshtein distance that allows to filter out the text appearing in multiple frames and extract the most relevant information presented in a video.

The remainder of this paper is organized in the following manner: In Sect. 2, we discuss related works. Sect. 3 presents our system and in Sect. 4 we evaluate its performance against baselines. We conclude the paper in Sect. 5.

2   Related Work

A significant amount of research focused on addressing the problem of text detection and recognition in images [4,12,14,17]. The work [17] presents a fully convolutional neural network that is trained for pixelwise classification of text regions in natural scene images. Text recognition is performed with a CRNN model inspired by [12], which is further improved through a dictionary based correction. In our system, we also rely on a spellcheck dictionary-based functionality to improve the output of our system. Another approach to text detection in images is presented in [14], where the authors use a fast cascade boosting technique to detect single characters. The characters are then merged into lines with min-cost flow network in a post-processing step, similarly to our rectification module. Although the selection of text detection and recognition methods presented above is far from complete, in this work we focus on extracting textual overlays from videos, not images and we review below related works that address this exact problem.

Detecting and recognizing blocks of text in videos has also gained significant attention from the research community [5,11,15]. In [11], Sato *et al.* present an approach based on extracting and classifying hand-crafted features using a computer vision method. They rely on specific properties of letters to detect blocks of text, segment it into characters and recognize them individually using template matching. To enhance the quality of the input, they leverage temporal consistency of the text blocks displayed across several frames of video using time-based minimum pixels value search. Although fairly effective for videos with high contrast, where the color of textual characters is significantly different then the background, the main limitation of the method is lack of robustness against less contrastive frames. As presented in Fig. 1, this is often not the case for social

(a) Standard frame with text

(b) Superimposed subtitles

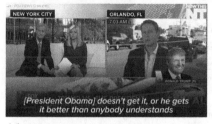

(c) Multiple text blocks with various fonts and sizes

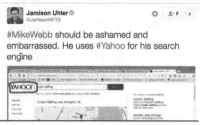

(d) Text displayed as a part of a background

Fig. 1. Sample frames extracted from social media videos with textual overlays displayed in challenging conditions.

media videos where various font colors are used and the contrast against the background cannot be guaranteed.

A recent work [15] presents a method that, similarly to [11], uses a computationally efficient text detection method, in this case the maximally stable external regions (MSER) [2], to generate a set of candidate regions. The regions are then filtered using a binary classifier based on a convolutional neural network architecture and text recognition is done using a similar neural network model. The system is capable of providing real-time OCR recognition in videos. Nevertheless, its main drawback is that the frames are processed individually, hence discarding temporal consistencies that are useful for getting stable and robust overlay detection and recognition system. Furthermore, processing videos on a frame-by-frame basis introduces a significant computational overhead in the context of overlay extraction - the exact problem we address in this paper. This is mainly due to the fact that the goal of overlay extraction is to output a set of phrases or sentences that do not have a significant overlap between each other, *i.e.* can be read as a single block of text spread across several scenes. In our approach, we tackle this problem using additional post-processing step that focuses on text rectification and proves its effectiveness through a set of qualitative results.

The problem of video overlay extraction is also tackled in [5], where Kannao and Guha propose to detect entire lines of text instead of single words. To decrease the computational cost of detection and recognition, they use temporal tracking across multiple frames. For the recognition, they train the Tesseract OCR model [13] with synthetically generated images. Inspired by this approach, we also generate part of our training data synthetically, however, we use the resulting dataset to improve the performance of several of our system's modules and not a Tesseract engine. Furthermore, contrary to the results presented in [5], our text recognition engine that relies on a convolutional recurrent neural network architecture [12] significantly outperforms the competing methods, including the baseline Tesseract method.

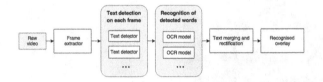

Fig. 2. Architecture of the system for textural overlays extraction.

3   Overlay Extraction System

In this section, we present our system whose goal is to extract complete sequences of text split across several frames of a social media video. An overview of the system is also shown in Fig. 2. The proposed solution comprises several components, starting from the frame extractor through the text detector to the text recognizer and rectifier. Below, we outline the main features of those components along with the method for generating a synthetic dataset used to improve the performance of text recognition model. We conclude this section with a description of post-processing step that allows us to avoid redundancies in the overlays returned by our system. We present sample results in Fig. 3.

Fig. 3. Results of text detection (**left**) and text recognition (**right**) modules used in the proposed framework.

3.1 Frames Extractor

The goal of this component of our system is the extraction of all frames containing unique overlays. Extracting too few frames leads to an information loss and extracting unnecessarily too many frames with overlapping overlays increases the processing time. Our frames extraction step is therefore an essential part of the whole system.

We use the functionality provided as a part of the ffmpeg codec[1] as a frame extractor. More specifically, we input a video and extract intra-coded frames, the so-called I-frames, used by the codec as benchmark frames. According to the codec specifications, I-frames are stored as complete images, in contrary to the P and B predictive frames which are encoded only through differences with respect to the benchmark I-frames. Although, there may be some cases, where the overlay text is visible only through the encoded P-frames, our preliminary results indicated that using only I-frames in those cases does not lead to a significant reduction in the information conveyed in the video.

Several alternative approaches to the problem of informative frame extraction exist. Since the overlays are typically changed when the video shot changes, selecting the last frame from every scene can be a viable solution. Unfortunately, a significant portion of our database videos consists of only one scene with multiple overlays, which reduces the applicability of this method in our use case. Another approach for frame extraction relies on a more complex method for highlight extraction based on neural network architectures [16]. Our initial experiments indicated, however, that this approach is too computationally expensive and therefore reduce the usability of the entire system. We therefore rely on our frame extraction on the ffmpeg codec which provides an efficient and effective method for selecting important video frames.

3.2 Text Detection

Our text detection component uses the TextBoxes method [8] based on an end-to-end trainable Single Shot Detector (SSD) [9]. Multiple layers of the network return coordinates of word bounding boxes along with a prediction score of text presence. Then, a non-maximum suppression algorithm is used to obtain optimum bounding box coordinates for each word. The publicly available implementation[2] we use detects only horizontal text. Therefore the text blocks that are less likely to be part of the typically horizontal overlays are automatically filtered out. In general, vertical texts are rarely used as overlays in social media videos and this is confirmed within our evaluation dataset. Modifying the solution to also detect vertical text blocks can therefore lead to a higher rate of misclassifications and ultimately reduced accuracy of our system.

---

[1] https://www.ffmpeg.org/.
[2] https://github.com/MhLiao/TextBoxes.

3.3   Text Recognition

Our method for text recognition is based on the Convolutional Recurrent Neural Network (CRNN) model [12]. We use the architecture with seven convolutional layers followed by two Bidirectional LSTM layers. Probability of a sequence is given by a Connectionist Temporal Classification layer [3]. As an input, the model takes an image displaying a single word. The image must be scaled to a fixed height while the width of the image can vary. Sequences that are input to recurrent layers are generated by concatenating columns of feature maps produced by convolutional layers.

Although the text detection module based on the CRNN performs well in general scenarios, its performance can be further improved by adjusting the training dataset to the application scenario. In our case, the goal is to recognize textual overlays presented in social media videos. Those videos often contain text blocks with special characters and are frequently displayed in challenging conditions (various backgrounds, font colors and sizes, etc.). To address those challenges, we propose to improve the recognition model based on the CRNN by fine-tuning the network on a synthetically generated dataset. Below, we outline the details of a dataset generation procedure which, as shown in Sect. 4 leads to significant performance improvements.

Generation of a Synthetic Dataset. As shown in [4], training a text recognition model with synthetically generated datasets can improve its results. Furthermore, due to a specific application of our system for text recognition in social media videos, existing datasets typically used for training text recognition models may not be sufficient, as they mostly contain natural images, very much different from those published in social media. Therefore we propose to synthetically generate a dataset that can simulate the conditions observed in social media, such as diversified background of text blocks and various fonts and colors of the text displayed in the images. The generation of a synthetic dataset can be split into the following steps:

Text. We prepare transcripts of overlays from over 100 social media videos collected from several Facebook profiles and a list of 5000 most frequent words in the Corpus of Contemporary American English [1] to create a set of unique single words for rendering on images. This dataset was augmented with digits and special characters, such as hyphens, commas and question marks. This augmentation is especially important, since the original CRNN model was trained on a dataset of alphanumerical characters only and its performance is significantly decreased on a dataset of social media videos, as shown in Table 2.

Background Images. To increase the diversity of the synthetically generated dataset, we superimpose text blocks over various backgrounds. To increase the diversity of those backgrounds, we use 50 frames from randomly selected videos and manually extract regions without blocks of text. We ensure that the extracted regions represented a wide range of used colors, intensity values and texture types. We also extract regions whose dimensions are large enough that we can randomly crop them to increase the pool of potential background images.

Fonts. We collect 71 fonts out of 30 font-families with Calibre font being the most popular one. The other fonts are picked to mimic the distribution of similar fonts in social media based on general guidances for editors. We present full list of font-families used below.

1. Alegreya	11. Chivo	21. Neuton
2. Aleo	12. Cormorant	22. OldStandard
3. AnonymousPro	13. CrimsonText	23. OpenSans
4. Archivo	14. Dosis	24. PlayfairDisplay
5. Arvo	15. Helvetica	25. Poppins
6. BioRhyme	16. Karla	26. Raleway
7. Bitter	17. Libre	27. Roboto
8. Cabin	18. Lora	28. SourceSans
9. Calibre	19. Merriweather	29. SpaceMono
10. Cardo	20. Montserrat	30. Spectral

Random Sampling. For each word in our dataset, we generate 100 samples by selecting random font, size and color. Then, based on the size of the text, we crop randomly selected background image and superimpose the text on the cropped image. All images are resized to 100×32px with anti-aliasing and saved in jpeg format. Figure 4 shows a comparison between real and synthetically generated frames with text.

Fig. 4. Comparison of sample images extracted from real videos (**left column**) and synthetic images generated with the same text block (**right column**).

Fine-Tuning. We use the synthetically generated dataset to fine-tune our CRNN model. We experiment with three different variants of the CRNN tuning procedure:

1. We modify the dimensions of the last LSTM layer to adapt it to the extended set of characters. Only the last LSTM layer is initialized with random weights and the parameters of all other layers are frozen.

2. We modify output dimensions of the last LSTM layer but the weights of both LSTM layers are initialized with random weights, while the other parameters are frozen.
3. We initially load weights from pretrained model and change output dimensions of the last LSTM layer. All network parameters are updated during training.

The comparison of the results obtained with different variants is shown in Sect. 4.

3.4   Text Merging and Rectification

Although our frame extraction component is fairly robust, it does not prevent the text extracted from text overlays to overlap across consecutive frames. We propose novel yet simple method for filtering out such overlaps. We can assume that components of a single overlay appear gradually and last until the end of a scene. Therefore, the version containing the greatest number of characters can be considered the final one. We sort the extracted overlays by the time of their appearance in a reverse order. We then compare consecutive texts of overlays using normalized Levenshtein distance. If the result is below a given threshold we consider that overlays are overlapping and disregard the one with fewer characters. We also use an autocorrection toolkit[3] to further improve the results of the OCR model.

4   Evaluation

In this section, we present the results of the evaluation of our method on a benchmark dataset. We first present the evaluation dataset along with the evaluation metrics. We then show the experimental results obtained for different pre-processing steps. Finally, we show the comparison of the results obtained with our method against the results of the system based on Tesseract of CRNN models.

4.1   Dataset

To measure the accuracy of the OCR component of our system we extract frames from 100 videos published on Facebook between June 2017 and January 2018 on NowThisNews, NowThisPolitics, NowThisHer, thedodosite and SeekerMedia channels using ffmpeg codec, as described in Sect. 3.1. Then, using the method presented in Sect. 3.2, we detect and extract single word images from a random subset of frames. We discard images with less than 20px height. We also exclude images with less than 3 characters as well as images that are part of a media brand logo as they would introduce overlaps in our test set. We randomly select 1000 of the remaining images and manually annotate them to use as the final

---

[3] https://github.com/phatpiglet/autocorrect/.

testing set. To measure end-to-end performance of the OCR and the text detection components, we annotate 100 randomly selected frames with 1128 words displayed in total. For each frame, we mark the location of the text and we transcribe all the words shown in the frame. The set of videos we have used to extract those frames was separate from the set that we used to select the list of words for generating synthetic images. We have not explicitly excluded repetitions of other words. We assume that random selection of frames and words taken from them is enough to prevent including two identical images in our testing set.

4.2 Evaluation Metrics

To evaluate our system and compare it with the baseline, we follow the evaluation protocol of [6], and compute several metrics: average precision, recall and f1 score of the system output. We also compare targets with the predictions using similarity metric based on normalized Levenshtein distance [7]. All metrics are calculated on a word level. Similar metric was used in [10] to evaluate OCR accuracy on distorted images which also may be the case in our task due to the frame extraction process.

The metrics are computed according to the following formulas:

$$recall = \frac{|labels \cap predictions|}{|labels|} \qquad precision = \frac{|labels \cap predictions|}{|predictions|}$$

$$f1 = 2 \cdot \frac{recall \cdot precision}{recall + precision} \qquad similarity = 1 - \frac{Levenshtein(labels, predictions)}{max(|labels|, |predictions|)}$$

4.3 Preprocessing Methods

The detection and recognition modules of our system expect grayscale images as their input and we evaluate several preprocessing methods that aim to improve the quality of grayscale images text recognition. To that end, we test the following preprocessing methods with a pretrained CRNN model [12] and the Tesseract OCR Engine [13]:

- No preprocessing: raw, grayscale images are input to the recognition component.
- Otsu's binarization: binarization method based on dynamic thresholding. We use OpenCV[4] implementation.
- Gaussian blurring with $5 \times 5px$ kernel followed by Otsu's binarization: Additional blurring step can potentially increase the robustness of the system.
- Gaussian blurring with Otsu's binarization and opening: by adding the morphological opening observation, we expect to reduce the amount of noise in the images.

---

[4] http://www.opencv.org.

- Max-RGB filter: we flat the color channel space by selecting a maximum pixel value from each channel and using it as the output image pixel. This preprocessing method is based on the assumption that text and background have different color and using this filter should lead to an improved contrast of the image.

Table 1 shows the results of the experiments with preprocessing methods. For the Tesseract OCR the best pre-processing method is Otsu's binarization, yet identical result was obtained without the preprocessing. However, for the CRNN model, which we use in our system in practice, the best results are obtained when using max-RGB filtering. Nevertheless, the performance improvement achieved by the best preprocessing method is negligible. The conclusion of this experiment is that the convolutional layers of the CRNN module are able to learn optimal transformations to increase the system performance and therefore fully substitute preprocessing steps. One can also see that the neural network based model significantly outperforms the traditional Tesseract OCR system.

Table 1. Word level recognition accuracy for the Tesseract OCR engine [13] and pre-trained CRNN model [12] when given preprocessing method was applied.

Preprocessing method	Tesseract	CRNN model
None	57.8%	75.4%
Gaussian blur + Otsu	52%	65.9%
Gaussian blur + Otsu + opening	57.2%	67.4%
Otsu	57.8%	69.1%
Max RGB	56.3%	**75.7%**

4.4   Results

Accuracy tests performed with the original model and its fine-tuned versions presented in the Table 2 show improvement for cases where only parameters for LSTM layers were updated during training. It means that the generated set may be too small for training the entire network without overfitting. At the same time updating parameters of both LSTM layers turn out to be better than modifying parameters of only the single last layer. It shows that features encoded by the penultimate LSTM layer are not generic enough and that our synthetic training set is sufficient to learn new features specific to the task. The best model allowed to reduce the word recognition error by 20%.

Evaluation of text detection and recognition presented in Table 2 shows that all fine-tuned models perform better than the original version for this specific task. Using the fine-tuned CRNN model leads to a 20% increase of precision, recall, F1 score and similarity metrics compared to a generic CRNN model.

End-to-end results show that the text detection component plays an important role in the system. Imperfect detection lowers the quality of CRNN input

Table 2. Performance comparison of baseline, original and fine-tuned models.

Model	Recognition	Detection with recognition			
	Accuracy	Precision	Recall	F1	Similarity
Tesseract [13]	57.8%	0.284	0.266	0.274	0.42
CRNN [12]	75.7%	0.368	0.343	0.352	0.52
Fine-tuned CRNN (all parameters)	74%	0.40	0.375	0.386	0.59
Fine-tuned CRNN (last LSTM layer)	76.6%	0.406	0.378	0.389	0.59
Fine-tuned CRNN (both LSTM layers)	**80.1%**	**0.45**	**0.42**	**0.432**	**0.62**

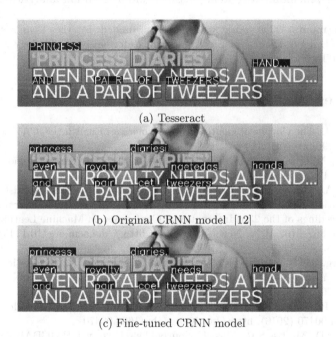

(a) Tesseract

(b) Original CRNN model [12]

(c) Fine-tuned CRNN model

Fig. 5. Results of text recognition using different models.

which translates into a decrease in recognition accuracy. However, from a practical point of view the system can be already used to extract meaningful information from social media videos. Overlays can be further processed using presented rectification methods.

To further evaluate different models used for text recognition, we visualize the outputs of various methods on a sample video frame with the overlay. The results are shown in Fig. 5. Those qualitative results confirm the numerical evaluation performed above - our fine-tuned CRNN model provides the most accurate transcription of the overlay.

5   Conclusions

In this paper, we presented a comprehensive system for video overlay text extraction that comprises several components: keyframe extraction, text detection, recognition and rectification. The system is specifically designed and evaluated in the context of social media videos where textual overlays appear in particularly challenging conditions. Using synthetically generated dataset allowed us to reduce recognition error of our neural network-based text recognition model by over 20%. Overall, the proposed system provides an effective and robust method for video overlay extraction. It has been successfully implemented and integrated into a complex social media video analysis engine and is actively used as part of many services, including a content classifier and a retention analytics engine.

Acknowledgments. This work was partially funded by the Dean's Grant nr II/2017/GD/1 of the Faculty of Electronics and Information Technology at Warsaw University of Technology.

References

1. Davies, M.: The Corpus of Contemporary American English (COCA): 560 million words, 1990-present (2008)
2. Donoser, M., Bischof, H.: Efficient Maximally Stable Extremal Region (MSER) tracking. In: CVPR (2006)
3. Graves, A., Fernández, S., Gomez, F., Schmidhuber, J.: Connectionist temporal classification: labelling unsegmented sequence data with recurrent neural networks. In: Proceedings of the 23rd International Conference on Machine Learning, ICML 2006, pp. 369–376. ACM, New York (2006). http://doi.acm.org/10.1145/1143844. 1143891
4. Jaderberg, M., Simonyan, K., Vedaldi, A., Zisserman, A.: Synthetic data and artificial neural networks for natural scene text recognition. arXiv preprint arXiv:1406.2227 (2014)
5. Kannao, R., Guha, P.: Overlay text extraction from TV news broadcast. CoRR abs/1604.00470 (2016). http://arxiv.org/abs/1604.00470
6. Karatzas, D., Mestre, S.R., Mas, J., Nourbakhsh, F., Roy, P.P.: ICDAR 2011 robust reading competition - challenge 1: reading text in born-digital images (web and email). In: 2011 International Conference on Document Analysis and Recognition, pp. 1485–1490, September 2011. https://doi.org/10.1109/ICDAR.2011.295
7. Levenshtein, V.I.: Binary codes capable of correcting deletions, insertions and reversals. Sov. Phys. Dokl. **10**, 707 (1966)
8. Liao, M., Shi, B., Bai, X., Wang, X., Liu, W.: TextBoxes: a fast text detector with a single deep neural network. CoRR abs/1611.06779 (2016). http://googlebooks. byu.edu/
9. Liu, W., et al.: SSD: single shot multibox detector. CoRR abs/1512.02325 (2015). http://arxiv.org/abs/1512.02325
10. Lundqvist, F., Wallberg, O.: Natural image distortions and optical character recognition accuracy. Ph.D. thesis, KTH, School of Computer Science and Communication (2016)

11. Sato, T., Kanade, T., Hughes, E., Smith, M., Satoh, S.: Video OCR: indexing digital news libraries by recognition of superimposed caption. In: ACM Multimedia Systems Special Issue on Video Libraries, February 1998
12. Shi, B., Bai, X., Yao, C.: An end-to-end trainable neural network for image-based sequence recognition and its application to scene text recognition. CoRR abs/1507.05717 (2015). http://arxiv.org/abs/1507.05717
13. Smith, R.: An overview of the Tesseract OCR engine. In: Proceedings of the Ninth International Conference on Document Analysis and Recognition - Volume 02, ICDAR 2007, pp. 629–633. IEEE Computer Society, Washington, DC (2007). http://dl.acm.org/citation.cfm?id=1304596.1304846
14. Tian, S., Pan, Y., Huang, C., Lu, S., Yu, K., Tan, C.L.: Text flow: a unified text detection system in natural scene images. CoRR abs/1604.06877 (2016). http://arxiv.org/abs/1604.06877
15. Yang, H., Wang, C., Bartz, C., Meinel, C.: SceneTextReg: a real-time video OCR system. In: Proceedings of the 2016 ACM on Multimedia Conference, MM 2016, pp. 698–700. ACM, New York (2016). http://doi.acm.org/10.1145/2964284.2973811
16. Yang, H., Wang, B., Lin, S., Wipf, D.P., Guo, M., Guo, B.: Unsupervised extraction of video highlights via robust recurrent auto-encoders. CoRR abs/1510.01442 (2015)
17. Yao, C., et al.: Incidental scene text understanding: recent progresses on ICDAR 2015 robust reading competition challenge 4. CoRR abs/1511.09207 (2015). http://arxiv.org/abs/1511.09207

Choosing an Optimal Bracketing Sequence for HDR Imaging

Paweł J. Łubniewski[(✉)] and Wojciech S. Mokrzycki

Faculty of Mathematics and Natural Sciences, School of Exact Sciences,
Cardinal Stefan Wyszyński University in Warsaw, Warsaw, Poland
{p.lubniewski,w.mokrzycki}@uksw.edu.pl

Abstract. In this paper we present a new concept of selecting a subset of significant images from a large sequence of multi exposure bracketing photographs, used for HDR imaging. Presented algorithm picks up several frames from a sequence taken with increasing exposure and use them to generate high dynamic range image. The choice allows us to obtain the photos with important data and to discard the images with redundant or deformed visual information, like overburned or dark areas. We have tested the presented technique by selecting $n = 7$ significant frames from the bracketing sequence of 49 elements. The chosen photos have been used to compose an HDR image which contains a maximum insight of the scene with a minimal presence of luminous deformations.

Keywords: HDRI · HDR image · Bracketing · LDR sequence
Image processing · Image optimization

1 Introduction

The *human visual system* is able to detect photon radiation in range $0.38\,\mu m - 0.76\,\mu m$ of wave length, which is called *light*. It is also sensible to 14 logarithmic levels[1] of the lightness (intensity) changes [1,6]. However, only four levels of lightness can be seen at once (Fig. 1) and the change of seeing range is caused by a mechanism of *luminance adaptation*. In such process, the human visual system moves the window of lightness perception range about the luminance axis and the adaptation is determined by the lightness of one degree solid angle, in the direction of looking [2]. Therefore, the human eye receives visual information in four logarithmic levels of lightness and the image defined in this range is called *high dynamic range* (HDR) image.

In this paper we present the LDR and HDR images in Sect. 2; our proposition for choosing optimal appropriate images from a bracketing sequence for HDR imaging is described in Sect. 3. The results and implementation details are given in Sect. 4.

---

[1] Subjective lightness perceived by an eye is expressed in the logarithmic scale.

© Springer Nature Switzerland AG 2018
L. J. Chmielewski et al. (Eds.): ICCVG 2018, LNCS 11114, pp. 300–307, 2018.
https://doi.org/10.1007/978-3-030-00692-1_26

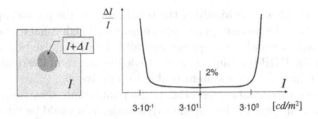

Fig. 1. Weber curve defines the ability of detecting different lightness levels by the human eye [7].

2   LDR and HDR Images

2.1   LDR Images

Most of the devices such as photography cameras and video recorders are unable to acquire the full range of lightness variability, even in the range perceived by the human visual system. Likewise, such hardware cannot generate or visualize an image composed of full luminance and color ranges. A conventional digital image (photograph) contains an amount of information about the scene recorded by a camera. In effect, when taking a photo of a silhouette against a lit window, it should be decided which parts of the image can be overexposed (overburned) and which area can be underexposed (crushed shadows) due to inability to register very light and dark regions at the same time. Particularly, the cameras and the monitors can process images of small range of luminance, called *low dynamic range* (LDR) images. Typical digital photograph, with narrow lightness dynamics is referred as *LDR image*.

The EV units[2] for the natural scene and some basic devices are the following:

- natural scene: 26 EV,
- human eye: 10 – 14 EV,
- digital camera sensor: about 11 EV,
- LCD display: about 9 EV,
- JPEG file format: 8 EV.

Similar problem concerns the colors: a conventional digital photo contains only 50–60% of the human perceptible color range.

2.2   HDR Images

An HDR image can be obtained by merging several photographs of the same frame, taken for different exposure parameters[3]. The correct fusion of the LDR

---

[2] In photography, EV (*exposure value*) is a unit measuring the difference of acquired light; 1 EV corresponds to doubled light intensity.

[3] Such a technique is called *bracketing* and contains both underexposed and overexposed images.

images sequence allows one to adjust the tonal range of the photographed scene and thus to obtain the desired quality of exposure and high tonal dynamic range. The HDR image is capable of representing all colors recognized by the human eye, therefore the HDR technique permits to define images of the quality at least as good as the human visual system is able to perceive [6].

HDR images are digital representation of a photograph; they cannot be characterized by a real range of the lightness dynamics, as it could be measured by a sensor. However, it is possible to interpret them as a dynamic range of an image displayed on a hypothetic monitor with sufficient technical parameters (comparable to the human-observed scenes) [10]. The HDR imaging domain has been well explored [6] and is currently under active development [11]. Several techniques of the HDR composition have been proposed for single photograph [9] and multi exposure images [3,5]. The problem of transforming HDR to LDR images by tone mapping is also important [6].

While the most common technique of the HDR image acquisition bases on multi exposure photographs, it demands some important knowledge and manual setup of the camera parameters. We propose, in the following Section, an algorithm which chooses best frames of a full bracketing images sequence.

3   Concept

In this work, we present our method of selecting the frames of a multi exposure sequence of photographs in order to generate an HDR image. We want to obtain the resulting high dynamic range image with maximal visual information available, therefore wide range of exposures should be used. Unlike most typical HDR cases, where small number of bracketed frames is taken (usually 2 to 3), we base on a large series of bracketing exposures (49 frames). Such large number of photographs contains the full range of luminance, but is also to big to use in practice for HDR imaging.

Not all of the frames from the bracketing sequence can be useful: especially the photos containing deformed information, characterized by under- or overexposed pixel regions. Our approach allows us to define a range of frames, which can be used to generate the HDR image with minimal lightness deformation.

Moreover, the images from above mentioned range can hold redundant information, which is the case if the exposure differences are small (e.g. below 1 EV). Thus, we perform a selection of frames holding significant data. Eventually, the full bracketing sequence allows us to pick up the frames characterized by minimal deformation and substantial color information.

As a result, we merge the selected photos into one HDR image by summing up the corresponding pixel values and performing a non-normalized gamma correction. Such a correction decreases the resulting image depth without loosing important information in the lower intensity range. The results, as presented in this paper (Fig. 3) are finally mapped to fit the standard display 24 bit pixel range.

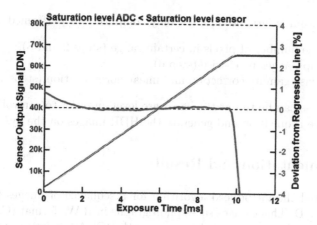

Fig. 2. Electrical characteristics of a CCD camera sensor. Boundary values $f_{\min}$ and $f_{\min}$ can be observed on the Sensor Output Signal graph (see Sect. 3.1).

3.1   Algorithm

The following algorithm selects appropriate frames from bracketing sequence and uses them to generate HDR image. It uses hardware dependent minimal and maximal signal values $f_{\min}$ and $f_{\max}$, which can be interpreted as the levels of minimum threshold and saturation of camera sensor (Fig. 2).

Bracketing Frames Selection and HDR Generating Algorithm:

1. Take image with the shortest possible exposure B_i, $i \leftarrow 0$.
2. Compute m_i, number of pixels exceeding $f_{\min}$ value.
3. If $m_i \geq pN$ (N – number of pixels), go to step 5.
4. Otherwise, take next image with longer exposure B_i, $i \leftarrow (i+1)$ and go to step 2.
5. Create HDR image H and initialize it to 0 (black).
6. Sum up B_i with HDR image $H \leftarrow H + B_i$.
7. Take next image with longer exposure B_i, $i \leftarrow (i+1)$.
8. Compute n_i, number of pixels exceeding $f_{\max}$ value.
9. If $n_i \geq qN$, go to step 11.
10. Otherwise, go to step 6.
11. Apply pixel-wise gamma correction to HDR image $H \leftarrow H^\gamma$
12. Create LDR version of H as $H_L = (2^L - 1) \cdot (H - f_{\min})/(f_{\max} - f_{\min})$, where L is desired color depth.

There are two adjustable parameters p and q in the algorithm. The former $0 \leq p \leq 1$ controls the amount of minimal light acceptable for selected sequence (step 3). The latter $0 \leq q \leq 1$ allows us to break the series at certain number of overburned pixels (step 9).

The algorithm is fast, because the only computations performed are:

- counting the number of pixels in certain range (steps 2 and 8),
- summing up images pixel-wise (step 6),
- one pixel-wise gamma correction and linear normalization (steps 11 and 12).

The full process can be run at the hardware level, in order to control the bracketing sequence acquisition and generate the HDR images on the fly.

4   Implementation and Results

We have tested the introduced algorithm for a sequence of images taken with Canon EOS 80D. This camera saves photographs in RAW format (Canon CR2) in 14 bits depth. We developed the images with DCRAW software, without any pixel values modifications (linear scale, no gamma correction, no white balance). The photos has been then stored in 16 bit TIFF format.

The full bracketing sequence consisted of 49 frames, from 1/8000 s to 8 s exposure time; succeeding frames differed by 1/3 EV (exposure value). Figure 4 presents the relative number of blacked and overburned pixels for all images. Our algorithm has been run for that sequence and selected a subset of 7 photographs (Fig. 3).

The following assumptions have been made:

1. The frame sequence contains extremely underexposed images,
2. The frame sequence contains extremely overexposed images,
3. An image contains significant visual information if the number of pixels exceeding f_{min} is greater than 0.1%, therefore $p = 0.001$,
4. An image contains deformed visual information if the number of pixels exceeding f_{max} is greater than 0.1%, therefore $q = 0.001$,
5. The gamma parameter is set to $\gamma = 0.6$.

The images extracted from the bracketing sequence are shown in Fig. 3 (all pictures except the right bottom one). We can observe the succeeding frames with increasing luminosity, where full visual information of the scene (subtle details) cannot be seen on any image at the same time.

The generated HDR image (flattened to $L = 8$ bit for the cause of printing in Fig. 3, right bottom) presents the full range of perceptual information. The gamma value, used for the HDR correction has been chosen experimentally and holds $\gamma = 0.6$.

4.1   Comparison

We have compared the obtained results with a default HDR image of the same scene, generated from a standard market bracketing setup: a sequence of 3 photographs with the exposure chosen automatically by the camera. The difference between the images has been set to 2 EV.

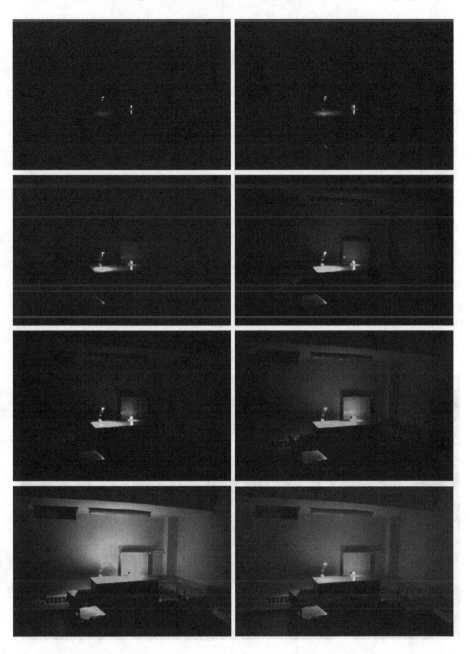

Fig. 3. Selected frames from the full bracketing sequence (ordered left-right, up-down). The last image is the resulting flattened HDR image (bottom right).

Figure 5 presents selected close ups of the photographs from the sequence (two columns on left) and the comparison between the default 3-bracketed HDR image and the HDR image issued from our algorithm (two columns on right).

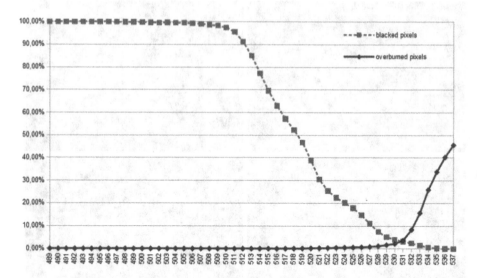

Fig. 4. Relative number of blacked and overburned pixels (red and blue graphs respectively) for the full bracketing sequence of 49 photos. (Color figure online)

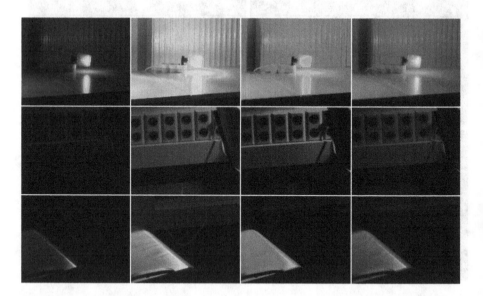

Fig. 5. Close ups of the images fragments. 1st and 2nd columns on the left are extracted from the second and last but one frames relatively; 3rd column contains the result of a default bracketing generated image. 4th (right) column presents our approach based HDR image (as in Fig. 3); one can observe some subtle details, unnoticeable for the default technique (3rd column), e.g. the lamp cloche shape, the seat texture.

Both high dynamic range images contain the scene details in dark and bright regions, but the default one is slightly overexposed for the lamp and the seat close ups. The overall darkness of the scene induced wrong exposure parameters chosen by the camera. Thus, it was not capable of capturing the full range of luminosity in lower bound.

5   Conclusions

We have presented our concept of choosing an optimal sequence of bracketed photographs for generating HDR images. Important aspect of our approach is to capture maximum amount of visual information from the scene. Consequently, we propose an algorithm which picks up the images containing important data and rejects photos with redundant, deformed or insignificant information. Our approach allows us to perform a fast selection of frames used to compose some HDR data. The results are promising as the final HDR image contains maximum visual information from the scene and has acceptable pixel depth due to non-normalized gamma correction.

We are planning further improvements of our method, especially the automatic choice of the parameters and the analysis of the colors relatively to the exposure.

References

1. Ferwerda, J.A., Pattanaik, S.N., Shirley, P., Greenberg, D.P.: A model of visual adaptation for realistic image synthesis. In: Proceedings of the 23rd Annual Conference on CG&IT, pp. 249–258. ACM, New York (1996)
2. Hood, D.C.: Lowel-level visual processing and models of light adaptation. Ann. Rev. Psychol. **49**, 503–535 (1998)
3. Goshtasby, A.A.: Fusion of multi-exposure images. Image Vis. Comput. **23**(6), 611–618 (2005)
4. Riggs, R.: The Magic of HDR Imaging. http://mentalfloss.com/article/20157/magic-hdr-imaging
5. Gelfand, N., Adams, A., Park, S.H., Pulli, K.: Multi-exposure imaging on mobile devices. In: Proceedings of ACM Multimedia, pp. 823–826 (2010)
6. Reinhard, E., Wart, G., Devebec, P., Pattanaik, S., Heidrich, W., Myszkowski, K.: High Dynamic Range Imaging, 2nd edn. Morgan Kaufman, San Francisco (2010)
7. Mokrzycki, W.S.: Wprowadzenie do przetwarzania informacji wizualnej. Tom II: Dyskretyzacja Obrazu, operacje pikslowe, morfologiczne i przekształcenia obrazowe. EXIT (2012)
8. Mantiuk, R.: HDR image. http://fotohdr.zut.edu.pl/?page_id=34
9. Banterle, F., Artusi, A., Debattista, K., Chalmers, A.: Advanced High Dynamic Range Imaging: Theory and Practice. CRC Press, New York (2011)
10. Hulusica, V., Debattista, K., Valenzisec, G., Dufauxc, F.: A model of perceived dynamic range for HDR images. SPIC **51**, 26–39 (2017)
11. Kottayil, N.K., Valenzise, G., Dufaux, F., Cheng, I.: Blind high dynamic range quality estimation by disentangling perceptual and noise features in images. IEEE Trans. Img. Proc. **27**(3), 1512–1525 (2018)

Detection of Pollen Grains in Digital Microscopy Images by Means of Modified Histogram Thresholding

Dariusz Frejlichowski[(✉)]

Faculty of Computer Science and Information Technology,
West Pomeranian University of Technology, Szczecin,
Żolnierska 52, 71-210 Szczecin, Poland
dfrejlichowski@wi.zut.edu.pl

Abstract. The paper describes and investigates the application of the algorithm for the detection and extraction of pollen contour shapes in digital microscopic images. This is the first step in the process of identification of pollen grains in order to obtain a method for automatic or semi-automatic analysis of air samples. The final approach is supposed to support this process by recognizing pollen types in digital microscopic images. The applied segmentation approach is based on the Modified Histogram Thresholding, previously employed in the extraction of red blood cells for the automatic diagnosis of certain diseases based on the erythrocyte shapes.

1 Introduction

Aerobiology is a science that studies organic particles transported by the air. In a wider context, it is connected with biology, as it is one of its subdisciplines. The air contains plenty of various particles, but amongst them, pollen grains and fungal spores attract particular attention, since the knowledge about their presence and number for particular species is especially important for people suffering from allergies. Nowadays, the pollen forecast is watched with great interest by many people, since it helps them in everyday life. There are many people allergic to pollen, for whom it is especially important to know when allergenic pollen grains are present in the air, and this is why air samples are analyzed. This process can be supported by automatic (or semi-automatic) analysis of digital microscopic images by means of image processing and recognition algorithms.

The paper describes the first stage of the approach used for the recognition of some selected pollen types. The goal is to localize and extract single pollen shapes for further identification by means of low-level shape or greyscale descriptors and classification algorithms. The segmentation and localization is applied to greyscale microscopic images and it is based on the Modified Histogram Thresholding, a method that was previously applied successfully for the localization of erythrocytes in microscopic human blood images [1]. The reason for choosing this algorithm for the task analyzed in the paper was the noticeable

© Springer Nature Switzerland AG 2018
L. J. Chmielewski et al. (Eds.): ICCVG 2018, LNCS 11114, pp. 308–315, 2018.
https://doi.org/10.1007/978-3-030-00692-1_27

similarity of the image appearance and properties between microscopic blood and pollen images, represented in greyscale. An example of the discussed similarity is provided in Fig. 1.

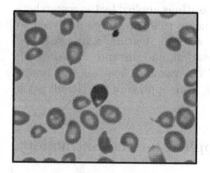 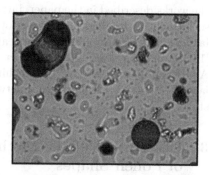

Fig. 1. The similarity between digital microscopic images of human blood (on the left) and pollen (on the right) in greyscale.

The remaining part of the paper is organized as follows. The second section provides a brief discussion on the related works. The third section describes the applied algorithm. The fourth section provides some exemplary results of its application to the digital microscopic images of pollen. Finally, the last section concludes the paper and provides the discussion about future plans.

2 Related Works

There are some works described in literature devoted to the problem of detecting pollen grains within digital microscopic images. The first decision that has to be made is the selection of the image type which will be subject to processing. Some of the approaches work on greyscale images (e.g. [2,3]), similarly to the assumption made in the method described in this paper, whilst others use color images (e.g. [4,5]). Later, more specific methods of processing can be applied. In [3] the Otsu algorithm in a multilevel form was applied for this task. In [2] the segmentation was based on thresholding with use of two selection criteria: the "triangle" to obtain a coarse segmentation, and the "isodata" for the refined result. The above-mentioned approaches are similar to the one adopted for the purposes of the research work described in this paper, although some other segmentation techniques are also used, e.g. split and merge [5], Hough transform [6] and the method based on the Principal Component Analysis [4]. In some applications the detection of the pollen border is also performed. For this purpose the edge detection algorithms have been applied so far, e.g. Canny algorithm [6] or snakes [7].

The pre-processing and segmentation are usually not the main topics of the works described in literature, since most of the scientific community members working on the problem are mainly interested in the identification of the extracted pollen types. Sometimes it is assumed that the subimage covering the objects of interest was earlier localized and that it constitutes the input for the analyzed algorithms. The authors tend to focus on the later stages of the whole approach—feature representation and classification. These are not the subjects of the works described in the paper, but some algorithms applied by the researchers so far can be recalled here. Some of the elements that have been analyzed so far include for example geometric features [8], color [9], texture [8,10–12], shape [10,12] and greyscale [13] for object representation, and distance measures [9], AdaBoost [14], support vector machines [12,13], ensemble classifiers [15], multi-layer perceptron [11] and neural networks [10] were applied in the classification stage.

3   Description of the Method Applied for the Extraction of Pollen Shapes

As it was already mentioned, the algorithm for image segmentation applied here was previously successfully used in the segmentation of blood cells in order to enable automatic diagnosis of certain diseases [1]. The reason for choosing this method was the similarity between digital microscopic images of human blood cells and pollen grains. An exemplary result of the application of the Modified Histogram Thresholding obtained for microscopic human blood images is provided in Fig. 2.

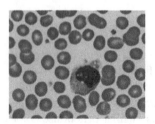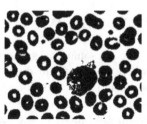

Fig. 2. Exemplary result of the Modified Histogram Thresholding obtained in previous works for the segmentation of erythrocytes [1]. The similarity between digital microscopic images of human blood and pollen grains gave the reason for the application of this approach in the segmentation of pollen.

The input images of pollen grains are represented in greyscale. Hence, the first stage is the binarisation of the input image. For this purpose the Modified Histogram Thresholding is applied, i.e. an algorithm that starts with the derivation of the histogram function $h(l_k)$:

$$h(l_k) = \sum_{k=1}^{m} b(k, l_k), \tag{1}$$

where:

$$b(k, l_k) = \begin{cases} 1, & \text{if } k = l_k \\ 0, & \text{if } k \neq l_k \end{cases}. \tag{2}$$

When the histogram representation is obtained, the process of smoothening is performed by means of bins averaging using a window whose length is derived using the following formula:

$$c(j) = \frac{\sum\limits_{i=j-m}^{j+m} h(i)}{2m+1}, \tag{3}$$

where:

j — number of a bin,

$c(j)$ — averaged histogram value for bin,

$h(i)$ — histogram value before averaging,

m — number of bins taken in left and right neighborhood of j-th bin.

The smoothened histogram constitutes the basis for calculating the threshold. This can be performed easily, because the obtained histogram for digital microscopic images of pollen is composed of two distinct peaks. The first one is connected with the objects of interest—the pollen grains, and the second one results from the lighter background. Hence, the threshold is derived between them. Depending on the number of non-zero bins v in the histogram obtained for the processed image two different steps are performed. If v exceeds 15 then the threshold t is calculated as the minimum value in the interval:

$$t \in \left(c_{\max} - \left\lfloor \frac{v}{4} \right\rfloor, c_{\max}\right), \tag{4}$$

where:

c_{max} — number of the highest bin,

v — number of grey-levels found in particular image (number of non-zero bins in histogram).

If v is smaller or equal to 15 then t is calculated as the minimum value in the following interval:

$$t \in \left(c_{\max} - \left\lfloor \frac{v}{4} \right\rfloor, c_{\max} - 20\right). \tag{5}$$

Using the derived value t the binarisation is performed—values smaller than t become 0, and those higher or equal to t become 1.

After the binary image is obtained, the localization of particular objects can be performed by means of tracing regions of separate objects in the image. For every object, the first pixel differing from the background is found and then the maximal boundaries of the object to which it belongs are searched for. After the extraction of the coordinates, the object is replaced with background pixels in order not to be studied later. The maximum coordinates of the shape in each direction are stored. Also, objects placed on boundaries are not taken into consideration, since their later recognition would be difficult. Moreover, the analysis of the microscopic images containing pollen leads to the conclusion that there are numerous small objects present in the image that should be removed. In order to solve this problem after the thresholding process, the obtained small black areas were not taken into consideration.

The strategy for tracing every pollen grain's contour is presented pictorially in Fig. 3.

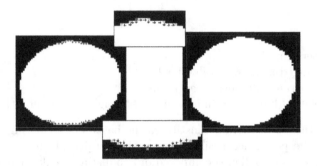

Fig. 3. An example of the coordinates extraction for a pollen grain by means of tracing the contour. The arrows in the middle part of the image show the directions of tracing.

4 Experimental Results

The algorithm described in the previous section was tested on twenty microscopic images containing pollen grains, in greyscale. Some examples of the images used in the experiment are presented in Fig. 4. The most important criterion for the evaluation of the approach was the number of correctly localized pollen shapes in comparison to the input greyscale image.

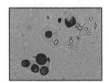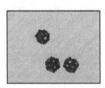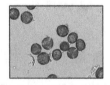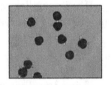

Fig. 4. Examples of the microscopic images used in the experiment.

Some results of the experiment are provided in Fig. 5. They are very promising, since the pollen shapes were in most cases properly localized and extracted. The assumption that neither the small shapes nor those present on the image boundaries are analyzed resulted in the rejection of those cases, as they should not be recognized in further steps. However, some problems occurred. Amongst them, the most important was the occlusion. The microscopic image covers the planar projection of a three-dimensional scene. Hence, in several cases the objects of interest overlapped with each other. The solution to this problem is to add certain other steps, such as morphological operations, to the algorithm. Additionally, assuming that the resolution of the input images is constant, the analysis of the shape area would easily provide the decision, if additional split should be applied.

The noise on the obtained contours is the second distortion that occurred in some cases. However, this problem should be solved by using an appropriate algorithm for object representation. This can be done both on shape and greyscale description, for example using the UNL-Fourier Descriptor [1] for the first case or the Polar-Fourier Greyscale Descriptor [16] for the second one. Another solution is to apply an additional image denoising step during the pre-processing stage.

Finally, the analysis of the microscopic images covering pollen leads to the conclusion that there are numerous small objects in the image that should be removed.

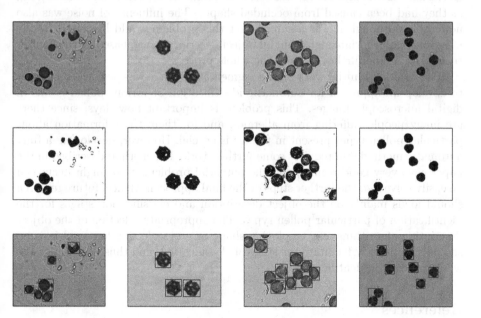

Fig. 5. Results of the experiment obtained for the images presented in Fig. 4.

In more specific terms, the obtained results were as follows. In 87% of the objects the localization worked perfectly well. It means that the pollen grains were detected correctly. Only in 2% of analyzed objects the result was wrong, i.e. an object was detected that was not pollen. Finally, in 11% the result of the approach was an object composed of several pollen grains combined into one larger object as a result of the occlusion (in all cases the obtained object was composed of two occluded pollen grains).

Further work was performed. During the second experiment, the proposed idea of rejecting the large objects as a potential result of occlusion, was applied. It worked perfectly well, as all instances of that kind were rejected. Thanks to this the efficiency of the analyzed method increased to 98%.

5   Conclusions and Future Plans

The aim of this paper was to describe and investigate experimentally a method for localization and extraction of pollen grains. The approach is based on the application of the Modified Histogram Thresholding, an algorithm that was previously applied with success for the segmentation of digital microscopic human blood images.

The obtained results were promising. The total efficiency of the approach was equal to 98%. However, there were two important problems to consider. Occlusion was the first one. It was easily overcome by rejecting too large objects, as they had been caused from occluded shapes. The influence of noise was also noticeable, although it was assumed that this problem would be solved by the usage of an appropriate algorithm for object description, e.g. based on the Fourier transform, at the further steps of the whole process.

The described initial work on the segmentation stage was performed in order to develop an approach for automatic identification of various pollen grains in digital microscopic images. This problem is important nowadays, since there are many people suffering from allergies, and for them the information about particular pollen types present in the air is crucial. However, developing a fully automatic method still requires some further work. The method described in the paper gave very good results, and the potential problems that might occur can be easily solved on the further steps of the final approach. Hence, future research should focus mainly on the object description and classification stages for the identification of particular pollen types. The appropriate selection of the object description algorithms, e.g. employing shape or greyscale as a low-level feature, should significantly facilitate the stage of classification, and thus, eventually, the whole process of identification.

References

1. Frejlichowski, D.: Pre-processing, extraction and recognition of binary erythrocyte shapes for computer-assisted diagnosis based on MGG images. In: Bolc, L., Tadeusiewicz, R., Chmielewski, L.J., Wojciechowski, K. (eds.) ICCVG 2010. LNCS, vol. 6374, pp. 368–375. Springer, Heidelberg (2010). https://doi.org/10.1007/978-3-642-15910-7_42
2. Chen, C., et al.: Feasibility study on automated recognition of allergenic pollen: grass, birch and mugwort. Aerobiologia **22**(4), 275–284 (2006)

3. Damian, M., Cernadas, E., Formilla, A., Otero, P.M.: Pollen classification of three types of plants of the family Urticaceae. In: Proceedings of 12th Portuguese conference on pattern recognition, Aveiro (2004)

4. Kumar, S., Ong, S.H., Ranganath, S., Chew, F.T., Ong, T.C.: Segmentation of microscope cell images via adaptive eigenfilters. In: Proceedings of International Conference on Image Processing, ICIP 2004, vol. 1, pp. 135–138 (2004)

5. Boucher, A.: Development of a semi-automatic system for pollen recognition. Aerobiologia **18**(3–4), 195–201 (2002)

6. Ronneberger, O., Wang, Q., Burkhardt, H.: Fast and robust segmentation of spherical particles in volumetric data sets from brightfield microscopy. In: Proceedings of 5th IEEE International Symposium on Biomedical Imaging: From Nano to Macro, ISBI 2008, pp. 372–375 (2008)

7. Ronneberger, O., Wang, Q., Burkhardt, H.: 3D invariants with high robustness to local deformations for automated pollen recognition. In: Hamprecht, F.A., Schnörr, C., Jähne, B. (eds.) DAGM 2007. LNCS, vol. 4713, pp. 425–435. Springer, Heidelberg (2007). https://doi.org/10.1007/978-3-540-74936-3_43

8. Travieso, C.M., Briceno, J.C., Ticay-Rivas, J.R., Alonso, J.B.: Pollen classification based on contour features. In: Proceedings of 15th International Conference on Intelligent Engineering Systems, Poprad, Slovakia, pp. 17–21 (2011)

9. Bonton, P., et al.: Colour image in 2D and 3D microscopy for the automation of pollen rate measurement. Image Anal. Ster. **21**(Suppl. 1), 25–30 (2001)

10. Holt, K., Allen, G., Hodgson, R., Marsland, S., Flenley, J.: Progress towards an automated trainable pollen location and classifier system for use in the palynology laboratory. Rev. Palaeobot. Palynol. **167**(3–4), 175–183 (2011)

11. Li, P., Flenley, J.R.: Pollen texture identification using neural networks. Grana **38**(1), 59–64 (1999)

12. Lagerstrom, R., et al.: Pollen image classification using the classifynder system: algorithm comparison and a case study on New Zealand honey. In: Sun, C., Bednarz, T., Pham, T.D., Vallotton, P., Wang, D. (eds.) Signal and Image Analysis for Biomedical and Life Sciences. AEMB, vol. 823, pp. 207–226. Springer, Cham (2015). https://doi.org/10.1007/978-3-319-10984-8_12

13. Ronneberger, O., Burkhardt, H., Schultz, E.: General-purpose object recognition in 3D volume data sets using gray-scale invariants — classification of airborne pollengrains recorded with a confocal laser scanning microscope. In: Proceedings of the IEEE 16th International Conference on Pattern Recognition, vol. 2, pp. 290–295 (2002)

14. Nguyen, N.R., Donalson-Matasci, M., Shin, M.C.: Improving pollen classification with less training effort. In: Proceedings of IEEE Workshop on Applications of Computer Vision (WACV), pp. 421–426 (2013)

15. Arias, D.G., Cirne, M.V.M., Chire, J.E., Pedrini, H.: Classification of pollen grain images based on an ensemble of classifiers. In: Proceedings of 16th IEEE International Conference on Machine Learning and Applications (ICMLA), pp. 234–240 (2017)

16. Frejlichowski, D.: Identification of erythrocyte types in greyscale MGG images for computer-assisted diagnosis. In: Vitrià, J., Sanches, J.M., Hernández, M. (eds.) IbPRIA 2011. LNCS, vol. 6669, pp. 636–643. Springer, Heidelberg (2011). https://doi.org/10.1007/978-3-642-21257-4_79

Medical Image Analysis

U-CatcHCC: An Accurate HCC Detector in Hepatic DCE-MRI Sequences Based on an U-Net Framework

Anna Fabijańska[1]([✉]), Antoine Vacavant[2], Marie-Ange Lebre[2],
Ana L. M. Pavan[4], Diana R. de Pina[4], Armand Abergel[2,3], Pascal Chabrot[2,3],
and Benoît Magnin[2,3]

[1] Institute of Applied Computer Science, Lodz University of Technology,
18/22 Stefanowskiego Street, 90-924 Łódź, Poland
anna.fabijanska@p.lodz.pl

[2] Université Clermont Auvergne, SIGMA Clermont, CNRS, Institut Pascal,
63000 Clermont-Ferrand, France
antoine.vacavant@uca.fr

[3] Centre Hospitalo-Universitaire, Clermont-Ferrand, France
pchabrot@chu-clermontferrand.fr

[4] Department of Physics and Biophysics, São Paulo State University,
Botucatu, São Paulo, Brazil
drpina@fmb.unesp.br

Abstract. This paper presents a novel framework devoted to the detection of HCC (Hepato-Cellular Carcinoma) within hepatic DCE-MRI (Dynamic Contrast-Enhanced MRI) sequences, by a deep learning approach. In clinical routine, radiologists usually consider different phases during contrast injection (before injection; arterial phase; portal phase for instance) for HCC diagnosis. By employing a U-Net architecture, we are able to identify such tumors with a very high accuracy (98.5% of classification rate at best) for a small cohort of patients, which should be confirmed in future works by considering larger groups. We also show in this paper the influence of patch size for this machine learning process, and the positive impact of employing all phases available in DCE-MRI sequences, compared to use only one.

1 Context and Motivation

Liver cancer is the second leading cause of death by cancer worldwide with more than 700,000 deaths in 2012 according to the World Health Organization (WHO) [16]. This cancer is particularly aggressive and its mortality rate is still increasing since the 90s in the World. Hepatocellular Carcinoma (HCC) is the most common liver cancer (90%), and the WHO estimated the number of new cases per year at 704,000 in the World in 2012. HCC occurs in liver cirrhosis at 80%, and due to a late diagnosis, the 5-years overall survival is of about 10%. HCC nodules are hypervascularized and their growth can be unifocal (as a single mass) or multifocal (several nodules). Patients suffering from HCC are 30–50,

© Springer Nature Switzerland AG 2018
L. J. Chmielewski et al. (Eds.): ICCVG 2018, LNCS 11114, pp. 319–328, 2018.
https://doi.org/10.1007/978-3-030-00692-1_28

and associated cirrhosis may be influenced by many factors: alcohol, hepatitis B/C or even diabetes [13].

For any patient follow-up, detection and diagnosis of HCC are conducted by radiologists who analyze medical images such as those provided by MRI (Magnetic Resonance Imaging), CT (Computed Tomography)-scanning or ultrasound (US) imaging. From a general point of view, MRI provides more information for diagnosis purposes, the exam is without ionizing radiation compared to CT, and has a better quality than US. Furthermore, DCE-MRI (Dynamic Contrast-Enhanced MRI) is getting a lot of attention, since it improves again the visualization of HCC tumors, thanks to the injection of a contrast agent (gadolinium-based). More precisely, the vascular profile of any suspicious liver nodule can be determined during three main phases of DCE-MRI acquisition: (1) before contrast injection, (2) at arterial phase (*e.g.* 30 sec. after injection), and (3) at late phase (*e.g.* 3 min after injection) [13]. Following this procedure, a HCC tumor should have same signal intensity and slightly different texture as healthy tissues in phase 1, then it should be enhanced in arterial phase and produce hypo-signal during late phase wrt. surrounding tissues. In general, imaging techniques have still a low performance for nodules smaller than 2 cm; as an illustration, sensitivity of MRI in detecting HCC is about 30% [4]. Hence, computer aided diagnosis (CAD) can be of great interest for HCC, and follows the popularization of machine learning approaches for tumoral tissue detection in medical images such as Radiomics [9].

In a recent work, a complete CAD framework has been proposed in [13] for the detection of HCC lesions in DCE-MRI images. To our knowledge, this is the first attempt in developing such an approach supported by this kind of data. Indeed, other researches have focused on classifying liver disorders or hepatic nodules within different tumor classes from CT or ultrasound images [1,8]. Some algorithms have been designed specifically for HCC, but concerns only CT data [2,6]. In [13], the authors have reached a classification rates of 80% approximately, with a very few false detection rate. They have also presented how to extend their patch-based approach toward a multi-processor architecture.

In parallel to this scale-up of CAD developments, deep learning has gained a lot of attention in medical image analysis tasks, and increased accuracy of many CAD systems. In particular, introduction of CNN (Convolutional Neural Networks) in [10] and augmentation of computer power have popularized the use of deep learning in medical image-based technologies [12,17].

In this article, we propose a novel HCC detection framework, called U-CatcHCC, and based on a deep learning approach by employing an adapted U-Net architecture [15]. This is the very first proposal aiming at identifying HCC nodules within DCE-MRI sequences based on such approach. We also show that U-CatcHCC detects accurately HCC by achieving a classification rate about more than 90%, by combining the three DCE-MRI phases.

The rest of the paper is organized as follows: Sect. 2 presents the material employed in this study, and the way we have pre-processed them. We then expose in Sect. 3 the U-Net-based architecture we have developed in order to detect HCC in DCE-MRI. Finally, various experimental results are conducted numerically and visually in Sect. 4, before conclusion (Sect. 5).

2   Material and Data Preprocessing Steps

2.1   Dataset

We have retrospectively selected 9 patients who underwent hepatic MRI in our department as standard of care for their cirrhosis. They all suffer from HCC diagnosed in the MRI by a radiologist, according to EASL criteria [3]: known cirrhosis (according to clinical, biological and imaging data), focal lesion of at least 1 cm, hypervascular in the arterial phase with washout in the portal venous or delayed phases. MR exams were performed on a 1.5 T Optima (General Electric Healthcare, Milwaukee, WI) with a phased array coil. It consisted of axial T2 Single Shot Fast Spin Echo (SSFSE), axial T2 FatSat Propeller, axial diffusion weighted imaging and multiphase 3D Fast Spoiled Gradient Echo T1 LAVA before and while injection of $0.2\,\mathrm{mL/kg}$ of gadobenate dimeglumine (MultiHance®, Bracco). MR images were obtained in the axial plane with a section thickness of 4 mm, a 2 mm intersection gap, matrix of 512×512 and a field of view of 420×420–$500 \times 500\,\mathrm{mm}^3$, which covered the whole liver. In this study, only T1 images were used to detect HCC.

2.2   Liver Volume Segmentation

To extract the complete liver volume within DCE-MRI images, we have applied an automatic model-based segmentation, described in [11]. To do so, we have first constructed a statistical model based on liver shape variability thanks to expert segmentations provided by public datasets: SLIVER07 [5], SHAPE2015 [7] and the last one provided by IRCAD [14]. We have then registered this *a priori* model into MRI volumes in order to localize the liver within patient's data.

After this localization, we have then calculated the largest liver surface and determined the associated slice by considering intensity histograms. After intensity-based thresholding operation and contour enhancement, we have employed the prior statistical model to initialize an active contour method based on a fast marching framework. A sample result of this algorithm is depicted in Fig. 1, for a single slice, and a 3D faithful reconstruction of the liver volume obtained afterward.

2.3   Phases Normalization

Input DCE-MRI volumes have been then processed by normalizing the three phases I_{p1} (before contrast injection), I_{p2} (arterial phase) and I_{p3} (late phase) with respect to each-other. Particularly, intensities of the phase images were linearly transformed to 8-bit grayscale, providing that the brightest region within all three phase images receives the highest intensity (*i.e.*, 255) and the darkest

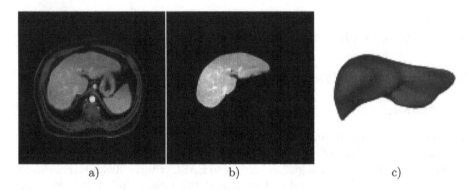

a)   b)   c)

Fig. 1. For a MRI slice (a) is presented the result of our automatic liver segmentation algorithm (b). A faithful 3D representation of the whole liver can be then obtained (c).

one receives the lowest intensity (*i.e.*, 0). This kind of preprocessing allowed to keep information about the DCE enhancement between the considered phases.

The normalized phase data was next used to compose a volumetric 3-channel image $I = [I_{p1}, I_{p2}, I_{p3}]$ where each channel stores a single phase data. Sample slices extracted from phase images and the corresponding 3-channel image are shown in Fig. 2.

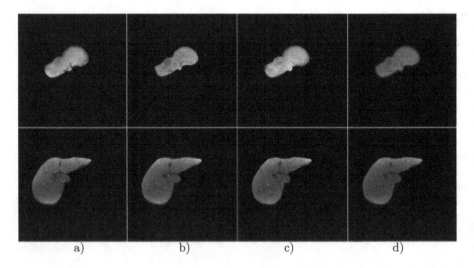

a)   b)   c)   d)

Fig. 2. The three consecutive phases of DCE-MRI of liver considered in this study: before contract injection (a), arterial phase (b), late phase (c). The corresponding 3-channel image composed from the phases is also exposed in (d).

The preprocessed data was next analyzed slice-by-slice to extract slices containing a cancerous regions. The obtained DCE-MRI slices and the corresponding ground truths were randomly divided into a training (50% of the slices) and testing sets (50% of the slices). As a result a total of 133 slices were extracted, 66 of which were included into a training set. The remaining 67 slices were used for testing. No data augmentation techniques were used.

3 U-Net-Based Classification of HCC

In this study a U-Net-based convolutional network [15] of the architecture shown in Fig. 3 was applied to detect the cancerous regions within the liver. In opposition to other popular CNN architectures, the U-Net can be effectively trained with only a few images and requires a limited amount of training samples. The network works in a tile-to-tile strategy, which means that it takes as input a patch of an image and outputs a patch with the corresponding predictions for all pixels within it.

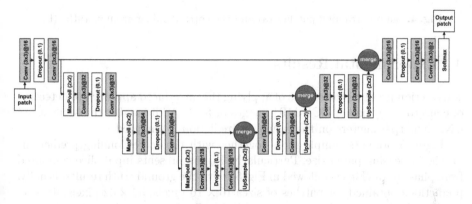

Fig. 3. The architecture of the U-Net network applied in this study.

The U-Net was applied in a slice-by-slice manner to input 3-channel images $I = [I_{p1}, I_{p2}, I_{p3}]$ composed of the three DCE-MRI phases. Prior training all three phases were averaged to produce a grayscale image. An application followed a tile-overlap strategy. Particularly, consecutive patches of an image (overlapping by a stride of 5 pixels in vertical and horizontal direction) were processed. The predictions obtained for the overlapping patches were next averaged to generate the final prediction of the input image.

The network was trained for 100 epochs, unless an early stopping condition (*i.e.* 10 iterations with no improvement) was reached. A total of 60,000 patches (80% for training and 20% for validation) were used for training. A batch size was equal to 320. The patches of a size 48×48 pixels were used. This patch size provided the highest CNN classification accuracy and was selected experimentally (see Fig. 5 and Table 1). The patches were extracted randomly with an equal sampling from the training images, but providing that each patch contains a cancerous region. Sample patches and the corresponding ground truths are shown in Fig. 4.

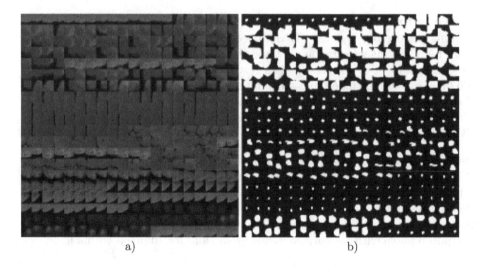

a)   b)

Fig. 4. Sample training patches (a) and the corresponding ground truths (b).

4   Experimental Results

This section presents the results of applying the introduced approach to detection of cancerous regions in DCE-MRI images of liver. Additionally, the influence of CNN hyperparameters on the resulting prediction is analyzed.

Figure 5 presents sample slices together with the corresponding predictions for the increasing patch size. Particularly, Fig. 5a presents input slice composed from phase data. This is followed in Fig. 5b with the ground truth results. Finally, predictions obtained for patches of sizes 16×16 pixels, 32×32 pixels, 48×48 pixels and 64×64 pixels are presented in Fig. 5c–f respectively.

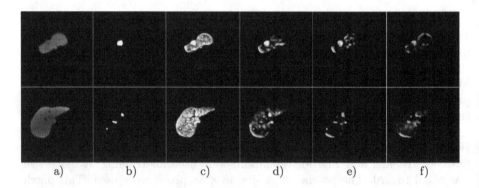

a)   b)   c)   d)   e)   f)

Fig. 5. The influence of a patch size on the resulting CNN prediction; (a) sample input images; (b) the ground truths; (c) prediction, patch 16×16 pixels; (d) prediction, patch 32×32 pixels; (e) prediction, patch 48×48 pixels; (f) prediction, patch 64×64 pixels.

Table 1. The influence of the patch size on the HCC prediction accuracy with our system.

Patch size	SEN	SPC	PREC	ACC	DIC
16 × 16	0.969	0.938	0.172	0.939	0.260
32 × 32	0.919	0.970	0.249	0.970	0.357
48 × 48	0.909	0.980	0.375	0.980	0.482
64 × 64	0.827	0.984	0.357	0.983	0.455

The numerical assessment of the results averaged over whole testing set is presented in Table 1. These include sensitivity (SEN), specificity (SPEC), precision (PREC), accuracy (ACC) and dice (DIC) of the results obtained for the increasing patch size. Prior to comparison the resulting cancer-likelihood maps were binarized with a local, adaptive thresholding performed with respect to a local mean value. We also compare these numerical results with the ones obtained by the related work presented in [13] (see Table 2), based on the same dataset. We can observe the superiority of our novel approach, in terms of sensibility, specificity and accuracy.

Table 2. The influence of the patch size on the HCC prediction accuracy, results obtained by [13].

Patch size	SEN	SPC	PREC	ACC	DIC
16 × 16	0.733	0.800	0.250	0.794	0.372
32 × 32	0.800	0.756	0.301	0.764	0.437
64 × 64	0.798	0.830	0.556	0.825	0.655

Figure 6 presents how the phase selection influences the final results. The consecutive subfigures of Fig. 6 present cancer-likelihood predictions obtained for phase 1 (Fig. 6a), phase 2 (Fig. 6b), phase 3 (Fig. 6c) and all three phases used together after averaging (Fig. 6d). The original images and the ground truths are shown in the corresponding rows of Fig. 5. Since, from Table 1 one can see that the bigger the patch, the more accurate prediction, unless the patch size is not bigger than 48 × 48 pixels. For this patch size the best results are obtained, which manifest themselves by the highest dice value. Precision and specificity were also the highest in the latter case. Therefore, the patch of size 48 × 48 pixels was also used when investigating the influence of phase selection on the accuracy of the prediction. When using patches of size 64 × 64 pixels the accuracy of the HCC prediction decreased. The effect was probably caused by an excessive averaging of cancerous regions that were smaller than the patches.

The numerical assessment of the single-phase-based results averaged over whole testing set is presented in Table 3.

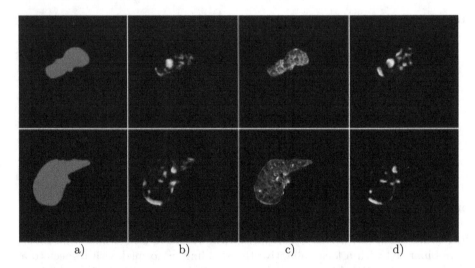

Fig. 6. The influence of a phase used for network training on the resulting CNN prediction (patch size: 48 × 48 pixels); (a) prediction, phase 1; (b) prediction, phase 2; (c) prediction, phase 3; (d) prediction, all three phases. The corresponding images of phases are shown in Fig. 2

Table 3. The influence of the phase selection on the HCC prediction accuracy (patch size 48 × 48 pixels).

Patch size	SEN	SPC	PREC	ACC	DIC
Phase 1	0.602	0.953	0.113	0.949	0.175
Phase 2	0.803	0.989	0.408	0.988	0.493
Phase 3	0.594	0.975	0.205	0.972	0.271
Phases 1–3	0.909	0.980	0.375	0.980	0.482

Figure 6 clearly shows, that the significance of the phases for the resulting prediction is different. When single phases are used it can be seen that the phase 2 is the most influential. Phase 1 alone seems to be useless, similarly to phase 3. However, when all three phases are considered, the best results are obtained and the cancerous regions are visibly highlighted in the predicted image. The visual impression is also confirmed by the numerical assessment. The results shown in Table 3 clearly show, that although the second phase is the most influential, the best prediction is obtained when all three phases are used together. This manifests itself mainly by the highest sensitivity, since for three phases used together over 90% of the cancerous region was correctly identified. This measure was about 10% lower when only the second phase was considered.

5   Conclusion and Future Works

In this paper the possibility of HCC detection in DCE-MRI images of liver using a deep learning approach was investigated. It was shown, that by applying the U-Net convolutional neural network it was possible to accurately predict the cancerous regions. The influence of the patch size on the resulting prediction was also investigated providing guidelines for future studies. We have also shown that our novel system overtakes recent work presented in [13], in particular for the overall accuracy (more than 98% against 82.5% for patches of size 64×64 pixels).

In this dataset, we have selected DCE-MRI sequences with a high contrast enhancement for HCC tissues, leading to a high impact of this phase in this machine learning process. We are also investigating the analysis of image sequences wherein HCC is more difficult to distinguish, only by considering phase 2. In this study, we hope to confirm that processing all phases is a benefit in HCC detection by our framework.

Although the training of the U-Net architecture with DCE-MRI phases took few hours (ranging from about 90 s per epoch for a patch of size 16×16 pixels, to about 400 s per epoch for a patch size 64×64 pixels), the prediction was also reasonably fast and took below one second per slice (GTX TITAN X 12 GB GDDR5) which makes the method available for a clinical routine. By increasing the size of our dataset, we expect a high increase of the learning phase of our system. We thus plan to investigate a parallel approach, by constructing a multi-processor code architecture, to speed-up our framework.

Acknowledgement. This work was co-financed by the Lodz University of Technology, Faculty of Electrical, Electronic, Computer and Control Engineering as a statutory activity (Project no. 501/12-24-1-5428).

References

1. Alvarez, M., de Pina, D.R., Romeiro, F.G., Duarte, S.B., Ricardo de Miranda, S.A.: Wavelet-based algorithm to the evaluation of contrasted hepatocellular carcinoma in CT-images after transarterial chemoembolization. Radiat. Oncol. **9**(1), 166 (2014)
2. Conze, P.H., et al.: Scale-adaptive supervoxel-based random forests for liver tumor segmentation in dynamic contrast-enhanced CT scans. Int. J. Comput. Assist. Radiol. Surg. **12**(2), 223–233 (2017)
3. European Association for the Study of the Liver: EASL-EORTC clinical practice guidelines: management of hepatocellular carcinoma. J. Hepatol. **4**(56), 908–943 (2012)
4. Gomaa, A.I., Khan, S.A., Leen, E.L., Waked, I., Taylor-Robinson, S.D.: Diagnosis of hepatocellular carcinoma. World J. Gastroenterol. **11**(15), 1301–1314 (2009)
5. Heimann, T., et al.: Comparison and evaluation of methods for liver segmentation from CT datasets. IEEE Trans. Med. Imaging **28**(8), 1251–1265 (2009)
6. Khalilinezhad, M., Dellepiane, S., Vernazza, G.: Detecting HCC tumor in three phasic CT liver images with optimization of neural network. Int. J. Med. Health Biomed. Bioeng. Pharm. Eng. **9**(3), 277–282 (2015)

7. Kistler, M., Bonaretti, S., Pfahrer, M., Niklaus, R., Buchler, P.: The virtual skeleton database: an open access repository for biomedical research and collaboration. J. Med. Internet Res. **15**(11), e245 (2013)

8. Krishnan, K.R., Radhakrishnan, S.: Hybrid approach to classification of focal and diffused liver disorders using ultrasound images with wavelets and texture features. IET Image Process. **11**(7), 530–538 (2017)

9. Lambin, P., Rios-Velazquez, E., Leijenaar, R., Carvalho, S., van Stiphout, R.G., Granton, P.: Radiomics: extracting more information from medical images using advanced feature analysis. Eur. J. Cancer **48**, 441–446 (2012)

10. Lecun, Y., Bottou, L., Bengio, Y., Haffner, P.: Gradient-based learning applied to document recognition. In: Proceedings of the IEEE (1998)

11. Lebre, M.-A., et al.: Medical image processing and numerical simulation for digital hepatic parenchymal blood flow. In: Tsaftaris, S.A., Gooya, A., Frangi, A.F., Prince, J.L. (eds.) SASHIMI 2017. LNCS, vol. 10557, pp. 99–108. Springer, Cham (2017). https://doi.org/10.1007/978-3-319-68127-6_11

12. Litjens, G., et al.: A survey on deep learning in medical image analysis. Med. Image Anal. **42**, 60–88 (2017)

13. Pavan, A.L.M., et al.: A parallel framework for HCC detection in DCE-MRI sequences with wavelet-based description and SVM classification. In: Annual ACM Symposium on Applied Computing (2018)

14. Research Institute against Digestive Cancer. IRCAD dataset. http://www.ircad.fr/research/3d-ircadb-01/

15. Ronneberger, O., Fischer, P., Brox, T.: U-Net: convolutional networks for biomedical image segmentation. In: Navab, N., Hornegger, J., Wells, W.M., Frangi, A.F. (eds.) MICCAI 2015. LNCS, vol. 9351, pp. 234–241. Springer, Cham (2015). https://doi.org/10.1007/978-3-319-24574-4_28

16. World Health Organization: Liver Cancer. Estimated Incidence, Mortality and Prevalence Worldwide in 2012 (2012). http://globocan.iarc.fr/old/FactSheets/cancers/liver-new.asp

17. Zhou, S.K., Greenspan, H., Shen, D.: Deep Learning for Medical Image Analysis. Academic Press, Amsterdam (2017)

Unsupervised Caries Detection in Non-standardized Periapical Dental X-Rays

Darren Osterloh and Serestina Viriri[✉]

School of Mathematics, Statistics and Computer Science,
University of KwaZulu-Natal, Durban, South Africa
{209501289,viriris}@ukzn.ac.za

Abstract. Dental caries are currently one of the most prevalent diseases in the modern world. Early detection and diagnosis of the disease is the best treatment available to dental healthcare professionals and is crucial in preventing advanced stages of decay. This paper presents an effective model for caries detection across a variety of non-uniform X-rays using individual tooth segmentation, boundary detection and caries detection through image analysis techniques. The tooth segmentation is implemented using integral projection and an analytical division algorithm. The boundary detection is implemented through the use of top and bottom hat transformations and active contours. Finally the caries detection was achieved through the use of blob detection and cluster analysis on suspected carious regions. The cluster analysis generates its results relative to the image being analyzed and as such, forms the unsupervised evaluation approach of this paper. The viability of this unsupervised learning model, and its relative effectiveness of accurately diagnosing dental caries when compared to current systems, is indicated by the results detailed in this paper, with the proposed model achieving a 96% correct diagnostic.

Keywords: Dental X-rays · Tooth segmentation
Boundary detection · Caries identification

1 Introduction

Despite advances in oral healthcare, dental caries remain the most widespread of oral diseases, with approximately 36% of the world's population showing signs of the infection [1]. This has led to many attempts to improve the detection rate of caries in order to prevent more serious oral diseases from developing. Traditionally, dental X-rays have been used by oral healthcare professionals to assess unobservable areas of the tooth and make a diagnosis through observation [2]. Newer advancements in computer vision have led to the development of Computer-aided Diagnosis systems in order to assist in the identification and

© Springer Nature Switzerland AG 2018
L. J. Chmielewski et al. (Eds.): ICCVG 2018, LNCS 11114, pp. 329–340, 2018.
https://doi.org/10.1007/978-3-030-00692-1_29

diagnosis process. Unfortunately these systems have a high false positive rate at identifying caries and as such have not been usable as standalone systems [3].

The goal of this paper is to propose a caries detection model to assist in the treatment of dental caries. The proposed model aims to rectify the shortcomings of existing models and provide more accurate results by implementing a new approach to the diagnostic algorithm.

Several factors have led to the unfavourable identification results with respect to caries diagnosis. Firstly, dental X-rays are noisy and low in contrast due to the low dosage rates in the capture process [4]. These low dosage rates can also affect the visibility of caries due to the X-rays not fully penetrating the teeth. There is no workaround for this as the low dosage rates ensure the health of the patient [5], thus image enhancement techniques must be utilized to assist in computer vision. Secondly, the majority of segmentation research focuses on tooth segmentation for the purposes of human identification. As a result, features required for caries detection are lost in favour of preserving crown shape in order to match teeth. Finally, current caries detection algorithms use a supervised learning model as the basis of their comparative model. Suspected caries regions are compared against a set of classifiers which are obtained from a learning set where the presence of caries is known. If there are similarities between the test image and the classifiers, the algorithm provides a positive caries diagnosis.

There have been varying degrees of research into optimizing the each of the specific aspects of radiograph processing. Ahmad et al. [6] tested the effects of four image enhancement techniques, namely adaptive histogram equalization (AHE), contrast adaptive histogram equalization (CLAHE), median adaptive histogram equalization (MAHE) and sharp contrast adaptive histogram equalization (SCLAHE) in an attempt to determine which provided better results in terms of improving X-ray quality. Further research by Bharathi et al. [7] looked at the effectiveness of median, finite impulse response (FIR) and Gaussian filters in reducing noise levels.

Research with regards to tooth segmentation alternates between the use of integral projection or active contours. Nomir et al. [8] proposed a method adapted from the works of Hu et al. [9]. A mask of the initial image was obtained by performing an iterative and adaptive threshold. Integral projection was performed on this mask based on the assumption that most, if not all, of the non teeth related pixels have been removed. This method was used again by Nomir et al. [10] for human identification. Lin et al. [11] also used an adaptation of the method presented in Ref. [8] for use in human identification. Jain et al. [12] and Frejlichowski and Wanat [13] further developed this method to incorporate a probability model. Segmentation through active contours was used by Zhou et al. [14] as well as Oliveira [15]. Rad et al. [16] compiled an evaluation of these various segmentation methods.

Not much research has been done with respect to caries identification itself. Solanki et al. [17] used an unsupervised learning approach where the shape contour of each tooth was analyzed. Oprea et al. [18] proposed a binary threshold be applied on a high contrast image. A subsequent rule check was performed to determine if any black pixel groups occurred within the tooth or along its boundary and flagged these as caries. Oliveira [15] made use of a supervised learning approach and developed a set of classifiers for caries detection. Finally, Zhang et al. [19] used a blob detection method to isolate potential dental caries for 3-D rendering and assessment.

In order to achieve the goal of an improved caries detection model using an unsupervised learning approach, this paper presents a unique diagnostic model. This model is comprised of both adapted algorithms from previous research and novel algorithms which reduce the inaccuracies inherent to current methods.

2 Segmentation

The segmentation of the X-rays into individual teeth was achieved through a three stage process. This process consists of pre-processing and image enhancement, adaptive and iterative thresholding and separation line selection using a novel algorithm.

2.1 Pre-processing

The diagnostic rate of the algorithm detailed in this paper was improved by optimizing the quality of the images being processed. This optimization was achieved through the implementation of image enhancement techniques which were used to remove nosie from the image and improve the overall image quality. To ensure the best outcome of the image enhancements, a preliminary cleanup process was implemented to remove any abnormalities present in the images due to the radiograph process.

Image Enhancement. Following the removal of all non-organic structures barring dental fillings, the image contrast was enhanced in order to provide better definition of the dental structures. To preserve feature detail, noise reduction obtained from blur filters was avoided. Following research conducted by Yoon et al. [20] which suggested that Adaptive Histogram Equalization provided a greater contrast improvement for computer vision, a combination of a median filter followed by histogram equalization was implemented.

2.2 Thresholding

Iterative Thresholding. Due to the similarities in the X-Ray images being processed, the model proposed in [8] was adapted as the basis for the thresholding implementation. A canny edge detector was used to obtain the general outline of the teeth in each X-ray image. A morphological dilation was then applied to these edges in order to obtain the pixels in the area assumed to be the tooth boundary. Approximately half of the pixels obtained this way corresponded to the teeth pixels whilst the rest were of the jaw bone and other background objects. The initial threshold value was calculated from the average pixel value of the assumed teeth pixels and the background pixels and subsequent thresholds were calculated as follows:

$$\mu_D^i = \frac{\sum_{(i,j)\in dental} f(i,j)}{\#dental\_pixels}, \tag{1}$$

$$\mu_B^i = \frac{\sum_{(i,j)\in dental} f(i,j)}{\#background\_pixels}, \tag{2}$$

$$T_{i+1} = \frac{\mu_B^i + \mu_D^i}{2}. \tag{3}$$

where f(i, j) is the grayscale value of a pixel at point (i, j), μ_D^i and μ_D^i are the mean grayscale values for their respective regions and T_i is the threshold value for the whole image calculated from the average values of the background and teeth pixels.

This step was repeated until the iterative threshold value did not change in subsequent re-evaluations or until a hard limit was reached. It was determined in Ref. [8] that convergence occurred within four to ten iterations for their set of images. Following several tests it was determined that convergence occurred within seven to fifteen iterations for the images discussed in this paper, so a maximum iteration limit of fifteen was used.

Once a final value had been determined for the iterative thresholding portion of the greater thresholding method, a mask of the X-ray was produced by isolating all teeth pixels whose grayscale value equaled or exceeded the iterative value.

Adaptive Thresholding. In order to correctly identify teeth pixels from miscellaneous background, jaw and gum pixels, an adaptive thresholding method was implemented. The adaptive thresholding method proposed by [8] determined the threshold value for an image as such; following standard adaptive threshold implementation, a pixel undergoes thresholding if, with it being the centre pixel of a window of size I × J pixels, its grayscale value is less than the mean value of all non-zero pixels within the window. The formula for this is thus

$$T(i,j) = \frac{\sum_{s=-\frac{I}{2}}^{\frac{I}{2}} f(i+s,j+t)}{\#nonzero\_pixels} \tag{4}$$

In order to account for the varying exposure rates of the X-Rays being tested, where some teeth would appear darker than background tissue, as well as the presence of darker regions in teeth which contained dental caries, the threshold value unique to each image could not be used. Likewise, a general threshold value for the entire dataset could not be used due to the varying brightness intensities in each X-Ray arising from the presence of dental fillings or caps.

A hybrid approach was therefore implemented to generate a threshold value which correctly removed as much of the non-teeth pixels as possible. A global threshold was determined by applying the adaptive threshold to the mask images of 40 images. The average of these thresholds was used to establish the global threshold value. The same process was applied to each image when it underwent thresholding to obtain its personal threshold. A final threshold value was obtained from the weighted sum of these two values where the distribution of the pixel intensity affected the weights. The initial weight for each threshold was set to 0.5 on the basis that the global threshold represented the average intensity trend for the dataset and that the personal threshold corrected any slight deviations. If there was a discrepancy between the two values, such that a 10% deviation or greater was present, the following rule was applied:

$$FT(i,j) = \begin{cases} 0.6PAT + 0.4GAT, & \text{if } 1 - \frac{PAT}{GAT} >= 0.1 \\ 0.4PAT + 0.6GAT & \text{if } 1 - \frac{GAT}{PAT} >= 0.1 \end{cases}$$

where FT is the final threshold, PAT is the personal adaptive threshold and GAT is the global adaptive threshold.

2.3   Tooth Separation

Tooth separation was handled in two parts. The potential separation lines are initially generated through integral projection, which determines the gap regions between identified teeth. Following this, an evaluation algorithm determines the line of best fit.

Integral Projection. Integral projection is able to analyze pixel intensities across an image and detect regions of darker pixels. As such, it provided the best solution for the detection of gaps between teeth, where the spaces between two adjacent teeth are easily identifiable from the thresholded mask obtained in the previous stage. Areas where clusters of black pixels were present between pairs of adjacent clusters of white pixels were identified as valleys.

Line Selection. Separation lines were calculated using the gap clusters as training points for a linear regression model. Two variations of the simple linear regression algorithm were used. The first algorithm was the standard formula defined as follows:

$$\hat{\beta} = \frac{\sum_{i=1}^{n} (x_i - \bar{x})(y_i - \bar{y})}{\sum_{i=1}^{n} (x_i - \bar{x})^2}, \tag{5}$$

$$= \frac{\sum_{i=1}^{n} x_i y_i - \frac{1}{n} \sum_{i=1}^{n} x_i \sum_{j=1}^{n} y_j}{\sum_{i=1}^{n} x_i^2 - \frac{1}{n} \left(\sum_{i=1}^{n} x_i\right)^2}, \tag{6}$$

$$= \frac{\bar{xy} - \bar{x}\bar{y}}{\bar{x^2} - \bar{x}^2}, \tag{7}$$

$$\hat{\alpha} = \bar{y} - \hat{\beta}\bar{x}. \tag{8}$$

where n denotes the number of points, β denotes the gradient of the slope and α denotes the y-intercept.

The second formula was a weighted linear regression model which proved effective in generating a correct separating line in cases where cluster distribution was favoured in one direction. In cases where there was an equal distribution of points around the median then the simple linear regression model was used. If the distribution of points was greater or less than the median then the value of n in the above equation was calculated to be half the total number of points.

In order to determine the best separation lines, the algorithm proposed by Frejlichowski and Wanat [13] was adapted to work on periapical X-Rays. The original algorithm determined separation lines based on the nature of panoramic X-rays, where all teeth are in view. It uses the uniform nature of teeth sizing to determine spacing across the entire row of teeth. Due to the nature of the X-rays being analyzed, where the number and types of teeth present in each X-Ray varied across each image, the adapted algorithm was required in order to achieve correct results. By combining the rotation algorithms used in [8,12] with an altered probability model derived from [13], the new segmentation algorithm was developed which incorporated both rotational and probabilistic functions.

For segmentation lines where the number of intersection points is equal to, or greater than, a previously determined optimal line, a new set of acceptance criteria were introduced. Based on the probability formula implemented in [12], vertical lines have a higher probability of generating successful segmentation results. The weighting system judged potential line candidates by using slope gradient and intersection point percentage relative to the total separation line. The probability of a line being the best segmentation line was determined by

$$P = |nW_T + \frac{W_I}{IP_{deep}} - J| \tag{9}$$

where P was the probability of the line being correct, n was the number of already segmented teeth, WT was the assumed width of the previous teeth, WI was the width of the image, IP are the number of integral projection points representing gaps between the teeth and J was the projected point of the segmentation line. The desire of the algorithm was to minimize the value of P where P actually represents the probability of a line being incorrect. Lines which fall on the projected segmentation value have a P rating of 0 meaning there is close to 0 probability of it being incorrect. As segmentation lines move away from the projected point the value of P increases resulting in unfavourable selection chances.

To accommodate for acceptance of separation lines for impacted or extremely close adjacent teeth, a second algorithm was used. If more than 60% of the separation line intersected with teeth pixels then the line was discarded and the gap was regarded as a space between molar roots.

3   Caries Detection

Caries detection was handled in two stages. Potential regions of interest were first identified using an edge detector which highlighted all locations where dark spots, and by extension possible caries, were present. Once a region of interest had been defined a novel algorithm was applied to the area in question in order to assess the validity of the caries flag.

3.1   Blob Detection

After testing several methods, a blob detector was implemented for the detection of potential caries in the demarcated search space. Regions of possible decay appeared substantially darker when compared to the surrounding tooth matter, due to the high contrast of the image from the top and bottom hat transformation performed during the boundary detection phase. Blob detection algorithms were able to capitilize on this, owing to their ability to locate local maxima. The blob detection model proposed by Lindeberg [21] was implemented as it was not affected by scaling issues which arose from the varying sizes of the teeth being processed. The model used a Laplacian of the Gaussian approach to detect darker regions, which was defined as a convolution kernel of the form

$$LoG = \frac{x^2 + y^2 - 2\sigma^2}{\sigma^4} e^{-\frac{x^2 = y^2}{2\sigma^2}} \tag{10}$$

where σ was the width of the kernel. This was approximated to a 5×5 kernel for the purposes of implementation defined as

$$LoG = \begin{bmatrix} 0 & 0 & 1 & 0 & 0 \\ 0 & 1 & 2 & 1 & 0 \\ 1 & 2 & -16 & 2 & 1 \\ 0 & 1 & 2 & 1 & 0 \\ 0 & 0 & 1 & 0 & 0 \end{bmatrix}$$

The use of a 4-connected kernel resulted in some loss of definition around the edges of the caries clusters which negatively impacted the diagnostic method, therefore the 8-connected kernel was implemented.

3.2   Caries Analysis

Region of Interest Generation. To achieve the goal of diagnosing whether dental caries were present with a non-supervised assessment model, image analysis techniques were implemented in order to assess the regions of interest using standard dentistry techniques. The depth of the search region was already known relative to the tooth, falling between 10–15% of the overall width. Teeth were approximated to fall between 7.5–9.0 mm in width as defined by Chu [22]. Due to the images being periapical X-rays and not panoramic, the exact tooth being analyzed was unknown as the X-Rays were taken of varying locations. In order to approximate the width, the following formula was proposed:

$$W = Tmax - \frac{T_{variance}(P_{max} - P_{calculated})}{P_{variance}} \tag{11}$$

where W was the estimated width, T was the width of the tooth and P was the percentage depth of the search space, determined to be 10–15%. $T_{variance}$ was obtained by calculating the difference of the maximum and minimum tooth width values and was determined to be 1.5. The value for $P_{variance}$ was calculated to be 5 following the same process. This formula was derived using the probability that teeth which required smaller analysis regions represented the narrower spectrum of teeth, whereas teeth with wider search regions represented the wider spectrum.

Cluster Analysis. Positive classification of caries from flagged regions of interest required that several acceptance variables were met. A threshold value was obtained by calculating the mean pixel value of the cluster region. A second threshold value was also generated by calculating the mean pixel intensity of the area surrounding the suspected caries region. Due to caries originating in the enamel of the tooth, the search space was constrained to this region. This was done primarily to avoid incorrect caries classifications resulting from the darker dentin region interfering with the assessment algorithm. Calculations were based on enamel thickness varying from 0.87–1.45 mm as defined in Ref. [23]. The search space was obtained by creating an elliptical region centered along the perpendicular of the cluster with width equal to double its height and height defined by:

$$H = E_{max} - \frac{E_{variance}(T_{max} - T_{calculated})}{T_{variance}} \tag{12}$$

where H was the height of the ellipsis, E was the width of the enamel and T was the width of the tooth. $E_{variance}$ was obtained by calculating the difference of the maximum and minimum enamel width values and was determined to be 0.58.

By restricting the search space to this elliptical region, the second threshold value was calculated from neighbouring pixels contained within the enamel region. The two threshold values were compared to determine if there was a sizeable difference between the suspected caries cluster and the surrounding pixels. If the cluster was less than 5% darker than the surrounding area the cluster was discarded and no caries were identified. If the cluster region had a mean more than 15% darker than the surrounding area the cluster was identified as a caries region. If the cluster mean was between 5–15% darker, the algorithm proceeded to determine if the cluster represented a darkening of the X-ray itself or a site of early caries development. A Sobel operator with a kernel size of 3 was applied to the elliptical region in order to detect significant gradient changes within the region. By limiting the kernel size to the minimum possible, it was possible to apply the operator to any sized region of interest. In order to deal with the inaccuracies inherent to 3×3 Sobel kernels, the Scharr function [24] was used, defined as two kernels of the form

$$G_x = \begin{bmatrix} -3 & 0 & +3 \\ -10 & 0 & +10 \\ -3 & 0 & +3 \end{bmatrix} \qquad G_y = \begin{bmatrix} -3 & 10 & -3 \\ 0 & 0 & 0 \\ +3 & +10 & +3 \end{bmatrix}$$

These kernels were applied to all pixels within the analysis region, resulting in the transformation of

$$G = |G_x| + |G_y| \tag{13}$$

where G was the value of the new pixel. If no edges were detected using this algorithm, it implied that there were no regions of significant pixel intensity change within the search region. As such, the cluster was regarded as a darkening of the X-ray which was initially flagged due to the enhanced contrast brought on by the top and bottom hat transformations. If, however, an edge was detected, this represented a region of pixel intensity change not in line with the surrounding area. As such these areas were denoted as caries.

4   Experimental Results

4.1   Segmentation Results

The success rate of the segmentation method was evaluated based on its ability to correctly separate teeth in the upper and lower jaw regions individually as well as the combined results of both regions. This provided both specific results as to whether the algorithm performed better on a particular jaw region, as well as a holistic view as to how well it performed on average when looking at both jaw regions.

Teeth were considered correctly separated if the separation line did not cause partial separation or division of the teeth. Teeth which were already partial as a result of being at the edge of the X-ray were considered correctly separated if no further partiality was caused. Teeth which were not correctly segmented were either caused as a result of extremely poor contrast in the original image, where the enhancement techniques could not establish a distinction between teeth and non-teeth structures, or due to impacted teeth.

A comparison of the results on a jaw specific basis are presented in Table 1. The results obtained by Oliveira and Nomir and Abdel-Mottaleb are used as a comparison, due to the similarity of the implemented methods used to achieve dental segmentation.

Table 1. Region specific segmentation results comparison

	Upper Jaw	Lower Jaw
Oliveira [15]	72%	72%
Nomir and Abdel-Mottaleb [8]	84%	81%
Proposed approach	**85%**	**90%**

As can be seen, with a combination of the adapted and novel algorithms discussed in this paper, the segmentation results improved over existing methods.

Table 2. Overall segmentation results comparison

	Accuracy (%)	Implementation
Nomir and Abdel-Mottaleb [8]	82.5	Thresholding
Said et al. [25]	83	Thresholding
Shah et al. [26]	58.1	Active contour
Phong-Dinh et al. [16]	77.23	Thresholding and integral projection
Oliveira [15]	71.91	Active contour without edge
Lai and Lin [27]	83	Region growing
Proposed approach	**87.5**	**Thresholding and integral projection**

Table 2 provides a comparison of the proposed method to other implementations of the segmentation process, as described in Ref. [16].

These results indicate that the method proposed in this paper offers a noticeable improvement on existing models. Furthermore, it indicates the diagnostic algorithm received the greatest quantity of correctly segmented images for evaluation.

4.2   Caries Detection Results

A collection of ground truth data was used to evaluate the success rate of the detection method. The data contained markers for the location of identified caries, as well as the locations of false positive regions. The false positive regions were defined as locations along the boundary of each tooth where caries were incorrectly identified. This occured due to a misinterpretation of the region, either due to the contrast of the X-ray, or because a partial set of caries identifiers were present which led to the algorithm interpreting the results as a caries location.

To determine whether these rates fall within acceptable limits, a comparison was done against the different diagnostic methods available. These comprised of caries detection performed by dentists using the Logicon Caries Detector system, as discussed by Tracy et al. [28], unassisted caries diagnosis by dentists, as discussed by Dykstra [29], and caries detection preformed by a supervised learning model, using the method proposed by Oliveira [15]. The results of this comparison can be seen in Table 3.

Table 3. Caries identification results comparison

	Correctly categorized (%)	False positives (%)	Missed caries (%)
Tracy [28]	94	-	6
Dykstra [29]	60	20	20
Oliveira [15]	98	-	2
Valizadeh et al. [30]	90	-	10
Proposed approach	96	2	2

5   Conclusion

In this paper an unsupervised learning model for caries detection was presented. The proposed model is implemented using a segmentation method to separate the X-rays into individual teeth, a boundary detection method to determine the edges of the teeth for caries analysis and finally a diagnostic algorithm that assesses the boundary using image analysis techniques. Both the proposed segmentation method and caries detection algorithm obtained favourable results when compared to similar models due to the novel approaches described in this paper. As such, the caries detection model outlined in this paper provides a viable alternative to existing models for use in caries detection.

References

1. Vos, T., et al.: Years lived with disability (YLDs) for 1160 sequelae of 289 diseases and injuries 1990–2010: a systematic analysis for the global burden of disease study 2010. Lancet **380**(9859), 2163–2196 (2013)
2. Booshehry, M.Z., Fasihinia, H., Khalesi, M., Gholami, L.: Dental caries diagnostic methods. DJH **2**(1), 1–12 (2011)
3. Amaechi, B.T.: Emerging technologies for diagnosis of dental caries: the road so far. J. Appl. Phys. **105**(10), 102047 (2009)
4. Noor, N.M., Khalid, N.E.A., Ali, M.H., Numpang, A.D.A.: Fish bone impaction using Adaptive Histogram Equalization (AHE). In: 2010 Second International Conference on Computer Research and Development, pp. 163–167. IEEE (2010)
5. Sakata, M., Ogawa, K.: Noise reduction and contrast enhancement for small-dose x-ray images in wavelet domain. In: 2009 IEEE Nuclear Science Symposium Conference Record (NSS/MIC), pp. 2924–2929. IEEE (2009)
6. Ahmad, S.A., Taib, M.N., Khalid, N.E.A., Taib, H.: An analysis of image enhancement techniques for dental x-ray image interpretation. Int. J. Mach. Learn. Comput. **2**(3), 292–297 (2012)
7. Bharathi, K.K., Muruganand, S., Periasamy, A.: Digital image processing based noise reduction analysis of digital dental xray image using matlab. J. NanoScience NanoTechnology **2**(1), 198–203 (2014)
8. Nomir, O., Abdel-Mottaleb, M.: A system for human identification from x-ray dental radiographs. Pattern Recogn. **38**(8), 1295–1305 (2005)
9. Hu, S., Hoffman, E.A., Reinhardt, J.M.: Automatic lung segmentation for accurate quantitation of volumetric x-ray CT images. IEEE Trans. Med. Imaging **20**(6), 490–498 (2001)
10. Nomir, O., Abdel-Mottaleb, M.: Human identification from dental x-ray images based on the shape and appearance of the teeth. IEEE Trans. Inf. Forensics Secur. **2**(2), 188–197 (2007)
11. Lin, P.-L., Lai, Y.-H., Huang, P.-W.: Dental biometrics: human identification based on teeth and dental works in bitewing radiographs. Pattern Recogn. **45**(3), 934–946 (2012)
12. Jain, A.K., Chen, H.: Matching of dental x-ray images for human identification. Pattern Recogn. **37**(7), 1519–1532 (2004)
13. Frejlichowski, D., Wanat, R.: Automatic Segmentation of digital orthopantomograms for forensic human identification. In: Maino, G., Foresti, G.L. (eds.) ICIAP 2011. LNCS, vol. 6979, pp. 294–302. Springer, Heidelberg (2011). https://doi.org/10.1007/978-3-642-24088-1_31

14. Zhou, J., Abdel-Mottaleb, M.: A content-based system for human identification based on bitewing dental x-ray images. Pattern Recogn. **38**(11), 2132–2142 (2005)

15. Oliveira, J.: Caries Detection in Panoramic Dental X-ray Images (2009)

16. Rad, A.E., Mohd Rahim, M.S., Rehman, A., Altameem, A., Saba, T.: Evaluation of current dental radiographs segmentation approaches in computer-aided applications. IETE Tech. Rev. **30**(3), 210–222 (2013)

17. Solanki, A., Jain, K., Desai, N.: ISEF based identification of RCT/filling in dental caries of decayed tooth. Int. J. Image Process. (IJIP) **7**(2), 149–162 (2013)

18. Oprea, S., Marinescu, C., Lita, I., Jurianu, M., Visan, D.A., Cioc, I.B.: Image processing techniques used for dental x-ray image analysis. In: 2008 31st International Spring Seminar on Electronics Technology, pp. 125–129. IEEE (2008)

19. Zhang, H., Boyles, M.J., Ruan, G., Li, H., Shen, H., Ando, M.: Xsede-enabled high-throughput lesion activity assessment. In: Proceedings of the Conference on Extreme Science and Engineering Discovery Environment: Gateway to Discovery, p. 10. ACM (2013)

20. Yoon, J.H., Ro, Y.M.: Enhancement of the contrast in mammographic images using the homomorphic filter method. IEICE Trans. Inf. Syst. **85**(1), 298–303 (2002)

21. Lindeberg, T.: Feature detection with automatic scale selection. Int. J. Comput. Vis. **30**(2), 79–116 (1998)

22. Chu, S.J.: Range and mean distribution frequency of individual tooth width of the maxillary anterior dentition. Pract. Proced. Aesthetic Dent. **19**(4), 209 (2007)

23. Vellini-Ferreira, F., Cotrim-Ferreira, F.A., Ribeiro, J.A., Ferreira-Santos, R.I.: Mapping of proximal enamel thickness in permanent teeth. Braz. J. Oral Sci. **11**(4), 481–485 (2012)

24. Scharr, H.: Optimal operators in digital image processing, Ph.D. dissertation (2000)

25. Said, E.H., Nassar, D.E.M., Fahmy, G., Ammar, H.H.: Teeth segmentation in digitized dental x-ray films using mathematical morphology. IEEE Trans. Inf. Forensics Secur. **1**(2), 178–189 (2006)

26. Shah, S., Abaza, A., Ross, A., Ammar, H.: Automatic tooth segmentation using active contour without edges. In: 2006 Biometrics Symposium: Special Session on Research at the Biometric Consortium Conference, pp. 1–6. IEEE (2006)

27. Lai, Y.H., Lin, P.L.: Effective segmentation for dental x-ray images using texture-based fuzzy inference system. In: Blanc-Talon, J., Bourennane, S., Philips, W., Popescu, D., Scheunders, P. (eds.) ACIVS 2008. LNCS, vol. 5259, pp. 936–947. Springer, Heidelberg (2008). https://doi.org/10.1007/978-3-540-88458-3_85

28. Tracy, K.D., et al.: Utility and effectiveness of computer-aided diagnosis of dental caries. Gen. Dent. **59**(2), 136–144 (2010)

29. Dykstra, B.: Interproximal caries detection: how good are we? Dent. Today **27**(4), 144–146 (2008)

30. Valizadeh, S., Goodini, M., Ehsani, S., Mohseni, H., Azimi, F., Bakhshandeh, H.: Designing of a computer software for detection of approximal caries in posterior teeth. Iran. J. Radiol. **12**(4) (2015)

Localizing Characteristic Points on a Vertebra Contour by Using Shape Language

Marzena Bielecka[1(✉)] and Andrzej Bielecki[2]

[1] Chair of Geoinformatics and Applied Computer Science,
Faculty of Geology, Geophysics and Environmental Protection,
AGH University of Science and Technology,
Al. Mickiewicza 30, 30-059 Kraków, Poland
bielecka@agh.edu.pl
[2] Chair of Applied Computer Science, Faculty of Electrical Engineering, Automation,
Computer Science and Biomedical Engineering, AGH University of Science
and Technology, Al. Mickiewicza 30, 30-059 Kraków, Poland
azbielecki@gmail.com

Abstract. In this paper, X-ray images are analysed by using the shape language. The algorithm combines syntactic and geometric approach. The geometric features of the contour are described by using syntactic approach. The points on the contour, where pathological changes can occur are localised effectively by the algorithm.

Keywords: X-ray imaging · Shape language · Bone contours
Vertebra · Syndesmophytes

1 Introduction

X-ray imaging has its specificity. On the one hand, this investigation is cheap and provides crucial information about pathological changes inside the body, first of all in bones and joints. On the other hand, however, it is hard to extract all possible pieces of information from an X-ray image and only an experienced radiologist can do this. Additionally, small details on the image should be noticed by the physician. The great number of X-ray images and a small number of radiologists cause demand for a computer system which can automatically analyse images or at least can aid the specialist [1, 7, 12, 14, 17, 20–22]. Therefore, development of efficient methods for the retrieval of medical information is very crucial. Various types of artificial intelligence systems [11] are applied to this task [15, 18].

In this paper, the algorithm of finding characteristic points in the vertebra contours is described. This topic is important because spine diseases limit the

The work of the first author was supported by the AGH - University of Science and Technology, Faculty of Geology, Geophysics and Environmental Protection as a part of the statutory project.

© Springer Nature Switzerland AG 2018
L. J. Chmielewski et al. (Eds.): ICCVG 2018, LNCS 11114, pp. 341–348, 2018.
https://doi.org/10.1007/978-3-030-00692-1_30

mobility of the patients and, as a consequence, their functionality. On the other hand, spine diseases are common in the contemporary societies. The algorithm combines the syntactic [10] and geometric approach and is based on the shape language that was introduced by Jakubowski [13] and recently used for X-ray image analysis [4,6]. A shape of a vertebral contour is relevant to study pathological changes. It is crucial to localise the pathological changes as early as it is possible. It means that the regions, where the changes can appear should be scrutinised. The described algorithm allows us do localise of the regions the particular interest automatically.

Thus, the proposed formalism allows us to determine the crucial points in the contour. Such points are utilized in the specific representation of the analysed contour. The approach is used in image retrieval, also in the context of bone contours [20–22].

The paper is organised in the following way. In the next section, the motivations are discussed. Then, the algorithm and the results are presented in Sect. 2.

2   Motivations

As it has been aforementioned, diseases of the spine significantly limit the patient functionality including professional activities, family life and leisure time. Especially, chronic inflammatory diseases, such as ankylosing spondylitis, psoriatic arthritis, reactive arthritis, arthritis in inflammatory bowel diseases and undifferentiated spondyloarthritis, produce pathological bone formations that cause remodelling of the spine. As a result, the spine becomes stiff and inflexible. Therefore, adequate early diagnosis is demanded because it provides a good chance for effective therapy. Plane radiography remains among basic techniques for inflammatory disease of the spine [2].

The bone medulla, that occurs in the vertebral bodies of the spine, affected by the inflammation interacts with the immune system. The syndesmophytes, formed at the vertebral corners, are the morphological effect of the immunological activation of the affected vertebra. The size and the shape of the syndesmophytes correlate with the activity of the disease. Therefore, they are regarded as the crucial predictive factors that allow the physician to assess the disease dynamics and prognosis. That is why careful monitoring of the shape of vertebral bodies, as well as the growth of the syndesmophytes, have important clinical meaning [3, 8,9,19]. The decision of continuation, modification or discontinuation of, usually expensive, therapy of the patient that suffer from inflammatory spine diseases is based on the response to the treatment assessment that answers whether the therapy inhibits new bone progression.

The syndesmophytes can be detected by using X-ray imaging. It is crucial, however, to recognise early stage of the disease which means that even the small changes in the regions of the interest should be detected effectively. To do it automatically by using a computer algorithm, first of all, the regions of the interest have to be localised.

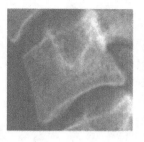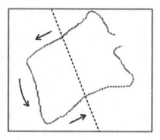

Fig. 1. The example of a vertebra and its contour received by using SDA algorithm.

3   The Algorithm and the Results

There are a few possible approaches to the analysis of the shape of contours. The analysis of the geometric features of the fragments of the contour is one of them. Such an approach works well if distinct features of the contours are searched. Therefore, it can be used efficiently for detecting visible pathological changes in bones such as advanced osteophytes, syndesmophytes and erosions [4–6]. Finding characteristic points of the contour is another possible approach. The points localisations and spatial relations between them can be the basis for the analysis of the contour properties [20,21]. It should be stressed, however, that the method proposed in this paper is different. The shape of the whole contour is analysed, and the characteristic points are found as a result of the analysis. The points determine the regions of the vertebra in which syndesmophytes can occur. These regions can be then analysed carefully by specialised algorithms.

A shape in medical images is one of the essential features that effectively describes different pathology diagnosed by medical experts. Lesions occurring within the vertebrae are syndesmophytes and osteophytes. The X-ray images analyzed in this paper were acquired from the University Hospital in Kraków, Poland. The set consists of 166 examples of vertebrae, 33 of them were diagnosed as affected by syndesmophyte. The analyzed vertebra contours have been obtained by using Statistical Dominance Algorithm (SDA for abbreviation) preprocessing method [16] which is dedicated for preprocessing of X-ray medical images - see Fig. 1. The SDA determines statistically whether the point belongs to an object or not. In the chosen neighborhood the points which dominate over the central point are calculated. That one, which has a bigger value of brightness belongs to the object. The main advantage of the algorithm is low sensitivity to the variance of the pixel values because the algorithm accounts only the relation between pixels. This allows us to omit the local thresholding. Such approach enables the impact of noise and uneven illumination in the image to be reduced.

The places where bone lesions can appear are marked in red - see Fig. 2.

To obtain a description of an interesting fragment of a contour the shape language was applied - see [5,6]. The analysis starts at the point A and ends at the point B - see Fig. 2. For spine shapes, the interesting pathologies on the spine X-ray images can be found along the vertebral boundary. Focusing

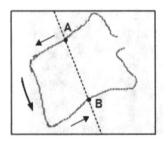

Fig. 2. The contour of a vertebra with marked places of possibly lesions such as syndesmophyte or osteophyte. Points A and B determine the part of the contour that is analyzed. (Color figure online)

on finding the entire shape of the vertebrae is unnecessary and often impossible, mainly because of the low quality of the images. The pathologies such as anterior osteophytes and syndesmophytes are of the main interest of the radiologists. They can be found just between the points A and B - see Fig. 2 and [20]. In the proposed shape language in every point z of a contour a four-component vector $\mathbf{c}(z) = [c_t(z), c_c(z), c_x(z), c_y(z)]$ is calculated. The first two elements, c_t and the c_c are the first and the second derivative. It was assumed that only the signs of these values are taken into consideration. Therefore they can be equal to "+", "−" and "0". However, in the case when the derivative denominator is equal to zero, the value of these components is denoted by "V". The c_x and c_y inform about the X and Y coordinate increments along a curve. These components can be positive, negative or equal to zero and they are marked by "+", "−" and "0", respectively. Then the contour is divided into fragments that consist of points with the same characteristics of the vector c. Each of these fragments is a primitive, which we denote by p_{ij}, $i, j \in \{1, 2, 3, 4\}$. The index i corresponds to geometrical features of the primitives, whereas the index j corresponds to the number of a quadrant of the Cartesian plane. There exist sixteen such primitives and each of them is an equivalence class with the equality relation. As a result of the division of the outline into primitives, we can present it in the form of a string of sinquads. Sinquad is a fragment of contour which consists of primitives with the same value of the index j. The examples of contours with division into sinquads are presented in Fig. 3. Every two consecutive sinquads form a biquad. Thus, a contour is encoded by a key, that informs about transitions between sinquads. Points between successive sinquads are called switches. They are very vital for the shape of the vertebra. In particular, they uniquely identify places where lesions such as syndesmophytes and osteophytes can appear. The vertebrae in the data set were described by proposed shape language. A few examples of received sinquads and switches are shown in Fig. 3.

For healthy vertebrae and those with small changes the following keys were obtained: 34.41 or 34.43.34.41. The possible lesions occur between $3 - sinquad$ and $4 - sinquad$ or between $4 - sinquad$ and $1 - sinquad$. In the first case, this is an upper corner of a vertebra, in the second one this a lower corner of the

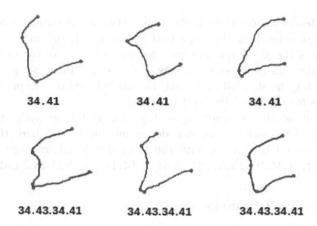

Fig. 3. Contours of vertebrae with marked sinquads received by using proposed shape language. Under each contour there is a key which describes transitions between sinquads.

vertebra. The switch is the point where the last primitive from the first sinquad and the first primitive from the next sinquad meets. The angle between these primitives informs us whether the analyzed vertebra is healthy or not. In Fig. 3 and 4, both red and yellow points denote the switches. The red ones correspond to the case when the vertebra is healthy, or changes are at an early stage. The yellow ones correspond to the case in which the vertebra is heavily changed as a result of the disease. In the case of large deformations of the cervical vertebrae, the form of the key changes. However, also this time the switches set points characteristic for the shape of the cervical vertebrae - see Fig. 4.

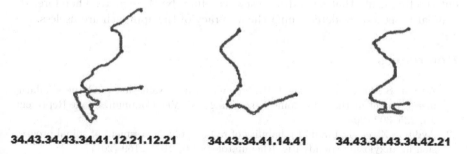

Fig. 4. Contours of vertebrae with large deformations and marked sinquads. In yellow are marked switches that appear in the place of deformations. (Color figure online)

To sum up, lesions that can be detected in the case of spine vertebrae are found in its lower and upper corner. Therefore, finding switches is synonymous with determining the place of occurrence of these changes. However, the measure of whether a lesion has occurred is the angle between the sinquads. Since a sinquad consists of primitives, the angle that interests us is the angle between the last primitive of the given sinquad and the first primitive of the next sinquad. Hence, the detection of a lesion consists of two steps. First, we get a contour description using the sinquad and, next, the angle based on the previously calculated values for the primitives is determined.

As a result of the comparison of keys for vertebrae without deformation and with deformations, one can determine the place where the changes occur. The received keys along with the marked deformations are as follows: 34.43.34.**43.34.41.12.21.12.21**; 34.43.34.41.**14.41**; 34.43.34.**43.34.42.21**.

4   Concluding Remarks

The proposed method allows us to localise the important regions of the analysed vertebrae boundaries automatically. By dividing the contour into sinquads, at the first stage of the contour analysis, explicitly indicate the places where early lesions may appear. It turned out that the possibilities of the shape language implied for its mathematical foundations constitute the efficient tool for finding the regions of the vertebra in which pathological changes can occur.

The regions in which pathological changes can occur are determined by using medical knowledge. They are situated at the corners of vertebrae. On the other hand, the corners constitute switches of the contour which is implied directly by the properties of the used shape language. Thus, the very idea of the task is to determine the regions in which the pathological changes can occur and then to use the angle between the sinquads in order to settle whether they exist indeed. As it has been mentioned, the changes can be in various stages of development, including the very early stages. In such cases, it cannot be settled unequivocally whether the change already exists or not. Nevertheless, the algorithm points out the fragments that should be tested carefully by the expert. Therefore, the standard methods of determining the accuracy of the approach are useless.

References

1. Antani, S., Lee, D.J., Long, L.R., Thoma, G.R.: Evaluation of shape similarity measurement methods for spine X-ray images. J. Vis. Commun. Image Represent. **15**, 285–302 (2004)
2. Aydin, S.Z., et al.: Limited reliability of radiographic assessment of spinal progression in ankylosing spondylitis. Rheumatology **56**, 2162–2169 (2017)
3. Baraliakos, X., et al.: Progression of radiographic damage in patients with ankylosing spondylitis: defining the central role of syndesmophytes. Ann. Rheum. Dis. **66**, 910–915 (2007)
4. Bielecka, M., Bielecki, A., Korkosz, M., Skomorowski, M., Wojciechowski, W., Zieliński, B.: Modified Jakubowski shape transducer for detecting osteophytes and erosions in finger joints. In: Dobnikar, A., Lotrič, U., Šter, B. (eds.) ICANNGA 2011. LNCS, vol. 6594, pp. 147–155. Springer, Heidelberg (2011). https://doi.org/10.1007/978-3-642-20267-4_16

5. Bielecka, M., Piórkowski, A.: Optimization of numerical calculations of geometric features of a curve describing preprocessed X-ray images of bones as a starting point for syntactic analysis of finger bone contours. In: Chmielewski, L.J., Datta, A., Kozera, R., Wojciechowski, K. (eds.) ICCVG 2016. LNCS, vol. 9972, pp. 365–376. Springer, Cham (2016). https://doi.org/10.1007/978-3-319-46418-3_32

6. Bielecka, M., Korkosz, M.: Generalized shape language application to detection of a specific type of bone erosion in X-ray images. In: Rutkowski, L., Korytkowski, M., Scherer, R., Tadeusiewicz, R., Zadeh, L.A., Zurada, J.M. (eds.) ICAISC 2016. LNCS (LNAI), vol. 9692, pp. 531–540. Springer, Cham (2016). https://doi.org/10.1007/978-3-319-39378-0_45

7. Bielecki, A., Korkosz, M., Wojciechowski, W., Zieliński, B.: Identifying the borders of the upper and lower metacarpophalangeal joint surfaces on hand radiographs. In: Rutkowski, L., Scherer, R., Tadeusiewicz, R., Zadeh, L.A., Zurada, J.M. (eds.) ICAISC 2010. LNCS (LNAI), vol. 6113, pp. 589–596. Springer, Heidelberg (2010). https://doi.org/10.1007/978-3-642-13208-7_73

8. Creemers, M., Franssen, M.J., van't Hof, M.A., Gribnau, F.W., van de Putte, L.B., van Riel, P.L.: Assessment of outcome in ankylosing spondylitis: an extended radiographic scoring system. Ann. Rheum. Dis. **64**, 127–129 (2005)

9. El Maghraoui, A., Bensabbah, R., Bahiri, R., Bezza, A., Guedira, N., Hajjaj-Hassouni, N.: Cervical spine involvement in ankylosing spondylitis. Clin. Rheumatol. **22**, 94–98 (2003)

10. Flasiński, M.: Syntactic pattern recognition: paradigm issues and open problems. In: Chen, C.H. (ed.) Handbook of Pattern Recognition and Computer Vision, pp. 3–25. World Scientific, New Jersey-London-Singapore (2016)

11. Flasiński, M.: Introduction to Artificial Intelligence. Springer, Cham (2016). https://doi.org/10.1007/978-3-319-40022-8

12. Howe, B., Gururajan, A., Sari-Sarraf, A., Long, L.R.: Hierarchical segmentation of cervical and lumbar vertebrae using a customized generalized Hough transform and extensions to active appearance models. In: Proceedings of the 6th IEEE Southwest Symposium on Image Analysis and Interpretation (2004)

13. Jakubowski, R.: A structural representation of shape and its features. Inf. Sci. **39**, 129–151 (1986)

14. Long, L.R., Thoma, G.R.: Use of shape models to search digitized spine X-rays. In: Proceedings of the 13th IEEE Symposium on Computer-Based Medical Systems, pp. 255–260 (2000)

15. Ogiela, M.R., Tadeusiewicz, R., Ogiela, L.: Image languages in intelligent radiological palm diagnostics. Pattern Recogn. **39**, 2157–2165 (2006)

16. Piórkowski, A.: A statistical dominance algorithm for edge detection and segmentation of medical images. In: Piętka, E., Badura, P., Kawa, J., Wieclawek, W. (eds.) Information Technologies in Medicine. AISC, vol. 471, pp. 3–14. Springer, Cham (2016). https://doi.org/10.1007/978-3-319-39796-2_1

17. Sharp, J., Gardner, J., Bennett, E.: Computer-based methods for measuring joint space and estimating erosion volume in the finger and wrist joints of patients with rheumatoid arthritis. Arthritis Rheum. **43**, 1378–1386 (2000)

18. Tadeusiewicz, R., Ogiela, M.R.: Medical Image Understanding Technology: Artificial Intelligence and Soft Computing for Image Understanding. Studies in Fuzziness and Soft Computing, vol. 156. Springer, Heidelberg (2004). https://doi.org/10.1007/978-3-540-40997-7

19. Tan, S., Wang, R., Ward, M.M.: Syndesmophyte growth in ankylosing spondylitis. Curr. Opin. Rheumatol. **27**, 326–332 (2015)

20. Xu, X., Lee, D.J., Antani, S., Long, L.R.: A spine X-ray image retrieval system using partial shape matching. IEEE Trans. Inf. Technol. Biomed. **12**, 100–108 (2008)
21. Xu, X., Lee, D.J., Antani, S., Long, L.R.: Localizing contour points for indexing an X-ray image retrieval system. In: Proceedings of the 16th IEEE Symposium on Computer-Based Medical Systems, New York, pp. 169–174, 26–27 June 2003
22. Zamora, G., Sari-Sarraf, H., Long, R.: Hierarchical segmentation of vertebrae from X-ray images. In: Proceedings of SPIE, Medical Imaging 2003: Image Processing, vol. 5032, p. 631 (2003)

Lytic Region Recognition in Hip Radiograms by Means of Statistical Dominance Transform

Marcin Kociołek[1]($^{(\boxtimes)}$)(iD), Adam Piórkowski[2], Rafał Obuchowicz[3],
Paweł Kamiński[4], and Michał Strzelecki[1](iD)

[1] Institute of Electronics, Łódź University of Technology,
ul. Wólczańska 211/215, 90 924 Łódź, Poland
marcin.kociolek@p.lodz.pl

[2] Department of Geoinformatics and Applied Computer Science, AGH University
of Science and Technology, A. Mickiewicza 30 Avenue, 30–059 Cracow, Poland

[3] Department of Radiology, Jagiellonian University Collegium Medicum,
Cracow, Poland

[4] Cracow Centre of Rehabilitation and Orthopaedics, Cracow, Poland
http://eletel.p.lodz.pl

Abstract. Total hip replacement is the accepted treatment procedure of the end stage degeneration of the hip joint. Instability of the prosthesis might be recognized on the radiographic images as area of bone radio - lucency adjacent to the prosthesis pin. However, the very important issue of radiological recognition of periprosthetic lucent areas reflecting the lysis remains a challenge. Small dimensions and fuzzy borders of the lytic areas makes them difficult regions to recognize. Additional factors as high BMI of the patients and/or radiograms taken through a mattress can make the evaluation even more difficult, while small lucent areas might be additionally blurred and of very low contrast. The paper presents a new approach for quantitative recognition of preprothetic lytic areas. We have proposed a multistep algorithm utilizing Statistical Dominance Transform for detection of lytic areas on digital radiograms. Preliminary results are quite promising. It was demonstrated that location and shape of the detected lytic region is in good agreement with assessment by radiologists.

Keywords: Staistical Dominance Transform · X-ray radiograms
Image analysis · Lytic region

1 Introduction

Total hip replacement (THA) is the accepted treatment procedure of the end-stage degeneration of the hip joint. Prosthesis are fixed in the femur either with use of cement or cementless systems. In the second case, mechanical stability of the prosthesis depends on trabecular bone ingrowth into prosthesis porosities.

© Springer Nature Switzerland AG 2018
L. J. Chmielewski et al. (Eds.): ICCVG 2018, LNCS 11114, pp. 349–360, 2018.
https://doi.org/10.1007/978-3-030-00692-1_31

Instability of the prosthesis might be recognized on the AP radiography as a lytic lesion - a region of decreased bone density (bone loss). Such region is more radiolucent than the surrounding bone tissue, therefore it appears on radiograms as a dark area close to the prosthesis. Radiolucent areas wider than 2 mm are recognized as an important sign of instability of the prosthesis and an early sign of implant failure [1]. Pattern of distribution of the lytic areas were analyzed by Gruen and zones describing the locations of the lytic areas were named after him and consecutively numbered from 1 to 7 [9]. The very important issue of radiological recognition of periprosthetic lucent areas reflecting the lysis remains a challenge. Small dimensions and fuzzy borders of the lytic areas make them difficult to recognize. Radiograms taken in patients with high BMI or through a mattress are even more difficult in evaluation while small lucent areas might be additionally blurred and of very low contrast.

Image texture reflects properties of visualized tissues; texture analysis is already a well developed and reliable technique used for the quantitative analysis of a large variety of biomedical images acquired by different modalities, such as CT [11], MRI [7], ultrasound [4], and optical [6]. For radiogram imaging the bone shape descriptors are used e.g. for musculoskeletal diseases diagnosis [2] and for assessment of surgical and orthodontic treatment outcomes [3]. Methods which potentially increase the sharpness of the edges and highlight contrast of the lesion are expected by the medical community with potentially high practical usability. Implementing of those techniques which allows for repeatable recognition of areas of similar intensity may assist medical professionals in recognition of potentially hidden information in radiographic pictures.

The aim of the presented study was to develop a technique of analysis of hip radiograms which would allow for a more confident and quantitative recognition of preprothetic lytic areas. It was demonstrated, that analysis of preprocessed radiographic texture can be used for characterizing the trabecular texture patterns on pelvic images for osteolysis and normal total hip arthroplasty cases [12]. Also, image analysis of CT scans enabled the location and estimation of the volume of periacetabular osteolysis. This study was performed on human pelvic cadavers, where bilateral total hip replacements were implanted and osteolytic lesions of varying sizes were created [5]. However, there have been no attempts to estimate lytic areas in hip radiograms. The proposed method implements a new approach that performs an image transform to emphasize the lytic region and enable its segmentation from the prosthesis and image background. Such method was described in Sect. 2, Sect. 3 presents the investigated images and the applied image processing techniques. The last two Sections discuss the obtained results and conclude the paper.

2   Statistical Dominance Transform (SDT)

Accurate processing of images with different brightness values and dynamic ranges is a demanding task. To do this, the values must be normalized to the same range. Stretching and histogram equalization transformations may be insufficient. This paper proposes the use of the Statistical Dominance Transform, which a special case of the previously developed Statistical Dominance Algorithm [10]. This algorithm transforms the gray scale of the image from the domain of intensity (translucency in the case of radiographs) to the domain of statistical intensity dependencies of pixel and its neighborhood. For every pixel in the resultant image a number of neighboring pixels with a higher intensity than the intensity of the given pixel is assigned. The neighborhood is defined as a circle with a radius R. The algorithm can be described by the following code:

```
for (x = N; x < SX - N; x++)
   for (y = N; y < SY - N; y++)
   {
       imgout[x,y] = 0;
       for (i = -N; i <= N; i++)
          for (j = -N; j <= N; j++)
             if (i * i + j * j <= R * R)
                if (imgin[x + i, y + j] >= imgin[x, y])
                   imgout[x, y]++;
   }
```

where:

> $imgin$ - input image,
> $imgout$ - output image,
> SX, SY - width and height of input/output image,
> R - radius of neighborhood,
> N - (integer) size of neighborhood mask (also size of mirror margin, not presented here), $N = \lceil R \rceil$.

A characteristic feature of this algorithm is the determination of how much the number of central pixel dominates its neighborhood, equally trapping pixels with different (small or large) contrast. Due this, it is possible to transform images with different brightness and its dynamics into a standardized form, preserving the topological features of objects and their shapes (Fig. 1).

The statistical dominance transform is independent of the mean image brightness, which is a very desirable feature in the case of analysis of biomedical images. A method for selection of the radius R is still to be determined. However it should be pointed out that the values for the desired lysis areas do not change significantly in certain ranges of R (Fig. 2), exact discussion is required before using the algorithm in clinical trials.

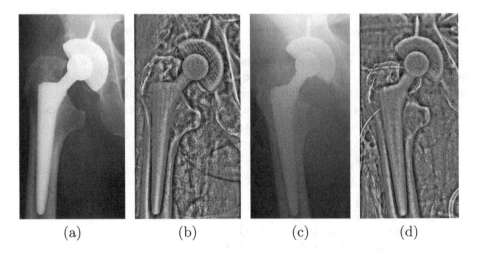

Fig. 1. Two examples of SDT radiograph processing. (a) high contrast radiographic image, (b) SDT with $R = 40$ for image (a), (c) low contrast radiographic image, (d) SDT with $R = 40$ for image (c).

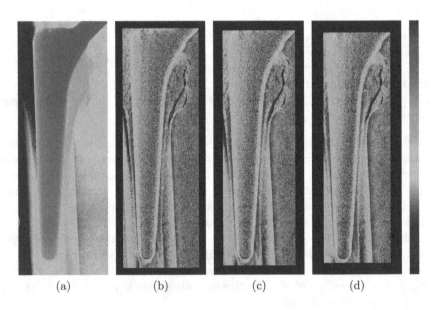

Fig. 2. An example of SDT radiograph processing for different values of R. (a) Input image, (b) SDT $R = 30$, (c) SDT $R = 40$, (d) SDT $R = 50$. Images are displayed in pseudocolors, according to the scale shown on the right(image: dark blue = 0, dark red = 4095, SDT $R = 30$: dark blue = 0, dark red = 2915, SDT $R = 40$: dark blue = 0, dark red = 5157, SDT $R = 50$: dark blue = 0, dark red = 7991). Maximal displayed value for SDT images corresponds to the max value of SDT for given radius R. (Color figure online)

3   Materials and Methods

Retrospectively collected radiographs made for clinical purposes were used as input data. They were acquired in the Center for Orthopedics Surgery and Rehabilitation in Cracow. Images were taken with peak tube voltage 80 kVp, and mean tube current 12 mAs with mean dose of 10 miligrays absorbed. Technique of anterio–posterior exposition with central radius 2 cm above symphysis was used. The obtained radiographs were stored in the lossless DICOM format using A/C 12 bit resolution; The image resolution was most often 2010 × 2446 pixels, with pixel spacing parameter of 0.175 mm × 0.175 mm. Sample images are presented in Fig. 3. The original images were cropped so that only the fragment containing the implant and adjacent bone tissue is visible.

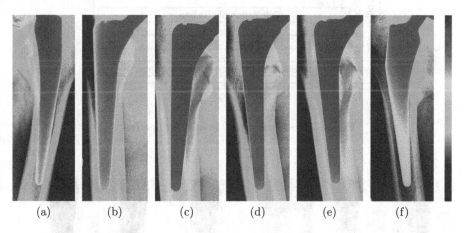

(a)   (b)   (c)   (d)   (e)   (f)

Fig. 3. Examples of images under consideration. For better visualization, images are displayed in pseudocolors, according to the scale shown on the right (dark blue = 0, dark red = 4095). (Color figure online)

To detect the lytic areas, we developed a multistep algorithm shown in Fig. 4. There are two main sections of the algorithm: the Implant region identification and lytic region identification.

The input to the algorithm are X-ray images containing the hip area with the implant and surrounding it bone tissue (Fig. 5(a)). As it can be easily seen in Fig. 5(a), the implant area has significantly higher intensities than the surrounding bone tissue. On the other hand, there is a clearly visible difference between intensities of the upper, thicker, part of the implant than the lower, thinner, part. Thus, simple thresholding will not allow for identification of the implant area and a multistep algorithm is needed.

The first step is the thresholding of the input image with a relatively large threshold value to get the implant seed (Fig. 5(b)). Then the morphological gradient image is calculated (Fig. 5(c)). Thresholding the gradient image produces

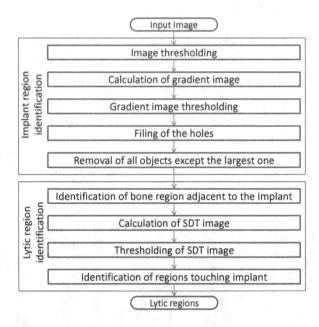

Fig. 4. Algorithm of lytic area identification.

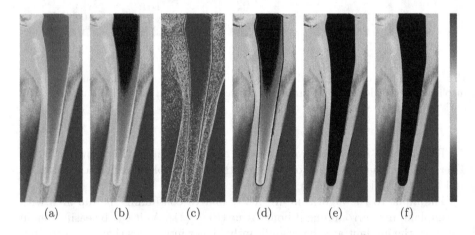

   (a)   (b)   (c)   (d)   (e)   (f)

Fig. 5. Results of consecutive steps of implant region identification. (a) input image, (b) result of thresholding, (c) gradient image, (d) gradient image thresholding result (added to the image (b)), (e) result of the hole filling procedure, f) result of the small regions removal procedure. Images are displayed in pseudocolors, according to the scale shown on the right(image: dark blue = 0, dark red = 4095, gradient: dark blue = 0, dark red = 800). Black area superimposed on the input image represents region area obtained in the given step of the algorithm. (Color figure online)

closed boundaries around the implant. The resulting region is added to the region obtained from the thresholding of the original image (Fig. 5(d)). Then the holes inside the closed object are filled (Fig. 5(e)). In the next step, all consistent regions are labeled and all but the largest are removed. This leads to the implant area identification (Fig. 5(f)).

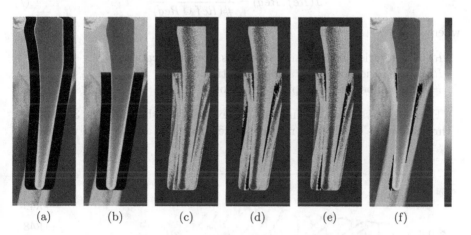

(a)   (b)   (c)   (d)   (e)   (f)

Fig. 6. Results of consecutive steps of lytic region identification. (a) expansion of the mask area, (b) cropping of the expansion mask, (c) SDT image calculation, (e) SDT image thresholding, (d) removal of regions which do not have contact points with the implant, (e) output superimposed on SDT image, (f) output regions superimposed on input image. Images are displayed in pseudocolors, according to the scale shown on the right (image: dark blue = 0, dark red = 4095, SDT: dark blue = 0, dark red = 4095). (Color figure online)

The next step is the expansion of the mask to identify the region of bone tissue adjacent to the implant (Fig. 6(a)). The top of the prosthesis is cropped to omit from the region of interest areas which do not contribute in the analyzed area of loosening (Fig. 6(b)). Due to computational intensity, the SDT transform is calculated only for the implant and its adjacent region (Fig. 6(c)). Thresholding of the SDT image (Fig. 6(d)) followed by removing regions which do not touch the implant allows for lytic area identification (Figs. 6(e) and (f)).

4   Results and Discussion

To investigate the accuracy of the proposed algorithm in a function of radius R in the SDT transform and the applied threshold value, the following test was performed. For a given image the lytic region detection algorithm was applied with neighborhood radius for SDT calculation equal to 40. The threshold for SDT image was selected manually by a trained physician. The obtained regions were treated as a reference. Then for the radius of the region for SDT calculation ranging from 30 to 50 with step of one an optimal threshold was found. Brute force approach was executed where threshold values from 0 to size of neighborhood area for SDT calculation with step equal to 5 were tested. The comparison of reference and resulting area was performed by means of Jaccard (J) index given by Eq. (1)

$$J(Ref, Reg) = \frac{\#(Ref \cap Reg)}{\#(Ref \cup Reg)} \tag{1}$$

where:

Ref - the region representing true lysis size and location,
Reg - the region obtained as segmentation result,
$\#$ - the number of image pixels in region.

Figure 7 shows plot of estimated J index for image shown in Fig. 3(a) against a threshold value for different radii of the neighborhood area for SDT calculation.

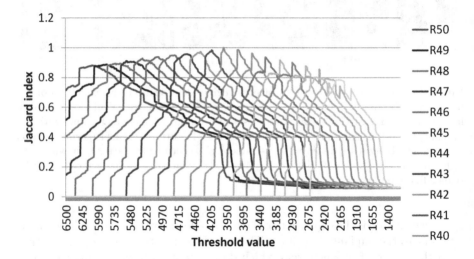

Fig. 7. Jaccard index plotted against the threshold value for different radii used in the SDT calculation.

The conducted test shows that the proposed method is sensitive to the changes in the radius of region for SDT calculation as well as to the selection of the threshold. For larger radii ($R = 43$–50 $pixels$) the method is less sensitive to the changes of the threshold value. Figure 8 shows Jaccard index for optimal threshold plotted against radius of region for SDT calculation.

Plots were obtained for images shown in Fig. 3 The reference analysis was performed for radius equal to 40. As it could be seen for investigated range of radii Jaccard index stays above 0.8. Figure 9 shows optimal threshold, according to the minimal Jaccard index criterion, plotted against radius of region for SDT calculation.

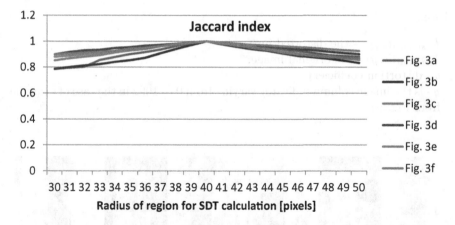

Fig. 8. Jaccard index for optimal threshold plotted against radius of region for SDT calculation. The reference analysis was performed for radius equal to 40. Plots were obtained for images shown on Fig. 3.

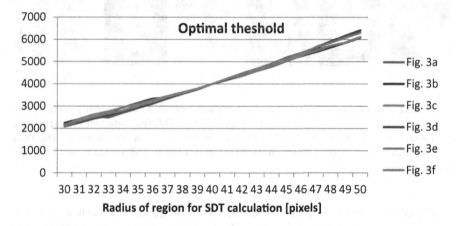

Fig. 9. An optimal threshold plotted against radius of region for SDT calculation. Plots were obtained for images shown on Fig. 3.

For the investigated range of radii there is almost a linear relation between optimal threshold value and radius of the region for SDT calculation. Anyway, for each radius tested it is possible to set the threshold for SDT image which leads to identification of lytical regions accepted (confirmed) by a trained physician. Another interesting property of the SDT transform is its robustness to gray level intensity changes. To show such robustness an experiment was designed, where the original image brightness was linearly distorted according to the Eq. (2)

$$I_{distorted}(x, y) = I_{original}(x, y) + y \cdot b \qquad (2)$$

where:

$I_{distorted}(x, y)$ - the distorted image,
$I_{original}(x, y)$ - the original image,
b - distortion coefficient.
y - is the image column indicator varying from 0 to 1092 in the case of example from Fig. 3(a).

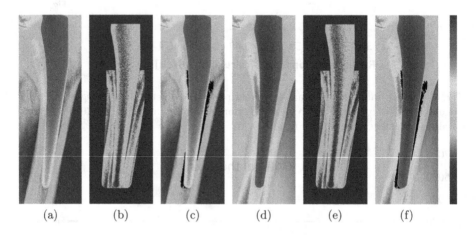

(a)   (b)   (c)   (d)   (e)   (f)

Fig. 10. 11 Robustness of SDT to the intensity artifact: original image (a), its SDT (b), detected lytical regions (c). Distorted image (d), its SDT (e), detected lytical regions (f). Images are displayed in pseudocolors, according to the scale shown on the right (image: dark blue = 0, dark red = 4095, SDT: dark blue = 0, dark red = 4095). (Color figure online)

Figure 10 shows the results of the analysis for distortion coefficient $b = 1$. The introduced intensity artifact has a limited impact on resulting SDT images (Fig. 10(b) and (e)). Thus size and shape of the identified lytical regions for both images remain similar (Fig. 10(c) and (f)) Table 1 shows the Jaccard index and the size of the lytical region found for three intensity coefficient values.

Table 1. Jaccard index value and the identified lytical region size after image intensity distortion according to the Eq. (2)

b	Jaccard index	Lytical region size [pixels]
0 (no artifact)	1	9707
1	0.97	9494
2	0.96	9466
3	0.93	9456

As it can be easy seen low level intensity fluctuations have a limited influence on results of the proposed method outcome. This is the result of application in the SDT of a threshold equal to zero, thus any monotonic variation of image background nonuniformity does not influence the result of the SDT. This is quite important since this reduces the nonuniformity artifact which is quite common in biomedical images [8], biasing results of the quantitative analysis.

One of the drawbacks of the proposed approach is the time of calculation of SDT image especially for large radiuses. The algorithm is not especially computationally intense but it requires high memory bandwidth. For cropped image containing the implant and surrounding bone region SDT image calculation (radius 50) takes roughly 5–6 s. For the original image it will take around a minute (one thread on i7 6700 16 GB of memory). However, this is not a big issue for static X-ray images where SDT image can be calculated prior the analysis.

5 Conclusions

The paper presents a new approach to quantitative recognition of preprothetic lytic areas in hip radiograms. Preliminary results are promising. It was demonstrated that SDT is able to convert radiographic bone texture into a map where the intensity codes the radiolucent area close to the prosthesis pin. Estimated location and shape of the detected lytic region is in good agreement with radiologist's assessment. However, the implemented technique should be verified on a larger database including images acquired in different medical units. Further works will be focused on method automation, e.g. on automatic selection of the optimal radius in the SDT and threshold selection for image segmentation. Moreover, the proposed method will be tested on various classes of biomedical images to exploit the potential of the developed Statistical Dominance Transform.

References

1. Bauer, T.W., Schils, J.: The pathology of total joint arthroplasty. Skelet. Radiol. **28**(9), 483–497 (1999). https://doi.org/10.1007/s002560050552
2. Bielecka, M., Korkosz, M.: Generalized shape language application to detection of a specific type of bone erosion in X-ray images. In: Rutkowski, L., Korytkowski, M., Scherer, R., Tadeusiewicz, R., Zadeh, L.A., Zurada, J.M. (eds.) ICAISC 2016. LNCS (LNAI), vol. 9692, pp. 531–540. Springer, Cham (2016). https://doi.org/10.1007/978-3-319-39378-0_45
3. Bogusiak, K., Kocinski, M., Lutkowski, A., Materka, A., Arkuszewski, P.: Changes in measurements of segner-hasund analysis in patients with mandibular prognathism after orthognathic surgery. Dent. Med. Probl **53**(1), 13–21 (2016)
4. Chrzanowski, L., Drozdz, J., Strzelecki, M., Krzeminska-Pakula, M., Jedrzejewski, K., Kasprzak, J.: Application of neural networks for the analysis of histological and ultrasonic aortic wall appearance-an invitro tissue characterization study. Ultrasound Med. Biol. **34**(2008), 103–113 (2008)
5. Claus, A.M., Totterman, S.M., Sychterz, C.J., Tamez-Peña, J.G., Looney, R.J., Engh Sr., C.A.: Computed tomography to assess pelvic lysis after total hip replacement. Clin. Orthop. Relat. Res. **422**, 167–174 (2004)

6. Kropidłowski, K., Kociołek, M., Strzelecki, M., Czubiński, D.: Model based approach for melanoma segmentation. In: Chmielewski, L.J., Kozera, R., Shin, B.-S., Wojciechowski, K. (eds.) ICCVG 2014. LNCS, vol. 8671, pp. 347–355. Springer, Cham (2014). https://doi.org/10.1007/978-3-319-11331-9_42

7. Larroza, A., Bodí, V., Moratal, D.: Texture analysis in magnetic resonance imaging: Review and considerations for future applications. In: Assessment of Cellular and Organ Function and Dysfunction Using Direct and Derived MRI Methodologies. InTech (2016)

8. Materka, A., Strzelecki, M.: On the importance of MRI nonuniformity correction for texture analysis. In: Signal Processing: Algorithms, Architectures, Arrangements, and Applications (SPA) 2013, pp. 118–123. IEEE (2013)

9. Mjöberg, B.: The theory of early loosening of hip prostheses. Orthopedics 20(12), 1169–1175 (1997)

10. Piórkowski, A.: A statistical dominance algorithm for edge detection and segmentation of medical images. In: Piętka, E., Badura, P., Kawa, J., Wieclawek, W. (eds.) Information Technologies in Medicine. AISC, vol. 471, pp. 3–14. Springer, Cham (2016). https://doi.org/10.1007/978-3-319-39796-2_1

11. Thevenot, J., et al.: Trabecular homogeneity index derived from plain radiograph to evaluate bone quality. J. Bone Mineral Res. 28(12), 2584–2591 (2013)

12. Wilkie, J.R., Giger, M.L., Engh, C.A., Hopper, R.H., Martell, J.M.: Radiographic texture analysis in the characterization of trabecular patterns in periprosthetic osteolysis. Acad. Radiol. 15(2), 176–185 (2008)

Motion Analysis and Tracking

Aggregation of Binary Feature Descriptors for Compact Scene Model Representation in Large Scale Structure-from-Motion Applications

Jacek Komorowski$^{(\boxtimes)}$ and Tomasz Trzciński

Warsaw University of Technology, Warsaw, Poland
jacek.komorowski@gmail.com, t.trzcinski@ii.pw.edu.pl

Abstract. In this paper we present an efficient method for aggregating binary feature descriptors to allow compact representation of 3D scene model in incremental structure-from-motion and SLAM applications. All feature descriptors linked with one 3D scene point or landmark are represented by a single low-dimensional real-valued vector called a *prototype*. The method allows significant reduction of memory required to store and process feature descriptors in large-scale structure-from-motion applications. An efficient approximate nearest neighbours search methods suited for real-valued descriptors, such as FLANN [19], can be used on the resulting prototypes to speed up matching processed frames.

1 Introduction

In recent years a number of methods was published aimed at constructing 3D point cloud models from video sequences or large collections of images using structure-from-motion techniques [2,9,24]. In a typical incremental structure-from-motion pipeline [23] keypoints are detected on each image in a video sequence and local feature descriptors are computed. Feature descriptors in different images are matched which allows estimating camera poses. 3D scene model, in the form of a sparse point cloud, is constructed by triangulating matching feature descriptors. Position of reconstructed 3D points and camera poses are iteratively refined using bundle adjustment [26] method. For each 3D scene point, so called landmark, a list of feature descriptors used to construct it is kept. This is necessary to allow recognizing previously visited places and for loop closure. When a new frame is processed, feature descriptors detected on the frame are matched with descriptors linked with previously reconstructed landmarks. This is usually done by searching for the nearest descriptor (in the descriptor space, Hamming for binary descriptors or Euclidean for real-valued descriptors) and taking the corresponding landmark. Such 2D (feature descriptor) to 3D (landmark) correspondence is noisy and contains a large number of incorrect matches. Robust parameter estimation methods such as RANSAC [8]

© Springer Nature Switzerland AG 2018
L. J. Chmielewski et al. (Eds.): ICCVG 2018, LNCS 11114, pp. 363–374, 2018.
https://doi.org/10.1007/978-3-030-00692-1_32

are used to estimate the absolute pose of the new video frame with respect to the 3D scene model.

In large scale structure from motion applications tens of thousands or millions [10] of images are processed and few hundred local feature descriptors are usually detected on each processed image. This produces very large datasets consisting of millions or hundreds of millions of feature descriptors. Although the size of an individual feature descriptor is small, storing millions of descriptors requires significant storage which can be problematic on mobile devices.

Floating-point descriptors, such as SIFT [20], typically offer better performance but at a higher computational cost. Their binary competitors, such as FREAK [3], are significantly faster to compute. In this work we focus our attention on feature binary descriptors. Due to their computational efficiency, they are often chosen in practical structure-from-motion applications on mobile devices with limited hardware resources.

In this paper we propose an efficient method for compressing scene models in incremental structure-from-motion applications by aggregating binary feature descriptors linked with each reconstructed landmark. Our approach is based on the idea of computing a compact *prototype* representing all binary feature descriptors linked with each landmark. Only this compact *prototype* is stored and used in further processing to match feature descriptors from subsequent frames. Original binary feature descriptors are discarded to free up the memory. The *prototypes* are iteratively updated, as new feature descriptors from subsequent frames are matched with corresponding landmarks. The method allows significant reduction of memory required to store feature descriptors from previously processed frames and speeds up matching feature descriptors from new frames. Our method was inspired by prototypical networks [25] which were proposed for few-shot learning domain.

2   Related Work

Due to an increasing number of practical applications of large scale structure-from-motion and SLAM methods, a number of research papers was published on efficient storage and compression of 3D scene models.

One approach is to compress large scene maps constructed in a structure-from-motion application by selecting representative 3D scene points (landmarks). [18] proposes a method to compress 3D scene model by storing and processing only a small subset of representative landmarks. The method selects a minimal set of landmarks that sufficiently cover the scene visible on processed images. The problem is formulated as a set covering problem and the smallest subset of points covering all processed images is selected. A greedy algorithm finding an approximate solution is proposed. [6] uses more sophisticate approach to produce the reduced scene description. The method selects landmarks taking into account their distinctiveness and coverage of the scene. A greedy algorithm is used to incrementally create a compact subset of landmarks. The method tries to balance two goals: maximize the probability of registering a new image while minimizing the number of points selected. Authors claim they can summarize a structure-from-motion model with as little as 3% of original landmarks while keeping reasonable image registration performance. Above methods differ from our approach, as they aim at selecting representative landmarks (3D points) that can be used to reliably match subsequent frames. Our method aggregates feature descriptors linked with an individual landmark. It is complementary to these methods and can be used in conjunction to further reduce the memory required to store 3D scene model.

Efficient compression methods are proposed for real-valued feature descriptors such as SIFT. Mean-shift clustering is used in [13] to compress SIFT descriptors linked with each landmark. Authors report 50% reduction in memory footprint without adversely affecting matching performance. However this method is not directly applicably to binary feature descriptors as clustering-based methods perform poorly in binary spaces [27]. [14] proposes a general feature descriptor compression method using tree coding technique. The method allows fast descriptor matching without requiring decompression. However it's aimed at real-valued descriptors such as SIFT, SURF or GLOH.

[5, 21, 22] propose compression methods aimed at minimizing the bandwidth required to transmit feature descriptors. These methods can be used for efficient transmission of feature descriptors and are not directly applicable in a structure-from-motion reconstruction pipeline.

A few methods [1, 12] try to solve the solve the problem of a compact image representation by aggregating local feature descriptors in the image. Quantization or aggregation techniques are used to generate summarization of all the extracted features in one image. This allows representing an image by a single global descriptor rather than hundreds of local feature descriptors. Our method, in contrast, tries to solve a different problem – how to compactly represent similar feature descriptors from multiple images linked with a single landmark.

[17] investigates if data-dependent hashing methods can be applied to find more compact representation of binary feature descriptors. A representative sample of recent unsupervised, semi-supervised and supervised hashing methods is experimentally evaluated on large datasets of labelled binary FREAK feature descriptors. The results prove that hashing methods cannot be effectively used to find compact representation of binary feature descriptors without sacrificing nearest neighbours search precision.

3 Method

This section presents a method to efficiently compress a scene map constructed in large-scale incremental structure-from-motion applications. It is based on the simple idea of calculating a compact representation, so called *prototype*, of all descriptors linked with each landmark (3D scene point). Feature descriptors used to construct the *prototype* are discarded and removed from the memory. The *prototype* is then used to match feature descriptors from subsequent frames. During incremental processing of the video sequence, the *prototype* is updated when new feature descriptors detected on new frames, are linked with the corresponding landmark. Suppose, in incremental structure-from-motion pipeline we initially construct the landmark by triangulating three keypoints detected in three frames. *Prototype* is initially computed using these three corresponding feature descriptors. Then, when new keypoint from some subsequent frame is linked with the landmark, its *prototype* is updated to take into account the new feature descriptor.

The simplest approach would be to compute the *prototype* as a mean of feature descriptors linked with one landmark. Then, the mean will be iteratively updated, when new descriptors, from subsequently processed frames, are linked with the landmark. However, when using binary feature descriptors, such approach is not feasible. Calculating and storing the real-valued mean of binary descriptors will increase memory requirements multiple times. For each bit of a binary descriptor we would need to store its real-valued mean. Alternatively, we can calculate mean value of each bit and threshold it at 0.5, to produce a binary-valued quantized mean vector. But this approach does not allow interactive updating. If a new feature descriptor in some subsequent frame is linked with the landmark, we would not known how to update the quantized mean with values of the new feature descriptor.[1] Therefore such approach cannot be used in an incremental structure-from-motion processing pipeline.

Our method works by using a neural network to compute low dimensional, real-valued embedding of binary feature descriptors. Then, the *prototype* is calculated as an arithmetic mean of real-valued embeddings of all descriptors linked with one landmark. This produces the low dimensional, real-valued *prototype* representing all descriptors linked with a landmark. We can then discard values of all feature descriptors used to calculate the *prototype*, freeing up the memory. The only additional data that needs to be stored for each landmark, in addition to the *prototype*, is the number of feature descriptors used to compute the mean. This allows updating the *prototype* as feature descriptors linked with the same landmark are detected on new frames. Usually the number of descriptors linked with a landmark is not bigger than 255, so one byte per landmark is sufficient.

Formally, let $\mathbf{p}_i \in \mathbb{R}^k$ denote a k-dimensional prototype linked with i-th landmark (3D scene point). n_i is a number of feature descriptors used to construct the prototype $\mathbf{p_i}$. $\mathbf{x} \in \{0,1\}^b$ is a b-dimensional binary feature descriptor ($b = 512$ for FREAK) and $\mathbf{y} = f(\mathbf{x}) \in \mathbb{R}^k$ is a low-dimensional, real valued, embedding of a feature descriptor $\mathbf{x}$ computed by a the neural network. Initially a *prototype* $\mathbf{p}_i$ is computed as a mean of real-valued embeddings of feature descriptors used to construct the i-th landmark:

$$\mathbf{p}_i = \frac{1}{n_i} \sum_{j=1}^{n_i} f(\mathbf{x}).$$ (1)

---

[1] Suppose the first bit of a quantized mean is 0 and first bit of a new feature descriptor is 1. As original feature descriptors used to construct the quantized mean are discarded, we cannot determine if the first bit in an updated quantized mean should remain 0 or be changed to 1.

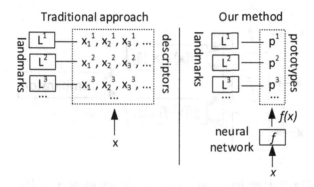

Fig. 1. (Left) In a traditional approach a feature descriptor $\mathbf{x}$ detected on a new frame is matched with all features linked with reconstructed landmarks. In our method (Right) an embedding $f(\mathbf{x})$ of a feature descriptor is computed using the neural network f. Then the embedding is matched with prototypes linked with reconstructed landmarks. Single prototype per each landmark is stored.

When a new frame is processed, for each feature descriptor $\mathbf{x}$ detected on the frame, its real-valued embedding $\mathbf{y} = f(\mathbf{x})$ is computed. Then we use the embedding $\mathbf{y}$ to search for the nearest neighbour, in Euclidean distance sense, in a set of landmark prototypes. The landmark linked with the closest, in Euclidean distance sense, prototype is retained as a putative match. The search can be efficiently done using fast approximate nearest neighbour search method such as FLANN [19]. Next, the robust parameter estimation method, such as RANSAC [8] is used to estimate the absolute pose and orientation of the new video frame with respect to the 3D model and to filter out putative matches. When a new keypoint is linked with the i-th landmark, its *prototype* is updated using the formula:

$$\mathbf{p}'_i = \frac{n_i}{n_i + 1}\mathbf{p}_i + \frac{1}{n_i + 1}f(\mathbf{x}). \tag{2}$$

This calculates the new prototype as a weighted average of the previous prototype and embedding of the new feature descriptor. See Fig. 1 for visualization of our method.

In practice, in addition to prototypes linked with each landmark, we need to keep all feature descriptors detected in few previously processed frames. This allows constructing new landmarks by triangulating matching feature descriptors in subsequent frames and provides initialization to our method.

We consider two approaches to train the neural network to compute low-dimensional embeddings of binary feature descriptors: Triplet Networks [11] and Prototypical Networks [25].

Triplet Networks [11] consist of three identical modules with shared weights that compute embeddings of the input data. High-level architecture of Triplet neural network is depicted on Fig. 2. During the training triplets of elements are presented to the network. The triplets are in the form of $(\mathbf{x}, \mathbf{x}^+, \mathbf{x}^-)$, where

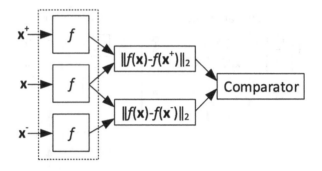

Fig. 2. High-level architecture of the triplet network [11].

$\mathbf{x}$ in an anchor element randomly sampled from a training set, $\mathbf{x}^+$ is a positive example from the same class and $\mathbf{x}^-$ is a negative example from a different class.

Input elements in a triplet are processed by an embedding module f which computes their embeddings $f(\mathbf{x})$, $f(\mathbf{x}^+)$ and $f(\mathbf{x}^-)$. The embeddings are used to compute the triplet loss, as formulated in [4]:

$$L(\mathbf{w}) = \frac{1}{N} \sum_{i=1}^{N} \max\{d_{\mathbf{w}}(\mathbf{x}_i, \mathbf{x}_i^+) - d_{\mathbf{w}}(\mathbf{x}_i, \mathbf{x}_i^-) + \text{margin}, 0\}, \qquad (3)$$

where $d_{\mathbf{w}}(\mathbf{x}, \mathbf{y}) = \|f_{\mathbf{w}}(\mathbf{x}) - f_{\mathbf{w}}(\mathbf{y})\|_2$ is an Euclidean distance between learned embeddings and $f_{\mathbf{w}}$ a function computed by an embedding module of the Triplet network parametrized by a weight vector $\mathbf{w}$.

The training is done using a classical mini-batch gradient descent approach. The training procedure optimizes the weights of the network, so that for each triplet the distance from an embedding of an anchor element $\mathbf{x}$ to the embedding of a negative example $\mathbf{x}^-$ is greater by a margin than a distance to an embedding of a positive example $\mathbf{x}^+$.

Prototypical Networks [25] work differently, as their loss function models directly results of the nearest neighbour search in a prototype space. Prototypical networks compute M-dimensional representation $\mathbf{c}_k \in \mathbb{R}^M$, called *prototype*, for each class using an embedding function $f_{\mathbf{w}} : \mathbb{R}^N \to \mathbb{R}^M$ parametrized by a weight vector $\mathbf{w}$. Training episodes are formed by randomly selecting a subset of classes from the training set. Then a subset of examples from each class forms a support set and the remaining ones serve as query points. Prototypical networks produce a distribution $p_{\mathbf{w}}$ over classes for each query point $\mathbf{x}$ based on a softmax over distances to the prototypes build using embeddings of elements from the support set.

$$p_{\mathbf{w}}(y = k|\mathbf{x}) = \frac{\exp\left(-d\left(f_{\mathbf{w}}\left(\mathbf{x}\right), \mathbf{c}_k\right)\right)}{\sum_{k'} \exp\left(-d\left(f_{\mathbf{w}}\left(\mathbf{x}\right), \mathbf{c}_{k'}\right)\right)}, \qquad (4)$$

where $\mathbf{c}_k$ is a *prototype* for each class calculated as a mean vector of the embedded support points from the class: $\mathbf{c}_k = \sum_{\mathbf{x}_i \in S_k} f_{\mathbf{w}}\left(\mathbf{x}_i\right) / |S_k|$ and S_k is a support set for class k. The loss L minimized during the training using stochastic gradient descent is defined as the mean negative log-probability of the true class k for all elements from the query set: $L(\mathbf{w}) = \sum_k \sum_{\mathbf{x} \in Q_k} - \log p_\mathbf{w}(y = k|\mathbf{x})$, where Q_k is a query set for class k. For details of the training procedure see [25].

4   Experimental Evaluation

Datasets: All experiments are conducted using data acquired with structure-from-motion solution embedded in a Google Tango tablet. The device produces datasets containing keypoints and feature descriptors detected in the input video sequence. Camera poses and scene structure, in the form of sparse 3D point set, are reconstructed using reliable structure-from-motion methods. They are used as the ground truth during the network training and performance evaluation. The training sequence consists of over 4 million FREAK descriptors detected in almost 10 thousand keyframes. The validation sequence, used to choose the best network architecture, consists of almost 2 million FREAK descriptors detected in approximately 5 thousand keyframes. The test sequence, used to measure the final performance of our method, consists of over 2 million FREAK descriptors detected in approximately 5 thousand keyframes.

Performance Metric: In order to choose the best embedding network architecture and evaluate performance of the resulting prototypes we simulated one step in a typical structure-from-motion pipeline. The evaluation set is split into two parts. 90% of keyframes are randomly chosen and form the support set. They simulate frames already seen and processed in a structure-from-motion processing pipeline. Based on the ground truth data, we compute embeddings of all descriptors linked with each landmark using the network being evaluated and compute prototypes using Eq. 1. Then unaggregated feature descriptors are discarded and only one computed prototype per each landmark is retained. Remaining 10% of keyframes form a query set. They simulate new frames that are being matched to the scene model reconstructed using previously seen frames. We randomly sample 10 thousand descriptors from the query subset. For each sampled descriptor we compute its embedding using the network being evaluated and find the closest, in Euclidean distance sense, prototype in the support set. If the prototype found is linked with the same landmark as the sampled descriptor, we declare a correct match otherwise we have a failure. The *precision* is defined as a proportion of correct matches to all search attempts. The procedure described above simulates matching descriptors from new frames with landmarks in a 3D model of the scene constructed using previously processed frames.

Network Training: We systematically evaluate wide range of neural network architectures to find the best performing one. We expect that prototype networks yield the best performance, as the their loss function directly models results of the nearest neighbour search in a prototype space. Loss function for Triplet networks aims at computing embeddings that preserve semantic similarity, so the elements from the same class are mapped to close elements in the embedding space; and elements from different classes are mapped to embeddings further apart. It's expected that averaging embeddings of elements from one class would produce good prototypes, but this is not directly modelled in the loss function.

In all experiments the network is trained using the same approach. Initial learning rate is fixed at 0.001. Adam [15] optimizer is used, as it gives reasonable results without the need to fine-tune training parameters. If the training stagnates and the loss on validation set doesn't decrease for a pre-defined number of epochs, the learning rate is reduced by a factor of 0.1. We fix the size of the resulting embedding to $k = 16$, to keep the amount of memory required to store a single prototype similar to the size of one FREAK descriptor.

Network Architectures Evaluation: To find the best architecture of an embedding module, computing the function f in Eqs. 1, 2, 4 and 3, we evaluate two types of fully-connected network architectures, named 'fat' and 'funnel'. In 'fat' architecture all layers, but the last one, have the same number of units, equal to the input dimensionality, and the last layer has $k = 16$ units. E.g. three layer 'fat' network consists of 512, 512 and 16 units. In 'funnel' architecture the first layer has the number of units equal to the dimensionality of an input vector. Each subsequent layer has half of the units of the previous layer, and the last layer has $k = 16$ units. E.g. three layer 'funnel' network consists of layers with 512, 256 and 16 units. Each liner layer, except for the last one, is followed by SeLU [16] non-linearity.

The results are presented in Fig. 3. Surprisingly, networks trained with a triplet loss consistently outperform prototypical networks. The best performance is achieved by relatively shallow three layer embedding networks trained with a triplet loss. Performance of 'funnel' and 'fat' architectures trained with the triplet loss is very similar.

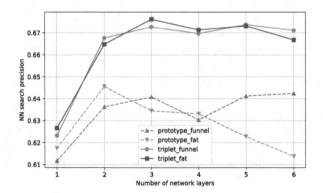

Fig. 3. Nearest network search precision on the validation set as a function of an embedding network architecture. Networks trained with a triplet loss [11] consistently outperform prototypical networks [25]. The best performance is achieved by relatively shallow three layer embedding networks trained with a triplet loss. Performance of 'funnel' and 'fat' architectures trained with the triplet loss is very similar.

We also investigate the dependency of the nearest neighbour search precision on the dimensionality of the prototypes constructed using our method. We evaluated the best performing embedding network from previous experiments (three layer fully connected network with 'funnel' architecture trained with triplet loss) modifying the number of neurons in the output layer. This produces prototypes of different size. The results are shown in Fig. 4. When dimensionality of embeddings produces by the network decreases from 16 to 8, the nearest neighbour search precision drops rapidly from 0.65 to 0.40. When dimensionality increases, the search precision goes up to 0.75 for 32 dimensions and 0.79 for 64 dimensions. However this is at expense of the memory required to store resulting prototypes. Instead of storing all feature descriptors linked with a landmark, usually between 3 and 15, we can only keep one prototype. 16-dimensional prototype requires storage compared to a single FREAK descriptor. This allows reducing memory footprint a few times. Using 32-dimensional prototypes also leads to significant memory savings, with moderate performance gap (0.796 for unaggregated descriptors versus 0.750 for 32-dimensional prototypes). When using 64-dimensional prototypes we can achieve performance comparable to using unaggregated feature descriptors. However the memory requirements, compared to 16-dimensional embeddings, quadruple.

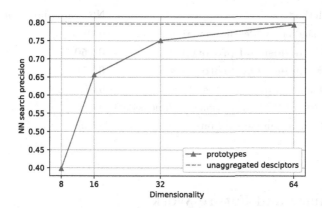

Fig. 4. Nearest network search precision on the test set as a function of prototype dimensionality. The precision grows as the size of the embedding increases, reaching the performance on raw unaggregated binary descriptors for 64-dimensions.

Final Evaluation: For the final evaluation we choose the best performing embedding network from previous experiments: three layer fully connected network with 'funnel' architecture (with 512, 256 and 16 neurons in each layer) trained with triplet loss. The evaluation is done on a separate test set, not used during network architecture evaluation. To benchmark the performance of the proposed method, we computed nearest neighbour search precision using alternative approaches. Results of the evaluation are given in the Table 1. As expected, nearest neighbour search precision using unaggregated feature descriptors is the highest (0.796). By aggregating feature descriptors linked with each landmark to 32-dimensional prototypes we can get minimally worse search precision (0.750). Using 16-dimensional prototypes the search precision drops to 0.676. Similar search precision (0.671) can be achieved by a straightforward approach of computing an arithmetic mean of feature descriptors linked with each landmark and quantizing it at 0.5 ('quantized mean'). However, as discussed in the Sect. 3, such approach cannot be used in an incremental structure-from-motion processing pipeline. For comparison we use principal component analysis (PCA) instead of the neural network to compute low dimensional, real-valued representation of binary descriptors. First 16 principal components are taken and their mean is used as a landmark prototype. The results are significantly worse than our method (0.581). Naive approach of taking as a prototype one random feature descriptor from a list of descriptors linked with a landmark yield even lower precision (0.526).

Table 1. Benchmark of performance of the proposed method. Using 32-dimensional prototypes gives good performance with small gap to raw unaggregated data. See Sect. 4 for description of evaluated methods.

Method	NN search precision
Unaggregated feature descriptors	0.796
32-dimensional prototypes	**0.750**
16-dimensional prototypes	**0.676**
Quantized mean (512 bits)	0.671
Mean of PCA projection (16 dimensions)	0.581
Random sample (512 bits)	0.526

5   Summary and Future Work

In this paper we presented an effective method for aggregation of binary feature descriptors. The method allows compact scene model representation in large scale structure-from-motion applications. This is achieved by computing a single prototype representing all feature descriptors linked with a landmark. The prototype can be iteratively updated, as additional feature descriptors detected in new frames are linked with the landmark. The size of the resulting prototype can be chosen as a trade-off between the required compression ratio and search precision. 32-dimensional prototypes offer very good performance, with small gap to unaggregated feature descriptors, and require the storage similar to the size of two 512-bit FREAK descriptors. Taking into account that a few feature descriptors are linked with each landmark, usually between 3 and 15 in practical applications, significant memory savings can be achieved.

Another advantage is that our method allows speeding-up of one of the key steps in the structure-from-motion pipeline, that is matching descriptors from a new frame with descriptors linked with landmarks in reconstructed 3D scene model. First of all, there are much less class prototypes than unaggregated feature descriptors, so the search can be performed faster. Secondly, descriptor embeddings and class prototypes are relatively low-dimensional real valued vectors. This allow to use very efficient approximate nearest neighbour search methods, such as FlANN [19], which are work very well in real-valued spaces.

As a future work we'd like to investigate if using and encoding additional information provided by a keypoint detector (e.g. scale and orientation) can improve the search precision. Traditionally keypoints are matched by searching using the nearest neighbour using feature descriptor values. In practice we often have additional information, such as scale and orientation, estimated by the keypoint detector. Using neural networks it should be possible to combine this information with raw binary descriptor to compute more discriminative prototypes.

Acknowledgement. This research was supported by Google Sponsor Research Agreement under the project "Efficient visual localization on mobile devices".

The Titan X Pascal used for this research was donated by the NVIDIA Corporation.

References

1. Giuseppe, A., Fabrizio, F., Vadicamo, L.: Aggregating binary local descriptors for image retrieval. Multimedia Tools Appl. **77**(5), 5385–5415 (2018)
2. Agarwal, S., et al.: Building Rome in a day. Commun. ACM **54**(10), 105–112 (2011)
3. Alahi, A., Ortiz, R., Vandergheynst, P.: Freak: fast retina keypoint. In: 2012 IEEE Conference on Computer Vision and Pattern Recognition, pp. 510–517 (2012)
4. Balntas, V., Riba, E., Ponsa, D., Mikolajczyk, K.: Learning local feature descriptors with triplets and shallow convolutional neural networks. In: BMVC, vol. 1, no. 2 (2016)
5. Baroffio, L., Ascenso, J., Cesana, M., Redondi, A., Tagliasacchi, M.: Coding binary local features extracted from video sequences. In: IEEE International Conference on Image Processing (ICIP), pp. 2794–2798 (2014)
6. Cao, S., Snavely, N.: Minimal scene descriptions from structure from motion models. In: 2014 IEEE Conference on Computer Vision and Pattern Recognition (CVPR), pp. 461–468 (2014)
7. Chandrasekhar, V., et al.: Survey of SIFT compression schemes. In: Proceedings of the International Workshop Mobile Multimedia Processing, pp. 35–40 (2010)
8. Fischler, M., Bolles, R.: Random sample consensus: a paradigm for model fitting with applications to image analysis and automated cartography. Readings Comput. Vis., 726–740 (1987)
9. Frahm, J.-M., et al.: Building Rome on a cloudless day. In: Daniilidis, K., Maragos, P., Paragios, N. (eds.) ECCV 2010. LNCS, vol. 6314, pp. 368–381. Springer, Heidelberg (2010). https://doi.org/10.1007/978-3-642-15561-1_27
10. Heinly, J., Schönberger, J.L., Dunn, E., Frahm, J.M.: Reconstructing the world in six days. In: Proceedings of the IEEE Conference on Computer Vision and Pattern Recognition, pp. 3287–3295 (2015)

11. Hoffer, E., Ailon, N.: Deep metric learning using triplet network. In: Feragen, A., Pelillo, M., Loog, M. (eds.) SIMBAD 2015. LNCS, vol. 9370, pp. 84–92. Springer, Cham (2015). https://doi.org/10.1007/978-3-319-24261-3_7

12. Husain, S., Bober, M.: On aggregation of local binary descriptors. In: IEEE International Conference on Multimedia Expo Workshops (ICMEW) (2016)

13. Irschara, A., Zach, C., Frahm, J.M., Bischof, H.: From structure-from-motion point clouds to fast location recognition. In: 2009 IEEE Conference on Computer Vision and Pattern Recognition, pp. 2599–2606 (2009)

14. Johnson, M.: Generalized descriptor compression for storage and matching. In: Proceedings of the British Machine Vision Conference (2010)

15. Kingma, D., Ba, J.: Adam: a method for stochastic optimization. arXiv preprint arXiv:1412.6980 (2014)

16. Klambauer, G., Unterthiner, T., Mayr, A., Hochreiter, S.: Self-normalizing neural networks. In: Advances in Neural Information Processing Systems, pp. 972–981 (2017)

17. Komorowski, J., Trzciński, T.: Evaluation of hashing methods performance on binary feature descriptors. Image Process. Commun. Chall. 9, 88–98 (2017)

18. Li, Y., Snavely, N., Huttenlocher, D.P.: Location recognition using prioritized feature matching. In: Daniilidis, K., Maragos, P., Paragios, N. (eds.) ECCV 2010. LNCS, vol. 6312, pp. 791–804. Springer, Heidelberg (2010). https://doi.org/10.1007/978-3-642-15552-9_57

19. Muja, M., Lowe, G.: Scalable nearest neighbor algorithms for high dimensional data. IEEE Trans. Pattern Anal. Mach. Intell. 11, 2227–2240 (2014)

20. Lowe, D.: Distinctive image features from scale-invariant keypoints. IJCV 60(2), 91–110 (2004)

21. Van Opdenbosch, D., Oelsch, M, Garcea, A., Steinbach, E.: A joint compression scheme for local binary feature descriptors and their corresponding bag-of-words representation. In: IEEE Visual Communications and Image Processing (VCIP) (2017)

22. Redondi, A., Baroffio, L., Ascenso, J., Cesano, M., Tagliasacchi, M.: Rate-accuracy optimization of binary descriptors. In: 20th IEEE International Conference on Image Processing (ICIP), pp. 2910–2914 (2013)

23. Schonberger, J.L., Frahm, J.M.: Structure-from-motion revisited. In: 2016 IEEE Conference on Computer Vision and Pattern Recognition (CVPR), pp. 4104–4113 (2016)

24. Snavely, N., Seitz, S., Szeliski, R.: Photo tourism: exploring photo collections in 3D. ACM Trans. Graph. 25(3), 835–846 (2006)

25. Snell, J., Swersky, K., Zemel, R.: Prototypical networks for few-shot learning. In: Advances in Neural Information Processing Systems, pp. 4080–4090 (2017)

26. Triggs, B., McLauchlan, P.F., Hartley, R.I., Fitzgibbon, A.W.: Bundle adjustment—a modern synthesis. In: Triggs, B., Zisserman, A., Szeliski, R. (eds.) IWVA 1999. LNCS, vol. 1883, pp. 298–372. Springer, Heidelberg (2000). https://doi.org/10.1007/3-540-44480-7_21

27. Trzcinski, T., Lepetit, V., Fua, P.: Thick boundaries in binary space and their influence on nearest-neighbor search. Pattern Recogn. Lett. 33(16), 2173–2180 (2012)

Shallow Convolutional Neural Network and Viterbi Algorithm for Dim Line Tracking

Przemyslaw Mazurek$^{(\boxtimes)}$ (ID)

West Pomeranian University of Technology Szczecin,
26. Kwietnia 10 St., 71126 Szczecin, Poland
przemyslaw.mazurek@zut.edu.pl

Abstract. The estimation of line is important in numerous practical applications. The most difficult case if the line is dim, even hidden in background noise. The application of Track–Before–Detect algorithms allows the tracking of such line. Additional preprocessing using shallow neural network trained for the detection of line features is proposed in this paper. Four variant of data fusion from neural network are compared. Direct output of neural network that works as a classifier gives best results for Mean Absolute Error (MAE) metric. Similar results are obtained if output of neural network is used as a mask for input image. Monte Carlo test are used for unbiased results. Test shows improvement of MAE about two times. The application of binary output from neural network is wrong solution and the error is largest. The influence of the number of convolutional layer neurons is not significant in this test.

Keywords: Neural networks · Viterbi algorithm · Line estimation
Line tracking

1 Introduction

Line tracking algorithms are important for image analysis in robotic [6,8,9] and medical applications typically [15]. Numerous algorithms are proposed for the estimation of straight lines like Hough Transform, but curved lines require the tracking or pattern matching.

Special case that is important in real scenarios is the dim line estimation. There are numerous edge detectors that could be applied for line visibility improving what is essential for tracking or pattern matching. Some of them uses fixed filter mask, some of them are adaptive or uses pattern recognition algorithm for improving visibility of line. The selection of them depends on the line contrast and brightness. Dim lines could be not visible for human even after global contrast/brightness modifications, but the estimation of them is possible using advanced tracking algorithms.

Line tracking uses the algorithm that estimates the position of line based on the previous measurement and model of position changes of line. There are

© Springer Nature Switzerland AG 2018
L. J. Chmielewski et al. (Eds.): ICCVG 2018, LNCS 11114, pp. 375–384, 2018.
https://doi.org/10.1007/978-3-030-00692-1_33

two important problems for tracking. The first problem is the initialization of algorithm. Some advanced algorithms (like particle filters [5]) do not work well with dim lines, because they require proper initialization. The second problem is related to input data requirements for tracking algorithm. Most algorithms, like the Kalman filter require preprocessed data by thresholding. It is not possible to use threshold in any form if line is dim, because a lot of false measurements are observed and finding a proper measurement related to the line is not possible in most cases. Some tracking systems, that are based on multiple line tracking allow the processing such cases for small amount of false observations [1,3].

Alternative approach based on TBD (Track-Before-Detect) approach allows the processing of dim signals [4,16]. The processing cost is high, because all possible trajectories are processed. The best trajectory or trajectories are selected as a result after the tracking. TBD algorithms allows processing of raw data, so all available information is used what is essential for accumulation of values related to trajectory and further detection. The detection based on threshold in conventional systems (not in TBD) looses information about the signal and it is an important source of tracking problems.

Pattern matching could be used for the detection of line using processing of part of image. Large images are processed using moving window of analysis. If this window is over the line a small part of image is extracted and processed by the pattern matching algorithm. The estimation of line is possible even for dim cases, because the detection is based on accumulation of values from multiple pixels.

Combining of pattern matching as a preprocessing algorithm and TBD algorithm is promising concept. Schematic of such system is shown in Fig. 1.

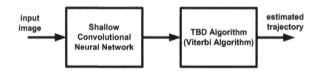

Fig. 1. Tracking system with input image preprocessing using neural network.

There is a lot tracking algorithms applied in civil and military applications [4]. Radon and Hough Transforms could be applied for straight line tracking [7]. Viterbi algorithm could be applied directly to line tracking [11].

Different preprocessing schemes are possible including convolutional neural networks. Deep learning approach for line tracking is considered in [12].

1.1 Content and Contribution of the Paper

The solution for the estimation of dim line using shallow convolutional neural network is proposed in this paper. Four different variants of line estimation are compared for different data fusion schemes. The evaluation is based on Monte

Carlo approach for achieving unbiased results. Viterbi algorithm is applied for line tracking and the improvement of detection.

The solution is described in Sect. 2. Evaluation methodology is considered in Sect. 3. Example results for single tracking case are presented in Sect. 4. This section shows results of Monte Carlo results also. Discussion is presented in Sect. 5. Final conclusions and further work are considered in Sect. 6.

2 Proposed Method

The tracking part of the system uses Viterbi algorithm [2,17]. This algorithm uses transition model (Markov model) between particular pixel and neighborhood pixels in next row. Transitions are descried by trellis and there a two main phases of algorithm. The first phase uses forward processing for the finding path with maximal value. The second phase is backward phase for the calculation of the most probable starting position (single pixel of starting row). The number of processed rows is a depth of analysis and influence on tracking results significantly. The window of analysis moves to next starting row and the process is repeated. Results from previous computation steps are not reused, so there is large and fixed effort for the estimation of single position for particular row. Details of the algorithm for line tracking are considered in [13] and are omitted in this paper. Single trajectory is obtained from Viterbi algorithm.

Input image could be processed directly by Viterbi algorithm, but it is not optimal solution in many cases. The spatial relations between pixels and states of algorithm could be not direct. An example lack of this relation is the line with width larger then one pixel. All pixels that are related to line should contribute to maximization of local and global detection probability. Preprocessing allows the spatial accumulation of values and denoisng of image for improving of line visibility.

Direct solution is copy of input image X to Viterbi input image V_{in}:

$$V_{in}(x,y) = X(x,y), \tag{1}$$

where x and y are pixel coordinates.

Different preprocessing algorithms are possible, including directional filters [14]. The problem of selection of filter masks is important as well as for data fusion from filters outputs. There are N filters with N outputs that should be merged together for Viterbi algorithm. Machine learning, using convolutional neural network [10] could be applied for the computation of filter mask as well as data fusion. Such neural network is a classifier with single output (E1) or with usually two complementary outputs (E1 and E2) and is shown in Fig. 2.

The output $E1$ could be used as input of Viterbi algorithm, so input image X is processed using shallow convolutional neural network and sliding window approach. The size of window 11×11 is assumed in this paper. This is the second variant of the line estimation.

$$V_{in}(x,y) = E1(x,y). \tag{2}$$

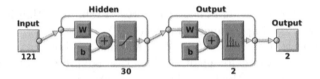

Fig. 2. Schematic of neural network.

Next algorithm for the line estimation uses binary output:

$$V_{in}(x,y) = E1(x,y) > E2(x,y), \tag{3}$$

but this solution is usually not a best, because raw data should be processed by TBD system like Viterbi algorithm.

The output $E1$ is related to input image X but it is enhanced as well as distorted version. The last considered algorithm is a 'Mask' approach and $E1 > E2$ logic gives the binary mask. This mask is used for masking input image X pixels and obtained image is processed by Viterbi algorithm

$$V_{in}(x,y) = (E1(x,y) > E2(x,y)) \cdot X(x,y). \tag{4}$$

This solution uses original input data.

3   Experimental Evaluation

Monte Carlo approach allows testing algorithm without bias. Transitions of Markov model are assumed: $g \in \langle -2, -1, 0, +1, +2 \rangle$. The application of generator of synthetic line allows testing algorithms under different conditions.

Line is generated with pixel value from $\langle 0-1 \rangle$ range randomly. The width of this line is extended by the application of 3×3 mask with uniform values and 2D filter. Image is distorted by Gaussian noise with zero mean and standard deviation 1.

There are 200 cases for particular depth and number of convolutional filters. Every case is obtained using 10000 training and testing 11×11 images, with random selection to training and validation groups (50%/50%). There are 5000 images that are related to random positions and 5000 images related to part of line. Weights are randomly selected and SCG (Scaled Conjugate Gradient) algorithm is applied for training.

The most important error value is MAE (Mean Absolute Error) that is calculated for horizontal direction and is used for evaluation of results.

CPU is applied for training purposes using Matlab Neural Network Toolbox. Tan–sigmoid transfer function is used for convolutional layer. Softmax transfer function is used in output layer.

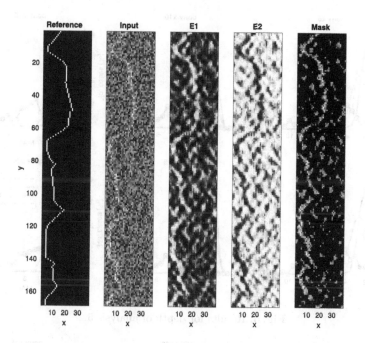

Fig. 3. Exemplary tracking - input and output images.

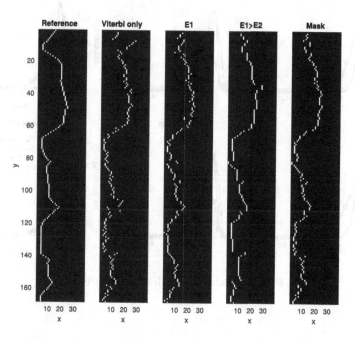

Fig. 4. Exemplary tracking - reference and outputs of Viterbi algorithm for different input images.

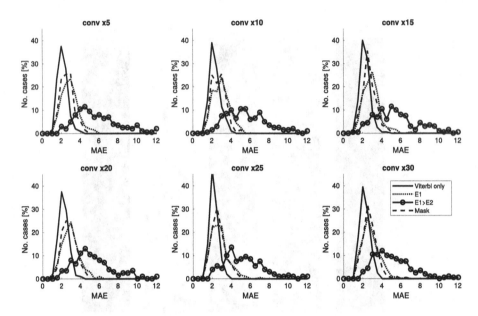

Fig. 5. Results for depth of analysis 5.

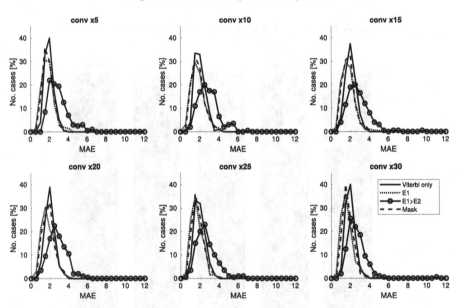

Fig. 6. Results for depth of analysis 10.

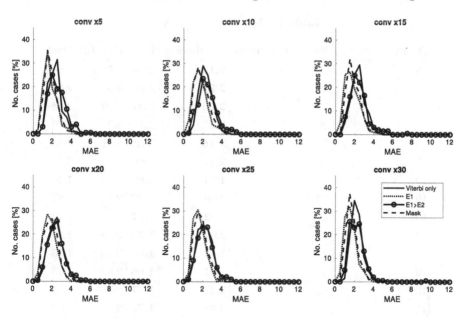

Fig. 7. Results for depth of analysis 15.

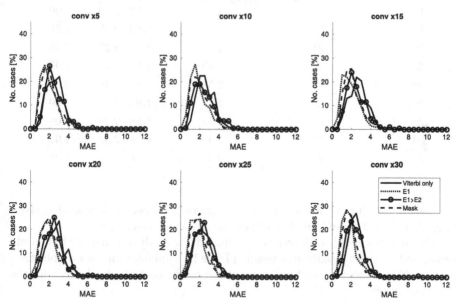

Fig. 8. Results for depth of analysis 20.

4   Results

Exemplary tracking case is shown in Figs. 3 and 4. Images are cropped uniformly for the comparison of results. Reference image depicts middle of line. Maximal contrast enhancement is applied for all images.

Table 1. Mean values for MAE

Depth of analysis	No. conv. neurons	Viterbi only	E1	E1 > E2	Mask
5	5	**2.15**	2.88	5.76	2.60
5	10	**2.29**	2.91	5.64	2.68
5	15	**2.23**	2.90	5.39	2.68
5	20	**2.22**	2.91	5.27	2.79
5	25	**2.16**	2.72	5.31	2.62
5	30	**2.19**	2.81	5.03	2.71
10	5	1.95	**1.80**	2.92	**1.80**
10	10	2.00	**1.77**	2.85	1.82
10	15	2.02	**1.77**	2.81	1.79
10	20	2.00	**1.75**	2.78	1.85
10	25	1.92	**1.66**	2.62	1.75
10	30	1.94	**1.66**	2.62	1.73
15	5	2.27	**1.77**	2.50	1.81
15	10	2.28	**1.73**	2.44	1.88
15	15	2.35	**1.75**	2.44	1.90
15	20	2.36	**1.77**	2.40	1.90
15	25	2.22	**1.64**	2.27	1.78
15	30	2.22	**1.65**	2.27	1.78
20	5	2.60	**1.89**	2.47	1.96
20	10	2.58	**1.87**	2.46	2.05
20	15	2.67	**1.91**	2.48	2.09
20	20	2.72	**1.96**	2.46	2.08
20	25	2.49	**1.78**	2.32	1.92
20	30	2.55	**1.78**	2.36	1.91

Results for all cases are shown as histograms for different depths of analysis (Figs. 5, 6, 7 and 8) and number of neurons is convolutional layer.

The analysis could be descriptive or quantitative. Mean value of MAE could be applied for the comparison of results (Table 1). Minimal values are emphasized using bold typeface and such value is related to the best obtained result for the same conditions.

5   Discussion

The application of shallow convolutional neural network is promising solution, but requires fitting of Viterbi algorithm. Too small depth of analysis, e.g. 5 leads to opposite results - neural network reduces tracking quality and results from Viterbi only solution is better. It is well visible in Table 1 for six first rows. Large depth of analysis provides to smaller MAE results for all four considered data fusion solutions, so the proper choice of this value is 10, 15 or 20. Extending depth of analysis for Viterbi only variant reduces performance. Almost fixed performance is obtained for preprocessed images for depth larger then 10. The best results are for 'E1' solution, but similar results are obtained for 'Mask' solution. Binary outputs from '$E1 > E2$' solution are highest - it is expected behavior, because TBD algorithm prefers raw data not binary.

The comparison of distribution for 'E1' and 'Mask' shows similarity. The application of another metric instead of MAE could provide to preference 'Mask' solution in a place of 'E1'. Shapes of the distributions are smooth so parameters of Monte Carlo are correctly estimated. The distribution of errors is similar to Rayleigh distribution.

There are no significant differences for the selected number of convolutional filters in the first layer, so for selected testing parameters 5 convolutional neurons are sufficient. This result do not proof that small number of them should be used in all cases. It could be result of too small training data set and rather straight line used in training.

6   Conclusions and Further Work

Proposed solutions using shallow neural network for preprocessing of image and Viterbi algorithm improves the quality of tracking about two times. The reduction of MAE error is obtained even for quite small values of depth that is important from computational point–of–view.

Different parameters could be modified and influence of window size will be considered in further work.

The most important property of proposed solution is the application of well known Viterbi algorithm. This algorithm has good theoretical foundations and is deterministic. The application of neural network solutions without separate tracking is much more difficult, because the verification of properties is very complex. Deterministic behavior is very important for reliable applications.

Acknowledgment. This work is supported by the UE EFRR ZPORR project Z/2.32/I/1.3.1/267/05 "Szczecin University of Technology – Research and Education Center of Modern Multimedia Technologies" (Poland).

We gratefully acknowledge the support of NVIDIA Corporation with the donation of the Titan X GPU used for this research.

References

1. Bar-Shalom, Y.: Multitarget-Multisensor Tracking: Applications and Advances, vol. II. Artech House, Norwood (1992)
2. Bertsekas, D.: Dynamic Programming and Optimal Control, vol. I. Athena Scientific, Belmont (1995)
3. Blackman, S.: Multiple-Target Tracking with Radar Applications. Artech House, Norwood (1986)

4. Blackman, S., Popoli, R.: Design and Analysis of Modern Tracking Systems. Artech House, Norwood (1999)
5. Boers, Y., Ehlers, F., Koch, W., Luginbuhl, T., Stone, L.D., Streit, R.L.: Track before detect algorithms. EURASIP J. Adv. Sig. Process. **2008**, 2 pages (2008). Article ID 413932, https://doi.org/10.1155/2008/413932
6. Chen, Z., Ellis, T.: Automatic lane detection from vehicle motion trajectories. In: Workshop on Vehicle Retrieval in Surveillance (VRS) in conjunction with 2013 10th IEEE International Conference on Advanced Video and Signal Based Surveillance, pp. 466–471 (2013)
7. Deans, S.R.: The Radon Transform and Some of Its Applications. Wiley, New York (1983)
8. Dupois, J.F., Parizeau, M.: Evolving a vision-based line-following robot controller. In: Proceedings of the 3rd Canadian Conference on Computer and Robot Vision (CRV 2006), p. 75 (2006)
9. Golightly, I., Jones, D.: Visual control of an unmanned aerial vehicle for power line inspection. In: 12th International Conference on Advanced Robotics, ICAR 2005, pp. 288–295, July 2005
10. LeCun, Y., Kavukcuoglu, K., Farabet, C.: Convolutional networks and applications in vision. In: Proceedings of 2010 IEEE International Symposium on Circuits and Systems, pp. 253–256, May 2010
11. Matczak, G., Mazurek, P.: History dependent Viterbi algorithm for navigation purposes of line following robot. Image Process. Commun. **20**(4), 5–11 (2016)
12. Matczak, G., Mazurek, P.: Dim line tracking using deep learning for autonomous line following robot. In: Silhavy, R., Senkerik, R., Kominkova Oplatkova, Z., Prokopova, Z., Silhavy, P. (eds.) CSOC 2017. AISC, vol. 573, pp. 414–423. Springer, Cham (2017). https://doi.org/10.1007/978-3-319-57261-1_41
13. Mazurek, P.: Line estimation using the Viterbi algorithm and track-before-detect approach for line following mobile robots. In: 2014 19th International Conference on Methods and Models in Automation and Robotics (MMAR), pp. 788–793, September 2014
14. Mazurek, P.: Directional filter and the viterbi algorithm for line following robots. In: Chmielewski, L.J., Kozera, R., Shin, B.-S., Wojciechowski, K. (eds.) ICCVG 2014. LNCS, vol. 8671, pp. 428–435. Springer, Cham (2014). https://doi.org/10.1007/978-3-319-11331-9_51
15. Scott, T.A., Nilanjan, R.: Biomedical Image Analysis: Tracking. Morgan & Claypool, San Rafael (2005)
16. Stone, L., Barlow, C., Corwin, T.: Bayesian Multiple Target Tracking. Artech House, Norwood (1999)
17. Viterbi, A.: Error bounds for convolutional codes and an asymptotically optimum decoding algorithm. IEEE Trans. Inf. Theory **13**(2), 260–269 (1967)

Fast-Tracking Application for Traffic Signs Recognition

Abderrahmane Adoui El Ouadrhiri[1,2](✉) , Jaroslav Burian[2] ,
Said Jai Andaloussi[1] , Rachida El Morabet[3] , Ouail Ouchetto[1] ,
and Abderrahim Sekkaki[1]

[1] Department of Mathematics and Computer Science,
Faculty of Science, LR2I, FSAC, Hassan II University of Casablanca,
B.P 5366, Maarif, Casablanca, Morocco
{a.adouielouadrhiri-etu,
said.jaiandaloussi,ouail.ouchetto,abderrahim.sekkaki}@etude.univcasa.ma
[2] Department of Geoinformatics, Faculty of Science, KGI,
Palacky University, 17. listopadu 50, 771 46 Olomouc, Czech Republic
jaroslav.burian@upol.cz
[3] Department of Geography, Faculty of Arts and Humanities LADES,
CERES, FLSH-M, Hassan II University of Casablanca,
B.P 546, Mohammedia, Morocco
rachidaelmorabet@yahoo.fr

Abstract. Traffic sign recognition is among the major tasks on driver
assistance system. The convolutional neural networks (CNN) play an
important role to find a good accuracy of traffic sign recognition in order
to limit the dangerous acts of the driver and to respect the road laws.
The accuracy of the Detection and Classification determines how powerful of the technique used is. Whereas SSD Multibox (Single Shot Multi-
Box Detector) is an approach based on convolutional neural networks
paradigm, it is adopted in this paper, firstly because we can rely on
it for the real-time applications, this approach runs on 59 FPS (frame
per second). Secondly, in order to optimize difficulties in multiple layers
of DeeperCNN to provide a finer accuracy. Moreover, our experiment
on German traffic sign recognition benchmark (GTSRB) demonstrated
that the proposed approach could achieve competitive results (83.2% in
140.000 learning steps) using GPU parallel system and Tensorflow.

Keywords: Traffic sign recognition · Deep learning
Multibox detector · Tensorflow · GPU parallel computing

1 Introduction

Traffic sign recognition is a part of the required researches today; recently, it has
drawn considerable attention to limit the dangerous acts of the driver.

Despite the traffic signs are designed with simple geometric shapes and basic
colors, the blurry image, the speed of the vehicle and the light conditions make

© Springer Nature Switzerland AG 2018
L. J. Chmielewski et al. (Eds.): ICCVG 2018, LNCS 11114, pp. 385–396, 2018.
https://doi.org/10.1007/978-3-030-00692-1_34

the recognition process difficult [14]. Thereby, the challenge is to recognize them quickly by the computer. Neural networks methods are able to open up a huge research prospect, especially in the driver assistance field. Therefore, the transition from the traditional methods of traffic signs to the advanced one forms a historical milestone. Thus, we find firstly HOG (Histogram of Oriented Gradients), HOF (Histogram of Oriented Flow), etc. that are based on the orientation histogram, and Viola-Jones pattern (Haar features) that makes the detection task more flexible with some instructions and constraints. Secondly, we mention that Convolutional neural networks have created a framework to make the traffic signs recognition very easy, with consideration, the accurate, the scalable, and the fault-tolerant [2,3,8,17,19].

In general, the traffic signs paradigm depends on two major aspects: detection and classification. The object detection approaches are selective search and deformable part model [5,20]. Recently we find the sliding windows and region proposal classification [9,11] that are built in objective to find a fast detection. On the other side, in the classification and in some cases, the methods indicated previously are hybridized with machine learning paradigm (Logistic Regression, Kernel-SVM, PCA, kNN, etc.) in order to identify a good classification/clustering system [13,21]. The simple example that we can present is R-CNN [6] and its extension Fast R-CNN.

Although the deeper neural networks are difficult to learn proportionally with a high number of layers, the residual networks has led to very deep networks training without problems of vanishing or exploding gradients [7]. Thus, Zeng et al. [22] utilized CNN and they achieved 99.40% accuracy on the GTSRB dataset using ELM (Extreme Learning Machine). Even the accuracy reached a good result, but the limit defined of this approach is that the last convolution layer has 200-dimensional as output. Thus, 2.916.000 output parameters with a small platform of CPU/GPU could make this approach hard to utilize. Indeed, the work of this paper was influenced significantly by the recent revolution of the neuron network to provide an extra help to the driver.

In this paper, we chose Single Shot MultiBox Detector [12] firstly because the tasks of object localization and classification are done in a single forward pass of the network. Secondly, the matching strategy of boxes could combine different input size of objects. And thirdly, the system runs at 59 FPS. On the other hand, it outperforms the Fast R-CNN (7 FPS) [16] and YOLO (45 FPS) [15], and it can operate even with 4K clips. Our application is implemented on TensorFlow architecture using Jetson TX2 AI supercomputer. This paper is not yet based on the final results, the research is still in progress. As results, our approach claims to be correct on 83.2%.

To summarize, our main contributions are as follows: the model is described in Sect. 2. Section 3, the experimental results and the conclusion is given in Sect. 4.

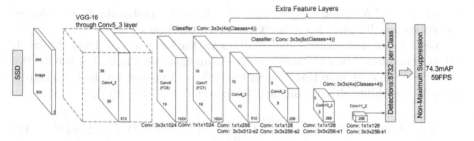

Fig. 1. Single Shot MultiBox Detector model [12].

2   The SSD MultiBox Model

SSD MultiBox architecture (Fig. 1) is based on VGG-16 network (*a feed forward CNN*) and it produces a fixed size series of bounding boxes. Moreover, the usage of multiple layers of SSD leads to the ability to learn, much more during the training phase, and provides a finer accuracy with different scales by the knowledge acquired.

SSD detection utilizes the anchor boxes (Fig. 2(d)) for generating RoIs (*Region of Interest*) with differing resolutions to capture the invariance size of objects (Fig. 2(a)).

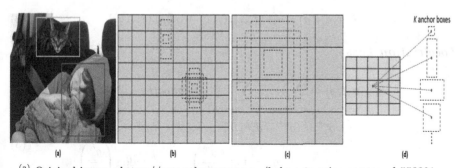

(a) Original image : https://www.thespruce.com/help-cats-enjoy-car-travel-553891

Fig. 2. Input image[a] and Ground Truth boxes.

The simple scaling and aspect ratios of SSD play a major role to get the appropriate "Ground Truth" dimensions which lead to calculate the default boxes for each pixel [10] (Eq. (1)).

Besides $38 * 38$ feature map of *VGG-16* network on SSD architecture, some layers are added, firstly, to produce feature maps of sizes $19*19, 10*10, 5*5, 3*3$, and $1 * 1$, and secondly to predict the bounding boxes.

Furthermore, $scale_{min} = 0.2$, $scale_{max} = 0.9$, and m represents the feature maps of prediction [12]. For each RoI, SSD classification uses $3 * 3$ receptive fields. At the first, to estimate the 4 localization offsets (*center* $- x$,

$center - y, width, height\ (\Delta\,(cx, cy, w, h)))$. Second, to estimate the confidences categories for all object from the "Ground Truth" boxes.

We indicate that $conv4\_3$ and $conv11\_2$ are the key parts to detect the smallest and the biggest objects, respectively. As an example, Fig. 2, it is noteworthy on the $8 * 8$ feature map that the cat (object) has one matched box (Fig. 2(b)), none for the child (object). But it is the case for $4 * 4$ (Fig. 2(c)).

$$Scale_k = scale_{min} + \frac{scale_{max} - scale_{min}}{m - 1}\,(k - 1)\,, k \in [1, m] \tag{1}$$

Thus, the default box on each cell will connect to each other to form the output of this network [12] that is presented as follow:

- A probability vector of length c, where c are the number of object classes plus the background class that indicates no object.
- A vector with four elements $(x, y, width, height)$ representing the offset required move the default box position to the real object.

In the training part, a combined Multibox Loss Function is calculated as a combination of localization and classification error [4] which measures how far off the prediction "landed" and α balances the contribution of the different loss terms.

The details are best-explained below:

$$L(x, c, l, g) = \frac{1}{N}\,(L_{conf}(x, c) + \alpha L_{loc}(x, l, g)) \tag{2}$$

Localization Loss

$$L_{loc}(x, l, g) = \sum_{i \in Pos}^{N} \sum_{m \in \{cx, cy, w, h\}} x_{ij}^p smooth_{L1}(l_i^m - \hat{g}_j^m)$$

$$\hat{g}_j^{cx} = (g_j^{cx} - d_i^{cx})/d_i^w \qquad \hat{g}_j^{cy} = (g_j^{cy} - d_i^{cy})/d_i^h$$

$$\hat{g}_j^w = \log\left(\frac{g_j^w}{d_i^w}\right) \qquad \hat{g}_j^h = \log\left(\frac{g_j^h}{d_i^h}\right) \tag{3}$$

$$smooth_{L1}(x) = \begin{cases} 0.5x^2 & if\ |x| < 1, \\ |x| - 0.5 & otherwise \end{cases}$$

Classification Loss

$$L_{conf}(x, c) = -\sum_{i \in Pos}^{N} x_{ij}^p log(\hat{c}_i^p) - \sum_{i \in Neg} log(\hat{c}_i^0)\quad where\quad \hat{c}_i^p = \frac{exp(c_i^p)}{\sum_p exp(c_i^p)} \tag{4}$$

- l: the predicted box,
- g: the ground truth box,
- c_{xy}: offsets center (cx, cy),

– x: an indicator for matching the i-th default box to the j-th ground truth box of category p, $x_{ij}^p = \{0,1\}$ and $\sum_i x_{ij}^p \geq 1$,
– d: the default bounding box,
– c: classes confidences
– w: width,
– h: height,
– N: the number of matched default boxes, if $N = 0$ than $L = 0$.

By this mechanism, the aim is to find the parameter values that most optimally reduce the loss function, thereby bringing the predictions closer to the ground truth. In general, the model detects as many as possible the objects by categories. Then, in the prediction, non-maxima suppression algorithm is utilized to filter the multiple boxes per object, that may identify in all layers, and it produces the final detections. Finally, the model presents an object similarity percentage.

This model was trained on the GTSRB dataset [18]. The implementation script is written in Python language running on Tensorflow architecture, on a supercomputer AI, Jetson TX2, with GPU NVIDIA Pascal, 256 CUDA cores, CPU HMP Dual Denver 2/2 MB L2 + Quad ARM A57/2 MB L2, and for the memory 8 GB 128 bit and LPDDR4 59.7 GB/s. The GPU is large arrays of small processors designed to process images in video cards of Nvidia.

3   Experimental Results

The main of our experiment is based on the study of the performance of SSD approach to recognizing the traffic signs using the GTSRB dataset. GTSRB contains more than 50,000 images, 39.209 (training) and 12.630 (testing); they were recorded in Germany under various weather conditions with image sizes between 15 * 15 and 250 * 250 pixels.

The GTSRB dataset is adapted to our system with little modifications. Thus, the annotation file of the dataset will be represented by this format: (*Filename, Width, Height, ClassName, ROI.x1, ROI.y1, ROI.x2, ROI.y2*) (Fig. 3). We also extended the GTSRB dataset (43 classes[1]) by adding two traffic signs classes (Pedestrians crossing, No motor vehicles) Figs. 4 and 5, typical traffic signs in the Czech Republic (the images are collected from different regions of

---

[1] Speed limit 20 km/h, Speed limit 30 km/h, Speed limit 50 km/h, Speed limit 60 km/h, Speed limit 70 km/h, Speed limit 80 km/h, End of speed limit 80 km/h, Speed limit 100 km/h, Speed limit 120 km/h, No overtaking, No overtaking by lorries, Junction with minor roads, Main road, Give way, Stop and give way, No entry for vehicles (both directions), No lorries, No entry for vehicles, Other hazard, Curve to the left, Curve to the right, Double curve, first to the left, Bumpy road, Danger of skidding, Road narrows (right side), Roadworks, Traffic lights ahead, Caution for pedestrians, Caution school, Caution for bicyclists, Be careful in winter, Wild animals, End of all prohibitions, Turn right ahead, Turn left ahead, Ahead only, Ahead or right only, Ahead or left only, Keep right, Keep left, Roundabout, End of no-overtaking zone, End of no-overtaking zone for lorrie.

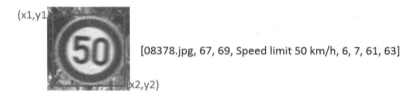

[08378.jpg, 67, 69, Speed limit 50 km/h, 6, 7, 61, 63]

Fig. 3. Annotation of Traffic sign image.

Fig. 4. No motor vehicles 99%.

Fig. 5. Pedestrians crossing 77%.

city "*Olomouc*"), with 400 images of training, 100 images of testing, the image sizes are between 100 * 100 and 600 * 600 pixels.

At the side of batch size 24, Smooth L1 (localization loss), Non-Maximum Suppression with "Jaccard overlap" of 0.45 per class, and Softmax as a neuron's activation function (confidence loss) with learning rate 10^{-3}. We were preserving the top 100 detections per image in the learning phase.

Table 1. Accuracy recognition of traffic signs

Batch size/Learning steps	5.000	45.000	70.000	100.000	140.000
Batch size: 12	0.4%	32.1%	61.3%	74.2%	77.5%
Batch size: 24	0.9%	46.5%	67.4%	78.8%	83.2%

In Table 1, we presented just 5 periods of training as a first result (5K, 45K, 70K, 100K, 140K). In the phase of training, the images are resized to 300 * 300 pixels, every learning step takes in average around 4 s.

According to our experiment and the curves of Figs. 6, 7, 8 and 9, no clear detection indicated at 5 K learning steps, while at 10 K learning steps, the localization curve begins to decline, it means that the determination of the location of the objects begins to improve. Thus, it converges towards 0 with high steps. In a parallel manner, the classification presents the significant results in the interval [1, 2] at 20K steps, and interesting results in [0.5, 1.5] with 45K. We notice that for getting a high recognition accuracy, the system requires more learning steps. As results, at 140 K learning steps, the accuracy of recognition is 83.2%.

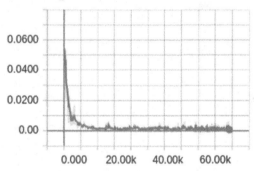

Fig. 6. Curve of localization 70k steps

In comparison with the Alexander Shustanov and Pavel Yakimov experiment [1], our approach runs at 59 FPS and our accuracy of recognition is 83.2% (not final results) and it could outperform [1] with more training steps.

In Table 2, we indicate the first results in comparison with previous Traffic signs recognition methods.

At the end of these results, the good results rely on the improvement of the classification; because the classes of the traffic signs which have the same shape (triangle, circle, etc.) with very small dimensions (e.g. 15 * 15) can't identify in a reliable way the extra shape inside road sign. Thus, the results of different shapes are more efficient than the closest ones (e.g. *No overtaking* and *No overtaking by lorries*, or *Road narrows (both sides)* and *Road narrows (right side)*). Well,

Loss/classification_loss

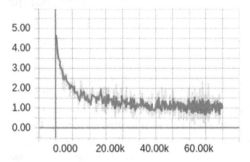

Fig. 7. Curve of classification 70k steps

regularization_loss

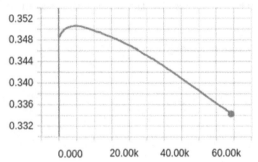

Fig. 8. Curve of regularization 70k steps

TotalLoss

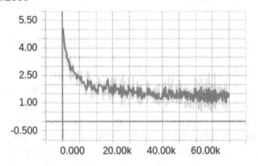

Fig. 9. Curve of Total Loss 70k steps

Table 2. Comparison of accuracy and performance of TSR methods.

TSR methods	Accuracy	FPS
HOG	70.33%	20
Viola-Jones	90.81%	15
Modified GHT with preprocessing + CNN [1]	99.94%	50
SSD 140K (proposed approach)	83.2%	59

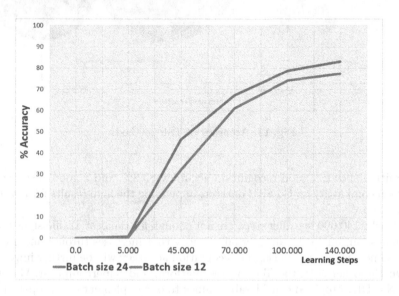

Fig. 10. Accuracy by batch sizes.

this kind of weakness shows only on small objects. For that, our prospect is to exclude the noisy images, which are misclassified by the network (*threshold dimension:* under of 100 * 100 pixels) or that they cannot present the objects clearly (bad quality) in the training/testing dataset. Thus, we will replace them with other road signs that will be pre-prepared in advance with high quality to understand how much each ingredient impacts on the final results. After that, we will test the system with different types of image quality and angles of view.

In addition, this study presents the first results (Figs. 10 and 11), and our perspective is to run it in 200K steps. Thereby, theoretically, this approach can outperform the other results indicated in Table 2. On the other side, it will be great to relate this system with other big data components like GPS, street mapping values, traffic signal timing and the edges of the road.

4 Conclusions and Perspectives

In this paper, the automatic model is allowing to evaluate decisions, where SSD Multibox is a base architecture of our experiment. Our model of traffic signs

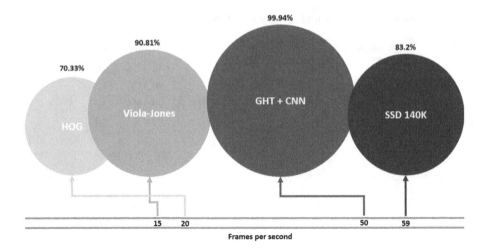

Fig. 11. Accuracy of TSR methods.

recognition shown a good recognition accuracy 83.2%, and a good cost of computation complexity on GTSRB dataset, in pending the final results for real-time application.

Clearly, 140.000 learning steps are not enough for the best Traffic signs recognition system, but, with an internal memory that increases through more experiences and the new database, the recognition accuracy will be further improved.

On the other side, the TensorFlow platform and Supercomputer AI Jetson TX2 NVIDIA provided considerable values to our implementation, especially in computation time. Besides, our prospect is to improve this work and apply it to autonomous vehicles adapting the "behavior of driver/car" to new specific situations we face and not be standard.

References

1. Shustanov, A., Yakimov, P.: CNN design for real-time traffic sign recognition. Procedia Eng. **201**, 718–725 (2017)
2. Caglayan, A., Can, A.B.: An empirical analysis of deep feature learning for RGB-D object recognition. In: Karray, F., Campilho, A., Cheriet, F. (eds.) ICIAR 2017. LNCS, vol. 10317, pp. 312–320. Springer, Cham (2017). https://doi.org/10.1007/978-3-319-59876-5_35
3. Ciregan, D., Meier, U., Schmidhuber, J.: Multi-column deep neural networks for image classification. In: 2012 IEEE Conference on Computer Vision and Pattern Recognition, pp. 3642–3649, June 2012. https://doi.org/10.1109/CVPR.2012.6248110
4. Erhan, D., Szegedy, C., Toshev, A., Anguelov, D.: Scalable object detection using deep neural networks. In: Proceedings of the IEEE Conference on Computer Vision and Pattern Recognition, pp. 2147–2154 (2014)

5. Felzenszwalb, P., McAllester, D., Ramanan, D.: A discriminatively trained, multi-scale, deformable part model. In: 2008 IEEE Conference on Computer Vision and Pattern Recognition, pp. 1–8, June 2008. https://doi.org/10.1109/CVPR.2008.4587597

6. Girshick, R., Donahue, J., Darrell, T., Malik, J.: Rich feature hierarchies for accurate object detection and semantic segmentation. In: Proceedings of the 2014 IEEE Conference on Computer Vision and Pattern Recognition, CVPR 2014, pp. 580–587. IEEE Computer Society, Washington, DC (2014). http://dx.doi.org/10.1109/CVPR.2014.81

7. He, K., Zhang, X., Ren, S., Sun, J.: Deep residual learning for image recognition. CoRR abs/1512.03385 (2015). http://arxiv.org/abs/1512.03385

8. He, K., Zhang, X., Ren, S., Sun, J.: Delving deep into rectifiers: surpassing human-level performance on ImageNet classification. In: Proceedings of the 2015 IEEE International Conference on Computer Vision (ICCV), ICCV 2015, pp. 1026–1034. IEEE Computer Society, Washington, DC (2015). http://dx.doi.org/10.1109/ICCV.2015.123

9. Hosang, J.H., Benenson, R., Schiele, B.: How good are detection proposals, really? CoRR abs/1406.6962 (2014). http://arxiv.org/abs/1406.6962

10. Kosub, S.: A note on the triangle inequality for the Jaccard distance, December 2016

11. Lampert, C., Blaschko, M., Hofmann, T.: Beyond sliding windows: object localization by efficient subwindow search. In: CVPR 2008, pp. 1–8. Max-Planck-Gesellschaft, IEEE Computer Society, Los Alamitos, June 2008. Best paper award

12. Liu, W., et al.: SSD: single shot multibox detector. In: Leibe, B., Matas, J., Sebe, N., Welling, M. (eds.) ECCV 2016. LNCS, vol. 9905, pp. 21–37. Springer, Cham (2016). https://doi.org/10.1007/978-3-319-46448-0_2

13. Martinović, A., Glavaš, G., Juribašić, M., Sutić, D., Kalafatić, Z.: Real-time detection and recognition of traffic signs. In: The 33rd International Convention MIPRO, pp. 760–765, May 2010

14. y. Nguwi, Y., Kouzani, A.Z.: A study on automatic recognition of road signs. In: 2006 IEEE Conference on Cybernetics and Intelligent Systems, pp. 1–6, June 2006. https://doi.org/10.1109/ICCIS.2006.252289

15. Redmon, J., Divvala, S., Girshick, R., Farhadi, A.: You only look once: Unified, real-time object detection. In: 2016 IEEE Conference on Computer Vision and Pattern Recognition (CVPR), pp. 779–788, June 2016. https://doi.org/10.1109/CVPR.2016.91

16. Ren, S., He, K., Girshick, R., Sun, J.: Faster R-CNN: towards real-time object detection with region proposal networks. In: Cortes, C., Lawrence, N.D., Lee, D.D., Sugiyama, M., Garnett, R. (eds.) Advances in Neural Information Processing Systems, vol. 28, pp. 91–99. Curran Associates, Inc. (2015). http://papers.nips.cc/paper/5638-faster-r-cnn-towards-real-time-object-detection-with-region-proposal-networks.pdf

17. Simonyan, K., Zisserman, A.: Very deep convolutional networks for large-scale image recognition. CoRR abs/1409.1556 (2014). http://arxiv.org/abs/1409.1556

18. Stallkamp, J., Schlipsing, M., Salmen, J., Igel, C.: The German traffic sign recognition benchmark: a multi-class classification competition. In: IEEE International Joint Conference on Neural Networks, pp. 1453–1460 (2011)

19. Szegedy, C., et al.: Going deeper with convolutions. In: 2015 IEEE Conference on Computer Vision and Pattern Recognition (CVPR), pp. 1–9, June 2015. DOI: https://doi.org/10.1109/CVPR.2015.7298594

20. Uijlings, J.R.R., van de Sande, K.E.A., Gevers, T., Smeulders, A.W.M.: Selective search for object recognition. Int. J. Comput. Vis. **104**(2), 154–171 (2013). https://doi.org/10.1007/s11263-013-0620-5

21. Zaklouta, F., Stanciulescu, B.: Real-time traffic sign recognition in three stages. Robot. Auton. Syst.**62**(1), 16–24 (2014). https://doi.org/10.1016/j.robot.2012.07. 019, http://www.sciencedirect.com/science/article/pii/S0921889012001236 new Boundaries of Robotics

22. Zeng, Y., Xu, X., Fang, Y., Zhao, K.: Traffic sign recognition using deep convolutional networks and extreme learning machine. In: He, X., et al. (eds.) IScIDE 2015. LNCS, vol. 9242, pp. 272–280. Springer, Cham (2015). https://doi.org/10. 1007/978-3-319-23989-7_28

Embedded Vision System for Automated Drone Landing Site Detection

Patryk Fraczek[1], Andre Mora[2], and Tomasz Kryjak[1](✉)

[1] Faculty of Electrical Engineering, Automatics Computer Science and Biomedical
Engineering, AGH University of Science and Technology, Krakow, Poland
vakii@student.agh.edu.pl, tomasz.kryjak@agh.edu.pl
[2] Computational Intelligence Group of CTS/UNINOVA,
FCT, University NOVA of Lisbon, Caparica, Portugal
atm@uninova.pt

Abstract. This paper presents an embedded video subsystem used to
classify the terrain, based on an image from a camera located under
the drone, for the purpose of an automatic landing system. Colour and
texture features, as well as decision trees and support vector machine
classifiers were analysed and evaluated. The algorithm was supported
with a shadow detection module. It was evaluated on 100 test cases
and achieved over 80% performance. The designed video system was
implemented on two embedded platforms – a Zynq SoC (System on Chip
– Field Programmable Gate Array + ARM processor system) and a
Jetson GPU (Graphic Processing Unit + ARM processor system). The
performance achieved on both architectures is compared and discussed.

Keywords: Unmanned Aerial Vehicle (UAV)
Safe landing site detection · Decision Trees (DT)
Support Vector Machine (SVM) · Machine learning
Digital image processing · FPGA · Zynq · GPU

1 Introduction

Recently, so-called unmanned aerial vehicles (UAVs), also known as drones, have
become increasingly popular. Once used only as military equipment (especially
developed by the USA army), nowadays they can be found in vast number of
commercial applications. From simple quadcopter controlled by an application
in a smartphone, through drones used in the film, television or photo industry
with mounted cameras for recording or taking pictures from the bird's eye view,
to scientific and research applications. These devices are also used in precision
agriculture (crop spraying and inspection), as well as in surveying and inspection.

More ambitious projects concerns courier drones or medical drones sent to
accidents or delivering AED defibrillators to people with sudden cardiac arrest.
Furthermore UAVs can be used in the search and rescue of missing persons, as
urban police patrol units or searching for criminals or protecting the country's
borders – generally speaking ensuring better security.

© Springer Nature Switzerland AG 2018
L. J. Chmielewski et al. (Eds.): ICCVG 2018, LNCS 11114, pp. 397–409, 2018.
https://doi.org/10.1007/978-3-030-00692-1_35

Those rather sophisticated drones have one thing in common – they are fully autonomous, which means they fly without any human control. It is a really challenging task to achieve, and one of its important aspects is an automatic landing procedure. Not only a safe landing must be ensured in the case of normal conditions, but what is more important (considering reliability) in the event of emergency situations (components failure, low battery, strong wind or other poor weather conditions, etc.).

In this research the process of detection and selection of an area suitable for such a landing manoeuvre was considered. Firstly, it should be a flat surface without any significant slopes. Secondly, the type of that surface is also important. For the UAV is better to choose a pavement, path or lawn than to land in the middle of a busy road or on a lake's surface. Also, information about the current altitude and size of the drone is helpful when it comes to choosing a landing zone. Thirdly, it was assumed that a good system should also take into account the level of battery charge and thus the range of the flight. In general the closest suitable locations should be preferred.

The presented research involved two steps: algorithm modelling and implementation on an embedded computing platform – a Jetson TX2 board with an embedded GPU (Graphic Processor Unit) and a Zynq SoC (System on Chip) device.

The main contributions of this paper are:

- a methodology for terrain classification based on a monocular RGB camera,
- an algorithm that allows to locate UAVs safe landing site,
- performance comparison between Zynq SoC (hardware-software) and embedded GPU implementations.

The rest of this paper is organized as follows. In Sect. 2 previous work on drone landing is presented. In Sect. 3 the proposed algorithm is discussed and evaluated. In Sect. 4 embedded implementation of the system on Zynq SoC and Jetson TX2 platforms are presented. The paper ends with a conclusion and possible further research directions.

2   Previous Works on Drone Landing Site Selection

In recent years several approaches have been developed to detect safe landing sites for UAV. In the work [5] a solution based on texture operators was described. Randomly selected squares in the image are enlarged in each iteration and a texture factor is determined. This process ends when the factor from the successive iterations is below a predefined threshold. Each area obtained in this process is then classified based on the naive Bayes method using texture and geometric features.

A different solution, based on machine learning, is presented in the paper [10]. The authors analyzed 5 features: RGB and HSV colour spaces, Local Binary Patterns (LBP), Canny edge detector and a Sobel filter. Several combinations of these features have been tried in a classification system based on the Support Vector Machine (SVM).

The Canny's method has also found its application in the work [6]. It is used in the first stage of the proposed solution. Then, a dilation is performed with a 5 × 5 structural element and detection of compact areas (squares of predefined size) containing no edges – they correspond to the size of the required terrain for a safe landing manoeuvre. The final stage involves an analysis of the brightness of the detected areas and choosing a suitable landing zone.

A similar approach was described in [3]. The first 3 steps of the algorithm coincide with those presented in [6]. Then an advanced classification algorithm based on neural networks is applied. The process was divided into a few stages, which allowed to distinguish between several types of classes, including: water, grass, trees, buildings, concrete and asphalt. The mean, variance and median of components of the HSV colour space and the mean and median of the image filtered by a Gabor filter set (the so-called bank) were used as a input to the classifier. The obtained classification accuracy was 97.12%.

Although, some of the works presented satisfactory results, to our knowledge none of these were implemented on an embedded platform that could be on-board of a drone. The only, known to the authors, quite similar paper describes an FPGA implementation of a landing controller [2]. However, no terrain classification module is implemented. The contribution involves a pre-detected landing site tracking algorithm and video based optometry.

3 The Proposed Algorithm

As it was mentioned before, choosing a safe landing site is a multi-criteria decision problem. It should be a flat surface without slopes, with small or without vegetation. Water should be avoided, as well as, moving objects, trees and rooftops. It is assumed that the algorithm should use just an on-board camera (a conventional RGB image sensor) to derive landing suitability degree maps and then choose the safest landing site. The approach used for locating safe landing sites for drones, was derived from the work on hazard avoidance for landing spacecrafts [8,13,15], where a data/image fusion algorithm was applied, gathering information from slopes, terrain roughness, scientific interest and fuel consumption to generate a hazard map.

The scheme of proposed algorithm is shown in Fig. 1. Four modules can be distinguished: pixel classification, shadow detection, reachability map and data fusion. They have been described in the next subsections.

3.1 Pixel Classification

In our solution, a machine learning approach was used to classify the type of terrain. In the first place, set of videos acquired by UAVs on-board cameras available on YouTube were prepared as source of video data. Then, basing on preliminary experiments and taking into account the limited amount of resources on the FPGA and GPU platforms, the size of the considered contexts was determined as 7 × 7, 9 × 9 and 11 × 11 pixels. Finally, samples were manually selected

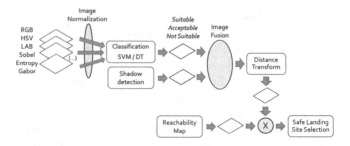

Fig. 1. The proposed safe landing site selection architecture

from each video frame. To speed up this process, it was decided to use initially 21×21 pixels samples, which allowed to obtain 9 separate feature vectors from every sample, for each of the three context sizes.

A summary of the identified terrain classes with the number of collected samples is shown in Table 1. Three classes of landing suitability were distinguished. Soil and asphalt/concrete (class 2) were considered as best landing sites. As second alternative, landing can take place on grass areas (class 1). Other surface types were considered as not suitable for landing (class 0). In total, 3079 training samples were used in the experiment. It is worth noting that the usage of a large number of patches containing water was dictated by the desire to correctly classify this surface type. Choosing a landing site on water would most likely result in the destruction of the UAV.

Table 1. Number of used samples for each landing suitability class.

No.	Terrain class	Number samples	Landing suitability class
1	Soil	298	2
2	Trees	392	0
3	Grass	451	1
4	Asphalt/concrete	228	2
5	Objects	231	0
6	Shrublands	300	0
7	Water	1179	0

Throughout the first stage of the research, a wide range of features was selected as input to the classifiers, based on research presented in [3,6,10] and authors previous works [7,9]. The initial collection contained features like:

1. **Pixel Colour** – 12 features; each component of RGB, YCbCr, HSV, CIE Lab colour spaces
2. **Pixel Neighborhood Colour** – 60 features; minimum, maximum, median, mean and standard deviation of colour spaces (same as in point 1.)

3. **Pixel Neighborhood Texture** – 45 features; calculated from luminance component Y:
   - Sobel 3×3 – sum, mean and standard deviation of neighbourhood,
   - bank of Gabor filters – 3 widths and for each one the maximum of four rotations ($45°$ each) was used,
   - Local Binary Patterns – in a 3×3 pixel neighbourhood [11],
   - Gray-Level Co-Occurrence Matrix (GLCM) [4],
   - Entropy,

In total 117 features were considered, some of them strongly correlated, but with different computational complexity (which is especially important during hardware implementation). Next, using the CART's variable importance measure [1] the discriminative factor of each feature was assessed with a distinction between 3 neighbourhood sizes (7×7, 9×9 and 11×11).

The 9×9 neighbourhood was selected as a compromise between the classification accuracy and implementation complexity. The features with very low importances were not considered for the final classifier. This led to the final set of features evaluated in the 9×9 neighborhood:

1. **Colour** – mean, minimum and maximum from all four colour spaces (without L component),
2. **Texture** – mean from Sobel 3×3,

The number of features considered was eventually 34. All the data was then normalized, so it would fit in range [0; 255] and could be represented by 8-bit number. This procedure significantly improved the later hardware implementation. The feature vectors were then used to train and test the Support

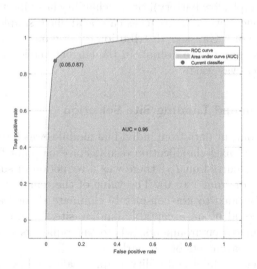

Fig. 2. ROC curve for the DT classifier

Vector Machines (SVM) and Decision Trees (DT) classifiers. They were evaluated using cross-validation and DT achieved the most accurate results (92.1%), while SVM performed at only 83.7%. For the DT classifier a ROC plot is presented in Fig. 2. It was obtained after merging class 1 and 2. The classifier is represented by red dot. It is sightly under the "cut-off" point which means the sensitivity (ca. 87%) is lower in favor of higher specificity (ca. 95%).

3.2 Shadow Detection

Detection of shaded places is an important component of the automatic landing system. First of all, because the correct classification of the ground can not be done for this type of area. Secondly, the presence of a shadow indicates that there is an object nearby (tree, car, building) that can be potentially dangerous to the drone. During software experiments the following approaches were considered:

- global binarization with a threshold determined by the Otsu method,
- global binarization with a threshold determined on the basis of the mean and standard deviation of the brightness of the image (Y component)
- global binarization with a threshold determined on the basis of histogram analysis (first local minimum after first local maximum).

It turned out, that the third approach provides better results, as usually the first local maximum in the histogram corresponded to dark (shaded) areas.

3.3 Reachability

Since the safe landing site selection is mainly designed to be used in emergency situations (for example, low battery), the reachability layer intends to prefer locations closer to drone. Several approaches can be applied: simple urban distance, Euclidean distance or a Gaussian distribution centred on the image (higher priority for locations close to the drone). In the current version of the system the Euclidean approach was used.

3.4 Data Fusion and Landing Site Selection

In the final stage, output data from individual modules was fused. The basis was the map I_c with the pixel classification result. For each point from I_c for which shadow detection occurred on I_{sh}, there was a reduction of suitability class by 1 (i.e. from 2 to 1 or from 1 to 0). The value of the remaining points was not modified. It was decided to not completely eliminate shaded areas, because in some cases they could be an acceptable landing site. Examples of such places can be found in urban environments, where tall buildings may cast shade on significant areas of pavements or car parks.

After obtaining the final suitability map, a safe landing site should be in the centre of the largest suitable area. The proposed solution was designed for a hexacopter type drone, so the landing site should be approximately shaped as a square with a side with a length of 1m. In the case of plane type drone, this shape should be modified to rectangular area with appropriate size and orientation (possibly considering wind direction).

This landing site detection can be conducted for a drone located at different heights above the ground, considering using a fixed-zoom on-board camera. Therefore, the area of $1\,\mathrm{m} \times 1\,\mathrm{m}$ will be represented by a different number of pixels depending on the altitude of the UAV. This relationship is described by the formulas:

$$D_v = \frac{d_v}{2H \tan \frac{\alpha_v}{2}}, \qquad D_h = \frac{d_h}{2H \tan \frac{\alpha_h}{2}} \tag{1}$$

where:

α_v, α_h – camera angle range in each directions (48.8° i 62.4°)
H – the altitude of the drone (e.g. obtained from a LIDAR sensor)
d_v, d_h – camera sensor resolution (1280 × 720)
D_v, D_h – landing site dimensions in pixels

Several approaches were considered for finding suitable areas:

- connected component labelling and centroid computation – the most straight-forward, however with serious drawbacks – in some cases the centroid could be outside the suitable area or near the boarder.
- modified connected component labelling – rectangular areas were tracked. This solution is also inefficient due to large possible number of rectangles present in the image.
- "brute force" search – moving a rectangular or square window along the image – due to large window sizes very inefficient,
- integral image to simplify the "brute force" approach. The use of a integral image allows a significant reduction of operations required for computing the number of pixels in a given area. However, it also turned out to be inefficient.
- distance transform – this approach turned out the most suitable and efficient in the initial experiments and was therefore used.

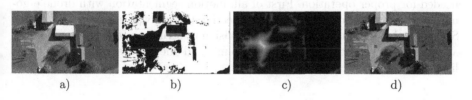

a)   b)   c)   d)

Fig. 3. (a) Original image; (b) Classified Image (c) Distance Transform; (d) Final safe location (red dot). (Color figure online)

The distance transform [12] allows to create a map, without plateaus, where each pixel is a function of its value and the distance to the closest plateau border (Fig. 3). This property allows to find circular areas of selected radius.

In the current version this threshold is fixed, however if a 1D LIDAR device would be used, this value should depend on the current altitude.

Finally, the distance transform map is analysed and locations exceeding the threshold are stored in a priority queue sorted against the distance to the image centre (i.e. to the drone). The first location in the queue is considered as the landing place.

It should be noted that the above described procedure is applied in two stages. First, only class 2 ground are considered. Then, if no landing place in detected, classes 2 and 1 are fused, and the distance transform computed again.

3.5   Evaluation

The proposed system has been evaluated on 100 images obtained from the sequences available on YouTube. A valid (acceptable) landing spot or information about its absence was obtained in 83 cases. For the remaining ones, the results were incorrect. Examples of such situations are shown in Fig. 4.

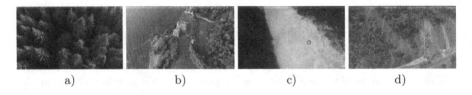

a)   b)   c)   d)

Fig. 4. Incorrect landing site detection. (a) bright tree; (b) a wall of a building; (c) flowing water; (d) cliff.

When assessing the effectiveness of the system, it should be noted that the landing procedure is a process during which a number of images are analysed (at least a few per second). Thus, the initially selected location is verified multiple times and can be changed. In addition, it seems that two more subsystems are needed for proper operation. First of all, motion segmentation with drone ergomotion compensation, would prevent selecting flowing water as a landing place. Secondly, the 3D sensor (LIDAR, stereovision or structure from motion), would allow to determine the slope of the ground and therefore eliminate situations like selecting the site on a cliff or a wall.

4   Embedded Implementation in FPGA and GPU

The described system was verified on two hardware platforms: Zynq SoC (Arty-Z7 20) and on the embedded GPU platform NVIDIA Jetson TX2.

4.1   Zynq SoC

The Arty-Z7 20 development platform is build around the Zynq System-on-Chip device – Zynq-7000 XC7Z020-1CLG400C. It consists of a 2 core ARM Cortex-A9 processor and reconfigurable logic (Field Programmable Gate Array device – containing 53,200 LUT elements, 106.400 flip-flops, 630 KB block RAM memory and 220 DSP blocks). The platform has also a DDR RAM and I/O HDMI ports (one input and one output) that are very useful when it comes to hardware tests of a vision system. Programming and configuration of the device was conducted using the Xilinx Vivado 2017.4 IDE.

In the first implementation step, the algorithm was split into a hardware and software part. The proposed architecture is shown in Fig. 5.

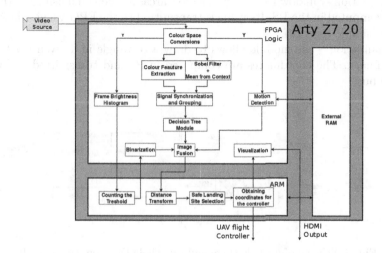

Fig. 5. Scheme of the proposed hardware-software implementation of the algorithm in Zynq SoC

In the programmable part (FPGA) the following modules were implemented (the Verilog hardware description language was used):

- Colour Space Conversions – the input RGB video stream is converted into and YCbCr, HSV, CIE Lab.
- Colour Feature Extraction – for particular colour components the mean, maximum and minimum values in a 9 × 9 context are computed. The required context is generated using the well-known delay line approach (circular buffer).
- Sobel Filter + Mean from Context – the Sobel filter consist of two filters (horizontal and vertical). Then the magnitude is computed as sum of absolute values for both filters. Finally, the mean value in a 9 × 9 context is computed.
- Signal Synchronization and Grouping – the module is responsible for delaying selected values, so that they are synchronized for a particular pixel (the above mentioned modules have different latencies).

- Decision Tree Module – pipeline implementation of a decision tree classifier (based on [14]). The scheme is presented in Fig. 6. In the left part, a single stage is visualized. The key element is the address which controls the behaviour of the structure. First, the threshold and attribute (feature) number are extracted from a table (Read-Only Memory). The both values are compared and the result used to generate a new address. The whole classifier consist of 8 stages, as presented in the right part of the image. It should be noted the this solution is very efficient and easy to parallelize.
- Image Fusion – classification and shadow detection results are fused.
- Frame Brightness Histogram – the histogram of the Y component is computed for every frame. The result is send to the ARM processing system (PS) via AXI4 bus.
- Binarization - Shadow Detection – shadow areas are detected using the threshold computed in the PS. Its value is transmitted to the FPGA logic via AXI4-Lite (simple register).
- Visualization – the module allows to draw a rectangle in a given position in the image. The coordinates are computed in PS and transmitted vis AXI4-Lite bus.

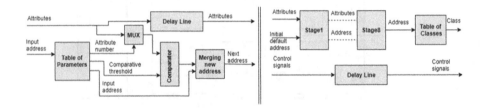

Fig. 6. Scheme of a single stage and the whole Decision Tree module.

In the ARM processing system the following procedures were implemented (in C++):

- Counting the Threshold – used for shadow detection.
- Distance Transform – used for selecting the landing sites (as discussed in Sect. 3.4). The implementation available in the OpenCV library was used (after some minor modifications to avoid using OpenCV structures like cv::Mat). The input image was obtained from the FPGA part via a Video Direct Memory Access (VDMA) module (direct transfer from FPGA to external RAM, from which it could be accessed by the processor).
- Safe Landing Site Selection and Obtaining the coordinates for the controller.

Resource utilization for the FPGA part is summarized in Table 2.

In the current version the system uses about 60% of the available resources and therefore some additional components could be implemented. However, the BRAM (on-chip local memory) utilization is quite high – mainly due to many

Table 2. Resource utilization for the FPGA part of the Zynq SoC.

Resource	Resource utilization	% of available
LUT	33270	62.54 %
FF	58569	55.05 %
BRAM	122	86.79 %
DSP	22	10.00 %

context operation and some buffers (e.g. in the VDMA module). The system was designed to process a 1280 × 720 video stream. In the FPGA part all operations are performed in real-time – 60 frames per second. However, the distance transform and landing site detection on the ARM core requires 200–400 ms for a single execution. From a practical point of view this is not a big problem, as tracking the landing site location few times per second is acceptable. On the other hand, implementing the distance transform in hardware should allow to obtain real-time processing, even for higher image resolutions. The power usage estimated by the Vivado tool is about 3.5 W (FPGA + ARM processor).

4.2 Jetson TX2

The NVIDIA Jetson TX2 is an embedded system designed to deliver a high performance on artificial intelligence applications (especially deep learning). It combines in single board a CPU complex composed by a dual-core NVIDIA Denver2 and a quad-core ARM Cortex-A57, running both at 2 GHz; an integrated 256-core Pascal GPU; 8 GB 128-bit LPDDR4 delivering 59.7 GB/s and a full package of I/O and network interfaces. It is announced a power consumption of 7.5 W under typical load. The software was implemented in C++ and profiled using NVIDIA Nsight IDE. The mean processing time for a single 1280 × 720 image was 1.2 s. One reason for the quite low performance were two custom CUDA functions (not from OpenCV). However, even without them only 8 frames per second could be processed.

5 Summary

In this paper an algorithm for the detection of landing sites for an autonomous drone was presented. The proposed solution has been verified on 100 test images and in over 80% cases provided a correct result. The system has been implemented on two embedded platforms: Zynq SoC and Jetson TX2. The performance comparison showed that for this application the Zynq SoC is a better solution, as it offers greater computing performance with less energy usage. On the other hand, creating applications for a GPU system (C++/CUDA) is easier than implementing hardware modules in the Verilog language.

As part of the further development of the system, it is planned to add a moving object segmentation module (with drone ergo-motion compensation).

The system should also be supplemented with 3D information. Implementations on embedded platforms could be further optimized – e.g. moving the calculation of distance transform to the FPGA part of the Zynq SoC. Moreover, the usage of High Level Synthesis tools should also be considered, as they allow to fasten the design of a hardware-software system. Finally, a challenge would be to run the system for a 4K image in real-time.

Acknowledgements. The work presented in this paper was partially supported by the National Science Centre project no. 2016/23/D/ST6/01389 and Fundação para a Ciencia e a Tecnologia under the grant SFRH/BSAB/135037/2017.

References

1. Breiman, L., et al.: Classification and Regression Trees. Wadsworth International Group, Belmont (1984)
2. Din, A., et al.: Embedded low power controller for autonomous landing of UAV using artificial neural network. In: 10th International Conference on Frontiers of Information Technology, Islamabad, pp. 196–203 (2012)
3. Fitzgerald, D., Walker, R., Campbell, D.: A vision based emergency forced landing system for an autonomous UAV. In: Proceedings Australian International Aerospace Congress Conference, Melbourne, Australia (2005)
4. Haralick, R.M., Shanmugam, K., Dinstein, I.: Textural features for image classification. IEEE Trans. Syst. Man Cybern. **SMC–3**(6), 610–621 (1973)
5. Li, X.: A software scheme for UAV's safe landing area discovery. AASRI Procedia **4**, 230–235 (2013)
6. Mejias, L., Fitzgerald, D.: A multi-layered approach for site detection in UAS emergency landing scenarios using geometry-based image segmentation. In: 2013 International Conference on Unmanned Aircraft Systems (ICUAS), pp. 366–372. IEEE (2013)
7. Mestre, D., Fonseca, J., Mora A.: Monitoring of in-vitro plant cultures using digital image processing and random forests. In: ICPRS - IET 8th International Conference on Pattern Recognition Systems (2017)
8. Mora, A.D., et al.: A fuzzy multicriteria approach for data fusion. In: Fourati, H. (ed.) Multisensor Data Fusion From Algorithms and Architectural Design to Applications, pp. 109–126. CRC Press, Boca Raton (2015)
9. Mora, A., et al.: Land cover classification from multispectral data using computational intelligence tools: a comparative study. Information **8**(4), 147 (2017)
10. Mukadam, K., Sinh, A., Karani, R.: Detection of landing areas for unmanned aerial vehicles. In: 2016 International Conference on Computing Communication Control and automation (ICCUBEA), pp. 1–5. IEEE (2016)
11. Ojala, T., Pietikäinen, M., Harwood, D.: A comparative study of texture measures with classification based on feature distributions. Pattern Recognit. **29**(1), 51–59 (1996)
12. Paglieroni, D.: Distance transforms: properties and machine vision applications. Comput. Vis. Graph. Image Process. Graph. Model. Image Process. **54**(1), 57–58 (1992)
13. Ribeiro, R.A., et al.: FIF: a fuzzy information fusion algorithm based on multicriteria decision making. Knowl.-Based Syst. **58**, 23–32 (2014)

14. Saqib, F., Dutta, A., Plusquellic, J., Ortiz, P., Pattichis, M.S.: Pipelined decision tree classification accelerator implementation in FPGA (DT-CAIF). IEEE Trans. Comput. **64**(1), 280–285 (2015)
15. Simoes, L., Bourdarias, C., Ribeiro, R.: Real-time planetary landing site selection-a non-exhaustive approach. Acta Futur. **5**, 39–52 (2012)

Human Face, Gestures and Action Analysis

Silhouette-Based Action Recognition Using Simple Shape Descriptors

Katarzyna Gościewska$^{(\boxtimes)}$ and Dariusz Frejlichowski

Faculty of Computer Science and Information Technology, West Pomeranian University of Technology, Szczecin, Żołnierska 52, 71-210 Szczecin, Poland
{kgosciewska,dfrejlichowski}@wi.zut.edu.pl

Abstract. This paper presents human action recognition method based on silhouette sequences and simple shape descriptors. The proposed solution uses single scalar shape measures to represent each silhouette from an action sequence. Scalars are then combined into a vector that represents the entire sequence. In the following step, vectors are transformed into sequence representations and matched with the use of leave-one-out cross-validation technique and selected similarity or dissimilarity measure. Additionally, action sequences are pre-classified using the information about centroid trajectory into two subgroups—actions that are performed in place and actions during which a person moves in the frame. The average percentage accuracy is 80%—the result is very satisfactory taking into consideration the very small amount of data used. The paper provides information on the approach, some key definitions as well as experimental results.

Keywords: Action recognition · Simple shape descriptors
Binary silhouette sequences

1 Introduction

Vision-based human action recognition is aimed at labelling image sequences with action labels. It is applicable in several domains such as video surveillance, human-computer interaction, video retrieval, scene analysis and automatic video annotation for efficient searching. The topic has been attracting many researchers for recent years—it is especially seen in constantly updated surveys and reviews (e.g. [1–6]) as well as growing number of methods and algorithms. According to [3] the main task in action recognition is feature extraction, and features can vary in complexity. Action recognition can include low-level features and interests points or higher level representations such as long-term trajectories and semantics, as well as silhouettes seen as a progression of body posture [4]. When a frame or sequence representation is available then action recognition is considered as a classification problem [2].

Motion recognition can be related to elementary gestures, primitive actions, single activities, interactions or complex behaviours and crowd activities. This

© Springer Nature Switzerland AG 2018
L. J. Chmielewski et al. (Eds.): ICCVG 2018, LNCS 11114, pp. 413–424, 2018.
https://doi.org/10.1007/978-3-030-00692-1_36

paper focuses only on actions and does not consider any other information except full body shape of object's binary silhouette. This excludes the recognition of single gestures. Moreover, action recognition should not be confused with gait recognition which identifies personal styles of movement. Action recognition also excludes the use of context information about background and interactions with objects or other people. Action recognition in which we are interested in can be seen as a non-hierarchical approach that is aimed to recognize primitive, short and repetitive actions [7], among which are jumping, walking or running. These actions are also classified as heterogeneous actions [8]. The most popular benchmark datasets consisting of these type of actions are KTH [9] and Weizmann [10].

Some silhouette-based state-of-the-art solutions are discussed in Sect. 2. Section 3 contains a description of the proposed method—consecutive processing steps together with the type of input data and applied algorithms are explained in detail. Section 4 includes information on the experimental conditions and results. Section 5 concludes the paper.

2   Related Works on Silhouette-Based Human Action Recognition

This section gives a short overview on some methods and algorithms which belong to the same category as our method, i.e. relate to action recognition based on sequences of binary silhouettes corresponding to simple actions such as running, bending or waving.

Bobick and Davis [11] proposed a technique that uses silhouettes to generate motion energy images (MEI) depicting where the movement is, and motion history images (MHI) to show how the object is moving. Hu moments are then extracted from MEI and MHI, and the resultant action descriptors are matched using Mahalanobis distance. Hu moments are also applied in [12] and calculated using modified MHI which stands as a feature for action classification. The modification involves a change in decay factor—instead of constant linear decay factor an exponential decay factor is used which emphasizes the recent motion and increases recognition accuracy. Hidden Markov Model (HMM) is applied for classification. The combination of modified MHI and HMM can achieve 99% accuracy which exceeds the results when the HMM is used for silhouettes only.

Silhouette features can also be identified by model fitting, e.g. using a star figure which helps to localize head and limbs [13]. In turn, Gorelick et al. [10] proposed to accumulate silhouettes into three-dimensional representations and to employ Poisson equation to extract features of human actions. The opposite to this is to use only selected frames, so called key poses (e.g. [14–16]). For example, the authors of [14] proposed simple action representation method based only on key poses without any temporal information. Single silhouette—a pose—is represented as a collection of line-pairs. A matching scheme between two frames is proposed to obtain similarity values. Then authors use a method for extracting candidate key poses based on k-medoids clustering algorithm and learning algorithm to rank the potentiality of each candidate—candidate key frames with the highest potentiality scores are selected as final key poses. Action sequence classification step requires the comparison of each frame with key poses to assign a label. A single sequence is then classified based on the majority voting.

The authors of [17] proposed two new feature extraction methods based on well-known Trace transform, which is employed for binary silhouettes that represent single action period. The first method extracts Trace transforms for each silhouette and then a final history template is created from these transforms. The second method uses Trace transform to construct a set of invariant features for action sequence representation. The classification process carried out with the use of Weizmann database and Radial Basis Function Kernel SVM gave percentage results exceeding 90%.

In [18] various feature extraction methods based on binary shape are investigated. The first group contains approaches using contour points only, such as Cartesian Coordinate Features, Fourier Descriptor Features, Centroid-Distance Features and Chord-Length Features. Other approaches use information about all points of a silhouette, and these are Histogram of Oriented Gradients, Histogram of Oriented Optical Flow and Structural Similarity Index Measure. All experiments in cited paper are based on space-time approach and above-mentioned features are extracted from Aligned Silhouettes Image, which is an accumulation of all frames in one video. That gives one image per sequence capturing all spatial and temporal features. Action sequences are classified using K-Nearest-Neighbour and Support Vector Machine. The highest correct recognition rate was obtained for Histogram of Oriented Gradients feature and K-Nearest-Neighbour classifier with Leave-One-Video-Out technique.

There are also some recent papers published in 2018 that still rely on KTH and Weizmann datasets in the experiments. The authors of [19] proposed the integration of Histogram of Oriented Gradients and Principal Component Analysis to obtain feature descriptor which is then used to train K-Nearest-Neighbour classifier. Such combination of methods enabled to achieve average classification accuracy exceeding 90%. In [20] a new approach for action recognition is presented. Human silhouettes are extracted from the video using texture segmentation and average energy images are formed. The representation of these images is composed of shape-based spatial distribution of gradients and view independent features. Moreover, Gabor wavelets are used to compute additional features. All features are fused to create robust descriptor which together with SVM classifier and Leave-One-Out technique resulted in recognition accuracy equal to 97.8% for Weizmann dataset.

3   Proposed Method

In the paper we suggest a processing procedure which uses binary silhouette sequences as input data for human action recognition. Our solution is based on simple shape parameters and well-known algorithms which are composed in several consecutive steps enabling to obtain satisfactory classification accuracy while preserving low-dimensionality of representation at the same time. To obtain that goal we employ various simple shape descriptors—shape measurements or shape factors—that characterize shape by a single value. Simple geometric features are often used to discriminate shapes with large differences, not as a standalone shape descriptors. However, in our method we combine shape representations of many frames in one vector and then transform it into sequence representation. This paper is a continuation of the research presented in [21,22].

In our experiments we use the Weizmann database and therefore the explanation of the proposed method is adapted to it. The Weizmann database for action classification purposes contains foreground binary masks (in Matlab format), extracted from 90 video sequences (180 × 144 px, 50 fps) using background subtraction [10]. Therefore, the original images are 180 × 144 pixels in size and one image contains one human silhouette (see Fig. 1 for example).

Fig. 1. Exemplary aligned silhouettes of running action taken from the Weizmann database for action classification.

3.1 Processing Steps

The proposed method includes following steps:

1. Each silhouette is replaced with its convex hull which is aligned with respect to its centroid in the image centre. A convex hull is the smallest convex region containing all points of the original shape. Single input image has background with black pixels and the foreground object consisting of white pixels. Image size equals to 144 × 144 pixels.
2. Each shape is represented using a single value—a shape measurement or shape ratio, so called simple shape descriptor. The reason for using different shape descriptors is the necessity to experimentally select such a shape feature that will result in the highest classification accuracy.
3. For each sequence, all simple shape descriptors are combined into one vector and values are normalized to interval [0,1].
4. Each vector has different length due to various number of frames. In order to equalize them all vectors are transformed into frequency domain using periodogram or Fast Fourier Transform (FFT) for vectors which were zero-padded to the maximum sequence length. Both approaches are used separately or combined. Each transformed vector becomes a sequence representation.
5. A pre-classification step is introduced which divides the database into two subgroups—actions that are performed in place and actions during which a person changes location. To do so, the information about centroid trajectory is used. Then, the following step is performed in both subgroups separately.

6. Final sequence representations are matched with the use of leave-one-out cross-validation technique to obtain classification accuracy. For comparison, we use three matching measures—standard correlation coefficient, C1 correlation [23] and Euclidean distance. The percentage of correctly classified action sequences indicates the effectiveness of the proposed approach.

3.2 Simple Shape Descriptors

The simplest measurements such as area A and perimeter P may be calculated as the number of pixels of shape's region or contour respectively [24]. Another basic shape feature is its diameter, which can be expressed using Feret diameters (Feret measures): X Feret and Y Feret which are the distances between the minimal and maximal coordinates of a contour, horizontal and vertical respectively. The X/Y Feret is the ratio of the X Feret to Y Feret, and Max Feret is the maximum distance between any two points of a contour.

Another six shape factors are compactness, roundness, circularity ratio, circle variance, ellipse variance and the ratio of width to length. Compactness can be computed as the ratio of the square of the shape's perimeter to its area. The most compact shape is a circle. The roundness is a measure of a shape's sharpness and is based on two basic shape features, i.e. the area and perimeter. The circularity ratio defines the degree of similarity between an original shape and a perfect circle. It can be calculated as the ratio of the shape's area to the square of the shape's perimeter. The ellipse variance is defined as the mapping error of a shape fitting an ellipse that has an equal covariance matrix as the shape [25]. The ratio of width to length is based on the distance between the shape's centroid and its contour points. It is computed as a ratio of the maximal distance between the centroid and the contour points to the minimal distance.

A minimum bounding rectangle (MBR) is the smallest rectangular region containing all points of the original shape. The area, perimeter, length and width of MBR can be used as measurements. Moreover, they can be combined either with the area of an original shape or with each other to create three different shape factors—rectangularity, eccentricity and elongation. Rectangularity is the ratio of the area of a shape to the area of its MBR. Eccentricity is calculated as the ratio of width to length of the MBR, whereby length represents the longer side of the MBR and width the shorter one. Elongation is then the value of eccentricity subtracted from 1 [25]. The calculation of width and height of a single bounding rectangle is quite obvious. For width we detect the shorter rectangle side—the distance between two certain rectangle corners. During the analysis of several bounding rectangles in a sequence we cannot constantly use the same points. As silhouette is changing, a shorter MBR side, calculated constantly for the same two points, can become a longer one. It affects experimental results therefore in our experiments we always consider the shorter side as MBR width.

Principal axes are two unique line segments that cross each other orthogonally within the centroid of a shape. The computation of eccentricity and elongation comprises several steps. Firstly, the covariance matrix C of the contour shape is calculated. Secondly, the lengths of the principal axes are equivalent to the eigenvalues λ_1 and λ_2 of the matrix C. Furthermore, the eccentricity is the ratio of λ_2 to λ_1, and the elongation is the eccentricity value multiplied by 2. We use the eccentricity value only.

4   Experimental Conditions and Results

4.1   Database

Binary silhouettes are usually obtained from the background subtraction process. Due to possible segmentation problems there is a risk of artefacts occurrence—obtained silhouettes may be disturbed by excess pixels or the lack of some (noisy data). Most common background subtraction drawbacks come from variable scene conditions: moving background, moving shadows, different lighting, foreground/background texture and colour similarity, etc. Another problematic issue is associated with the action itself—different people can perform a specific action in a different way and with different speed. We should also emphasize the importance of the manner how the video sequences were captured—lighting, camera point of view, resolution, video duration, etc. Despite several difficulties there are still many characteristics which enable the differentiation of actions. It is crucial to find shape features, or a combination of some, which are distinctive for a particular action.

In our research we use the Weizmann dataset [10] for action classification that contains binary masks in Matlab format. The original binary masks were obtained by background subtraction process from 90 video sequences (180×144 px, 50 fps). In our approach we change an original silhouette to its convex hull, centred in 144×144 pixel size image. Such change resulted in classification improvement by several percent. Exemplary convex hulls of silhouettes from a running action are depicted in Fig. 2.

Fig. 2. Exemplary convex hulls for running action—the person ran from the right to the left.

The actions under recognition belong to two subgroups. Actions performed in place are: bend, jump in place on two legs, jumping jack, wave one hand and wave two hands. In turn jump forward on two legs, run, gallop sideways, skip and walk are actions during which a person changes location.

4.2   Experimental Conditions

The aim of the experiments was to indicate the best combination of algorithms to be employed in the proposed method that results in highest classification accuracy. In each experiment the approach was tested using a different combination of algorithms for sequence representation and matching measures for classification. For shape representation we use 20 various simple shape descriptors, namely: area, perimeter, X Feret, Y Feret, X/Y Feret, Max Feret, compactness, roundness, circularity ratio, circle variance, ellipse variance, ratio of width to length, rectangularity, MBR elongation, MBR eccentricity, MBR area, MBR width, MBR length, MBR perimeter and PAM eccentricity. All shape descriptors were tested in each combination.

During the experiments each silhouette was represented using one simple shape descriptor and all descriptors for one sequence were combined into one vector. Such vector was transformed into final sequence representation using one of the following methods:

1. FFT's magnitude and periodogram.
2. FFT and periodogram.
3. Periodogram only.
4. FFT's phase angle and periodogram.
5. FFT for zero-padded vectors.
6. FFT for zero-padded vectors, but only half of the spectrum is taken.

All sequences were pre-classified into two subgroups—actions that are performed in place (static) and actions during which a person changes location (moving). The division is made using centroid location on the following frames. For example, for the second subgroup, the centroid would change its location on every frame while in the first subgroup the centroid trajectory would be very short. These trajectories are obtained using original, unaligned silhouette data.

The next step is performed in each subgroup separately. We take one sequence representation and match it with the rest of representations to indicate the most similar one by calculating similarity using correlation coefficient (or C1 correlation) or dissimilarity using Euclidean distance. The correct classification is when a tested representation is considered the most similar to other representation belonging to the same class. The percentage of correct classifications (in each subgroup and averaged) is a measure of the effectiveness of the experiment. The experiments were carried out using Matlab R2017b.

4.3   Results

The experimental results are presented in the following tables. Table 1 gives information on the highest percentage accuracy in each experiment that was obtained using a specific simple shape descriptor. The results are averaged for both subgroups (static and moving actions). It turned out that the best results are achieved when a combination of MBR width for shape representation is used, sequence representations are zero-padded to the maximum sequence length and

Fast Fourier Transform is applied, and subsequently transformed representations are classified using Euclidean distance. In this case the highest average classification accuracy equals 80.2%, whereof for actions performed in place the accuracy is 83.3% and for actions with silhouettes that change locations—77.1%.

Table 1. Highest average percentage accuracy for each experiment with the indication of the applied simple shape descriptor.

	Correlation coefficient	C1 correlation	Euclidean distance
FFT's magnitude and periodogram	60.1% perimeter	60.4% X/Y Feret	62.4% X/Y Feret
FFT and periodogram	45.1% MBR width	55.5% MBR width	52.4% MBR width
Periodogram only	69.4% MBR width	72.0% MBR width	73.2% MBR width
FFT's phase angle and periodogram	29.2% compactness	26.0% compactness	29.3% compactness
FFT for zero-padded vectors	70.5% PAM eccentricity	74.6% width/length ratio	80.2% MBR width
As above, but half the spectrum	69.6% MBR width	73.8% PAM eccentricity	77.2% PAM eccentricity

Figure 3 contains a graph illustrating percentage classification accuracy for all simple shape descriptors used in the experiment that brought the best results. Bars refer to the average classification accuracy, the dashed line shows the accuracy for action sequences on which a person performs an action in place, and the continuous line refers to the accuracy obtained for action sequences in which a silhouette is changing location within consecutive frames.

Due to the fact, that all sequences were pre-classified into two subgroups we are able to analyse the results separately, as if we had two datasets—with static and moving actions. Tables 2 and 3 contain percentage classification results obtained in each experiment together with the indication which shape feature was used. It turned out that the best results are obtained when we use different simple shape descriptors—MBR width should be used for actions performed in place (83.3%) and PAM eccentricity for actions during which a person changes location (85.4%). However, in both cases, it may be accepted to use the FFT for zero-padded vectors to obtain sequence representations, and Euclidean distance in classification step.

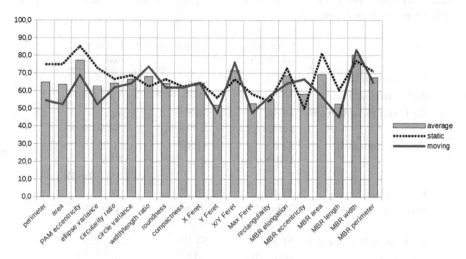

Fig. 3. Percentage classification accuracy for the best experiment using zero-padded vectors, Fast Fourier Transform and Euclidean distance. The highest accuracy is obtained when MBR width is used as a shape descriptor.

Table 2. Highest percentage accuracy for static actions with the indication of the applied simple shape descriptor.

	Correlation coefficient	C1 correlation	Euclidean distance
FFT's magnitude and periodogram	66.7% X/Y Feret	66.7% X/Y Feret	71.4% perimeter
FFT and periodogram	54.8% MBR width	57.1% PAM eccentricity	61.9% MBR width
Periodogram only	69.1% circle variance	76.2% width/length ratio	71.4% width/length ratio
FFT's phase angle and periodogram	35.7% MBR width	26.2% PAM eccentricity	35.7% compactness
FFT for zero-padded vectors	71.4% MBR width	76.2% width/length ratio	83.3% MBR width
As above, but half the spectrum	69.1% MBR width	76.2% width/length ratio	78.6% PAM eccentricity

Table 3. Highest percentage accuracy for moving actions with the indication of the applied simple shape descriptor.

	Correlation coefficient	C1 correlation	Euclidean distance
FFT's magnitude and periodogram	62.5% MBR width	62.5% MBR area	62.5% Max Feret
FFT and periodogram	45.8% perimeter	56.2% X Feret	52.1% MBR area
Periodogram only	79.2% MBR width	81.3% area	81.3% PAM eccentricity
FFT's phase angle and periodogram	33.4% Y Feret	37.5% circularity ratio	29.2% circularity ratio
FFT for zero-padded vectors	83.4% perimeter	83.4% PAM eccentricity	85.4% PAM eccentricity
As above, but half the spectrum	85.4% perimeter	83.4% PAM eccentricity	85.4% PAM eccentricity

5 Summary and Major Conclusions

The paper covered the topic of action recognition based on simple shape features. The proposed approach represents binary silhouettes using simple shape parameters or ratios to create sequence representations, and then classify these representations into action classes in two steps. Firstly, action sequences are pre-classified using the information about centroid trajectory into two subgroups— actions that are performed in place and actions during which a person moves in the frame. Secondly, action representations in each subgroup are classified using leave-one-out cross-validation technique. The highest percentage of correct classifications indicates the best combination of algorithms that should be applied in the proposed approach.

During the experiments it turned out that the best results are obtained when vectors are composed of the MBR width values, transformed using Fast Fourier Transform and then matched using Euclidean distance. The average percentage accuracy is 80.2%, whereof for actions performed in place the accuracy equals 83.3% and for actions with silhouette displacement—77.1%. However, in the second subgroup with moving actions it is more effective to use PAM eccentricity instead of the MBR width because the classification accuracy increases to 85.4%. Ultimately, due to the very small amount of information used for shape representation the results are very satisfactory and promising.

Future plans include the investigation of other sequence representation techniques which would eliminate the influence of unusual silhouettes disturbing the typical action characteristics and would help to ease classification process by making representations equal in size. It is also worth checking some combinations of simple shape measures that would help to make shape representations more discriminative and invariant. Moreover, further research will focus on other classification methods as well.

References

1. Moeslund, T.B., Hilton, A., Krüger, V.: A survey of advances in vision-based human motion capture and analysis. Comput. Vis. Image Underst. **104**(2), 90–126 (2006)
2. Poppe, R.: A survey on vision-based human action recognition. Image Vis. Comput. **28**(6), 976–990 (2010)
3. Weinland, D., Ronfard, R., Boyer, E.: A survey of vision-based methods for action representation, segmentation and recognition. Comput. Vis. Image Underst. **115**(2), 224–241 (2011)
4. Borges, P.V.K., Conci, N., Cavallaro, A.: Video-based human behavior understanding: a survey. IEEE Trans. Circ. Syst. Video Technol. **23**(11), 1993–2008 (2013)
5. Cheng, G., Wan, Y., Saudagar, A.N., Namuduri, K., Buckles, B.P.: Advances in human action recognition: a survey. CoRR (2015)
6. Herath, S., Harandi, M., Porikli, F.: Going deeper into action recognition: a survey. Image Vis. Comput. **60**, 4–21 (2017)
7. Vishwakarma, S., Agrawal, A.: A survey on activity recognition and behavior understanding in video surveillance. Vis. Comput. **29**(10), 983–1009 (2013)
8. Chaquet, J.M., Carmona, E.J., Fernández-Caballero, A.: A survey of video datasets for human action and activity recognition. Comput. Vis. Image Underst. **117**(6), 633–659 (2013)
9. Schuldt, C., Laptev, I., Caputo, B.: Recognizing human actions: a local SVM approach. In: Proceedings of the 17th International Conference on Pattern Recognition, vol. 3, pp. 32–36 (2004)
10. Gorelick, L., Blank, M., Shechtman, E., Irani, M., Basri, R.: Actions as space-time shapes. IEEE Trans. Pattern Anal. Mach. Intell. **29**(12), 2247–2253 (2007)
11. Bobick, A.F., Davis, J.W.: The recognition of human movement using temporal templates. IEEE Trans. Pattern Anal. Mach. Intell. **23**(3), 257–267 (2001)
12. Alp, E.C., Keles, H.Y.: Action recognition using MHI based Hu moments with HMMs. In: IEEE EUROCON 2017–17th International Conference on Smart Technologies, pp. 212–216 (2017)
13. Chen, D.Y., Shih, S.W., Liao, H.Y.M.: Human action recognition using 2-D spatio-temporal templates. In: 2007 IEEE International Conference on Multimedia and Expo, pp. 667–670 (2007)
14. Baysal, S., Kurt, M.C., Duygulu, P.: Recognizing human actions using key poses. In: 2010 20th International Conference on Pattern Recognition, pp. 1727–1730 (2010)
15. Chaaraoui, A.A., Climent-Pérez, P., Flórez-Revuelta, F.: Silhouette-based human action recognition using sequences of key poses. Pattern Recogn. Lett. **34**(15), 1799–1807 (2013)
16. Islam, S., Qasim, T., Yasir, M., Bhatti, N., Mahmood, H., Zia, M.: Single- and two-person action recognition based on Silhouette shape and optical point descriptors. Sig. Image Video Process. **12**(5), 853–860 (2018)

17. Goudelis, G., Karpouzis, K., Kollias, S.: Exploring trace transform for robust human action recognition. Pattern Recogn. **46**(12), 3238–3248 (2013)
18. Al-Ali, S., Milanova, M., Al-Rizzo, H., Fox, V.L.: Human action recognition: contour-based and Silhouette-based approaches. In: Favorskaya, M.N., Jain, L.C. (eds.) Computer Vision in Control Systems-2. ISRL, vol. 75, pp. 11–47. Springer, Cham (2015). https://doi.org/10.1007/978-3-319-11430-9_2
19. Jahagirdar, A.S., Nagmode, M.S.: Silhouette-based human action recognition by embedding HOG and PCA features. In: Bhalla, S., Bhateja, V., Chandavale, A.A., Hiwale, A.S., Satapathy, S.C. (eds.) Intelligent Computing and Information and Communication. AISC, vol. 673, pp. 363–371. Springer, Singapore (2018). https://doi.org/10.1007/978-981-10-7245-1_36
20. Vishwakarma, D.K., Gautam, J., Singh, K.: A robust framework for the recognition of human action and activity using spatial distribution gradients and Gabor wavelet. In: Reddy, M.S., Viswanath, K., K.M., S.P. (eds.) International Proceedings on Advances in Soft Computing, Intelligent Systems and Applications. AISC, vol. 628, pp. 103–113. Springer, Singapore (2018). https://doi.org/10.1007/978-981-10-5272-9_10
21. Gościewska, K., Frejlichowski, D.: Action recognition using silhouette sequences and shape descriptors. In: Choraś, R.S. (ed.) Image Processing and Communications Challenges 8, pp. 179–186. Springer, Cham (2017). https://doi.org/10.1007/978-3-319-47274-4_21
22. Gościewska, K., Frejlichowski, D.: Moment shape descriptors applied for action recognition in video sequences. In: Nguyen, N.T., Tojo, S., Nguyen, L.M., Trawiński, B. (eds.) Intelligent Information and Database Systems, pp. 197–206. Springer, Cham (2017). https://doi.org/10.1007/978-3-319-54430-4_19
23. Brunelli, R., Messelodi, S.: Robust estimation of correlation with applications to computer vision. Pattern Recogn. **28**(6), 833–841 (1995)
24. Yang, L., Albregtsen, F., Lønnestad, T., Grøttum, P.: Methods to estimate areas and perimeters of blob-like objects: a comparison. In: Proceedings of IAPR Workshop on Machine Vision Applications, pp. 272–276 (1994)
25. Yang, M., Kpalma, K., Ronsin, J.: A survey of shape feature extraction techniques. In: Yin, P.-Y. (ed.) Pattern Recognition, pp. 43–90. INTECH Open Access Publisher (2008)

Landmark-Based Re-topology
of Stereo-Pair Acquired Face Meshes

Eric Patterson[1](✉), Jessica Baron[1](✉), and Devin Simpson[2]

[1] Clemson University, Clemson, SC 29634, USA
{ekp,jrbaron}@clemson.edu
[2] Microsoft, Redmond, WA 28052, USA
devincsimpson@gmail.com

Abstract. Believable, detailed digital faces are desired for both film and game production as well as research applications. A high-resolution mesh of a face is acquired often with structured light and stereo computer-vision methods. In production for visual effects or games, the acquired mesh is "re-topologized" by an artist using software to draw a new edge layout in order to simplify and prepare a mesh for animation. For building models of facial population and expression for research, meshes often undergo a similar process to find correspondence among face models, although in the past the desired layout has not been designed for effective facial animation. We propose a process using images accompanying a 3D scan to locate dense 2D facial landmarks automatically to re-topologize meshes with the particular goal of creating models that deform well for facial animation. The technique also allows real-time editing of the re-topology relationship if modifications are desired.

Keywords: Re-topology · Polygon edge layout · Landmarking
FACS · Blendshapes

1 Introduction

Photo-realistic representations of the human face are desired for many applications. This poses challenges depending on budget and rendering times, but the capability to produce convincing facial appearances has arguably been reached in recent visual-effects film-making, and real-time pipelines are nearing similar levels of quality. This has only been done so, however, with extensive labor [11]. A high-resolution polygonal mesh of a performer's face is acquired, usually via laser scan, structured-light, or photogrammetry, then used to create a new mesh. The purpose of devising this new mesh layout is multi-fold. Firstly, the new mesh follows the musculature of the human face, assisting in creating a character rig that can deform believably during animation. Secondly, conforming meshes facilitates other goals such as uniform layout of material maps used during rendering. Thirdly, an overly dense mesh may be reduced to a lower polygon count so that it can perform in a reasonable manner. Lastly, the new mesh is a vehicle for

© Springer Nature Switzerland AG 2018
L. J. Chmielewski et al. (Eds.): ICCVG 2018, LNCS 11114, pp. 425–437, 2018.
https://doi.org/10.1007/978-3-030-00692-1_37

creating blend-shape, or morph, targets in a corresponding format that can be used to pose facial expressions for animation. The process of creating the simplified, production-ready mesh from the acquired mesh is termed "re-topology" and is usually meticulously performed by an artist using software such as 3DCoat, ZBrush, or Maya. It may take a significant amount of time as the artist draws and refines the edge layout on top of the initial mesh.

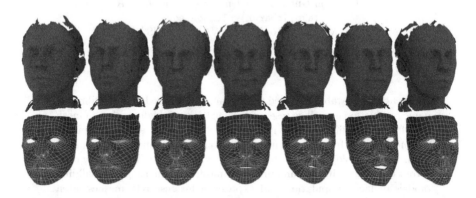

Fig. 1. Polygonal meshes acquired with a 3DMD capture device and auto-re-topologized to a designed layout.

With 3D acquisition technology and face databases becoming more available, much facial research now uses three-dimensional models [5,9,12,13,19]. To build models of face shape and texture, though, it is necessary to find a correspondence between acquired meshes. A variety of methods have been adopted and are summarized in the background section of this paper. Similarly to face acquisition for games and visual effects, if a standardized polygon layout is used to re-topologize meshes captured for research, the layout could be a system of correspondence across expressions and individuals.

The goals of correspondence, designed edge flow, and data reduction could be achieved via the same re-topology method, and accurately automating this could facilitate the use of high-quality digital faces in many applications. We propose a process using 2D-image, face-landmark-fitting methods to enable automatic re-topology of polygonal meshes of the face that were acquired via stereo-pair, structured-light scan with the new approach of deriving a mesh designed specifically for face animation. This paper describes two approaches that make use of landmarking techniques to automate re-topologizing 3D face meshes acquired using a 3DMD face-capture system, the second using a novel multi-step interpolation to dense landmarks. A set of Facial Action Coding System (FACS) based captures is used to demonstrate the potential of this approach. An interactive editing system that allows real-time editing of the automated re-topology is also discussed. The next section presents related background material and is followed by a section describing details on the process. Results are discussed in

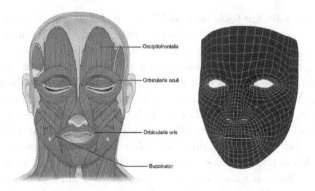

Fig. 2. On the left, several major muscles that pose the face; on the right, a template mesh designed with an edge flow that allows deformation to match muscle movement.

the fourth section of the paper. The authors conclude with discussion of the merits and drawbacks of the techniques as well as suggested future work.

2   Background

2.1   Polygonal Mesh Acquisition

Methods such as laser-scan, structured-light stereography, and photogrammetry have been devised for acquiring detailed meshes of the face. Commercial systems include such as marketed by Cyberscan, 3DMD, Arctec, and others. Photogrammetric solver packages such as PhotoScan by Agisoft and CaptureReality by Reality Capture are also in growing use, and studios have built large systems of camera arrays to capture the images needed. Many of these leverage 2D images in order to construct their 3D representations. Estimated depth information from multiple images is used to build a 3D point-cloud which can yield a polygonal mesh via a stitching algorithm. With capture technology available, a variety of 3D face databases have also been collected using like devices. Some include the USF, BU-3DFE, BU-4DFE, Bosphorous, Frav3D, GavabDB, and Mein3D. Meshes acquired as above or included in the publicly available databases often suffer from dense geometry, no known vertex ordering nor correspondence, no semantic associations for geometry, and no topological flow in the mesh design. Goals of this work include automating topological re-formation to solve these weaknesses, maintaining accurate facial likenesses, and preparing meshes ready for rigging for animation as an artist might for a digital production.

2.2   Facial-Mesh Correspondence

To work with multiple meshes, it is necessary to establish correspondence. To create blend-shape targets, a template layout of vertex location and edge association may be used to guide re-topology. This could be manually constructed or assisted with software tools such as Wrap3. In facial research correspondence has often been sought as a preliminary step to create a morphable model – a statistical representation of shape and texture of a sample of faces [3]. This correspondence problem has been solved with a few primary techniques but with little attention to conforming to a mesh matching human musculature.

Blanz and Vetter found a correspondence among meshes by projecting them into a cylinder, flattening to a 2D texture-layout, and using image registration via optical flow [3]. Patel and Smith manually labeled similar cylindrical projections of meshes then used thin-plate splines [4] to complete correspondence registration also in texture-layout (UV) space [24]. Cosker et al. manually labeled certain images from an image sequence acquired over time in order to build an Active Appearance Model (AAM) to find similar correspondence landmarks for one individual [8]. Others such as Paysan et al. have used a variant of the Iterative Closest Point (ICP) algorithm [1] to complete alignment of scans [25]. In 2013 Ichikari et al. proposed their Vuvuzela system, a semi-automated system that also works in texture space; a user selects specific landmarks and meshes are triangulated and matched via optical flow. Then a variety of texture maps are used to find dense correspondence that is reported at the sub-millimeter level [12]. Booth et al. proposed a system where various camera projections are used along with automated face-finding and annotation algorithms [2,5,15,22]. Most correspondence work has used alignment within 2D texture space using landmarks or optical flow, 3D space using an ICP variant, or a combined approach as in the recent large-scale morphable model system [5]. Li et al. also used a non-rigid ICP method for aligning scanned meshes [18]. Weise et al., investigated aligning depth-captures to avatar meshes but did not specifically target re-topologizing a high-resolution mesh [27]. The two methods presented here are most similar to those of [8,24] but have several differences, a primary being the target design.

The first technique here is performed in the image space of the original 2D photos acquired during the structured-light capture and uses a registration technique of very dense landmarking automatically located via Active Appearance Model (AAM). The second technique presented here uses a more recent landmarking technique, ensemble of regression trees, to locate sparse 2D landmarks on images but also leverages a novel multi-pass application of thin-plate-spline (TPS) interpolation to improve registration around difficult areas such as the nostrils and mouth. Finally this work is novel in that it is inspired by production workflows to re-topologize automatically into a mesh that is ready to deform for facial animation.

2.3   Re-topology of Acquired Scans

A main purpose for re-topology of an acquired face capture is to enable effective deformation in the direction of major muscle movement. Figure 2 illustrates these muscles [23] along with the template mesh layout that was used for this work designed to match muscle flow. Note the vertical lifting of the occipito-frontalis which are matched by largely horizontal and vertical edges in the forehead region,

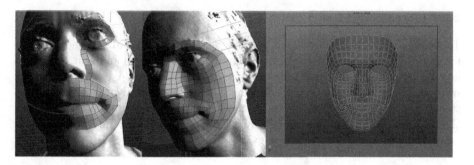

Fig. 3. Manual re-topology using 3DCoat to create a deformable mesh within Maya.

the orbicularis oculi which are matched by concentric circles leading out from the eye sockets in the mesh, the orbicularis oris which are also matched by concentric circles leading out from the mouth, followed by an area on the cheeks where the curves align and also follow the buccinator muscle. A variety of software packages such as 3DCoat, ZBrush, Maya, and others have fairly mature toolsets to complete re-topology, but the process is still largely manual and can take hours or longer. Figure 3 shows an example of a re-topology being completed in 3DCoat, a software tool that has been used at high-end visual-effects studios for this process. This work attempts to automate the like process effectively.

2.4 Automatic Landmark Fitting

A large variety of work has been completed regarding the location of faces and landmarking of specific features. With a longer history of development and simpler data and computation, many 2D algorithms are more effective than current 3D ones for locating points on a human face. The first re-topology technique that the authors present uses AAM fitting. AAMs use statistical shape and texture models combined in an appearance model, and the fitting algorithm iteratively updates parameters to reduce the residual of a synthesized estimate and original image pixels. This search continues until convergence with the goal of matching the location of an object in an image [6,7,21].

The second technique presented here uses a rendered frontal-face view of the acquired mesh and a multi-pass process for different regions of the face. The ensemble of regression tree technique [2,14,15,17] is used to landmark a sparse set of particular points on different regions of the face such as the eyes, nose, and mouth. Separate steps of thin-plate spline interpolation are then applied per region to determine dense 2D landmarks of the face. This multi-pass landmark labeling and regionally targeted TPS interpolation is novel and results in improved results around difficult regions such as the nose, nostrils, and lips.

2.5   Interactive Mesh Editing

Techniques have been developed for live manipulation of 3D meshes, where, for example, a user can perform quadrangulation of meshes and edit the quad-layouts [20,26] or paint in 2D for textured results in 3D renders [16]. Such software aims for interactivity via real-time editing, supported by geometric data structures. Here we use a KD-tree for accelerated search of landmarks and store the computed mapping, updating only as necessary. This live interaction allows artist-friendly updates to re-topology layouts as needed.

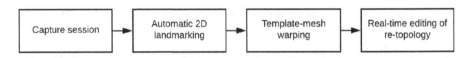

Fig. 4. Flowchart of the main process for our re-topology method.

3   Procedure

Figure 4 illustrates the main flow of our approach to re-topology. Dense, high-resolution facial meshes were captured using a 3DMD structured-light face system. Color photos from the left and right cameras are included with the mesh. Each mesh contains over 50,000 vertices triangulated in whatever order they were stitched from the sampled point cloud. The goal is to transform a designed template mesh of just over 1,000 vertices (described further below) with specifically deformable edge layout to the shape of the acquired mesh. As previously mentioned in Sect. 2.4 on Automatic landmark fitting, two methods were tried for 2D landmarking. Once 2D landmarks are located, a reverse search from texture-space to the acquired 3D mesh finds the vertex closest to that 2D landmark. The template-mesh vertex matching the 2D landmark is transformed to the 3D location on the acquired mesh, and this is repeated over all template-mesh vertices.

3.1   2D Landmarking Techniques

The first technique demonstrated employs an AAM and works directly from 3DMD frontal photos acquired during a capture session. The second could work with any acquired meshes and has potential to out-perform the first method on difficult regions such as the nostrils and lips due to its multi-pass method for landmarking and interpolation to dense locations on the face.

Photo-Pair Method: In this approach, the symmetry of the human face is leveraged to build one Active Appearance Model for auto-fitting. The authors use the AAM implementation of the Menpo Python library [22].

During model training, a sparse set of landmarks is used for identifying key regions of half-face images to label unknown faces more quickly. This sparse set acts as control points for interpolation via thin-plate-spline (TPS) warping, resulting in the placement of all 2D landmarks relating to template-mesh vertices for half of the face. An AAM is built upon this dense set of landmarks and is then used for fitting landmarks to new photos. The photo for one side of the face is flipped to employ only one AAM during fitting. A complete set of landmarks results after taking the union of the landmarks for the two half-face images; these landmarks are used in the remaining part of the process in a reverse-lookup via texture coordinates to acquired mesh vertices for warping the template mesh (Fig. 5).

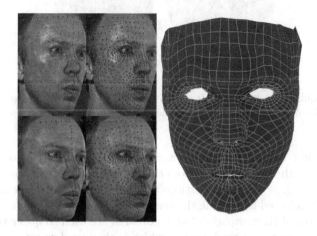

Fig. 5. Sparse and dense landmarkings of both sides of the face (top row being the subject's right side and the bottom being the left-side flipped horizontally) of a single capture, using the Photo-Pair Method, and the respective re-topology.

Frontal-Face-Projection Method: This method of automatic landmarking focuses on iteratively placing all template-mesh landmarks on a new texture-map image. First, a front-facing, image of the subject's face is generated via a projection rendering where the projection mapping from 3D to 2D is stored. 2D template-mesh-related landmarks are placed using an ensemble of regression trees (Dlib implementation [15]) and TPS interpolation to dense labeling in multiple passes of the eyes and face, the region around the nostrils, and the region around the lips. This multi-pass process aims to improve interpolation on difficult regions where a broader fitting process may perform worse.

3.2   Template-Mesh Warping

A template mesh was chosen that was designed with an edge layout that follows the musculature of the face and fulfills deformation concepts presented in the background section. This mesh is shown in Fig. 2 aside a diagram of facial muscles. Along with the desire to allow facial deformation for animation, the mesh was also chosen with a polygon count that is fairly minimal to still create a high-quality face shape that may be rendered smoothly (Fig. 6).

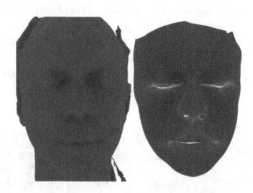

Fig. 6. An acquired mesh on the left with a subdivided re-topologized version, via the AAM method, on the right. Note appearance likeness is preserved.

The template mesh is ultimately warped to match the shape of the 3DMD scanned mesh with the landmarks from the previous step, as shown in the right-most mesh of Fig. 7. The scan vertices that are nearest to the template-mesh landmarks are selected by loading the vertex data into a KD-tree data-structure. The coordinates of the template-mesh landmarks are used to query the KD-tree to locate the nearest scan-mesh vertex, which is then used to set a new location of the current template-mesh vertex. Running this procedure on the entire set of template-mesh landmarks results in a template mesh that is fully warped to the shape of a 3DMD acquired face mesh.

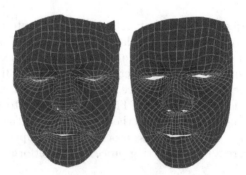

Fig. 7. A resulting warped mesh from the 3DMD photo-pair and frontal-face approaches.

Figure 10 displays the reduced meshes of one capture section with their corresponding color texture maps re-calculated to match.

3.3   Interactive Editing

We developed a platform-independent tool to use for re-topology and interactive editing. It is written in Python and uses PyQt5 bindings with the Qt5 user-interface library; OpenGL 4.x and GLSL are accessed through Qt5 for state-of-the-art, shader-based graphics processing that allows flexibility for displaying quad-mesh layout topologies and other features. Figure 8 is a screenshot of this interactive re-topology tool. The software's focus is providing 2D and 3D viewports that can support user interaction and real-time rendering, making the tool artist-friendly and also ready to build plug-ins for various research projects. Automatic calls to the reverse-lookup, mesh-warping method described earlier are triggered with each transformation of landmarks in the 2D image view to see immediate re-meshing results. Successive calls minimize calculations by updating only the vertices in the warped mesh that match the changed landmarks.

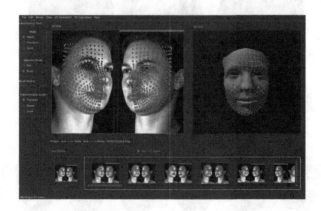

Fig. 8. Screenshot from the interactive software tool for 3D mesh re-topology.

4   Results

For visual effects or game development, an actor may perform a variety of facial expressions during mesh acquisition that illustrate the range of motion to be matched. These are often based on, or inclusive of, Facial Action Coding System (FACS) action units [10]. With the goal of testing representation of a variety of facial poses, similar capture sessions covering most FACS action units for two individuals was completed using a 3DMD two-pod acquisition setup. All of the 31 acquired meshes per individual were re-topologized using both of the aforementioned automated methods. For the first auto-landmarking technique, because no training model had been previously built (and half-face AAMs are not common), color photos acquired during mesh acquisition were manually landmarked and used to build an AAM. Sparse landmarking was completed within a few hours, using only twenty half-face images, and thin-plate-spline interpolation provided dense landmarks to build an AAM used for the final fitting of the remaining 21 mesh image pairs. For the second auto-landmarking technique, ensemble of regression trees trained using the iBug 68-point landmark scheme as included and one using the HELEN 194-point landmark scheme trained on HELEN.

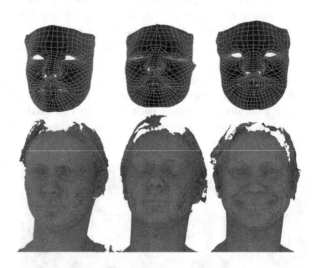

Fig. 9. Re-topologized meshes of second individual.

Fig. 10. Re-topologized meshes with transfered color texture map.

Acquired meshes could be processed directly after a frontal projection image was rendered, and the multi-pass landmarking and TPS interpolation was used to densely mark the same FACS-capture meshes. Both landmarking methods resulted in auto-landmarking on the millisecond or fraction of a millisecond time order per face mesh.

Figure 1 shows several meshes that represent some variation in facial expression from the FACS capture sessions. Figure 9 shows meshes re-topologized from a second individual's FACS capture session. Figure 10 illustrates the full set with texture transfer warped via the front-projection, regression-tree approach.

5   Discussion and Conclusion

Both approaches yield re-topologized meshes based on a uniform template mesh that match the shape of original, acquired face meshes as desired. Figure 7 shows the same mesh re-topologized via the two methods and illustrates some visible differences that may be generally noted between the two techniques at this point.

The 3DMD photo-pair method initially produces meshes that are less smooth but do match the shape of the acquired mesh well in most cases, even trained on this small AAM. More sophisticated methods could be added to regularize the mesh. A drawback to the photo-pair technique, however, is the necessity of dealing with the texture-coordinate seam between the two images. The multi-pass method seems to result in meshes that are slightly more rounded, likely due to the current projection method, perhaps not matching the brow, nose, and cheek bones quite as well, but does have the advantage of performing better in many cases on the difficult region of the nostrils, frustum, and lips.

There are a variety of areas related to this work for future consideration. The first is expanding and testing the method on a larger population of individuals and a wider variety of FACS expression captures that include both subtle (A) and more extreme (E) expression poses for each action unit. Along with calculating color-maps and normals to associate with re-topologized meshes, normal maps and displacement maps may be calculated to improve quality of renders with the reduced-poly-count mesh. Non-Rigid Iterative Closest Point (NICP) and Optical Flow registration techniques could possibly improve the consistency and alignment between re-topologized meshes. Multiple "camera-view" renders of an acquired mesh and focused landmarking models, trained on specific regions, could also potentially improve template-mesh warping in more difficult topological regions of the face and ensure that these regions map well across a wide variety of faces.

References

1. Amberg, B., Knothe, R., Vetter, T.: Optimal step nonrigid ICP algorithms for surface registration. In: IEEE International Conference on Computer Vision and Pattern Recognition (2007)
2. Antonakos, E., Alabort-i-Medina, J., Tzimiropoulos, G., Zafeiriou, S.: Hog appearance models (2014)
3. Blanz, V., Vetter, T.: A morphable model for the synthesis of 3D faces. In: SIGGRAPH International Conference on Computer Graphics and Interactive Techniques, pp. 187–194 (1999)
4. Bookstein, F.: Principal warps: thin-plate splines and the decomposition of deformations. IEEE Trans. Pattern Anal. Mach. Intell. **11**, 567–585 (1989)
5. Booth, J., Roussos, A., Zafeiriou, S., Ponniahy, A., Dunaway, D.: A 3D morphable model learnt from 10,000 faces. In: 2016 IEEE Conference on Computer Vision and Pattern Recognition (CVPR), pp. 5543–5552 (2016)
6. Cootes, T.F., Edwards, G.J., Taylor, C.J.: Active appearance models. In: Burkhardt, H., Neumann, B. (eds.) ECCV 1998. LNCS, vol. 1407, pp. 484–498. Springer, Heidelberg (1998). https://doi.org/10.1007/BFb0054760
7. Cootes, T.F., Kittipanya-ngam, P.: Comparing variations on the active appearance model algorithm. In: British Machine Vision Conference, pp. 837–842 (2002)
8. Cosker, D., Krumhuber, E., Hilton, A.: A FACS valid 3D dynamic action unit database with applications to 3D dynamic morphable facial modeling. In: Proceedings of the IEEE International Conference on Computer Vision (2011)
9. Debevec, P.: The light stages and their applications to photoreal digital actors. In: SIGGRAPH Asia, Singapore (2012)
10. Ekman, P., Friesen, W., Hager, J.: Facial Action Coding System: Second Edition. Paul Ekman Group (2002)
11. Enstice, T.: The curious case of Benjamin Button. In: ACM SIGGRAPH 2009 Computer Animation Festival, SIGGRAPH 2009, pp. 36–37. ACM, New York (2009)
12. Ichikari, R., Alexander, O., Debevec, P.: Vuvuzela: a facial scan correspondence tool. In: ACM SIGGRAPH 2013 Posters, SIGGRAPH 2013, p. 89:1. ACM, New York (2013)
13. Jo, J., Choi, H., Kim, I.J., Kim, J.: Single-view-based 3D facial reconstruction method robust against pose variations. Pattern Recognit. **48**(1), 73–85 (2015)
14. Kazemi, V., Sullivan, J.: One millisecond face alignment with an ensemble of regression trees. In: Proceedings of the 2014 IEEE Conference on Computer Vision and Pattern Recognition, CVPR 2014, pp. 1867–1874. IEEE Computer Society, Washington, DC (2014)
15. King, D.E.: Dlib-ml: a machine learning toolkit. J. Mach. Learn. Res. **10**, 1755–1758 (2009). http://dl.acm.org/citation.cfm?id=1577069.1755843
16. Lambert, T.: From 2D to 3D painting with mesh colors. In: ACM SIGGRAPH 2015 Talks, SIGGRAPH 2015, p. 72:1. ACM, New York (2015)
17. Le, V., Brandt, J., Lin, Z., Bourdev, L., Huang, T.S.: Interactive facial feature localization. In: Fitzgibbon, A., Lazebnik, S., Perona, P., Sato, Y., Schmid, C. (eds.) ECCV 2012. LNCS, vol. 7574, pp. 679–692. Springer, Heidelberg (2012). https://doi.org/10.1007/978-3-642-33712-3_49
18. Li, H., Adams, B., Guibas, L.J., Pauly, M.: Robust single-view geometry and motion reconstruction. ACM Trans. Graph. **28**(5) (2009). Proceedings SIGGRAPH Asia 2009

19. Ma, M., Peng, S., Hu, X.: A lighting robust fitting approach of 3D morphable model for face reconstruction. Vis. Comput. **32**(10), 1223–1238 (2016)
20. Marcias, G., et al.: Data-driven interactive quadrangulation. ACM Trans. Graph. **34**(4), 65:1–65:10 (2015)
21. Matthews, I., Baker, S.: Active appearance models revisited. Int. J. Comput. Vis. **60**(2), 135–164 (2004)
22. Alabort-i-Medina, J., Antonakos, E., Booth, J., Snape, P., Zafeiriou, S.: Menpo: a comprehensive platform for parametric image alignment and visual deformable models. In: Proceedings of the ACM International Conference on Multimedia (2014)
23. OpenStax: OpenStax Anatomy and Physiology. Rice University (2017). https://cnx.org/contents/FPtK1zmh@8.25:fEI3C8Ot@10/Preface
24. Patel, A., Smith, W.: 3D morphable face models revisited. In: Proceedings of the IEEE Conference on Computer Vision and Pattern Recognition, pp. 1327–1334 (2009)
25. Paysan, P., Knothe, R., Amberg, B., Romdhani, S., Vetter, T.: A 3D face model for pose and illumination invariant face recognition. In: IEEE International Conference on Advanced Video and Signal-Based Surveillance (2009)
26. Peng, C.H., Zhang, E., Kobayashi, Y., Wonka, P.: Connectivity editing for quadrilateral meshes. In: Proceedings of the 2011 SIGGRAPH Asia Conference, SA 2011, pp. 141:1–141:12. ACM, New York (2011)
27. Weise, T., Bouaziz, S., Li, H., Pauly, M.: Realtime performance-based facial animation. ACM Trans. Graph. **30**(4) (2011). Proceedings SIGGRAPH 2011

A Kinematic Gesture Representation Based on Shape Difference VLAD for Sign Language Recognition

Jefferson Rodríguez[1,2,3](✉)(iD) and Fabio Martínez[1,2,3]

[1] Grupo de investigación en ingeniería biomédica (GIIB), Bucaramanga, Colombia
[2] Motion Analysis and Computer Vision (MACV), Bucaramanga, Colombia
[3] Universidad Industrial de Santander (UIS), Bucaramanga, Colombia
{jefferson.rodriguez2,famarcar}@saber.uis.edu.co

Abstract. Automatic Sign language recognition (SLR) is a fundamental task to help with inclusion of deaf community in society, facilitating, noways, many conventional multimedia interactions. In this work is proposed a novel approach to represent gestures in SLR as a shape difference-VLAD mid level coding of kinematic primitives, captured along videos. This representation capture local salient motions together with regional dominant patterns developed by articulators along utterances. Also, the special VLAD representation allows to quantify local motion pattern but also capture shape of motion descriptors, that achieved a proper regional gesture characterization. The proposed approach achieved an average accuracy of 85,45% in a corpus data of 64 sign words captured in 3200 videos. Additionally, for Boston sign dataset the proposed approach achieve competitive results with 82% of accuracy in average.

Keywords: Motion analysis · Sign recognition
Mid-level representation · VLAD representation

1 Introduction

Deaf community and people with some auditive limitation around world is estimated in more than 466 millions according to world health organization (WHO) [3]. This community had achieved to structure different natural sign languages as spatio-temporal gestures, developed by articulated motions of upper limbs that together with facial expressions and trunk postures allows communication and interaction. Sign languages are as rich and complex as any spoken language, being the automatic recognition a tool that allows to include deaf community in society. Nevertheless, the automatic interpretation of deaf languages remains as an open problem because the multiple inter and intra signers variations and also external variations produced by culture, history and particular interpretations according to regions. Such variations implies great challenges to understand and associate semantic language labels to spatio-temporal gestures.

© Springer Nature Switzerland AG 2018
L. J. Chmielewski et al. (Eds.): ICCVG 2018, LNCS 11114, pp. 438–449, 2018.
https://doi.org/10.1007/978-3-030-00692-1_38

Also, typical video processing problems are present such as illumination changes, perspective of signers, occlusion of articulators during the deaf conversation, among many others. Such related problems limits the use of automatic learning methodologies, the usability of multimedia tools and puts deaf community in disadvantage to explore much of information in multimedia platforms.

The sign recognition has been addressed in literature by multiple approaches that include global shape representations that segment all articulators of language but with natural limitation due to occlusions and dependences of controlled scenarios [17]. Other strategies have developed analysis of gestures from local representations that include the characterization of interest points [11,16] and the analysis of appearance and geometrical primitives to capture shape of gestures in videos [12]. For instance, Zahedi et al. [19] proposed a SLR by computing descriptors of appearance that together with gradient of first and second order characterize particular signs. Such approach is however dependent of signer appearance and perspective in video sequence. An extension of this work developed the analysis of multi-modal information to recover shape from RGB-D sequences and also compute trajectories from accelerometers to complement sign description [17]. Despite the advantages of 3D analysis the depth sequences are limited to controlled scenarios and the external accelerometers can alter the natural motion of gestures.

Motion characterization have been fundamental to develop strategies to recognize gestures being robust to appearance variance and illumination changes [10,11]. For instance, in [10,16] utterance sequences were characterized from firs order relationships of appearance velocities captured from Lukas-Kanade motion field. This approach is however prone to errors because the flow sensibility to little camera displacements and also the sparse nature of the approach capture few displacement points that difficult any statistical analysis. In same line, Konecný et al. [10] integrates local shape information with histograms of an optical flow to describe gestures. This approach achieved a frame-level representation but lose local and regional information to represent gestures. Wan et al. [16] proposed a dictionary of sparse words codified from salient SIFT points and complemented with flow descriptors captured around each point. This representation achieve a proper performance of sign recognition but remains limited to cover much of the variability gestures. In [11] was obtained a local motion description at each frame of a particular SL by computing motion trajectories along the utterance. Nevertheless, this approach lost spatial representation of signs because the nature of the bag of words representation.

The main contribution of this work is a regional mid level representation of kinematic primitives that achieve a local description but also a regional coding representation of gestures during utterance sequences. The proposed approach is robust to describe sign from incomplete utterance representations being efficient in on-line applications. For doing so, a set of salient motion patches are characterized with kinematic histogram features like speed and motion boundaries and also regional features such as rotational and divergence were computed. Such volumes are coded in a shape difference VLAD that recover main centroids described by the means and variance of motion. This representation allows to recover partial gestures and robustly describe different gestures in a particular sign language. Finally the obtained motion descriptor is mapped to a Support vector machine and validated with respect to both LSA64 and Boston public corpus.

2   Proposed Approach

In this work is presented an automatic strategy to recognize gestures from a kinematic mid-level representation. The herein proposed approach achieves a robust local description of signs by considering several motion features. Then a classical dictionary approach allows to cluster volumetric patches to represent the signs. The mid-level representation allows to capture local kinematic similarities of patches but also is able to recover the shape of descriptor distribution from a shape difference VLAD [7] representation. The pipeline of the proposed approach is illustrated in Fig. 1.

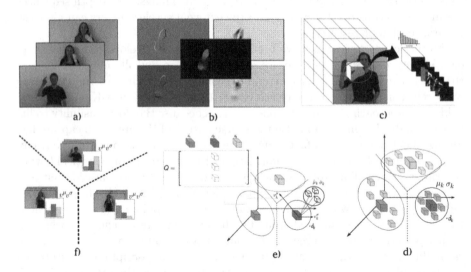

Fig. 1. Pipeline of the proposed approach to SLR. A set of utterance sign samples (a) are codified from a set of motion primitives (b). Then kinematic primitives are computed in utterance sequences (c) and coded as a local volumetric patch description. A dictionary of patches (d) is obtained and finally a coding representation is obtained using Hard assignment and SD-VLAD. The computed descriptor is mapped to a previously trained SVM to recognize the gestures (f)

2.1   Computing Kinematic Features

The motion characterization had proven to be fundamental to analyzing atomic symbols in gesture recognition applications. A fundamental task in this kind of applications is to quantify large motion regions developed by independent actuators, such as arm, hands, face or even shoulders. In this approach we compute a set of kinematic primitives to describe gestures independent of appearance. The set of set of computed features are described as follows:

- **Dense flow velocity fields**
  A first kinematic primitive herein considered was the dense appearance field produced among consecutive frames. Typical approaches remain limited to quantify large displacements because the assumption of smooth motion in local neighborhoods. To avoid these limitations, herein was implemented a robust optical flow approach able to capture dense flow fields but considering large displacements of gestures [2]. In this approach is considered classical flow assumptions in which color $E_{color}(w)$ and gradient $E_{gradient}(w)$ changes remain constant among consecutive frames. Likewise, it is also included a local criteria of field smoothness, expressed as:

$$E_{smooth}(w) = \int_\Omega \Psi(|\nabla u|_{t_{i+1}} + |\nabla v|_{t_i})d\mathbf{x} \tag{1}$$

where Ψ represents the atypical values that are penalized in a specific neighborhood and Ω is the region analyzed. Finally a non-local criteria is considered in this approach that allows the estimation of coherent large displacements. In this case, a sift matching is carried out among consecutive frames, and then the flow regions of such interest matched regions are measured to find flow similar patterns $\mathbf{f}_{t_i}(\mathbf{x})$, described as:

$$E_{desc}(w_1) = \int_\Omega \delta(\mathbf{x}) \, \Psi(|\mathbf{f}_{t_{i+1}}(\mathbf{x} + w_1(\mathbf{x})) - \mathbf{f}_{t_i}(\mathbf{x})|^2)d\mathbf{x} \tag{2}$$

with $\delta(\mathbf{x})$ as step function that is active only for regions where exist interest points. The sum of whole restrictions are minimized from a variational Euler-Lagrange approach.
- **Divergence fields**
  Additionally to velocity field description, in this work was also considered the physical pattern of divergence over the field. The feature result from the derivative of flow components (u, v) at each point x along spatial directions (x, y), described as:

$$div(p_t) = \frac{\partial u(p_t)}{\partial x} + \frac{\partial v(p_t)}{\partial y} \tag{3}$$

This feature capture a local expansion of field, and result useful to characterize independent body actuators along a sign description.
- **Rotational fields**
  The rotational measures of flow field was also herein considered. From each local point of estimated field is measured the rotation around of a perpendicular axis [1,8]. This rotational patterns stand out circular gestures, commonly

reported in sign languages. Also, this measure estimate the flow rigidity, useful to distinguish articulated motions. The rotation of field can be expressed as:

$$curl(p_t) = \frac{\partial v(p_t)}{\partial x} - \frac{\partial u(p_t)}{\partial y} \tag{4}$$

– **Motion limits**
First spatial derivative in flow components are also estimated [6] as kinematic information of signs, coding the relative motion among pixels. The gradient of flow remove constant motion information, while remain the changes of velocity. This primitive also highlight main articulator motions.

2.2 Coding Motion Gesture Patches

A main drawback of global gesture characterization is the sensibility to occlusion of articulators, and scene perturbations while the sign is described. The herein proposed approach is based on a local gesture representation, from which, a set of local motion patches can represent the temporal description of a sign gesture. Because the proposed representation is mainly based in motion patches, a first step was to remove background patches with poor motion information. For doing so, we compute the average background of the video as: $B(\hat{x}, y) = \frac{1}{t} \sum_{t=1}^{t} f_t(x, y)$ for each t frames and then foreground pixels are get by a simple subtraction w.r.t the background $|f_t(x, y) - B(\hat{x}, y)| > \tau$. Differences larger than τ (experimentally obtained value) are considered static pixels and removed. For on-line purposes, the average background can be built from a recursive mean estimator. To remove relative static patches also improve the computational efficiency of the approach (see in Fig. 2).

2.3 Kinematic Patch Description

In this work, a particular sign is defined as a set of n spatio-temporal patches $S = \{p_{1...n}^{(c,j)} : j \in [t_1 - t_2]; c \in [x_1, x_2]\}$ bounded in a temporal interval j and spatially distributed in a c region. Each of these volumetric patches are described using the motion local information, coded as kinematic histograms. Then, for every kinematic primitive considered in the proposed approach a local histogram representation was considered, as:

$$h(p) = \sum_{\mathbf{x} \in p} R_b(\mathbf{x}) W(\mathbf{x}), b = \left\{ 1, 2, \cdots, \frac{2\pi}{\Delta\theta} \right\}$$

$$R_b(x, y) = \begin{cases} 1 \ if \ (b-1)\Delta\theta \leq \theta(\mathbf{x}) < b\Delta\theta \\ \\ 0 \ elsewhere \end{cases} \tag{5}$$

where $R_b(\mathbf{x})$ is an activation function that determine the particular bin that code the local kinematic feature, while the $W(\mathbf{x})$ corresponds to the particular weight that sum in the histogram bin. Particularly, for orientation flow

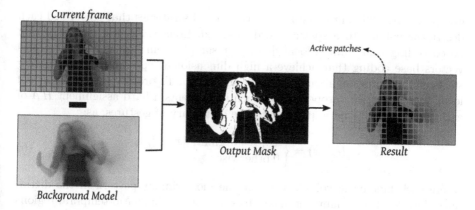

Fig. 2. An efficient kinematic patch representation is achieved by only considering patches with relevant motion information. To remove static pixels is herein considered a simple but efficient background model.

histograms (**HOOF**) the bins b correspond to orientations, while the $W(\mathbf{x})$ is defined by the norm of each vector, as proposed in [5]. Likewise, the motion limits are codified as MBH histograms, quantified for each x, y components as proposed in [6]. For divergence and curl the primitives are statistically cumulated by defining the bins as: $\{\max, \frac{\max}{2}, 0, \frac{\min}{2}, \min\}$. In such case the curl histogram (**HCURL**) quantify the main motion around perpendicular axis, while divergence histogram (**HDIV**) summarize the main moments of divergence present around each spatio-temporal patch. For divergence a simple occurrence counting is carried out while for rotational the occurrence is weighted according to angular speed. The final descriptor for each patch is formed as the concatenation of all histogram herein considered.

2.4   Mid Level Gesture Representation

Gesture Dictionaries. Each volume is coded with kinematic histograms that represent different local and regional primitives. The relationships among such volumes along the video highlight predominant patterns to describe gestures. Such patterns are the local representation to compute SLR from motion characteristics. To build a volumetric dictionary, a set K representative volumes: $D = [d_1, d_2, ...d_k] \in \mathbb{R}^{d \times K}$ are recovered from a set of N volumetric patches described by a d-*dimensional* descriptor $X = [x_1, x_2, ...x_N] \in \mathbb{R}^{d \times N}$ using a classic k-*means* algorithm, where $K \ll N$. Under the assumption of patch density, we consider that a set of K patches are sufficient to represent particular gestures and that each articulator is form by a set of these mean patches.

Gesture Coding. The computed dictionary is used as reference to code a global representation of registered sign along the video. The codification strategies are group in three different classes: (1) voting based strategies that associated each descriptor volume to a specific word in the dictionary, (2) the reconstruction based coding that built a local descriptor sample from inputs and (3) super-vectors base coding that achieve a high dimensional representation by adding statistical information about descriptor shape [13]. To preserve independence of local description, the proposed approach implements a hard assignment HA of each computed kinematic patch w.r.t the dictionary of gestures, as:

$$HA(x) = \begin{cases} 1 \ if\ i = \operatorname{argmin}_j \|x - d_j\|_2 \\ 0 \ \text{otherwise} \end{cases} \tag{6}$$

where each kinematic volume vote for the most similar pattern in the dictio-nary. This kind of assignment allows to stand out main spatio-temporal regions associated with salient learned patches in the dictionary. Eventually, such rep-resentation can border similar gestures in regional salient details recovered.

Shape Difference VLAD. Classical Bag of Words (BoW) codify occurrences using simple occurrence strategies that lost information about descriptor and particular details of gestures, which can be dramatical in SLR [16]. Currently, the codification Vector of Locally Aggregated Descriptors (VLAD) have shown advantages w.r.t mid level representations by considering statistics of first order about computed cluster descriptors [9]. In such representation, the difference among local descriptors and predominant patterns are cumulated in a local char-acteristic vector. The whole difference vectors for each clusters form the video descriptor, denoted as: $v_k^\mu = \sum_{j=1}^{n_k}(x_j - D_k)$ with dimensionality of $K \times d$. This particular strategy achieves gesture description from dominant kinematic pat-terns by capturing similarities sign motions w.r.t centroid dictionaries and adding variance informations. In clusters with low variability, the resultant vectors has mainly zero values. Such fact result interesting to differentiate kinematic patterns with dynamic and spatial similarities along utterances. Nevertheless, this strat-egy is limited to capture the local distribution of the motion descriptor and is variant w.r.t. symmetric motions. For instance, same features vectors can result from different kinematic gestures. Hence, the standard deviation of each clus-ter can be aggregated to complement statistical information of signs, recovering regional relationships of patches that form a cluster [7]. To achieve this variance cluster representation, firstly, the characteristic vectors of each cluster proposed in [9] are weighted by their respective standard deviations and normalized by the number of descriptors as:

$$v_k^\mu = \frac{1}{n_k} \sum_{j=1}^{n_k} \frac{(x_j - D_k)}{\sigma_k} \tag{7}$$

where the normalization n_k is a pooling carried out to VLAD descriptors. To highlight the calculation of the variance descriptor, a new cluster $\hat{D}_k$ is estimated with projected samples of particular test utterances what are assigned to the pattern D_k. Then, the variance of the means is defined as the difference between the new $\hat{D}_k$ estimated centroid and the dictionary centroid D_k, as:

$$\bar{v}_k = \frac{1}{n_k}\sum_{j=1}^{n_k}(x_j - D_k) = \frac{1}{n_k}(\sum_{j=1}^{n_k}(x_j) - n_k D_k)$$

$$= \frac{1}{n_k}\sum_{j=1}^{n_k}(x_j) - D_k = \hat{D}_k - D_k \tag{8}$$

From same analysis, a new representation is added to descriptor by computing differences among standard deviation, such as:

$$v_k^\sigma = \hat{\sigma}_k - \sigma_k = \left(\frac{1}{n_k}\sum_{j=1}^{n_k}(x_j - D_k)^2\right)^{\frac{1}{2}} - \sigma_k \tag{9}$$

where $\hat{\sigma}_k$ is the standard deviation of assigned local descriptors in VLAD and σ_k is the standard deviation of assigned descriptors D_k. Such difference recover shape information of descriptor. The SD-VLAD descriptor is form by the concatenation of vectors v^μ and v^σ. Finally is applied a normalization at each dimension of the descriptor as suggested in [14] as: $f(\mathbf{p}) = sign(\mathbf{p})|\mathbf{p}|^{\frac{1}{2}}$

2.5   SVM Sign Recognition

The recognition of each potential sign is carried out by a Support Vector Machine (SVM) [4] classifier since this constitutes a proper balance between accuracy and low computational cost. The present approach was implemented using a *One against one SVM multi-class classification* with a Radial Basis Function (RBF) kernel. Here, the classes represent the particular signs coded as SD-VLAD descriptors and optimal hyperplanes separate them by a classical max-margin formulation. For m motion classes, a majority voting strategy is applied on the outputs of the $\frac{m(m-1)}{2}$ binary classifiers. A (γ, C)-parameter sensitivity analysis was performed with a grid-search using a cross-validation scheme and selecting the parameters with the largest number of true positives.

3   Evaluation and Results

A public corpus of a sign language LSA64 [15] was herein used to evaluate the proposed approach. Such corpus describe a total of 64 signs that correspond to the Argentinian Sign language performed by 10 non-expert signers. Each sign is developed 5 times by each signer by a total of 3200 utterance videos. The spatial resolution is 1920×1080 at 60 frames per second. The selected signs involve articular motions, the use of one or both hands, and evident displacements in space and time. The corpus was captured in different scenarios, with some illumination changes. Several challenges are present in some different gestures with dynamic

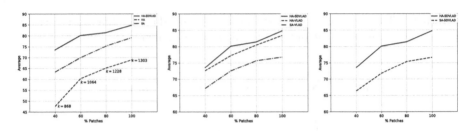

Fig. 3. On the left is illustrated the average performance using the common approaches Hard and Soft assignment from different dictionaries computed from $K = \left(\frac{patches}{2}\right)^{\frac{1}{2}}$. In middle is illustrated the performance of VLAD version while on the right is illustrated the SD-VLAD computed over Hard and Soft assignments with $K = 64$. For all experiments we used partial information, from 40% to 100%.

and geometric similarities during the sequences except in some localized spatio-temporal regions. For experimental evaluation, the dataset was spatially resized to 346×194, since proposed approach is mainly based in kinematic features captured from temporal correlations. The whole experiments were computed with volumetric patches of $15 \times 15 \times 5$ with kinematic histograms of 7 bins for HOOF and 14 bins for MBH (both directions) and 5 bins for HDIV y HROT features. A total of 31 scalar values constitutes the dimension for each considered patch. Regarding, the ASL64 corpus the recognition strategy was validated by using a k-fold cross validation with a $k = 10$. At each iteration, a signer was tested while other 9 signers were used for training model.

In a first experiment, were evaluated different mid-level representation with different coding strategies over the LSA64 corpus. In whole experiments was considered only patches that have motion information, i.e., patches computed mainly from foreground signers. In order to evaluate the capability of representations to recognize partial and incomplete utterances, several incremental sub-set of input patches were considered to built the dictionary. In Fig. 3 is illustrated the performance of different representation and codings. In Fig. 3-left is shown the proposed HA-SDVLAD w.r.t classical bag of words representation using hard and soft assignment representation. As reported, the SD-VLAD representation achieved a better description of utterances and its able to represent partial signs with 80% of accuracy using only the 60% of information. In Fig. 3-middle is reported several configuration for VLAD representation. As expected, the best performance is achieved by the hard assignment (HA) in SDVLAD because the proper codification of salient sign patterns in both local and regional characterization. At Fig. 3-right is observe the contribution for hard assignment (HA) coding in the proposed representation achieving 85% of accuracy for complete utterances. Also, it should be mentioned that the proposed strategy is able to capture partial utterance only using the 60% of information and even with the 40% of information achieved plus of 70% of accuracy.

In a second experiment (see in Fig. 4) was evaluated the performance of proposed approach in individual signers using different representations. In whole

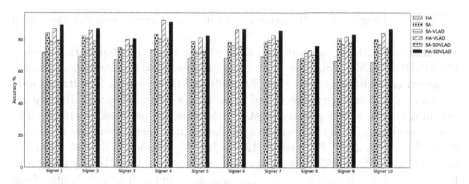

Fig. 4. A individual signer analysis is carried out from different mid-level representations for LSA64.

signers performance the HA-SDVLAD approach achieve the best representation of signs, thanks to shape representation of kinematic clusters. Particularly for signer 8 there exist some limitations because strong noise variation in temporal recording such as hair movement. Other noise artifacts occupy more than 25% of spatial video area.

A complete analysis of analyzed gestures is reported in confusion matrix of Fig. 5. As expected the proposed approach is able to recognize almost perfectly whole considered sign gestures with some limitations in particular gestures that share more than the 90% of dynamic gesture information. For instance the particular sign "realize" is misclassified w.r.t to sign "buy" because in almost whole

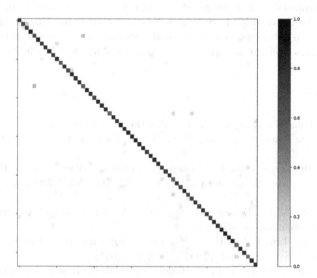

Fig. 5. The confusion matrix obtained with the LS64 dataset. The proposed approach achieves an average score close to 85% for the multi-class recognition

utterance the gestures are the same except in a local finger action at the end of gestures.

Additionally, the proposed motion descriptor was evaluated in the classical RWTH-BOSTON50 [18]. This dataset has widely used to test strategies in realistic scenarios, containing more than 50 words and three signers. The frames were recorded at 30 frames per second and frame size is 195 × 165 pixels. To compare obtained results, it was selected a set of utterance like proposed in [18,20]. The considered words (with the respective number of utterances) are: *can* (19), *something* (12), *house* (12), *Possession* (12), *ix far* (12), *woman* (8), *break-down* (5), *new* (7), *not* (7), *like*(6). The recognition strategy was validated by using a k-fold cross validation with a $k = 10$. The proposed approach achieved outperform conventional approaches obtaining an average accuracy of 82%.

4   Conclusions

In this work was proposed a novel approach to describe gestures from a shape difference VLAD representation of kinematic volumes. The proposed approach is relative invariant to appearance, robust to occlusion and recover salient regions of the gestures coded in the computed dictionary. From a corpus with more than 3000 utterance videos and five signers, the proposed method achieved 85% of accuracy in average. Also the proposed approach was evaluated over a classical Boston dataset obtaining a 82% of accuracy in average. Future works include continuous representations of gestures to achieve on-line translation in SLR and frame-level evaluation to built a grammatically more complex models.

Acknowledgments. The authors acknowledge the Vicerrectoría de Investigación y Extensión of the Universidad Industrial de Santander for supporting this research registered by the project: Análisis de movimientos salientes en espacios comprimidos para la caracterización eficiente de videos multiespectrales, with VIE code 2347"

References

1. Ali, S., Shah, M.: Human action recognition in videos using kinematic features and multiple instance learning. IEEE Trans. Pattern Anal. Mach. Intell. **32**(2), 288–303 (2010)
2. Brox, T., Bregler, C., Malik, J.: Large displacement optical flow. In: IEEE Conference on Computer Vision and Pattern Recognition, CVPR 2009, pp. 41–48. IEEE (2009)
3. WHO Media Centre: Deafness and hearing loss, March 2018. http://www.who.int/mediacentre/factsheets/fs300/en/
4. Chang, C.C., Lin, C.J.: LIBSVM: a library for support vector machines. ACM Trans. Intell. Syst. Technol. (TIST) **2**(3), 27 (2011)
5. Chaudhry, R., Ravichandran, A., Hager, G., Vidal, R.: Histograms of oriented optical flow and Binet-Cauchy kernels on nonlinear dynamical systems for the recognition of human actions. In: IEEE Conference on Computer Vision and Pattern Recognition, CVPR 2009, pp. 1932–1939. IEEE (2009)

6. Dalal, N., Triggs, B., Schmid, C.: Human detection using oriented histograms of flow and appearance. In: Leonardis, A., Bischof, H., Pinz, A. (eds.) ECCV 2006. LNCS, vol. 3952, pp. 428–441. Springer, Heidelberg (2006). https://doi.org/10. 1007/11744047_33

7. Duta, I.C., Uijlings, J.R., Ionescu, B., Aizawa, K., Hauptmann, A.G., Sebe, N.: Efficient human action recognition using histograms of motion gradients and vlad with descriptor shape information. Multimedia Tools Appl. **76**, 22445–22472 (2017)

8. Jain, M., Jegou, H., Bouthemy, P.: Better exploiting motion for better action recognition. In: Proceedings of the IEEE Conference on Computer Vision and Pattern Recognition, pp. 2555–2562 (2013)

9. Jégou, H., Douze, M., Schmid, C., Pérez, P.: Aggregating local descriptors into a compact image representation. In: 2010 IEEE Conference on Computer Vision and Pattern Recognition (CVPR), pp. 3304–3311. IEEE (2010)

10. Konecnỳ, J., Hagara, M.: One-shot-learning gesture recognition using HOG-HOF. J. Mach. Learn. Res. **15**, 2513–2532 (2014)

11. Martínez, F., Manzanera, A., Gouiffès, M., Braffort, A.: A Gaussian mixture representation of gesture kinematics for on-line sign language video annotation. In: Bebis, G., et al. (eds.) ISVC 2015. LNCS, vol. 9475, pp. 293–303. Springer, Cham (2015). https://doi.org/10.1007/978-3-319-27863-6_27

12. Paulraj, M., Yaacob, S., Desa, H., Hema, C., Ridzuan, W.M., Ab Majid, W.: Extraction of head and hand gesture features for recognition of sign language. In: International Conference on Electronic Design, ICED 2008, pp. 1–6. IEEE (2008)

13. Peng, X., Wang, L., Wang, X., Qiao, Y.: Bag of visual words and fusion methods for action recognition: comprehensive study and good practice. Comput. Vis. Image Underst. **150**, 109–125 (2016)

14. Perronnin, F., Sánchez, J., Mensink, T.: Improving the Fisher Kernel for large-scale image classification. In: Daniilidis, K., Maragos, P., Paragios, N. (eds.) ECCV 2010. LNCS, vol. 6314, pp. 143–156. Springer, Heidelberg (2010). https://doi.org/ 10.1007/978-3-642-15561-1_11

15. Ronchetti, F., Quiroga, F., Estrebou, C.A., Lanzarini, L.C., Rosete, A.: LSA64: an Argentinian sign language dataset. In: XXII Congreso Argentino de Ciencias de la Computación (CACIC 2016) (2016)

16. Wan, J., Ruan, Q., Li, W., Deng, S.: One-shot learning gesture recognition from RGB-D data using bag of features. J. Mach. Learn. Res. **14**(1), 2549–2582 (2013)

17. Zafrulla, Z., Brashear, H., Starner, T., Hamilton, H., Presti, P.: American sign language recognition with the kinect. In: Proceedings of the 13th International Conference on Multimodal Interfaces, pp. 279–286. ACM (2011)

18. Zahedi, M., Keysers, D., Deselaers, T., Ney, H.: Combination of tangent distance and an image distortion model for appearance-based sign language recognition. In: Kropatsch, W.G., Sablatnig, R., Hanbury, A. (eds.) DAGM 2005. LNCS, vol. 3663, pp. 401–408. Springer, Heidelberg (2005). https://doi.org/10.1007/11550518_50

19. Zahedi, M., Keysers, D., Ney, H.: Appearance-based recognition of words in American sign language. In: Marques, J.S., Pérez de la Blanca, N., Pina, P. (eds.) IbPRIA 2005. LNCS, vol. 3522, pp. 511–519. Springer, Heidelberg (2005). https://doi.org/ 10.1007/11492429_62

20. Zaki, M.M., Shaheen, S.I.: Sign language recognition using a combination of new vision based features. Pattern Recogn. Lett. **32**(4), 572–577 (2011)

Security and Protection

Camera Sensor Traces Analysis in Image Forgery Detection Problem

Andrey Kuznetsov[1,2]([envelope]) [iD]

[1] Samara National Research University, Samara, Russia
kuznetsoff.andrey@gmail.com
[2] Image Processing Systems Institute of RAS – Branch of the FSRC
"Crystallography and Photonics" RAS, Samara, Russian Federation

Abstract. One of the most frequently used types of image forgery is embedding another image fragment in some part of the image. In this article a methods for this type of forgeries detection is proposed. The method is based on the analysis of traces introduced by the camera sensor used to obtain an image. The analyzed image is divided into blocks, for each block we calculate a criterion valued determining the probability of presence/absence of CFA artifacts and, as a consequence, the probability of whether the block is a forgery is calculated. In the experimental part of the work, the accuracy of the detection of the embedded regions is analyzed. We also analyze the robustness of the proposed algorithm to various types of distortions: additive Gaussian noise, JPEG compression and linear contrast enhancement. The results of the experiments showed that the method makes it possible to detect embedded regions of various nature, shape and size, and is also robust to additive Gaussian noise and linear contrast enhancement for a given range of distortions parameters, but is not robust to JPEG compression. A distinctive feature of the method is the ability to identify embedded regions with a minimum size of 2×2 pixels.

1 Introduction

A large number of digital devices used to obtain images has led to a decrease in their cost and, as a consequence, to their wide availability for everyone. At the same time the number of software tools for image processing has increased significantly. All this influenced a widespread image forgery creation. In the modern world any user can make changes in the image, which can not be detected by an expert. In addition, if it comes to professional forgery, then even existing software tools for verifying the authenticity of images can not detect it. There are many examples in military and political spheres, in media and many other areas where image forgeries were detected. They were created for committing crimes, concealing some facts or receiving public resonance. In this regard, the issue of image protection and verification of their authenticity was sharply raised.

Depending on the intended purpose of forgery creation, images can be distorted by retouching or copy-move attack. The methods of retouching detection

© Springer Nature Switzerland AG 2018
L. J. Chmielewski et al. (Eds.): ICCVG 2018, LNCS 11114, pp. 453–463, 2018.
https://doi.org/10.1007/978-3-030-00692-1_39

are proposed in [1], and copy-move detection algorithms are presented in [2]. Another frequently used forgery type is embedding of areas from another image to the source image, also called photomontage [3].

To protect images from this type of forgery, it is possible to embed a digital watermark in them [4]. However, this method has several pros and cons. For example, its application is limited, since authentication in this case can only be done by the owner of the data.

Other solutions have been developed that do not require the embedding of additional information into the image. In particular, they include those methods that analyze the characteristics of the camera sensor to detect the forgery. One of these characteristics is the color filter array (CFA), which is used in most modern recording devices. It is a part of the photosensitive matrix of the photodetector, which performs spatial color separation of the image with the help of photo sensors - pixels of the matrix located behind filters of different colors. The presence of a CFA filter in the device leads to the fact that the images obtained with it, contain artifacts, also called CFA artifacts [5]. In other words, CFA artifacts are local image distortions caused by the presence of a CFA filter in the recording device with which the image was obtained. CFA-artifacts are unique for each recording device.

For example, in [6], a method for CFA artifacts detection in an image is described. Within the framework of the method, a map of the probability of CFA artifacts presence is calculated for the image, then the Fourier transform (FT) is calculated for this map. The analysis of FT peaks leads to changed areas detection. With small modifications, the method can be used to detect distortions in an image of a size of 256×256 or more.

Similarly, based on the fact that CFA artifacts have a periodic structure, in [7] the authors present an algorithm for image forgery detection and to determine whether it was obtained with a digital device or artificially generated. The work of the method is also based on the analysis of Fourier spectrum. The absence of CFA artifacts indicates that the area has been altered, artificially generated, or the CFA filter is not used in the recording device. This method is applicable for detection of distortions on images of size 64×64 or more, which is due to the use of Fourier transform.

This paper is devoted to the investigation of one of the methods for detecting embeddings in images based on the analysis of CFA artifacts. One can detect distortions with a minimum size of 2×2 using the proposed solution. The result of applying the proposed method is the image distortion probability map, which is a two-dimensional array, each element of which contains the distortion probability of the corresponding local area in the image. At the same time the designed algorithm has low computational complexity.

2   Color Filter Array (CFA)

In most modern cameras, a color filter array is used to obtain a color image. There are a number of types of CFA filters, the most frequently used is the Bayer filter, which is shown on Fig. 1.

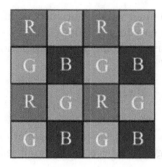

Fig. 1. Bayer filter

When light flows through the CFA filter and the sensor, a RAW file is created. Each pixel of this file contains only one color channel data (it is usually a green channel), which means that only one third of the color information of the image is presented in the RAW file. In addition, this file stores EXIF data, containing information about the snapshot creation date and time, the recording device, the parameters of the image obtaining, etc. Since RAW contains only one color channel data a demosaicing algorithm is used to obtain a color RGB image. This leads to a correlation between pixels within each channel or CFA-artifacts which are in fact local image distortions determined by the camera characteristics [8].

A schematic view of the green image channel (red and blue channel are processed likewise) after interpolation is presented on Fig. 2. A corresponds to the values obtained during image registration (acquired), I corresponds to the values calculated by means of interpolation or demosaicing algorithm (interpolated).

Fig. 2. Green image channel (A - acquired pixels, I - interpolated pixels)

When using bilinear interpolation green channel values $s(x, y)$ are calculated as follows:

$$s(x,y) = \begin{cases} G_A(x,y), & (x,y) \in A \\ G_I(x,y) = \sum_u \sum_v h(u,v) \times G_A(x-u, y-v), & (x,y) \in I \end{cases} \quad (1)$$

where $G_A(x, y)$ - green channel values obtained in image registration process, $G_I(x, y)$ - interpolated green channel values, $h(u, v)$ - interpolation kernel. In the proposed solution we use the following interpolation kernel:

$$h(x, y) = \frac{1}{4} \times \begin{bmatrix} 0 & 1 & 0 \\ 1 & 4 & 1 \\ 0 & 1 & 0 \end{bmatrix} \tag{2}$$

During forgery creation process the pixels correlations introduced by interpolation are violated or changed. This is a major point leading to forgery detection algorithm development.

3 The Proposed Forgery Detection Method

3.1 Theoretical Justification

Let $s(x)$ be a 1D green channel of an image. It is calculated according to (1). Odd values of x correspond to acquired pixel values, even x values correspond to interpolated values. Prediction error can be calculated as follows:

$$e(x, y) = s(x) - \sum_u k(u)s(x + u), \tag{3}$$

where $k(u)$ is a prediction kernel. It should be mentioned that if $h(u)$ of the recording device is known then $k(u) = h(u)$ and prediction error equals to 0. If we substitute 1D form of (1) in (3) we receive the following prediction error equation:

$$e(x) = \begin{cases} G_A(x) - \sum_u k(u)s(x + u), & x(\mathrm{mod}\ 2) = 0 \\ \sum_u h(u)G_A(x + u) - \sum_u k(u)s(x + u), & x(\mathrm{mod}\ 2) \neq 0 \end{cases} \tag{4}$$

In practice when we calculate prediction error only even u values are meaningful for error value estimation. According to this assumption (4) can be evaluated as follows:

$$e(x) = \begin{cases} G_A(x) - \sum_u k(u) \sum_v h(v)G_A(x + u + v), & x(\mathrm{mod}\ 2) = 0 \\ \sum_u (h(u) - k(u))G_A(x + u), & x(\mathrm{mod}\ 2) \neq 0 \end{cases} \tag{5}$$

Assuming that pixel values are independent and equally distributed with mean μ_G and variance σ_G^2, prediction error mean can be calculated as follows:

$$E[e(x)] = \begin{cases} \mu_G - \mu_G \sum_u k(u) \sum_v h(v), & x(\mathrm{mod}\ 2) = 0 \\ \mu_G \sum_u \big(h(u) - k(u)\big), & x(\mathrm{mod}\ 2) \neq 0 \end{cases} \tag{6}$$

The variance for x values is calculated as follows:

$$Var[e(x)] = \begin{cases} \sigma_G^2\left[\left(1 - \sum_u k(u)h(-u)\right)^2 + \sum_t \left(\sum_u k(u)h(t-u)\right)^2\right], & x - odd \\ \sigma_G^2 \sum_u \left(h(u) - k(u)\right)^2, & else \end{cases}$$

$$(7)$$

On the basis of the above calculations, it can be concluded that the prediction error variance is proportional to the variance of the values obtained during image registration. However, if the prediction kernel and the interpolation kernel are the same, then the variance of the error for acquired pixels values is significantly higher than the variance of the error for interpolated values.

3.2   Forgery Detection Algorithm Development

In case the image was not obtained by applying the demosaicing algorithm or was changed, the demosaicing artifacts are violated, so the variance of the prediction error for both types of values (acquired and interpolated) will have close values within a certain range of ϵ. Therefore, in order to identify the presence or absence of these interpolation artifacts, it is necessary to calculate the variance of the prediction error for acquired and interpolated values.

Let prediction error be stationary in a window $(2K+1) \times (2K+1)$, $c = 1 - \sum_{i=-K}^{K} \sum_{j=-K}^{K} \alpha^2(i,j)$ - scaling factor, $\mu_e = \sum_{i=-K}^{K} \sum_{j=-K}^{K} \alpha(i,j)e(x+i,y+j)$ - locally-weighted mean of prediction error, $\alpha'(i,j) = W(i,j)$ if $e(x+i,y+j)$ and $e(x,y)$ are values of the same type, W - Gauss smooth filter with size $(2K+1) \times (2K+1)$ with mean square deviation $\sigma_W^2 = \frac{K}{2}$. Then locally-weighted variance of prediction error is calculated as follows:

$$\sigma_e^2(x,y) = \frac{1}{c}\left(\sum_{i=-K}^{K} \sum_{j=-K}^{K} \alpha(i,j)e^2(x+i,y+j) - \mu_e^2\right), \tag{8}$$

where $\alpha(i,j) = \frac{\alpha'(i,j)}{\sum_{i=-K}^{K} \sum_{j=-K}^{K} \alpha'(i,j)}$.

3.3   Main Criterion Calculation

After evaluation of the locally-weighted variance of the prediction error, a criterion that characterizes the ratio of variances of the prediction error in the acquired and interpolated pixels is calculated. Based on the obtained criterion values, it is possible to determine the presence or absence of CFA artifacts in the image.

Let the size of the analyzed image be $N \times N$, then we can calculate the criterion for each of the disjoint image fragments of size $B \times B$. The block value must be related to the size of the Bayer filter, with a minimum allowable block size 2×2. The matrix of the obtained values of prediction error variance is divided into blocks of size $B \times B$ Each block $B_{k,l}$ contains variance values of acquired and interpolated pixels, which we will denote as $B_{k,l}^A$ and $B_{k,l}^I$ respectively.

In order to form a criterion to determine distorted or undistorted block, we will use the geometric mean of locally-weighted variances of the prediction error within the selected image fragment. It is worth noting that you can also use any other averaging measure, for example, the arithmetic mean to get some characteristic value of fragment distortion.

Let $GM_A(k, l)$ be the geometric mean value of prediction error variance for acquired pixels A in the block $B_{k,l}$ and is calculated as follows:

$$GM_A(k, l) = \Big[\prod_{i,j \in B_A(k,l)} \sigma_e^2(i, j) \Big]^{\frac{1}{|B_{k,l}^A|}}, \tag{9}$$

$GM_I(k, l)$ be the geometric mean value of prediction error variance for interpolated pixels I in the block $B_{k,l}$ and is calculated as follows:

$$GM_I(k, l) = \Big[\prod_{i,j \in B_I(k,l)} \sigma_e^2(i, j) \Big]^{\frac{1}{|B_{k,l}^I|}}, \tag{10}$$

then the criterion value is evaluated using the following equation:

$$L(k, l) = ln \Big[\frac{GM_A(k, l)}{GM_I(k, l)} \Big]. \tag{11}$$

If there are CFA artifacts in the image block $B_{k,l}$ and it was obtained as a result of applying the demosaicing algorithm, then the variance value will be higher for acquired pixels A, so the value of the criterion $L(k, l)$ will be positive. However, if the image was obtained in another way, then the prediction error variance for the two types of pixels will have close values within a certain range ϵ, hence the value $L(k, l)$ will be close to zero within the selected ϵ range.

If some image part was distorted, then in order to make the forgery more realistic, it is accompanied by other processes: smoothing, compression, etc. All this steps violate the artifacts caused by the interpolation process and as a consequence leads to the violation of CFA artifacts. Therefore, the values of L criterion in the changed image will be non-uniform: in some areas these value will be much higher than zero, which is a consequence of the presence of CFA artifacts, and in other areas where CFA artifacts are absent, the criterion value will be close to zero within the selected neighborhood. This fact can be used to detect distortions in images by evaluating the probability of CFA artifacts presence in each block using criterion values. This is why it is possible to determine the probability map of CFA artifacts presence. To solve this problem the Expectation-Maximization (EM) algorithm is used. However, this step is out of scope of the current paper and will not be described in details.

4 Experimental Results

We took 4 RAW files from the database [9] to carry out research experiments. The selected images were obtained from 4 different cameras that use Bayer filter:

Canon EOS 450D, Nikon D50, Nikon D90 and Nikon D7000. The type of filter used is taken from technical documentation of these cameras. To obtain an RGB TIFF image from a RAW file, we used dcraw tool. Images used in investigations have sizes 3000 × 2000 pixels.

Two types of embedded fragments were used to create forgeries: artificially created images and images taken from sources, which have different interpolation artifacts. Figure 3 shows an example of an image with an arbitrary shape insert and the corresponding distortion probability map computed for a block size 8×8. The embedded area was obtained by another camera.

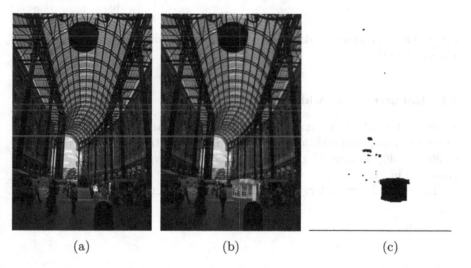

(a)   (b)   (c)

Fig. 3. Initial image (a), forgery (b), probability map computed for a block size 8×8 (c)

It should be noted that the algorithm is able to detect distortions of very small sizes, so the probability distortion map can be calculated for blocks with a minimum size 2×2. Let the size of the region to be embedded in the image equals $M \times M$. The dependency of forgery detection quality from the embedded region size is shown in Fig. 4. We use true positive and false positive measures to estimate the quality of the proposed solution: $R_{TP}(M)$ and $R_{FP}(M)$ respectively.

The results of the experiments showed that with the increase in the size of the embedded area, the detection quality increases also and reaches a maximum value of 1 at size 512×512, however with a minimum checked embedding size 32× 32 $R_{TP} = 0.93$, which characterizes a high detection quality. At the same time, the number of false detected undistorted image blocks increases insignificantly and at size of the embedded area 1024 × 1024 reaches $R_{FP} = 0.0133$.

We also carried out research on robustness of the proposed solution to different types of distortions of embedded areas: additive Gaussian noise and JPEG compression.

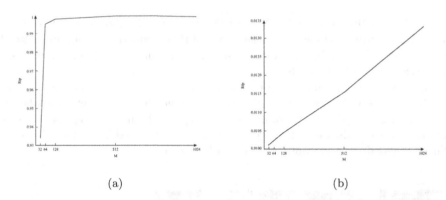

(a)   (b)

Fig. 4. The dependency of detection quality from embedded area size: $R_{TP}(M)$ (a) and $R_{FP}(M)$ (b)

4.1 Robustness to Additive Gaussian Noise

We fixed the embedded area size 128×128 and created 40 test forgery images. Every test image was additionally distorted with additive noise with SNR equals to 30, 35, 40, 45 and 50 dB. The results of the experiment carried out are presented in Figs. 5 and 6.

The dependency of forgery detection quality from SNR values is shown in Fig. 6.

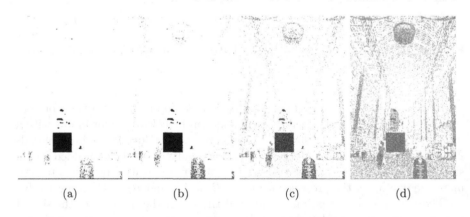

(a)   (b)   (c)   (d)

Fig. 5. Probability maps for SNR = 50 (a), 45 (b), 40 (c), 35 (d)

The results of the experiment showed that the number of true detected distorted blocks in the image is large for a given range of SNR values, but at $SNR = 35$ dB or less, the number of false detected blocks increases, so we can say that the proposed method works for $SNR > 35$ dB.

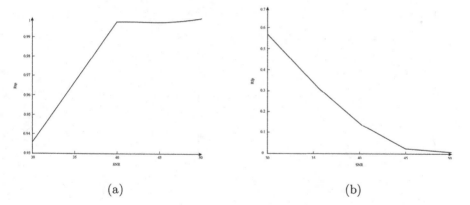

(a)   (b)

Fig. 6. The dependency of detection quality from SNR values: $R_{TP}(M)$ (a) and $R_{FP}(M)$ (b)

4.2   Robustness to JPEG Compression

We then applied JPEG compression to the forgery image with different values of compression quality Q. In Fig. 7 probability maps are shown for Q equals 100, 98, 96 and 94.

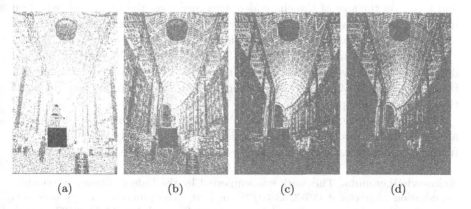

(a)   (b)   (c)   (d)

Fig. 7. Probability maps for Q = 100 (a), 98 (b), 96 (c), 94 (d)

The dependency of forgery detection quality from compression quality Q values is shown in Fig. 8.

From the results obtained, it can be seen that the proposed method is not robust to JPEG compression - even at high quality parameter values the number of false detections is high for $Q = 92$ and equals to $R_{FP}(Q) = 0.803$. Such a result can be considered a confirmation of the obvious assumption. The use of JPEG algorithm violates interpolation artifacts on the image, which leads to a rapid increase in false detected image fragments.

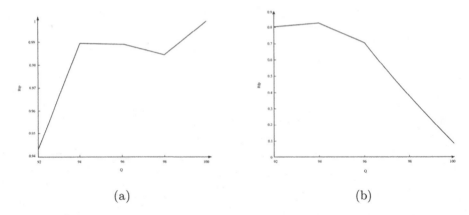

(a)   (b)

Fig. 8. The dependency of detection quality from compression quality Q values: $R_{TP}(M)$ (a) and $R_{FP}(M)$ (b)

5 Conclusion

The method for image forgery detection is proposed in this paper. The algorithm is based on CFA artifacts analysis in images. During the conducted researches it was established that it allows to detect embedded areas of various nature and form. As the size of the embedded area increases, the quality of detection increases, and the number of false positives increases slightly. The minimum size of embedded area that can be detected is 2×2.

Experimental studies also showed that the algorithm is resistant to such distortions as additive Gaussian noise with $SNR > 35$ dB. However, the method is not robust to JPEG compression. Even for high values compression quality Q the number of false positives is high.

The proposed method can be used to verify the authenticity of images. It allows to find embedded areas of very small sizes, but its use is limited and further investigations in this field are needed.

Acknowledgements. This work was supported by the Federal Agency of scientific organization (Agreement 007-3/43363/26) in part "The proposed forgery detection method" and by the Russian Foundation for Basic Research (no. 17-29-03190) in part "Experimental results".

References

1. Choi, C., Lee, H.: Estimation of color modification in digital images by CFA pattern change. Forensic Sci. Int. **226**, 1013–1015 (2013)
2. Evdokimova, N., Kuznetsov, A.: Local patterns in the copy-move detection problem solution. Comput. Opt. **41**(1), 79–87 (2017)
3. Burvin, P.S., Esther, J.M.: Analysis of digital image splicing detection. IOSR J. Comput. Eng. (IOSR-JCE) **16**(2), 10–13 (2014)

4. Snigdha, K.M., Ajay, A.G.: Image forgery types and their detection. Int. J. Adv. Res. Comput. Sci. Softw. Eng. **5**(4), 174–178 (2015)
5. Ferrara, P., Bianchi, T., Rosa, A., Piva, A.: Image forgery localization via fine-grained analysis of CFA artifacts. IEEE Trans. Inf. Forensics Secur. **7**(5), 1566–1577 (2012)
6. Popescu, A., Farid, H.: Exposing digital forgeries in color filter array interpolated images. IEEE Trans. Signal Process. **53**(10), 3948–3959 (2005)
7. Gallagher, A., Chen, T.: Image authentication by detecting traces of demosaicing. In: IEEE Computer Society Conference on Computer Vision and Pattern Recognition Workshops, pp. 1–8 (2008)
8. Li, L., Hue, J., Wang, X., Tian, L.: A robust approach to detect digital forgeries by exploring correlation patterns. Pattern Anal. Appl. **18**(2), 351–365 (2015)
9. Bayram, S., Sencar, H., Memon, N., Avcibas, I.: Source camera identification based on CFA interpolation. IEEE Image Process. **3**, 63–72 (2005)

Barcoding in Biometrics and Its Development

Nazym Kaziyeva[1]([⊠]), Georgy Kukharev[2], and Yuri Matveev[1]

[1] ITMO University, Saint Petersburg 197101, Russia
kaznaz@list.ru, matveev@mail.ifmo.ru
[2] State Electrotechnical University "LETI", Saint Petersburg 197376, Russia
kuga@gmail.com
http://www.ifmo.ru/

Abstract. The problems of using barcoding in biometrics and its applications are discussed. An overview of the existing solutions to this problem is presented for the different biometric modalities: face, iris, fingerprints, DNA, voice, etc. It is shown that the factor limiting the use of barcoding in biometrics was the low capacity of barcodes. It is noted that at present this problem is being solved within the framework of color barcodes. In this case, the problems of barcoding in biometrics and its applications can be solved in a new way, and examples of these solutions are given in the article.

Keywords: Biometrics · Biometric modalities · Barcoding · Linear Two-dimensional and color barcodes

1 Introduction

In recent years, barcodes have been widely included in our everyday life, we read them on streets, on checks in shops and payment orders in banks, on the goods and products bought, tags of clothes and luggage, in registration coupons, we introduce ourselves on badges and stickers, etc.

The barcodes "live their own independent life" and rapidly "grab" more and more new applications. At first, simple linear barcodes were transformed into composite (composed of several linear) codes, then into two-dimensional barcodes (readable in any directions), and now three-layer and multi-layer color barcodes have already appeared.

Among applications of barcoding, biometrics and its applications - medicine and criminalistics - are of interest. So in medicine, barcodes are used in information systems for registration, recording and tracking patients of medical institutions, drawing up medical records and referrals to procedures, extracts and prescriptions. And, since the appropriate barcodes are used in such document circulation, the identification of patients, the compilation of all documents is implemented very quickly. At the same time in biometrics, and especially in facial biometrics and related criminalistics, barcoding is used less actively and,

© Springer Nature Switzerland AG 2018
L. J. Chmielewski et al. (Eds.): ICCVG 2018, LNCS 11114, pp. 464–471, 2018.
https://doi.org/10.1007/978-3-030-00692-1_40

as practice shows - literally in single examples. At the same time, the need to use barcodes in biometrics has been noted since the end of the last century, as exemplified by an article written 20 years ago [1].

In view of the foregoing, the purpose of this article is to review the known solutions to the barcoding in biometrics according to its basic modalities: the face and its phenotype, the iris of the eye, fingerprints, DNA, voice, etc.

2   Overview of Barcoding Solutions in Biometrics

In the information systems of various companies, barcodes are used when issuing confirmation documents (route receipt, air tickets, transaction documents, etc.), names of Internet sites for purchasing goods, a register of unique identifiers of scientists (ORCID), etc. These examples of barcoding are related to the mobility of people, their professional activities and current affairs, which is also associated with the identification of people in their daily lives.

A more complete and detailed overview of barcoding solutions directly related to biometrics is presented below.

The first application of linear barcodes for the identification of persons during electronic transactions was presented in [2]. The barcode was placed on the person's hand, but in fact it was not his biometric identifier. And, here it should be noted that biometric information about a person is quite big in size and specific in the way it is presented and received. Therefore, its storage and use in the form of the linear barcodes was almost impossible.

The problem of capturing persons biometric information and reducing the amount of this information is still relevant, as evidenced by the publication [3]. The authors of this publication suggested to store information about the shape and phenotype of a persons face in a two-dimensional barcode, which required a substantial simplification of all information about a person's phenotype. Applications of this method in practice aren't known.

The second example, related to the large amount of biometric information, is given in [4], which presents an approach to human identification based on a genetic barcode. The method is not standard and, therefore, the authors of [15] translated the nucleotide sequence from [4] to the QR code shown on the right side. In this case, all information including the nucleotide sequence is easily decoded from the QR code. An example of the "direct degeneration" of a fingerprint into a linear barcode is shown in [5]. And, although the solutions in [5] are original, they don't use standard barcodes and, therefore, have not been developed further.

In [6], a method is presented for transforming a person's signature into the format of a signature reference and recording this reference into a QR code. The high efficiency of this approach is noted even at change of dynamic parameters of a signature. It is not known whether this method is applied in practice.

In [7,16], the authors developed the idea of a "humans biological barcode" and showed a method for recording the phenotype of a person's face in the form of linear barcodes EAN-8 and EAN-13. This allows us to identify the face even in its daily and age changes. However, the solutions proposed have not been used due to the limited capacity of EAN-8 and EAN-13 codes and the inability to store symbolic information and special signs. The downside of using EAN-8 and EAN-13 codes is also the need to use the first three barcode characters as a service information (country of the manufacturer of a product) or as a loose barcode with a "200–299 prefix". The further development of this approach can be done with the use of Code 128, as well as color linear and two-dimensional barcodes, as noted in [15]. In grounding of interest in the phenotype, we note that if we do not know the phenotype of the persons face we are looking for, we cannot find and recognize faces in a crowd and even in not very large face databases.

In [8], it is shown how to store minutiae triplets of fingerprints in the QR code. Obviously, this method is promising because it uses traditional human's identification by fingerprints and at the same time the standard way of storing information in the QR code.

In [9], the idea of a compact (after compression) representation of the iris image in the form of a nonstandard barcode is discussed. However, it is widely known that the iris image is easily converted into "own barcode" by its transforming into a polar coordinate system.

In [10], a method for encoding a speech signal into a binary code and recording it in a QR code format is shown. It is not known, however, how wide this approach is applied in practice.

In [11], a representation of full-size images of faces and fingerprints (represented in the GRAY scale) in the lower bits of the black strokes of the PDF417 barcode, represented by three slices is presented. The recording is implemented using the watermarking method. However, the addresses of the pixels of the PDF417 barcode for writing and reading embedded information in them must also be transferred or calculated again at the "reception the end", which significantly complicates the use of the method [11].

The characteristics of the above barcodes can be found on the website [12]: "Barcode Comparison Chart"-
http://www.makebarcode.com/specs/barcodechart.html.

Table 1 shows the dynamics of barcode capacity growth for the recording of alphanumeric characters over the past 40 years [12,13]. The details of the barcode solutions discussed above in biometrics are presented in Table 2.

Table 1. Capacity growth (alphanumeric information) of barcodes

Type/Year	1D/1977	1D/1981	2D/1991	2D/1991	2D/1994	2D/2013
Name	EAN-13	Code 128	PDF 417	Data matrix	QR code	Color QR code
Capacitance	13	128	1850	2335	7089	3x7089

Recently, color barcodes (Color 2D barcode [13]) are used for barcoding, which "solve problems of the barcode capacity" and, thus, open up new

Table 2. Characteristics of barcodes in biometrics

Biometric modality	Initial data	Proposed solution	Barcode standard	Source
DNA	Sequence of nucleotides	Recording into a linear barcode	No solutions	[4]
		QR code		[15]
Face	Color image in YCbCr format	Simplification of a color palette	QR code	[3]
	Full-size face image in GRAY format	Face phenotype - brightness histogram or gradients of brightness	EAN-8, EAN-13	[7]
		Watermarks embedded into the dark regions of the PDF 417 barcode	PDF 417	[11]
Fingerprint	Full-size fingerprint in GRAY format	Fingerprint converts into a specific linear barcode	No solutions	[5]
		Image compression and pixel-by-pixel recording	No solutions	[9]
	Parameters of Minutiae: coordinates and direction of popilary lines	The triplets of minutiae matrix is used as a message in the QR code	QR code	[8]
Iris	Iris image	Image compression and pixel-by-pixel recording	No solutions	[9]
Signature	Signature on a tablet	Preprocessing, features extraction and selection, creation of signature templates	QR code	[6]
Voice	Speech signal	Binarization of a speech signal	QR code	[10]

possibilities for using barcoding in biometrics and its applications. Color 2D barcodes may contain 3 or more layers. For example, a color QR code with three layers is, in fact, a color image, each layer of which is a separate QR code. The capacity of such a barcode is 3x7098 alphanumeric characters.

In [14], it is shown how to embed a digital image into a QR code and/or QR code into a digital image. However, the method in [14] has some drawbacks: the QR code in the image leads to a certain decrease in the probability of detecting read errors. The capacity of a color image is inefficiently used (all three layers of the image are "nested" with the same message). But, it is important to note that the image of a person's face with a QR code embedded in it is an almost ready solution for barcoding in biometrics if the image and the contents of the barcode embedded in it represent information of the same person. At the same time, the visibility (accessibility) of a facial image can be both a plus (for example, for a badge) and a minus, as the coding (or hiding) of a facial image automatically leads to invisibility (inaccessibility) of this image embedded in the barcode.

3   New Solutions for Biometrics and Its Applications

As an example of a new solution, in the Fig. 1 shows a QR code containing anthropometric points of a face, obtained in computer interactive mode. This system is designed for integration into mobile devices (smartphone).

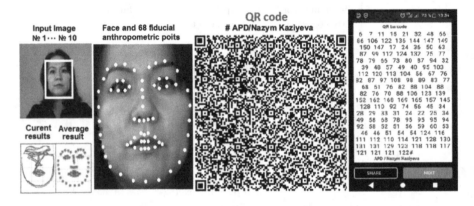

Fig. 1. The QR code that stores anthropometric points of the facial image

The QR code is generated online using a set of coordinates of anthropometric points (APP) on the persons facial image and information about the person. The following tasks are implemented: entering a user information (NAME) in dialog with the user; online face detection in frames of a video sequence from a camera; detecting APP coordinates in each frame; averaging the APP coordinates over several frames; composing a message with the averaged APP coordinates and NAME information; embedding the message into a standard QR code; saving the QR code into computer memory; controlling decoding of the stored QR code and extracting the message from it; displaying and comparing the generated and decoded messages. The screen of the smartphone presents the coordinates of the values of APPs, received from the QR code. Such QR code can be used in ID-systems, in medicine, in criminology. Search 68 APP is based on the procedures of the library "dlib". Algorithms for encoding and decoding QR code uses the library "zxing".

Examples of color barcodes for biometrics and their applications (based on the solutions shown above) are shown in Fig. 2.

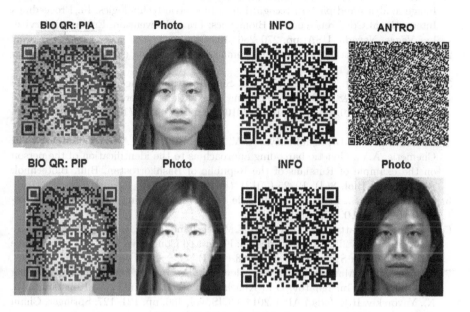

Fig. 2. Examples of QR codes for biometrics (BIO QR [15])

Generally, color QR codes for biometrics and its applications contain at least one layer with a QR code and some additional layers with any complementary information (for example, GRAY scale images).

4   Conclusion and Recommendations

The paper reviews the solutions of barcoding for biometrics. From the presented review it is clear that the problem of barcoding in biometrics is practically not solved. New solutions for biometric barcoding and related tasks should be sought in the use of color QR codes. At the same time, the hottest tasks are the barcoding in facial images; adaptation of digital facial anthropometry to barcoding; development of the ideas of a person's phenotype within the framework of barcoding; the use of color 2D barcodes as a media of large capacity; development of software for modeling appropriate barcode generators and solving applied problems with their use.

Acknowledgement. This work was financially supported by the Government of the Russian Federation (Grant 08-08).

References

1. Soldek, J., Shmerko, V., Phillips, P., Kukharev, G., Rogers, W., Yanushkevich, S.: Image analysis and pattern recognition in biometric technologies. In: Proceedings International Conference on the Biometrics: Fraud Prevention, Enhanced Service, Las Vegas, Nevada, USA, pp. 270–286 (1997)
2. Heeter, T.W.: Method for verifying human identity during electronic sale transactions. Patent US, no. 5878155 (1999)
3. Jung, E., Kim, J., Woo, S., Kim, S.: Simplification of face image using feature points. In: SCIS & ISIS 2010, Okayama Convention Center, Okayama, Japan, 8–12 December 2010, pp. 1071–1073 (2010). https://doi.org/10.14864/softscis.2010.0.1071.0
4. Garafutdinov, R.R., Chubukova, O.V., Sahabutdinova, A.R., Vakhitov, V.A., Chemeris, A.V.: Genetic barcoding approach as to the identification of the person on the example of Russians of the Republic of Bashkortostan. Bull. Biotechnol. Phys. Chem. Biol. **8**(3), 19–25 (2012). (in Russian)
5. Bhattacharya, S., Mali, K.: A bar code design and encoding for fingerprints. Procedia Technol. **10**, 672–679 (2013)
6. Querini, M., Gattelli, M., Gentile, V.M., Italiano, G.F.: Handwritten signature verification with 2D color barcodes. In: Federated Conference on Computer Science and Information Systems, pp. 701–708 (2014)
7. Kukharev, G., Matveev, Y., Shchegoleva, N.: A gradient method for generating facial barcodes. In: Ignatov, D.I., Khachay, M.Y., Panchenko, A., Konstantinova, N., Yavorskiy, R.E. (eds.) AIST 2014. CCIS, vol. 436, pp. 121–127. Springer, Cham (2014). https://doi.org/10.1007/978-3-319-12580-0_12
8. Ambadiyil, S., Soorej, K., Pillai, V.: Biometric based unique ID generation and one to one verification for security documents. Procedia Comput. Sci. **46**, 507–516 (2015). International Conference on Information and Communication Technologies (ICICT)
9. Buchmann, N., Rathgeb, C., Wagner, J., Busch, C., Baier, H.: A preliminary study on the feasibility of storing fingerprint and iris image data in 2D-barcodes. In: International Conference of the Biometrics Special Interest Group (BIOSIG), pp. 281–288 (2016)
10. Lee, J., Ruan, Sh., Lin, Ch.: VoiceCode: a 2D barcode system for digital audio encoding. In: 2016 IEEE 5th Global Conference on Consumer Electronics (GCCE 2016), pp. 303–305 (2016)
11. Noore, A., Tungala, N., Houck, M.: Embedding biometric identifiers in 2D barcodes for improved security. Comput. Secur. **23**(8), 679–686 (2004)
12. Barcode Comparison Chart. http://www.makebarcode.com/specs/barcodechart.html
13. Nesson, C.: Encoding multi-layered data into QR codes for increased capacity and security. Research Experience for Undergraduates, Final - Report 4, 22 (2013)
14. Garateguy, G., Arce, G., Lau, D., Villarreal, O.: QR images: optimized image embedding in QR Codes. IEEE Trans. Image Process. **23**(7), 2842–2853 (2014)

15. Kukharev, G.A., Kaziyeva, N., Tsymbal, D.A.: Barcoding technologies for facial biometrics: current status and new solutions. Sci. Tech. J. Inf. Technol. Mech. Opt. **18**(1), 72–86 (2018). https://doi.org/10.17586/2226-1494-2018-18-1-72-86. (in Russian)
16. Matveev, Y., Kukharev, G., Shchegoleva, N.: A simple method for generating facial barcodes. In: Proceedings of the 22nd International Conference in Central Europe on Computer Graphics, Visualization and Computer Vision, WSCG 2014, Communication Papers Proceedings - in co-operation with EUROGRAPHICS Association, pp. 213–220 (2015)

Digital Image Forensics Technique for Copy-Move Forgery Detection Using DoG and ORB

Patrick Niyishaka[(✉)] and Chakravarthy Bhagvati

University of Hyderabad, Hyderabad 500046, India
niyishakapatrick@gmail.com, chakcs@uohyd.ernet.in
http://scis.uohyd.ac.in/~mc14pc21/, http://scis.uohyd.ac.in/~chakcs/

Abstract. Copy–Move forgery or Cloning is image tampering or alteration by copying one area in an image and pasting it into another area of the same image. Due to the availability of powerful image editing software, the process of malicious manipulation, editing and creating fake images has been tremendously simple. Thus, there is a need of robust PBIF (Passive–Blind Image Forensics) techniques to validate the authenticity of digital images. In this paper, CMFD (Copy–Move Forgery Detection) using DoG (Difference of Gaussian) blob detector to detect regions in image, with rotation invariant and resistant to noise feature detection technique called ORB (Oriented Fast and Rotated Brief) is implemented, evaluated on different standard datasets and experimental results are presented.

Keywords: Blobs · CMFD · DoG · ORB · PBIF

1 Introduction

Digital images as visual elements are a leading source of information in many applications and one of the key characteristics of digital images with a discrete representation is its flexibility to manipulation. Image tampering is defined as changing or removing some important features from an image for malicious purposes without leaving any noticeable trace of forgery [1] and can be divided into three main categories listed below.

Copy-Move forgery or **Cloning**, a part of an image is copied and pasted to another part of the same image [14].

Cut-Paste forgery or **Splicing** forgery technique involves composition or merging of two or more images changing the original image significantly to produce a forged image [15,16].

Image Retouching, retouching operation is carried out mostly to enhance or reduce the image features but the subject of the image remains same [14,16].

Digital image forensics deals with the detection of traces of forgeries in digital images [17]. PBIF (Passive-Blind Image Forensics) refers to passive ways of

© Springer Nature Switzerland AG 2018
L. J. Chmielewski et al. (Eds.): ICCVG 2018, LNCS 11114, pp. 472–483, 2018.
https://doi.org/10.1007/978-3-030-00692-1_41

evaluating image authenticity to perceive hints of tampering in a given image without prior information or security codes [1,13]. In this paper, we focus on CMFD (Copy-Move Forgery Detection).

CMFD methods are either block-based methods or keypoint based methods [5].

Block-based approach: Image is divided into small overlapping or non- overlapping blocks. The blocks are compared against each other in order to see which blocks are matched. Best to detect forgery under Gaussian noise and JPEG compression attacks.

Keypoint based approach: Compute the feature vectors for regions with high entropy in an image without any image subdivision then feature vectors within the image are matched to find the copied regions. Best to detect image forgery under scaling and rotation attacks.

Copy–Move forgery detection major challenges are robustness against geometric transformations like rotation, scaling and common image processing operations like compression, noise addition and time complexity.

2   Related Work

Recently different techniques were proposed to encounter the Copy–Move forgery. To distinguish between normal and forged images, they used ORB features with a classification method using SVM (Support Vector Machine) [1]. Obtention of feature vectors from the forged image is achieved using ACC (Auto Color Correlogram), which is a low complexity feature extraction technique [2]. A detection technique based on SIFT (Scale Invariant Feature Transform) has been proposed and determines the geometric transformations applied to perform tampering [4]. A method based on Gabor wavelets, where only magnitudes are used is proposed [3]. In PCA (Principal Component Analysis) based technique, image blocks are organized lexicographically and PCA is used to represent the dissimilar blocks in a substitute mode [8]. In DCT (Discrete Cosine Transform) based detection method, the image is divided into overlapping blocks, DCT coefficients are used for feature extraction of these blocks then DCT coefficients of blocks are lexicographically sorted, comparable squares are distinguished and forged regions are found [9]. In a copy-move image forgery detection method based on LBP (Local Binary Pattern) and neighborhood clustering, image is decomposed into three color components. Then, calculating LBP histograms from each component overlapped blocks and retain shortest one-fourth of total block-pairs. Extract block-pairs that are common in the three components and find duplicate regions [7]. A detection method based on local invariant feature extracts local feature using Scale Invariant Transform algorithm, then it locates copied and pasted regions by matching feature points [10]. A technique to detect Copy–Move Forgery based on SURF (Speeded Up Robust Features) and KD-Tree for multidimensional data matching was proposed in [11].

3   Proposed Method

Implementation steps and algorithm are discussed in this section.

There are three main steps: Sobel edge detection (Sect. 3.1), feature extraction DoG and ORB (Sect. 3.2) and feature matching (Sect. 3.3).

To tackle the Copy–Move forgery detection Major challenges, we aim to combine block-based and keypoint based detection techniques in a single model.

Block-based techniques exhibit some limitations, selecting the size of the block is difficult, the matching process becomes computationally intensive with small blocks, larger blocks cannot be used to detect small forged areas, and uniform regions in the original image will be shown as duplicates. To cope with the above limitations, we use blobs instead of image blocks.

For many keypoint based techniques, to eliminate false matches after keypoints are matched, RANSAC (Random Sample Consensus) algorithm is applied. Our approach avoids the use of RANSAC to remove false matches (Sect. 3.3).

Images used as input to evaluate our model are from standard datasets known in the literature, and large images are reduced to have a maximum size of 1000×1000 pixels.

3.1   Sobel Edge Detection

A 2D spatial gradient measurement is performed on an image using Sobel edge detector [25, 26]. The resultant image (Sobel image) is 2D map of the gradient at each point, the areas of high gradient visible as white lines. We use Sobel image as the input of blob detector to enhance blob localization.

3.2   Feature Extraction

Feature extraction process is performed at this stage, that is blob detection and ORB feature detection.

3.2.1   DoG

(Difference of Gaussian) is a blob detector, blob detection methods are aimed at detecting blobs which are regions in a digital image that differ in properties, such as brightness or color, compared to surrounding regions [18]. To detect Blobs we are using DoG method [12]. But we also used Laplacian of Gaussian (LoG) [23] for evaluating the model. DoG is the difference between two images convolved with two Gaussian filters $g(x, y, \sigma k)$ and $g(x, y, \sigma)$ as shown in Fig. 1.

$$g(x, y, \sigma) = \frac{1}{2\pi\sigma^2} e^{\left(\frac{-x^2 + y^2}{2\sigma^2}\right)} \qquad (1)$$

$$DoG = g(x, y, \sigma k) * I(x, y) - -g(x, y, \sigma) * I(x, y) \qquad (2)$$

$g(x, y, \sigma)$ is gaussian filter, * is convolution operator, k is a scale variable, σ is standard deviation and I(x, y) is image.

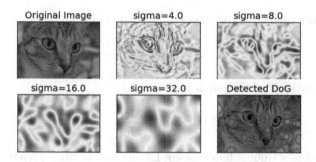

Fig. 1. DoG blob detection, k = 1.6.

3.2.2   ORB

(Oriented Fast and Rotated Brief) is a fast robust local feature detector [6] as shown in Fig. 2(b). ORB is the fusion of oriented FAST keypoint detector and rotated BRIEF descriptor and is much faster than SURF and SIFT [6]. As such, it is preferred for real–time applications. In FAST (Features from Accelerated Segment Test), the pixel P is a corner if there exists a set of n = 12 contiguous pixels in the Bresenham circle of 16 pixels with radius of 3 units as shown in Fig. 2(a) [21], which are all brighter than Ip + t or all darker than Ip – t, t is a threshold.

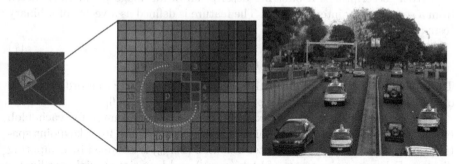

Fig. 2. (a) FAST keypoint detector. (b) ORB feature detection.

A high speed test is performed to exclude a large number of non corners, this test examines only the four pixels at 1, 9, 5 and 13. Since FAST does not compute the orientation, ORB came up with following modification for an orientation compensation mechanism. Given image patch $I(x, y)$, patch moments are defined as:

$$M_{pq} = \sum_x \sum_y x^p y^q I(x, y) \qquad (3)$$

With the above moments, the center C of the patch is found

$$C = \frac{M_{01}}{M_{00}}, \frac{M_{10}}{M_{00}} \tag{4}$$

The orientation θ of the patch is given by :

$$\theta = Tan^{-1}\frac{M_{01}}{M_{00}} \tag{5}$$

BRIEF (Binary Robust Independent Elementary Features) is a binary feature descriptor such as LBP (Local Binary Pattern), it only performs simple binary comparison tests [19,20]. Building a binary descriptor, it is only necessary to compare the intensity between two pixel positions located around the detected interest points. This allows to obtain a representative description at very low computational cost. BRIEF takes smoothened image patch and selects a set of $n(x, y)$ location pairs [22], then some pixel intensity comparisons are done on these location pairs. Considering a smoothed image patch P, a binary test τ is given by:

$$\tau(P; x, y) := \begin{cases} 1 : P(x) < P(y) \\ 0 : P(x) \geq P(y) \end{cases} \tag{6}$$

where $P(x)$ is intensity of P at point x and $P(y)$ is intensity of P at point y.

BRIEF descriptor is a bitstring description of an image patch constructed from a set of binary intensity tests. The feature is defined as a vector of n binary tests ($n = 256$).

$$fn(P) := \sum_{1 \leq i \leq n} 2^{i-1}\tau(p; x_i, y_i) \tag{7}$$

To achieve rotation invariant, ORB steers BRIEF (rBRIEF) according to the orientation of keypoints and uses pyramid scheme for scale [6].

For feature localization, we extract 2D spatial coordinates for each blob (x_b, y_b, r) and for each ORB keypoint (x_k, y_k). The distance from keypoint spatial coordinates (x_k, y_k) to the center of a blob (x_b, y_b) is obtained by computing distance D between the center of blob (x_b, y_b) and keypoint spatial coordinates (x_k, y_k).

$$\sqrt{(x_k - x_b)^2 + (y_k - y_b)^2} = D \tag{8}$$

The keypoint (x_k, y_k) is inside the blob if $D < r$, on the blob if $D = r$, and outside the blob if $D > r$. **r** is the radius of the blob and it is given by the sigma of Gaussian kernel used to find the blob.

3.3 Feature Matching

For feature matching, the hamming distance metric is used to determine the similarity between two descriptor vectors. Hamming distance D_h between i^{th} and j^{th} descriptor vectors of the same length is the number of positions in which the corresponding symbols are different and can be computed very efficiently with a bitwise XOR operation followed by a bit count [22]. Let v_k be the kth element of the ith descriptor.

$$D_h(i, j) = \sum_{k \leq 256} XOR(v_k(i), v_k(j)), \tag{9}$$

$$v_k(i) = v_k(j) \Rightarrow 0 \tag{10}$$

$$v_k(i) \neq v_k(j) \Rightarrow 1 \tag{11}$$

Then D_h is normalized such that $D_h \in (0, 1)$. A match is found between the two interest points If D_h is smaller than a predefined threshold T, that is

$$D_h \leq T \; where \; T \in (0, 1) \tag{12}$$

To deal with false matches, we noticed that if there is a copy–move forgery, the original region and moved region always resulted in different blobs. Thus, to remove false matches, we only match ORB features from different blobs.

To highlight a match we use a straight line joining the two matched interest points spatial locations. Figure 3(a) shows the combination of DoG and ORB, whereas Fig. 3(b) shows ORB feature matching between different blobs.

Fig. 3. (a) Blobs and ORB Feature detection. (b) Feature matching.

4   Experimental Results

Evaluation metrics used to assess our technique are p_r (Precision), r_c (Recall) and f_1 score [5]. Precision denotes the probability that a detected forgery is truly a forgery, while recall or true positive rate shows the probability that a forged image is detected. $f1$ score is a measure which combines precision and recall in a single value.

$$p_r = \frac{tp}{t_p + f_p}, \quad r_c = \frac{tp}{t_p + f_n}, \quad f_1 = 2\frac{p_r r_c}{p_r + r_c} \tag{13}$$

Algorithm 1. CMFD based on DoG and ORB feature

Result: Image with CMFD results

1   I : Input Image;
2   Gi : Compute grayscale of I ;
3   Si : Apply sobel edge detector to Gi;
4   $Di_{(x_b, y_b, r)}$: Extract DoG feature and spatial coordinates from Si;
5   $Oi_{(x_k, y_k)}$: Extract ORB feature and spatial coordinates from Gi;
6   $List_1 = empty$;
7   **for** $Blob$ in $Di_{(x_b, y_b, r)}$ **do**
8     $List_2 = empty$;
9   **for** $Keypoint$ in $Oi_{(x_k, y_k)}$ **do**
10   **if** $\sqrt{(x_k - x_b)^2 + (y_k - y_b)^2} \leq r$ **then**
11         $list_2.\text{append}(Keypoint)$;
12   **else**
13   continue;

14   **if** $list2 \mathrel{!=} empty$ **then**
15       $List_1.\text{append}(List2)$;
16   **else**
17   continue;

18   **for** i in $range(0, len(List_1) - 1)$ **do**
19   **for** $desc_1$ in $List_1[i]$ **do**
20   **for** j in $range(i + 1, len(List_1))$ **do**
21   **for** $desc_2$ in $List_1[j]$ **do**
22           $D_H = \text{distance.hamming}(desc_1, desc_2)$;
23   **if** $D_H \leq T$ **then**
24   print 'Match found';
25   drawline(keypoint($desc_1$),keypoint($desc_2$));
26   **else**
27   continue;

---

where forged images correctly detected are t_p. Images wrongly detected as forged are termed as f_p. Tampered images that are falsely missed are termed as f_n.

The experiments have been launched using python 2.7.12 and OpenCV 3.0 on a machine with Intel Core i5 processor with 8 GB RAM and running time analysis results are reported in Table 4.

4.1 Experiment

To set the operating point properly; the experiment is done on 400 images as reported in Table 1 and illustrated in Fig. 4, and to compare our method with other methods known in the literature [2] and results are reported in Table 6.

Table 1. Experimental results on 400 images (100 originals and 300 forged) randomly selected from dataset CoMoFoD [24] and T values between 0.1 and 0.9 to set the proper operating point.

Threshold (T)	t_p	f_p	f_n	p_r (%)	r_c (%)	f_1 (%)
0.1	97	1	203	98.97	32.33	48.73
0.2	126	2	174	98.43	42.00	58.87
0.3	185	7	115	96.35	61.66	75.19
0.4	253	8	47	96.93	84.33	90.19
0.5	274	10	26	96.47	91.33	**93.82**
0.6	278	23	22	92.35	92.66	92.50
0.7	283	52	17	84.47	94.33	89.12
0.8	288	89	12	75.06	96.00	84.24
0.9	289	100	11	74.29	96.33	83.88

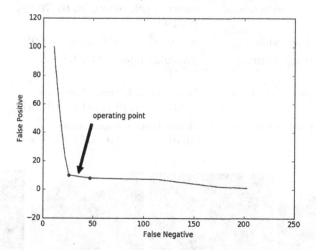

Fig. 4. The proper operating point of threshold T is obtained using the results from Table 1 where T is approximated to be 0.5 and f_1 score is 93.82%.

Using $T = 0.5$ we performed the following robustness tests and reported results in Table 5. **Test 1** is done on simple copy-move as shown in Fig. 5 with geometric transformations parameters reported in Table 2.

Test 2 is done on multiple cloning as shown in Fig. 5, on 24 images from dataset $C3\_$nikon [5] (12 multiple cloning tampered images and 12 originals with maximum size 3039×2014 pixels) and 8 tampered images from dataset MICC–F8multi [4] with maximum size of 2048×1536 pixels.

Test 3 is done on post–processing operations as shown in Fig. 6 with parameters reported in Table 3.

Table 2. The rotation θ in degrees and the scaling factors S_x, S_y applied to the x and y axis of the cloned image patch of size 1.2% of the whole image on 100 images (50 originals and 50 forged) selected randomly from dataset MICC-F220 [4].

Attack	θ	S_x	S_y	Attack	θ	S_x	S_y
A	0	1	1	F	0	1.2	1.2
B	10	1	1	G	0	1.3	1.3
C	20	1	1	H	0	1.4	1.2
D	30	1	1	I	10	1.2	1.2
E	40	1	1	J	20	1.4	1.2

Table 3. Parameters for post–processing operations on selected 400 images (100 originals and 300 forged) of size 512×512 from dataset CoMoFoD [24].

Methods	Parameters
Jpeg compression	factor = [20, 30, 40, 50, 60, 70, 80, 90, 100]
Noise adding	$\mu = 0$, $\sigma^2 = [0.009, 0.005, 0.0005]$
Image blurring	averaging filter = [3×3, 5×5, 7×7]
Brightness change	(lower bound, upper bound) = [(0.01, 0.95), (0.01, 0.9), (0.01, 0.8)]
Contrast adjustment	(lower bound, upper bound) = [(0.01, 0.95), (0.01, 0.9), (0.01, 0.8)]

Fig. 5. Rotated tampered image and multicopies scaled tampered images are shown in the first row, while the detection results are reported in the second row.

Fig. 6. Blurred and noisy tampered images are shown in the first row, while the detection results are shown in the second row.

Table 4. Processing time in seconds (average per image) per number of ORB features extracted from image.

Number of ORB features	100	500	1000
CoMoFoD : Time [s]	0.8	2	5.5
MICC-F220, MICC-F8, $C3$_nikon : Time [s]	1.41	3.45	9.20

Table 5. Detection results for robustness tests against geometric transformations, multicopies forgeries and post–processing operations.

Robustness tests	t_p	f_p	f_n	p_r (%)	r_c (%)	f_1 (%)
Test 1	48	1	2	97.95	96.00	97.46
Test 2	14	1	6	93.33	70.00	80.00
Test 3	274	10	26	96.47	91.33	93.82

Table 6. Comparative results between the proposed model and other methods known in the literature [2].

Feature extraction methods	p_r (%)	r_c (%)	f_1 (%)
DCT [9]	78.69	100	88.07
PCA [8]	84.21	100	93.20
SURF [11]	91.94	89.58	90.53
ACC [2]	95.65	91.67	93.62
Proposed DoG & ORB	96.47	91.33	93.82

5   Conclusion

A new model for Copy–Move Forgery Detection based on DoG blobs detector and ORB feature detection has been proposed. The proposed technique shows effectiveness to diverse operative scenarios such as multiple copy–move forgeries in same image and geometric transformations including rotation and scaling. Since original region and moved region always resulted in different blobs, we only matched ORB feature descriptors from different blobs, hence computational time, the number of features to match and false matches reduced considerably. Combining DoG and ORB feature merges the advantage of block-based and keypoint based forgery detection methods in a single model. Future work will be mainly dedicated to the elimination of human interpretation of the output of Copy–Move Forgery Detection techniques to enable performance evaluation on very large datasets.

References

1. Dhiman, N., Kumar, R.: Classification of copy move forgery and normal images by ORB features and SVM classifier. In: ICITSEM 2017, pp. 146–155 (2017)
2. Malviya, A.V., Ladhake, S.A.: Pixel based image forensic technique for copy-move forgery detection using auto color correlogram. Procedia Comput. Sci. **79**, 383–390 (2016)
3. Lee, J.-C.: Copy-move image forgery detection based on Gabor magnitude. J. Vis. Commun. Image Representation **31**, 320–334 (2015)
4. Amerini, I., Ballan, L., Caldelli, R., Del Bimbo, A., Serra, G.: A SIFT-based forensic method for copy-move attack detection and transformation recovery. IEEE Trans. Inf. Forensics Secur. **6**(3), 1099–1110 (2011)
5. Christlein, V., Riess, C., Jordan, J., Riess, C., Angelopoulou, E.: An evaluation of popular copy-move forgery detection approaches. IEEE Trans. Inf. Forensics Secur. **7**(6), 1841–1854 (2012)
6. Rublee, E., Rabaud, V., Konolige, K., Bradski, G.: ORB: an efficient alternative to SIFT or SURF. In: ICCV, pp. 2564–2571 (2011)
7. AlSawadi, M., Ghulam, M., Hussain, M., Bebis, G.: Copy-move image forgery detection using local binary pattern and neighborhood clustering. In: EMS (2013)
8. Popescu, A., Farid, H.: Exposing digital forgeries by detecting duplicated image regions. Dartmouth College, Computer Science, Technical report, TR 2004-515 (2004)
9. Fridrich, J., Soukal, D., Lukas, J.: Detection of copy-move forgery in digital images. In: Digital Forensic Research Workshop, Cleveland, OH, pp. 19–23 (2003)
10. Jing, L., Shao, C.: Image copy-move forgery detecting based on local invariant feature. J. Multimed. **7**(1), 90–97 (2012)
11. Shivakumar, B.L., SanthoshBaboo, S.: Detection of region duplication forgery in digital images using SURF. IJCSI Int. J. Comput. Sci. Issues **8**(4), 199–205 (2011)
12. Lowe, D.G.: Distinctive image features from scale-invariant keypoints. Int. J. Comput. Vis. **60**(2), 91–110 (2004)
13. Ng, T.-T., Chang, S.-F., Lin, C.-Y., Sun, Q.: Passive blind image forensics. In: Multimedia Security Technologies for Digital Rights Management, pp. 383–412 (2006)

14. Gupta, C.S.: A review on splicing image forgery detection techniques. IJCSITS, **6**(2), 262–269, (2016)
15. Mushtaq, S., Hussain, A.: Digital image forgeries and passive image authentication techniques: a survey. Int. J. Adv. Sci. Technol. **73**, 15–32 (2014)
16. Rathod, G., Chodankar, S., Deshmukh, R., Shinde, P., Pattanaik, S.P.: Image forgery detection on cut-paste and copy-move forgeries. Int. J. Adv. Electron. Comput. Sci. **3**(6) (2016). ISSN: 2393–2835
17. Redi, J., Taktak, W., Dugelay, J.: Digital image forensics: a booklet for beginners. Multimed. Tools Appl. **51**(1), 133–162 (2011)
18. Lindeberg, T.: Detecting salient blob-like image structures and their scales with a scale-space primal sketch: a method for focus-of-attention. Int. J. Comput. Vis. **11**(3), 283–318 (1993)
19. Calonder, M., Lepetit, V., özuysal, M., Trzcinski, T., Strecha, C., Fua, P.: BRIEF: computing a local binary descriptor very fast. IEEE Trans. Pattern Anal. Mach. Intell. **34**(7), 1281–1298 (2012)
20. Hassaballah, M., Abdelmgeid, A.A., Alshazly, H.A.: Image features detection, description and matching. In: Awad, A.I., Hassaballah, M. (eds.) Image Feature Detectors and Descriptors. SCI, vol. 630, pp. 11–45. Springer, Cham (2016). https://doi.org/10.1007/978-3-319-28854-3_2
21. Audi, A., Pierrot-Deseilligny, M., Meynardand, C., Thom, C.: Implementation of an IMU aided image stacking algorithm in a digital camera for unmanned aerial vehicles. Sensors **17**(7), 1646 (2017)
22. Calonder, M., Lepetit, V., Strecha, C., Fua, P.: BRIEF: binary robust independent elementary features. In: Daniilidis, K., Maragos, P., Paragios, N. (eds.) ECCV 2010. LNCS, vol. 6314, pp. 778–792. Springer, Heidelberg (2010). https://doi.org/10.1007/978-3-642-15561-1_56
23. Kong, H., Akakin, H.C., Sarma, S.E.: A generalized Laplacian of Gaussian filter for blob detection and its applications. IEEE Trans. Cybern. **43**(6), 1719–1733 (2013)
24. Tralic, D., Zupancic, I., Grgic, S., Grgic, M.: CoMoFoD - new database for copy-move forgery detection. In: Proceedings of 55th International Symposium ELMAR-2013, pp. 49–54 (2013)
25. Irwin, S., Gary, F.: A 3 x 3 Isotropic Gradient Operator for Image Processing. The Stanford Artificial Intelligence Project, pp. 271–272 (1968)
26. Vincent, O.R., Folorunso, O.: A descriptive algorithm for Sobel image edge detection. In: Proceedings of Informing Science & IT Education Conference (InSITE) (2009)

Pattern Recognition and New Concepts in Classification

Does the Research Question Structure Impact the Attention Model? User Study Experiment

Malwina Dziśko[1]([⊠]), Anna Lewandowska[1], and Anna Samborska-Owczarek[2]

[1] Faculty of Computer Science and Information Systems,
West Pomeranian University of Technology, Szczecin, Poland
{mdzisko,atomaszewska}@wi.zut.edu.pl
[2] FRIS® - Thinking Styles (Style Myslenia), Szczecin, Poland
anna@FRIS.pl

Abstract. The main purpose of this work is to analyse the influence of questions given in perceptual experiments on the reliability of received results. The problem have been investigated in literature, however in a form of theoretical discussion rather than quantitative evaluation. Therefore in the paper in include quantitative evaluation and results visualization. Nevertheless the main novelty is employment of human cognitive style for research questions problem. The analysis was supported with FRIS® [7] that is a psychometric model and also an inventory for cognitive styles measurement. We conduct the user study in order to investigate the way the observers understand research question given during the experiment execution. Therefore two kinds of questions were employed to the experiment: the one not suggesting a response or the one suggesting an answer. In researches we focused on the images' objects that attach observer's attention dependent on a structure of a given question. The obtained results were submitted to statistical analysis that proved that correctness of experimental results is highly correlated to the way the research question is designed. The questions that suggesting the answer affects the outcome of the perceptual experiment and make them unreliable. The results confirmed that the human cognitive style is highly correlated with the research questions interpretation.

1 Introduction

Introducing a new imaging algorithm, there is often a need to compare the results with the state-of-the-art methods. The most reliable way of assessing the quality of an image is by its subjective evaluation. From last years, there is a strong new trend to support the visual results by user studies [13,14,20]. One of the drawbacks of perceptual experiments is a proper design of research questions given to the experiment participants. Ill-defined research task affects the observer's understanding. In the case of a question that suggesting the answer, the experiment will be pointless. If we lead the subject to the answer, the subject is likely to mark the suggesting object and not what he would consider a correct

L. J. Chmielewski et al. (Eds.): ICCVG 2018, LNCS 11114, pp. 487–498, 2018.
https://doi.org/10.1007/978-3-030-00692-1_42

answer. The literature assumes that a good question means question producing similar answers [5]. Moreover according to Fowler [5] one of the properties of good question is that it means the same thing to every respondent. Nevertheless the psychologists reports that respondents may differ from each other because of their cognitive styles [18,19]. It means that their interpretation of the questions may be different [7]. According to that assumption, we consider the property of good question should be formulate rather as the question that is understandable to every respondent but its interpretation can be different. That seems more correct as the goal of perceptual experiments is the human preferences collection. Therefore the human cognitive style should be investigated during the problem analysis, what is one of the paper purposes.

Analysis of the observers' perception while exposed to different types questions (not suggesting or suggesting the answer) and difference in obtained results is the main goal of the paper. The observers perception would be obtained by observers' gaze points tracking and analysed from a perspective of the way the observers responded to the given questions. The gaze points tracking can be obtained using eye-tracker device.

Correctly stated questions for the experiment allow us to precisely determine what we expect from the subject. This is very important from the point of view of computer graphics research and perceptual experiments. Often the same question modified with only one word, may result in a different interpretation and conduction of the experiment by the observers. In the paper the investigation of the correspondence between gaze points fixation maps given by an eye-tracker and observers preferences is included. In our investigations we analyse the human responses not only in relation to question structure, but also from exploration of human cognitive style. We believe that such approach may deliver new interesting findings on image perception domain.

According to cognitive psychology the way an individuals perceive the world is dependent on their cognitive style that is his natural property [11]. The term 'cognitive style' refers to a psychological dimension representing consistencies in an individual's manner of cognitive functioning [1]. Therefore cognitive styles are considered stable attitudes and preferences that determine individuals' modes of information perceiving and processing, thinking, decision making and problem solving habitual strategies [16]. As human cognitive styles influence the way an individual perceives information and thus make a judgement about image quality, the relation between the style, image perception and objects attention should be investigated.

A human attention dependent on structure of a given question is analyzed according to FRIS® Thinking Styles Inventory, which is psychometrically reliable and valid [7]. The inventory offers multidimensional description of user's thinking preferences thus is suitable for variety of perceptual experiments.

In the paper we examined how the asked question affects perceptual responses during experiments. The main research question was: *Does the structure of a question given to the image affects a different observer answer?*

A description of the assumptions for conducting the experiment is described in Sect. 2. Section 3 introduces to Human Cognitive Style. In Sect. 4 the experiment description is presented. The results and analysis we included in Sect. 5. The paper ended with a conclusion in Sect. 6.

2 Related Work

Proper asking questions while conducting perceptual experiments has an impact on the results of experiments [10]. From the point of view of computer graphics and perceptual experiments, an important aspect is to formulate questions clearly, because it is a kind of communication process that allows to obtain information that is necessary to and increase knowledge about human perception [2].

Proper preparation of questions that appear in the perceptual experiment make it possible to acquire the knowledge we need. That is the condition of the questions or tasks constructed in such a way as this directly express our view and lead to the designated goal [4]. The questions contained in the experiment should first of all be unambiguous and understandable for the observer, moreover should not suggesting a response. In the opposite case, the observer will interpret the question in his own way. In addition, it is worth paying attention to the distribution of logical questions [12]. In the literature one can found also the principles of a good question. The first is to consistently understand the question, second, design the answers to accurately describe what the respondents have to say [6].

A correctly formulated question is the key to the good results. An example are two images depicted different types of trees: real one and made of blocks. Giving the command: 'Select trees', the observers should select real tree or both trees. In the case of a question: 'Select real trees', the observers should select only image with real tree, except those made of blocks. It means that structure of research question has crucial influence on communication between the researcher and the observers [15]. This is evidence that conducting research without taking into account knowledge about observers cognitive styles can lead to distortions of results [21]. The relationship between the difference in the stated questions and the given answers are very important from the perspective of learning associated with computer graphics and perception [3] as they translates into other experiments and research and precisely determines what researchers expect from the user [17]. Floyd points out a similar problem in his publication [6]. However, its polemics are theoretical and are not supported by quantitative experiments. Floyd also does not include human cognitive styles in his article. Correlation between the cognitive style and preferences is a new issue in the field of computer graphics research. Therefore the problem of properly constructed research questions with taking into account the observer cognitive style is the subject of the paper.

Fig. 1. Test images used to conduct the experiment.

3 Human Cognitive Style

There are many approaches to human cognitive styles description and most of them define one or more bipolar scales, such as: reflectivity vs impulsivity, concrete vs abstract, relational vs analytical or field-dependence vs field-independence etc. [18]. Nevertheless, even the cognitive styles are considered to be fundamental individual differences as long as temperamental types, there is no standard model or finite list of cognitive scales [19]. Some of the most widely used cognitive styles are measured by formal questionnaires or inventories. In our experiment in order to demonstrate that a correctly formulated research question differentiates responses, every observer was described by FRIS® Thinking Styles Inventory [8] that is a psychometric questionnaire measuring individual's preference ranking of 4 cognitive perspectives (cognitive styles metacategories) defined by FRIS® Model [7]:

- F: fact-based thinking (concrete, sequential, logical thinking),
- R: relation-based thinking (intuitive, field-dependent, relational thinking),
- I: idea-based thinking (abstract, lateral, global thinking),
- S: structure-based thinking (field-independent, reflective, analytical thinking).

FRIS® Thinking Styles Inventory [8] is psychometrically reliable, valid, normalised and standardised [7]. The 6 factors of the inventory are bipolar scales discriminating between pairs of cognitive perspectives: F vs I, F vs R etc. with internal consistency $0.76-0.82$ Cronbach's α. The 4 superfactors' internal consistency is $0,82(F)$, $0,88(R)$ $0,88(I)$ $0,88(S)$ Cronbach's α. In our experiment we used 1 nominal variable TS Thinking Style - the dominant (maximal) cognitive perspective of the subject (one from the set): $TS = \{F, R, I, S\}$.

4 Subjective Experiment

The main aim of the paper is an investigation whether different asking questions to the same images will affect the different responses by the observers. Therefore to conduct the experiment, a research stand was prepared.

Display Conditions. The experiments were run on display: NEC with, 1050 × 1680 pixel resolution. The display responses were measured with the Minolta CS-200 colorimeter and Specbos 1201 spectroradiometer. The measurements were used to calibrate the displays and ensure that all images were reproduced in the sRGB colour space.

Test Images. In the experiment we used six images (see Fig. 1) displayed twice, with differently formulated research questions. Images were displayed in random manner. Every image was attached with two different research questions: not suggesting a response or suggesting the answer. Images with the same scene and different questions were not displayed one by one. Between displayed images, middle-grey display was presented.

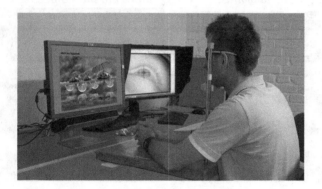

Fig. 2. The research stand for perceptual experiment supported with eye-tracker device.

Observers. To the experiment we invited 43 observers with normal or corrected to normal vision. The observers task was to mark the object visible of the image according to the given question. Lack of the answer was also an answer. The research was carried out in accordance with the rules described in ITU report (*International Telecommunication Unit*) [9]. After the experiment, for every observer his cognitive style was identified by FRIS® Thinking Styles Inventory [8].

The observers may have reported implausible impression scores because they misunderstood the experiment instruction or did not engage in the task and gave random answers. If the number of participants is low, it is easy to spot unreliable observers by inspecting the plots. However, when the number of observers is very high or it is difficult to scrutinise the plots, the [9] standard, Annex 2.3.1,

Q: *Mark the ladybirds.*   Q: *Mark the the silhouettes of ladybirds.*

Fig. 3. Test image *flybirds* used in the experiment. Left: The gaze map and objects marked for a not suggesting a response question (white dots) and Right: The gaze map and objects selected (white dots) for a suggesting an answer question. Results obtained from an example observer.

Q: *Mark the ladybirds.*   Q: *Mark the the silhouettes of ladybirds.*

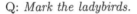

Fig. 4. Fixations paths given for a test image *flybirds*. Left: for not suggesting a response question (white dots) and Right: for a suggesting an answer question. Results obtained from an example observer.

provides a numerical screening procedure. We performed this procedure on our data and found no participants whose data needed to be removed.

Experimental Procedure. We collected our data through the two techniques: the forced-choice experiment and observer interaction with the observed image by indicating the included objects by mouse clicks. There was no time limit or minimum time in which to make the task according to a given question. The experiment was conducted together with an eye-tracker to analyze the way the observers perceive displayed images (see Fig. 2).

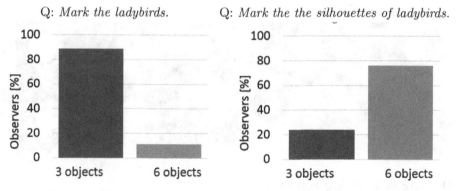

Fig. 5. The graph shows the number of observers (in percentage) that indicated 3 (left bar) and 6 (right bar) objects in the image *ladybirds* Left: for question that does not suggesting an answer. Right: for questions that suggesting a response.

5 Results and Analysis

The experiments were followed by statistical analysis. First we analyzed how the observers interpreted and performed the research task given in the experiment, dependent on the question type: question not suggesting a response and question suggesting an answer respectively. The analysis was conducted based on observers clicks number and gaze points data. An example of such answers given for *ladybirds* image was depicted in Figs. 3 and 4. An example question not suggesting a response was: *Mark the ladybirds* (see Fig. 3 Left and Fig. 4 Left). In opposite, a question suggesting an answer was: *Mark the the silhouettes of ladybirds* (see Fig. 3 Right and Fig. 4 Right).

If the question was asked quite generally (not suggesting a response), approximately 89% of users marked three objects in the image (see Fig. 5 Left). In case a question suggesting a response, about 76% of users indicated more than three objects in the image, including the ladybugs reflection in the water (see Fig. 5 Right).

The analyses carried out showed that people interpret images differently (see Figs. 6 and 7). For test image *butterflies*, the questions to the image were *Mark butterflies* and *Mark butterflies if you see any* accordingly. For the first question about 70% of the observers did not mark anything and 30% of them marked flowers suspended in the air (see Fig. 8 Left). In case a question suggesting a response, all of the observers did not mark anything 100% (see Fig. 8 Right). It means that all observers properly identified flowers as flowers not butterflies.

In the next stage of our analysis we checked whether observer choose objects on which they direct gaze. Dependent on its cognitive style (described by FRIS® questionary), the observers first looked at the image and then selectively rejected the unnecessary data and focused on specific objects. To identify the objects we used an eye-tracker device. It turned out that in the case when the question not suggesting an answer, the observers got theirs attention on the objects according

Q: *Mark butterflies.*

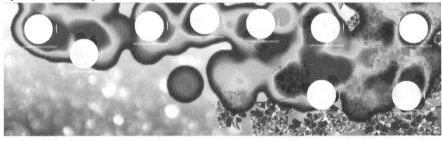

Q: *Mark butterflies if you see any.*

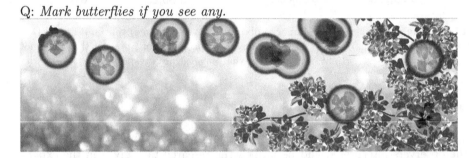

Fig. 6. Test image *butterflies* used in the experiment. Top: The gaze map and objects marked for not suggesting a response question (white dots) and Bottom: The gaze map and objects selected (white dots) for a suggesting an answer question. Results obtained from an example observer.

to their preferences (see Fig. 3 Left, Fig. 4 Left, Fig. 6 Top and Fig. 7 Top). In case of the question suggesting a response, users paid attention also to the remaining objects (mirror images) (see Fig. 3 Right and Fig. 4 Right) or did not mark anything (see Fig. 6 Bottom and Fig. 7 Bottom).

Additionally we identified subjects' thinking styles by FRIS® questionary [8]. We used the questionary as a tool to show that a correctly formulated research question differentiates responses. During analysis we found that for suggesting a response question there is no significant difference between observers ($p = 0.6232$) (see Fig. 9 Bottom). It implies that such type of questions produce less significant results when analysing individual perception preferences of the subjects. Introducing to the experiment such kind of questions enable the author to influence on the final results according to their intention and make the results unreliable.

In the case of results obtained for not suggesting an answer question we found a statistical significance between results obtained for relation-based and rest of cognitive thinking groups (idea-, structure-, fact-based thinking) with $p = 0.0353$ (see Fig. 9 Top). The means distribution of the results for different cognitive styles is depicted in Fig. 10.

Q: *Mark butterflies.*

Q: *Mark butterflies if you see any.*

Fig. 7. Fixations paths given for a test image *butterflies*. Top: for not suggesting a response question (white dots) and Bottom: for a suggesting an answer question. Results obtained from an example observer.

Q: *Mark butterflies.*   Q: *Mark butterflies if you see any.*

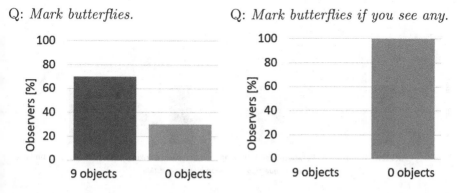

Fig. 8. The graph shows the number of observers (in percentage) that indicated 9 (left bar) and 0 (right bar) objects in the image *butterflies*. Left: for question that does not suggesting an answer. Right: for questions that suggesting a response.

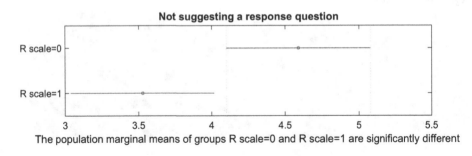

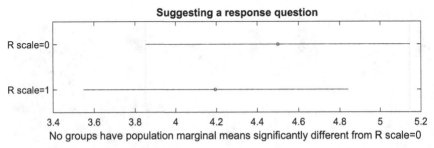

Fig. 9. Statistical significance between relation-scale (R = 1) and F, I and S-based thinking groups of cognitive styles (R = 0): Top: for not suggesting a response questions, Bottom for suggesting an answer questions respectively.

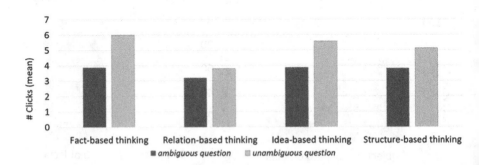

Fig. 10. Mean difference between relation-based and idea-, structure-, fact-based human cognitive styles given for conducted experiment.

The reason of the significance in differences between observers with different cognitive styles results from the fact that relation-based thinking style people have more trouble separating the hidden form from its surrounding context [19]. However, here such explanation is not our intention. The key is that not suggesting questions used for perceptual experiment enable to obtain valuable results that can not be obtained if the answer is suggested.

6 Conclusions

The main purpose of this work was to analyze the impact of questions given in perceptual experiences on the reliability of the results obtained with taking into account the observer cognitive style.

This research was conducted to check whether the structure of a research question used in a perceptual experiments affects the observers answer. After the analysis, it has been proved that to get reliable answers, the research questions used for the experiment should be formulated in a way that not suggesting an answer. Otherwise, the satisfactory results will be got, but they will be manipulated and therefore will not be reliable. The analysis also proved that people who looked at a given object usually pointed it out. This is confirmed by the generated fixation maps from the experiment. It is evident that in the case of questions not suggesting a response, observers looked at and marked objects that exist, while in the case of questions suggesting an answers, observers behaved according to the experiment authors expectation.

Additionally we identified the observers cognitive style by FRIS® Thinking Styles Inventory [8] and analyzed the results received from our experiments according to observers cognitive styles. We found that results obtained from properly design experiment (with not suggesting questions but clear and understandable) can be differentiate and provide valuable information that could be used later according to requirement. In opposite, the results obtained from the experiment designed with the question suggested an answer come out not significantly different. Moreover, received from our analysis results suggest that to proper analysis of perceptual experiments results the human thinking style recognition should be taken into account. We received statistical significance between the responses of people with relationships and without relationships.

Acknowledgement. We would like to give a special thanks to Marcelina Ginalska for helping us in conducting perceptual experiment.

References

1. Ausburn, L.J., Ausburn, F.B.: Cognitive styles: some information and implications for instructional design. Educ. Commun. Technol. **26**, 337–354 (1978)
2. Berry, D.C., Broadbent, D.E.: Interactive tasks and the implicit - explicit distinction. Br. J. Psychol. **79**(2), 251–272 (1988)
3. Carpenter, P.A., Shah, P.: A model of the perceptual and conceptual processes in graph comprehension. J. Exp. Psychol. Appl. **4**(2), 75–100 (1998)

4. Clark, C.M.: Asking the right questions about teacher preparation: contributions of research on teacher thinking. Educ. Res. **17**(2), 5–12 (1988)

5. Floyd, F.J.: Improving Survey Questions: Design and Evaluation, vol. 38. Sage, Thousand Oaks (1995)

6. Floyd, F.J.: Survey Research Methods. Sage Publications, Thousand Oaks (2013)

7. Samborska-Owczarek, A.: FRIS Thinking Styles Inventory, January 2018. https://fris.pl/FRIS-validity-data.eps

8. Samborska-Owczarek, A.: FRIS Thinking Styles Inventory. https://fris.pl

9. ITU-R.REC.BT.500-11: Methodology for the subjective assessment of the quality for television pictures (2002)

10. Jacoby, L.L., Dallas, M.: On the relationship between autobiographical memory and perceptual learning. J. Exp. Psychol. Gener. **110**(3), 306 (1981)

11. Kozhevnikov, M.: Cognitive styles in the context of modern psychology: toward an integrated framework of cognitive style. Psychol. Bull. Am. Psychol. Assoc. **133**(3), 464–481 (2007)

12. Levin, D.T.: Race as a visual feature: using visual search and perceptual discrimination tasks to understand face categories and the cross-race recognition deficit. J. Exp. Psychol. Gener. **129**(4), 559–574 (2000)

13. Mantiuk, R.K., Mantiuk, R., Tomaszewska, A., Heidrich, W.: Color correction for tone mapping. Comput. Graph. Forum **28**, 193–202 (2009)

14. Mantiuk, R.K., Tomaszewska, A., Mantiuk, R.: Comparison of four subjective methods for image quality assessment. Comput. Graph. Forum **31**(8), 2478–2491 (2012)

15. McLeod, S.A.: Perceptual set (2007). https://www.simplypsychology.org/perceptual-set.html. Accessed 19 Jan 2018

16. Messick, S.: Personality consistencies in cognition and creativity. In: Messick, S. (ed.) Individuality in Learning, pp. 4–23. Jossey-Bass, San Francisco (1976)

17. Reber, R., Winkielman, P., Schwarz, N.: Effects of perceptual fluency on affective judgments. Psychol. Sci. **9**(1), 45–48 (1998)

18. Riding, R.J., Rayner, S.G.: International Perspectives on Individual Differences: Cognitive Styles. Ablex Publishing, Stamford, CT (1998). (Riding, R.J., Staley, A.)

19. Sternberg, R.J., Zhang, L.: Perspectives on Thinking, Learning, and Cognitive Styles. Educational Psychology Series. Taylor and Francis, UK (2001)

20. Tomaszewska (Lewandowska), A.: Scene reduction for subjective image quality assessment. J. Electron. Imaging **25**(1), 013015-1–013015-13 (2016)

21. Lewandowska, A., Samborska-Owczarek, A., Dzisko, M.: Contrast perception across human cognitive style. In: Campilho, A., Karray, F., ter Haar Romeny, B. (eds.) ICIAR 2018. LNCS, vol. 10882, pp. 345–352. Springer, Cham (2018). https://doi.org/10.1007/978-3-319-93000-8_39

Pattern Recognition Method for Classification of Agricultural Scientific Papers in Polish

Piotr Wrzeciono[(✉)] and Waldemar Karwowski

Faculty of Applied Informatics and Mathematics,
Warsaw University of Life Sciences – SGGW, Warsaw, Poland
{piotr_wrzeciono,waldemar_karwowski}@sggw.pl

Abstract. Calculation of text similarity is an essential task for the text analysis and classification. It be can based, e.g., on Jaccard, cosine or other similar measures. Such measures consider the text as a bag-of-words and, therefore, lose some syntactic and semantic features of its sentences. This article presents a different measure based on the so-called artificial sentence pattern (ASP) method. This method has been developed to analyze texts in the Polish language which has very rich inflection. Therefore, ASP has utilized syntactic and semantic rules of the Polish language. Nevertheless, we argue that it admits extensions to other languages. As a result of the analysis, we have obtained several hypernodes which contain the most important words. Each hypernode corresponds to one of the examined documents, the latter being published papers from agriculture domain written in Polish. Experimental results obtained from that set of papers have been described and discussed. Those results have been visually illustrated using graphs of hypernodes and compared with Jaccard and cosine measures.

1 Introduction

Today, most of the publications, like books, articles, and other documents are available in digital form; a significant source of such publications is the Internet. Very often we look for papers about a specific topic, or we want to find documents with a similar subject. Of course, if a publication has an explicitly specified title, the first information about the document is contained in that title, but it is not always sufficient. Scientific publications usually contain an abstract and keywords making it much easier to find an interesting work. Summary of content of a document and its keywords are of course very useful. However, they are not always telling enough about all issues considered in the document. Sometimes, we look for aspects not covered by the authors in their abstracts or lists of keywords. Naturally, documents contain much information in their text body, and it is essential to find all interesting issues, often well- hidden in them. A usual way to uncover interesting content is to employ search engines, but the quality of the results is very often not quite satisfactory, so that additional analysis is needed. To improve the quality of search in documents related

© Springer Nature Switzerland AG 2018
L. J. Chmielewski et al. (Eds.): ICCVG 2018, LNCS 11114, pp. 499–511, 2018.
https://doi.org/10.1007/978-3-030-00692-1_43

to a given subject we can use natural language processing method on set preselected by search engines. We have to note that search engines work relatively
well in the case of English-language documents but much worse in less popular languages such as Polish. Additionally, search engines are general-purpose
tools; they are not dedicated to particular domains like agriculture. Our goal
has been to analyze preselected documents written in the Polish language in the
field of agriculture. We have intended to discover the connections between the
documents which result from their whole contents, and not just from their titles
and lists of keywords. The proposed approach attempts to overcome the limitations of the *bag-of-words* [1] model in measures of similarity between documents.
This is done by creating *artificial sentences* which are based on features selected
from the text and utilize syntactic and semantic rules in the Polish language.
Moreover, we have grouped analyzed documents into separated clusters based on
artificial sentence pattern. The main body of the paper is organized as follows:
in Sect. 2 the pattern recognition methods for text classification are presented,
and then in Sect. 3 the concept of a similarity between documents is discussed.
In Sect. 4 the *artificial sentence* pattern is introduced and described. In Sect. 5
similarity analysis and results for a set of scientific papers written in Polish are
presented. In Sect. 6 distances between analyzed documents are discussed. We
finish with a summary and concluding remarks in Sect. 7.

2   Pattern Recognition Methods for Text Classification

According to Encyclopaedia Britannica [2], pattern recognition is about the
imposition of identity on input data, such as speech, images, or a stream of text,
by the recognition and delineation of patterns it contains and their relationships.
Pattern recognition is most commonly considered as a branch of machine learning, but it may also refer to identification of faces, texts or other objects [3–5].
Pattern matching in texts, although close to pattern recognition, is a distinct
process of finding exactly the same text in different documents. In the case of
pattern recognition, extraction of features for the defining attributes, and comparison with known patterns to determine a match or mismatch, is an important stage [2,6]. The most popular methods for text analysis adopted term-based
approaches. However, they usually suffer from the problems of polysemy and syn-
onymy. There has been intense work to overcome that limitation. For big corpora
of texts, methods based on statistical models have been proved effective. Firstly,
feature extraction co-occurrence between words and documents is the basis of
statistical language models with embedded latent semantic knowledge [7]. Unfortunately, such methods are not suitable for smaller sets of documents. Secondly,
many interesting methods that utilize graph structures have been developed.
It is possible to use them even on small sets of texts. For instance, weighted
directed multigraph method for text pattern recognition has been discussed in
[8]. The weights of edges were treated there as distances between the keywords,
and a keyword-frequency distance-based algorithm was designed, which not only
utilizes the frequency information of keywords but also their ordering information. An interesting approach that employs grammatical relations to establish

the weights of various terms in a text document was presented in [9]. A graph model was used there to encode the extracted relations, and the term weighting scheme was applied to text classification. A short survey of frequent pattern mining algorithms based on n-grams and phrases is presented in [10]. The methods of text representation discussed there used a structure in the form of a graph, with frequent sequences represented by nodes. A different pattern discovery technique in text documents has been presented in [11]. To improve the effectiveness of using and updating discovered patterns for finding relevant and interesting information, two innovative processes, namely pattern deploying and pattern evolving were utilized. In [12], an approach based on iterative relaxation labeling has been presented. It can be combined with either Bayesian or SVM classifiers on the feature spaces of the given data items. That approach considers the neighborhood of data items in a graph structure.

3   Similarity Between Documents

To talk about the similarity of documents we have first to determine what the similarity is. It is easier to define this concept in mathematics; in particular, it is precisely defined in geometry. In the case of texts, it is not easy to define similarity, and many definitions have been formulated. For instance, distance between strings of characters can be defined as Hamming distance, i.e., the number of positions at which the corresponding symbols are different [13]. Another well-known related measure is the Levenshtein distance [1] between words which is, roughly speaking, the minimum number of single-character insertions, deletions or substitutions required to change one word to the other. Unfortunately, these measures, although very effective in text searching with errors like spelling correction, or in bioinformatics for comparing of sequence similarity, are not useful in the analysis of similarity of general texts. We are interested instead in the texts similarity on a semantic level. Such sentence similarity is the basis of many natural language tasks such as information retrieval, question answering or text summarization. Many similarity measures are discussed in [14,15]. If we have relatively significant text corpus, we can use methods based on building word frequencies from a specific corpus. A well- known and effective method is the Latent Semantic Analysis (LSA) [16,17]. If a set of documents (corpus) is rather small and we want to compare documents, pairwise LSA is not very useful, however. The general intuition about the similarity of the texts is the following: it should be proportional to the size of a part of the text they have in common and related to the size of the texts.

In [15], Lin has formulated the basic intuitions and six assumptions about similarity from the information theory point of view and, finally, formulated Similarity Theorem in the general form (1):

$$\text{sim}(A, B) = \frac{\log P(\text{common}(A, B))}{\log P(\text{description}(A, B))} \tag{1}$$

The similarity between A and B is measured by the ratio between the amount of information needed to state the commonality of A and B and the information needed to fully describe A and B. This measure is applicable as long as the domain has a probabilistic model and has become a point of reference and a basis for many other measures. The above equation, in general, shows how the similarity between the texts can be defined.

The most basic similarity measure is, however, that based on the Jaccard index. We take into account only the occurrence of a term in the texts and ignore how often the term occurs. The similarity is expressed in the form (2):

$$\text{sim}(A, B) = \frac{|A \wedge B|}{|A \vee B|} \tag{2}$$

In other words in Jaccard index documents are represented as vectors where each dimension corresponds to a separate term and 0 means that term is not present and 1 otherwise. A generalization of this simple measure is the Vector Space Model [1,18]. Documents are represented as vectors $(a_1, ..., a_n)$ and $(b_1, ..., b_n)$ of features which are typically terms that occur in both documents. The value of each feature is called the feature weight and is usually taken as the frequency of appearance of that term in the document. From the Vector Space Model formulation the similarity measure between documents which uses cosine similarity between representing vectors (3) emerges quite naturally:

$$\text{sim}(A, B) = \frac{\sum_{i=1}^{n} a_i \cdot b_i}{\sqrt{\sum_{i=1}^{n} a_i^2 \cdot \sum_{i=1}^{n} b_i^2}} \tag{3}$$

We have to note that the Euclidean distance is not useful in this situation, because it does not take to account the size of documents. The Jaccard index and cosine measure are handy, but they treat the text as a bag-of-words which are usually nouns. That means that we lose information originated from the sentence syntax and semantics. During the process of preparing vectors of words (nouns), we can remove non-essential words. Some semantics can be added if we have the vocabulary, i.e., a set of predefined terms, connected with the specific domain; then representing vectors consist only of terms from the vocabulary.

4   Artificial Sentence and Hypernode

Since our goal is to define a distance measure for documents written in Polish, we first describe main issues connected with the text processing in that language. A method of analysis of the scientific texts in Polish has been presented and described by us in [20]. Our method consists of several steps; the first of these is a special preprocessing of an analyzed text. In the beginning, to overcome the issues associated with inflection, the custom stemming algorithm is applied, and words are reduced to their base form. In the Polish language, the verbs, the nouns, and the adjectives all have inflection. The number of possible forms is enormous. For example, the verbs have about one hundred inflection forms, including the past and passive participle with their grammar rules. Because we cannot use algorithms specific for the English language the stemming is based on the dictionary of Polish [19]. That freely available dictionary consists of words with the inflection forms. Based on it, together with the stemming, we prepared methods of parts of speech tagging [20]. After such preprocessing, during indexing some parts of speech, like particles or pronouns are removed. As a result of the indexing process, we obtained a set of words classified as particular parts of speech together with the number of their occurrence. Representing vectors are not limited to nouns, they contain verbs, and adjectives as well. Thanks to this fact our method uses not only the word statistics but also the syntactic and semantic features of the text.

In the kind of language as Polish, a basic sentence is constructed with the three parts: a subject (S), a verb (V) and an object (O). According to that, in [20] we observed an interesting connection among the most frequent noun, the most frequent verb, and the second most frequent noun; they often form the main thesis of the paper. A short sentence built from these three words we called *artificial sentence* (see [20]).

As we can see, an *artificial sentence* is based on a grammar of the natural language; the subject and object belong to the noun category. Accordingly, we created a semantic network with three types of nodes. The word node represents one word. The second type is the article node which represents a particular document (paper) and is connected with different words in that paper.

The third type is hypernode, the node which contains *artificial sentence*, the three most important words from the paper (most frequently occurring noun, most frequently occurring verb and the second most frequently occurring noun). Example of such semantic network we presented and discussed in [20].

In this work we expand our artificial-sentence approach by including another type of sentence. That new kind of analyzed sentence in the natural language is the adjective sentence. It is used for describing a state of the object, e.g., "A tomato is red." Naturally, there is yet another aspect of the phrase grammar which is the order of its parts. The most common order in the Polish language is the SVO pattern, but because the inflection of that language is rich and complicated, any permutation of SVO is admissible. To model this kind of relations and construct *artificial sentence* it is necessary to choose one verb, one adjective, and two nouns from the vector of words of the analyzed text. The verb is needed for the standard SVO phrase and the adjective for the adjective sentence. We used the most frequent word in each category (noun, verb, adjective) as a basis to choose the words for creating a hypernode. We have taken the most frequent noun (marked as the subject), the most frequent verb, and the most frequent adjective for the adjective sentence. The second most frequent noun is tagged as an object. Each analyzed text has only one hypernode containing two *artificial sentences*.

5   Experimental Results

To test our modified *artificial sentence* method small database of the agriculture scientific papers in Polish was prepared. The selected publications in Polish were taken from Agricultural Engineering Journal (Inżynieria Rolnicza - IR), and are related to the cultivation and processing of maize or potato. "A0" is "Assessment of the operation quality of the corn cobs and seeds processing line" (J. Bieniek, J. Zawada, F. Molendowski, P. Komarnicki, K. Kwietniak: "Ocena jakości pracy linii technologicznejdo obróbki kolb i ziarna kukurydzy". IR 2013 Nr 4); "A1" is "Methodological aspects of measuring hardness of maize caryopsis" (G. Czachor, J. Bohdziewicz: "Metodologiczne aspekty pomiaru twardości ziarniaka kukurydzy". IR 2013 Nr 4); "A2" is "Evaluation of results of irrigation applied to grain maze" (S. Dudek, J. Żarski: "Ocena efektów zastosowania nawadniania w uprawie kukurydzy na ziarno". IR 2005 Nr 3); "A3" is "Extra corn grain shredding and particle breaking up as a method used to improve quality of cut green forage" (A. Lisowski, K. Kostyra: "Dodatkowe rozdrabnianie ziaren i rozrywanie cząstek kukurydzy sposobem na poprawienie jakości pociętej zielonki". IR 2008 Nr 9); "A4" is "Comparative assessment of sugar corn grain acquisition for food purposes using cut off and threshing methods" (M. Szymanek: "Ocena porównawcza pozyskiwania ziarna kukurydzy cukrowej na cele spożywcze metodą odcinania i omłotu". IR 2009 Nr 8); "A5" is "Information system for acquiring data on geometry of agricultural products exemplified by a corn kernel" (J. Weres: "Informatyczny system pozyskiwania danych o geometrii produktów rolniczych na przykładzie ziarniaka kukurydzy". IR 2010 Nr 7); "A6" is "A decision support system in maize silage production" (A. Zaliwski, J. Hołaj: "System wspomagania decyzji w produkcji kiszonki z kukurydzy". IR 2007 Nr 2); "A7" is "Application of computer image processing to determine the physical properties to potato tubers" (P. Kiełbasa, P. Budyń: "Zastosowanie techniki wideo-komputerowej przy wyznaczaniu cech fizycznych bulw". IR 2005 Nr 8); "A8" is "New technology of the potatoes production – the bed tillage" (K. Jabłoński: "Nowe technologie produkcji ziemniaka – uprawa zagonowa". IR 2005 Nr 1); "A9" is "The impact of microwave irradiation on growth dynamics of potato germs" (T. Jakubowski: "Wpływ napromieniowania mikrofalowego na dynamikę wzrostu kiełków bulwy ziemniaka". IR 2008 Nr 5); "A10" is "Evaluation of selected physical properties of potato bulbs" (P. Kiełbasa: "Ocena wybranych cech fizycznych bulw ziemniaków". IR 2005 Nr 6); "A11" is "The impact of potato plantation irrigation on selected physical attributes of tubers which are significant in crop separation and sorting process" (K. Klamka, M. Rad: "Wpływ nawadniania plantacji ziemniaka na wybrane cechy fizyczne bulw istotne w procesie separacji i sortowania plonu". IR 2008 Nr 11); "A12" is "Evaluation of yield, chemical composition and quality of tubers of medium early, medium late and late starch potato cultivars" (M. Kołodziejczyk, A. Szmigiel, B. Kulig, A. Oleksy, A. Lepiarczyk: "Ocena plonowania, składu chemicznego i jakości bulw wybranych odmian ziemniaka skrobiowego". IR 2013 Nr 3 T.2); "A13" is "The impact of selected agrotechnical factors on the quantitative characteristics of potato tuber crop" (B. Krzysztofik, N. Marks, D. Baran: "Wpływ wybranych czynników agrotechnicznych na ilościowe cechy plonu bulw ziemniaka". IR 2009 Nr 5); "A14" is "Using the canvassing of the image to assessing losses in the nursery of the potato" (J. Rut, K. Szwedziak:

"Zastosowanie akwizycji obrazu do szacowania strat w uprawie ziemniaka". IR 2008 Nr 7); "A15" is "Relations between tuber density growth and selected potato properties during storage" (Z. Sobol, D. Baran: "Relacje pomiędzy przyrostem gęstości bulw a wybranymi właściwościami ziemniaka w okresie przechowywania". IR 2007 Nr 9); "A16" is "Assessment technique and statistic modelling of the degree of potato damage caused by Colorado beetle" (K. Szwedziak, J. Rut: "Technika oceny i modelowanie statystyczne stopnia uszkodzeń ziemniaka przez stonkę ziemniaczaną". IR 2008 Nr 6); "A17" is "Design Parameters of a roller-type potato cleaning separator" (W. Tanaś: "Parametry konstrukcyjne rolkowego separatora czyszczącego do ziemniaków". IR 2008 Nr 10); "A18" is "Potato as a cultivated plant – fragments of history" (P. Zalewski: "Ziemniak jako roślina uprawna – fragment historii". IR 2009 Nr 5). The created hypernodes are shown in Table 1. That table contains the found subject, verb, object and adjective. It also presents the translation of the *artificial sentences* from Polish to English.

We have found the resulting *artificial sentences* entirely satisfactory. However, we have also notices some erroneous results stemming from misidentification of the adjective, for example in A0, A2 and A18 "były" is the past form of verb "być" (to be) but at the same time it means "former" in Polish. In A0 the second adjective is "seminal" and it should be added. In A10 in Polish there is one word for "to rub" and act of fractioning. In A11 noun group "wskaźnik wypełnienia gabarytowego" which means an indicator of dimensional fill, has been extracted only partially, i.e., "gabarytowy". This result means that entire phrases should be taken into account. In the A14 and A16 "potato" is subject, but also is connected with the object because in Polish language a Colorado beetle larva is something like potato beetle larva ("larwa stonki ziemniaczanej"). In A17 the adjective "spiral" should be connected with the phrase roller-type cleaning separator. We can conclude that the simplest sentence patterns are not enough. The predicate sometimes is more complicated than merely verb plus object. We can have a noun phrase as subject and a verb phrase as predicate. Additionally, the word order in the sentence in Polish can be more differentiated than in English. Apparently, some important words are left out that are not found in the selected four words. These insights allow us to conclude that the *artificial sentence* should sometimes be corrected. Instead of two very simple sentences, we can create one more complex *artificial sentence*. The following sentences can be proposed for more complicated cases:

– A0 Grain (from) cob was (seminal material).
– A1 Time is (needed for preparing) maize seminal (material).
– A2 A maize grain (depends on whether the fields) were irrigated.
– A3 Working (factor) of maize grain fragmentation.
– A4 Carry (out research on) a sugar maize grain.
– A5 A mesh for (modeling) agricultural product.
– A6 Direct (economic) model for maize is (constructed).
– A7 The influence of clay (soil) for tubers were tested (for many) varieties.
– A8 A potato bed cultivation planting.

Table 1. Words in hypernodes

Paper	Subject	Verb	Object	Adjective
A0	ziarno (grain)	być (to be)	kolba (cob)	były (former)
A1	czas (time)	być (to be)	ziarniak (kernels)	nasienny (seminal)
A3	ziarno (grain)	rozdrobnić (to fragmentize)	kukurydza (maize)	roboczy (working)
A4	ziarno (grain)	pzeprowadzić (to carry)	kolba (cob)	cukrowy (sugar)
A5	produkt (product)	być (to be)	siatka (mesh)	rolniczy (agricultural)
A6	kukurydza (maize)	być (to be)	model (model)	bezpośredni (direct)
A7	bulwa (tuber)	badać (to test)	odmiana (variety)	gliniasty (clay)
A8	uprawa (cultivation)	sadzić (to plant)	ziemniak (potato)	zagonowy (bed)
A9	bulwa (tuber)	promieniować (to irradiate)	dawka (dose)	mikrofalowy (microwave)
A10	bulwa (tuber)	trzeć (to rub)	odmiana (variety)	istotny (significant)
A11	bulwa (tuber)	nawadniać (to irrigate)	ziemniak (potato)	gabarytowy (dimensional)
A12	bulwa (tuber)	być (to be)	odmiana (variety)	średni (average)
A13	plon (yield)	nawozić (to fertilize)	bulwa (tuber)	handlowy (commercial)
A14	ziemniak (potato)	być (to be)	larwa (larva)	komputerowy (computer)
A15	bulwa (tuber)	przechowywać (to store)	ziemniak (potato)	przechowalniczy (connected with storage)
A16	ziemniak (potato)	być (to be)	larwa (larva)	statystyczny (statistical)
A17	bulwa (tuber)	być (to be)	ziemniak (potato)	spiralny (spiral)
A18	ziemniak (potato)	być (to be)	roślina (plant)	były (former)

- A9 A tuber irradiated (by) microwave dose.
- A10 A significant friction value (for) tuber.
- A11 A potato irrigation (changes) dimensional (factor) of tuber.
- A12 A tuber average (starch content) for variety.

– A13 Potato fertilizing is significant (for) yield.
– A14 Potato (beetle) larvae were (studied) by computer.
– A15 Tuber of potato was stored in storage (utilities).
– A16 Potato is (damaged by) potato (beetle) larvae.
– A17 Potato tubers were (cleaned) in cylinder (with) spiral.
– A18 Potato is a plant (which) were cultivated (for a long time).

After manually correcting the *artificial sentences*, we have found the result
to be entirely satisfactory. The main subject of every paper has been recognized
correctly.

6 Measure of Distance Between Different Texts

Each of analyzed scientific papers has its own hypernode. Although not every
simple *artificial sentence* based on the hypernode is appropriate, we can arrange
four words from that hypernode into a legitimate *artificial sentence*. It means
that only hypernodes are needed to compare the texts. The result of comparison
has to provide information about the differences between hypernodes in terms
of weights. The smaller is the value of weights, the closer two analyzed texts are.
Our measure of distance stresses a little more the syntax than the semantics.
We propose the following values of the weights while comparing two documents:

– 0 – two texts have the same words in their hypernode.
– 0.5 – the adjectives in both hypernodes are different, but the subject, the
  verb, and the object are the same.
– 0.75 – the object and the adjective are the same in both hypernodes.
– 1.0 – the object and the subject are the same in both hypernodes.
– 1.5 – the subject in the first hypernode is the object in the second and vice
  versa.
– 2.0 – the hypernodes have the same subject or the object,
– 2.5 – One of the hypernodes has the same subject as the object in the other.

We present the results of our calculations of the distances between the pairs
of hypernodes from the agricultural scientific articles (specified above) in the
form of a non-directed graph (Fig. 1).

The dependency graph of our semantic net is divided into two separate parts
and additional two single nodes. The first group of texts (A0, A2, A3, A4, A6)
is related to the cultivation of maize. A6 is about decision support system and
has the connection only with the paper A2 about assessing the impact of irrigation. They are related by yield estimation discussion in both of them. Separate
node A5 is formally about maize, but in practice, it is instead about the technical aspects of data collection system for geometry properties (mesh models) of
agricultural objects. The second separate node A1 is for paper connected with
maize, but it is devoted to the physical parameters of maize grain. Our method
has successively separated these two nodes. The second group (A7, A8, A11,
A12, A13, A14, A15 A16, A17, A18) is generally speaking about potatoes. The

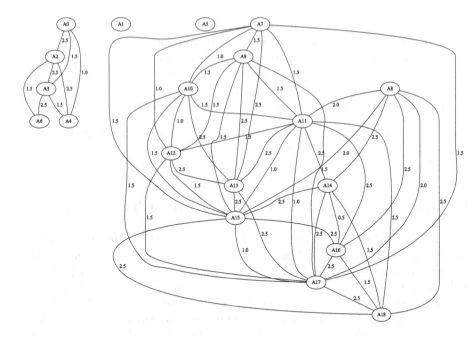

Fig. 1. The non-directed graph of distance between analyzed papers

papers A14 and A16 are very close; the reason is obvious because both papers have the same authors. The papers A11, A15, and A17 are relatively close; all of them are about properties of potato tubers described by physical parameters. We can observe that those nodes have highest vertices degrees 11. It means that they have the connection with every member of the second group and form a kind of center.

We have also generated graphs based on the distances obtained using the Jaccard index (Fig. 2) and the cosine measure (Fig. 3) to compare the obtained results. In both cases, the representative vectors have been built only from nouns. The appropriate distance for Jaccard has been obtained as the difference $1 - Sim_J$ where Sim_J is defined in (2). To obtain the measure from cosine similarity, the arc cosine of the similarity value has been computed and normalized. The method based on Jaccard similarity has turned out to connected the paper about maize A2 with papers about potatoes. Moreover, other papers about maize have turned out to be poorly connected. The human-made analysis of texts performed by specialists showed that method based on cosine measure has given much better results but has been worse than the method based on the *artificial sentence*.

Another test of the results obtained from ASP has been performed by using two popular web search engines: Google and Bing. We have used the words from the hypernodes and searched for scientific articles by the above-mentioned web services. The conditions have been as follows: the web browsers have worked

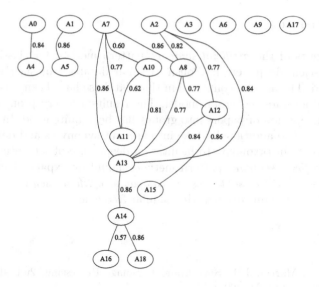

Fig. 2. The non-directed graph of Jaccard weights

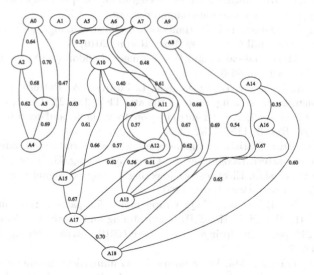

Fig. 3. The non-directed graph of cosine weights

in private mode and two languages, Polish and English, have been used. The translation of the words came from Table 1. The scientific papers found (both in Polish and English), have had the same subjects as the papers from which the hypernodes have been extracted. This fact is very promising because it suggests, that the hypernodes generated in the one language, e.g., Polish, can be easily translated and used to create hypernode in other languages.

7   Conclusion

To perform tests of the *artificial sentence* pattern method for classification of agricultural scientific papers in Polish, a small database of such papers has been prepared. The articles contained in that database have been classified with the help of a non-directed graph model. The results are very promising in the sense that the division of papers into groups has been quite good. In the future research, we plan to additionally take into account synonyms and dependencies between concepts in taxonomy to facilitate a deeper use of semantics. What is more, our *artificial sentence* pattern method should be expanded into the set of two or three *artificial sentences*, or *compound artificial sentence*, especially when several main nouns occur with a similar frequency.

References

1. Jurafski, D., Martin, J.H.: Speech and Language Processing, 2nd edn. Prentice Hall, Englewood Cliffs (2008)
2. Encyclopedia Britannica: Pattern recognition. https://www.britannica.com/technology/pattern-recognition-computer-science
3. Indurkhya, N., Damerau, F.J.: Handbook of Natural Language Processing, 2nd edn. Chapman & Hall CRC Press, Boca Raton (2010)
4. Kornai, A.: Mathematical Linguistics. Springer, London (2008). https://doi.org/10.1007/978-1-84628-986-6
5. Kocaleva, M., Stojanov, D., Stojanovik, I., Zdravev, Z.: Pattern recognition and natural language processing. State of the art. TEM J. **5**(2), 236–240 (2016)
6. Clopinet, I., Elisseeff, A.: An introduction to variable and feature selection. J. Mach. Learn. Res. **3**, 1157–1182 (2003)
7. Bellegarda, J.R.: Statistical language models with embedded latent semantic knowledge in pattern recognition. In: Chou, W., Juang, B.-H. (eds.) Speech and Language Processing. Electrical Engineering & Applied Signal Processing Series, 1st edn. CRC Press, Boca Raton (2003)
8. Wu, Q., Fuller, E., Zhang, C.Q.: Graph model for pattern recognition in text. In: Ting, I.H., Wu, H.J., Ho, T.H. (eds.) Mining and Analyzing Social Networks. SCI, vol. 288, pp. 1–20. Springer, Heidelberg (2010). https://doi.org/10.1007/978-3-642-13422-7_1
9. Huynh, D., Tran, D., Ma, W., Sharma, D.: Grammatical dependency-based relations for term weighting in text classification. In: Huang, J.Z., Cao, L., Srivastava, J. (eds.) PAKDD 2011. LNCS (LNAI), vol. 6634, pp. 476–487. Springer, Heidelberg (2011). https://doi.org/10.1007/978-3-642-20841-6_39
10. Ożdżyński, P., Zakrzewska, D.: Using frequent pattern mining algorithms in text analysis. Inf. Syst. Manag. **6**(3), 213–222 (2017)
11. Zhong, N., Li, Y., Wu, S.T.: Effective pattern discovery for text mining. IEEE Trans. Knowl. Data Eng. **24**(1), 30–44 (2012)
12. Angelova, R., Weikum, G.: Graph-based text classification: learn from your neighbors. In: SIGIR 2006 Proceedings of the 29th Annual International ACM SIGIR Conference on Research and Development in Information Retrieval, pp. 485–492 (2006)

13. Hamming, R.W.: Error detecting and error correcting codes. Bell Syst. Tech. J. **29**(2), 147–160 (1950)
14. Atoum, I., Otoom, A., Kulthuramaiyer, N.: A comprehensive comparative study of word and sentence similarity measures. Int. J. Comput. Appl. **135**(1), 10–17 (2016)
15. Lin, D.: An information-theoretic definition of similarity. In: ICML 1998 Proceedings of the Fifteenth International Conference on Machine Learning, pp. 296–304. Morgan Kaufmann (1998)
16. Deerwester, S., Dumais, S., Landauer, T., Furnas, G., Harshman, R.: Indexing by latent semantic analysis. J. Am. Soc. Inf. Sci. **41**(6), 391–407 (1990)
17. Landauer, T.K., Foltz, P.W., Laham, D.: Introduction to latent semantic analysis. Discourse Process. **25**, 259–284 (1998)
18. Manning, C.D., Raghavan, P., Schütze, H.: Introduction to Information Retrieval. Cambridge University Press, Cambridge (2008)
19. The Polish language dictionary (Słownik Języka Polskiego) Homepage. sjp.pl. Accessed 10 Mar 2018
20. Wrzeciono, P., Karwowski, W.: Automatic indexing and creating semantic networks for agricultural science papers in the Polish language. In: 2013 IEEE 37th Annual Computer Software and Applications Conference Workshops, COMPSACW 2013, Kyoto, Japan, 22–26 July 2013, pp. 356–360 (2013)

Pattern Recognition in Financial Data Using Association Rule

Krzysztof Karpio[(✉)] and Piotr Łukasiewicz

Warsaw University of Life Sciences, Nowoursynowska 166, 02-787 Warsaw, Poland
krzysztof_karpio@sggw.pl
http://www.sggw.pl

Abstract. The paper is devoted to study patterns between the world's financial markets. The classical Association Rules method was adopted to study the relations between time series of stock market indices. One revealed the comovement patterns are predominant over the anti comovement ones. The strength of the relations depends on the distance between markets. One extracted the strongest patterns what allowed to distinguishing the groups of financial markets. The strongest links between Polish and other stock markets were discovered.

Keywords: Data mining · Association rules · Stock market indices
Pattern recognition

1 Introduction

Association Rules (AR) is one of the most interesting and frequently used data mining techniques. Origin of this method dates back to the problem of discovering dependencies in the context of the so called analysis of the shopping cart (MBA - Market Basket Analysis). In the classical MBA problem the method yields the results in the form: "when product A is purchased then product B is also purchased" called association rules. Nowadays AR is used in the wide range of branches of science where big data sets are analyzed, from natural sciences to management and business [1,2], banking [3], medicine (medical diagnosis) [4,5], technology [6], and others.

We applied this method to study the patterns between financial time series [7–9]. In the first of the cited papers, we used AR to study relations between the return rates of the assets on the Warsaw Stock Exchange (WSE). The results yielded by AR were compared to the reference model. The reference data were constructed based on the real data by randomly choosing daily return rates. That allowed us to measure the statistical significances of the discovered patterns. In next paper [8] we adopted AR method to explore the comovement between sector indices listed on the WSE. The measures describing discovered rules were calculated and strong rules were selected. Based on the discovered strong rules the relations between parts of the Polish economy were presented. In [9] we

© Springer Nature Switzerland AG 2018
L. J. Chmielewski et al. (Eds.): ICCVG 2018, LNCS 11114, pp. 512–521, 2018.
https://doi.org/10.1007/978-3-030-00692-1_44

incorporated new way of calculating support and measuring rules' qualities which were taking into account various periods the studied assets were traded. That allowed us to analyze financial data in a wide range of time. The results were compared to those obtained using the traditional approach. We observed higher values of measures and smaller errors for a majority of the rules.

The relations between main stocks indices in Europe, USA, Brazil, and Japan were also investigated by Pan et al. in [10]. Na and Sohn were forecasting changes in the Korea Composite Stock Price Index based on its relations to various worlds' stocks indices [11]. In this paper the AR data mining technique is used to discover patterns in comovements between main indices of the selected world's stock markets. The analysis has been performed in the wide range of time, the various time periods the indices were traded has been taken into account. Rules of types: up-up, down-down, up-down and down-up were being searched. The statistical significance of the results has been evaluated using the Monte Carlo method and errors of the rules' measures were calculated using the bootstrap method. We used our own algorithm, implemented in MATLAB system and based on the classical Apriori algorithm [12]. The Apriori is the iteration algorithm of the AR, which in subsequent steps generates ever-increasing frequent itemsets [13,14].

2 Association Rules and Their Measures

The association rules are defined as in [12]. Let $I = \{i_1, i_2, \ldots, i_m\}$ be a set of binary attributes called items. By transaction T we understand every non-empty subset of I ($T \subset I$ and $T \neq \emptyset$). A set of all transactions is called the database and is denoted by D. An association rule is any relation of the form $X \to Y$, where $X \subset I$, $Y \subset I$ and $X \cap Y = \emptyset$. A support value of the set $A \subset I$ is the ratio of the number of transactions T such as $A \subset T$ to the number of all transactions in the database D. A support of the set A will be denoted by $supp(A, D)$. We define the support and the confidence of the rule $X \to Y$ in the following manner:

$$Supp(X \to Y) = supp(X \cup Y, D), \tag{1}$$

$$Conf(X \to Y) = supp(X \cup Y, D)/supp(X, D). \tag{2}$$

A number of discovered rules might be very big, so it is crucial to select those which are the most usefull. The selection is usually done based on both the minimum support $minSupp$ and the minimum confidence $minConf$. There are cases when rules with high supports and confidences are not interesting [15]. That's why the selected rules are also checked for satisfying the inequity: $Lift > 1$, where $Lift$ of the rule: $X \to Y$ is defined as

$$Lift(X \to Y) = supp(X \cup Y, D)/(supp(X, D) \cdot supp(Y, D)). \tag{3}$$

The measures which were described above can be expressed in the terms of random events [12]. Let E_X be a set of transactions containing X, thus $E_X = \{T \in D : X \subseteq T\}$, and $supp(X, D) = |E_X|/|D| = P(E_X)$, then:

$$Supp(X \to Y) = P(E_X \cap E_Y),\tag{4}$$

$$Conf(X \to Y) = P(E_Y|E_X),\tag{5}$$

$$Lift(X \to Y) = P(E_X \cap E_Y)/(P(E_X) \cdot P(E_Y)).\tag{6}$$

Support of the rule $X \to Y$ is a proportion of the transactions containing $X \cup Y$ in the database D. Support is a frequency the rule occurs and it reflects a proportion of the rules in the database. Confidence is an estimate of the conditional probability $P(E_Y|E_X)$ that is the probability of observing Y given X. Confidence measures strength and reliability of the rule. Support of the rule is often described as the measure of its usefulness.

3   Data and Selections

The analyzed data regards daily return rates of the main stock market indices from various countries. The indices, their trading periods, and countries of origin are listed in Fig. 1. The analyzed period of time starts from 1970-01-01 and ends at 2017-10-16, what corresponds to 12388 trading days. The longest traded indices are: DJIA, NIKKEI, and SP500, on the other hand SASESLCT starting from 2003-01-03 has the shortest period of trading time.

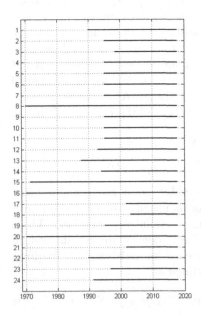

1	ALL_ORD	Australia
2	AMEX MAJ	USA
3	B SHARES	China
4	BOVESPA	Brasil
5	BUX	Hungary
6	CAC40	France
7	DAX	Germany
8	DJIA	USA
9	DJTA	USA
10	DJUA	USA
11	EOE	Holland
12	FT SE100	UK
13	HANGSENG	China
14	MEXICIPC	Mexico
15	NASDAQ	USA
16	NIKKEI	Japan
17	RUSSEL 2000	USA
18	SASESLCT	Chile
19	SMI	Switzerland
20	SP500	USA
21	TOPIX	Japan
22	TSE 300	Canada
23	BUENOS	Argentina
24	WIG_POLAND	Poland

Fig. 1. Indices with time periods when they were traded.

Distributions of the return rates of the indices are similar to each other. They are symmetric and concentrated around zero [8]. We set the limit for each index equal to of its return rates' standard deviation. The return rates with its absolute value smaller than the limit is considered to be consisted with zero. On the other hand, we consider the return rates outside the limits as significantly positive or negative. This procedure leads to the 1516 (about 12%) 'empty trading days' (days with no indices with positive or negative return rates). We studied coincidences among the significant positive and negative return rates in the form of: up-up, down-down, up-down, and down-up rules. We perform the analysis in the whole range of time and we took into account different period of times the indices were traded [9].

We analyzed the set of indices originated from various parts of the world and countries of different levels of economy. We shall therefore expect a weak or no mutual interactions between some those indices. On the other hand, we chose the subset of the indices originated from USA, which are related to the same country and economy and sometimes contain return rates of the same companies. In that case we should face the strong rules, at least between some of them.

4   Comovement and Anti Comovement Patterns

Based on the processed data we evaluated rules: $X^\uparrow \to Y^\uparrow$ (up-up), $X_\downarrow \to Y_\downarrow$ (down-down), $X^\uparrow \to Y_\downarrow$ (up-down) and $X_\downarrow \to Y^\uparrow$ (down-up). Numbers of the rules were: 552, 552, 551, and 551 respectively. Measures for all discovered rules were estimated and their errors were calculated using the bootstrap method. Lift vs support is presented in Fig. 2 and lift vs confidence is in Fig. 3. Mean and maximum values of the measures for all four types of the rules are presented in Table 1.

Table 1. Mean and mamsimum values of the rules' measures.

Rule's type	Supp		Conf		Lift	
up - up	0.108	0.227	0.425	0.939	1.693	3.882
down - down	0.097	0.205	0.435	0.945	1.968	4.344
up - down	0.031	0.071	0.123	0.264	0.498	1.299
down - up	0.031	0.071	0.140	0.291	0.639	1.694

The obtained results were compared to a reference model. The reference data were constructed based on the real data by randomly permuting daily return rates. This procedure conserves distributions of the return rates of each index but destroys correlations between then. That allowed us to compare the measures of the real rules with measures of the rules which were raised by statistical coincidences. The rules in the area of the statistical unimportance are indicated by open circles in Figs. 2 and 3.

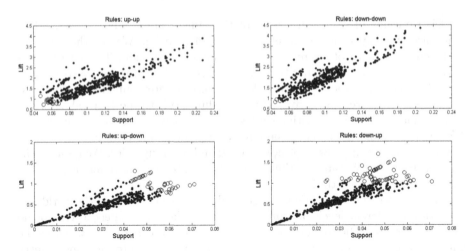

Fig. 2. Lift vs support of the discovered rules. Open circles: statistically insignificant rules.

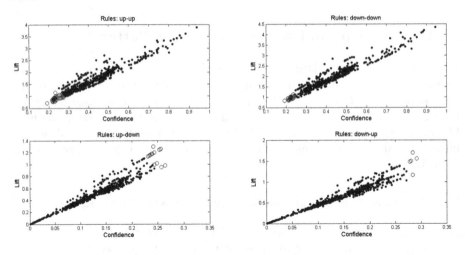

Fig. 3. Lift vs confidence for discovered rules. Open circles: statistically insignificant rules.

The statistically important up-up and down-down rules are characterized by $Lift > 1$. According to the lift definition, its value around 1 indicates on mutual independence of a predecessor and a successor of the rule. Such a rule can occur by accident and is of no usage. The rules having lift much greater than one are most important because they indicate a comovement of the index pairs. The greater lift the greater co-movement. On the other hand up-down and down-up rules can be identified by $Lift < 1$. That means the rise of the one index and drop of the other in the same day occur much less often than in the case of the absence of any correlations between the indices. Moreover, those rules occur seldom and are weak ($Supp < 0.065$, $Conf < 0.28$). This behavior further supports the previous observation: indices exhibit global alignment patterns. These results confirm well known observation of global comovement of financial markets.

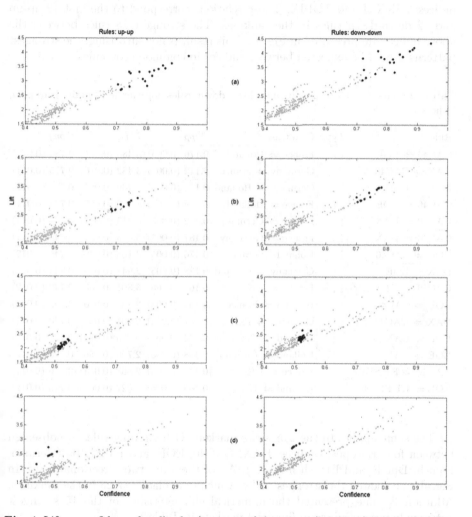

Fig. 4. Lift vs confidence for all rules (gray point) for up-up (left plots) and down-down rules (right plots). The black points indicate the strongest (a) rules among USA indices and among Japanese indices, (b) rules among German, French, Holland, and British indices, (c) intercontinental rules (d) rules between Polish and other indices.

The rankings of the up-up and down-down rules based on confidence were built. A ranks based on lift are similar because both measures are strongly correlated to each other. Implementing the requirement $Lift > 1.5$, what corresponds roughly to $Conf > 0.4$, we excluded the weakest rules. There were 285 up-up rules and 312 down-down rules remaining. Those rules are shown in Fig. 4, where the groups of rules described below are distinguished.

We observe the strongest relations between US indices: AMEX_MAJ, DJIA, DJTA, DJUA, NASDAQ, RUSSEL 2000, SP500 as well as between two Japanese indices: NIKKEI and TOPIX. Those relations correspond to the first 12 up-up and 12 down-down rules in the rankings. The strongest 18 rules between the above indices are presented in Fig. 4a. This result is not surprising; the strongest patterns should be expected between indices in common economies.

Table 2. The strongest up-up and down-down rules for the four main European indices.

Rule	Type	Countries	$Supp$	$Lift$	$Conf$
CAC40 ⇒ EOE	↓↓	France ⇒ Holland	0.176 (0.005)	3.488 (0.071)	0.784 (0.011)
DAX ⇒ CAC40	↓↓	Germany ⇒ France	0.172 (0.005)	3.482 (0.076)	0.775 (0.011)
DAX ⇒ EOE	↓↓	Germany ⇒ Holland	0.172 (0.005)	3.469 (0.069)	0.772 (0.012)
CAC40 ⇒ EOE	↑↑	France ⇒ Holland	0.192 (0.005)	3.090 (0.057)	0.771 (0.011)
CAC40 ⇒ DAX	↓↓	France ⇒ Germany	0.172 (0.005)	3.415 (0.077)	0.767 (0.011)
CAC40 ⇒ DAX	↑↑	France ⇒ Germany	0.187 (0.005)	3.003 (0.052)	0.749 (0.011)
EOE ⇒ CAC40	↓↓	Holland ⇒ France	0.176 (0.005)	3.153 (0.070)	0.745 (0.012)
DAX ⇒ EOE	↑↑	Germany ⇒ Holland	0.188 (0.005)	2.948 (0.055)	0.744 (0.012)
CAC40 ⇒ FT_SE100	↓↓	France ⇒ UK	0.167 (0.005)	3.301 (0.065)	0.742 (0.012)
EOE ⇒ CAC40	↑↑	Holland ⇒ France	0.192 (0.005)	2.861 (0.060)	0.742 (0.011)
DAX ⇒ CAC40	↑↑	Germany ⇒ France	0.187 (0.005)	2.931 (0.060)	0.740 (0.011)
EOE ⇒ DAX	↓↓	Holland ⇒ Germany	0.172 (0.005)	3.075 (0.071)	0.727 (0.013)
EOE ⇒ DAX	↑↑	Holland ⇒ Germany	0.188 (0.005)	2.796 (0.056)	0.725 (0.012)
CAC40 ⇒ FT_SE100	↑↑	France ⇒ UK	0.179 (0.005)	2.868 (0.054)	0.716 (0.011)
EOE ⇒ FT_SE100	↓↓	Holland ⇒ UK	0.169 (0.005)	3.027 (0.066)	0.715 (0.012)

The same applies to the European markets. Other strong rules are observed between four European indices: DAX, CAC40, EOE, and FT_SE100 (German, French, Dutch, and British markets). All of them are two directional rules. In Fig. 4b one showed the strongest rules, which take places 13–23 in the rankings. Additionally, one presented the numerical characteristics of the 15 strongest patterns between European financial markets in Table 2.

Next rules in the rankings are primarily two-directional relations between main European indices and Swiss financial market (SMI index) as well as between US indices and two markets: Canadian (TSE_300) and Mexican (MEXICIPC). Intercontinental patterns exist in both rankings starting from ranking position 65. The strongest rules among them are between indices in North America (USA, Canada, Mexico) and South America (Brasil, Chile) as well as between the four main European indices and North American indices. The lower positions in the rankings are occupied by rules reflecting the comovement patterns among Asian and Australian markets. The 20 strongest rules are presented in Fig. 4c.

Table 3. The strongest up-up and down-down rules between Polish and other financial markets

Rule	Type	Countries	$Supp$	$Lift$	$Conf$
WIG ⇒ EOE	↓↓	Poland ⇒ Holland	0.093 (0.004)	2.876 (0.063)	0.517 (0.016)
WIG ⇒ BUX	↓↓	Poland ⇒ Hungary	0.100 (0.004)	2.565 (0.053)	0.508 (0.014)
WIG ⇒ DAX	↓↓	Poland ⇒ Germany	0.091 (0.004)	2.814 (0.063)	0.506 (0.016)
WIG ⇒ SASESLCT	↓↓	Poland ⇒ Chile	0.076 (0.004)	3.340 (0.062)	0.504 (0.015)
WIG ⇒ BUX	↓↓	Poland ⇒ Hungary	0.090 (0.004)	2.777 (0.067)	0.499 (0.016)
WIG ⇒ SMI	↓↓	Poland ⇒ Switzerland	0.089 (0.004)	2.761 (0.060)	0.496 (0.016)
WIG ⇒ CAC40	↓↓	Poland ⇒ France	0.089 (0.004)	2.751 (0.066)	0.494 (0.016)
WIG ⇒ EOE	↓↓	Poland ⇒ Hungary	0.097 (0.004)	2.483 (0.050)	0.492 (0.015)
WIG ⇒ FT_SE100	↓↓	Poland ⇒ UK	0.089 (0.004)	2.723 (0.059)	0.492 (0.016)
WIG ⇒ DAX	↓↓	Poland ⇒ Germany	0.097 (0.004)	2.466 (0.057)	0.489 (0.016)
WIG ⇒ SMI	↓↓	Poland ⇒ Switzerland	0.096 (0.004)	2.444 (0.049)	0.484 (0.015)
WIG ⇒ SASESLCT	↓↓	Poland ⇒ Chile	0.085 (0.004)	2.713 (0.041)	0.480 (0.015)

The rules containing WIG_POLAND index are in positions starting from 97. The 13 up-up and down-down rules are in Fig. 4d. Values of support are in the range 0.07 ÷ 0.10. All rules except one are of the form WIG_POLAND ⇒ Y. These are the rules binding the Polish market and the four largest European markets. The relationship between the Polish market and the Hungarian one (WIG_POLAND ⇒ BUX and BUX ⇒ WIG_POLAND) and the Chilean one (WIG_POLAND ⇒ SASESLCT) can be explained. Economic relations between Poland and Hungary are close. The last rule can be related to the activity of Polish company KGHM, whose the largest foreign investment is in Chile. The strongest rules are listed in Table 3.

5 Conclusions

In this paper the use of Association Rules method to discover patterns between main indices of the world's stock markets. There are three main differences in comparison to the classical market basket analysis: (1) there are three states of financial assets: price could increase, decrease or stay; (2) empty baskets exist, i.e. trading days with no increases/decreases; (3) various assets debuted at different times, what should be taken into account. There is more on these issues in [9].

One distinguished four types of the rules: up-up, down-down, up-down, and down-up. One showed that anti comovement patterns occur seldom and are weak. They are below the expected frequencies and strength as in the case of the lack of correlations. World's stock markets are characterized by significant dominance of the mutual comovement over anti comovement; even they are far away from each other. The strongest patterns exist within USA, Japan, and big European markets. These relations are two-directional of up-up and down-down types. The intercontinental patterns are weaker but still characterized by high values of their measures and decreasing with geographic distance of the financial markets. The Polish market is the strongest link to the big European markets. One also discovered its strong relations with Hungary and Chilean markets.

Our works indicate on the two directions of the future studies. Values of classical measures of the rules are strongly correlated to each other. This is the result of their definitions; confidence and lift are determined by the rules' support. It would be beneficial to develop a new measure that would allow to efficiently differentiating the rules. The studies show the up-up and down-down rules often coexist in the financial markets; the positions of these rules' pairs are close to each other in the rankings. It seems to be useful to study the comovement patterns based on the merged rules and elaborating ways to measure them.

References

1. Huang, Z., Lu, X., Duan, H.: Mining association rules to support resource allocation in business process management. Expert Syst. Appl. **38**(8), 9483–9490 (2011)
2. Moreno Garcia, M.N., Román, I., Garcia-Peñalvo, F.J., Toro Bonilla, M.: An association rule mining method for estimating the impact of project management policies on software quality, development time and effort. Expert Syst. Appl. **34**(1), 522–529 (2008)
3. Sánchez, D., Vila, M.A., Cerda, L., Serrano, J.M.: Association rules applied to credit card fraud detection. Expert Syst. Appl. **36**(2, Part 2), 3630–3640 (2009)
4. Nahar, J., Imam, T., Tickle, K.S., Chen, Y.P.P.: Association rule mining to detect factors which contribute to heart disease in males and females. Expert Syst. Appl. **40**(4), 1086–1093 (2013)
5. Chaves, R., Ramirez, J., Górriz, J.M., Puntonet, C.G.: Association rule-based feature selection method for Alzheimer's disease diagnosis. Expert Syst. Appl. **39**(14), 11766–11774 (2012)
6. Han, H.K., Kim, H.S., Sohn, S.Y.: Sequential association rules for forecasting failure patterns of aircrafts in Korean airforce. Expert Syst. Appl. **36**(2, Part 1), 1129–1133 (2009)
7. Karpio, K., Łukasiewicz, P., Orłowski, A., Ząbkowski, T.: Mining associations on the warsaw stock exchange. Acta Phys. Pol. A **123**(3), 553–559 (2013)
8. Karpio, K., Łukasiewicz, P., Orłowski, A.: Associations rules between sector indices on the warsaw stock exchange. In: Řepa, V., Bruckner, T. (eds.) BIR 2016. LNBIP, vol. 261, pp. 312–321. Springer, Cham (2016). https://doi.org/10.1007/978-3-319-45321-7_22
9. Karpio, K., Łukasiewicz, P.: Association rules in data with various time periods. In: Gruca, A., Czachórski, T., Harezlak, K., Kozielski, S., Piotrowska, A. (eds.) ICMMI 2017. AISC, vol. 659, pp. 387–396. Springer, Cham (2018). https://doi.org/10.1007/978-3-319-67792-7_38
10. Pan, Y., Haran, E., Manago, S., Hu, Y.: Co-movement of European stock markets based on association rule mining. In: Proceedings of 3rd Data Analytics 2014, Rome, Italy, pp. 54–58 (2014)
11. Na, S.H., Sohn, S.Y.: Forecasting changes in Korea composite stock price index (KOSPI) using association rules. Expert Syst. Appl. **38**, 9046–9049 (2011)
12. Agrawal, R., Imieliński, T., Swami, A.: Mining association rules between sets of items in large databases. In: Proceedings of the 1993 ACM SIGMOD International Conference on Management of Data, New York, USA, pp. 207–216 (1993)

13. Agrawal, R., Srikant, R.: Fast algorithms for mining association rules. In: Proceedings of the 20th VLDB, Santiago, Chile, pp. 487–499 (1994)
14. Agrawal, R., Shafer, J.: Parallel mining of association rules. IEEE Trans. Knowl. Data Eng. **8**(6), 962–969 (1996)
15. Azevedo, P.J., Jorge, A.M.: Comparing rule measures for predictive association rules. In: Kok, J.N., Koronacki, J., Mantaras, R.L., Matwin, S., Mladenič, D., Skowron, A. (eds.) ECML 2007. LNCS (LNAI), vol. 4701, pp. 510–517. Springer, Heidelberg (2007). https://doi.org/10.1007/978-3-540-74958-5_47

Ulam Spiral and Prime-Rich Polynomials

Arkadiusz Orłowski[(✉)] and Leszek J. Chmielewski[(✉)]

Faculty of Applied Informatics and Mathematics (WZIM), Warsaw University of Life Sciences (SGGW), ul. Nowoursynowska 159, 02-775 Warsaw, Poland
{arkadiusz_orlowski,leszek_chmielewski}@sggw.pl
http://www.wzim.sggw.pl

Abstract. The set of prime numbers visualized as Ulam spiral was considered from the image processing perspective. Sequences of primes forming line segments were detected with the special version of the Hough transform. The polynomials which generate the numbers related to these sequences were investigated for their potential richness in prime numbers. One of the polynomials which generates the numbers forming the 11-point sequence was found exceptionally prime-rich, although it was not the longest sequence found. This polynomial is $4n^2 - 1260n + 98827$ and it generates 613 primes (20 of them with the minus sign) for the first 1000 non-negative integers as arguments. This is more than generated by some other well-known prime-rich polynomials, the Euler one included.

Keywords: Ulam spiral · Line segment · Prime-rich · Polynomial
Hough transform

1 Introduction

The set of prime numbers is a subject of intensive research and is still hiding mysteries (cf. [20]). It is interesting from the point of view of many subdomains of mathematics, including the theoretical number theory on one side and the practical cryptography on the other. One of the ways the prime numbers can be visualized is the Ulam spiral, first devised in 1963 [21] and published in 1964 [17]. It is also called prime spiral [19]. The spiral containing the prime numbers and the remaining numbers forming a square, with the number 1 in the center, will be called the Ulam square.

The visual appearance of lines, mostly diagonal, and forming an asymmetric pattern, is a striking feature of the Ulam spiral. This feature became the subject of our studies. We were interested in whether the lines which seem to be visible with a human eye were actually present there, and if so, what were their properties. We wanted to check for the presence of sequences of immediately neighboring points as well as those mutually placed at a longer range, forming sequences of points, or lines, inclined at a specified angle. We wished not to limit the search to lines inclined by such specific angles as 0, 45 or 90°, but to search for lines at arbitrary angles realizable on the square grid. Therefore, we

© Springer Nature Switzerland AG 2018
L. J. Chmielewski et al. (Eds.): ICCVG 2018, LNCS 11114, pp. 522–533, 2018.
https://doi.org/10.1007/978-3-030-00692-1_45

actually went beyond the limit imposed by the noticeability of lines to a human eye. However, we wished to apply image processing techniques, to objectivize the visual effects characteristic to humans.

To detect and describe line segments the Hough transform (HT) can be used. The Ulam square is a strictly defined mathematical object, not a projection of a real-world object containing physical lines. Therefore, a special version of HT should be used. The analysis of digital lines with the HT was described in [7,12], where all the lines, being digitizations of a mathematical straight line representable in an image, were considered. This *digital* HT was compared to te conventional *analog* HT in [11]. Our approach was different, due to that the lines in the Ulam square are not approximations, but are the sequences of points having strictly specified ratios of coordinate increments. For such lines, we have proposed a relatively simple detection method in [3].

In this paper we shall shortly remind our previous findings, in order to pass to new results concerning the problem of looking for prime-rich polynomials, which we have found as a side-effect of looking for long sequences of points uniformly displaced in the Ulam square. With each sequence, a quadratic polynomial which generates its primes is connected. It occurred that one of the sequences found by us has a polynomial which is, in some sense, more rich in primes than some well-known polynomials which can be found in the literature.

At this point let us clarify the terminology. We shall call the *line* a set of points in the Ulam spiral forming a straight line, irrespectively of whether perceivable or not. A set of points located at fixed intervals and belonging to a line inclined at a specified angle will be called the *segment*. A segment has a limited number of points, naturally. We shall refer to this number as the *length* of the segment, in spite of that it is not the length in typical sense. The prime numbers corresponding to the points of the segment will be called the *sequence*. Conveniently, the *length* of this sequence is the same as the *length* of its segment. These terms will be further specified in the following.

The remainder of this paper is organized as follows. In Sect. 2 the method of detecting lines in the Ulam square will be outlined. In Sect. 3 the properties of the segments known until now will be described: their lengths and numbers in Sect. 3.1, directionality in Sect. 3.2, relation of number of segments to number of primes in Sect. 3.3, and some results for larger numbers and more directions in Sect. 3.4. These Sections contain a brief recapitulation of the results from our previous works on Ulam spiral, according to their sequence in time: [2–4,6]. In Sect. 4 we shall present our new findings concerning the prime-rich polynomials which we have come upon during the study. In the last Section the paper is summarized and concluded.

2 Detection of Segments

Let us very briefly describe the basics of the applied line detection method proposed in [3]. Its description was partly repeated in [2,4–6]. We shall summarize and abbreviate the explanation from [2].

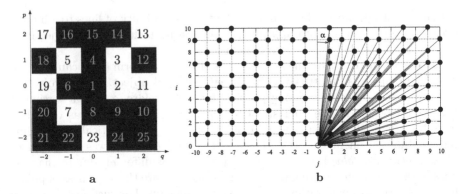

Fig. 1. (a) The central part of the Ulam spiral for dimensions 5×5 with coordinates (p, q). Primes: black on white, other numbers: grey on black. (b) Directional vectors represented by the *direction table* D with elements D_{ij} containing increments $(\Delta p, \Delta q) = (i, j)$. Each vector has the initial point at the empty circle $(0, 0)$ and the terminal point at one of the black circles (i, j), $\neg(i = 0 \land j = 0)$. Angle α is the angle between the line segment and the vertical axis. From [2,3], with permissions.

Let us remind first the structure of the Ulam spiral shown in Fig. 1a. It starts with 1 as the center and goes on right, up, left, down and so on. Prime numbers are marked (here, in white). Other numbers remain on black. Some line segments present in the square are shown in Fig. 2a.

To specify such objects let us establish a coordinate system Opq centered in the number 1. Let us consider three points corresponding to numbers $23, 7, 19$ which form a contiguous segment. Its slope, or direction, can be described by the differences in coordinates between its ends: $\Delta p = p(19) - p(32) = 2$ and $\Delta q = q(19) - q(32) = 2$. The directions are be stored in the table shown in Fig. 1b called the *direction table*, denoted D, with elements D_{ij}, where $i = \Delta p$ and $j = \Delta q$. The considered segment can be described by the directional vector $(i, j) = (-2, 2)$, which can be reduced to $(-1, 1)$ and stored in D. The offset of the segment can be represented by q of its section with axis Oq, in this case $q(19) = -2$. In table D it is possible to represent slopes expressed by pairs $i \in [0 : N]$ and $j \in [-N, N] \setminus \{0\}$. Now let us consider points $23, 2, 13$ which form a segment inclined by $(i, j) = (2, 1)$, with offset $q(2) = 1$. These points are not neighbors in the normal sense, but they are the closest possible at this direction; hence, the segment formed by them will be denoted as *contiguous*. The angle can take as many different values as is the number of black circles in Fig. 1b, shown with thin lines.

The direction table can be used as an accumulator in the Hough transform for straight lines passing exactly through the points in the Ulam spiral. The vote is a pair of points, so this is a two-point HT. The neighborhood from which a second point is taken for each first point, is related to the dimensions of D (doubling the pairs should be avoided). During the accumulation process, in each D_{ij} a one-dimensional data structure is formed. For each vote the line offset and

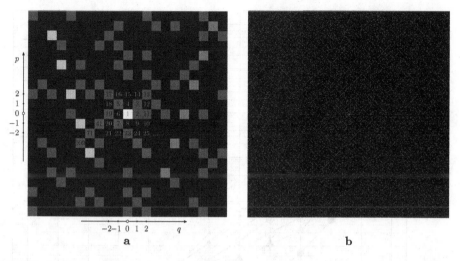

Fig. 2. (a) Central part of the Ulam spiral of dimensions 21 × 21 and with segments of lengths 5 and 6 marked in colors. Coordinates as in Fig. 1a. Primes: black on grey or color background; other numbers: grey on black or white. Blue: two segments of length 5, slopes $(\Delta p, \Delta q) = (1, 1)$ and $(1, -1)$, respectively, with one common point corresponding to prime number 19 marked with darker blue. Cyan: segment of length 5, slope $(\Delta p, \Delta q) = (3, -1)$. Magenta: segment of length 6, slope $(3, 1)$. From [5], with permission. (b) The longest, 16-point segment in 301 × 301 square, in green. From [4], with permission. (Color figure online)

the locations of two voting points are stored and the pairs and their primes are counted. After the accumulation, the accumulator can be analyzed according to the need, for example, to find long segments or to find the dominating directions of lines. As an example, in Fig. 2b the long segment having 16 primes and slope $(i, j) = (3, 1)$ is shown.

3 Properties of the Detected Segments

3.1 Number and Length

It can be expected that short segments are more numerous in the Ulam square than long ones. Questions arise, how many segments of various lengths are there? Is there a limit on segment length? A partial answer to these and other questions can be seen in Fig. 3.

In general, the number of segments falls down with their length, not very far from linearly in log scale. It is interesting to see that there are no longer segments than 16 points, and that in the investigated set there are no segments of length 14 and 15 points [4] (this gap will be briefly addressed in Sect. 3.4).

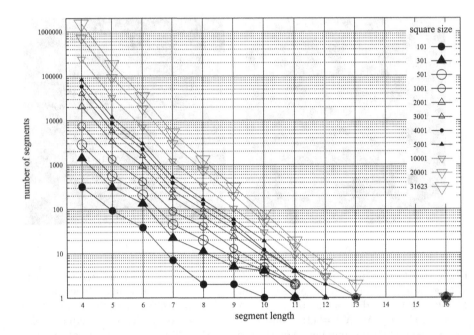

Fig. 3. Number of segments versus length of the segment for various sizes of the Ulam square, for direction array $N = 10$. If the number of lines is zero the data point is absent. The black lines show the results up to the largest prime 25 009 991 [4], the red ones – those for primes up to 1 000 014 121 [2]. From [2], with permission. (Color figure online)

3.2   Directionality

It is known that there are more lines inclined at $(i, j) = (1, -1)$, angle $\alpha = -45°$ than at $(i, j) = (1, 1)$, $\alpha = 45°$ (angle α has been marked in Fig. 1b). This observation has been checked in [6].

The stronger the line is, the more voting pairs has voted for it. In Fig. 4 the numbers of votes on all the lines in the given direction are graphed. The numbers are normalized so that the maximum is one.

It can be seen that the value for $\alpha = -45°$ is the largest, and that for $\alpha = 45°$ is the second large. The values for vertical ($\alpha = 0°$) and horizontal lines ($\alpha = 90°$) are smaller. It has been also checked if the directional structure of the Ulam square is indeed so specific, by comparing it with that of a random dot square, with the number of points corresponding to that of the Ulam square of the same size (cf. Fig. 6). It can be seen in the graphs in Fig. 4 that the random square has a different directional structure. One of the clearly visible differences is that the direction $\alpha = -45°$ is not privileged.

It has been also shown in [6] that the graphs in Fig. 4 stabilize quickly with the growing size of the square. The results for random data are practically

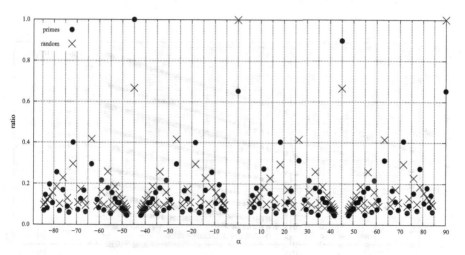

Fig. 4. Normalized numbers of votes (pairs of primes) on all the lines in the given direction, for Ulam square with primes and for random square with point density as in the Ulam one. From [6], modified, with permission.

indiscernible for their various realizations. Here, the results for squares 1001∗1001 are shown.

3.3   Number of Segments, Number of Primes

The primes are decreasingly dense in the set of natural numbers, as expressed by the function $\pi(n)$ [1,18]. It can be expected that the lesser the primes, the lesser the segments. The question arises whether the number of segments fall down quicker or slower than the number of primes decreases [5]. This relation is shown in Fig. 5 for all the lengths of segments present in the images.

It can be seen that this relation is always close to linear in the double log scale, provided that the number of segments involved is large. The longest segments are rare and for them the relation does not hold.

Regular structures necessitate not only for the presence of the primes, but also for the existence of some constant relations between them. This is a restrictive demand, so it might well be expected that at some point the number of regular structures could fall down. No such phenomenon is observed in the range of primes investigated until now.

The human eye has a tendency of seeing regularities even in a random image. It is interesting whether the regularities just presented could not emerge from mere abundance of data. Random images having the density of dots very close to that observed in the Ulam square [5] (Fig. 6) can be subjected to the same analysis as the Ulam square.

The results for randomized data can be seen in the Fig. 5. The sets of graphs appear different. Let us point out just two differences.

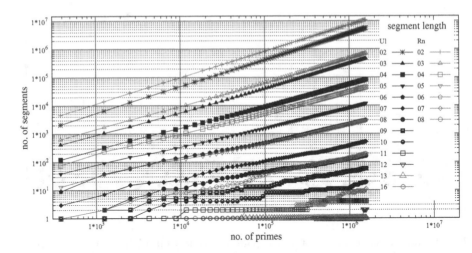

Fig. 5. Number of segments vs. number of primes in the Ulam square (Ul: thick blue or green lines, full symbols for lengths present also in random squares) and in random square (Rn: thin red lines, empty symbols). From [5], with permission. (Color figure online)

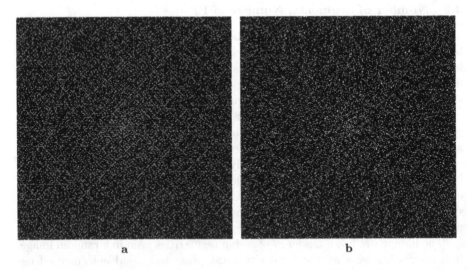

a   b

Fig. 6. (a) The actual Ulam square of size 351 × 351 and (b) one of its randomized realizations with density of white points corresponding to that in the Ulam square. The structure of the randomized square differs from that of the actual one even in visual inspection. From [5], with permission.

The longest segment in the Ulam square has 16 points, while in the considered realizations of the random square it has 8 points. This suggests that in the Ulam square the regularity is stronger than that in a random square.

In the random square the numbers of shorter segments (with 2 and 3 points) are larger than those in the Ulam square, while the numbers of the longer segments (with 4, 5, 6 points) is smaller, independently from the size of the squares. This suggests the existence of some factor which promotes the appearance of longer structures in the Ulam square.

It has been checked [5] that the results are stable for shorter segments, although the locations of segments in the subsequent realizations are entirely different.

The described observations suggest that the structure of the set of the prime numbers might contain long-range relations which do not depend on the scale.

3.4 Larger Numbers, More Directions

All the above described experiments (except those shown in red in Fig. 3) were carried out for the square of 5001×5001, hence for numbers up to approx. 25×10^6, and for the directions limited by the number $N = \max(i, j) = 10$. This was due to memory limits in the software and hardware. With the new equipment, the previously found tendencies were confirmed in [2] where numbers up to approximately 10^9 were analyzed. After extending the graphs from Fig. 5 to larger numbers the same tendencies were confirmed (see [2] for details). New interesting results have been found when the limit for the number of directions, previously set with the dimensions of the direction table $N = 10$, were relaxed by setting to $N = 50$ (with the size of the square 5001×5001, as it was in the first experiments). The results are shown in Fig. 7.

Several observations can be made. There are three new segments having 14 points. Two of them emerged near 3×10^5, and the third one for the primes over 10^6. Consequently, the gap between the segments with 13 and 16 points has been partly filled. There are also more segments with 13 points. Their points are much farther from each other than in the segments previously found.

Further, the close-to-linear shape of the graphs became less apparent in parts of the graphs. The linearity seems to hold for numbers over 10^5, quite similarly as it was in the case of less directions. Extending the calculations to larger numbers could reveal the validity of the experimental asymptotic tendency in this case.

4 Prime-Rich Polynomials

It is quite easy to verify that many sequences of prime numbers of a given length (say l) discovered in the Ulam square, i.e., forming a segment of a detected line, can be generated by a special class of quadratic polynomials. In other words, there is a function of the form

$$f(n) = 4n^2 + bn + c,$$

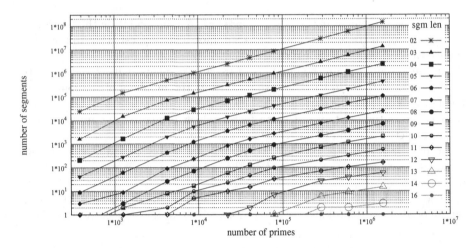

Fig. 7. Number of segments versus number of primes in the square, for direction array $N = 50$. From [2], with permission.

where b and c are some integer numbers, producing prime numbers belonging to the considered sequence for consecutive values of non-negative integers n from the range $0 \le n \le l - 1$. For example, one of our detected sequences of eleven primes: 97571, 96323, 95083, 93851, 92627, 91411, 90203, 89003, 87811, 86627, 85451, which belongs to a line with the directional vector $(i, j) = (3, 1)$, is generated for non-negative integer numbers $0 \le n \le 10$ by the following quadratic polynomial:

$$a_{11}(n) = 4n^2 - 1260n + 98827.$$

Finding polynomials (or any function, for that matter) generating prime numbers for subsequent values of arguments (being natural or integer numbers) is a very important problem for its own sake and its origins have nothing to do with the Ulam square, see, e.g., [9,14–16,20] and references therein. There is a famous example, known as the Euler quadratic polynomial

$$e(n) = n^2 + n + 41$$

that produces 40 different primes for non-negative integer numbers $0 \le n \le 39$. It is somewhat interesting that exactly this polynomial was invented by Lagrange, not Euler, original Euler's invention being a similar function: $g(n) = n^2 - n + 41$. In spite of the slightly different form both generate the same 40 distinct primes (in the latter case we should take $1 \le n \le 40$). As far as we know there is no other quadratic polynomial that improves over the Euler one in producing more than 40 different primes for subsequent values of non-negative integer arguments. However, it can happen that there are other quadratic polynomials that generate more primes in any given range of arguments than the Euler polynomial, if we relax the requirement that all these primes must come for subsequent values of arguments within that range. In fact, searching for such rich in primes quadratic polynomials has a long and exciting history.

Let us denote by $P_f(N)$ the number of primes generated by a given polynomial $f(n)$ for non-negative integer arguments $0 \le n \le N$. It is interesting to observe that for $N = 1000$ our polynomial $a_{11}(n)$ gives $P_{a_{11}}(1000) = 613$ primes (20 of them come with the minus sign) what is not only better than provided by the Euler polynomial $e(n)$, which gives $P_e(1000) = 582$, but better than several other well-known prime-rich polynomials like, e.g., all three so-called Beeger polynomials: $b_1(n) = n^2 + n + 19421$ (with $P_{b_1}(1000) = 558$), $b_2(n) = n^2 + n + 27941$ (with $P_{b_2}(1000) = 600$), and $b_3(n) = n^2 + n + 72491$ (with $P_{b_3}(1000) = 611$). Asymptotically, for larger N, our polynomial loses in this respect to the two latter polynomials, still beating both the Euler one and the first Beeger one [8,10,13]. Preliminary computations suggest that our polynomial has higher formally defined prime density than the Euler one and many other prime-rich polynomials. This is remarkable, especially taking into account the fact that polynomials discovered just by looking at segments of primes in the Ulam square were in no way optimized for that purpose, which follows from the descriptions given in the previous Sections. Of course not all quadratic polynomials generating sequences of primes forming line segments have these properties. Nevertheless the fact that starting from image analysis and pattern recognition perspectives we can obtain some potentially interesting results related to the number theory is, in our opinion, worth to be emphasized.

5 Conclusions

The set of prime numbers was considered from the perspective of its visualization in the form of the Ulam spiral. The objects of particular interest were the line segments, some of them perceivable with the human eye, and all detectable with image processing techniques. The detection method used was a specially designed version of the Hough transform. The search included the segments inclined at angles defined by ratios of integers up to 50, and the integers were up to approximately 10^9.

The results described in the previous papers were briefly recapitulated, including the numbers and lengths of the segments, their directionality, and the relation of their numbers to the number of primes.

It was shown that among the polynomials which generate the numbers forming the sequences found, at least one is exceptionally rich in primes. This polynomial generates one of the 11-point segments. This segment is not the longest segment found (the longest segment has 16 primes), and from the point of view of its appearance in the Ulam square it is not specific in any way. Its polynomial is $a_{11}(n) = 4n^2 - 1260n + 98827$ and among the numbers it generates for integer n, $0 \le n \le 1000$, there are 613 primes, including 20 of them with the minus sign. This is more than the number of primes generated by some other well-known prime-rich polynomials, like the Euler one and the three Beeger ones, for example. Asymptotically, this polynomial is more prime-rich than the Euler one and the first Beeger one. This is remarkable, because it has been discovered by looking for long segments in the Ulam square and not by optimizing its richness in primes.

This indicates that approaching the problem related to the set of prime numbers from the image analysis and pattern recognition perspective can lead to interesting results related to the number theory.

References

1. Caldwell, C.K.: How many primes are there? In: Caldwell, C.K. (ed.) The Prime Pages (2018). http://primes.utm.edu/howmany.html. Accessed 15 July 2018
2. Chmielewski, L.J., Janowicz, M., Gawdzik, G., Orłowski, A.: Contiguous line segments in the Ulam spiral: experiments with larger numbers. In: Rutkowski, L., Korytkowski, M., Scherer, R., Tadeusiewicz, R., Zadeh, L., Zurada, J. (eds.) ICAISC 2017. LNCS (LNAI), vol. 10245, pp. 463–472. Springer, Cham (2017). https://doi.org/10.1007/978-3-319-59063-9_41
3. Chmielewski, L.J., Orłowski, A.: Hough transform for lines with slope defined by a pair of co-primes. Mach. Graph. Vis. **22**(1/4), 17–25 (2013). http://mgv.wzim.sggw.pl/MGV22.html#1-3
4. Chmielewski, L.J., Orłowski, A.: Finding line segments in the Ulam square with the Hough transform. In: Chmielewski, L.J., Datta, A., Kozera, R., Wojciechowski, K. (eds.) ICCVG 2016. LNCS, vol. 9972, pp. 617–626. Springer, Cham (2016). https://doi.org/10.1007/978-3-319-46418-3_55
5. Chmielewski, L.J., Orłowski, A., Gawdzik, G.: Segment counting versus prime counting in the Ulam square. In: Nguyen, N., Tojo, S., et al. (eds.) ACIIDS 2017, Part II. LNCS (LNAI), vol. 10192, pp. 227–236. Springer, Cham (2017). https://doi.org/10.1007/978-3-319-54430-4_22
6. Chmielewski, L.J., Orłowski, A., Janowicz, M.: A study on directionality in the Ulam square with the use of the Hough transform. In: Kobayashi, S., Piegat, A., et al. (eds.) ACS 2016. AISC, vol. 534, pp. 81–90. Springer, Cham (2016). https://doi.org/10.1007/978-3-319-48429-7_8
7. Cyganski, D., Noel, W.F., Orr, J.A.: Analytic Hough transform. In: Proceedings of the SPIE. Sensing and Reconstruction of Three-Dimensional Objects and Scenes, vol. 1260, pp. 148–159 (1990). https://doi.org/10.1117/12.20013
8. Fung, G.W., Williams, H.C.: Quadratic polynomials which have a high density of prime values. Math. Comput. **55**(191), 345–353 (1990). https://doi.org/10.1090/S0025-5718-1990-1023759-3
9. Guy, R.K.: Unsolved Problems in Number Theory. Springer, New York (1994). https://doi.org/10.1007/978-0-387-26677-0
10. Jacobson, M.J., Williams, H.C.: New quadratic polynomials with high densities of prime values. Math. Comput. **72**(241), 499–519 (2002). https://doi.org/10.1090/S0025-5718-02-01418-7
11. Kiryati, N., Lindenbaum, M., Bruckstein, A.M.: Digital or analog Hough transform? Pattern Recogn. Lett. **12**(5), 291–297 (1991). https://doi.org/10.1016/0167-8655(91)90412-F
12. Liu, Y., Cyganski, D., Vaz, R.F.: Efficient implementation of the analytic Hough transform for exact linear feature extraction. In: Proceedings of the SPIE. Intelligent Robots and Computer Vision X: Algorithms and Techniques, vol. 1607, pp. 298–309 (1992). https://doi.org/10.1117/12.57109

13. Mollin, R.A.: Prime-producing quadratics. Am. Math. Monthly **104**(6), 529–544 (1997). https://doi.org/10.1080/00029890.1997.11990675
14. Narkiewicz, W.: The Development of Prime Number Theory: From Euclid to Hardy and Littlewood. Springer, Heidelberg (2000). https://doi.org/10.1007/978-3-662-13157-2
15. Ribenboim, P.: The Book of Prime Number Records, 2nd edn. Springer, New York (1989). https://doi.org/10.1007/978-1-4684-0507-1
16. Riesel, H.: Prime Numbers and Computer Methods for Factorization. Progress in Mathematics, vol. 126, 2nd edn. Springer (Birkhäuser, Basel), New York (1994). https://doi.org/10.1007/978-1-4612-0251-6
17. Stein, M.L., Ulam, S.M., Wells, M.B.: A visual display of some properties of the distribution of primes. Am. Math. Monthly **71**(5), 516–520 (1964). https://doi.org/10.2307/2312588
18. Weisstein, E.W.: Prime counting function. From MathWorld-A Wolfram Web Resource (2018) http://mathworld.wolfram.com/PrimeCountingFunction.html. Accessed 15 July 2018
19. Weisstein, E.W.: Prime spiral. From MathWorld-A Wolfram Web Resource (2018) http://mathworld.wolfram.com/PrimeSpiral.html. Accessed 15 July 2018
20. Wells, D.: Prime Numbers. The Most Mysterious Figures in Math. Wiley, Hoboken (2005)
21. Wikipedia: Ulam spiral – Wikipedia, The Free Encyclopedia (2018). https://en.wikipedia.org/wiki/Ulam_spiral. Accessed 15 July 2018

Author Index

Printed in the United States
By Bookmasters

Printed in the United States
By Bookmasters